BACKWARD RAN SENTENCES

The Best of Wolcott Gibbs
from *The New Yorker*

Wolcott Gibbs

Foreword by P. J. O'Rourke

Edited and Introduced by
Thomas Vinciguerra

B L O O M S B U R Y
New York   Berlin   London   Sydney

Published by Bloomsbury USA, New York

All of the pieces in this collection originally appeared in
The New Yorker, except the following:
"In Defense of Dermathermy" and "Non-Graduates, We are
Gathered Here . . ." appeared in *Cosmopolitan*.
"The Kingdom of the Blind" appeared in the *Saturday Review of Literature*.
"Little Sureshot" appeared in *Life*.
"Robert Benchley: In Memoriam" appeared in the *New York Times*.
"Stuff and Nonsense, Mr. C." appeared in the *New York Herald Tribune*.
"Theory and Practice of Editing *New Yorker* Articles" appeared in *The Years
With Ross* by James Thurber (Little, Brown, 1959).

All papers used by Bloomsbury USA are natural, recyclable products made
from wood grown in well-managed forests. The manufacturing processes
conform to the environmental regulations of the country of origin.

LIBRARY OF CONGRESS CATALOGING-IN-PUBLICATION
DATA HAS BEEN APPLIED FOR.

ISBN: 978-1-60819-550-3

First U.S. Edition 2011

1 3 5 7 9 10 8 6 4 2

Typeset by Westchester Book Group
Printed in the U.S.A. by Quad/Graphics, Fairfield, Pennsylvania

BACKWARD RAN
SENTENCES

CONTENTS

THEY WRITE AS I PLEASE: *Parodies*

SOME TROUBLES I'VE SEEN: *Casuals*

WOUNDS AND DECORATIONS:
Theater and Film Criticism

THOUGHTS ON INFINITY:
Personal and Professional Essays

Coda

Notes

A NOTE ON THE SELECTIONS

Despite his voluminous magazine output, Wolcott Gibbs published a mere five books, only three of which comprised selections of his *New Yorker* work. (The fourth, a 1931 effort called *Bird Life at the Pole*, was a comic novel about the polar explorations then making headlines. The fifth was the book of his Broadway play, *Season in the Sun*.) His own most strident critic, Gibbs put between hard covers only those pieces that particularly pleased him. "It is a fortunate author," he wrote in the foreword to his first collection, *Bed of Neuroses*, "who can reread what he has written at the end of six months without loathing."

In assembling this volume, I have tried to convey the fullest possible range of Gibbs's oeuvre. Certain classic and often reprinted pieces, such as his iconic, parodic profile of Henry Luce, were obvious candidates. However, given his sheer productivity, much ruthless culling was necessary. Nonetheless, included herein are a number of overlooked treasures that have not seen the light of print since they first appeared. The chapter headings are borrowed from Gibbs's original anthologies.

All contents were first published in *The New Yorker*, except as noted on the copyright page. To those parties who granted reprint permission, I am most grateful. I am especially indebted to Gibbs's literary heirs—his granddaughter, Susan Ward-Roncalli, and above all his son, Tony—for their inexhaustible support and kind encouragement.

—T.V.

FOREWORD
The Top Ten Reasons Why We Should Still Read Wolcott Gibbs
(and the Top Ten Reasons Why We Don't Anymore)

P. J. O'ROURKE

I. THE TOP TEN LIST

Wolcott Gibbs may be said to have invented the admonitory Top Ten list, if we don't count God's stand-up monologue to Moses. A few thousand years later, but long before David Letterman, Gibbs wrote a pair of comic theater columns for *The New Yorker* in which he listed the top ten behavioral characteristics of successful drama critics and the top ten journalistic techniques of successful drama criticism.

All such lists, the Commandments included, sneer at common human shortcomings. But today we consider the sneer to be an end in itself, sufficient, if we "get it," as proof that we are a cut above the common golden calf–worshiping herd. A different opinion was held by Gibbs and God (with whom Gibbs shared, judging by the King James Bible, a striking talent for prose composition).

A list, a sneer, a burning bush—they're just bits of stage business to draw the audience's attention to larger ideas such as a chosen people's sacred covenant or how play reviews get so filled with b.s.:

> Too often dramatists, a cynical crew, are in the racket merely for the dough and write plays as barren of moral or political content as Fannie Farmer's cookbook. It is up to the conscientious critic to remedy this situation . . . The best trick . . . is to credit the play with a secondary level on which the author's real purpose becomes apparent. The discovery that this neat little bedroom farce is in reality a ringing denunciation of capitalistic morality may astonish the innocent author, but this obviously isn't the critic's fault.

That's not quite the Top Ten list as we know it, in fact it continues for 56 ½ column inches. Not to overdo the comparison of Gibbs and God, but neither would be welcome on modern late night television—they go on too long.

2. A DIVINE, AS PREVIOUSLY NOTED, STYLE

Here is a sample, chosen almost at random, from Gibbs's contributions to "The Talk of the Town," this one from 1932:

> The other night we rode out to the country in one of the Long Island Railroad's new double-decked cars. Descriptively, in our time, we have dealt with a lot of man's ingenious devices for making his neighbor's life insupportable, doing these things up as brown as the good Lord has given us the strength to do, but we are baffled by this new horror. One hundred and twenty commuters instead of seventy-six (these are the figures) sharing the meager air; standees' feet parading by your face, if you sit on the lower tier; their faces, unexpected and strange, at your elbow, if you sit on top; downstairs, the sense of life, heavy heavy, over your head; upstairs, the uneasiness that goes with any variation of a familiar ritual . . . altogether, an old ordeal, now made intolerable.

Compare the majestic language here to the next whiney Tweet you get from some Facebook friend stuck on a train to the Hamptons. Alas, majestic is exactly the problem for the modern reader—*lèse majesté* being our contemporary motto in language as it is in taste and manners. Or it would be if we knew what the French phrase meant. Majesty of language offends us today. We're in charge here. Communication is a lowly servant to be beaten, abused and humbled in every text message. LOL if that makes this particular neighbor's life insupportable.

P.S. Eighty years on, the Long Island Railroad is worse than ever.

3. HE WAS NOT FOOLED BY MODERNISM

Gibbs demystified Samuel Becket's *Waiting for Godot* with a few keystrokes on the drama critic's typewriter. The play, he said, *does* have a meaning:

> . . . and it seems to me that the most likely is also the simplest. Gogo and Didi, then, represent the great mass of lost men, and the savior who never comes for them is God . . . All I can say, in a critical sense, is that I have seldom seen such meager moonshine stated with such inordinate fuss.

This simple, old-fashioned detection of bunk is not welcome now. We moderns are, after all, by definition modernists. If we can't fool ourselves, who can we fool?

4. HE WAS NOT FOOLED BY TALENT

Here is Gibbs describing that most talented of modern actors, Marlon Brando, portraying Stanley Kowalski in *A Streetcar Named Desire* by that most talented of modern playwrights, Tennessee Williams: ". . . this character emerges as almost subhuman—illiterate, dirty, violent . . . Mr. Williams attempts, though the evidence on stage is against him, to portray Kowalski as a man of enormous sexual attraction . . ."

Many of us moderns were fooled by Marlon almost until his last bloated moment, and more of us remain fooled by the overdramatized neuroses of Tennessee. The least little talent, or none at all, is enough to fool us: witness YouTube. In the twenty-first century, we like to fool and be fooled, otherwise why surround ourselves with political, economic, and entertainment foolery?

People who aren't fooled are annoying. They make us feel foolish.

5. HE WAS NOT FOOLED BY MUCH

Gibbs, though he spent a large part of his professional life reviewing entertainments, was not very fond of being entertained. He
resented the deceptions involved. "The reason I approach the theatre as I do, with suspicion and a cold foreboding," Gibbs explained, was a result of early childhood exposure to theatricality.
In a stage production of *The Wizard of Oz*, "Dorothy, although she
wore a parody of the costume in the book, was definitely grown-
up; not perhaps quite as antique as my parents, but certainly old
enough to be excluded from any world in which I had the slightest
part or interest." And the cowardly lion "was a miserable fake, incapable of making anybody (except conceivably an adult) believe
that he was anything more than just an actor dressed up."

Illusions are poor things. Yet today we live in an almost wholly
illusionary world. There is the illusion that a thousand cable chan-
nels bring the world to us, the illusion that the Internet brings us to
the world, the illusion that media is social, the illusion that social
media is a medium for thought or deed.

Gibbs had few illusions, and he was not the man to whom you'd
want to serve a virtual martini.

6. HE UNDERSTOOD OUR
POPULAR CULTURE—TOO WELL

In 1951 Gibbs described television for once and all time: "The machine operates constantly; the deadly surge of creation goes on night
and day." And he described the role of the television critic: "He is employed to look at, listen to, and write about stuff that usually appears
to him to be the work of half-wits."

If we substitute "blog" for "write," we have today's idea of a deeply
cultured man. And what was culture doing, anyway, before it got
popular?

7. HE PREDICTED WHERE OUR POPULAR CULTURE
WOULD LEAD US

In 1941 Gibbs wrote:

Keeping in step with the times, Director Wagner Schlesinger of the Fels Planetarium, in Philadelphia, has replaced the classic symbols of the constellations with characters out of Disney. Ursa Major and Cygnus, the Swan, have turned into Pluto the Pup and Donald Duck, respectively. Boötes is Madame Upanova, the ostrich ballerina in *Fantasia*, and Gemini, the Twins, are Mickey and Minnie Mouse.

And now we wonder what he was talking about. Didn't Ursa Major star in the 3-D remake of *10*? Is Cygnus a cell phone app? I think Boötes makes those big plastic shoes with the holes in them that the kids all wear. And was Gibbs a Gemini? Me, too!

8. HE WAS A BRILLIANT PARODIST

But the line between parody and contemporary life's customary baloney has become so blurred that we are confused when we read Gibbs's take on a boarding school catalogue:

The students are supervised at all times by a capable faculty consisting of Professor F. Dwight Bohn, Amherst '88, Princeton '88, Harvard '88, D.D., LL.D., M.D., Ph.D., who has many years' experience as an educator in the row of beautiful pines which flank the campus. It is from these pines that the Hanover Country School takes its name.

And we think, "Do our kids stand a chance of getting in?"

9. HE WAS FUNNY

But the wit of Gibbs was dry. The following appeared in "The Talk of the Town" in the middle 1930s:

> A Japanese "cultural mission" is on its way to the United States with a membership including a vocalist, a reader of Japanese poetry, a musician, and an expert on flower arrangement. We admire the versatility of a nation that can distribute culture with one hand and operate a bombing plane with the other. The flower arrangements, we feel sure, will be equally suitable for the table or the grave.

These days, wit's all wet.

10. HE WAS SERIOUS

Gibbs was able to deal with earnest matters in an earnest voice:

> As we write this, four hours after the British Prime Minister declared war, it is still hard to understand what the headlines mean. Unless there is a miracle, ten million more young men will die (very few of them especially heroically or quickly); millions of children will die (very few of whom had time to form very strong or dangerous political opinions); cities that rose proudly and slowly over the centuries will be ugly ruins between a morning and a night. The thought that built them, the thought of life, was turned off at six o'clock today . . . from now on, and for how long no man can know, there will be only the thought of death.
>
> The best minds of the world will now think continuously and cleverly of death . . .

These days the earnest voice is extinct. We can be damn serious. But to be earnest would require a kind of honest weighing-up of our feelings and beliefs that . . . We're too busy! Bring on the over-the-top emotions! Bring on the tears! Enough with this gentility—show us some rage, Gibbs!

INTRODUCTION

THOMAS VINCIGUERRA

WHENEVER NOSTALGIA-MINDED ADMIRERS of *The New Yorker* recall the magazine's glory years, certain names invariably crop up. Leading the pack is founding editor Harold Ross, the rough-hewn newspaperman from Colorado, who in 1925 created the definitive weekly chronicle of smart metropolitan life. There are the acknowledged masters of long-form nonfiction (Joseph Mitchell, A. J. Liebling, St. Clair McKelway), the star short story writers (John O'Hara, J. D. Salinger, Jean Stafford), and the legendary fixtures of the Algonquin Round Table (Robert Benchley, Dorothy Parker, Alexander Woollcott). There is the gentle philosopher E. B. White and the manic humorist James Thurber.

And then there was the shadowy, thin, lonely man who was once mentioned in the same breath as these giants, and who in his prime contributed more words and more different kinds of pieces than any of them. His death made the front page of the *New York Times*. But today he is almost completely forgotten.

Meet Oliver Wolcott Gibbs.

Of all *The New Yorker*'s leading lights, Gibbs probably came closest to being its Indispensable Man. Harold Ross, who never offered praise unless absolutely warranted, pegged him as "one of the best goddam [*sic*] editors in the world." Gibbs's veteran colleague, Brendan Gill, declared that there was "simply nothing on the magazine that he couldn't do well." P. G. Wodehouse, referring to *The New Yorker* as a whole, called it "the dullest bloody thing ever published"—that is, "except for Wolcott Gibbs."

Yet today, Gibbs is just barely remembered for a single article: "Time . . . Fortune . . . Life . . . Luce," his celebrated 1936 profile of Henry Luce, which doubled as a satire of *Time* magazine. More specifically, he is remembered for a single quip, which memorably spoofed *Time*'s weirdly inverted syntax: "Backward ran sentences until reeled the mind."

A good line, certainly, but the present obscurity of his countless others is baffling. For Gibbs was, in many ways, the ideal *New Yorker* talent. He embodied the magazine's archetypal combination of blunt honesty, sly wit, exacting standards, and elegant condescension. He was uniquely productive and versatile; by his midthirties he had contributed, by his own estimation, more than a million words to the magazine.

Starting as a copy editor, Gibbs would ultimately exert an influence felt throughout *The New Yorker*. He published scores of stories, both humorous and serious. He was a superb parodist. He reviewed the press, books, and nightlife. He edited both fiction and nonfiction and for years evaluated thousands of cartoon submissions. When the draft seriously depleted *The New Yorker*'s ranks during World War II, Gibbs continued to churn out copy while serving as both drama critic and, for a time, movie reviewer. And from E. B. White he inherited the "Notes and Comment" department, effortlessly assuming the graceful yet offhand collective editorial voice that his predecessor had established.

Gibbs worked with many leading contributors, including F. Scott Fitzgerald, John Cheever, and his good friend John O'Hara, who named the fictional setting of many of his classic stories—Gibbsville, PA—in his honor. But no matter how famous the author, he could be ruthless when editing. If a piece was particularly long and convoluted, he would book a hotel suite, lay out the article page by page on the floor, cut it into paragraphs with scissors, rearrange them, write transitions, and then line-edit the result from beginning to end.

Gibbs was equally merciless as a writer. His profiles were derisive gems. So critical was his depiction of New York Governor Thomas Dewey that Dewey became convinced that Gibbs was in the employ of the Democrats. He responded by impounding Gibbs's bank account. Gibbs's three-part takedown of Alexander Woollcott—a mainstay of *The New Yorker* and one of its first advisors—was so sly that Woollcott took the piece as a sort of love letter. Then his friends told him to read more carefully. Thereupon relations between

Woollcott and Harold Ross, which had always been tempestuous, pretty much disintegrated altogether, and Woollcott never printed another piece in the magazine. (Gibbs, for his part, made no apologies. He regarded Woollcott as "one of the most dreadful writer who ever existed.")

Gibbs truly hit his stride in his eighteen years as *The New Yorker's* chief drama critic, frequently issuing damning pronouncements that were entertainments in themselves. As one reader remarked, "He reviews plays in the manner of a little boy plucking the wings off a nasty insect." Many was the time that he left a show before the finale, deeming it pointless to continue watching the wretched proceedings. At his best—that is, his most condemnatory—Gibbs was hilariously mocking:

> The only other production my schedule permitted me to consider this week was an unpleasant little specimen called "Lady, Behave!" at the Cort. Its producer was Hugh Bennett, its star was Pert Kelton, and it demonstrated the really incredible amount of vulgarity an ingenious mind can work into a farce about psychoanalysis. (1943)

> It was dirty and feeble-minded in about equal doses. (*The Girl From Nantucket,* 1945)

> Total imbecility is something rarely achieved, even on Broadway, but I think that "Second Best Bed," a sort of rigadoon on Shakespeare's grave, can modestly claim to have come very close to it. (1946)

> [A] desolate little comedy . . . The verbal humor took the form either of bone-crushing innuendo or else of pre-adolescent epithet, the comic situations usually involved the discovery by one character of two others grappling on the sofa, and the acting was loud and desperate. (*Grandma's Diary,* 1948)

With prose like that, he couldn't help but make enemies. Irwin Shaw wrote that Gibbs had "a firm resolve to learn nothing about the theater and to treat it like a garrulous mother-in-law who will stay the winter if given any encouragement." Fellow reviewers blasted him as well. Stanley Kauffmann called him "a complete critical non-entity." Eric Bentley said he was "egregious," that he cloaked his "barbarism in the sheep's clothing of a dilettante," and that "his special contribution is an attempt to legitimize philistine prejudice." *Village Voice* critic and Yale professor Gordon Rogoff wrote, "Gibbs, notably lacking in ideas or a subject he could call his own, passed himself off as a sophisticated wit by hating all the plays of Shakespeare."

By contrast, Jacques Barzun praised Gibbs as "a man of courage" for speaking his mind. And one admirer remarked, "God, he's brilliant, he doesn't like *anything*." To which Harold Ross replied, "Maybe he doesn't like anything, but he can do everything."

And yet, although Gibbs could ostensibly do everything (except, as he once said, write about "women's fashions and horse racing"), he was one of *The New Yorker's* most elusive figures. Edmund Wilson recalled that he "glided past like a ghost. His eyes always seemed to be closed." Another colleague, Frank Modell, never saw him smile. Because he preferred to work from home, many of his co-workers didn't even know what he looked like. Once, when he dropped by to see Ross, an unrecognizing receptionist asked, "Whom shall I say is calling?" Gibbs turned on his heel and fled to the elevator.

Physically, he was not an imposing figure. Although he stood five feet, nine inches tall, he weighed only 130 pounds. A *Time* writer called him "wispy, waspy Wolcott Gibbs." He did look the part of a literary man, complete with glasses, delicately trimmed moustache, and well-cut suits, often worn with a tattersall vest. A chain smoker, he would compose his reviews in his head while pacing his living room on East Fifty-first Street in his dressing gown, three cigarettes burning in as many ashtrays. He would approach one, take a puff, put it back, and proceed to the next.

A major neurotic, Gibbs regarded the world askance, with disdain and supercilious suspicion. Frequently he would assume a cynic's pose, squinting one eye and cocking the brow of the other, as if all he beheld was beneath contempt (after reviewing each week's crop of cartoons, said art editor James Geraghty, Gibbs "always felt he should wash his hands with a strong soap"). Crowds and gatherings were torture for him. Once, at a meeting of the New York Drama Critics' Circle, he stood up suddenly and declared to his baffled neighbor, "I will not be talked to like that!" He turned to another member at random and said, "How dare you insult my wife, sir!" Whereupon he left.

In short, Gibbs was a curmudgeon and he knew it. "I wonder if there is something the matter with me that I can't like anybody for long," he confessed. "The first couple of times almost anybody seems interesting, and then you always begin to run into gaps in their humor or their taste or their perception or something, and they just get tiresome." On another occasion he observed, "I spend half my own life writing letters to sons of bitches I don't like about things that don't interest me at all. They usually answer, too. That makes it worse." He did find one way to escape this drudgery: To anyone who questioned his judgment, he would send a form response that read, "Dear Sir [or Madam]: You may be right. Sincerely, Wolcott Gibbs."

THERE WAS A good reason why Gibbs was so shy and so rude. It was because he was so sad. He rarely believed in his work or himself. He called writing "a ludicrous pastime" and theater criticism "a silly occupation for a grown man." Upon giving fiction editor Gus Lobrano one of his casuals, he said, "I wouldn't have my name on it for anything in the world, and if I were an editor I would reject it quicker than the human eye." At a time when *The New Yorker* was arguably the most prestigious general-interest periodical in America, Gibbs considered it basically a comic magazine. "I should really be writing novels," he would grouse, "not 'Talk of the Town' pieces."

Yearning to be regarded as a man of letters, Gibbs determined to be a playwright. He was envious of his friend O'Hara's smash Broadway version of *Pal Joey,* and wrote the book for his own musical, *Sarasota Special,* expecting that O'Hara would write the lyrics. He also wrote the first treatment of a musical fantasy with gossip

columnist Dorothy Kilgallen.★ For a while he tried to hammer out
a stage version of his idol Max Beerbohm's *Zuleika Dobson*. At various intervals he worked on an original play that he called *Diana*.
In 1947, he approached Charles Addams about a possible collaboration involving the clan of macabre characters he had created in
his *New Yorker* cartoons. "Something really ought to be done about
that haunted house bunch," he wrote, "and if you haven't made any
other arrangements, I'd love to try a play with you . . . There's never
been material so rich in sight gags, characters, atmosphere, and perfect curtain lines." Of course, Gibbs was right; the "Addams Family"
was later brought to life in multiple TV series and movies and, in
2010, a Broadway musical. But at the time, all of his efforts came to
nothing.

Gibbs did have one theatrical triumph, in 1950, when he became
probably the country's first major critic to have a production on
Broadway. It was an autobiographical comedy called *Season in the Sun*,
based on nine *New Yorker* stories he had published a few years before. The rest of the New York critics waited to see the result with
sharpened pens. But they seemed both genuinely impressed and
pleasantly surprised: *Season* received uniformly good notices and
ran for ten months. With his usual self-deprecation, though, Gibbs
said his success proved only "that damn near anybody can write anything." More than once he said that if he had personally reviewed
the show, he would have panned it because it was little more than "a
bunch of vaudeville routines, hooked together by some crap about
whether a guy writes a novel or paragraphs, a non–existent dilemma
if ever I heard of one."

Success though it was, *Season* still didn't register with Gibbs as a
major achievement. He was apparently incapable of taking joy in
his own particular talents. "I suppose he was the unhappiest man I've

---

★The show eventually ran for twenty-eight performances on Broadway in 1944 as
Dream With Music, but Gibbs disassociated himself from the project early on. "I
can sum up the whole show in one phrase," he recalled. "It's the phrase that Miss
Kilgallen opened up every one of our story conferences with: 'Wouldn't it be cute
if . . .'" According to George Jean Nathan, Gibbs also "blanched" at many of Kilgallen's lowbrow lines, e.g. "I'd hate to lose my head; I'm attached to it."

ever known," said his friend Sam Behrman. "I used to talk to him endlessly about his impressive gift. It made no impression on him." Fiction editor Katharine White, under whom Gibbs worked for more than a decade, called him "one of the few really tragic heroes in my life."

IF GIBBS WAS a tragic figure, it was in part because his family had fallen so far. The Gibbses had made a fortune in shipping in the eighteenth century. Gibbs's great-great-grandfather, Oliver Wolcott, was a signer of the Declaration of Independence and governor of Connecticut. Gibbs's great-grandfather also served as governor of the state, and later as John Adams' Treasury Secretary. On his mother's side, Gibbs was directly descended from Martin Van Buren. Unfortunately, most of the family wealth evaporated before Gibbs was born. "Grandfather Gibbs bought something like 1,000 acres of land out in New Jersey," he recalled. "He was wrong. They are kind of under water."

Gibbs's father, Lucius, was an engineer for George Westinghouse and Thomas Edison, but he aspired to be an inventor like Edison himself. After Wolcott was born in Manhattan in 1902—on March 15, the Ides of March—Lucius moved the family all over the Northeast, pursuing his dream of perfecting the electric car. But his business soon collapsed, and he died of pneumonia when his son was only six. Relatives took young Wolcott and his baby sister, Angelica, away from their mother. As an adult, Gibbs would refer to himself as "a longstanding orphan." Throughout his life he tried to recapture some kind of security but never did. He channeled his disillusion into his work, wounding others in print. "Do unto others before they do unto you" was his unofficial motto.

From an early age, Gibbs distinguished himself as bookish and cerebral. He attended a series of prep schools, among them Horace Mann, Riverdale, and Hill, and published several stories and poems, notable for their precocious sophistication, in Hill's school literary journal. His classroom performance was another matter. Teachers found him "erratic," with a "tendency to dream." With perverse pride, Gibbs claimed he once received a score of 17 ½ out of a possible 100 on a geography test because he had mistakenly studied a text on geology. In 1919 he was expelled from Hill for "smoking in Alumni Chapel, smoking in a near by [*sic*] cemetery, where very unworthy behavior was indulged in by his friends and himself, and his complicity in the persecution of younger and less quick-witted boys in his Form." Although he later completed his secondary school requirements at what is now the Cheshire Academy, in Connecticut, his formal education ended there. "I got fed up," he explained, "and didn't pass those college board exams."

So he got a job through his uncle George, a pioneering railway engineer who had helped build the New York City subway system, Pennsylvania Station, and Grand Central Terminal. George Gibbs started his nephew out on the lowest rung of the family business, as a brakeman on the Long Island Rail Road. For several years, Gibbs floated freight cars across the harbor between the Pennsylvania Railroad yards in Bay Ridge, Brooklyn, and Jersey City. Although the experience inspired some short stories and provided the basis for his unrealized musical *Sarasota Special*, he regarded the LIRR as "a pretty comic kind of railroad" and the time he spent on it as "utterly wasted."

Then in 1925 his cousin, the feminist author Alice Duer Miller, thinking railway work beneath him, got him into journalism. For two years, Gibbs wrote for and edited the Long Island newspapers owned by Lloyd Carpenter Griscom, a cousin by marriage. Griscom's holdings—the *East Norwich Enterprise*, the *North Hempstead Record,* and the *Nassau Daily Star*—were unexceptional suburban broadsheets. But Gibbs had plenty of editorial freedom: Besides covering local politics, zoning plans, the social scene, and similar small-town topics, he turned out whimsical vignettes, essays, and light poetry. Eventually he learned his trade well enough for Miller, an advisory editor at *The New Yorker* from its outset, to secure him a job at the magazine. Recalling his first meeting with Harold Ross, Gibbs quoted the notoriously plain-spoken editor as telling him, "I don't give a damn what else you do, but for God's sake, don't fuck the contributors." It was, Gibbs said, "the closest approach to a coherent editorial policy I ever discovered."

Regardless of the coherence of its policies, *The New Yorker* quickly became the most stable thing in the longstanding orphan's life.

Certainly Gibbs never found real domestic tranquility; he was married three times, and each wife brought a different kind of heartache. His first marriage took place during his newspaper days, to a nineteen-year-old Elmira College student, Helen Marguerite Galpin, who lived near him in Oyster Bay. Their impulsive wedlock lasted only briefly and was so clearly a mistake that neither of them spoke of it afterward. Indeed, in *Here at The New Yorker*, Brendan Gill mistakenly identified Helen as the daughter of a fellow railroad worker (her father was actually an English butler for the wealthy Schiff family). And Gibbs and Helen's children from subsequent unions grew up never knowing the names of their parents' first spouses.

Gibbs's second marriage, in 1929, was to Ada Elizabeth Crawford of Detroit, a *New Yorker* promotion writer. A popular member of the staff, she committed suicide eight months after the wedding by jumping out of their seventeenth-story apartment in Tudor City. Accounts of the tragic end of that marriage are conflicting. Some say Elizabeth leaped when Gibbs was talking with O'Hara and the men wouldn't let her join in the conversation. Others believe she was driven to kill herself after Gibbs cruelly and repeatedly mocked her attempts to be a writer. The official account, from newspaper and police reports, was that Elizabeth had become morbidly obsessed with the play *Death Takes a Holiday* following a recent viewing. A week later, when Gibbs, Elizabeth, and Gibbs's sister Angelica were all lunching in the apartment, Elizabeth excused herself to the bedroom. When she didn't return after a few minutes, Gibbs looked out the window and saw her on the pavement.

Whatever the circumstances, Elizabeth's death shattered him. But in 1931, he met the woman who was by every indication the love of his life. Nancy Hale was an early short story writer for *The New Yorker,* and Gibbs her editor. Hale was elegant, distinguished, frank—and beautiful. It wasn't long before he fell for her. Over many letters, with uncharacteristic passion, he poured out his heart: "You're going to have to take me, because I am absolutely incapable of getting through a day without seeing you. Today, for instance. It seems very likely that I am going to die at about four o'clock this afternoon unless you telephone." And again: "Do you know that I probably love you more than Yahweh, the God of Israel? I want to be married as soon as possible for several reasons—principally because I think it would be pleasant only to have to get up and walk eight feet to sit on the edge of your bed."

Unfortunately, Nancy was married, with a baby boy. She entered into an affair with Gibbs but never seriously considered leaving her husband. The adultery went on for months; finally, Hale insisted that they separate. Again, Gibbs was devastated. "Darling," he wrote, "I've spent two days now just on the edge of putting my head down and howling like a dog. Oh darling whatever happens, I'm so damn glad that you have slept with me, and I have something to remember. I think you're the only person I ever loved in my life, and I always will. I don't think I'm going to be able to get over you."

But he did. In 1933, O'Hara introduced Gibbs to Elinor Mead Sherwin. The daughter of a Manhattan architect, Elinor had attended Brearley and Wellesley (she dropped out of the latter because she didn't like the food). She then made a living for several years as a model and a silent film actress. So captivating was she that a Hollywood producer reportedly named a seventy-foot schooner for her. After just a few months of acquaintance, she and Gibbs eloped.

On the surface, it seemed like an ideal match. Gibbs's friend and colleague St. Clair McKelway called them the most beautiful couple in New York. Elinor shared her husband's irreverent nature, so much so that her nickname was "Flip." Cosmopolitan and urbane, she was also flighty: She read mystery novels through a lorgnette, dealt with bills by stashing them in a shoebox in her closet, and fed the family's many cats by opening cans of pet food and putting them under the couch.

Gibbs and Elinor shared a genuine love, but their marriage had plenty of strife. They could both be a tad too brittle, a bit too cutting. There were whispers of mutual infidelity. What is undeniable is that both were alcoholics.

Gibbs's alcoholism defined his entire adult life. "There is no such thing as *one* martini," he liked to say, and his conduct while under the influence ran the gamut from the amusing to the pathetic. Once, while he was slicing a steak in a restaurant, it slipped off his plate. Cursing, he got down on his knees and carved it on the floor. When he ended up prostrate in a nightclub, playgirl Leonore Lemmon yelled at him, "Hey, Wolcott! You're out three days before your magazine!" He mangled seven of his fingers jumping down a flight of stairs on a drunken bet. "At a party Gibbs was good for about two hours," recalled David Cort, foreign editor of *Life*. "After that he didn't fight, he dissolved, and had to be carried."

His addiction also tainted his work. All too often, the critic would arrive at the theater intoxicated and collapse in his seat. At the opening of *The Crucible,* Gibbs had to be carted into his chair in full public view. It was rumored that Elinor sometimes had to write his reviews for him. Lillian Hellman was so outraged by his inebriation when he reviewed her play *Another Part of the Forest* in 1946 that she wrote him, "Serious critics should treat writing seriously . . . [Y]ou did not do that. Because I respect you as a writer, I am more sympathetically sorry for that than you would probably believe."

Gibbs's alcoholism made him miserable. As he confided to his friend Sam Behrman after one ten-day bender, "Son of a bitch if I know how these things happen to me because they're always poison, or anyway no damn fun and the pieces nearly impossible to put together again afterwards. The big trouble with getting soused, really soused, is that you give too many awful people an edge on you."

Still, he felt convinced that alcohol was somehow integral to his persona. He told Nancy Hale, "Most of the time I lie on the sofa and think about you and what a god damn bore I'll be when I've been sober for six months." That is precisely the scenario in his casual piece "A Man May Be Down," wherein a fellow named Munson gives up drinking only to find it "a tiresome mistake" because "the gift of repartee left Munson the day he drank his last Martini." Similarly, in *Season in the Sun,* a stage direction describes the effects of the first drink that Gibbs's alter ego, George Crane, has had in five months: "It is an amazing metamorphosis. This is probably the first time we've seen the fundamental George."

Like many of his *New Yorker* brethren, Gibbs visited a number of genteel sanitariums in attempts to dry out, with varying degrees of success. "I feel much better already," he wrote Elinor during one stay, "but tremendously depressed, or maybe humiliated. It's miserable to think that I can't cope with life any better than these other lunatics, and worse to realize that it's a regular thing with them—a week at

Foord's every year to put your character together again. I can't face a prospect like that, if I have to spend the rest of my life on the wagon." In spite of this humiliation, his sobriety never stuck.

THERE WAS ONE thing in Gibbs's life that made him genuinely happy. That was Fire Island. He first explored the fragile barrier beach off the South Coast of Long Island when he was a child, sailing there with his cousins from Merrick before World War I. Years later, he bought a place at Ocean Beach that he called "The Studio" and cherished it for twenty years. He loved the sun, the ocean, the sand, and the freedom they all represented. For many years there were no phones on Fire Island, only a telegraph office, so Gibbs could fully escape his work—and his demons. He would drink, but he would also simply sit on the beach, his knees tucked up under his chin, soaking up the rays. In "Dark Cloud in the Sky," he writes explicitly of his love for the place through his character, George Crane:

> I guess I really like it here better than any place in the world, he thought, and for the moment his delight in Fire Island, in this one place where life could be slowed to the almost forgotten tempo of childhood seemed as much as he could bear. The distance from New York, by train and boat, was only fifty terrestrial miles, but in spirit it was enormous. You ate and slept in the dark, untidy little houses that lay along the dunes between the sea and the bay, but most of your life was spent on the loveliest beach in the East, a narrow, sunny shelf that ran thirty miles along the Atlantic, from Babylon to Quogue, and here you just lay in the sun, and all the staggering complexity of your relations with others, the endless, hopeless bookkeeping of your personal morality with too many people, could be put aside for a little while. It was a state of wonderful irresponsibility, a time in which you belonged to nobody but yourself, on which there were no immediate claims from the world.

"I am a child of the sun," he wrote to Nancy Hale, "and in the summer I am happy, singing from morning till night, but when it gets cold I die."

In 1954, with his friends Bill Birmingham and Herman Wechsler, Gibbs founded the *Fire Islander,* a weekly summer newspaper. As he had almost a generation before, Gibbs edited a small broadsheet for a local readership. This time, though, he was the boss, and the *Fire Islander* was one of his proudest achievements. He declared in his first issue:

> We worked once on a Long Island weekly where the lady in charge of social notes saved herself a good deal of time and bother by confining herself almost exclusively to the activities of a Mr. and Mrs. Gil Manifold and their charming daughter, Belle, all of whom happened to be cousins of hers. The subscribers were told practically everything about this pleasingly named family, right down to what they ate for breakfast, but they heard very little about anybody else. It was generally felt that the Manifolds got a little monotonous. *The Fire Islander* will try to avoid this kind of reporting. It will, in fact, try not to concentrate on any one group. . . . What we hope to do, in short, is give you a complete picture of what goes on in this village. Our reporters will be instructed to get around. There are usually twenty little communities in any community. It will be their job every week to get in touch with a representative member of each of them and come back with the facts, upon which the editors will then superimpose grammar.

Gibbs's editorial philosophy reflected his devotion to the island. During the time he edited the *Fire Islander,* he eschewed his usual misanthropy and concentrated on the life of the residents, improving it wherever possible. Among his causes were the protection of the dunes, the construction of tennis courts, and the building of a new yacht basin. He also attacked the commercial interests who cast their nets in the bay, thus threatening "to make rod and line fishing extinct." He inveighed against the low-flying military jets that disturbed the peace. When asked why he had taken on this civic minded and often tedious job, Gibbs answered, "I'm in love with the goddam beach."

For three summers, Gibbs made the *Fire Islander* an eagerly awaited institution. To give it a more cosmopolitan flair, he courted contributions from friends like Thurber, O'Hara, Addams, Fred Allen, Herman Wouk, William Steig, Nathaniel Benchley, and John Lardner, paying everyone in lunch. But it was hard work, probably a little too hard, on top of his *New Yorker* responsibilities. "I have been mixed up in a lot of suicidal enterprises in my life," he wrote, "but nothing like this." After forty issues, Gibbs handed his brainchild over to a new team.

The newspaper might have reinvigorated, for a time, a man already in decline. But when Gibbs let go of the *Fire Islander,* something seemed to go out of him. For some years, he had been feeling isolated in what was perceived as a more "serious" atmosphere at the postwar *New Yorker,* epitomized by the devotion of an entire issue in 1946 to John Hersey's "Hiroshima." The neuroses of the new Cold War were not exactly hospitable to Gibbs's role as comic exploder of pretense, pomposity, and bunk in general. "I had an idea [that] humor was supposed to be against the rules around here," he wrote E. B. White in 1947. "The moral climate is against it. Right at this minute there is a son of a bitch down the hall ([John] Bainbridge) writing a thirty-two-part Profile of Stalin."

Gibbs was in poor health, as well; a 1947 operation for pleurisy, which involved removing portions of his rib cage, left him with a physical slump so pronounced that his clothes had to be altered accordingly. Then, with the death of Ross in 1951, Gibbs lost the closest thing he had to a father. Not long after Ross passed away, McKelway confided to Behrman about Gibbs's increasingly dramatic mood swings:

> I've been worried about him off and on for years. He goes through these bad periods and then suddenly and unaccountably turns some kind of corner, cheers up, and does a lot of work. I don't know what we can do for him . . . I heard from Charlie Addams that Elinor had said she was more worried about him now than she had ever been before . . . Gibbs being the man he is, I wouldn't be at all surprised to hear that, since I last talked to him on the phone, he has completed his new play and has written a novel comparable to *War and Peace.* On the other hand,

the fact that his success with *Season,* and the security that should have come to him . . . have not made him less anxious but seem to have made him more so, and more melancholy, suggests to me that his trouble may be deeper than I ever thought.

"My own feeling about *The New Yorker* is that it is deteriorating at almost exactly the right rate for me," Gibbs wrote to Thurber toward the end. "I seem to be wearing very thin as a writer and the theatre stuff I'm doing now would be embarrassing in the magazine we used to know." In fact, in his last couple of years he did almost nothing but publish theater criticism, increasingly lengthy and less quotably barbed. He rarely came to the office. Staff members called his cubicle "The Shrine" and kept it untouched. In 1956, young editor William Murray was installed in the Shrine. In two years, he never saw its previous occupant once. Publicly, Gibbs talked about resigning. But when he mentioned this to an actress friend, Pat Collinge, she implored him, "Oh please, please don't. We *need* you."

Gibbs died on Fire Island on September 16, 1958. It was Elinor who found him, in bed, with an advance copy of his last book, *More in Sorrow*—and, according to legend, a cigarette still lodged between his fingers. The official cause was congestion and cyanosis of the lungs. But the attending physician falsified the death certificate, claiming that an autopsy had been performed when in fact none had. The fakery was apparently in deference to a distraught Elinor, who suspected suicide.

Privately, O'Hara decided that Gibbs had drunk himself to death. "I had hoped, without much hope, that he might last out this phase and be one of my old-age cronies as he had been of my youth," he wrote. "But the whole business of life was stacked against Gibbs. I know of no one who had better reasons for being soured, and he is all the proof you need that things do not even up in the end. They never evened up for him."

Nonetheless his work, long neglected, endures. Eulogizing him in *The New Yorker,* E. B. White recalled one of Gibbs's funniest casuals, "Ring Out, Wild Bells," about the time he played the role of Puck in a Riverdale Country School version of *A Midsummer Night's Dream.*

Gibbs's mother had made him a jester costume, covered in tiny bells. The director told him, "I want you to be a little whirlwind," and Gibbs was exactly that, bouncing and dancing all over the stage— and thereby drowning out much of the dialogue. "He was, in all truth, a whirlwind," wrote White, "and in these offices can still be heard the pure and irreplaceable sound of his wild bells."

More than half a century after Gibbs's death, his unique tintinnabulation rings out from these pages as well.

The Editorial We

*"Notes and Comment" and
"The Talk of the Town"*

THE SOUND NEWSREELS, whatever else they do, certainly confirm America's worst suspicions about foreigners. Because of the necessity of introducing noise into the reel, practically all news events are accompanied either by speech or by music. Audiences therefore always see Europeans gathered in groups, listening to something. In general this confirms what the audiences have believed all along—that foreigners are characterized by a persistent lethargy and a desire for free entertainment. Most of the recent shots from France, for example, are of peasants singing in their vineyards, or of musical goings-on among the art students—both views bearing out the common notion that the French are occupied largely with making wine and singing dirty songs. Shots from England invariably show the guard being changed (ta ta ta-ta) at Buckingham Palace, or passing in review before the Prince of Wales—proving that the English, though lazy, are warlike and we better keep a big navy. Italians are always standing under balconies, listening to Mussolini and being heated into a nation of firebrands. Germans drink beer and sing while they drink, confirming our fear that they still don't realize how badly they were defeated. Spiggoties dance the tango and kill bulls. All, in other words, is just as everybody surmised, and foreigners are after all just a bunch of foreigners.

July 26, 1930

★ ★ ★

A GENERAL BLURRING of the critical faculty is, of course, one of the first symptoms of the mood for war. A little while ago we were reading a book about the Spanish revolution in which the author, musing over a battlefield, remarked, "There is always a certain nobility about our dead." This sentence, which would have seemed fantastic to everybody back in 1920, was quoted by several critics who apparently endorsed the proposition that a corpse can be ennobled or degraded in appearance by the political opinions it used to hold. The most astonishing example of the whole thing, however, came to us in a newsreel which showed the Armistice Day celebration in London when the King laid a wreath on the Cenotaph in memory of the dead while the living soldiers lined the square. "Suddenly," to quote the announcer, who spoke with horror and dismay, "a madman broke through the ranks, shouting, 'This is hypocrisy! You are preparing for war!'" There is no doubt that the man was crazy, but certainly his comment was grimly apposite, with the rather devastating humor of a family scandal revealed by a child. The audience we watched, however, didn't laugh, and as far as we know, the newspapers treated the incident without irony, but rather as a tribute to the royal serenity under trying circumstances. Both these things are funny, ladies and gentlemen, funny little things that can happen in twenty years.

December 11, 1937

★ ★ ★

WE WONDER, IN fact, how closely tragedy and rapture balance for the average child at Christmas. The lovely things—the excitement and insomnia, the stocking shapeless with mystery, the tree trimmed and lit—are as familiar as "The Night Before Christmas." The heartbreak is less easily recalled, but at the time it can outweigh all the rest. We remember, for instance, one Christmas when a scheming publisher put out a special edition of "Treasure Island," disagreeably illustrated in color, and we got three copies of it. It was explained to us, of course, that they could all be exchanged, but a child lives in an immediate world and anyway he has no faith in the mysterious readjustments of commerce. Those books were a dead loss and they ruined our holiday. They were not quite as bad, however, as the present which for years had always been the most magnificent of all and then somehow, one Christmas, was basely transmuted into a twenty-dollar gold piece and salted away, as far as we knew, forever in a bank. Never again did we feel quite the same about Christmas, or, for that matter, about banks.

December 25, 1937

★ ★ ★

DOWN IN ATLANTA, where anything may happen, a painting of a battlefield has been wired so that distant sounds of conflict issue from the canvas when you push a button. A Dr. Orestes H. Caldwell, who has some left-handed connection with this miracle, reports that it is only a beginning.

"For example," he says, "the famous masterpiece of Rosa Bonheur, 'The Horse Fair,' might be given an accompaniment of clattering hoofs, adding to its pulsing realism. Family portraits could be fitted up with the voices of the departed. Paintings of statesmen might be wired for sound, with recordings of their most stirring orations."

Dr. Caldwell's prophecy is as grim and complete as a skull, and there isn't much we can add to it. There is not much, indeed, to be said to any man who wishes to rig up his ancestors for sound. We wondered for an uneasy minute what plans the radio engineers might be meditating for "The Last Supper." On the whole, perhaps, we'd rather not be told.[1]

March 26, 1938

★ ★ ★

WE ARE ALWAYS astonished when returning natives tell us about the political fury of the screen writers on the Coast. Except for the few hours a month when he tries to think how a giant pie containing five hundred gorgeous dames might logically be introduced into the screen version of "Oedipus Rex," the writer devotes most of his life to protests of one kind or another. Nowhere is the outcry against Fascism so passionate or articulate; nowhere is "Tory" a term of such cold and dreadful contempt. We wonder why these fortunate people, whose meanest thought is worth a million dollars, should be so cross. It is commendable but mysterious, since the land of the lotus-eaters is traditionally barren soil for revolt. Perhaps the troubled artist turns to protest only because he finds insufficient emotional outlet in his work. Or perhaps his ardor is just the wistful quest for thought in a land where thought is dead. It is quite possible that neither of these explanations is the right one. We only know that it delights us to think of a large group of people profitably engaged in degrading the public taste and at the same time hotly determined to elevate the public welfare. This strangely contradictory ideal is, we imagine, one of the reasons that Hollywood continues to baffle the social historian, who goes out confidently to report a minor phenomenon and comes back babbling in an unknown tongue.

May 7, 1938

★ ★ ★

NERVOUS CITIZENS HAVE complained that their minds are being unsettled by the mournful toot of river and harbor shipping, especially between four and five in the morning, when their vitality is at its ebb. Much of this tumult is unnecessary, says Henry H. Curran, the Deputy Mayor; it is nothing more than "conversation" between the captains of inland craft. Necessity in this case is probably a matter of opinion. What does Mr. Curran know of the inward necessity of a tugboat captain adrift at dawn below the sleeping city, how desperate his urge to reach out through the gloom for others of his kind? That hoarse cry from the river, murdering sleep in Tudor City, may come from the heart of a lonely man. Who, safe in bed, can gauge his need or grudge him fellowship?

July 30, 1938

★ ★ ★

THE CAMERAMEN HAD to wait eleven hours but the next day every New York paper, with the exception of the *Times* and the *Herald-Tribune*, was able to print one or more pictures of the body of a suicide as it fell from the seventeenth floor of the Gotham Hotel. We regard these photographs as in cruelly and inexcusably bad taste. The practice of publishing gratuitously offensive pictures started when the *Daily News*, to its perpetual shame, used one of the electrocution of Ruth Snyder. Since then, with the two exceptions noted above, all the papers and a great many magazines have followed the precedent set by the *News*, also to their shame. There is a reasonable justification, of course, for printing pictures of the dead in war and even of those who are killed in automobile accidents or strikes or under any circumstances in which publicity can serve a healthy purpose. There is no possible justification for printing pictures like those of the Warde suicide, beyond the contemptible one that readers demand such pictures and that each paper has to use them because all the others do. For all these papers, finally, to print these pictures and then in their news columns to comment virtuously on the morbidity of the crowds who gathered on the street seems to us the year's most distinguished example of journalistic hypocrisy. There is, as far as we know, nothing to prevent a general agreement among the newspapers of the city not to use such photographs, except the fear that it would be violated at the first opportunity by one of them. We refuse to believe that this is a valid excuse; that the press can't operate except on the level of its lowest practitioner. On the other hand, however, we are often very naïve.[2]

August 6, 1938

★ ★ ★

DAY AFTER DAY Laura Jean Schanze, a rather sinister little girl in the Clinton, New Jersey, public school, sat at her desk writing down the mistakes her teacher, a Miss Melick, made in English. Miss Melick said "poopils" when she meant "pupils" and "arn" when she meant "iron;" once, in an unexplained crisis, she exclaimed, "There aren't no Chinamens in here!" In the end Laura Jean's dark industry was rewarded and Miss Melick was dismissed by the school board. This episode illuminates a quality we have always felt in little girls— something derisive, watchful, and colder than the climate on the moon. For some reason it reminds us of a conversation we overheard on the beach the other day. Two young ladies, each perhaps fifteen, lay on the sand and talked of love.

"So," said one of them, "he told me he was giving up smoking for me. For *me*, for God's sake! He thinks I'm worried because he's stunting his nasty little growth or something."

"They all do," said the other, and the baby gorgons laughed together, a silvery music, ancient and terrible.

August 27, 1938

★   ★   ★

CELLOPHANE HAD ITS thirtieth birthday last week; for about a third of that time it has been a tremendous factor in our life. We try to remember what things were like before the wonder came. Was everything much damper then? Were there noticeably more germs in our food? We can't remember. It is the cross of science that men so quickly take her boons for granted, forgetting the barbarous past. The only thing we do remember is that in those days, before almost every article we bought had to be shelled out of its slippery envelope, it was a lot easier to get at things. We started to figure out how much time we had lost over ten years because of cellophane, but suddenly realized that there was a fallacy in our reasoning. We haven't lost a second. Science, cleverly anticipating exactly this point, has arranged to keep our account with time in perfect balance. The hours she has stolen from us with cellophane she has rendered back, unto the ultimate decimal, with the zipper, the dial telephone, and streamlined transportation. Peace, it's wonderful.

October 1, 1938

★   ★   ★

THERE IS A garden behind our new place on Fifty-first Street, full at the moment of strangled vines and prowling, angry cats, but capable, we suppose, of being made beautiful. We don't know what to do with it. There is something very silly about having a garden attached to the lower two floors of a converted brownstone house. It is absurd to be mowing your lawn under the level, derisive eyes of thirty-five ladies curling their hair in the windows of the great apartment building across the way. All the little chores, in fact, which might easily be pleasant enough outside the city limits take on a strong air of burlesque when conducted in the shadow of somebody else's washing. Even supposing that a man were self-possessed enough to plant and tend his foolish plot, it would be worth his life to sit in it with a thin rain of cigarette butts falling around him and an occasional tomato can winging down from the sixteenth floor. When the day comes, of course, we can use it for a bombproof shelter, but in the meantime there it is, full of the vines and the cats, a reproach every time we look out the window.

November 5, 1938

* * *

IT SEEMS TO us that little Orson Welles, rather painfully injured a while ago when a space rocket he had been playing with backfired on him, made his mistake not so much in the form of his experiment as in the technique with which he carried it out. In speaking about his embarrassing experience to the press, Mr. Welles said, "The broadcast was performed as if occurring in the future and as if it were then related by a survivor of a past occurrence." People anchored to the present listening to a future event described by an invisible man to whom it happened in the past are in a bad way to start off with, and are going to be uneasy no matter what is said. Combine this with chromium-plated Martians operating death rays, and you may easily get panic. Probably the lesson to be learned from all this is that it is unwise to deal with the time principles of J. B. Priestley over a mechanical device which in itself is still a little staggering to the common mind. Electricity and metaphysics, Orson, just don't mix. Also, as we said once before, a public that unhesitatingly accepts a ventriloquial act without wanting to see that there really is a dummy can accept practically anything, including the total destruction of the Atlantic seaboard.

November 12, 1938

★ ★ ★

LAST WEEK THE *Herald Tribune* sent one of its young men out with forty Jefferson nickels to learn what the city thought about their design. We read his story without reaching any especially valuable conclusions—some people thought the new coin was pretty, but most of them merely regarded it with the mild suspicion with which freeborn Americans look on all government innovations. One sentence, however, stuck in our mind. "The first stop," it said, "was in a bar at Greenwich and Cortlandt Streets." There was something familiar about this, an old echo, something we had read many times before, and suddenly we realized that practically every newspaper symposium we could remember had started off in a bar—sometimes in two or three bars. We don't know why this should be, unless it takes at least one quick one to put a man in the proper frame of mind to ask complete strangers feeble-minded questions. Nevertheless, it is obviously sound technique, having got results through the years, and we recommend it to professors of journalism, who, it often seems to us, devote too much time to how to write a story and too little to how to get the damn thing in the first place. It may be, though, that forty nickels is a lot to give a new man. Ten (five beers) is all we'd give any pupil of ours.

November 26, 1938

★ ★ ★

IN HIS BOOK about the Algonquin Hotel, Mr. Frank Case expresses his deep affection for writers, actors, and other public entertainers, and then goes on to propound one of the most disastrous theories we have ever heard. Chuckling, Mr. Case tells us about the time the late John L. Sullivan took his walking stick and knocked all the glasses off a shelf in back of the bar. This kind of behavior, it appears, has Mr. Case's whole approval and his episcopal blessing. "We should not," he says, "expect extraordinary folk to behave like commonplace folk . . . I think that gifted people should not only be tolerated but should be encouraged in their strange and tempera-mental antics." The literary or dramatic performer is hard enough to keep in order under the best conditions: six drinks will make practically any actor insufferable, and five can turn the gentlest poet into a spectacular nuisance. It is only because the rest of the world has always regarded people of artistic impulses with profound suspi-cion and has been prepared to deal violently with them that they have remained in even tolerable adjustment to society. A remark like Mr. Case's can undo the work of centuries. Let an actor or a writer know that it is O.K. for him to shout and throw glasses, and you are on your way to bedlam. We are not, we're afraid, going to be able to work up much sympathy about anything that happens in Mr. Case's bear pit during the next few weeks. You asked for tem-perament, sir, we shall say as the riot cars come screaming through Forty-fourth Street, and, lo, you've got it.

December 10, 1938

★ ★ ★

WE HAD LUNCH with an actor last Wednesday and it was one of the most unsettling experiences we can remember. What telephon-ing went on, a new handset brought to the table almost before he'd finished with the old one, what tender messages written on scraps of paper and carried by the waiter to beautiful women eating mixed green salads, what waves and bows and little visits round the room. It was like trying to talk to a man in a high wind.

"What's the matter with you?" we asked him finally. "What's the idea of all the *élan?*"

He smiled at Mrs. Tiffany Saportas and threw a kiss to Mrs. Jules Brulatour, who was wearing her Balenciaga black crêpe and the skins of several small animals.

"I beg your pardon," he murmured vaguely. "What did you say?"

"Never mind," we replied, "the hell with it," and pushing our *baba au rhum* in his lap, we went up to Central Park to look at the bears.

January 7, 1939

★ ★ ★

WHEN THE REVOLUTION starts, the first aristocrat will die in one of those shabby little bars in the theatre district, and it will happen on the night of a big opening—probably something with Tallulah Bankhead in it. For about three-quarters of the year these melancholy deadfalls represent home to the residents of the neighborhood. Earl the Gimp has his special place at Marty's bar; Dorthy puts nickels in the piano while she waits for something to turn up; Paul and the mob drop in for a glass of beer. There is talk and beer and plenty of room for everybody. Let the lights go up on the marquee across the street, however, and all that is changed. With the first intermission, Café Society, thirsty from too much concentration and far removed from 21, hits Marty's dump like a flock of homing peacocks. Earl finds himself pinned into a corner with his mouth clogged with ermine and his soul black with hate; Dorthy goes on sullenly playing the piano whenever she can get at it, although she knows she can't get anywhere against this kind of competition; Paul and his mob are elbowed away from the bar by the boys from the Racquet Club—all, generally speaking, younger and in better condition. Marty, a traitor to his class, can't be bothered with serving beer when people are calling for Seagram's and Courvoisier (there is only weak poison in the bottles he shoves over the bar, of course, but this is just a commercial expedient and has nothing to do with his political sympathies). The talk is loud and fashionable, and you couldn't get two bucks down on Mexita in the Fifth at Hialeah if you were Owney Madden himself. The joint smells like a girls' school.

One day this is going to go too far. Some guy in a silk hat is going to push Earl once too often, right across the thin line that separates him from homicide; some dame in a fur coat is going to talk out of turn to Dorthy and wind up on her ear; the Racquet Club boys will get too tough and find that Paul is not unarmed. It may be a year and it may be next week, but it will come. You can count on that. Don't say we didn't warn you.

February 4, 1939

★ ★ ★

IT IS HARD to say how much of the Bund's fury against Dorothy Thompson was political and how much was the irritation of any group of solemn men confronted with a lady laughing in a superior and exasperating manner for reasons that are mysterious to them.[3] Their feelings were probably not unlike the indignation and bewilderment of a Shriner who finds that his wife is amused by his singular hat, and to that extent the engagement at the Garden came down to a war of sex rather than ideology. Regardless of why Miss Thompson's laughter annoyed the Nazis, however, there can be no question that it had a healthy effect, and we would like to hear more such public merriment around the town. Merriment may not be precisely the word—after the meeting Miss Thompson said that her performance was not entirely spontaneous; the irony of Fascism invoking the Golden Rule seemed to her at least as shocking as funny—but in any case she laughed and it was more damaging to the composure of Herr Kuhn and his mob than all the angry clamor in the streets.[4]

We thought that there were several other occasions for this kind of wry and incredulous laughter during the same week. The D.A.R. has reached a point where it seems to be going out too diligently for its comic effects, but nevertheless there was a neat if rather elementary irony in its decision to bar Miss Marian Anderson, a distinguished Negro singer, from Constitution Hall, which, of course, takes its name from a document guaranteeing Miss Anderson freedom from racial discrimination. There was humor, too, in Governor Moore's appointment of Frank Hague, Jr., as a judge in the Court of Errors and Appeals, thus making the son an instrument of the law in a state where the father, by his own appointment, *is* the law. "It will make his dad happy," said Governor Moore. It makes us happy, too, in a peculiar sort of way.

We were also pleased to learn that ex-District Attorney Dodge had loved Jimmy Hines "like a mother loves her son." It is nice to think of the love, brooding and maternal though ungrammatical, which the public prosecutor bore for one of the merry boys in the back room. It is nice, too, to think of the four detectives who were so conscientious in guarding the public safety that they didn't hesitate to attack a small, elderly man who was lost in the subway. We even laughed a little at Mr. Lewis Mumford's book called "Men Must Act," in which he argued that the first step to be taken in the preservation of democracy is logically the abolition of free speech, and, in much the same spirit, we laughed when we read that Great Britain and France were anxious to give official recognition to one military dictatorship in order to frustrate two other military dictatorships.

All these things called for laughter, and from various portents we read in the sky many more will before the spring comes in. We live in merry times, Dorothy. Take care of your larynx.

March 4, 1939

★　★　★

STRUGGLING TO PUT down what we think about the World's Fair, we are conscious of our own inadequacy and, perhaps, impertinence. If what we write is occasionally bad-tempered, it is because the city that grew overnight on that desolate swamp is too dazzling for our eyes and the words for its splendors are not easy to find on our keyboard. The little mind, confronted by too great a dream come true, usually has to take its choice between levity and madness. When we laugh at the grandeur of some of the conceptions in Flushing (the cosmic ray illuminating the World of Tomorrow; the cosmic squirrel burying his nut for five thousand years), it is because we ourself have never dared to dream of anything more spectacular than getting a fifteen-cent magazine out on time with most of its pages right side up. When we speak flippantly of the miracles of order and beauty so casually wrought by Grover Whalen, it is with the secret envy of a group of men who for over fourteen years have been trying vainly to perfect a rational system for getting small pieces of paper from one end of a hall to the other.[5] Life will probably always be like that—the men of vision creating, the little men carping, with terror and amazement in their hearts.

WE SPENT AN hour in the library looking at pictures of old World's Fairs and reading what contemporary opinion had to say about them. It might all have come out of Flushing this week. How strange and gratifying, our fathers wrote, that civilization should have culminated in their lifetime, that *their* Fair should have been the stick in the sand to mark the highest reaching of the tide. How quaint, we said to ourself, looking at the scrolled and turreted buildings at the old Chicago Fair. How quaint, we suppose our grandson will say when he comes across pictures of this one in all its streamlined and functional majesty. We tried to think what *his* Fair will look like, fifty years from now, but our mind, too, wouldn't go beyond the miracles of the present. Perhaps, after all, we thought, 1939 will be remembered as the year when the human mind actually did reach the limit of its ingenuity, and Grover Whalen, the flower of a race, built the towers that could never be improved.

AS A MATTER of fact, it often seems to us that our own generation is the most arrogant and self-conscious of all. The men of the past were sure that they lived in the Golden Age, but they stopped short of considering themselves immortal and the small details of their culture as indispensable to posterity. The Time Capsule, buried on the assumption that our time of all others will be of peculiar interest to the historian of 6939, seems to us half wistful, half comic. The human anxiety to die but never be forgotten is touching, but the notion that in five thousand years the period between 1920 and 1940 will appear as any more than a little breathing space between two great wars strikes us as an almost perfect comment on the vanity of a strange day. We sometimes wish we could be there when the Capsule is finally opened and the men of tomorrow are confronted with the crumbling vestiges of a civilization.

"Where in hell did you dig *that* thing up?" we can hear the great archeologist ask fretfully, as the cockeyed films unroll.

April 29, 1939

★   ★   ★

WE WERE INTERESTED to learn how the King of England wants Mrs. Roosevelt to make his bed (two light-weight blankets covered with a silken coverlet and, at the foot, a down puff, not folded but pushed back in accordion pleats).[6] The *Daily News*, commenting on these instructions, is a little indignant about the whole thing. "The capital in general," it says, "is beginning to be irked by British emphasis on the prerogatives of royalty in a land which decided 150 years ago it wanted no part of said royalty." We are a great admirer of the *News*, and on the whole opposed to royal prerogatives, but here our sympathy is entirely with the King. The average guest-room bed in America is a terrible mess, and we are for anything that promises to make it better. The King's bed, we would like to inform every Connecticut and Long Island hostess, is the way a bed ought to be made, and the way we expect to find ours from now on. Please be especially careful with that puff.

May 27, 1939

★   ★   ★

A YOUNG MOTHER we know has sent us a song, or a chant, or a poem, or something that her four-year-old son made up and sings every evening in his bathtub.[7] It goes on practically forever, like the Old Testament, and she was able to copy down only part of it, but even this fragment seems to us one of the handsomest literary efforts of the year, as well as another proof that children are the really pure artists, with complete access to their thoughts and no foolish reticence. It is sung, she says, entirely on one note except that the voice drops on the last word in every line. We reprint it here because seldom, we think, has the vision of any heart's desire been put down so explicitly:

> *He will just do nothing at all,*
> *He will just sit there in the noonday sun.*
> *And when they speak to him, he will not answer them,*
> *Because he does not care to.*
> *He will stick them with spears and put them in the garbage.*
> *When they tell him to eat his dinner, he will just laugh at them,*
> *And he will not take his nap, because he does not care to.*
> *He will not talk to them, he will not say nothing,*
> *He will just sit there in the noonday sun.*
> *He will go away and play with the Panda.*
> *He will not speak to nobody because he doesn't have to.*
> *And when they come to look for him they will not find him,*
> *Because he will not be there.*
> *He will put spikes in their eyes and put them in the garbage,*
> *And put the cover on.*
> *He will not go out in the fresh air or eat his vegetables*
> *Or make wee-wee for them, and he will get as thin as a marble.*
> *He will not do nothing at all.*
> *He will just sit there in the noonday sun.*

July 1, 1939

★   ★   ★

AS WE WRITE this, four hours after the British Prime Minister declared war, it is still hard to understand what the headlines mean. Unless there is a miracle, ten million more young men will die (very few of them especially heroically or quickly); millions of children will die (very few of whom had had time to form very strong or dangerous political opinions); cities that rose proudly and slowly over the centuries will be ugly ruins between a morning and a night. The thought that built them, the thought of life, was turned off at six o'clock today with the speaking of a sentence in London; from now on, and for how long no man can know, there will be only the thought of death.

The best minds in the world will now think continuously and cleverly of death—planning new and better ways to annihilate an army in the open field (the planes will be very useful this time); planning ways to crush and stifle men in their impregnable shelters (it is a tribute to our ingenuity that no shelter these days remains impregnable very long); planning bombs that set incendiary fires which can't be put out (a much more economical way of destroying a city than the old-fashioned one of just trying to blow it up); planning death just as thoroughly and competently for old men and women and children as for the soldiers (this war will be quite impartial; it will play no favorites).

The war against the flesh will be a terrible thing, and the war against the spirit will be terrible, too—the hatred for a political idea turned almost imperceptibly into hatred for a race; the thought of killing turned adroitly from something shameful but necessary if freedom is to survive into an act beautiful and noble for its own sake; the mystical idea of God degraded into the likeness of an angry man, hating half the world.

It is hard to understand or believe any of these things now on Sunday morning in New York. The city from our window seems unutterably safe; the high buildings strong and invulnerable against the sky; the streets we grew up in quiet and almost deserted on a holiday. The plane flying low behind the R.C.A. Building toward the Hudson carries no threat to anyone (the children on their way to roller-skate in the Park don't even bother to look up at it); the voice on the radio speaks of a tennis game and not of war. "The Australians lead four games to two," it says.

We try to reconcile the cheerful and familiar details of our life with news that may well mean the end of all of them, but it is too soon. The ten million men who will die are still just an arbitrary figure, an estimate from another war; the children who will be starved or bombed belong to people we can never know; the bombs themselves will fall only on strange names on a map. It will be another day or perhaps another week before we realize fully the implications of what we've read this morning, before the horror is personal and real. As a matter of fact, though, there's no particular hurry. We'll all have plenty of time to get used to war. It's very likely that a good many of us will have all the rest of our lives.

September 9, 1939

★ ★ ★

WE SAW A man off the other day, on his way to be a war correspondent in Europe, on his way to keep a rendezvous with History. Where, we wanted to ask him, do you expect to meet this dame? How are you going to recognize her when you do? Mr. Ernest Hemingway, an old beau of hers, thought he recognized her in Spain, disguised as the basic conflict between Fascism and Communism. He had the wrong girl. Many have claimed they saw her in Moscow, a red angel of salvation. This apparently was a mistake, too. Within two years, she has turned up in Vienna, Munich, Prague, and Danzig, but few of the correspondents present on these occasions recognized her very clearly. They saw something hurrying through the fog, but whether it was History and what she was up to was any man's guess. She is sure to be around again soon—at the West Wall, or in Switzerland, Belgium, or even Italy. She may, in fact, show up practically anywhere, and in any disguise. It is going to be very hard to catch her for an interview. This is not the History that used to love to jump up on Richard Harding Davis's lap and whisper in his ear. This is another girl altogether.

October 14, 1939

★ ★ ★

CHEMICAL ENGINEERS MAKE the best husbands, only about ten per cent of the women who marry them being really miserable. They are closely followed by ministers, college professors, and football coaches. Among the worst husbands, on the other hand, are barbers, musicians, travelling salesmen, and plumbers, whose capacity

for annoying their wives is terrific. Dentists, lawyers, and advertising men are about halfway down the list—not good, not bad. Writers aren't mentioned at all, possibly because *their* records are just too
appalling for print. We learned these rather odd facts from a book
called "Predicting Success or Failure in Marriage," by a couple of
doctors named Burgess and Cottrell, who spent nine years and sent
out more than five hundred questionnaires in getting them together.
The reason ladies are happiest with people like teachers and ministers, the authors say, is that these men are apt to stay in one place,
where they can be watched, while the others drift around, getting in
jams. All this seems reasonable enough, but there is one other little
point that keeps on bothering us. How about the other side of the
picture? How about the boys who married all these confiding ladies? Are they happy? We doubt it. Show us, we say, a wife who will
fill in a questionnaire about her private life and mail it back to a couple
of strange doctors, and we will show you a husband who wishes he
were in the Foreign Legion.

October 21, 1939

★ ★ ★

FOR MORE THAN three years we have been watching a very
bothersome and heroic struggle in the publishing world—*Life* magazine trying to figure out a way to print a picture of a living, breathing
woman with absolutely no clothes on. The especial problem of *Life*,
of course, is that everything in it has to have the air of a respectable,
high-minded commentary on America. *Life*, that is, can't publish a
picture of a woman undressed over the caption "Woman Undressed."
It has to Say Something. We are glad to be able to tell you that in
their issue of February 12th, after years of frustration and seventeen
million angle shots that almost got there but not quite, the editors
have finally seen the answer. Like all truly great things, it was simple.
They merely photographed a life class at the Yale Art School. This
had Yale, it had Art, it had Class, it had America; it had everything,
including no clothes on. It was *Life's* dream come true—a girl who

had shucked (and no fooling) but had done it for her country. It was a tremendous relief to us. And a very interesting picture, too.[8]

March 2, 1940

★ ★ ★

IT IS HARD to say why Department of Sanitation men should have to be so much stronger than anybody else. In fact, we think it's a mistake. If there is one thing the matter with street-cleaners today, it is too much verve, too much agility, too much strength. Lying in our bed beside the murdered corpse of sleep, we have often listened to them as they threw the cans around or sluiced the street so merrily. In addition to these mechanical and necessary sounds, the air has usually been full of bits of song, fragments of anecdote, and loud and careless laughter. The effect has been unmistakably that of well men, happy at their work. The new standards of fitness, according to the N.Y.U. professor who thought them up, will make our street-cleaners about the most perfect physical specimens in the world, and we doubt very much if we are going to be able to stand it. Give us, we say, a group of soft, dyspeptic men who will lift the big cans cautiously and fight the struggling hose in grim silence, with no breath left over for song or conversation.

March 9, 1940

★ ★ ★

WE HAVE BEEN thinking off and on all week about Shirley Temple, who has retired at eleven with three million dollars. By almost any standards, Miss Temple has already lived a full life. She was the greatest box-office attraction of her time; she was on intimate terms with many powerful and fascinating people, including Bill Robinson and the President of the United States; she set fashions and established manners; her biography was printed in the *Saturday Evening Post*; her political opinions were even discussed in Congress.[9] To a certain extent, we are sorry for her now, since it is not going to be easy for her to adjust herself to the quiet rhythms of the classroom. We are even more sorry for her teachers. Miss Temple has a great deal of first-hand experience that will make her a tough one to impress with the usual facts and legends. A young woman who has grossed twenty million dollars at the box office in five years is not going to think very highly of Napoleon, who could only get fifteen for the entire Mississippi Basin. A girl who was accused of trying to overthrow the government before she was ten may easily wonder what was keeping Joan of Arc. "Pooh," we can hear her say, on learning that Juliet was full fourteen. "That hag!"

May 25, 1940

★ ★ ★

WENDELL WILLKIE, A Republican Presidential candidate as the result of some mysterious upheaval of nature, says that he is against the view of America as a free-lunch counter. At the same time, the Department of Agriculture announces that the average citizen on relief can legitimately spend $4.90 a month for food, or roughly five cents a meal. For this amount he can enjoy beef stew (two ounces of beef, a quarter of a carrot, a quarter of an onion, and half a potato), half a slice of bread with a pat of oleomargarine, a cup of coffee with milk, and a prune. In one paper, we saw a picture of Mrs. Franklin D. Roosevelt eating this tasty concoction, doubtless to demonstrate that it could actually be done. We mention these facts to correct what appears to be a slight misapprehension on Mr. Willkie's part. This nation, sir, is not a free-lunch counter. Hell, it's a banquet hall.

June 1, 1940

★ ★ ★

WE CAN HARDLY remember when we last looked a woman in the eye. The sunglasses, dark and almost opaque, that we used to see at Coney Island and Southampton have come into town, spreading

blackouts from ear to ear. "The smartest girls around town are having their own prescriptions made up," says *Mademoiselle*, showing us
pictures of "Nancy Van Vleck hiding behind giggly goggles at the
Pavilion Marguery," Patricia Suydam "in an anti-sun-glare pair,
up-swinging and pixilated," and Natalie Hyde in "oval, panda-eyed
specs." We don't know what the effect of all this will be. A girl who
always looks through green lenses is bound to see things in a dim
and bilious light; a girl accustomed to peering through amber will
be only mildly surprised when the world burns down. The effect on
men, we think, may be disconcerting, too; the relations between the
sexes worse than ever. Grandfather may not have known much about
a woman anatomically, but he had a better grasp of the whole problem than his grandson, who can see through almost all there is to a
girl except the windows of her soul. Many a youth, peering anxiously into his loved one's eyes to find out what the hell she is driving at, is going to come away with the wrong information or no
information at all. Many a grown man, baring his inmost heart to a
silent and apparently receptive girl all the long afternoon, will discover that she has merely been asleep.

August 10, 1940

★　★　★

WE CLOSED THE gray house on the beach last week with the
same feeling we have each year. It is always very sad to go. The last
time the colored umbrellas and the children's toys are brought up
from the beach and packed to go to town is the most melancholy of
our annual domestic rites. It always seems too soon to be going
back to the city. The air has an edge in September, but most of the
time the sky is washed a pale, clear blue and the water is warmer
than it was in June. At night the driftwood fire still keeps the living
room a bright and cheerful place in spite of the autumn wind off
the ocean; it is a better fire than the ones we'll lay in New York—
functional, not decorative, lit specifically to keep people warm.

It is always much too soon to be going back. Our excursions along
the hard, wet sand at the margin of the tide have taken us five miles

west to Fire Island Light and east as far as the colony of nudists, wild and shy as deer among their dunes, but there are wonders beyond these that we planned to see but somehow never did. Before the end of summer we meant to ride a surfboard in on the smooth, high-breaking waves or to hire a boat and fish for tuna out on the misty rim. We never did these things either; we never even reached that perfect shade of brown—something between the Emperor Jones and Sitting Bull—we could have had in just another week.

Theoretically, after spending three months in such a happy vacuum, we ought to be glad to get back to town and down to work. We aren't. As we came up out of Penn Station onto Eighth Avenue last Monday, it struck us that the old town had never looked worse. The idea of getting down to the office in the morning to bat out a living for our loved ones had seldom seemed more dismal or absurd.

September 14, 1940

★ ★ ★

"THIS BUILDING HAS been planned throughout for the convenience and comfort of our customers and the utmost efficiency in service," said an invitation we got from Tiffany's asking us to look over their new place up on Fifty-seventh Street. "It is equipped with the most advanced lighting and air-conditioning." Well, we can't help feeling that this is no way for a jewelry store to be. It reminds us of Woolworth's—no glamour, no intrigue. Let us buy even the crown jewels of Russia in such a high-class dump and we would come away depressed, convinced that we had merely exchanged a price nicely adjusted to the world market, with a reasonable profit to the management. If Tiffany's is interested, we have a dream store in the back of our mind. No scientific lighting, no comforts, no air-conditioning. You go in through a manhole, and a girl in a tight dress, smoking a reefer, takes you up to meet a clerk called the Professor, a man with a false beard, no eyebrows, and acid stains on his fingers. He takes you in the back room and unscrews a table leg, revealing a cunning cache. The rocks, glowing and slightly blood-stained, roll out in your trembling hand and you give him a wad of folding money. Just then the lights go up and down in a secret code and you peer through the dusty shutters to see a sinister man in a black hat and yellow shoes, lurking in front of Bonwit Teller's. Gathering up the ice, you escape hilariously through an underground passage that lets you out in the lobby of River House, your heart pounding like a hammer. That's *our* jewelry store. Send a man over with some secret ink, Tiffany, and we'll give you the rest of the dope.

November 2, 1940

★ ★ ★

A PIECE OF hot metal, about the size of a bean, fell from the sky and hit a Nebraska farmer sharply in the foot. Picking it up, he mailed it off to the American Meteorite Laboratory at Denver to find out if it was a meteor, a spent bullet, or perhaps just a fragment from some mysterious and distant explosion. In this tiny episode, we see somehow a symptom of what is wrong with the times. A simple man, ploughing his field, gets a clear sign from heaven. His grandfather would have accepted the miracle at its face value, as a divine warning or prophecy. He would have told his neighbors at meeting and the religious life of the countryside would have been richer for his experience. This man, however, ships the supernatural pellet to a laboratory for analysis. Skepticism, it seems to us, has reached its last frontier when every message from on high is promptly submitted to the scientists. There can be no more wonders when the first instinct of every citizen, confronted with the inscrutable, is to consult a research chemist or a psychoanalyst. Occasionally, at times like these, we understand dimly what the clergy is up against. We don't envy them.

December 7, 1940

★ ★ ★

EVERY YEAR WE go into the months of February and March with the same feeling of gloom and despair. It is the way we felt as a child when the Long Island trains suddenly dipped into their tunnel under the East River on their way to Pennsylvania Station—a chilly plunge into the long darkness, with the blood singing in our ears and sweat on our palms and never much hope of reaching Thirty-fourth Street alive. We can remember long, mysterious halts in the middle of the river when there was only an eggshell of steel and concrete between us and all the water in the Atlantic. We used to invent a thousand catastrophes—a nudge from one of those sharp keels overhead and then the water roaring and boiling against the windows; an explosion of deadly gas (in those days everybody knew that the tunnel was full of fumes only waiting for a spark); a head-on collision, hurling the cars through the walls of the tube as if they were paper. As we've said, it's always been the same way with the melancholy and dangerous journey through the next two months; we've never really hoped to see the spring. This year the chances for us and the world seem even more negligible than usual. The tunnel is darker than it ever was, the gas much thicker, and the walls are leaking like a sieve. God knows what's ahead on the track.

February 8, 1941

★ ★ ★

SOME OF OUR happiest hours were spent with the measles, we realized as we read that more than six hundred children in the city have been coming down with them every day for the past month or so. There is no form of escape quite like a disease which involves almost no suffering yet still calls for rigid quarantine, and it is a sad thing that few men are allowed to enjoy them more than once. We had ours when we were about twelve and away at boarding school. It was wonderful. The masters, being potential carriers, couldn't get at us, and we weren't supposed to do any studying anyway, on the ground that it was bad for our eyes. Life, in fact, resolved itself into a dreamy sequence of food, sleep, and long, beautiful thoughts, be-ginning and ending nowhere. The pleasures of childhood, generally speaking, have been greatly overrated by writers (almost invariably nervous and unpopular children), but too much can't be said for the measles. If we could go back to anything in our past, it would be to the quiet cot in the old infirmary, with our temperature at 99.2 degrees, spots on our stomach, and, outside the window, our less fortunate playmates slogging along to their classes in the thick March mud.

March 15, 1941

★ ★ ★

THE ANTI-SALOON LEAGUE, we learn, is on the march again. Already resolutions have been passed demanding that Congress stop the sale of the old devil's broth to soldiers and sailors; already a bill has been introduced which would give the Secretary of War power to declare "dry areas;" already the middle-aged furies are back on their broomsticks and the low-comedy statesmen are waiting in the wings. As a persistent and happy violator of the Constitution of the United States for over fourteen years, we look forward to the new foolishness with a good deal of enthusiasm. There was a lot to be said for life in New York under prohibition, in the dark rooms where strangers were drawn together in the commission of a universal and imaginary crime. Liquor had an extra flavor then, half creosote, half romance, and the men who sold it were more than bartenders. Joe and Tony and Bob were our visible assurance that other, fiercer men were riding armed trucks in the dark, shooting it out in dusty alleys, and corrupting the law with bloody century notes. Dining these nights in restaurants where nothing is violated except privacy and the most sinister figures are columnists gathering rubbish, we sadly miss the old hocus-pocus, and we are eager to welcome it back again. It isn't going to be hard to get the liquor business operating on the old illicit basis, not nearly as hard as it was last time, when there were no precedents and a man had to feel his way along. Right now the machinery is all there and ready. We estimate that there are at least twenty thousand places on the island that could be turned back into speakeasies simply by locking a door and hiring a man to watch it; there must be a hundred thousand potential federal agents itching to turn a crooked buck. As a matter of fact, most of the old cards that have been in our desk drawer for the past seven years, collecting dust and dreams, will probably soon be just as good as they ever were. The lovely, foolish past is right around the corner. We are ready for the Second Noble Experiment, just as we were ready for the Second World War. Ladies of the W.C.T.U., we expect every holy lunatic to do her duty.

April 5, 1941

★ ★ ★

STREAMLINING EVERYTHING, THE New York Central has laid off the last cowboy in New York—a man hired to carry a red flag on horseback in front of freight trains on Tenth Avenue. We can see that this represents progress, but spiritually it is going to take something out of us. As an institution, he was as anachronistic as Buffalo Bill or, for that matter, Ward McAllister, but as a symbol, we don't know what we are going to do without him.[10] It used to be nice, while we were swilling the drink and leering at women in some gilded dive, to know that over to the west a few blocks there was a man riding the range and looking at the clean stars, with his mind fastened on God and railroad presidents. It was very comforting, while the world went into its tailspin, to know there was a man over on Tenth Avenue keeping everything down to six miles an hour.

April 12, 1941

★ ★ ★

THE GREAT PARADOX about this age of perfect communication, of course, is that nobody knows anything about what's going on. We ourself read six newspapers every day, listen interminably to the radio, and spend a good deal of our time talking to industrious prophets who have just flown in from the warring cities and the capitals and the battle fronts. Our guess is that we know rather less about the state of the world than an ancestor of ours who lived in

Connecticut and depended for his information on old copies of *The Federalist* delivered occasionally by a man on a horse. He got his news late and in fragments, but in the end the picture in his mind was probably clear and sensible; we hear about everything the minute it happens, in staggering detail, and, generally speaking, it just adds up to balderdash.

This is not only because the stage these days is too big for any man to comprehend, or because an event described by ninety-five eyewitnesses is apt to be less satisfactory than the same thing reported on by one, or even because the current government spokesmen are sometimes apt to be rather coy about their facts. It is caused mostly by our own frantic state of continual reception. We are too busy listening to hear anything in particular, too overwhelmed by the parts to see any outline of the whole. History, to be understood at all, should be absorbed a very little at a time, in solitude, and always a step or two behind the actual march of events.

If we had the organization of this magazine to do over again, we would employ an elderly hermit to lie on a couch in a small, quiet room, perhaps eating an apple. He would read exactly one copy of the *Times* every month and then, whenever our editorial way grew dark, we'd drop in for a minute and ask him what the hell was really up.

June 7, 1941

★　★　★

OUR ESPIONAGE AGENT up at Columbia, a man who walks now in fear of his life, has sent us his belated report on why no novel was chosen for the Pulitzer Prize. It is in the form of a memorandum addressed by President Nicholas Murray Butler to the members of the jury, and it reads, "The trustees of Columbia University would never, under any circumstances, approve the awarding of the prize for Novel to so obscene, vulgar, and revolting a book as Ernest Hemingway's 'For Whom the Bell Tolls.'" The jury, our spy adds, agreed that it would be absurd to award the prize to anything else and futile to attempt to persuade Dr. Butler and his trustees to accept the Hemingway book. They just sighed and went home. This, of course, doesn't clear up any mystery, since it is about what everybody suspected all along. We just thought you might be interested in the actual documents in the case.

June 7, 1941

★ ★ ★

WHILE WE'RE ON espionage, we'd like to report that the Army's program of having Indians use their tribal dialects as an undecipherable code for communicating military messages has run into the inevitable snag—finding enough Indians who know their tribal dialects. The new plan is to use soldier slang, and we suspect that the same trouble is going to turn up. The Army's sample passage, released to the press, included a translation of "That little guy just arrived but he is going to quit playing marbles and start playing mumble-de-peg" as "The Thirtieth Infantry has just arrived in motors and is preparing to attack the resistance from all sides." We agree that this is guaranteed to baffle any foreign agent, but we are afraid it is just as sure to baffle any soldier, too. Occupational groups never really know their own technical jargon, we're convinced, the only people that do being ardent neophytes, trade-paper reporters, and H. L. Mencken. A soldier who tries to get a military message across to another soldier in terms of "that little guy" and "playing marbles" is going to run into the same kind of thing we once saw happen to an eager young man who asked a prominent jazz clarinetist a technical question larded with terms like "blackstick," "gutbucket," and "ride." The musician turned to him, honestly puzzled and very sweet. "I don't know much about that stuff," he said. "I just blow."[11]

September 20, 1941

★ ★ ★

THE NEW TAXES came in like a lion, and we suspect many lambs will go gambolling out before they do. Club dues, saxophones, clay pigeons, furs, and pinball machines are all taxed, as are pool tables and yachts. As a somewhat dubious consolation, the *Times* ran a scholarly article listing taxable things Congress had missed. The Russians, it seems, once taxed beards; the English took their cut on windows, hearths, butlers, and coats of arms; Rumania taxes dogs and funerals; Italy gets bicycles and bachelors; and Maryland taxed the vest John Brown wore at his hanging, valuing it at $50. We were not really much consoled, feeling that Congress will get around to most of them in the next tax bill, but another piece of news we picked up shames us into facing the situation with at least a semblance of good grace. The Papuan natives are so thrilled at being allowed to pay a tax that they dress in their cleanest clothes for the occasion, march down to the courthouse in a body, circle it ceremoniously once or twice, and walk in singing gaily to hand out their hard-earned dough.[12]

October 11, 1941

★ ★ ★

WE'VE BEEN THINKING all week about the man who drove his automobile, containing a radio, a typewriter, a set of lawbooks, and some golf clubs, into a creek and just left it there. "I was tired of fiddling with it," he told the police, "and I was tired of all that stuff in the car. It was my property and I had a right to get rid of it." Here, it seems to us, is the perfect rebel and the almost perfect selection of material for oblivion. An electrical device for plucking disaster and advertising matter impartially out of the sky; a noisy machine for writing very rapidly (but to whom, what, and, above all, why?); some rules for behavior based on the dusty precedent, arbitrary, unworkable; a bunch of sticks to hit a little ball out and back to where it started from—all these piled in the car, which was never fast enough to get its tired owner away from fiddling with things, and at last all soaked, dissolved, lost forever in the muddy creek. We admire this determined man. Multiply his strange dream of peace by a hundred million all over the world and you might very easily get the millennium.[13]

November 22, 1941

★ ★ ★

WAR CAME TO us with the ball in Brooklyn's possession on the Giants' forty-five-yard line. "Japanese bombs have fallen on Hawaii and the Philippine Islands," a hurried voice broke in to announce. "Keep tuned to this station for further details. We now return you to the Polo Grounds." No more than that. Twisting the dial, we got other voices: a cheerful voice singing the tune of "Jingle Bells" but different words ("Oh, have you seen those bridal suites at Busch's something stores?"), a sprightly voice crying "Listen, America! We bring you good news!," a courteous voice that wished to thank somebody for relinquishing fifteen minutes to Armageddon.

Gradually all the voices—in reality, one voice, the placid, rather foolish voice of America on Sunday afternoon—took up the incredible story from the Pacific. It came in slowly—disjointed, fragmentary, contradicting itself now and then. A man in a private plane over Diamond Head, just flying for fun, shot down by two planes coming in from the sea with the Rising Sun on their wings; Japanese parachute troops dropping on the beach at Waikiki; three hundred and fifty men killed by a direct hit on the barracks at Hickam Field, and a ship capsized and burning in Pearl Harbor; a transport loaded with lumber torpedoed and sunk a thousand miles west of San Francisco; an unidentified ship, probably an aircraft carrier, shelling the forts at Honolulu; fifty, a hundred, a hundred and fifty planes bombing Oahu; and all over this country—in Washington, New York, San Francisco, Dallas—the commentators talking rapidly but evasively, not yet knowing what to say about a catastrophe as sudden and preposterous as something contrived by Orson Welles, not yet able to believe that war had at last made the full circle of the world on Sunday morning.

We write this still not understanding anything very clearly ourself.

The difference between being a citizen of a nation even precariously at peace and one of a nation with its outposts already under fire is hard to grasp in the middle of a football game; the old nightmare of the Yellow Peril, a comic bugaboo almost as long as we can remember, is a strange thing to have come true in the early afternoon, with the radio on and the Sunday papers still only partly read. Like practically everybody else, we've been sure for a long time that war was bound to come, but we never thought that it would come like that.

December 13, 1941

★ ★ ★

EACH MAN WAS pretty much alone with his thoughts last week, turned inward, considering things privately. The man we met for lunch was preoccupied, adjusting his life to a new set of conditions, not yet completely understood. In their offices, on the street, at home, people met and talked as they always had, but they thought separately. Everybody exchanged military opinions based on what little information there was (it was a lovely season for clichés and false premises), but no one was very attentive, each busy with his own need to grasp the real dimensions of what had happened, to define his own relation to it.

Actually there was an uneasy duality in most men all that week. The realization of an absolute change from yesterday was never continuous. People waking up in the morning forgot for a little while, people working at their desks forgot, people shopping, reading, going to the movies, playing with children all forgot briefly that they were at war. This happy state was always brief. There was always something to bring back the consciousness of total separation from the past, putting familiar faces and scenes into sharp, unaccustomed focus, giving the man who looked at them a sense of valuing them precisely for the first time, changing the identity of the man himself.

ANY ATTEMPT TO tell how people felt in New York during the first days of war necessarily has a personal basis. Our own emotions covered quite a good deal of ground. We wish we could say that we looked forward to being bombed with the calm fatalism recommended by our London friends, but we didn't. Logic (and the military experts) told us there was no appreciable danger, but the peril was too far outside our experience—something that might come in from the sea without warning, very high and nearly silent, as impersonal as lightning. The wail of the sirens coming up thinly from the street, the controlled voice on the radio telling of destruction already conceivably on its way, even the drumming of our own planes patrolling the threatened city—none of these sounds was particularly reassuring. We weren't exactly afraid, but unlike one nerveless hero we met, we weren't exactly bored, either.

THERE WAS SOME indignation, too, some things we were ashamed of: an heiress anxious to learn if the bombs had damaged her Hawaiian estate (and also the society columnists who reported her anxiety with respectful sympathy); an ornament of night-club society exploiting the crisis to advertise a restaurant; a few ingenious radio sponsors quick to seize their opportunity to plug patent medicines along with patriotism; especially the realization of how little had been done, by us and everybody else, to prepare for all this two years ago, when there still was so much time.

On the other hand, there was a good deal more to be proud of: the President's magnificent speech on Tuesday night and the quick answer to it by a suddenly united nation; the brave men who died in the Pacific; the acceptance of the first bad news by everyone, without any illusions about its importance, but equally without discouragement or fear; the sense of civilian obligation, slow in coming but universal at last; the promise that boundless production was finally under way and not to be stopped until its certain purpose was accomplished. We felt some pride and confidence because of all these things.

IT MAY BE, however, that the strongest emotion we felt was relief. We were safe enough up to that disastrous Sunday afternoon, but it was an unsatisfactory kind of safety, humiliating to some, foolish to others, clearly temporary to all but a few. It was also a safety strongly mixed with fear. We're sure that a lot of very unpleasant things still

lie ahead of us, but we doubt if anything can be much more unpleasant than the uncertainty, frustration, and bitterness that lay between
Munich and Manila. On the whole, we'd say we feel much better
now.

December 20, 1941

★ ★ ★

CHRISTMAS, OF COURSE, is an anachronism in New York. It
belongs to non-converted brownstone houses and gaslights and
streets banked high with snow, to a day when there were still suburbs on Manhattan Island. The perpendicular city has no place for
it. We dig up this interesting thought about this time every year, but
we never get very far with it. As a matter of fact, it is one of those
circular and aimless meditations that take up too much of our time.
Christmas belongs to Old New York, we write confidently, but what
precisely do we mean by Old New York? The picturesque past is
attached to the thrusting present, like a barge to a tug, moving at a
constant interval with it through time. Actually, there is a string of
barges. Our father's Old New York is almost lost in antiquity; our
own has something to do with Steve Brody and steam engines on
the "L;" for a boy of six we know, New York was old in that lost,
mysterious, and forever fascinating period when his parents risked
their lives nightly in something called a speakeasy.[14] For each new
generation, the good old days move a little further forward in time;
the tug and its barges move eternally up the river.

The figure always develops neatly enough up to this point, but
that's as far as we go. When we try to imagine the time and the
people who will look back on the grotesque complexity of New York
in 1941 and say Christmas was really Christmas in those simple, far-
off times, our mind rejects the whole impossible picture. The terrible
unborn who are going to remember us as quaint and cheerful figures in an old daguerreotype are as unthinkable to us as men from
Mars. We give them up. In fact, we give up the entire complicated
analogy; as far as we're concerned, the tug and its barges will sink
with us. In the final perspective of history, it may well be that you

are enjoying a nice, old-fashioned Christmas right here and now. We leave you with this thought, for whatever comfort you may find in it, but it sounds like lunacy to us.

December 27, 1941

*   *   *

WE'VE BEEN TRYING to adjust our mind to the idea of a civilization without tin, and perhaps it won't be so tough after all. No more canned peas out of season, no more tubes for toothpaste, no more foil around cigarettes, no more beer in cans, possibly a certain reduction in the amount of reserve material a publication will be able to keep standing in type—the list is long, but these are a few of the items that struck us as especially applicable to our own life. Conceding that it has been agreeable to use metal in all these ways, we still doubt if we have been a better man for any of them. To a certain extent the pioneer has been lost in the sybarite. Our Spartan ancestor ate peas when they grew and would undoubtedly have suspected the whole idea of tampering with nature's cycles as the work of an atheist or a Frenchman; there was certainly no foil around his tobacco or metal sealing up his beer, and his teeth were cleaned without benefit of lead. He was able to confront the unprotected product, and so are we, or so we hope.

The greatest moral benefit we expect to derive from the shortage, however, lies in the possible curtailment of linotype metal. Things have been too easy for editors for many years. Confronted with a manuscript of dubious beauty, their tendency has been to get the darn thing set up in type and then to judge it at their convenience in this more legible form. Much of this material stood around for months while the editors mustered either enough spirit to reject it altogether or enough energy to rewrite it into some land of usable shape. Some of it stood around for years, bought but never edited, until it was pleasantly apparent to everybody that it was hopelessly out of date and there was nothing left to do but charge it off on the books. This was an immoral condition and worth clearing up, almost at the cost of a war. From now on, according to our dream, literary decisions will have to be immediate and absolute. With a faulty sonnet tying up almost enough metal for a small shell, the editor's duty is obvious.

January 10, 1942

★ ★ ★

ONE OF THE minor curiosities of this war is the fact that so far the artists have failed to produce anything recognizable as the typical German soldier. It was different, of course, in 1917. We were looking over a collection of old cartoons the other day, and there he was on almost every page—a fat-necked barbarian, wearing a spiked helmet and decorated with the Iron Cross; a monstrous baby with disgusting habits. No matter who drew him, he was always the same: his name was Fritz and the balloon that issued from his mouth contained vaudeville Dutch. He was drawn in many poses but most frequently either with one hobnailed boot on the body of a beautiful young woman labelled "Belgium" or else in comic surrender to a contemptuous athlete with a bayonet. We look in vain for any such foolish, reassuring composite today. The artists still draw Germans, but there is no agreement among them and out of all the faces comes no face at all. It occurs to us that the faceless men, the blank symbols of a race that has surrendered its identity, are better propaganda than the Hun at his bloodthirsty worst. They may even be a healthy symptom, indicating that we are outgrowing our political age of innocence.

February 7, 1942

★ ★ ★

WE TOOK AN out-of-town friend to Radio City Music Hall the other night—through the great lobby, up the infinite stairs, out into the stupendous auditorium. The steel sky above us was round and rifled; we were sitting in the barrel of some inconceivable gun, sighting the distant stage. Presently, from a cavern under the city, a giant platform rose, bearing an orchestra bathed in ghastly light and playing Rimski-Korsakov. There was a luminous pillar on the stage,

around which men and women danced, while in its heart strange
pagan figures swam in flame. This dimmed and sank, and the orchestra rumbled backward over the stage, lifted, hung suspended in
air, and then miraculously was enclosed by the walls of an ancient
city. We were in Mexico or Spain, and a gifted seal played "God Save
the King" while fifty precision dancers kicked as one. Prodigy followed prodigy, change change, until at last all split, dissolved, vanished, and there came the kindly night and Miss Katharine Hepburn
in "Woman of the Year." We'd been through such things before,
but we were interested in its effect on our friend, whose previous
cultural experience had been largely limited to Milwaukee, Wisconsin.

"Well, what do you think of it, George?" we asked.

His reply was dazed and irrelevant, but we found it comforting.

"Do you know," he said, "this is the first time I've been *really*
sure we couldn't lose this war."

February 28, 1942

★   ★   ★

WHEN THIS WAR is over, we wouldn't be surprised if two villains of it turn out to be Rudyard Kipling and Gary Cooper. Beyond
almost any question, they are the greatest authors of Anglo-Saxon
complacency, and it is hard to say which is worse. The Man from
Bombay, of course, got there first, establishing the ratio of white
supremacy at something like ten to one and inculcating forever in
British minds the notion that heathen races don't understand machinery. Mr. Kipling left his countrymen the bow-and-arrow delusion,
and we suspect that it cost them the Malay Peninsula. Mr. Cooper
belongs to the same school but he is a considerable refinement, the
message of his art having to do sheerly with morals rather than race
or equipment. He is dedicated to the theory that a virtuous man of
correct political principles is impervious to bullets, and we have
observed how *that* idea worked out at Pearl Harbor. We hate to
tamper with the comfortable old legends, but in the interests of national defense we feel we ought to bring the odds a little more up to

date. In our book, Sergeant York with a Bible and a squirrel rifle is no better than a six-to-five shot against Fuzzy-Wuzzy in a dive bomber, and the smart money is said to be on the colored boy.[15]

March 7, 1942

★ ★ ★

WE SPENT A good part of last week reading the new *Who's Who*, a feat requiring considerable strength and persistence. In many ways, it is our favorite book, though, like "The Magic Mountain," there is a good deal of it we don't quite understand. The theory seems simple enough. There are two kinds of people who get in *Who's Who*—"those who are selected because of special prominence in creditable lines of effort" and "those who are included arbitrarily on account of official position;" i.e., congressmen, bishops, generals, and such. We can grasp that all right, though regretting the cynicism which implies that members of the second class do not necessarily belong to the first. When we arrive at the listings themselves, however—the thirty thousand-odd men and women who have been tapped for posterity—we find things getting a little obscure.

The problem of the comparative amount of space devoted to the various subjects, of course, is an old one and has been adequately explained by the fact that each item is really an autobiography, only mildly edited by the management. It is interesting to note this year, for instance, that of the several Roosevelts listed, the President of the United States takes up thirty-five lines; his son James, thirty-four; and Theodore, Jr., forty-nine; while in the arts Ernest Hemingway is discussed in thirteen, as compared with thirty-nine for Kathleen Norris and forty-one for the late Albert Payson Terhune. These are pleasant facts, but not really mysterious.

What really fascinates us is the selection of material made by the exhibits themselves—great events dismissed in a parenthesis, absurdities expanded to half a column. Here are three men, each of whom has had four wives. What strange sense of obligation to the future historian compels them to list every one of these domestic mishaps, what curious pride? Here is Mickey Rooney. What cautious impulse leads him, of all the males we can find, to conceal the date of his birth? Here is Guy Lombardo, who contributes what is certainly an editorial opinion of himself to a book of facts—"Accorded recognition since 1930 by radio editors of U.S. and Can. as outstanding orchestra leader," and here, on the other hand, is William Saroyan, who confines himself austerely to the titles of his works. Here, finally, are all those whose names are marked with an asterisk, meaning that they have ignored requests from *Who's Who* for facts about themselves. What about them? Indifference? Modesty? Or the fiercest vanity of all?

Altogether, as we say, it's a great book, full of valuable information but richer still in its perpetual challenge to the inquiring mind.

STILL PREOCCUPIED WITH our thoughts about those who fill out questionnaires, we turned from *Who's Who* to the industrial-fitness quiz about to be mailed to registrants in the third draft, a group including us. Somewhere in the middle of this complex document, we came upon what seems to us one of the most ill-advised queries we've ever seen. "Job for Which You Are Best Fitted?" asks the government briskly, and then adds in smaller type, "Is this job the same as your present job?" Most men, as someone has said, lead lives of quiet desperation. Generally speaking, however, not only are their lives quiet but the victims may even confuse their desperation with a sort of dim contentment. The Army, in our opinion, is going out of its way to look for trouble—stirring up God knows what half-forgotten dreams, rekindling the embers of rebellions long since nearly dead. We don't know how most men are going to feel about this ruthless awakening of the past, but it left us sad and resentful. The job for which we are best fitted, we would like to inform our draft board, is playing juvenile leads opposite Miss Katharine Hepburn. It bears no resemblance whatever to our present employment. Further, gentlemen, how would you like to go to hell?[16]

April 11, 1942

* * *

WE ARE GOING to miss a lot of things along the South Shore of Long Island this summer, but none more strongly than the Sunday fishermen, bobbing up and down, fifty men to a boat, from Manhattan Beach to Montauk Point. They were perhaps the perfect symbols of everything most contemptible in totalitarian eyes—defiantly unregimented; irresponsibly criticizing the government and practically everything else; accomplishing little useful purpose, since they acquired few fish and even less health, what with the beer, the sun, and the wayward motion of the sea; and, returning at last to land, often making lamentable spectacles of themselves in the eyes of all decent and right-minded men. For a while Hitler has succeeded in eliminating the pleasures of a good many simple men and these urban mariners are by no means the least of his victims. When we think of them and the ships in which they sailed—Daisy and Maida and Alys II—we are sure, however, that it is only for a very little while. The ships were frail and overloaded and the crews were sometimes drunk, but there was something about them both that convinces us they will be triumphantly afloat when the last of the U-boats is scrap and the Scharnhorst has gone to join the Bismarck in her rusty grave.

May 16, 1942

★ ★ ★

HOW QUICKLY AND imperceptibly America has come to accept the idea of fantastic calamity, we thought as we read an article on air-raid shelters for the home in a great women's magazine. "Then even if the house comes tumbling down into the cellar, you will be comparatively safe," the author wrote cheerfully, unimpressed by the fact of the missing house. This point of view is probably encouraging, indicating a native aptitude for total war. "Home is where you fall down in the bathtub and break your leg," said an insurance pamphlet we got a couple of years ago. At the time we were struck by a certain unsentimental recognition of the facts of life in this statement. Now, when home is something that is likely to come tumbling down into the cellar, the voice is just as tranquil, just as matter-of-fact. The bomb has merely succeeded the bathtub as a threat to domestic security. The change is only one of degree. Don't give it a second thought.

May 23, 1942

★ ★ ★

THE DEATH OF John Barrymore made us think again for a minute of F. Scott Fitzgerald. They were very different men; a lot alike. Undoubtedly they both worked hard, but there was the same sense of a difficult technique easily mastered (too easily, perhaps); there was the same legend of great physical magnetism, working incessantly for its own destruction; there was the same need for public confession, either desperate or sardonic; and there was always a good deal of time wasted, usually accompanied by the sweet smell of grapes. We have seen Scott Fitzgerald when everything he said was a childish parody of his own talent, and the last time we saw John Barrymore he was busy with a sick and humiliating parody of his. The similarity probably ends there. Up to the day he died, we believe, Fitzgerald still kept his original and eager devotion to his profession, along, we like to think, with the confidence that he might still achieve the strict perfection that was so often almost his. Barrymore, on the other hand, had given up long ago. It is absurd, of course, to say that a man was never gifted on the ground that he has lent himself to a savage burlesque of his own gifts, but it is a good deal easier to accept his death. We mourned Scott Fitzgerald with a sense of waste and loss because, in spite of everything, he must have died with some hope still bright in his heart. We are going to miss John Barrymore, but it is hard to regret what surely must have remained of his career—a few more foolish jokes to be made over the radio, a few more cheap paragraphs to be written in the gossip columns, just a little while longer to pull down what was left of the hateful and magnificent past.

STILL REFLECTING ON John Barrymore, we've decided that this may be the time to revive an old campaign that a good many people have waged from time to time. Our version of it is divided into two parts.

First: Anybody who knowingly exploits a sick, senile, or merely irrelevant person of talent would be shot, automatically. This would include whoever cleverly gave Mr. Barrymore certain passages from "Hamlet" to speak in a play called "My Dear Children," whoever induced Mme. Sarah Bernhardt to play "Camille" at seventy-five with a wooden leg, whoever permitted a well-known prizefighter to go on fighting when he was clearly insane from being hit too often on the head, and perhaps various publishers who continue to extract books from authors who no longer have any idea what they're talking about. In the category of exploiting irrelevant genius, it would certainly include whoever convinced Ulysses S. Grant that he ought to be the President of the United States, the countless theatrical gentlemen who have persuaded countless celebrated prostitutes (not to mention an occasional murderess) that they ought to act on the stage, and conceivably the editors and politicians who are already grooming General Douglas MacArthur for the White House. This list is not complete; it is just a good beginning.

Second: Sick, senile, or irrelevant talent would be taken care of by the government whenever necessary, not on minute pensions but at a rate approximating the amount they made during the period of their greatest success. This, we feel, ought to square us with history, which, as things stand now, is going to want to know why the most famous men and women in this country, once past their immediate usefulness, were ever confronted with the choice of either starving to death in a dignified manner or else entering a vaudeville act of one kind or another, such as the Grant administration. So far we haven't made up our mind what agency would be responsible for deciding which ex-talents deserved a government subsidy, except that we're pretty sure it wouldn't be the Pulitzer Prize Committee. We feel, however, that this detail wouldn't be hard to work out. The whole project is obviously in the interest of the dignity of the human race.

June 13, 1942

★   ★   ★

AFTER A WINTER and spring spent largely in filling out forms of one kind and another, we pause briefly for station identification. We are, we believe, one of the most exhaustively catalogued men in the United States—every conceivable fact of our life cross-indexed and filed in triplicate in handsome steel cabinets in New York, Washington, Albany, and other far-flung cities. The simple details of our age, sex, race, weight, height, and the color of our hair and eyes are known to many, including the Motor Vehicle Bureau and the United States Customs, which also has our photograph. More intimate physical information is in the possession of two or three insurance companies, several doctors, dentists, and oculists, a marriage-license bureau, and, of course, our draft board. The intricate shape of our financial and domestic condition is common gossip with the state and federal income-tax authorities, the Social Security Administration, a couple of credit-rating bureaus, a lawyer, and again our draft board, which by now must be equipped to turn out a fairly definitive biography. There are tiny clues to the whole picture elsewhere. The police department of Hicksville, Long Island, knows (or once knew) something moderately interesting. An organization made up of people whose ancestors once fought together in another war has some rather dry genealogical data. Our present employer and several past ones are in possession of material of no possible use to anybody but an employer. The things our friends know about us, while amusing, are not matters of record. It is probably just as well. Reflecting on all the agencies to whom we are known, usually as a number (we once figured out that we had no less than twenty-two official numbers, all vital), we can't help feeling a mild glow of importance. Our simplest act, such as moving to a new address, would call for revisions on a hundred little cards. Our death would agitate bookkeepers from Maine to California, or anyway from Massachusetts to the District of Columbia. As a matter of fact, the American today has a special and restricted immortality. He never really dies, in the sense that his personality is finally obliterated. He is simply translated from one set of heavenly files to another.

July 11, 1942

★   ★   ★

WE CAME ACROSS one of our favorite sentences in English literature last week in an essay a child had written about the war.
"The battle," it said, "was getting ready to have itself." The peculiar
grievance of most writers is that they are at the mercy of editors and
proofreaders, who rearrange their syntax in a pure though high-
handed manner. Staring at the lovely confusion of words in this
essay, we wished we'd written them ourself. No living editor could
get anywhere with that sentence, we thought; with any kind of luck
it might even drive a lot of editors crazy.

September 18, 1943

★   ★   ★

THE MAN WHO had had the table before us had left his newspaper
behind, folded back to the feature section. We picked it up and saw
that he had been checking over a syndicated personality test, a series
of questions to be answered yes or no, designed to tell the reader in
decimals if he was happy with his lot. Following his marks, we
found that we were sitting in a chair still warm from a man content
at home and interested in his work, free from bad dreams, indigestion, boredom, and worry about the future, genial with children and
dogs, considerate of his servants and his inferiors at the office, a man
with a good hobby and some money in the bank. His total was only
ninety-five out of a possible hundred—he couldn't honestly say that
he always tried to keep up with old friends—but anyway, there it
was, written testimony to a life that had fallen only five points short
of all the world could hold. We ordered tomato juice and eggs and
coffee and ate them sitting in the chair just vacated by a lonely, most
uncertain man.

October 2, 1943

★   ★   ★

WE SAW OUR daughter off on the school bus for her first day at
kindergarten—a serious child, braced for the unknown, her nose

running a little with excitement. Her eight-year-old brother, an upper-classman, sat beside her, wearing a strained and rather distant expression. He was, we knew, very conscious of his responsibility for the public behavior of this most unpredictable member of the family. "Don't get the idea you can go whooping around at school the way you do here," he had told her severely at breakfast and, because he seemed concerned about her nose, we had pinned an extra handkerchief to her blouse. Now she was sitting as close to him as she could, but she had her hands in her own lap, having been instructed on this point and being anxious not to offend. The bus pulled away from the door and we waved, admiring her dignity and wishing her well. We went back to our own breakfast, touched by all the profound and immemorial banalities of the occasion. We'd found nothing to say except goodbye when the bus left, and even now we could think of nothing that might have been helpful to a little girl on her way to school, to her first experience with the gathering perplexities that beset a lady on her own. Just try to take it easy, kid, was really the only advice we had to give her on such a solemn moment in her life, but somehow it didn't seem quite suitable. It was wonderful advice, but as we knew from experience it had never been much use to anybody in a crisis.

October 9, 1943

*   *   *

THANKSGIVING WILL BE on us in a week, and thoughtfully we count our blessings. After nearly two years of war, this office, generally speaking, is holding up pretty well. The water runs a little warmer and more reluctantly from the coolers in the hall, strangling now and then on a big bubble; at the moment the bulb is burned out over the mirror in the men's room, and the paint is flaking away from the wall in the cubicle where one of the lesser editors sits alone with his lesser, flaky thoughts; the passage of memoranda from one man to another has been clogged by the fact that the messengers now are not very good at names, and lately the telephone service has been only approximate, so usually we get an outside wire when we ask for Mr. McGuire, a mechanical buzz instead of a living man; the ink in our well is often mud and dust, and the ersatz paper clips crumble away in our hands; the personnel, of course, is greatly changed, most of the rough work and heavy lifting being entrusted to tall girls, and creative thought to the elderly, the infirm, and the conclusively domestic. We realize how our reduced circumstances are apt to strike a man with a gun in a swamp, and we mention them really with thanksgiving and embarrassment. There is, in fact, so much to be thankful for. The magazine continues to come out, a small, impertinent miracle, it may be, in a world in which so much better writing has been stilled, and we who edit it live in more comfort and safety than we have any right to expect. Above everything else, however, we are grateful that all those who have gone from here into the armed forces are, as far as we know, still alive and well, wherever they may be. It is indeed a season of thanksgiving for us as long as that is so.

November 20, 1943

★   ★   ★

THERE IS A man working for Time, Inc., who has a very dangerous idea. We met this renegade in a saloon the other night and listened to him for a long while as he talked of life in Luce's clean, appalling tower. Looking nervously over his shoulder, he told us of an atmosphere as brisk and antiseptic and charged with muted suffering as a dental clinic, of a queer, lost race of men who have come to speak only upside down and backward, of vast and by no means impossible projects to remake the world beautifully in the image of Yale, of new schemes every day to put the lonely, desperate art of communication on a business basis, with Timen on the top. Most of all, however, he was troubled by a terrible air of omniscience that seemed to him to mark every man, woman, and child on the payroll, from the tiniest Timan to the boss himself. His eyes were wide and wild as he told us this, draining the green stuff in his glass. "It's all right, though," he said at last. "I know how to fix them. One of these days I'm coming out of my office and I'm going to stand in the hall and, as loud as I can, I'm going to shout, 'I don't *know!*'" He looked at us blankly, lost in his furious dream. "The whole damn thing will just come tumbling down," he said.[17]

April 15, 1944

★　★　★

LAST WEEK, ON the thin barrier of sand that separates Great South Bay from the Atlantic, we waited for the hurricane that never came. Sitting out the watch with us was our cat, who had ridden out the last one, just a year ago, all alone in an empty house facing directly on the uproarious sea. She had had quite a time. We were in town with our wife that day and the children and their nurse had been moved inland by the Coast Guard late in the afternoon, when the waves began to chew away the dunes. They looked for the cat, but she had found a private hideaway and they had to leave without her. In the night, after the dunes went, the sea tore off the porch, carried it out a little way, and then tossed it back, driving a hole through the side of the house big enough to take a freight car. We have no idea what awful sounds went with this crazy game. It was clear and calm in the morning, when the nurse and the children went back to see what was left. They found the beach lying flat from the edge of the sea right through the hole in the side of the house. They didn't find the cat at first, but there in the sand, in what had been a bedroom on the ground floor, were her prints, and they told a strange and terrible story. At some time during the night, it seemed, she had raced desperately back and forth in her perilous shelter, and she had not been alone, for mixed with her prints, overlapping and crossing them, were those of an enormous gull. What was the purpose or design of this mad dance in the dark, who was chasing whom, who ate or was eaten, wasn't clear from the tangled evidence, but it seemed obvious that a tragedy had taken place. She was quite an old cat, far past her normal span, and they decided that she had met a fearful but somehow glorious end. In a way, perhaps, they were a little let down when she turned up at noon from some secret recess, damp and blinking in the sun, and with a certain wildness in her eye, but whole and, as cats go, reasonably sane. The mysteries of the night— what she felt when the wind screamed and the house split and the man-high waves came riding in, where her weird visitor came from and what they did, and in the end what happened to him—remained her private property, hers and God's. Last week, when the storm from the south threatened again, we considered the cat and took comfort from her on the ground that no experience that lay in store for us could possibly compare with hers, whatever it had been. Her own expression, as she looked out on the furious and mounting sea, was supercilious and even bored.

April 29, 1945

★ ★ ★

THE TRUSTEES OF Mark Twain's estate went to law to prevent a couple of men, Lew D. Feldman and Allan Hyman, from publishing an unfinished manuscript of his called "A Murder, a Mystery, and a Marriage." The history of this manuscript is long and complicated, and we'll try to boil it down as much as we can. It was written in 1876, promptly rejected by the *Atlantic Monthly*, and then disappeared until Twain's death, in 1910, when it turned up among his effects, as the saying goes. Mr. Feldman and Mr. Hyman bought it at an auction in 1945, and subsequently proposed to bring it out as a book, conceivably inspired by the example of "Edwin Drood." In protesting to the court against this project, the trustees said, "The evidence shows that he [Mark Twain] was very particular about his unpublished manuscripts up to the time of his death. This . . . is quite sufficient to justify the holding that no intentional transfer of the manuscript for the purpose of publishing it was ever made by the author." Last week, the Appellate Division ruled in their favor, against allowing the material to be so used.

All this brings up a problem that has occupied us from time to time: What is a writer's real intention in regard to the rejected manuscript that he almost always has stashed away in the bottom drawer of his desk? The fact that the darn thing hasn't been thrown out would seem to indicate some doubt of the editorial judgment that decided against it, some stubborn hope that it might be a masterpiece after all. It is possible, of course, that the author intends to rewrite it on some distant day, when he has nothing more important on his mind. The chances are, however, that he really has no such design. Doing a piece over again, particularly a novel, is the writer's special purgatory, being essentially a matter of compromising with opinions for which he has nothing but derision and of a, considerable amount of rough manual labor. If an author rewrites a piece, he does so, in most cases, only out of stern financial necessity and he goes to work on it without delay, usually the minute he gets it back, along with the editor's half-witted suggestions. A manuscript that, like Twain's, has been lying around for thirty-four years is obviously not going to get rewritten. What, then, is it doing in the drawer? We believe that the almost invariable dream is that some upward shift in taste, either in his lifetime or after he is dead, will permit his stuff to be published exactly as he wrote it, in the only form that his own genius tells him is artistic and rational. People—sometimes heirs, sometimes interested bystanders like Mr. Feldman and Mr. Hyman— are often criticized for exhuming the unpublished works of a famous writer, on the ground that they are willing to sacrifice the great man's reputation for base, financial considerations. There is something in this charge, of course, but we can't help feeling that they are also carrying out the author's real, if never openly admitted, wish. We suspect that "A Murder, a Mystery, and a Marriage" is just as bad as the *Atlantic Monthly* said it was in 1876 (the title, certainly, is hardly reassuring), but just the same we're sorry Twain isn't finally going to get it printed. It could hardly have done anything to diminish his fame, and we like to think it might have gratified his amiable, disappointed ghost.

January 29, 1949

★ ★ ★

READING JOHN DICKSON Carr's biography of Sir Arthur Conan Doyle, we learned that Doyle had a very low opinion of

Sherlock Holmes. It was one of the happiest days of his life when he sent the great private eye hurtling down to the bottom of the Reichenbach Falls, locked in Professor Moriarty's deadly embrace, and he was disgusted when popular demand forced him to fish the old nuisance out again. Doyle's feeling was that the Holmes stories were no more than potboilers, and that their enormous success had a tendency to obscure his "better work," like "The White Company," "The Lost World," and quite a few books we'd never even heard of. Reflecting on this, we realized that a good many creative artists have been similarly afflicted, ranging all the way from Robert Louis Stevenson, who could never regard "Treasure Island" as an example of his best prose, to Al Capp, who has publicly expressed his distaste for the Shmoo. As a matter of fact, we have known the same puzzled indignation ourself: The only story we ever wrote that attracted any considerable attention struck us as, at best, a competently executed trick; the piece we liked most, a sad story of our lost youth, was admired only by a man now confined in an institution for the hopelessly insane. The writer (or painter or musician) who suffers from what he is bound to consider the degraded and irresponsible taste of his time is apt to comfort himself with the idea that posterity will correct all such errors. The weight of the evidence, however, is against him. Posterity, if she doesn't ignore him altogether, is far more likely to confirm and even to emphasize the vulgar judgment of his contemporaries, as she has done in the case of Doyle and Holmes. The most discouraging thought of all is that the silly bitch will probably be right.

February 12, 1949

★　★　★

It was considered unsuitable last week to play the National Anthem before a wrestling match at Madison Square Garden, presumably because the thing was an obvious fake and there was no chance that anybody would really get hurt. It is, however, still considered highly suitable to play it before all prizefights, presumably because these bouts—in theory, at least—are on the level and men often get quite badly hurt and sometimes even killed. The distinction here is too tough for us, and we report it only for the information of some future social historian interested in the minor tribal rites of a forgotten age.

March 5, 1949

Some Matters of Fact

Profiles

UP FROM AMHERST¹

BACK IN 1930, a clerk in some forgotten casting office discovered that she could sum up the qualifications of an actor whose full name was Oliver Burgess Meredith in exactly five words. On his card applying for any job at all, under the brief list of his performances up to that time, she noted: "Young. Homely. Large Head. Blond." This dispassionate entry remains one of the few unflattering comments made about Meredith during his seven years on the stage. It is true that Guthrie McClintic, while he was directing John van Druten's "Flowers of the Forest," felt obliged to complain that his young star played the part of a man suffering from cerebral hemorrhage as though he were rowing a boat, and certainly there must have been an empty moment when Meredith picked up the first paper on the morning after the opening of "Winterset" and found that although he had learned a part almost as long as Hamlet, the late Percy Hammond had neglected even to comment on his performance.

Opposed to these negligible brickbats, however, there has been a general ovation certainly remarkable when applied to an actor still under thirty. The newspaper critics, who obviously can't be expected to think up any new adjectives, have been profuse with the old ones. They have described Meredith's performances as "brilliant," "impressive," "heartbreaking," "vibrant," "eloquent," "sinewy," and, most often and most inevitably, "sensitive." A gentleman who, by what the cynical might have regarded as a fortunate coincidence, also happened at the time to be press agent for "Flowers of the Forest" hailed him in practically every paper of appetizing circulation as the "Hamlet of 1940." So often, indeed, has this modest estimate been printed that Meredith sometimes feels as if he ought to wear "Hamlet '40" on his sweater, like a quarterback. Probably the gaudiest tribute, however, came from a critic on the White Plains *Reporter*.

This lady—from the evidence, it seems permissible to deduce a lady, and a frantic one—wrote in June, 1930:

> A young man of remarkable genius walked out on the stage last night, and began creating a Marchbanks that became one of the most beautiful and poetic things seen in the theatre anywhere and anytime. So great was the flame of his creation that he fired into being the greatest production of George Bernard Shaw's "Candida" that this writer has ever seen. Burgess Meredith rose to the highest achievement in the theatre last night.

After adding that "the immortal Bernhardt never did a more perfect piece of work" than Miss Vera Allen, who played Candida, the writer closed with a rather peremptory suggestion that if Mr. Shaw had any sense, he would get right over to White Plains and see what was up before the miracle rolled on.

To anyone who has never seen Meredith on the stage, meeting him casually for the first time, this clamor is apt to seem more or less incomprehensible. The "young man of remarkable genius" is twenty-eight, five feet seven inches tall, weighs a hundred and thirty-five pounds, and his pointed face might more reasonably belong to a jockey. His clothes, especially his hats, have a crumpled, offhand air, and at the moment it has seemed to him suitable to let his ginger-colored hair grow long on top, so that in dimmer lights he looks rather like a chrysanthemum. His friends call him Buzz, or Bugs, and either of these in some vague way seems descriptive.

What he says might also seem misleading. Currently, Meredith has two tremendous enthusiasms: Ezra Pound, whose expatriate rhythms seem to him the most enduring thing in contemporary poetry, and Maxwell Anderson, the author of some fourteen plays, ranging from "What Price Glory?" to those successive prizewinners, "Winterset" and "High Tor." Meredith's regard for Pound is strong, but presumably temporary; his admiration for Anderson has been one of the most important things in his life. To a great extent, Anderson is both his literary guide and his social conscience, and this leads him into an eager defence of many strange propositions. He will tell you, for instance, that blank verse is the only rational dramatic form because it is permanent, holding whatever story is to be told in solution for posterity. You are invited in this connection to consider the Elizabethans. He will also tell you that the only possible cure for the world is the complete absence of formal government, although as to just what this means and why it is so, I'm afraid he's inclined to be a little vague.

In any case, Meredith's extraordinary success on the stage has practically nothing to do with what he looks like or with his momentary literary notions. In addition to his original talent, which I have no intention of trying to define, he has in the first place an acute sense of his own limitations. Once, in talking about a production in which he succeeded a famous, and certainly more robust, actor, he apologized for the lower key of his own performance.

"There was no use my trying to play it the way he did," he said. "When I go after power, I just sound boyish."

It has been a good thing for him to know, giving his work taste and reticence, and keeping it conspicuously free from overacting.

He also has the utmost faith in good direction, claiming that the less creative an actor is, or thinks he is, the better. He believes that the director's control should be absolute. Whether that is true or not, and it is at least debatable, he has been singularly fortunate in his own directors. A young actor could scarcely hope for better supervision than Meredith got from the very beginning—from Eva Le Gallienne, Howard Lindsay, and, most helpful of all, Guthrie McClintic, who has directed him in "The Barretts of Wimpole Street," "Flowers of the Forest," "Winterset," and "High Tor."

Strangely enough, however, it seems to me that almost as important as either of these qualities has been the effect of what one of his pre-theatre employers, with a restraint that must have brought him very close to apoplexy, has called "a somewhat disorganized life."

There wasn't so much disorganization in the beginning. Meredith was born in Lakewood, a suburb of Cleveland, on November 16th, 1908. His father was a doctor. His grandfather was a revivalist who, after spending half a lifetime shedding the chilly light of Methodism over the Middle West, settled down to a pastorate in Cleveland. There was, of course, an Uncle Jay Burgess in vaudeville, and an older brother, George, had had from time to time some casual connection with a jazz band. Also, after his mother's death, Meredith was astonished to learn from an old scrapbook that once, as a girl, *she* had run away from home and played ten months in stock. At the most, however, these were minor vagaries, noteworthy only in the light of the Methodist tradition.

Very early it developed that the boy had a remarkably true soprano, and before he was ten he was singing solos in a Methodist church. At eleven, against seventy-five other Cleveland competitors, he won a scholarship in vocal training at the Paulist Choir School in New York. At this point Methodism again took a hand in his career. Mrs. Meredith had apparently no objection to her son's winning a Catholic competition, but she certainly had no intention of letting him sing in a Catholic church. Instead, he came to New York to live with his married sister and enter the choir in the Cathedral of St. John the Divine.

In 1923, when he was fifteen and no longer a plausible soprano, he was sent to the Hoosac School, which for some obscure purposes of confusion is located at Hoo*sick*, near Albany. Little is remembered of this period except that in his senior year he was editor of a school paper called the *Owl*, which, under his casual regime, ran so far into debt that for several years after he had gone it survived only haggardly. In fact, so anemic were these subsequent issues that the embarrassed editors changed their paper's name to the *Owlet*.

By 1926, his father had been obliged to retire and there was no more money to be expected from Lakewood. An uncle, however, sent him to Amherst, and there he began a period of tremendous confusion. His tuition and a room in one of the dormitories had been paid for, but he had no money for food or books. He had come so late in the term that there were no jobs on the campus. For two weeks he lived on $25 which he had managed to borrow from what must have been a singularly gullible bank, and then he went to the dean and confessed that he couldn't go on. The dean was sympathetic, but obviously there was no provision at Amherst for such cases. He gave the boy a letter of recommendation and advised him to work for a year, save his money, and then come back. A month later Meredith was a reporter on the Stamford *Advocate*, where the legend persists that he was once sent out to investigate a suicide and came back with all the essential facts except the name of the victim.

Whether this story is true or not, performances very like it seem to have been typical, and in a little while the ex-reporter was on his way to Cleveland in a second-hand Star roadster that he had picked up for $50. Here he opened a haberdashery store with his brother, by that time divorced from the jazz band. It is reasonable to suppose that potential customers felt that nobody who dressed as negligently as these partners could conceivably have anything of interest for sale. At any rate, the customers remained potential and the venture collapsed. Brother George, who seems to have been versatile, took up the study of veterinary surgery. Still driving the Star, and with $50 in his pocket, all that remained after the bankruptcy sale, Meredith headed back for Amherst. It was the beginning of another year, and this time he was able to get a job taking care of a furnace, in return for which he was given a room, and a job washing dishes in a hotel, which accounted for his meals. On Sundays he got $4 for singing in a choir, which he optimistically imagined would cover books, and clothes, and "recreation." It wasn't life exactly, but it was possible to live.

From the beginning, Amherst seems to have had very little use for Meredith. If the college thought about him at all, which is doubtful, it must have considered him queer and rebellious, certainly incapable of conforming with rational campus and fraternity standards. It was probably right. Meredith's feeling about Amherst, on the other hand, was fiercely resentful. As late as 1935, he wrote an account of his year there, which astonishingly was published in the *Graduates' Quarterly*. In one place he spoke of the fraternity system:

> Then the rushing season began. I went from house to house. They looked at me. They talked at me. The Psi Upsilons bought my car for $40 cash! (What a wealthy crew that was!) I did not receive a single bid. Neither did the Negro boys. Nor the Jewish boys. I don't know why, but none of us did. It appalled me . . . that fierce indestructible social barrier, especially to youngsters full of hope, which was set up by the fraternity problem.

There was clearly no companionship for him on the campus, but there were speakeasies in Northampton, and he went there, the $4 from the choir just enough for carfare and gin and ginger ale. His marks went down, and the greasy dishes he had to wash in the hotel made him sick.

One day an exponent of the Oxford religious movement came to town. A "Buchmanite." He was impressed, he said, by my understanding, and would like to talk to me sometime. I agreed.

The ensuing conversation was remarkable, however you look at it.

He said, "Tell me your sins."
I said, "I've sinned in heart and mind and deed. . . ."
He said, "Have you sinned with your roommate?"
"I have no roommate."
"Well—with another man?"
"No, by God!" I said.
"Don't swear," he admonished. "Are you sure?"
"Absolutely."

This was alarming, and so were the righteous and gleaming eyeglasses, but the lonely boy was hysterically grateful at being noticed, even so embarrassingly as this. In the end he began to cry.

"*Now*," the "Buchmanite" said triumphantly, "you are ready for God."
"What will I do?"
"God will reveal," he advised.
My next thought was to ask whether God would get me into a fraternity . . . and this struck me as so funny—what with me on my knees and everything, confessing what must have been mild iniquities to an Oxford man—that I burst into laughter.

The Oxford man, however, must have been accustomed to levity and hard to discourage, because in a little while the mail brought

Meredith a check for $7. The Buchmanites wanted him to go to
Boston to testify at a meeting. He cashed the check and bought a
ticket to his first prom.

For a while he felt better, but soon things were just as bad as ever.
He tried for the dramatic club and was chosen at once.

> That could have been my triumph, my change of heart. But
> the office declared I was ineligible for extra-curriculum activi-
> ties because of my studies.

Determined to act, he went over to Northampton to play Sir Toby
Belch in "Twelfth Night" with the Smith Dramatic Club, and was
nearly dismissed when the dean heard about it. The debts mounted,
and the loneliness, and "the continuous blundering sadness" of his
undergraduate life. When the end of the year came, there wasn't
even money for carfare to get away. Providentially—a last-minute
Providence seems to have operated for him as usual—he heard about
an annual declamation prize of $50. With only one day to prepare, he
memorized the last scene of "Cyrano de Bergerac," bellowed it at the
judges, and won.

The last words on Meredith's Amherst days come from the editor of the *Quarterly*, who added a deprecating postscript to his contributor's narrative:

> I do not think that this story should be taken as an indict-
> ment of Amherst College . . . though there are certain implied
> criticisms of the fraternity system that will not go unnoticed . . .
> but if he [Meredith] fulfills the promise of his youth, we must
> be a bit hesitant about taking full credit for his success.

It seems something of an understatement.

IF AMHERST HAD been sad and blundering, what came next
was bedlam. With no money, no especial ties, and certainly no purpose whatever, Meredith joined that strange army of young men,
between twenty and thirty, who wander from town to town, doing
odd jobs, getting fired, wandering on again. Once, during the

Christmas rush, he turned up at Macy's, selling eighty-nine-cent neckties, and made there an occasional, unexpected profit through the very circumstance that his merchandise was so eccentrically priced. One day, in a desperate attempt to keep up with the rush of last-minute shoppers, he gave a hurried lady her eleven cents' change out of his own pocket, and absentmindedly pocketed her dollar. There was, of course, no official record of the transaction, and Macy's never missed the tie. Forgetting to turn the dollar in to the cashier was a mistake that anybody might make, especially a temporary clerk who had been hungry almost as long as he could remember. Thereafter he made it often. Again, he found himself at the complaint desk in the fur department at Saks-Fifth Avenue, which was mysterious because he knew nothing whatever about furs. That experience ended when he told a protesting customer that caracul was naturally expensive because it had been a cold winter, and the little things had retired shyly under the ice. In various cities he sold roofing, vacuum cleaners, and toilet articles, and for two months he was a runner in Wall Street. Once, to his considerable mystification, he found himself back in college, at a place called St. Stephen's in Annandale-on-Hudson, and another time he lived for a week on the free samples that the Shredded Wheat Company gives to visitors to its plant in Niagara Falls. A man, he says, can get very tired of Shredded Wheat. He lived for a while in Brooklyn with a genial salesman of pornography, and after that up on West End Avenue with three young men whose income depended on their dealings with dubious pawnbrokers. Most of the time, though, he lived with another persistent bankrupt over a plumbing shop on Hudson Street. When the electric-light company discontinued the service in their apartment, they tapped the current from a hall light with a long extension cord, but the rent, of course, had to be paid, and that they accomplished by giving "rent parties," at which, for $3 each, the fortunate guests were provided with a lethal punch (one part alcohol, one part red wine, one part water) and entertainment of sorts. After three glasses of the punch, as a matter of fact, it didn't especially matter about the entertainment.

All this had to end, of course, and for Meredith it ended, curiously enough, with an ocean voyage. He had shipped with the Munson

Line as a common seaman on a tramp. He made one trip uneventfully, but on the second the lights of some South American port
seemed full of promise and he overstayed his shore leave to investigate them. He was brought back to America under arrest, which on
a tramp steamer can be a condition of singular tedium. He relieved
it as far as possible by reciting out loud everything he could remember, to the deep mystification of members of the crew who happened
to be passing the brig. The prisoner himself, however, was pleased
with the sound, and although it had never seriously occurred to
him up to that moment, he decided to be an actor.

As any number of sad young men will tell you, it is almost impossible to get on the stage unless you've been on it before, but Meredith
was not discouraged for long. From a kindly man in the theatre he
got a letter of introduction to Eva Le Gallienne. This letter warmly
praised his qualifications as an actor, although it was careful not to
say just exactly what they were, and in December, 1929, Meredith
became a member of the Civic Repertory Company. He was engaged as an apprentice, without pay, but at any rate he was on the
stage. During that winter he lived with his married sister in East
Orange and hoped for the best. His first part was that of a servant to
Juliet's nurse, and he had one line to say. The parts after that were a
little better, though, and by the spring he was getting $20 a week.

For the next two years he alternated between Miss Le Gallienne's
company and summer stock. (It was during his first summer in stock,
incidentally, that he drove the critic in White Plains so nearly out of
her wits.) In the fall of 1931, Miss Le Gallienne left the stage for a year
and, except for his appearance in a slightly misguided production of
"People on the Hill," Meredith had no rôles. With his roommate,
he spent his time organizing something called the Stage Society.
This was a coöperative venture in which the two directors and an
acting company of unemployed players worked without salary, with
an expectation of sharing in the profits. The general idea was that
for a $5 fee, subscribers would be entitled to see five plays in the
course of the winter. Everybody happily expected this scheme to
revolutionize the American theatre, and indeed it might have if it
hadn't been for the highly capricious judgment of the play-readers.
Nobody now seems to be able to remember the plays that were put

on, but among those that were turned down were "One Sunday Afternoon," "Another Language," and "Men in White." The Society dissolved in March still owing its fifteen hundred subscribers one play, which, incidentally, it still owes them and undoubtedly always will.

Twice more Meredith tried to arrange permanent acting companies, operating on a profit-sharing basis, and both collapsed from what seems to have been general inertia. In spite of these discouragements, he still believes the idea is practicable, and hopes to do something about it one of these days.

In the spring of 1932, he went back to stock, and in a casual interval between performances married Mrs. Helen Berrien Derby, on the stage of the summer theatre at Cape May, N.J. Mrs. Derby was also a member of the company; to be exact, she took the tickets. They were divorced in September, 1935, just as "Winterset" began its run.

Miss Le Gallienne reopened the Civic Repertory Theatre in the fall, and Meredith went back to Fourteenth Street. After playing small parts in "Liliom" and "Peter Pan" (in which J. Edward Bromberg, to his profound disgust, was cast as a Newfoundland), he reached his greatest New York triumph by playing three parts at once in "Alice in Wonderland." For being the Duck, the Dormouse, and Tweedledee, each of which involved elaborate and rather painful makeup, he was paid $30 a week.

The discomfort of pushing himself around the stage with roller skates strapped to his knees, as the Duck, combined with the indignity of wearing an enormous papier-mâché head, as Tweedledee, seems to have been too much, and in March Meredith left repertory (leaving Miss Le Gallienne, incidentally, with three expensive costumes that wouldn't fit anybody else) and entered his first Broadway production. This was "The 3-Penny Opera," and it was so clearly a mistake that, after a week, he signed a contract to appear in Albert Bein's "Little Ol' Boy."

He was paid $75 a week for the "Opera," but "Little Ol' Boy" brought him the stupefying sum of $225. It was undoubtedly more money than he'd ever expected to make legitimately in his life.

"Little Ol' Boy," the tragic, biting story of a reform-school waif, was a critical success, and Meredith's own notices were remarkable.

Stark Young, whose prose can also be tart, wrote in the *New Republic* that his performance was "as near perfection as could be imagined;" that what he achieved "was worth a hundred performances up and down the town." Even Mr. Nathan seemed to be pleased. The play lasted nine days.

This personal triumph, however, had its inevitable consequences. After another summer in stock, on November 20th, 1933, he opened in Howard Lindsay's "She Loves Me Not."

The play was a prodigious success, and Meredith, tap-dancing to the balanced periods of a Walter Lippmann editorial, proved his versatility, if nothing else. When "She Loves Me Not" finally closed, however, he got mixed up in another project that must still trouble his dreams. In October, 1934, he signed a contract to broadcast a program called "Red Davis," sponsored by Beech-Nut Gum, for the National Broadcasting Company. Red Davis was described as "radio's typical American boy." He was an athlete and a woman-hater and he spoke with a homely, nasal drawl which his sponsors insisted was characteristic of adolescent America. "Hey, Maw, kin I go out an' play ball" may not have been an actual line in any script, but it was typical of all of them.

Meredith got $350 a week for this repellent performance. In his innocence, he imagined that he had signed to broadcast three times a week; actually, his contract stipulated that he was to appear three *nights* a week, which is something quite different. To his horror, he learned that there was a regular Eastern broadcast at 7:30, a rebroadcast for the states west of the Mississippi at 11:30; and after that a phonograph recording for smaller stations not on the regular network. Each ghastly episode, it seemed, had to be run through three times. As if this weren't enough, almost throughout the series he was appearing on the stage—in "Hipper's Holiday" and "Battleship Gertie" (neither of which can have been much solace to his outraged spirit) and finally in "The Barretts of Wimpole Street." In order to get from the theatre to the station in time for the rebroadcast, he hired a private ambulance for $15 a night and went clanging magnificently through the streets. In a way, however, this outlandish double life was a protection. As long as he was acting between 8:30 and 11, he didn't have much time to brood about Red Davis.

Disaster came only when one of the plays closed and he was temporarily without a part. Leaving the studios one night, after an especially wholesome Eastern broadcast, he wandered into a Sixth Avenue bar and sat down. While he thought darkly of the Typical American Boy, he availed himself of the hospitality of the house, and when he happened to look at the clock, it was long after midnight.

When Meredith appeared apprehensively at the studios the next day, however, he found the broadcasting executives almost too shocked to be outraged. It was possible that Mr. Meredith didn't realize the magnitude of the calamity. Not only had five million kiddies been deprived of their usual inspiration, but his defection, to put the thing as charitably as possible, had cost the studio just exactly $62,000. They had been obliged to put a paid advertisement in every newspaper west of the Mississippi, explaining that Red Davis had been suddenly taken ill. It was a national disaster. It was more than that. There was no predicting the effect this announcement might have on the immature mind; it was even possible that some skeptical infants might think he got that way from chewing Beech-Nut Gum.

Later this preposterous experience gave Meredith a queer, uncomfortable sense of power, but at the moment he simply waited dully for the words that would dismiss him in disgrace from the air. Incredibly, they never came. There can be no question that the executives would have *liked* to fire Meredith, but it seemed they couldn't. So firmly was his special version of the Davis accent fixed in the juvenile mind that any substitute would have been detected instantly. Regardless of its personal feelings, which were strong, the Beech-Nut Company couldn't quite bring itself to break so many childish hearts. Upon his promise to be more careful after that, Meredith was pardoned, and the program dragged uneventfully out to its conclusion. He was Red Davis for forty weeks. It is hard to believe that any actor has ever loathed his creation quite so much.

In comparison with Red, in fact, even his experience in making "Winterset" for the movies must have seemed almost a pleasure. But, in spite of the fact that he was paid $1,500 a week, it was bad enough. On his first day on the lot, he was puzzled when an assistant director gave him a suit of rubber underwear and told him to put it on under his costume. Its purpose was soon only too clear. For ten weeks he wore the rubber underwear while from perforated pipes overhead a thin, synthetic rain drifted over the set. Even this didn't satisfy the Hollywood realists, and from time to time a property man stepped forward and sprayed his face with Nujol from a Flit gun. These things were irritating, and so was the set of porcelain caps which a studio dentist slipped over his own teeth and which almost invariably fell out at the height of his most emotional scenes. The worst thing of all, though, was that the studio wouldn't let him fly an airplane in his spare time, but this somehow seems reasonable enough. Meredith is a student pilot, and neatly typed at the bottom of his licence is a peculiar sentence. "The student," it says, "has a tendency to see double."

In spite of those ten weeks, which might be expected to turn an actor against any play in the world, Mio, in "Winterset," remains his favorite part.

"It was the hardest, pleasantest, and most rewarding thing I ever played," he says. "Hard, because I had to overcome the immense technical hazard of presenting a great and poetic line spoken by a lowly person. Each line, each performance, was a challenge. Pleasant, because the play lifted people up. You felt that all the time you were on the stage."

"Winterset," of course, was also his greatest success. It was the first time he had been starred in any production—he took a picture of his name in lights the first night it went up—and when the play won the drama critics' award, it seemed somehow to guarantee him stature and permanence. Beyond that, it had an important effect on his personal life. Although he had been a featured player for some time, with an income ranging around $12,000 a year, his living arrangements had remained more or less haphazard. He had had an apartment in the Village, but most of the time he stayed at hotels, any hotel that was convenient. The grateful restaurateurs along Fifty-second Street knew him as a regular and prodigal customer. A month after "Winterset" opened, Maxwell Anderson, who seems to have been watching this gaiety with some misgivings, persuaded him to leave New York and take a house in Sneden's Landing, twenty miles up the Hudson. Here he met Margaret Perry, whose mother,

Antoinette Perry, has been associated with Brock Pemberton in producing several plays, including "Strictly Dishonorable" and "Ceiling
Zero." Her daughter had appeared in both these productions, but
she had agitated New York even more fiercely when she married
Winsor French of Cleveland in a ceremony which cost $18,000 and
involved entertaining two thousand people at a reception at the Park
Lane. By this time both Miss Perry and Meredith had been divorced,
and they were married at Piermont, New York, on January 10th,
1936. After that, they went to live in a remodelled farmhouse at
Mount Ivy, which is near Nyack, and not far from Maxwell Anderson's own house. They live there still. It is a pleasant, casual place,
designed apparently by a humorous architect, because no two rooms
are on the same level, or even approximately the same level, and the
unwary guest going from one to another takes his life in his hands.

Every night, or *almost* every night, after the curtain comes down
on "High Tor," Meredith drives out to Mount Ivy in a Packard operated by an Englishman called Wood, who transforms himself from
a dressing-room valet into a chauffeur instantaneously by the simple
device of putting on a chauffeur's cap. It was Wood, incidentally,
who paid his employer one of the most peculiar compliments of his
career. Once, at an early performance of "Winterset," a suburban
lady fainted from sheer rapture, and was removed. Wood dutifully
reported this to the star, and added, "Congratulations, sir. I don't believe that's happened in a New York theatre since Mr. Valentino
died."

Meredith's life at present must seem to him very nearly ideal.
The Andersons, the McClintics, and practically all the other people
he has known in the theatre come to Mount Ivy and talk until
morning about the abstractions that fascinate him. His wife is amiably
disposed to accept the fact that his conduct is, and always will be, a
little unpredictable. For the second time he is in the play that won
the critics' award. This summer he will make another picture; next
winter he would like to go to London and play at the Old Vic, or
else to do a play of Pirandello's called "One Does Not Know How"
in New York. His forty-two-page contract with R.K.O. calls for one
picture a year, any time he wants to make it, for eight years, and for
the final picture his salary will have risen to $3,500 a week. In

"Winterset," on the stage, he was paid $750 a week, and in "High Tor" he gets the same thing, plus five per cent of the box-office gross. Professionally and financially (his wife, incidentally, inherited a little over $600,000 from her father, who was Henry L. Doherty's partner), it would hardly seem that he has much to worry about, but Amherst and Macy's and most especially the diet of Shredded Wheat have left him with a mild pessimism.

"When I didn't have a dime for a cup of coffee," he says, "I didn't think *that* was going to last, and sometimes I'm not so sure that this is going to last either."

April 3, 1937

THE DIAMOND GARDENIA~I

Manhattan café society, of course, existed long before June 1st, 1934, but that was when it first came into open glory. Before that there had been only a life of rumor and hearsay. The little man of the suburbs was aware of this braver world, but it came to him dimly—the breath of it in the wistful gossip of his wife's friends; official confirmation of it when the press reported, for instance, that Belle Livingstone, a celebrated professional hostess of the era, had raced over the housetops in her pajamas, the prohibition agents buzzing angrily at her heels. As a matter of fact, Miss Livingstone's invitation to the opening of her Fifty-eighth Street Country Club in November, 1930, has survived, and it gives us an agreeable picture of that abundant though secret life:

> In an atmosphere of the piquant and beautiful it will be my aim to bring together the monied and the mental, both the aristocracy of Park Avenue and of the intellect; to bring back to our time something of the camaraderie and joyance of the Venetian carnivals, of the Florentian fiestas, days when an opulent and colorful aristocracy fraternized with the shining spirits that made the world beautiful through poetry, philosophy and art! My opening will mark a gesture to recover—for those qualified to appreciate or afford it—the spirit of unadulated [sic], unsynthetic and pristine joy!

Newspaper reports of the raid added that Miss Livingstone had gone to the rather unusual expense of installing a running brook in her clubrooms and stocking it with live eels. They were Bourbons and parasites themselves, those eels; they were not to eat.

After the heat had been applied to Miss Livingstone, the gesture to recover pristine joy collapsed for the moment. Certainly, how-

ever, this was the life. The only trouble was that the news of it was
sporadic and unsatisfying. Café society, in fact, needed a prophet,
and four years later, in the person of Lucius Morris Beebe, himself
of a piquant, beautiful, and even moderately Florentian aspect, it
got one. Starting in that enlightened June, his column, called "This
New York," was published every Saturday in the *Herald Tribune*,
and rapidly thereafter the world of fashion took form and substance.

Almost in the beginning Mr. Beebe pointed out that the old
order—the society of Mrs. Astor, Mrs. Fish, and the Four Hundred—
had had its day, though it might be that it still persisted dustily in
the boxes at the Metropolitan or lingered among the ghostly antiques at the Charity Ball. New York, however, had no further use for
an aristocracy postulated sheerly on family. Café society was the
thing.

"A general definition of café society," Mr. Beebe instructed the
multitude, "might be: an unorganized but generally recognized
group of persons who participate in the professional and social life
of New York available to those possessed of a certain degree of affluence and manners."

Students may note that this remark, though in rather less deliri-
ous prose, is exactly what Miss Livingstone said about the shining
spirits.

Coming down to the particular, Mr. Beebe provided some samples
of the manners and habits of the new order. Café society, he explained, meets almost invariably at night, although there are reports of
it at cocktails, and even at lunch, when, as its biographer notes with
fond amusement, it is pale and eats with loathing. At night, however, all this is changed. It is a lively aristocracy that meets at 21 for
dinner, rushes off to an opening, and gathers finally at El Morocco,
where at last it enters the full kingdom of Heaven.

"Inside the door," writes Mr. Beebe on a muffled keyboard, "there
are two or three hat-check girls of positively iridescent beauty. And
beyond them is Carino, most urbane of waiter captains . . . on whose
favors and discretion hang feuds and romances, careers, aspirations,
and the very foundations . . . of the social hierarchy. Fortunes and
professional careers have been made by sitting at the right table at
Morocco, believe it or not, and people have been known to leave

town because Carino had said that he was sorry, but all the tables were taken. . . . The café set of Manhattan firmly believes that if a given celebrity fails to show up at Morocco three or four times a week, he is dead."

This is the landscape; single figures in it are harder to discern. There is a group movement, a communal surge and flow, a frantic beating of the splendid wings. It is like trying to isolate a single butterfly in a lovely cloud of them:

Stanley Sackett pays $7.50 a pair for his French lisle socks . . . Doris Duke has nine Rolls-Royces . . . Ona Munson's drawing-room is quite littered with pianos . . . M. André Simon of the Wine and Food Society ordered a bowl of spring flowers removed because it infringed on the bouquet of the Château Latour '20 . . . Margaret Valdi Curtis, a relative of Lord Asquith, is around town singing Tahitian songs in a straw skirt . . . Mrs. Graham Fair Vanderbilt's butler is reported to have been dismissed for saying "O. K., madam" . . . Prince Kyril Scherbatoff, A. K. Mills and this department discovered the other day they were wearing identical suits. Tony Williams is a wretch to have duplicated them on us.

Sometimes the glass of fashion is clearer; the portrait almost three-dimensional:

Cecil Beaton, the languid photographer of folk who count, is back in town from London, and bravely carrying the torch for clothes that set Manhattan's lorgnons a'quiver. He showed up at the Colony for lunch last week in a little number Lanvin had run up for him in a pale shade of apple green, with a darker green waistcoat, double-breasted and buttoned with gold and emerald links. Everyone remarked how fine and brave he was.

In the end, though, it is useless. The movement is too swift and nervous, the colors too bright for the unaccustomed eye. We are told that Mr. Karl K. Kitchen, a celebrated gourmet, once swept a soufflé wearily to the floor because it was badly made; that Miss Virginia Faulkner, a fashionable *littérateuse*, gave a hungry cab-driver twenty-five dollars' worth of truffled *pâté de foie gras* in a Strasbourg crock; that an unidentified lady is in the habit of monopolizing a style by buying one hundred and forty-five identical hats at thirty-five dollars each; and that somewhere on Fifth Avenue a whimsical jeweller stocks gold ear-clips to pin a spaniel's ears over its head, out of its soup.

According to Mr. Beebe, there are no more than five hundred men and women in the United States of sufficient wealth, charm, and leisure to be considered members of café society. Furthermore, its leaders are hard to identify, since there are neither degrees in perfection nor rulers in Utopia. It is a grave responsibility to award the laurels, and Mr. Beebe himself approaches it warily. He supplies eleven names, but does not "by any means suggest that they are the ranking members." They are merely the names that come to him first, their frequency of public appearance having at least as much to do with it as any special and unearthly lustre. With this firmly understood, he names dread names: Mr. Dwight Fiske, Mrs. Tiffany Saportas, Mr. Alfred de Liagre, Mr. and Mrs. Harry Bull, Mrs. Brock Pemberton, Mr. Nicky de Molas, Miss Valentina Schlee, Miss Gloria Braggiotti, Mrs. James Finan, Miss Beatrice Lillie.

As you can see, the structure of the new society is not easy to understand, and there is little in Mr. Beebe's style to make it easier. Ingrained in his character, there is a profound nostalgia for dead elegance, and his prose is consequently heavy with Gothic ornament. Almost anything on wheels becomes a "herdic;" a serving dish is a "firkin;" "zounds" and "egad" break up the rolling periods. It is impossible for him to write "hat" or "street" or "policeman." They are transmuted into "chapeau," "faubourg," and "gendarme," and at one time the Gallic inspiration was so strong upon him that "success foolish" and "but incredible" threatened to unseat whatever was left of his readers' minds. Beyond all this, he has a hearty squire's contempt for spelling and syntax. Mr. Beebe has written "superceded" and "screetches;" he has written "pleural" when he was not referring to the thorax, and "illusions" when he must have meant "allusions."

The total effect might lead a critic to imagine some heavenly communion of Van Bibber, Philo Vance, and the author of "The Young Visiters."[1]

IT IS NECESSARY to go to the past to discover how Mr. Beebe got the way he is. The first recorded member of the family, a Northamptonshire yeoman, the grandson of a shoemaker, sailed for America in 1650. He died on the voyage, but five of his children, three sons and two daughters, landed at New London and took happily to the soil. The family did so well that by 1750 they were men of property in the Galsworthian sense and warmly Tory in their sympathies. One of them, indeed, had managed to ally himself with a lady who, if we may believe a genealogy compiled by one of her grateful descendants, was able to trace her line over the sea to Charlemagne.

In 1825 Junius Beebe sailed before the mast in a packet from Boston to New Orleans, where he eventually opened a waterfront warehouse, trading the produce of the farms and factories of New England for Southern cotton. Three of his brothers joined him almost at once, and as there was a handsome profit in it, it marked the final emergence of the Beebes as "warm men," in the pleasant old phrase.

Lucius, the second brother, was the travelling representative of the firm, and his business often took him back to the North. At last, in 1853, he settled in Wakefield, Massachusetts, and Junius, his ninth child, was born there the following year. Junius was a true descendant of the men who had gone before him, and by the time he was twenty-five, he was serving as a partner in the leather business which his father had bought in 1871. Later he became its president, and also held office at one time or another as president of the Wakefield Trust Company, president of the Brockton Gas Company, director of the Atlantic National Bank of Boston, and director of the Mutual Chemical Company of New York.

In 1886, he married Eleanor Harriet Merrick, of Walpole, Massachusetts, whose father was a professor of chemistry at Harvard and a close friend of Emerson, Thoreau, and other arresting literary monuments of the day. The subject of this investigation was Junius' fourth child. He was born at Wakefield on December 9th, 1902.

Here, very sketchily, is the heredity, and it can easily be seen that a child born of such a line would be brought up to a sense of security and permanence. He was also, since Wakefield was essentially a Beebe squirearchy (all the stores were closed the day old Lucius Beebe died), very apt to feel a little like God.

Lucius spent his early life on Beebe Farm, which takes in 140 pleasant acres on the outskirts of the town. He was sent to the local public school, early democratic immersion being a tradition in the family, and didn't especially like or dislike it. He remembers only that there were fist fights at recess and the immemorial smell of disinfectant in the corridors. The only man, in fact, whose influence can be traced in his later life was the licenced town blaster. He seems to have been a casual dynamiter, and left his stock in accessible places, so that Lucius, equipped with high explosives and a rudimentary knowledge of how to use them, was often a leader in the ancient rural pastime of blowing up outhouses. These forgotten explosions are significant only because they were the first of an endless series of practical jokes with which Lucius was to enchant, bore, and annoy his contemporaries for the next twenty years. They were the beginning of what persistently delayed adolescents in their thirties still call the Beebe Legend.

At fifteen, it was decided that he had outgrown the North Ward School, and he was sent to St. Marks in Southboro. His visit there was brief, culminating in another experiment with a homemade bomb. St. Marks, which apparently had its own New England respect for property, could discover no humor in this, and he was sent home. The next school was Berkshire, in Sheffield, and here more sinister activities were born. He was about seventeen, and he had discovered alcohol. He confined these first ventures to Boston, but the faculty found out about them anyway, and returned him politely to Wakefield. He was not especially appreciated, either, by his father, who, with the exception of a little claret at Christmas, had never allowed liquor to be served in his house. In a determined, but certainly misguided, attempt to insure discipline in the future, he decided that the place for his son was the Roxbury School in Cheshire, Connecticut, a few miles outside New Haven.

In 1920 Roxbury was beyond question the most efficient of the

New England tutoring schools, the ultimate hothouse for forcing talents elsewhere abandoned as dead on the vine. There is no especial record of him in Cheshire, and it was probably a time of quiet contemplation. Unconsciously, he may have been on the verge of discovering his life's work, because café society was there in microcosm, and he found it fascinating. It was while Lucius was at Roxbury, for instance, that Phil Plant, a celebrated schoolmate whose vivacity has diminished very little with the years, wrecked his car early one morning in the Bronx. Among his passengers was a "Follies" girl who suffered injuries which, in her subsequent suit against Plant, she estimated roundly at half a million dollars. These were spectacular doings. To a Boston boy of eighteen, it must have seemed that only in a fabulous world could such things happen to a contemporary, and it is reasonable to suppose that the conflict between heredity and environment started then, if it hadn't before. Whatever spiritual effect Roxbury had on him, however, it had the material one of making him decide to go to Yale, which was also the destination of most of his glittering classmates.

Yale was a larger field, and heterogeneous. You could, of course, go in for the pleasures of the world, but you could also be an athlete or a scholar or a politician; you could even be poor and worthy and industrious. Without hesitation, Lucius elected to be a scholar and a dandy. Even in those days, his clothes were remarkable. A friend remembers seeing him often on his way from New Haven to New York in the club car of the Knickerbocker Limited "immense and immaculate" in full dress, with a gold-headed cane. Sometimes he came back on the newspaper train and went to an 8 A.M. French class in the same attire. His three cutaways were a wonder of the college, and just before Junior Prom he was suddenly popular with large upperclassmen who had ideas about borrowing them. There is a legend that he introduced the first pair of white linen plus fours to the campus, and that Professor Chauncey B. Tinker, seeing them at a distance, complained irritably that the place was getting overrun with women.

"Don't look," he said, "but here come two of them right now."

The *Yale News* referred appreciatively to Lucius's "grey orchidaceous trousers" and "vine-crowned high hat," and added that "two hemispheres knew him at nineteen," which perhaps was a little excessive.

He lived alone in Durfee Hall in a style that was more or less commensurate with his wardrobe. Drawings by Picasso covered the walls; there was a roulette wheel that disappeared ingeniously when it seemed prudent; a bookcase revolved and became a bar. It was his boast that even in those days, when prohibition was at least semi-effective, he was equipped to make any drink a guest could name. Once a man who had ordered an especially peculiar mixture thought his host was baffled when he muttered and fumbled in the shelves.

"Of course, if you haven't got anisette . . ."

"Anisette, hell!" said Lucius petulantly. "We're out of ice."

An innocent freshman was surprised to learn that Mr. Beebe existed in the flesh. He had imagined that "Lucius Beebe" was simply the conventional password when you wanted to get into a speakeasy.

The culture, though, was the really formidable thing. A man who is still troubled when he thinks about it recalls that years ago, when he was an undergraduate, he was approached by an intense and fashionable stranger in a Chapel Street bar.

"You look," he said, "as if you'd be the only man here who'd be interested in knowing that I've just finished a *ballade à refrain redoublé*. I'll read it to you."

Which he did.

WHILE LUCIUS WAS still a freshman, he published a book of verse called "Fallen Stars," and contributed often to the *Yale Literary Magazine* and the *Record*, winning the Richard Memorial Prize for the best contribution to the latter during 1922–23. It is not charitable, of course, to investigate such early works too thoroughly. A casual examination indicates that they were of a rich and gloomy aspect, holding out little hope for a corrupt time. One of them was reviewed, in question-and-answer form, in the *News*:

Q. What is the theme?

A. Defeat, foreseen or expected, lying in wait for American materialism.

Q. What does the author indicate will remain after said defeat?
A. Nothing.

The first and last stanzas of the poem were also quoted:

I am weary of these times and their dull burden,
Sweating and laboring in the summer noontide,
And the hot stench of inland forges
Sickens my nostrils.

Soon there will be no more metals to plunder,
There will be no more forests to slash and dismember,
Then, O chosen people, nation of fortune,
Where is thy glory?

In the end, it was culture that undid him. In January, 1924, the *Yale News* published the result of a poll on prohibition among the students of the Divinity School, showing that these good young men stood 99 to 1 in favor of complete enforcement. Even the solitary dissenter was not wholly lost; he voted only for light wines and beer. For some reason, these innocent statistics infuriated the young Villon, and in a letter which combined the mannerisms of George Jean Nathan with those of a retired colonel writing to the London *Times*, he denounced them: "One of the obsolete institutions trading on the name of Yale . . . out of the colossal cavity of their ignorance . . . innocent device that proved a pleasure to Jesus Christ . . . exhibit their poltroonish idiocy . . . Such whim-wham we may look for in pretzel-varnishers . . . dodos and dinosaurs at large on the campus." It was signed "Petronius."

His fellow-rakehells were enchanted, but Professor Henry Hallam Tweedy, at the moment in charge of the Divinity School, was only pained. He gave the blasphemer a pamphlet listing the good works of Yale men in China, and reproved him for calling these potential martyrs cowards. Lucius, who had been under the dim impression that "poltroon" meant "fool," apologized in another letter to the *News*, but the holy rebuke apparently rankled.

Two weeks later the members of an audience at the Hyperion

Theatre were astounded to see a tall, extravagantly bearded figure rise in one of the stage boxes. Their first impression that he was part of the show was dispelled when he addressed them furiously.

"I am Professor Tweedy of the Yale Divinity School!" he shouted, and flung an empty bottle to the stage.

It took them a little while to remove Mr. Beebe, because he had been prudent enough to lock himself in, but almost no time at all for President Angell to make up his mind that such exuberance was not for Yale. Lucius left in the middle of his sophomore year, complaining that, as usual, his motives seemed to have been misinterpreted.

After he had spent a tiresome year as a reporter on the now defunct Boston *Telegram*, Harvard got him, and there is a story that President Angell took official notice of the transfer in a letter to President Lowell—"I apologize for sending you such a bad potato." At any rate, the practical-joke mill was still operating at full blast. We hear of him hiring an airplane and flying over the pleasure fleet at New London, festooning J. P. Morgan's Corsair with streamers of toilet paper. It was Lucius who circulated a ballot to determine whether it would be profitable for Harvard to trade President Lowell and three full professors for a good running backfield. The motion was barely lost—1,234 to 1,227—but the story was widely circulated. He also attracted quite a lot of attention when he counterfeited and sold a sheaf of tickets for the Hale House Ball, and was set free by the police only after he had persuaded his brother to post one of the family lots on Commonwealth Avenue for bail. One night he stood up in a box at Loew's State Theatre and responded graciously to the applause of an audience which had been led to suppose that he was Governor John Trumbull of Connecticut. On Christmas Eve, when the Locke-Ober Café seemed to him sadly lacking in atmosphere, he paid a pretty sentimental tribute to the day by hiring a newsboy to stand outside in the snow and press his nose hungrily against the pane.

In his quieter moments, Lucius lived very much as he had at Yale. There was usually a little trouble at the bank because of overdrafts, and enough rumors reached Wakefield to make things difficult there, too. However, he diverted himself on the whole with a fair amount of contentment. He lived for a time in a boarding house known as Mrs. Murphy's Summer Palace, and later in an apartment in Ridgely Hall which was convenient for his friends. When his father was amiable and funds were high, he ate magnificently at the Touraine—he wore a monocle, and was embarrassed when it fell into the soup and had to be fished out and dried by a waiter. When times were hard, he went to cafeterias and drank homemade gin.

Lucius was graduated from Harvard with the class of 1927, but remained in the Graduate School to study poetry under Professor John Lowes. He had already published a book about Villon, and another volume of verse, "Corydon and Other Poems," which netted him thirty-two dollars in royalties. He was at work on a thesis on the poetry of the late Edwin Arlington Robinson, whose habit of interpreting the New England scene in terms of Arthurian legend could not fail to charm a young man who had identified himself romantically with both these worlds.

Curiously enough, it was this sober and innocent work of scholarship which led to his downfall. In preparing his thesis, he had borrowed from Mr. Robinson the manuscript copy of a hundred and sixty-four lines of blank verse which the poet had deleted, as unbearably florid, from the final version of "Lancelot." The *Yale University Library Gazette* is authority for what followed:

Photographs were made of this manuscript, for they were to be bound in Mr. Beebe's thesis—where they now are. But before they were thus legitimately used, they served another purpose. For, from seeing them about, Mr. Beebe . . . one evening conceived the notion of having printed from them the rarest of all Robinson items, an edition of two copies of the fragment. Wrappers and title-page were printed at one establishment, the text at another. In order that there might be copies of record, however, seventeen and not two were assembled, folded, and trimmed by the clandestine editor. Some were sent to libraries in England and America, others were given to individuals; and thus one of the rarer of modern books had come into being. There are at the moment not more than seven copies in private hands. Only one copy has, to the best of the writer's knowledge,

been sold; for it was not a business venture—a fact which earned
for Mr. Beebe Mr. Robinson's forgiveness for the piracy.

Before he was forgiven, however, there were reproachful letters
from the poet, and Lucius thought often and irritably about the man,
another undergraduate bibliophile named Wetherby, who had first
called Mr. Robinson's attention to the theft. One night, after dining
handsomely in Boston, Lucius went to call on the traitor. There was
an argument, and in the course of it a heavy bookcase fell or was
thrown. Mr. Robinson's informant was taken to the infirmary, suspected of having a fractured skull, and for a time he was not expected
to live. Harvard, not unreasonably averse to being the scene of a trial
for manslaughter, acted promptly, and for the second time Lucius
was a martyr to culture.

He was not, however, especially depressed. He had enjoyed
Yale, but for some reason Harvard had seemed dull. Perhaps he had
outgrown the campus. The distillation of Boston and Babylon, of
recondite scholarship and grandiose frivolity, was coming to a slow
boil. "Nothing matters but the gallant gesture," he told a young
lady, who was so agreeably impressed that she embalmed it forever
in her diary. He had perfected an attitude. He was ready for the
world.

(This is the first of two articles on Mr. Beebe.)

WHEN LUCIUS BEEBE came to the *Herald Tribune* from the Boston *Transcript,* in June, 1929, he was twenty-seven years old, six feet four inches tall, and weighed in the neighborhood of a hundred and eighty pounds. His blond hair was closely cropped, and he looked strongly Germanic, like an especially rubicund officer in the Potsdam Guard. When he was introduced to Stanley Walker, the city editor, he clicked his heels and bowed from the waist. He said "sir" in a tone of booming deference, to the grateful amazement of the *Tribune* staff, which was not itself inclined to be punctilious.

Mr. Walker had never seen a reporter of such baroque design, but he was no man to recoil from the unknown, and he hired Beebe for thirty-five dollars a week. Thus began a career which may be tritely described as unique in American journalism, although it can never be said that Mr. Beebe was much of a reporter. He had an apathy about facts which verged closely on actual dislike, and the tangled wildwood of his prose was poorly adapted to describing small fires and negligible thefts. His splendid plumage and a certain jovial condescension in his manner were probably a source of either terror or indignation to the homely citizens who provide the bulk of routine news. We hear of him, in a top hat and opera cape, arriving fashionably late for the annual dinner of the Landscape Gardening Society, and there is a story that he attended a fire in a morning coat. Nor was he always very clear about his assignments. Told to cover a banquet of the New York Central Railroad Engineers, he appeared somehow at one sponsored by the Caledonian Club, and after lingering only long enough to get a prepared copy of the principal speech, went back to his office to report that the President of the Central had incomprehensibly chosen to talk to his men about Scotland. He was astonished by the clamor which the publication of this item aroused, being clearly of the opinion that one damn dull dinner was very much like another.

Only a sort of heroic obstinacy can have kept Mr. Beebe from resigning early in his career. He was a tower of Boston erudition and his social philosophy would have amused Marie-Antoinette, and yet he was being asked to wear out his life in vulgar trivialities. The martyrdom went on for two years, at the end of which he was transferred to the dramatic department, for which he reviewed occasional moving pictures and dubious plays and wrote interviews with the players. Even here he must have been something of a problem. He had his own opinion of Hollywood, calling it the "outhouse civilization of the world, full of preposterous mountebanks and bores who live in the most witless and spurious manner ever devised," and this Bourbon estimate was reflected in his work. It didn't matter so much about the plays, since most of them had been damned before they were born, and further abuse was superfluous. The interviews were all right, too, except that when they were printed, it could be observed that the subjects, both men and women, all spoke in an educated and haughty manner, rather reminiscent of Mr. Beebe himself.

It can reasonably be supposed that Harry Staton, the manager of the Herald Tribune Syndicate, spent the summer of 1933 brooding over the cinema, because in the fall he turned up with the conception of New York as Babylon-on-the-Hudson, sinful, extravagant, full of the nervous hilarity of the doomed. It was Mr. Staton's idea that a column could be written exploiting this point of view, and that that richly upholstered Babylonian, Lucius Morris Beebe, was the man to do it.

At first the column was tried out almost furtively; on September 9th, it appeared in the Philadelphia *Inquirer,* a little later in the Wyoming *Pioneer.* The readers of these two journals accepted it happily, their gaudiest suspicions about New York confirmed and amplified, but it was not until the first of the following June that the *Tribune* itself, which had been skeptical, decided to give it a try. In the outlands, the column had been called "So This Is New York!" and

"New York Speaking," but these were dismissed as rustic and collo-
quial. Thenceforth it appeared with simple austerity as "This New
York."

Almost from the beginning it was a success. The actual circle
Mr. Beebe wrote about was small, but its potential public was enormous. "This New York" was read with awe in the social twilight of
the upper West Side, and in the ineligible portions of Westchester
and Long Island; it even had its bitter nuisance value in Union Square,
where Mr. Kyle Crichton, the most persistently vocal of the oppressed, described its author as "a sort of sandwich-man for the
rich." Very soon Mr. Beebe had seven papers in addition to the
Tribune—in Cleveland, Kansas City, St. Louis; in all the cities, in
fact, where the society he wrote about existed in wistful miniature.
Boston and Washington, of course, remained aloof, and so did the
proud South. At one time, however, he had a paper in Ketchikan,
an Alaskan fishing community of 6,000 population, although this
was more or less accidental. The editor of this paper, in New York
on a vacation, was handsomely entertained by the members of the
Tribune staff, including Mr. Beebe, and he returned to Alaska unaware in his grateful daze that he had contracted to take "This New
York" for the next six months. He printed it dutifully, but apparently the doings of Miss Elsa Maxwell and the Grand Duchess Marie were matters of indifference to the sturdy fishermen, because the
contract was not renewed.

Mr. Beebe's eight papers reach a total of a million and a half
readers, and while this may seem trifling compared with such a co-
lossus of syndication as O. O. McIntyre, who has five hundred papers and is presumably read by every American who can spell, it is
sufficiently remarkable in view of the fact that "This New York"
deals almost exclusively with perhaps five hundred patrons in four
or five restaurants.[2]

At any rate he must be regarded as at least moderately successful.
Last winter, in response to a letter from San Simeon suggesting that
Beebe be lured into "the big league," King Features offered him a
contract for five hundred dollars a week to write for the twenty-
odd Hearst papers, plus fifty per cent of the gross sales to outside
sheets. Agents from Hollywood have approached him, and even

radio, which he regards as a medium "debased beyond the dreams of vulgarity," has made its timid advances. He has declined them all, feeling that the *Tribune* is the proper and inevitable vehicle for his talent, which perhaps it is.

Money is a more or less secondary interest, in any case. Mr. Beebe's father left no estate on his death in 1934, but he had previously set up a trust fund amounting to roughly $200,000, and Lucius also benefits from the terms of an insurance trust, which brings in about $2,000 a year. He is half-owner of the 140-acre Beebe farm at Wakefield, Massachusetts, and has substantial shares in other Beebe properties, including an apple orchard in the State of Washington, considerable real estate in Key West and Mineola, and Lucius Beebe & Son Leather Company. He estimates that these bring him roughly $12,000 a year, while market ventures in oil and Canadian gold have recently added $5,000 more. His salary from the syndicate and the dramatic department comes to about $7,500 annually, and usually he makes $5,000 more from books, lectures, and magazines. He made a small profit—less than a hundred dollars a week—during the time he had a quarter-interest in the American Music Hall, but sold his share back to John Krimsky last winter during the run of "Naughty-Naught." In spite of reports that he is worth at least a million dollars, however, he says that if he could liquidate everything he owns, it would come to rather less than $300,000.

Even at that he should be comfortable enough. He has always been a bachelor—his friends would be a little startled if he ever married—and that cuts down expenses. He lives on the seventh floor of the Hotel Madison, in a suite which was handsomely panelled by a former occupant. This apartment is not remarkable except for the photographs of its inmate, which lie under the glass tops of the bureaus and tables or stare robustly from a hundred frames. Most of them were taken by Jerome Zerbe, a fashionable gnome who has remarked that he almost *never* photographs people who go to second nights. His art has given us Mr. Beebe as perhaps he most often thinks of himself—the heir of a richer tradition, urbane, intolerant, a little tired.

Concealed in drawers and closets about these premises is probably the most industriously publicized male wardrobe outside Hollywood.

In February of this year, Lucius was chosen one of the ten best-dressed men in America by the National Merchant Tailors Association, an honor diminished only for the captious by the fact that the man who cuts Mr. Beebe's clothes happened to be president of it. Lucius has posed in fashion shows, and his picture has decorated countless articles in the glossy journals of the clothing trade. Once, when he went to Hollywood for a ten-day stay (and discovered to his horror that the natives ate baked grapefruit, grape soup, and hard-boiled eggs Gloria Swanson), he took seven pieces of luggage, containing, among other things, nine suits and seventy-two shirts.

He owns about forty suits at a time, ten of them formal outfits of one kind and another. His dress shirts are made for him in Boston from the same paper pattern, miraculously unfrayed, which was used for his father in the late seventies, and he usually goes home at midnight and puts on a fresh one. He has a good evening dress coat lined with mink and collared in astrakhan which he has insured for $3,000, and an old rag, also lined with mink, but with a sable collar, which didn't seem worth the bother. The jewels necessary to set off these splendors, or else to hold them together, include three gold cigarette cases (although he rarely smokes anything but cigars), valued at approximately $700 each; a cashmere sapphire cabochon ring worth $1,200; a single emerald stud at $500, and a platinum evening watch which cost $1,000. He estimates that any man can be as gallantly arrayed at a cost of about $1,200 a year, not including jewelry, and if you usher at as many fashionable weddings as he does, a lot of that is free. Mr. Beebe believes, or says he does, that dressing properly is with him a question of professional obligation rather than vain personal adornment.

"I wear formal clothes, morning or evening, whenever they are called for," he says, "and regard them quite literally as the livery of my business. As a reporter for the *Tribune*, I would no more think of appearing in a restaurant in the evening out of dinner dress than I would in swimming shorts."

But then, perhaps lest the *Tribune* grow unbearably proud, he adds an afterthought: "Also, of course, you get better tables and better service."

The only flaw in his total perfection would not be apparent to a casual observer: he never wears an undershirt.

MR. BEEBE's SOCIAL and professional life is not quite as ornate as his column might lead the innocent to suspect. He gets up early, usually at seven, an hour unheard of in Babylon; has breakfast in his suite; and reaches the *Tribune* by eight-thirty, working there until a quarter of one. He lunches at 21 or, with members of the staff, at Bleeck's Artists and Writers Restaurant, the *Tribune's* rather anxiously fostered version of the Mermaid Tavern. Then he goes to the Turkish baths at the Biltmore for a steam and rub (no exercise) in the solidly reassuring company of Alfred E. Smith, Walter P. Chrysler, and other men of property. His social life begins at six, after his nap, either with a large semi-public cocktail party or a gathering of friends in his own rooms. During the theatre season, he usually dines at 21 or the Colony, both of which reserve tables for him every night. After the theatre—he goes to about a hundred and fifty first nights a year—he drops in at El Morocco, where he picks up the bulk of the material for his column. He is almost always at home by two or three in the morning, and about once every two weeks he goes to bed at nine, turning off his telephone resolutely against the hunting call of the pack. During the year he makes many semi-professional trips to the hinterland, either to lecture to club ladies anxious to know how Manhattan débutantes manage to get along on nothing but gin and luminal, or else to investigate the struggling social life in the cities that take his column. He spends his vacations quietly recuperating on the family farm in Wakefield.

In addition to his column, Mr. Beebe writes quite a lot of other things, for in spite of the wear and tear of the fancy life, he is industrious. In his spare time during 1934, he wrote "Boston and the Boston Legend," a 100,000-word study of his native city of which five thousand copies were sold at $5 each. It had a mixed reception. Boston, generally speaking, was flattered to appear in such an expensive format—the illustrations by E. H. Suydam had a special *fin-de-siècle* elegance—but it was troubled because his references to the Watch and Ward Society and Mr. Emerson seemed lacking in reverence.

The social philosophers were infuriated by his contemptuous dismissal of the Abolitionists and his flippant treatment of the Sacco-Vanzetti case. Walter Pritchard Eaton wrote, "He betrays an incomprehension of moral fervor and high humanitarian purpose hardly reassuring in a historian."

Only here and there, however, was the frantic prose of the column in evidence, and the consensus of opinion seems to have been that as superficial social history, the book was both pleasant and competent. Before that, in 1934, he had contributed an introduction to Mr. Zerbe's book of photographs called "People on Parade," and in that, as one angry purist had occasion to remark, the writing was cloth of purest brass. Describing the opening of the Chicago World's Fair, through which Mr. Zerbe crept and snapped, he wrote in part:

> An ocean of plug hats and imperial sable tippets was cascading down the stairs, impeded only by a cross-current of persons smelling vaguely of Guerlain's Shalimar and Four Roses whiskey who were going to one of the seventeen bars . . . Approximately a million celebrities were falling on their faces or kissing the wrong people, and Mr. Zerbe had the screaming meemies with excitement.

Mr. Beebe's next major work, which will be published during the World's Fair in Flushing, seems likely to be pitched in much the same key. It is about café society, the true love of his life, and three installments which have appeared in *Cosmopolitan*—he writes for almost all the magazines that like nice things—are breathless chronicles of fur and precious stones.

At the moment he is at work on an album of about two hundred railroad and locomotive pictures, with forty or fifty thousand words of text, to sell for $5. This is not the unaccountable enterprise it might seem at first, because he has chosen to regard steam engines, like the hansoms at the Plaza, as symbols of the polite and vanishing past. He is, in fact, an authority on railroading, and at the "Parade of Years" at Cleveland in 1936, he spent much of his time, large, pink, and merry, driving Moguls and ancient Mason-built diamond-stackers around the exposition's private tracks.

His literary ambitions don't extend much beyond the things he does now. Depressed and confused by modern forms, he has given up poetry, and he says he is incapable of writing fiction, a comment which might conceivably amuse his associates at the *Tribune*.

On the whole, Mr. Beebe is probably well content to leave serious ambition to others, being sensible of the vulgarity which too often underlies the man of action. In his philosophy, it is a far better thing to contemplate and adorn a civilization than to plan a new one. In any case, he has the true Bourbon's profound hostility to change, looking much more affectionately on the decent past than on any raw new world to come. He is an overpowering gourmet, a member of Les Amis d'Escoffier, and he is most eloquent in his column when he is writing about staggering feasts he has attended. Although he spent $3,000 on a banquet for a recent bridegroom, the little dinners in his own suite are usually modest. The following one is typical:

Cream of green turtle soup
Grilled pompano, with Würzburger '29
Saddle of English venison, with
Clos de Vougeot '89
Field salad
Strawberry soufflé, with champagne
of an English cuvée
Coffee, with Cognac Grand Fine '65
Partagas cigars in the Rothschild size

He also enjoys his reputation for picturesque behavior. Every year for four years, with the first appreciable fall of snow, he bundled into one of the Plaza's surviving sleighs and raced to the Central Park Casino for the magnum of champagne which the management traditionally offered to the winner. There were technical flaws in this reenactment, since the sleigh was not driven by Mr. Beebe himself but by an Irish realist called Paddy Rafferty, who was heavily subsidized to keep an eye on the weather and wake up his patron when it was time to go. Nor was it precisely a contest, since nobody else's nostalgia was quite up to the strain, and Mr. Beebe raced against ghosts, his runners squealing, alone and eerie, over the snow. Nevertheless it was a solace to his old-fashioned spirit, and it was profitable to Rafferty, and they were both sad when a proletarian administration tore down the Casino.

Another attempt to ginger up the fashionable life turned out very badly indeed. In the fall of 1936, Marcus & Co., the jewellers, molded ten clusters of diamonds in the form of gardenias and presented them for sale at $10,000 each. It was their hope that gentlemen of wealth and discernment would take up the style, and as a form of direct advertising they offered Mr. Beebe to the public, wearing one, at the opening of Noel Coward's "Tonight at 8:30." During the first of the three plays, he glittered quietly in the darkness, an even more alluring figure than Mr. Coward, who was appearing on the stage in nothing more startling than a pair of silk pajamas; during the intermission, he was surrounded by an admiring group which unhappily also contained a practical joker whose wit was scarcely to be distinguished from kleptomania. She—for it was a lady, and one of formidable social position—gently detached the gardenia and went south with it. For about ten minutes Mr. Beebe thought poignantly of suicide, but during the second play the humorist was discovered and the gardenia returned. It was a little hard to persuade the police that the whole episode was just an example of aristocratic high spirits, for they were hoarsely determined to put somebody in the can, but in the end it was accomplished and they went away. However, he is still sensitive and avoids the subject whenever possible.

MR. BEEBE'S POLITICAL ideas are simple but definite, leaving inquirers no doubt about where he stands. Inevitably he supported Governor Landon, but the victorious Democrats have left him calm. He is sure the depression is over; certainly the cafés have never been so full of happy and prosperous people. Everything is perfect in a perfect world, or would be if theatre curtains went up at 9:30 so that civilized playgoers could finish their cognac in peace. He has no patience with any of the manifestations of organized labor, and is especially repelled by the American Newspaper Guild, whose heavy shadow has apparently threatened him even in his cloister at the *Tribune*.

"I am not a member of the Guild," he says, "and will never join any union unless a closed shop necessitates it, and then it would be a nearly even choice between my integrity and my job. I do not believe in gangs of any sort and a union is just that, organized for the benefit of the worthless, discontented, and incompetent to harass their betters and to prevent ambitious hardworking people from getting ahead. The Guild is, of course, nothing but a racket of the most patent order, and why newspaper writers should want to associate themselves with anything so shabby, degraded, and spurious, I'm damned if I know."

Mr. Beebe's philosophy, his art, and even his personal appearance have stirred various people in many ways. The earliest available report comes from a friend of his undergraduate days at Yale who found him "energetic, exuberant, and good-natured."

"There were quite a number of people who thought Lucius a bit *fin-de-siècle*," he adds, "but I never found him suffering from any *tædium vitae* . . . [he was] a saga of sartorial splendor and Elizabethan gusto which grew somewhat too vigorous for the anemia of academia, where an eighteenth-century leaning toward 'good taste' tended to rule out robustious activities Marlovian."

There is something about this prose which indicates the beginnings of Mr. Beebe's own style; the critic may be too closely allied to his subject to be allowed the last word. A Harvard classmate is more detached:

"He was intolerant, overbearing, inconsistent, and prejudiced in the Tory manner. Yet to his friends he was considerate, generous, and forever surprising with some gallant (and probably impractical) gesture. He was very much impressed by the outward signs of affluence and horribly bored by the attributes of honest worth that came to his attention."

Accepted literally, this would suggest that Mr. Beebe had hardened into his present mold before he was twenty, but that seems unlikely. It is more probable that in those days the Tory manner was deliberately, perhaps anxiously, cultivated, and it is even rather hard to tell to what extent Mr. Beebe's present icy façade is actually part

of the building and to what extent it is simply a false front run up
for the benefit of a world which has not, on the whole, been as respectful as he had once hoped.

There is pathos here; the lack of respect, and even the occasional
open derision, must be irksome. When the Boston book came out,
those of the Leftist critics who noticed it at all were either patronizing or rude. One of them called it "a pompous guide-book—usually
irritating, at best gracefully trite." Another critic, referring only to
his column, remarked that he wrote like an educated Negro. Once
O. O. McIntyre, meeting him at a cocktail party, tactlessly confused
him with that other, sub-marine Beebe, and asked if he'd been catch-
ing any interesting fish. It is Walter Winchell's irritating habit to call
him "Luscious Lucius." Even his social prestige has been impugned.
Winsor French, writing in the Cleveland *Press*, reproved him for in-
accuracies in reporting what went on at parties given by Libby Holman and Tallulah Bankhead.

"I might also add," he said with the comprehensible snappishness
of a rival, "that I have never seen him at *either* Miss Bankhead's *or*
Miss Holman's." Don Skene, a frail but lively journalist, has often
embarrassed Mr. Beebe by calling him either "Lou" or "Beeb," nick-
names which would have been equally suitable for one of the Elgin
marbles.

On the other hand, there have been many compensations. In
1925, Robert Hillyer, now Boylston Professor of Rhetoric at Harvard, was so impressed by Mr. Beebe's two books on Edwin Arlington Robinson that he nominated him for *Who's Who*, and he
was included. He was twenty-three, the youngest man in that year's
volume.

Many other people have been kind, especially interviewers in out-
of-town papers. One young lady from the Sanford (Florida) *Herald*
was startled almost out of her pretty wits when she met him: "It
seems impossible to think of a Pan with Puritan ancestry, but with
this Beebe nothing is impossible. I noticed his ears set tightly to his
head, not exactly pointed at the top, but with just a suggestion of a
faun's. I had the strange feeling that if he took his shoes off, maybe
his feet would be slightly cloven!"

She dismissed this indelicate thought rather hastily: "Suddenly I remembered that I wasn't there to gape but to get a famous gourmet's slant on citrus for the Florida exhibit at Rockefeller Center."

Whatever admirers or detractors say, however, one tribute must be paid. It takes cognizance of everything—of the long shadow of Boston, of cloistered study and splendid feasts, of Elsa Maxwell and the Boylston Professor of Rhetoric, even of the forty suits and the diamond gardenia. The words of it, with one tiny exception, are from a song made popular in his own time by Miss Ethel Merman, and they can be sung when he is gone: "Beebe had Class, with a capital K."

November 20 and 27, 1937

LADY OF THE CATS[1]

SINCE 1919, MISS Rita Ross has done her best to rid the city of half a million homeless cats which the S.P.C.A. estimates roam its streets. Almost singlehanded, during that period she has turned over more than two hundred tons of cats to the Society for painless destruction. Like the Post Office ideal, Miss Ross is deterred neither by snow, nor rain, nor heat, nor gloom of night on her round of deadly mercy. On Sundays and holidays, blown along by the high March wind or baked by August, in buildings rotten and sagging, through streets that crawl and smell, almost always among people who are hostile or derisive, she has followed her incomprehensible star. It is a bad day when she gets only six cats; it is a good one when she gets sixteen. Once, when the S.P.C.A. recklessly provided her with one of its wagons and a driver, she bagged fifteen hundred. She has the peculiar reputation of being able to move off under her own weight in cats.

Miss Ross, though a furious and indomitable woman, is also a small one. She is five feet two and a quarter inches tall, and without equipment she weighs only a hundred and one pounds. Her face is shrewd, her glance penetrating, with a sort of birdlike fixity, her manner self-possessed and bouncy. She talks a good deal—coyly about her cats, sardonically about the enemies she has routed on a thousand battlefields. She is around thirty-seven years old.

Every morning at seven-thirty she leaves her home, a small stucco one-family house in the Bay Ridge section of Brooklyn, and takes the subway to the east end of Brooklyn Bridge. Here she alights and proceeds on foot over the bridge, gathering in cats as she goes. She works an average of fourteen hours a day, and she always keeps herself in first-class condition. Once, when a gang of hoodlums tried to deprive her of forty cats, she routed them decisively, wielding an ashcan with murderous effect.

Of the agility which makes a seven-foot billboard only a negligible obstacle in her course, she says, "I studied acrobatic dancing when I was a chorus girl and that comes in handy in climbing. I can beat any man in the S.P.C.A. up a tree except Johnny Joule of the Brooklyn Shelter. He used to be a tree pruner for the Park Department and he is wonderful at getting up a tree."

This is no empty boast. Once Miss Ross was interrupted in her customary work on the third floor of a deserted Harlem tenement by a man who came in quietly and locked the door behind him. His manner was menacing and Miss Ross did not stop to question him about his intentions. She dissolved an untidy situation by scrambling through the transom.

Miss Ross's clothes are nondescript except for an enormous cone-shaped hat, which she wears to keep cobwebs and plaster out of her hair. Her equipment is bizarre. She carries more impedimenta than the average Red Cap: a big, homemade wire trap of the cage type, an animal case, and a good-sized market basket. The trap may contain as many as ten swearing cats, the animal case up to six more. In the market basket are tins of canned salmon, catnip, tin pie plates, a can opener, a flashlight, a police whistle, a ball of twine, and five burlap sacks, used to contain an occasional overflow from the trap and the animal case. Laden with these unusual devices and proceeding at an effortless lope that eats up the miles, Miss Ross is an arresting figure. She is even more so when a vague but cheerful impulse leads her to dye her black hair red, or to wear a yellow wig.

Cat-catching on the grand scale leaves little time for other interests. Miss Ross has none of the accepted vices. She neither smokes nor drinks and if she had her choice, she says emphatically, she would rather kiss a cat than the best man who ever walked on two feet.

WHILE MISS ROSS is unquestionably the champion cat woman, there are lesser ones, and occasionally she is accompanied by a Miss Marion Kane. Miss Kane is about thirty-three, short, Celtic, and a ferocious hitter with either hand. When she and Miss Ross roam the streets of Harlem at night, prudent residents take cover, for both ladies have hasty dispositions and would not hesitate to engage an army. Most of the time, however, Miss Ross prefers to hunt alone, having, like so many gifted people, a distaste for collaboration.

Her usual hunting grounds are the bleaker, poorer parts of town. There she operates with matchless precision and technique, as relentlessly as doom. Every day she speaks to about a hundred people on the street, asking them to be on the lookout for stray cats and to communicate with her by mail when they hear of any. One ally, who modestly prefers to be known only as "The Lady from Grantwood, N.J.," scarcely allows a day to pass without providing Miss Ross with the address of at least one underprivileged cat. Miss Ross carries the answers to these requests in her bag and they dictate roughly her course for the day. In addition, she cuts out bankruptcy notices from the papers, because small-store failures almost always result in homeless or locked-in cats. The greater part of her success, however, can be laid to simple vigilance. She penetrates sewers, elevator shafts, and cellars, and climbs to roof tops. She investigates freight yards, abattoirs, bridges, and cemeteries. She never passes a deserted building without making cat sounds, and it is a hard and cynical cat that can resist Miss Ross when she mews. She never allows any animal to be maltreated in her wide and various wanderings and can be almost as indignant about a horse whose teeth aren't clean as she can about one that is being beaten. While Miss Ross has room in her heart for the entire animal kingdom, she focusses principally on cats because she thinks they are victims of prejudice and bigotry.

"A dog has a million friends to a cat's one," she says. "Why, even *snakes* are sometimes praised!"

In a typical working day Miss Ross frequently covers between twenty-five and thirty miles; running like a flame through the Bronx, Brooklyn, Manhattan, and nearer New Jersey, stopping only reluctantly for food. In restaurants and lunchrooms her mystifying burden often arouses comment, but she is not embarrassed.

"They're just a little nervous," she says, referring to the ghostly heave and bounce of the containers at her feet.

The people among whom Miss Ross works always regard her with amazement and sometimes even with consternation, a lady so oddly possessed being a little upsetting to the simple-minded.

Once, accompanied by an admiring representative of this magazine, she entered a building at 447 Lexington Avenue to call for a cat. The building was being renovated and the only occupant was a moody Negro in spectacles, hoeing mortar in a tub. Miss Ross told him she had come for the cat.

"Whut cat?" he said. "I don't know of no cat."

"Listen," said Miss Ross, and she gave her celebrated cry. They listened, and from a dark tunnel in the rear of the basement there came an answering cry, soft and dolorous.

"Why you want that cat?" asked the colored man, nervously.

Miss Ross did not reply directly. She had put on her beehive hat and prepared a mess of salmon on a tin plate. She paused at the mouth of the aperture and looked at the colored man.

"I don't suppose you noticed whether it was a boy or girl?" she asked.

"No'm," he replied. "I don' recollect."

"Well," said Miss Ross, and disappeared, mewing softly.

When she came out, blurred with cobwebs, she was carrying a thin, exasperated cat which she thrust into her basket, already the prison of three others. Leaving the building, she spoke once more to the colored man, who had retreated behind a barrel of lime.

"If you see any more kitties, you be nice and play with them, won't you?" she said.

THE UNEASINESS INSPIRED by Miss Ross is by no means confined to the humble. There is no way of telling what the cats themselves think about her, though their gratitude is probably mixed with other emotions, but the S.P.C.A., that enlightened body of humanitarians, speaks of her with horror. The day in 1926 when she brought in fifteen hundred cats is still remembered as the darkest point in the Society's history, although Miss Ross dismisses her stupendous feat lightly. She had spotted colonies of cats around town too large to be handled by a lady on foot—there were eighty-seven in the basement of one deserted tenement—and she had dreamed of the day when she would be able to deal with them wholesale. The Society's wagon and driver gave her her glorious opportunity and she seized it fiercely. From dawn until deep night, driven furiously from the Battery to the Bronx, delivering fifty, sixty, a hundred cats at a clip to the stupefied officials, she accomplished the miraculous. The wagon and driver were withdrawn soon afterward. Miss Ross, disappointed but by no means daunted, went back to patrolling the streets on foot, and even with this handicap continued to tax the Society's facilities. She still does. Sydney Coleman, vice-president of the Society and not essentially a robust man, has barred his door against her in a pitiable effort to save his reason. The Society itself would like to have her restrained legally before it is engulfed in a living wave of cats. This, however, would mean a court suit and such an advertisement might easily be bad for the Society. Kindly people, unaware of the real nature of the crisis, would take Miss Ross's side; contributions would drop off. Last year an unofficial hearing was arranged before Magistrate Louis Brodsky in West Side Court. The judge told Miss Ross that the Society had a legal right to refuse cats in such staggering abundance. Miss Ross, with a ringing eloquence that made the representatives of the Society shudder, cried that it had no *moral* right before God or man to close its doors to sick or suffering animals. Magistrate Brodsky, a sanguine man, said in conclusion that he was satisfied that no further trouble would come up between Miss Ross and the Society. Miss Ross continued to use the Society's five borough shelters to deposit her cats.

The charge has arisen—and the Society would probably give its handsomest medal to the man who can prove it—that Miss Ross is indiscriminate in her choice of cats, that in the fever of the chase she has abducted cats whose home lives were by no means insupportable. One fall, a few years ago, the West End Fruit Market, the New Yorker Delicatessen Store, Schwartz Brothers Fruit Store, and other establishments on the upper West Side missed their cats after Miss Ross had passed that way, conceivably on a broomstick, but whether she had anything to do with these disappearances has never been proved. To accusations of this kind Miss Ross has a firm, invariable answer. Three kinds of cats are safe from her—well-fed cats, altered cats, and nursing mothers. The first two imply ownership, the third maternity. No one can say with certainty that she has ever violated this rule.

If nobody calls for them within forty-eight hours, the cats Miss

Ross brings in to the S.P.C.A. are placed in a lethal chamber and as-
phyxiated in fifteen seconds. That her love is deadly, her artful miaou
a siren song, does not concern Miss Ross too much. The stray cat in
New York, she feels, can look forward only to a life of great suffering and anxiety, a lonely and miserable end. The alternative is eu-
thanasia and, since he cannot make the choice himself, she does so
for him, merciful beyond pity or regret. Estimating that Miss Ross
has seduced an average of ten cats a day for nineteen years, she has
nearly seventy thousand souls on her conscience. They weigh lightly.

"It's a better death than most humans get," she says.

THE POLICE HAVE also met Miss Ross, and they look on her
with distaste mixed with a sort of stunned respect. She knows that
any citizen has a right to use a patrolman's box to call the station
house, and that a reported felony will bring two patrol cars; a murder, five. Several times when she has felt that things were getting a
little out of hand, Miss Ross has not hesitated to shout murder.

Innocent patrolmen have occasionally made the mistake of sum-
moning Miss Ross to court and charging her with disorderly conduct.
Not one of them has done so twice. She has an imposing courtroom
presence and an astonishing legal vocabulary, so her accusers are often
dismayed to learn that in the eyes of the law they have been either
brutal or incompetent or both. She has even been known to bring
departmental charges against patrolmen who have tried to thwart her
in one way or another, and this has made the force wary, since such a
charge remains on a man's record, proved or not. There are officers in
New York who would not arrest Miss Ross if they caught her setting
off a bomb.

Thoughtful policemen, in fact, have concluded that the best way
to deal with Miss Ross is to do what she says, even if it involves
situations not found in the Manual. Once she commandeered two
patrolmen from the Borough Park Station in Brooklyn and took
them to a deserted bakery which, she said, contained two cats. This
was true. The cats were plainly visible and painfully emaciated but,
as the policemen discovered when they had forced their way in,
Miss Ross had forgotten to mention that they were also insane. In
their delirium they mistook their rescuers for aggressors and leapt

furiously about the bakery. They were marvellously light from hunger and strain and for the better part of an hour they kept their freedom while Miss Ross and the patrolmen, all heavily floured, toiled irritably after them among the barrels. At last superior physical condition triumphed and the cats were captured and turned over to their nemesis. Miss Ross can be appreciative when the occasion seems to call for it. She wrote a letter of commendation to the Police Commissioner himself.

Probably the most striking example of the influence Miss Ross has with the police occurred some time ago in the Williamsburg section of Brooklyn. She was chased into the subway by a gang of boys trying to rescue a rather unwieldy dog which she had been given by one of their mothers and now carried under her arm. It was her plan to conceal the dog in the ladies' room until the excitement blew over, but she was thwarted by an officious guard. Undaunted, Miss Ross reversed her field, ran up another flight of stairs, and swung down the street to a stationery store. Once inside, to the owner's amazement she slammed the door and locked it.

"Don't open that door," she said sharply as he came from behind the counter.

"But Madam, this is a place of business."

"Don't open that door," repeated Miss Ross, and gave him the dog to hold. While he held the dog uncertainly, she went to the telephone and put in a murder call. Inside thirty seconds, five radio patrol cars, commanded by a Sergeant Kelly of the Canarsie Station, had rushed to the scene. The police dispersed the crowd, and Miss Ross emerged triumphantly with the dog.

"I demand protection against these ruffians," she said, and rode majestically in Sergeant Kelly's car to the nearest police station, where she left an order for an S.P.C.A. truck to come and pick up the dog. Then, as calmly as if such stirring things happened every day, she went out cat-gathering.

Miss Ross met Sergeant Kelly just the other day in the subway.

"Remember all that excitement in the stationery store, Rita?" he asked genially.

★ ★ ★

In spite of the truce which she has forced upon the Police Department, Miss Ross is still a familiar figure in the magistrates' courts. At least six times a year she appears against people who have maltreated animals or else have insulted her or hampered her in the performance of her duty. She is merciless with those who abuse animals. She has succeeded in having countless five-dollar fines imposed on tradesmen who beat their horses, and one Negro janitor who was convicted of burning cats alive in his furnace was sentenced to six months in jail. She has never lost a case, though sometimes the penalties have seemed to her soft and foolish beyond belief.

"My pet dislike is judges who are lenient in cruelty cases," she says, and probably only their judicial robes have saved many magistrates from the more tangible weight of her displeasure.

With those who harass her personality, she is more moderate, though no less effective. All she wants is an apology, and her courtroom manner is lucid, demure, and undoubtedly maddening to her opponents. Last summer Miss Ross summoned an Irene Mara before Magistrate Nicholas Pinto in Coney Island Court. This woman, aided and abetted by her mother, had used uncivil language in attempting to restrain Miss Ross from making off with a brood of cats. Unkind words had led to blows and in the end the embattled ladies had been separated by several patrolmen. A certain disarray in Mrs. Mara's appearance suggested that Miss Ross had had all the better of the skirmish. Nevertheless, the judge, influenced by the deceptive meekness in Miss Ross's manner, ruled that she was entitled to an apology.

"Me apologize to *her!*" cried Mrs. Mara incredulously, and started to flounce out of the courtroom. The judge had her brought back and, after a stern lecture, the apology was given.

"He called me a lady," Miss Ross says merrily, recalling this scene. "'You apologize to this lady,' he said. Me, a lady!"

Before the stray cats of the city so relentlessly took possession of her life, Rita Ross gave every promise of a successful career on the stage. Born Marion Garcewich, in the section of Harlem just

north of 110th Street, she was the daughter of the German-Jewish
proprietor of a gents' furnishing store. She attended Public School
170 in that neighborhood and eventually was graduated. In her
teens, her family moved to Brooklyn. For a while she was a salesgirl
for Loft's, and afterward a model for Galen Perrett, a commercial
artist, from whose studio at 51 West Tenth Street her likeness emerged
as the radiant face in the Bel-Ton Powder advertisements, displayed
throughout the transportation systems of the city. In 1919 she got a
job as a chorus girl in a road company of "So Long, Letty."

Unfortunately for her career, it was at this time that she fell under
the influence of her private daemon. Foreshadowing that remarkable pedestrianism which was later to wear down strong men, Miss
Garcewich (now, for theatrical purposes, Rita Ross) used to walk
across Brooklyn Bridge every day on her way to work in Manhattan. The cats of the lower East Side, degraded and mournful, attracted her strongly, and she got to picking up one or two of them
and taking them to an S.P.C.A. shelter on her way uptown.

It is hard to say how this merciful habit gradually became a compulsion. It appears that one cat simply led to another. Miss Ross herself has no explanation of it except in vague, humanitarian terms. It
is only clear that from a lady who could, on the whole, take a cat or
leave it alone, she was suddenly translated into the most prodigious
cat-catcher of our time. As her obsession grew, her other interests
inevitably suffered. She was no less fetching as a chorus girl, of
course, but she became a little embarrassing as an associate. In Salt
Lake City, she rescued an alley cat from a vivisectionist by beating
him severely over the head with her handbag. In Indianapolis, where
she had gone with "The Spice of 1922" company, she was dismissed
for picking up a dirty white poodle and installing it in her dressing
room.

By 1926, when she was playing in "The Song of the Flame" in
Chicago, her peculiarities were so generally recognized that she was
warned by the management not to bring any animals into the theatre. She wrestled heroically with temptation, but the habit had her
in an iron grip. One night she smuggled in two shivering kittens
and hid them in shoebags below her mirror in the general dressing
room. The cats, numb and grateful, remained as they were during

the first number. When, however, the chorus girls came back after the second number, clawed costumes covered the floor and the wardrobe mistress panted after two hilarious cats. Miss Ross returned to New York. She remained on the stage during the run and tour of Hope Hampton's "My Princess" in 1927, but her heart wasn't in it. When it closed, she retired to devote all her time to her cats.

"I'm not sorry I stopped the stage," she says. "This work is much more interesting. You never know what's going to happen."

She realizes that a professional cat-catcher cannot hope to be as immaculate as Mrs. Harrison Williams, and occasionally this causes her mild distress. Last summer she passed Arthur Hammerstein in Greenwich Village. Miss Ross was in full regalia and the producer looked firmly at something else.

"My, was I embarrassed! I just slunk past."

On the whole, though, she has never regretted her choice. The average chorus girl, she feels, is at least as peculiar as she is, and not in the direction of good works, either.

MISS ROSS NOW lives with her widowed mother, a brother, two sisters, and a nephew, all of whom regard their relative's habit of sleeping in a room crawling with cats as merely odd. These cats are transient, being ones that she has picked up too late at night to turn over to the S.P.C.A. She maintains only one cat of her own, a deaf, toothless antique named Tibby-Wibby Simpson Ross, the gift of an amiable colored woman Miss Ross met on Lenox Avenue. In addition to the usual handicaps of age, Tibby-Wibby has another, of an embarrassing nature.

"He'll never be a daddy," Miss Ross explains delicately.

Miss Ross is given her room and some of her meals by her family, and, since she is a vegetarian and a light eater anyway, the others don't cost much. Money for her clothes, her cat-trapping equipment, and the rest of her needs comes from well-wishers. She is supported at the moment by two anonymous ladies—one in Brooklyn and one in Manhattan—who send her a total of fifteen dollars a week in care of *Variety*, which still nervously handles her mail. At various times during her career, Miss Ross's patronesses have changed, but she has always been able to find ladies, generally prominent supporters of the S.P.C.A., who were anxious to continue her good, though unusual, work. Occasionally there are windfalls from anti-vivisectionists or people whom she has helped to rid of a plague of cats. In all, she receives about nine hundred dollars a year, which is ample for a woman who up to now has never even been able to find time to go to a talking picture.

Singular things have happened in the course of her career. Once, when she was rearranging her cats in a ladies' room in an "L" station, a habit she has when pressed for time, another passenger, alarmed by strange, thin cries from an adjoining booth, told the ticket agent that a child had just been born, and was barely restrained from sending for an ambulance. Again, in the old New York Hospital at Fifteenth Street and Sixth Avenue, Miss Ross was forced by a series of improbable circumstances to pursue a cat up from the basement and under a bed in the psychopathic ward. Doctors and nurses, coming in to find what they imagined to be a fully dressed patient down on her hands and knees mewing, tried to get her undressed and back into bed. Things looked fairly black until somebody discovered that there actually *was* a cat under the bed. Miss Ross, however, kept her poise.

As a matter of fact, she says she has been really at a loss only once. That was when a dozen of her cats escaped three summers ago while she was riding on the Third Avenue "L." Miss Ross was sitting quietly with her eyes closed, bothering no man. Suddenly, for some unexplained reason, the lid of her animal case flew open. A stream of cats, long pent and indignant, emerged and, with Miss Ross anxiously after them, leaped and gambolled down the aisle, springing over and upon the agitated passengers. When the train stopped, the cats, Miss Ross, and most of the passengers got off in a hurried flux. The passengers milled unhappily around on the platform. The cats, with Miss Ross pursuing the main body, scampered down both stairways. Baffled by their unfamiliar surroundings in the street, the cats darted perilously about in the traffic while Miss Ross sifted after them, like an image in an old moving picture cranked up to dizzy speed. In the end she got them all, but for once the situation threatened to be a little beyond her.

"I can tell you I blushed," she says, describing a vehicular chaos which must have compared very favorably with that immediately following the Wall Street explosion.

The future, like the past and present, holds for Miss Ross only a continuation of her singular crusade. The half-million cats still loose on the streets are a challenge to her genius and she cannot rest until the last one is trapped and riding to its doom. Even at her present spectacular rate, it is the work of a lifetime. She approaches it without misgiving.

May 14, 1938

BIG NEMO

I

A lady who loves him said once that Alexander Woollcott has eight hundred intimate friends. This may easily be true, because he leads a social existence that might have seemed exhausting to Catherine of Russia; it is also true that there is scarcely one of the eight hundred who has not spoken of him derisively. Edna Ferber, even before her first passion for him had cooled into loathing and he in turn had stopped dedicating his books to her, remarked that she was getting damn sick of this New Jersey Nero who mistook his pinafore for a toga. It was Miss Ferber, too, who, being asked by a frantic bookworm if Mr. Woollcott didn't seem exactly like a character out of Dickens, replied generously that he often seemed to her like *two* characters out of Dickens, both from the same book. This was "The Old Curiosity Shop," and the pair of whom Miss Ferber thought when she was reluctantly obliged to look at Mr. Woollcott were Little Nell and Quilp. Charles Brackett, a devoted admirer, described him in one of his novels as "a competent old horror with a style that combined clear treacle and pure black bile," while Harpo Marx spoke of his idol considered sheerly as an artist. "He is just a big dreamer," said Mr. Marx, "with a good sense of double-entry bookkeeping." Elsie Janis's mother, struggling to define the effect that Mr. Woollcott has on people who aren't altogether used to him, said that in many ways he was like a fine old olive, and S. N. Behrman, who twice permitted him to play himself on the stage, caused one of his heroines to express herself crossly. "Oh, Sig, Sig," she cried, "if you'd been a woman, what a bitch you would have made!" Back in 1921, George Jean Nathan wrote a scurrilous article about him in the *Smart Set* entitled "The Seidlitz Powder of Times Square," and once, Howard Dietz, afflicted by prose more beautiful than he could bear, called him Louisa M. Woollcott, thus speaking for thousands who had also been troubled without ever quite knowing what was the matter with them. These tributes for the most part have come from the more articulate of the eight hundred. The rest have usually contented themselves with describing him simply and passionately as a monster, or at the very least as a man of absurdly mixed ancestry.

The caricaturists have also been severe, which is probably ungrateful of them, for Mr. Woollcott is a persistently obliging model, one wartime associate on the *Stars and Stripes*, the A.E.F. weekly newspaper, even hinting that he was by no means above using his sergeant's chevrons to *compel* gifted privates to draw pictures of him. His face, of course, could not have been more helpfully designed for their purposes. Florence Atwater, one of Booth Tarkington's darkly observant little girls, once came close to his total effect, although at the time she was speaking of her grandfather's cook. "Her *face* is sort of small," she said, wrestling with the inexpressible, "but the other parts of her head are terribly wide." Mr. Woollcott's small features occupy the front part of a head which is at least wider than most. He has a rather beaked nose and a tight mouth and a negligible mustache, all closely grouped. His eyes are made strange and fierce by thick glasses. A clever child could easily draw him and, as a matter of fact, many have, although usually under the impression that they were turning out owls. The caricaturists, of course, have made the most of this resemblance, as well as of a body which suggests the anatomy of St. Nicholas in "The Night Before Christmas." A gallery of Woollcott portraits would include the work of almost every considerable black-and-white artist in the country and, while all the pictures would be very different, in some mysterious fashion they would all look precisely like Mr. Woollcott and all, naturally, rather like owls.

The average man might be embarrassed at finding himself the focus of quite so much hilarity and be inclined to swing on somebody. Mr. Woollcott, however, loves it, and often shakes with laughter when he comes on an especially damaging sample. The fact is that insult is a casual demonstration of regard with him, as it is with most of his friends. "Hello, repulsive" is a tender greeting under his roof and goodbye is said as sweetly. "I find you are beginning to disgust me, puss," the great man will say as his bedtime approaches. "How about getting the hell out of here?"

As far as his friends have been able to tell, in fact, the old fascinator is actually enraged only by two forms of misbehavior. He finds it very hard to forgive any man or woman who, through forgetfulness, drunkenness, or even simple disinclination, breaks an engagement with him, thus upsetting a social program as delicately assembled as a little watch; and he is furious with humorists who try to discredit his favorite philanthropies.

AS LONG AGO as 1926, growing rich through his dubious employment as a critic for the late Frank Munsey, he moved from the hovel which he shared with three penniless adventurers on West Forty-seventh Street and went to live at the Hotel des Artistes. These premises offered many advantages, including a remarkable chef, and Mr. Woollcott began to spread out socially, his little dinners becoming the talk of his circle, many of whom lived almost entirely on ham sandwiches in the back room at Tony's.[1] Everything at des Artistes was arranged with extraordinary care—the chef advised long beforehand what to cook and the instant when it must leap, brown and lovely, from the dumbwaiter. The guests were selected as carefully as the roast and expected to turn up as promptly. Informal people sometimes found so much ceremony oppressive, and, while admiring Mr. Woollcott for his other qualities, considered him a little peremptory as a host.

One man, born with a horror of having to be anywhere at any particular time, successfully dodged his fate for two weeks only to be pinned down at last for dinner a week from Tuesday. As his time drew near, despair overcame him and the afternoon of the great day found him in a speakeasy, nervously drinking Scotch. He was with friends and finally one of them, a Mr. Connelly, was persuaded to call up Mr. Woollcott and explain that his guest had been delayed.[2] "Dishere Mr. Smiff's body servant," said Mr. Connelly upon being connected with his party. "He say he cain't—"

The noise that came from the receiver was like the crackle of summer lightning, and after a while Mr. Connelly hung up and went back to his table.

"Well, I fixed it up all right," he said airily. "You don't have to go."

They went instead to the Algonquin and had been sitting in the lobby for some time, bothering nobody, when the door revolved to admit an object both fashionable and alarming. It was Mr. Woollcott in evening clothes. He was wearing a broad-brimmed black hat and a flowing cape, carrying a heavy, silver-headed cane, and on the whole he looked very much like Dracula. Afterward it developed that, having sent back the dinner (he was on a diet of toast and orange juice himself), he was now merely looking for someone to replace the unspeakable Smith as his guest at Walter Hampden's performance of "Caponsacchi." At the time, however, the guilty crew thought he had tracked them down and probably meant to do something nasty with the cane. His eye, in fact, did light on the little group and for a moment his face was contorted with pique, but instead of assassinating them, he whirled and flung out of the hotel, spinning the door so furiously that two little old ladies, standing near it, bowed in the wind.

The humorists were not content to let it go at that. Smith, encouraged by his associate demons, sent him a telegram which read, "If anybody asks you where I was last night will you say I was with you?" At first, on receiving this, Mr. Woollcott was somewhat mollified, having a pleasant sense of being mixed up in some kind of dirty work. Learning that it was merely an extension of the original insult, however, and that Smith had, in fact, been seen that night innocently amusing himself with friends at Hubert's Flea Circus, he came close to apoplexy and wrote a letter so vitriolic and unusual that it became a sort of museum piece and was ultimately acquired by a rich collector for twenty-five dollars. It is noteworthy that in moments of actual fury Mr. Woollcott has no use for the fancy epithet; his style then is simple and austere, almost Biblical. This valuable letter said what he wished to say in the bleakest terms. "I find," it began, "that you are a distinctly third-rate person."

In spite of many discouragements—for other people have also

objected to having their lives so arbitrarily arranged—his schedule remains elaborate. His itinerary is always laid out at least a month in advance, and his calendar, when he is in New York, is as precisely calculated as a dentist's.

MR. WOOLLCOTT'S ENTHUSIASMS are often apt to seem a little arbitrary, too. Critically, for instance, he was able to dismiss "The Children's Hour" as "gauche, implausible, and untidy," and "Strange Interlude" as an " 'Abie's Irish Rose' of the pseudo-intelligentsia," while finding in Mr. James Hilton a talent "as warming to the heart and nourishing to the spirit as any I can remember" and in Little Orvie, certainly one of Mr. Tarkington's glummer inspirations, a creation in many ways superior to Penrod. The truth is probably that he prefers to dig up his own crusades, finding no especial satisfaction in getting excited about something that excites everybody else. So, while most commentators have been busy with anti-Fascist demonstrations, labor disputes, and other community activities, Mr. Woollcott has found his own causes and stood up for them, vocal but alone. The Seeing Eye, which, thanks to him, probably needs no further identification, has received in print and on the air more publicity than has ever been given to any other organization dedicated to so special a purpose, and Hamilton College, which graduated him and of which he is a trustee, has also come into its just reward. He has not even neglected the Several Marx Brothers, an outfit which, from time to time, he appears to believe he invented himself. Journalistically, all this has been sound and profitable, since there are many people who feel that they have heard more than enough about the state of the world. It has also called forth a certain amount of criticism, a few serious thinkers being of the opinion that Mr. Woollcott's interests are rather peripheral, to put it mildly. There have even been moments of embarrassment when his protégés have backfired on him.

There was, for instance, the story of Sergeant Quirt, which is probably as good a name for him as any.[3] The saga of the Sergeant, who picked up his title as a member of the American Expeditionary Force, is practically endless. A literary though virile sort of man, he once worked for a newspaper syndicate, and there he was in the habit of returning a manuscript to its anxious author with a letter saying that it wasn't *quite* right, but that with a little professional advice, he was sure, it could be made to do. There was, now he happened to think of it, a literary agency that specialized in just that sort of thing and, if the author cared to send his manuscript to them, he felt confident that—for a small fee, of course—they could tell him what repairs were necessary. The literary agency, it turned out, was the Sergeant masquerading as a post-office box, and he made a very nice little thing out of it until something slipped up and he was fired. After that he caused a temporary confusion in the publishing world by setting up a McClure Syndicate to compete with the real McClure Syndicate simply by going into business with a man whose name happened to be McClure. A pretty ingenious fellow all around was Sergeant Quirt.

Mr. Woollcott and the Sergeant had worked together on the *Stars and Stripes*, where they shared heroic experiences and a strong bond grew up between them. Back in this country, the friendship persisted and Mr. Woollcott invited his buddy to come and live in his apartment. The Sergeant had not yet affiliated himself with the newspaper syndicate, or indeed with any other employer, and he was without visible means of support. Mr. Woollcott's kindness provided him with a roof and meals, of course, but the Sergeant wanted other things from life, including a little pocket money. His host had gone to Europe, leaving him alone in the apartment, so he turned to other friends of his army days. He was successful with them, so successful, in fact, that he made up his mind that he could afford to travel. Action always followed closely on decision with the Sergeant, and presently, handsomely dressed and equipped with fine luggage, he was on his way to the Coast in a bus. He rode in peace, busy, no doubt, with his innocent plans, until the bus reached a more or less desolate portion of the Western plains. Here an embarrassing thing happened. A pair of state troopers, appearing from nowhere, drew up beside the bus and announced grimly that they were looking for an escaped convict. Even as they spoke, a pale man in one of the front seats leaped to his feet and through an open window. Before the troopers could get clear of their roadster, Sergeant Quirt was in action. He, too, leaped through the window and took off across the desert. The convict ran fast, but virtue lent wings to Quirt and he brought the man down not a hundred yards from the highway. When Quirt came back with his catch, the troopers were grateful and admiring.

"It was nothing," said the Sergeant.

The officers soon departed, taking with them the convict and a suitcase he claimed to be his. The bus rolled on, with Quirt the object of much favorable comment. It had not gone many miles, however, before the same patrol car appeared beside it again and ordered the driver to stop. One of the troopers got out and stood in the highway. He was holding up a suitcase and he looked even more menacing than before.

"All right," he said, "*now* I want to know who in hell belongs to this bag."

Sergeant Quirt took one look at it and sighed.

"I do," he said.

"You?" said the trooper incredulously, recognizing the recent hero.

"Yes," said Quirt.

"O.K., buddy," said the trooper, though still doubtful. "Then I guess you better come along."

Quirt went, for he knew when he was licked, and he also knew that the suitcase, which fate had malignantly mixed up with the convict's, contained about as fine a set of plates for counterfeiting traveller's checks as you could buy east of the Alleghenies, as well as a neat bundle of Southern Pacific pay checks which he had turned out from time to time on a little press he happened to have kicking around the house.

When this news finally reached Mr. Woollcott, he was embarrassed. It was too bad, he cried; it was obviously just some innocent misunderstanding. In proof of all this, he would personally redeem every dollar's worth of false checks that could be shown to have originated with his virtuous friend. He even had his lawyer make an announcement to that effect, and this was a mistake, because several thousand dollars' worth of pay checks which had been issued by the Sergeant on previous business trips to the West were now joyfully presented for payment. Such a sum being somewhat be-

yond his means at the time, Mr. Woollcott was obliged to retract
his offer and leave the Sergeant to the mercy of the State of California, which apparently had the strongest claim on him, although
Oregon and Nevada were mildly interested, too. Mr. Woollcott, in
fact, withdrew from the whole matter after arranging with the war-
den of San Quentin to get the Sergeant a set of false teeth, his own
being in shocking condition.

Things like that hurt, because there can be little question that
Mr. Woollcott is one of the most sentimental men alive in spite of
his prickly exterior. At fifty-two, the world to him is still a strange
and glamorous place, with all its values heightened and transposed
as the appearance of a landscape is dramatized when it comes out in
Technicolor. Mr. Woollcott's world isn't perhaps very much like
anybody else's, but certainly he is happy there. It is a little remarkable that he should be so invincibly romantic and especially that he
should feel such an overwhelming affection for the past, because his
impressionable years were spent in what would appear to be more
or less discouraging places.

He was born in what had once been the *phalanstère* or head house
of a Socialistic community near Red Bank, N.J. This settlement,
commonly known as Phalanx, was an experiment in coöperative
living, based on the writings of Albert Brisbane, Arthur's father. It
was akin to Brook Farm and, though less celebrated, it was more successful. In 1855, however, it blew up—largely because none of the
disciples cared to act as garbage collector—and Woollcott's grandfather, who happened to be president at the time, came into possession of the enormous eighty-five-room building which his descendant
remembers as a "shabby, rambling caravansary, bleak as a skull." In
1887, when little Alexander was born, there were fourteen other
grandchildren infesting this barracks and the chances are that he
would have grown up quite happily there if it hadn't been for some
aching discontent with life that lay at the back of his father's mind.
Walter Woollcott, who came to America from England when he
was thirteen, was at various times and rather apathetically a lawyer,
an accountant, a government clerk, and a Stock Exchange member.
He also seems to have been one of the most accomplished escapists
in history. Once, in Germantown, he went to bed and stayed there

two years although there was nothing in particular the matter with him; most of the time he had to be on the move, hoping that in each new town he would find the power and glory that had just eluded him in the last. In the course of his marriage, accompanied by his docile though bewildered family, he turned up as a resident of such assorted places as Raleigh, Washington, Omaha, Fort Union, Pittsburgh, and Manchester (England).

In November, 1889, he took his brood to Kansas City, Mo. A lady who taught little Aleck when he was in the Second Grade there reports on him favorably:

> As a very young boy, Aleck was very frail-looking, with delicate features, blond hair, and the finest, keenest, intellectual face I have ever seen on such a young lad. His vocabulary, then as now, was marvellous. He was a constant reader—in fact, he read everything he could find in the family library, supplemented by first-class reading matter, such as *St. Nicholas*, the *Youth's Companion*, etc. Small and slender as he was, he held his own with the larger boys. I can see him now, walking with his chest out and trying to look strong and manly. He thirsted for knowledge and I realized even then that he would go far.

A surviving photograph, taken at this period, bears her out. It shows a frail, intent infant who, although as cute as a bug's ear, in the beautiful old phrase, exhibits nevertheless strong traces of that devouring curiosity which has brought the mature Woollcott far indeed from Kansas City.

The child played one of the Vinard children in a "Trilby" tableau given at the Coates Opera House, and Puck in the days when Mrs. Roswell Martin Field, a sister-in-law of Eugene Field, used to "do" Shakespeare in the Woollcott doorway while the audience looked on from the street. He sent his first composition, "The Adventures of a Shopping Bag," to the Kansas City *Star*, which rejected it impassively; he got his first complimentary seats to the theatre from Roswell Field. He was notable chiefly in the neighborhood, however, because when hurt, strong and manly though he might be, he would set up such an unbearably doleful cry that adults could be relied upon to pacify him with nickels. It got to be a practice among the larger boys to toss the little intellectual off the veranda onto his head and then, when he had wept and subsequently collected his nickel, to take it away from him.

In 1895, Walter Woollcott found that the Holy Grail was not in Kansas City and he moved his wife and five children (there were three other sons and a daughter, all older than the constant reader) back to Phalanx. They stayed there about a year and Aleck went to school. Then, for the mysterious search was never ended, they went to Philadelphia, where he finished his primary education and entered Central High School in the class of 1905. Woollcott was living by himself now, his father having wandered away again, this time alone, breaking up the family group forever. Aleck supported himself by reviewing books and doing similar odd and menial jobs for the *Evening Telegraph* and the *Record*. He won a gold medal for writing an essay and sold it, cash in his little damp hand being at the moment even more important than glory. Beyond the discovery, however, that he could turn a phrase with the next man, he didn't get much out of Central High School. He had met a nephew of Elihu Root's who had been to Hamilton College, at Clinton, N.Y., and, impressed by this man's worldly manner, young Woollcott decided to go there too.

Hamilton is a small college and in its student body of two hundred Alexander Humphreys Woollcott '09 was pretty conspicuous, having a busy little finger in practically everything except athletics, which he loathed. He was editor of the monthly magazine; he founded and directed the dramatic club and acted female parts in its productions; he did monologues with the glee club; he even drank a little from time to time, preferring absinthe because of its sinister reputation. He was rather bizarre in appearance, for he habitually wore corduroy trousers and a turtle-necked sweater and topped them off with a jubilant red fez, and he was already firmly prankish, fellow-members of Theta Delta Chi recalling that in "rushing season" he was accustomed to get himself up even more repulsively than usual and go and sit on the steps of rival fraternities as a horrible example of what

the prospective brothers might expect to find inside. Above everything else, however, he was a scholar (he made Phi Beta Kappa in his
junior year) and his chief concern was writing.

Of what he wrote, only one curious fragment has survived. It is
called "The Precipice: A Story of Bohemia" and the action takes
place at a New Year's Eve party in the Philadelphia equivalent of a
Greenwich Village studio. Nana, the heroine, it seems, is not exactly beautiful, but she has other charms which Woollcott '09 is too
delicate to specify. She is a virtuous girl, though given to swilling
Benedictine, but unfortunately she is infatuated with one Bonny, a
cad who operates from hansom cabs.

In the course of the party, this louse, a married man, arranges to
come back and meet her after the others have all gone.

"We'll see the old year out together," he says, brimming with
lechery.

"That will be joyous," says Nana, who has already been at the
Benedictine.

He leaves, and Nana, alone at last, really goes to work on the
bottle. She is, in fact, flat on her back, lighting matches and muttering away to herself about "playing with fire" when a messenger
comes in with a package and an explanatory letter for her. The letter
is from a man called Morton K. Enderby and Nana is in no shape to
cope with that, but the package contains her mother's picture and
its effect is very gratifying indeed.

"The great grey eyes looked at her reproachfully, accusingly, and
the girl cowered. She turned quickly and her glance fell on the ta-
bouret with its litter of cigarette ashes, and in the mess her glass
with the dregs of the Benedictine staining its sides. The sight sick-
ened her. There was a tremendous revulsion of feeling in her soul; a
shattering of the illusions of the past few weeks. The fair lights of
Bohemia were calcium; the gayeties tinsel; the beauties tawdry."

Nana was sober as an owl when she heard Bonny's footsteps on
the stairs. He was singing a questionable song and it was clear that
he thought everything was in the bag. He was too optimistic.

"For a moment she saw his figure outlined against the light: then . . .
she was flying down the dark stairway, one hand nervously feeling the
banister as she ran, the other pressing the picture to her bosom. The

little slippered feet sped along the streaming pavements, the crimson figure passed swiftly out of the great swinging circle of the creaking arc light and she was swallowed up in the darkness.

"'Just in time, mother,' she whispered. 'Just in time.'"

This excruciating piece of prose was actually bought by a magazine called *The Black Cat*, which paid twelve dollars for it, and it also won a twenty-five-dollar prize for the best piece of undergraduate writing of that year.

When the day came for Woollcott to leave Hamilton, he went sadly, for he had loved it. Furthermore, he had a nervous distaste for the world beyond the campus and for a while he dreamed of a cloistered life as principal of a high school. He even went to Hudson, N.Y., where he had heard a vacancy existed, but when he found that he would be expected to preserve discipline by violence if necessary and was shown a group of students any one of whom could have dissected him singlehanded, he abandoned the project as impracticable. He came instead to New York and went to work as a fifteen-dollar-a-week clerk in the Chemical National Bank, adding and subtracting, dreaming of the horrible day when he would be promoted to teller. Samuel Hopkins Adams, a trustee of Hamilton and, in fact, the man who had put up the prize won by "The Precipice," rescued him from finance by informing Carr Van Anda of the *Times* that a *Wunderkind* had come to town, a journalistic prodigy who would eclipse even the great Frank Ward O'Malley. This, it turned out, wasn't strictly true. There could be no question that the *Times'* new man could write very nicely, though in a strangely lacy and intricate fashion, but as a reporter he was exasperating. He wasn't exactly hostile to facts, but he was apathetic about them, and he liked a story to be neatly assembled in one place—a good cornerstone-laying, for instance—and not spread out untidily all over hell so that a man had to run himself ragged trying to get it together.

He was assigned to the sinking of the *Titanic*, the Equitable fire, the Rosenthal case, and even what might be called the aesthete's angle of one World Series, but his heart wasn't in it. Neither, apparently, was the *Times'*, for in 1914, after Woollcott had expressed his discontent by having a nervous breakdown, Van Anda made him dramatic critic. The reasons for this appointment are obscure. Detractors say it was a choice of getting young Woollcott off news or turning the paper into a weekly (the *Times* was beaten daily on the Rosenthal story before Mr. Woollcott retired in favor of a more curious and mobile man); admirers, on the other hand, claim that the management considered it wasteful to confine the most ornamental prose in New York to routine journalism. The subject of the whole controversy says modestly that *he* thinks it was only because Mr. Van Anda imagined that his employee looked like Thackeray.

It wasn't much of a job anyway. The *Times* was inclined to be haughty about the drama and considered reviews of it just barely fit to print. The column occupied a modest position and its author was paid sixty dollars a week. Nevertheless, Mr. Woollcott felt that at last he had come into his own, and when he was barred from all the Shubert theatres for wickedly denouncing almost everything he saw in them, it gave him an almost intolerable sense of power.

When he was first chosen, he wrote his mother and told her the magnificent news, but she wasn't especially impressed.

"*I* should think it would be very narrowing," she wrote back.

(This is the first of three articles on Mr. Woollcott.)

II

Alexander Woollcott, erstwhile dramatic critic for the *Times*, now risen to the estate of private in the United States Medical Corps, embarked for France on July 11, 1917, but his transport was rammed and sunk by the liner Panama halfway down New York Harbor. Mr. Woollcott, who didn't even get his feet wet, was extricated and put back on shore. A week after this anticlimax he sailed again, and this time, in spite of a skirmish with two U-boats off Belle Isle, he reached St.-Nazaire. From there he was sent to Base Hospital No. 8, in the village of Savenay in the Loire-Inférieure. For six rather exasperating months he lingered in Savenay, performing duties which would unquestionably have amused a great many actors back in New York if they could have seen him.

While he was engaged in this embarrassing fashion, the *Stars and*

Stripes, the weekly newspaper of the A.E.F., had been started in a crowded little office on the Rue Ste.-Anne in Paris. In those early days it was badly understaffed—the first few issues, in fact, were almost entirely written by one man—and soon the editor began to look around for American journalists in other branches of the service. When he telegraphed Savenay to ask if there was any reasonable objection to transforming one Alexander Woollcott from an orderly into a reporter, the colonel in charge of the hospital was on duty elsewhere and the message was given to his adjutant to deal with in his absence. This agreeable man called Woollcott—he was Sergeant Woollcott by now—into his office and allowed him to cook up his own answer.

"Sergeant Alexander Woollcott has done magnificent work here," wrote Sergeant Woollcott after a moment's thought, "but can be spared."

Woollcott the reporter for the *Stars and Stripes* wasn't really very different from Woollcott the dramatic critic for the *Times*. The war appeared to him in the light of an enormous and essentially rather good-natured melodrama, and he wrote about the men in the trenches with the same romantic intensity that he had once reserved for Mrs. Fiske. The atmosphere in the office on the Rue Ste.-Anne, and later in the one on the Rue des Italiens, was also not unlike that he had known in New York. His colleagues were rude men who preferred on the whole witnessing the confusion of one of their superior officers to any catastrophe that might overtake the Germans. Most of them were what might be called old-fashioned newspapermen, with a childish contempt for high-class prose, and when the former dramatic critic for the New York *Times* proudly reported for duty, their behavior must have been a little irritating. One of them, in fact, a barbarian who had worked on almost every paper in the United States, laughed so insanely that he had to be helped out of the room.

To some extent they got used to Sergeant Woollcott after a while and even came to respect him for the way he was able to adjust himself to a life that was wildly foreign to his nature, but he never stopped entertaining them. Woollcott was probably the most heavily burdened war correspondent in history, being festooned on his tours of the front with a collection of binoculars, cameras, gas masks, canteens, and other spare parts that would have weighed down Richard Harding Davis. In spite of all this fancy equipment, he always looked dismally non-military. Once he was dining in Paris with another member of the staff who had done no more than button up his blouse in honor of the occasion. A young lady who was with them studied Mr. Woollcott anxiously for a long time but clearly could identify him with nothing in her previous military experience. At last she gave him up and turned to her other companion.

"But you," she said timidly, "*you're* in the Army, aren't you?"

On another occasion he was with Elsie Janis and her mother when the news came that the draft age had been extended to take in men of forty-five.

"Goodness, Aleck," said both ladies as one woman, "that means *you'll* have to go, doesn't it?"

Altogether his appearance was so exotic that A. A. Wallgren, who drew a comic strip for the *Stars and Stripes* and usually employed his colleagues as models, liked to show Sergeant Woollcott carrying a single lovely rose. General Pershing, in fact, was probably the only man in the A.E.F. who ever mistook Mr. Woollcott for a soldier. This was long after the Armistice, on a day when several members of the editorial staff had just got their discharges and the only occasion on which Pershing ever visited the office. Sergeant Woollcott, still in uniform, was presented to the Commander in Chief together with the information that he had that day, after twenty-two months of service, at last become a civilian.

"Well, well," said the General, amid a stunned silence, "he doesn't look much like a civilian to *me*."

The old sergeant still likes to quote this inexplicable compliment along with another he received from the New Orleans *Times-Picayune*. In a review of one of Mr. Woollcott's books, this paper published an unusually hideous photograph of the artist. The caption under it, however, was what would have confounded every man who ever worked on the *Stars and Stripes*. "Soldier-Author," it said.

Even though the A.E.F.'s correspondent didn't look especially warlike, he saw a lot of the battlefield. He had a sort of roving commission from the paper and spent most of his time up close to the front lines, sending his dispatches back to Paris by courier. It is the general impression that Mr. Woollcott was imperturbable under fire, although one cynical man who knew him at the time has his own explanation.

"I thought he was a hero myself," says this small spirit, "until I found out he had something the matter with his eyes. Hell, he could get right up on top of a town without even knowing it was under fire."

Myopic or not, Woollcott occasionally found himself within range of the cannon, and witnesses say that it was a moving and pitiful sight to see him trying to get down on his stomach when he heard the scream of an approaching shell. Other men dropped where they were, but Mr. Woollcott weighed close to two hundred pounds exclusive of hardware and his descent was gradual and majestic, like a slowly kneeling camel. Even when he had got safely down, he was still far from flat, and it is one of the miracles of the war that he came through it unperforated. Unwieldy as he was, however, he was a conscientious reporter. There were even those who felt he was *too* conscientious, their number including one cross-grained sergeant who was bringing his platoon back from a tour of duty in the frontline trenches when he was accosted by Mr. Woollcott in his best New York *Times* manner.

"Sergeant," he said crisply, "I'm from the *Stars and Stripes,* and I'd like you to tell me exactly—"

"You go to hell, Willie," said the sergeant.

The *Stars and Stripes,* which had built up a weekly circulation of 550,000 and returned to the government a net profit of $700,000 in a little less than a year and a half, went out of existence on June 13, 1919. Things had been pretty dull in the seven months following the Armistice, and Mr. Woollcott was glad to get back to his job on the *Times.*

IN RETROSPECT IT is not very easy to evaluate him as a dramatic critic. He had enthusiasm, an honest love for the theatre, and a gift for the neat and deadly phrase. On the other hand, he was sentimental, partisan, and maddeningly positive about everything even before he had been a critic long enough to know much about anything. His style, which could be lucid and witty, could also be muddled and frantic, and reading him in this mood often made subscribers feel as if his hot breath was actually on their necks. The short space of writing time allowed by a morning paper, of course, had a lot to do with that, for the Woollcott style, pouring too richly from his heart, needed a great deal of skimming and straining before it was fit for public consumption. He was aware of this himself and once, when an admiring lady asked him how he ever wrote so much in such a short time—most of his reviews were turned out in less than an hour—he answered her reasonably.

"If I had twice as much time, my blossom," he said, "my pieces would probably be half as long."

The case against him was not too temperately stated by George Jean Nathan, then writing about the theatre for *Smart Set*. Mr. Nathan's performance had a fascination of its own, because in calling his rival unbearably dogmatic he exhibited the same quality in an even stronger degree, and in commenting on a style that seemed to him lush and juvenile he employed one that was tangled, multilingual, and indecently burdened with learned reference. It was not unlike Lady Godiva reproaching September Morn for not having enough clothes on, but it was not without some justice, either.

Mr. Nathan began by questioning some of the Woollcott judgments, which seemed to him rather in the nature of valentines. It struck him, for instance, as a little excitable to write the following about a fetching but by no means extraordinary young actress: "This most beguiling rôle . . . is played to incredible perfection by Lotus Robb, the April charm of whose delicate performance seemed . . . a thing which only lyric verse could adequately describe." Mr. Nathan was also pained to hear Jacob Ben-Ami, a strolling player of the period, described as a matchless world genius and *his* performance as so supernatural in every way that "some of us would crawl on our hands and knees to see it." So much indeed did this bonbon upset the little pundit that without half trying he reeled off the names of Arbatoff, Teliakovsky, Dalmatoff, Glagolin, Massalitinoff, Adelheim, Katchaloff, Moskvin, and Uraloff as a few of those who might be employed to teach this Ben-Ami the rudiments of acting. Alice Delysia, for whom Mr. Woollcott also entertained a respectful yen, provoked a similar outburst from Mr. Nathan, who this time listed no less than fifteen little-known French music-hall comediennes who were in every way her superior.

While Mencken's partner disapproved of much that Woollcott said, it was the *way* he said it that really made his head hurt.

"This style," he wrote sombrely, "is the particular bouquet I invite you to sniff. . . . It never strikes a mean; it is either a gravy bomb, a bursting gladiolus, a palpitating missa cantata, an attack of psychic hydrophobia, or a Roman denunciation, unequivocal, oracular, flat and final. . . . A style, in brief, that is purely emotional, and without a trace of the cool reflectiveness and contagious common sense suitable to criticism."

It is sometimes felt in the theatrical world, however, that nothing can possibly be half as bad as George Jean Nathan says it is, and certainly Mr. Woollcott had many passionate admirers. They conceded his faults—even his best friends were apt to murmur "Ben-Ami" in a thoughtful way whenever he turned up with a new world genius— but insisted that in spite of them his pieces had a life that was missing from those of his more austere competitors. There was an excitement, a quality of shared experience, of having been there and seen it yourself, which you couldn't get from anyone else.

There must have been something in what they said, because in 1922 the late Frank Munsey offered him the critic's job on his *Herald.* Like almost every newspaperman in New York, Mr. Woollcott loathed Munsey, but the *Times,* which had started him at $60 a week and now paid him $100, indicated clearly that it considered this figure more than ample for a man who had nothing more exhausting to do than inspect actors. Munsey offered him $15,000 a year, and in October, 1922, Mr. Woollcott went to work down the river. He stayed with Munsey nearly three years—on the *Herald* until it was sold to the *Tribune,* and then on the *Sun.* It was an unrewarding experience, for the *Herald* and the *Sun* were spiritless affairs, run by a clammy, ruthless man whose heart was really in the delicatessen business.

In 1925, Heywood Broun, succumbing to a combination of claustrophobia and a desire to rearrange the solar system, resigned as dramatic critic of the *World,* and Woollcott was chosen to succeed him. The pay was the same as it had been on the *Sun,* but the surroundings were vastly different. Financially the *World* was already sickening for its last illness, but editorially it was the most provocative paper in New York. The celebrated "opposite-editorial page," which was worshipfully read at almost every up-and-coming breakfast table, was a sort of five-ring circus. F.P.A. was doing the Conning Tower; Broun, though no longer a critic, was still writing It Seems to Me, Laurence Stallings and Samuel Chotzinoff dealt with books and music, respectively, and now Woollcott had come to do the theatre. On the day that the new dramatic critic went to work, it undoubtedly seemed to *him* that he could remain in the Pulitzer Building happily forever.

EVER SINCE HE came back from the war, Mr. Woollcott's social life had been expanding in a very satisfactory way. Before that, to most people he had just been a man who wrote dramatic criticism for the *Times* and signed to it a name that always looked like a typographical error. Now he began to emerge as a metropolitan character and a member of the group which firmly took charge of humor in America throughout the nineteen-twenties and early thirties.

They were a remarkable gang, however you look at them, and they have left us many legends, of which the most durable are the Round Table at the Algonquin Hotel, the Thanatopsis Literary and Inside Straight Club, .the back room at the West Side Tony's, and, conceivably, Herbert Bayard Swope. Franklin P. Adams was their official biographer, and it was a rare Saturday when his Pepys' Diary failed to mention A. Woollcott, H. Broun, G. Kaufman, M. Connelly, D. Parker, D. Stewart, I. Berlin, R. Sherwood, H. Dietz, E. Ferber, H. Swope, D. Taylor, F. Sullivan, N. McMein, C. MacArthur, R. Crouse, and one or more of the interminable Marx Brothers. This was the nucleus of the group, the permanent acting company. Others attached themselves to it briefly from time to time. Noel Coward and Beatrice Lillie belonged when they were in town and so did the Lunts; Thornton Wilder and S. N. Behrman, coming into glory rather later than the others, were more or less honorary members, and even Jed Harris sometimes hung around because in that dim yesterday several people were actually speaking to him.

Because of a certain patriarchal though not entirely benevolent aspect and a superior talent for abuse, Mr. Woollcott gradually became a sort of spiritual focus for the rest. It was he who played the parlor games of the period—Anagrams, Adverbs, Categories, Murder, and a dozen others—with the fiercest relish; it was he who won or lost at cards with the noisiest rejoicing and the blackest hate; it might even be said that it was he who, writing about his friends in almost every publication extant, earned against fairly stiff competition the title of the noblest logroller of them all. As a matter of fact, it was logrolling of a singularly high-minded and disinterested sort, for Mr. Woollcott, in his romantic way, had no doubt that he was entirely surrounded by genius, and every bouquet came from his heart. Nor was his generosity confined to print. He was passionately and even almost intrusively concerned with the private lives of all his acquaintances, and when catastrophe visited them, as it much too frequently did, he was usually the first to hear about it and his response was invariable. Dorothy Parker, who is not always so mellow, wrote an article about him in *Vanity Fair* in which she said, "He does more kindness than anyone I have ever known; and I have learned that not from him but from the people who have experienced it."

In 1920, the average age of the members of the Thanatopsis-Algonquin axis was somewhere around twenty-eight, and with one or two exceptions they were comparatively unknown. The next ten years, however, brought extraordinary wealth and celebrity to most of them. Kaufman and Connelly wrote "Dulcy" in 1921 and worked together on such successes as "To the Ladies," "Merton of the Movies," and "Beggar on Horseback" until they split up, in 1926, after which Connelly wrote "The Wisdom Tooth" and "The Green Pastures" alone, and Kaufman collaborated with many people, among them Edna Ferber ("The Royal Family"), Ring Lardner ("June Moon"), and Moss Hart ("Once in a Lifetime"). MacArthur wrote "Lulu Belle" with Edward Sheldon in 1926 and "The Front Page" in 1928 with Ben Hecht, the latter to the considerable profit of Jed Harris, who had already produced "Broadway" and "Coquette."

In the same period, Howard Dietz, until 1924 a not especially humble press agent, helped to turn out two "Little Shows" and

"Three's a Crowd." Behrman wrote "The Second Man" and adapted "Serena Blandish"; Sherwood came out with "The Road to Rome," "The Queen's Husband," and "Waterloo Bridge;" and Donald Ogden Stewart, after an initial success with "A Parody Outline of History" and three or four other books, wrote and acted in a profitable little play called "Rebound." The ladies were busy too, with Edna Ferber turning out "So Big" and "Show Boat," Dorothy Parker picking up a reputation as the most murderous book critic of her time while herself producing two books of verse and one of short stories, and Neysa McMein becoming recognized as about the best pastel artist in the business.

It was an exciting and gratifying time for everybody, but its very magnificence spelled the end of the Algonquin group as a local phenomenon. Hollywood got some of them and others moved to Connecticut, partly to escape the New York state income tax and partly under the sad old delusion that a man can write far more rapidly and beautifully while raising his own vegetables. Those who didn't move away were by now temperamentally unfit for the old close association, since there is nothing more enervating to the artist than the daily society of a lot of people who are just as famous as he is. The new conscience, born of dark doings abroad, also had some bearing on it. Mr. Woollcott's friends, who had no political convictions worth mentioning in 1920, began to think rather intensely and presently occupied conflicting positions ranging all the way from mild liberalism to the ultimate hammer and sickle.

They grew apart, meeting only occasionally and usually by accident. While they no longer knew one another intimately, however, almost all of them kept in pretty close touch with Mr. Woollcott. His apartment at 450 East Fifty-second Street, which Dorothy Parker in a spasm of rascality had named Wit's End, was a comfortable, untidy garret looking down on the East River, and long after the Round Table and the Thanatopsis Club were dead it was still a hangout for whatever members of the old mob happened to be in town. Sunday breakfast there lasted practically all day, with Mr. Woollcott, in rumpled pajamas and an ancient, rather horrible dressing gown, receiving his guests from a throne in one corner with an air that would have done credit to Queen Victoria.

"You kept thinking you ought to kiss his God damn hand," said one man who should never have been admitted to polite society in the first place and never was again.

Games of chance in which a careless gambler could easily lose four or five hundred dollars at a sitting went on day and night, and when that palled, they played croquet, at which most of them were ferociously expert, either on the green in Central Park or out at Herbert Swope's house in Sands Point.

It is hard to tell just exactly when Mr. Woollcott worked in the midst of all this revelry, but he did. He wrote his daily reviews and erudite pieces for the Sunday theatre section, which, incidentally, he and George Kaufman elevated from a press agents' clearing house to its present handsome and literary state. He even found time to turn out casual belles-lettres for many magazines. He was aided in all this by a succession of secretaries—intense, rather fragile young men, who protected their master from the vulgar public as reverently as if he had been a fine old tapestry. It is pleasant to report that most of them have passed on to artistic careers of their own, one man, indeed, now being known to millions as a gossip columnist on the *Daily News*, while another is visible nightly to thousands as a mandolin-player in "The American Way." The rest of Mr. Woollcott's domestic staff consisted of one dapper and mysterious young Negro, who had, to the best of anyone's knowledge, no other name than Junior. He was an imaginative man, given to inventing dramatic and unlikely pasts for himself, and he has gone down slightly to history for a comforting remark he made to Jed Harris, who, or so it seemed to Junior, was unduly conscious of his racial heritage.

"You take me now, sir," said Junior. "Why, my own grandfather was a Jew."

WITH THE CLOSE of the theatre season in the spring, Mr. Woollcott always left town. For a few years he experimented with houses on Long Island and in Westchester, but they were never very satisfactory. He dreamed of something more remote and inaccessible, a communal Eden—the theories of Brook Farm and Phalanx have never been far from his heart—free from the sights and sounds and disgusting little faces that haunted him in Times Square. In 1920 he found it in Neshobe, a seven-acre, beautifully wooded island in Lake Bomoseen, Vermont.

Neshobe was bought from its original owners about thirty years ago by a lawyer named Enos Booth, who built a small cottage there as a headquarters for hunting and fishing trips. Mr. Booth was apparently a simple man himself, but he had literary friends and just after the war a few of them began to come up for weekends. That wound up the hunting and fishing, but it also sent the island off on its career as the most relentlessly playful resort in New England. It wasn't long after the first artists came to Neshobe before the place was overrun with them. Eventually Mr. Booth decided to turn the island into a club and then, shortly after having made his contribution to American art and letters, he passed quietly from the scene.

In addition to Mr. Booth, the early members were Woollcott, Alice Duer Miller, Harpo Marx, Neysa McMein, Raymond Ives, George Kaufman, Dorothy Parker, Marc Connelly, and Charles MacArthur, and all but the last three, who turned out to be languid about their dues, now belong. The dues, still in force, were probably reasonable enough, all things considered. There was an initiation fee of $1,250, an annual charge of $150, and another charge of $7.50 for every day spent on the island. While the membership was restricted to ten, there were beds for sixteen and guests could be brought provided that their sponsors paid $7.50 a head for them and also that they were acceptable mentally to everybody. A young lady who went up there explained this matter clearly though rather forbiddingly in an article she subsequently wrote for a magazine. "There is no pat way to sum up the perfect guest on the island," she said. "Individuality and vitality of thought, quick wit, charm, and proficiency at games are desirable qualifications. . . . But if a guest can qualify simply as an engaging companion, he needs no additional social talents. For, contrary to rumor, talk on the island is not entirely badinage; it is anything and everything, as rich and unflagging a mixture as ever stemmed from an assortment of active, alert, and challenging minds. Sooner or later an opportunity to chime in comes to everyone who is there, but it is better to say nothing than to say something badly. Pleasant as they may be personally, bores are never tolerated."

She didn't explain what happens to the bores, and it is best perhaps just not to think about it.

In the beginning the island was actually coöperative, but by now it is half owned and almost wholly buffaloed by Mr. Woollcott. It is he who, grimly impatient for the games to begin, routs the rich, challenging minds up at seven-thirty every morning to go for a swim in the cold lake; it is he who, from morning to midnight, drives them ruthlessly from the lake to the croquet ground to the backgammon table; he who a year ago removed himself grandly from the community shack and built a fine stone house all his own, with marble baths and an open fire in every bedroom. The other members visit the island intermittently between May and October, but Mr. Woollcott spends almost all the summer there and even goes up alone in the dead of winter, crossing dangerously from the mainland on the ice. He loves Neshobe as proudly and jealously as young Bonaparte loved Corsica.

The island is a perpetual source of wonder to the simple Vermont natives who circumnavigate it cautiously in motorboats and observe the inmates, who are frequently to be seen lying like seals along the rocky shore. The general opinion apparently is that Neshobe is a sort of Hollywood nudist camp, and this leads to odd confusions. Thornton Wilder has been mistaken for Jack Benny, and MacArthur, sun-bathing in the nude, was once pleased to hear himself identified as Irving Berlin and sang "All Alone" loud and clear in gratitude. A few years ago, Mr. Woollcott himself, inadequately wrapped in a dressing gown and wearing a limp, enormous straw hat, was reading one day on the dock when a boatload of sightseers drifted by. Their voices came to him quite plainly over the water.

"Who on earth is *that?*" he heard one lady cry in startled and even rather horrified tones.

"I'm not sure," said another voice doubtfully, "but I *think* it's Marie Dressler."

Mr. Woollcott resigned from the *World* at the end of the 1928 theatre season. For a long time the physical discomfort and mental anguish of writing daily theatrical criticism had been wearing him down. He was not as thin as he once was, and the after-theatre congestion in Times Square was driving him crazy. He wrote his pieces in a little office in the Hotel Continental, where breathless couriers snatched the completed pages out of his typewriter and delivered them to a telegrapher. In the end even this got too hard, especially as the *World*, in a desperate effort to beat the other papers to the street, kept advancing his deadline until, unless Mr. Woollcott left before the curtain went down, he often had no more than twenty minutes to turn out his copy. It was not only nerve-racking to work under such pressure; he also felt that there was something vaguely absurd in making such a commotion about plays that nine times out of ten were of no conceivable interest to anybody.

"It was like engaging Balto to rush a relief supply of macaroons to Nome," he says, obviously pleased with the metaphor.[4]

He also felt in a dim way that perhaps he had got to be a dramatic critic too young. He still loved the theatre better than anything else, but somehow he couldn't imagine being a critic for fifteen or twenty years more. It was too long a time just to keep on doing the same thing. The prospect appalled him.

"A man can't take the job of his life at twenty-seven," he said once, trying to explain the almost panic restlessness he felt.

(This is the second of three articles on Mr. Woollcott.)

III

With his resignation as dramatic critic for the *World* in May, 1928, Alexander Woollcott entered the present phase of his career, a period of great, though rather jumbled activity. During the next ten years he was to be, often simultaneously, a Broadway star, a playwright, a contributor to the magazines, a radio performer, a moving-picture actor, a lecturer, an anthologist, a stock-market operator, and an advertising-copy writer for tobacco, whiskey, and fast automobiles. He was forty-one years old, and Walter Pitkin might well have used him for a frontispiece.

He had left the *World* because of the wear and tear on his nervous system caused by the demands of daily journalism. Looking around for something that would give him time to arrange his thoughts in a decent and leisurely fashion, his eye fell on the magazines and by

February, 1929, he was writing for them busily. Here, for the first time, he was able to deal with the things, unconnected with the theatre, which had been cluttering up his mind for years. He still paid an occasional fragrant tribute to Mrs. Fiske, Chaplin, and the Marx Brothers, of course, for these names write themselves almost automatically on his typewriter, but for the most part he dealt with his experiences in the larger world. The past played a considerable part in all this—memories of his early days in Phalanx, N.J., Kansas City, and Philadelphia; anecdotes about Hamilton College and the A.E.F.—but he covered the present, too, writing winsomely about the celebrated people he knows all over the world. Sometimes he spoke chillingly of murder and sometimes he published even more gruesome collections of Americana. He told about the books he liked and the ones he loathed, the games he played, the restaurants he ate in, and once he even described, though in rather evasive terms, his impressions of the Soviet Union. It was a remarkable potpourri and it was served with remarkable elegance. Newspaper deadlines had been hard on his style, but now it came into its own, a sort of heavenly compound of Dickens and Chesterton with perhaps a little earthly leaven of Booth Tarkington and even hellish prophecies here and there of Lucius Beebe, whose intolerably flossy column wasn't to make its appearance for nearly five years.

As other men fear and hate the dentist's drill, Mr. Woollcott is tortured by an unbalanced sentence. Adverbs and adverbial phrases ("oddly enough" is his favorite) and tender apostrophes to the reader ("my blossom," "puss," "my little dears") are judiciously inserted until the magic equilibrium is achieved. His mind is intricate and circuitous and thoughts often emerge from it in an arrangement of subordinate clauses that would have satisfied Henry James. Woollcott is romantic, and this can express itself in a tropic violence of description. He is in love with the dear past, and it lives again in his prose in words like "wraprascal," "gaffer," "tippet," and "minx." At its best, all this can have an admirable effect, charming the reader's ear and conveying the author's own emotion vividly to his mind; at its infrequent worst, when Mr. Woollcott is betrayed by his too easily accessible heart, it suggests to some extent the tormented prose of a sophomore writing to his girl.

Mr. Woollcott's relations with his various editors were amiable for the most part. He was prompt with his copy, which was typed with never a misspelling or an erasure on long sheets of delicately tinted paper, and he was agreeably reliable when it came to facts. The difficulties that arose were usually temperamental, resulting from a curious paradox in Mr. Woollcott's character. Although the innocent vulgarities of the advertising business horrified him—a product called Didy Panties almost did him in—he had a lingerie salesman's fondness for smoking-car anecdotes, the lower the better. About once a month a specimen would turn up which would usually not only be unprintable in any magazine not intended exclusively for the United States Marines but would also be drearily familiar to all worldly editors. Its removal from his copy was always the signal for a fierce battle, with Mr. Woollcott passing from blank astonishment that anyone could be virginal enough to object to such a pretty story, then to a vehement lecture on the subject of taste, and finally to the cold tendering of his resignation. On several occasions, when some editor had as usual proved adamant, he actually did resign and had to be won back with humble telephone calls and ardent letters. These lovers' quarrels turned up periodically and while they brought two or three editors close to nervous collapse, Mr. Woollcott enjoyed them thoroughly. Up in his topless tower on the East River, he sometimes felt as controversial and desirable as Helen of Troy.

ON THE MORNING of October 19, 1929, Mr. Woollcott was reasonably well off. He and his friends knew gifted people in Wall Street and with this professional assistance, or perhaps in spite of it, they had all done very nicely in the market. It was reflected in their lives. They spoke in the proud, mysterious language of finance, and they moved their poker game from the Algonquin to the Colony, where the check for refreshments was usually more than anybody had made in a week when the Thanatopsis Club began. Almost everybody bought a little place in the country. Like so much wealth of the period, however, their profits were entirely a matter of bookkeeping, and when the American dream abruptly turned into a nightmare, most of them were seriously damaged. In two days Mr. Woollcott had dropped more than $200,000. He was playing croquet out on Long Island when his broker telephoned to say that he was finally undone. Mrs. George S. Kaufman, who was playing with him and had herself had a fairly painful lesson in the folklore of capitalism, says that he came back to the croquet ground and finished his game without batting an eye.

Later he was even able to describe his broker genially as a man who could run your fortune into a shoestring, but in spite of this unearthly detachment his losses had been annoying. His income from his magazine writing was somewhere around $30,000 a year, but he had strong obligations to his family and to other people—he was putting a Vermont boy through Hamilton, for one thing—and his scale of living, with the New York apartment and the island in Lake Bomoseen, was not especially modest. Mr. Woollcott admires money as much as the next man and now, especially, a little extra would come in handy. He had been approached by the radio from time to time, but he had never paid much attention. In fact, he had never willingly listened to a broadcast in his life and regarded the unpleasant sounds he occasionally heard in his friends' houses as no more than childish attempts to upset him when he was concentrating on the cards. This, however, was no time to be proud, and by the end of October he had succumbed, going on the air one Sunday night in a fifteen-minute sustaining program called "The Town Crier." There wasn't a great deal of money in that, but by the following September he was being sponsored by the Gruen Watchmakers Guild and appearing two nights a week. At this time he also took over a sustaining program in which he reviewed books under the prettily whimsical title of The Early Bookworm, a choice which was more or less perplexing in view of the fact that he had once expressed horrified disgust upon learning that Mrs. Isabel Paterson of the *Herald Tribune* had decided to call *her* column "Turns with a Bookworm." He was off the air from March, 1931, until September, 1933, when he came back again as The Town Crier and was handsomely sponsored, first by the Cream of Wheat Company and then by Liggett & Myers, for whom he spoke admiringly of Granger Cut Plug. For a while he was being paid $3,500 a broadcast, which is probably not much as radio salaries go, but is not, on the other hand, just hay, puss.

Mr. Woollcott came to like the radio, there being something

about projecting himself into several million parlors at the same time which answered the special requirements of his spirit, and although his programs were a little advanced for the Amos 'n' Andy public, he was successful and popular. Like his magazine articles, his broadcasts covered a great deal of ground, touching on books and the theatre, furnishing affectionate bulletins about his friends, and carrying on his perpetual crusades for the Seeing Eye and Hamilton College. He was, if anything, more emotional than he was in print, and finally this led to one of the most maddening experiences of his life.

On the day following an especially rich performance, he was going over his fan mail when he came upon a letter written on ruled paper in a hand that shook a little but was fine and legible still—an old-fashioned hand, with curlicues. The letter bore no address and it was unsigned, but nevertheless there was something about it that afflicted its recipient with the same romantic melancholy he felt whenever he thought about Mrs. Fiske.

His correspondents, it appeared from the text, were two old ladies, sisters, and they lived somewhere near Albany. They didn't care to be more specific than that because they were afraid that Mr. Woollcott might want to help them and they couldn't take charity from anybody. The fact remained, however, that they had little left in life except their radio, to which they listened every night when the dishes were washed and the chores all done. They liked a lot of things they heard, but they thought Mr. W. was about the *best* thing in the world. He had no idea what comfort he'd brought into their lives, and for their part they didn't know what they'd do without him as they went down into the Valley of the Shadow. There was indeed a scriptural tone all through the letter, as might have been expected from two ladies whose only consolation, at least until The Town Crier came along, had presumably been Holy Writ.

Mr. Woollcott had photostatic copies made of the letter and sent them around to his friends, declaring that this was the greatest tribute he'd ever received. He also serenaded the sisters on the air, having the studio orchestra play what he felt sure must be their favorite tunes—the old simple songs, things like "Home, Sweet Home" and "Way Down Upon the Swanee River." These serenades, incidentally, had already gone out from The Town Crier to many people, among them ex-Justice Oliver Wendell Holmes, who died three days later, causing Charles MacArthur, a Baptist faun, to send Mr. Woollcott a brief wire. "One," it said pleasantly. Anyway, more letters came from the sisters and at last one that announced that the elder of them had died, died happily and confident of her salvation at the very moment he went off the air. It was a lot to ask, said the survivor, but next week, if he could spare the time, would Mr. Woollcott mind reading the Twenty-third Psalm over the radio. It would be a sort of requiem. Mind indeed! The next week, with a catch in his throat, Mr. Woollcott read the Twenty-third Psalm. It was a great emotional performance, judged by any standards. "He was right in the groove that night," says a musical friend admiringly.

Nothing was heard then for a week or two, but finally a letter came in another, younger hand. Both sisters were dead now, it said, and the last one had also died with gratitude to Alexander Woollcott in her heart. The sisters were gone, but their memory plagued him. He was determined to find out who they had been, where and how they had lived, anything at all about them. He exhausted all the possibilities, even sending an agent up to explore the country around Albany to see if anybody remembered two old ladies who had lived alone. A Catholic priest had been named in one of the letters—the only actual clue—but he proved as elusive as his parishioners and nothing came of him, either. Mr. Woollcott spent almost as much as he made from his broadcasts trying to beat the sisters out of the bush, but it was no good. Apparently they had left behind them no relatives, no graves, and, what was most curious of all, no death certificates.

Some of Mr. Woollcott's friends, who may have heard a little too much about the sisters while they were alive, began to ask if they had ever lived at all. Mightn't it be just a little joke? How else could you account for this strange vanishment? The case was never publicly proved one way or the other, but people who ought to know said that the weird sisters and their letters were in actual fact the work of a brooding author whose book Mr. Woollcott had dismissed too arrogantly as tripe. They knew this miserable man, they said, and had even listened to his shameless confession. Mr. Woollcott found it hard to accept this explanation. In spite of all the evidence, he couldn't believe that any human heart could be black enough for such villainy. Nor can he even now.

Mr. Woollcott still appears on occasional guest programs, although he hasn't had a regular hour of his own since July, 1937. A few weeks ago, as The Town Crier, he spoke over WEAF in behalf of political refugees (this was a triumph for him, since once he had resigned in disgust because they wouldn't let him criticize dictatorships), and more recently he might have been heard praising—of all things—the Hamilton College Choir. Some time ago he was on the Information Please Hour when it embarrassingly developed that, although Dickens is one of his most widely advertised enthusiasms, he had never finished reading "Bleak House," and the behavior of his colleagues on this occasion was so exasperating to him that one listener reported that he was the only man she had ever heard who could pout quite unmistakably over the air.

HIS CAREER IN the theatre began about the same time as his first venture on the radio. During the summer of 1929, he had been collaborating with George S. Kaufman on "The Channel Road," an adaptation of de Maupassant's "Boule de Suif," and it was put on at the Plymouth Theatre in the fall of that year. The critics, who may not have been precisely laying for Mr. Woollcott but certainly hadn't been weaving any garlands for him either, jumped it with glad little cries. It was a wordy, shapeless, amateurish piece, they said, and suggested that Mr. Woollcott go back to his fancywork. This vigorous reception was enough to discourage him until the fall of 1933, when, again in collaboration with Mr. Kaufman, he turned up with a pathological study in murder called "The Dark Tower." This was a little better, but not much. In spite of an unusual amount of villainy, it was a rather static play and the sight of Miss Margalo Gillmore wandering through most of it in a hypnotic trance seemed to have a rather stupefying effect on the audiences.

The reason for both these failures probably lay in a curious relationship between the authors. Mr. Kaufman, usually an acute and practical judge of scripts, with strong opinions of his own, was a helpless admirer of Mr. Woollcott's prose, which seemed to him to have a grace and felicity not entirely of this world. He had occasional misgivings about how some of the more elegantly sculptured lines would sound when offered on the stage as the casual speech of human beings, but his modest heart told him that this was Art and therefore not to be tampered with by the likes of him. The result was that Mr. Woollcott was played as written, and was presently playing largely to empty seats. The budding playwright's own opinion of both these ventures can be guessed at from his paragraph in *Who's Who*, which lists all his other occupations but says nothing to suggest that he ever wrote a play in his life.

His acting, of course, was something else. On November 9, 1931, Mr. Woollcott made his first appearance as a child actor of forty-five in S. N. Behrman's "Brief Moment." He opened before a first-night audience made up largely of his dearest friends, most of whom hoped, in an amiable way, that he would stink. They were disappointed. Woollcott, who spent the evening lolling around on a sofa and insulting people, was barely distinguishable from the Woollcott they knew in private life. Since this was just what Mr. Behrman had in mind, the performance, while not precisely acting, had to be regarded as adequate. The *Times'* Mr. Atkinson, clinging desperately to ancient standards, said that for Mr. Woollcott "acting consists in speaking rather more deliberately than he does in the aisles and lobbies" and added that he not only dislocated the couch on which he sprawled but also to a certain extent the play itself. This, however, can be dismissed as the remark of a classicist. Languidly horizontal, beautifully plump, and talking in that strangely precise voice, which still has sharp overtones of Kansas City, Mr. Woollcott was the hit of the show and it was he rather than Miss Francine-Larrimore, or even the author, who was responsible for the fact that it ran for thirteen weeks. His second appearance on the stage, in Mr. Behrman's "Wine of Choice" last winter, was a very similar performance, but since he had a lot more to do and was even asked to move around a little, it was not quite so successful. As an occasional choral effect he is admirable, but as a featured exhibit he can grow monotonous.

In spite of the fact that Mr. Woollcott's technique on the stage involved no more than playing himself, he took his acting pretty seriously. Once, during the run of "Brief Moment," he happened to see a special matinée of a play starring his old friends the Lunts, and its effect was immediately perceptible in his own next performance. Miss Larrimore, coming off after the first act, complained bitterly to Mr. Behrman. "He just lies there and mutters, Sam," she said. "I can't hear a damn word he says."

Tactfully questioned by Mr. Behrman, who asked him if he was unwell, Woollcott dissolved the mystery.

"I see everything now," he said. "I've been working too hard. God, you ought to see Alfred. Never raises his voice. It's marvellous."

He was also given to experimenting on his own hook and often came to Mr. Behrman or Guthrie McClintic, who directed him, for approval.

"Did you notice me in the second scene tonight?"

"You were swell, Aleck," they would say politely.

"I know, but that business with the cigarette, where I look at Larrimore and *then* light it instead of the way we had it before?"

"Sure. That's swell."

"I thought it kind of pointed the whole thing up myself," he would say with satisfaction.

These improvisations had a somewhat disturbing effect on the rest of the cast, who were never completely sure what Mr. Woollcott was liable to do next, and they were also handicapped by the fact that his performance moved at a tempo of its own which hadn't very much to do with anything else that was going on on the stage. It was in "Wine of Choice," however, that he startled them most. Somebody had given him a Spanish cape, a spectacular thing, richly lined with crimson silk. It was, his false friend said, exactly what was needed to give his part a little extra touch of color and romance. Mr. Woollcott, who is no man to resist beauty, wore the cape in the out-of-town tryouts and would undoubtedly have done so on Broadway if his colleagues hadn't protested in a body. Not only was he a vehement spot of color, they said, reducing the rest of them to pale ghosts; he was even bad for their nerves.

"Every time he comes on I think, 'Good God, it's Bela Lugosi,'" said the pretty ingénue rather wildly.

Mr. Behrman was chosen to express their discontent, and when he explained that the cape was disturbing everybody terribly, Mr. Woollcott gave up, although he still wore it around town and was frequently mistaken for an advertisement.

In spite of his dreamy passion for the theatre, he never lost his practical financial sense. At one time, when "Brief Moment" wasn't doing especially well, the whole cast was asked to take a twenty-five-per-cent cut, and, though sadly, they all at last agreed—all, that is, except Mr. Woollcott. It had been his contention from the beginning that he was miserably underpaid, and the proposal that he take even less infuriated him. Not only did he refuse to take the cut; he demanded a raise and a substantial one, too. He threatened to resign and he had them there, because there was no question by this time that it was the prospect of seeing Woollcott plain that got people into the theatre. His salary, which had been $400 a week, was nearly doubled, which was more than could be said for his popularity with the rest of the company.

ALL HIS FINANCIAL affairs, as a matter of fact, have gone nicely in the ten years since the crash wiped him out. His income from the radio varied widely, but it seems likely that he collected at least $200,000 for the four years he was on the air; his magazine work brought in about $125,000; and as an actor and playwright he must have made $50,000, including his percentage from the sale of "The Dark Tower" to the movies. "While Rome Burns," published in 1934, sold an amazing total of 290,000 copies and his royalties from that were $70,000, while the two "Woollcott Readers," issued in 1935 and 1937, although they didn't approach that figure, made together between $15,000 and $20,000.

These were his main sources of income, of course, but other tidy sums kept dropping in his lap. In 1935, for instance, he played himself for a brief, profitable moment with Noel Coward in a moving picture called "The Scoundrel," and, in 1934, he had made a short for R.K.O. about spelling games; out-of-town ladies were always delighted to hear him lecture, since he was known to be personally acquainted with all the bright, disreputable people in the world; and in his spare time he had drummed up a very satisfactory little trade in commercial endorsements (Woollcott collapsed bonelessly on the back seat of a Chrysler, Woollcott urging all his friends in a rather peremptory form letter to give him a bottle of Seagram's whiskey for Christmas, Woollcott in full color and waving a bell, saying Granger Cut Plug is good for you). His ten-year total was certainly well over $700,000, and while an income of $70,000 a year, about thirty per cent of which went to the tax-collectors and perhaps another ten to agents, isn't money in the Hollywood sense, it was doing all right for a man who on the whole had managed to devote his talent only to things that really interested him.

MR. WOOLLCOTT'S LIFE, while unquestionably ideal for him, sometimes makes morbid observers think of a spider in its web. Recently, whenever he hasn't been hibernating up on Lake Bomoseen, he has been living at the Gotham Hotel in a suite that has the same untidy but expensive air that clings about him personally. His friends drop in obediently when he sends for them, and he loots and insults them over the card table with the best nature in the world. He is also high-handed with the employees of the hotel, who have learned rather painfully that the usual rules don't apply to the old eccentric in 9B. The other day, for instance, the clerk at the desk telephoned him to say that Miss Ina Claire was downstairs.

"All right, send her up," said Mr. Woollcott.

"I can't, sir," said the clerk nervously. "She has a dog."

"Either Miss Claire's dog comes up or I'm coming down," said Mr. Woollcott, and added gently, "I'm in my pajamas."

Miss Claire's dog came up.

Although he is fascinated by other people's domestic arrangements, Mr. Woollcott has never come very close to getting married himself. He has admired many ladies and once his engagement was considerably announced for him by the tabloids, but the idea of a little woman sashaying around the house has never really appealed to him. He is, however, a terrific matchmaker—nothing delights him quite so much as throwing his startled acquaintances into one another's arms—and he is strongly attached to children. His four nieces, the daughters of his brother William, who lives in Baltimore, are proudly exhibited and handsomely entertained when they come to town, and he is godfather to many of his friends' children. He is always flattered when anybody asks him to take on these spiritual responsibilities, although not as flattered as he was last year when Harpo Marx, who once inserted a "Duer" in his own name as a tribute to a lady he adored, decided to call his adopted son William Woollcott Marx.

At the moment Mr. Woollcott's plans are a little vague. Sometime in May, if not before, he will go up to his island and, dressed in a few disgusting rags, spend the summer knocking croquet balls around and thinking up new ways to badger the other inmates. If he feels like it and there is still peace anywhere in the world, he may even decide to go travelling again, as he used to do whenever his friends' personalities got to seem more than he could bear. As a world traveller, he has covered a great deal of ground, skipping breathlessly from the polite and ancient splendors of Knole in Kent (where he was embarrassed to learn that he had spoken rudely of Lady Sackville when she was an American actress), to the Riviera (where Frank Harris, decaying in obscurity, tried to sell him an armful of books), and even turning up in Moscow (where the peasants were impressed by his royal stomach and Mme. Litvinoff asked him severely if, as an employee of *The New Yorker*, he wouldn't please find out why she hadn't been getting her magazine).

Mr. Woollcott likes to travel, but somehow he always comes back a little sooner than he had planned. He doesn't actually believe his friends are incapable of conducting their lives in his absence, but on the other hand they are peculiar and helpless people, and he feels happier when he is around where he can keep an eye on them.

JUST NOW MR. Woollcott's writing is confined largely to the stupendous correspondence he always carries on—a deluge of affectionate or indignant or blasphemous but always stylishly written bulletins that many of his friends are thriftily storing up for posterity. In a day when most letters aren't much more than hastily expanded telegrams, they are unique, and his correspondents are grateful to him—grateful, that is, except once in a while when they are apt to be a little startled by Mr. Woollcott's intricate sense of humor. When Beatrice Kaufman, for instance, gave her celebrated friend as a reference to the school in which she was entering her daughter, she received from him what for an uneasy moment she actually believed was a carbon copy of the letter he had sent the headmistress. "I implore you," it began, "to accept this unfortunate child and remove her from her shocking environment," and went on from there to describe the orgies which took place nightly in the Kaufman household. S. N. Behrman was also momentarily taken aback when he got a carbon of the letter to a real-estate agent in which Mr. Woollcott remarked that he was astonished to learn that the company was even remotely considering accepting as a tenant such a notorious drunkard, bankrupt, and general moral leper as his miserable friend Behrman. Mr. Woollcott's correspondents undergo another small strain because he seldom puts his own name to his letters, preferring to sign them "Richard Whitney" or "Charles Hanson Towne" or sometimes, fondly, just "The Prince Chap."

When he starts writing professionally again, he will probably go back to contributing to the magazines, for it is in them he finds the audience that suits him best. However, the theatre and the movies and the radio are always there waiting for him, and television, of course, is just around the corner. At the back of his mind, he has a rather vague but entirely magnificent project for writing a definitive biography of the late Oliver Wendell Holmes, whom he considers the greatest American of our time. He may get around to doing that. It doesn't really matter what he does. He will almost certainly be successful at it, but his greatest success will always lie, as it did when he was an actor, in his tireless, eloquent, and extraordinarily diverse performance of the character called Alexander Woollcott, a man whose influence and importance can be attributed only in part to the work he has actually done. "He is predisposed to like people and things, in the order named," Dorothy Parker wrote of him once, "and that is his gift from Heaven and his career."

March 18, March 25, and April 1, 1939

ST. GEORGE AND THE DRAGNET

Iᴺ ᴀ ɢʀᴇᴀᴛ many ways, Thomas Edmund Dewey is an impressive Presidential candidate. He was born in a typical American town (Owosso, Mich., pop., 14,496) and he came of sound American stock (the hero of Manila Bay was his grandfather's third cousin). In his virtuous youth, he belonged to the Boy Scouts, sang in the choir, and peddled the *Saturday Evening Post*, winning a bicycle. At one time he spent the summer working as a hired hand on a farm, and at another he learned to set type on his father's newspaper. He went to the local public schools and was never late or absent a day in his life. After he was graduated from the University of Michigan and had taken his LL.B. at Columbia, he was admitted to the bar, and presently emerged, at the age of thirty-three, as a fighting prosecutor and the terror of the underworld.

Obviously all this is in the most acceptable tradition—the saga of a more virile and melodious Coolidge, without the snobbish taint of Amherst or the sad comedy of the electric horse. Fortunate as he was in this personal background, however, he was even more fortunate in the times that produced him. Whatever else it accomplished, prohibition got the world ready for the coming of Dewey. The intense melodrama of the twenties accustomed people to the idea of an aristocracy of crime, to a superheated vision of America ruled by an outlaw nobility of vast and incalculable powers. Beer barons and vice lords were a dime a dozen; almost every thug was at least a king. In New York, there were kings of vice, poultry, dope, fur, policy, and artichokes, to mention a few, and each of them commanded a band of desperadoes capable of dealing with the United States Marines. It was wonderful. Even more wonderful were the names that some of these monsters and their mates obligingly bore. In addition to such celebrated figures as Lucky, Waxey, Dixie, Legs, and Lepke, there were Spasm Ison, Cokey Flo Brown, Stone-Faced

Peggy, Jenny the Factory, Crazy Moe, Abadaba, Gashouse Lil, Six-Bits, and Blue Jaw Magoon.

From almost the beginning of his political career, Dewey tangled with this demoniac royalty, and he made the most of it. If the voters were already inclined to believe that they were taking part in a moving picture, he did little to disillusion them. His private and public conversation always emphasized the menace of the underworld, omnipresent, almost omnipotent, crouched for a leap. "What do *you* know about the Unione Siciliana?" he asked a startled interviewer, and when it turned out that the man knew almost nothing, he described the fate of a prominent writer who offered to sell *Liberty* a story about its machinations and was shot down like a dog for his pains. "Never been in the papers!" whispered the District Attorney, rolling his eyes wildly. "No indictment. A terrific business! If you had seen men blanch as I have at its mere mention—its mere *mention*—you would know what terror it holds." He was no less alarming when addressing millions. "He has a Japanese butler," he said over the radio, referring to the king of something or other, "who—serves—him—well." He has prosecuted few cases in which he was unable to suggest that there were nameless forces at work, and this has sometimes irritated his critics. "No matter if it was only rolling a lush," said one of them in his homely way, "Dewey could always make it look wonderful on the record."

WHILE THERE ARE many things in favor of the District Attorney, almost an equal number oppose him. Physically, he is not majestic, or even especially bizarre, which is probably the next best bet. He is five feet eight and a half inches tall and he weighs a hundred and fifty-seven pounds stripped. His teeth, with centre gaps in both the upper and lower sets, are his most unfortunate feature; his eyes, next to the mustache and the voice, his most arresting. These are brown, with small irises surrounded by a relatively immense area of white, and Dewey has a habit of rotating them furiously to punctuate and emphasize his speech, expressing horror and surprise by shooting them upward, cunning by sliding them from side to side behind narrowed lids. At climactic moments, he can pop them, almost audibly. Lloyd Paul Stryker, who has had less occasion to admire them than most, says that they are the only piercing brown eyes he has ever seen.

Dewey has a jutting jaw, high cheekbones, a slightly bulbous nose, and thick eyebrows. His face, on the whole, has a compressed appearance, as though someone had squeezed his head in a vise. His suits are custom-made but uninteresting, and always seem a little too tight for him, although the Merchant Tailors and Designers Association of America chose him this year as one of the twenty-five best-dressed men in America. Altogether—smallish, neat, and dark—he looks like a Wall Street clerk on his way to work; unlike the late and magnificent Harding, he is a hard man to imagine in a toga.

Dewey is also unfortunate in the fact that people too close to him are usually either entertained by his super-cinema technique or else irritated by his proud, peculiar ways. One crisp hostess has said, "You have to know Mr. Dewey very well in order to dislike him," and the reporters in the Criminal Courts Building usually speak of him lightly as The Boy Scout or, more simply, just The Boy. One man, who frequently boycotts Dewey's press conferences for ten days at a stretch, explains his absence airily. "You got to rap The Boy on the knuckles once in a while," he says.

Lawyers, politicians, and others whose careers are directly affected by Dewey's activities are apt to be more portentous. An attorney for the Civil Liberties Union has compared him with Mayor Hague, though conceding Dewey a good deal more class, and a Republican leader, noting the candidate's petulant behavior at a Party dinner, observed gloomily to Mr. Kenneth Simpson that they seemed to have a problem child on their hands. He has been accused of bullying hostile witnesses and coddling favorable ones, demanding exorbitant bail, wire-tapping, condoning the use of perjured testimony, and even (in the case of Dixie Davis, who was allowed to leave the Tombs some eighty or ninety times in the course of three months to go up to a lady's apartment and change his shirt) of conniving at adultery. In this case, Dewey's answer was frank, if not precisely responsive or even in the best possible taste. "Well, gentlemen," he told the jury, "if Davis did not have . . . desires, he wouldn't be human . . ."

Some hecklers even go to the length of complaining that the

leading contributors to the Dewey campaign fund represent more wealth and special interest than seem quite consistent with his notorious enthusiasm for the underprivileged. Among these well-heeled angels are, it is claimed, Ruth Hanna McCormick Simms, a President-maker by inheritance and a Dewey Cabinet member by inclination; John Foster Dulles, a senior partner in the law firm of Sullivan & Cromwell, counsel to some of the biggest corporations in the country, including the North American Company, International Nickel, and Brown Brothers Harriman (Mr. Dulles might turn up as Secretary of State); Roger W. Straus, vice-chairman of the board of the American Smelting & Refining Company, who might land an ambassadorship; Artemus L. Gates, president of the New York Trust Company; S. Sloan Colt, president of the Bankers Trust Company; Robert H. Thayer, who has Standard Oil connections; and Francis Dwight Bartow, vice-president of J. P. Morgan & Co. Up to now, it is estimated that they have been largely responsible for raising between $250,000 and $300,000 for private Pullman cars, publicity, rental on campaign headquarters, and all the other expenses necessary in presenting a candidate appetizingly to the public.

Dewey's most serious handicap, however, is the fact that he was born as recently as March 24, 1902. It is difficult for a great many people to think seriously of a candidate who was sixteen years old at the end of the World War, ten when the Titanic went down, six when William Howard Taft entered the White House, and thirty-one before he could buy a drink legally at any bar in the United States. If he happened to be elected, Dewey, of course, would be the youngest President in history, four years younger than Theodore Roosevelt, thirty years younger than William Henry Harrison, and about sixteen years below the average age of his predecessors at the time of their inauguration. Mrs. Dewey, who will be thirty-eight on February 7, 1941, would not, however, be the youngest First Lady—Dolly Madison was thirty-six when she entered the White House and Mrs. Cleveland was a tot of twenty-two.

Critics, in an attempt to make these cold figures a little more picturesque, have pointed out that he is only eight months older than Lucius Beebe, the fashionable pamphleteer, and seven weeks younger than Colonel Charles A. Lindbergh, the aviator—two national phenomena who, although of almost equal prominence, are not generally regarded as quite ready for the Presidency. Dewey's detractors also like to quote Secretary Ickes' comment that the District Attorney of New York had finally thrown his diaper in the ring.

Beyond a slight and comprehensible annoyance, it is doubtful if the candidate pays much attention to these brickbats. Nobody believes that Thomas E. Dewey is better qualified to be President of the United States than Thomas E. Dewey. Last fall many Republican heavyweights were asked to sign a resolution which read in part:

> Convinced that he possesses above all other leaders in the country today the ability, temperament, training and ideals which the next President of the United States must have, we have determined to cooperate in the movement to elect Thomas E. Dewey President in 1940.
>
> This movement has in every sense originated with the people themselves. Mr. Dewey's record has inspired new efforts on behalf of good government throughout the country. It has evoked a spontaneous demand everywhere for his election to the Presidency. In him the people see a new hope for a better America.
>
> He has experienced judgment on public questions. He has vigor, executive ability, sincerity and devotion to duty. All these qualities have been proved by exceptional performance in the public service.
>
> New York will be a pivotal state in the 1940 national elections. We are convinced Mr. Dewey will carry not only New York but also the country at large next year against any opponent. . . . We extend to all citizens a cordial invitation to join us.

According to the best authorities, this document was not only circulated by the candidate, who would whip it out of his pocket like an automatic when he had his victim cornered, but was also written by the man of experienced judgment himself.

This version, picturing Mr. Dewey drafting himself almost singlehanded, differs a little from the District Attorney's own account of what went on. Shortly after his defeat by Governor Lehman, he says, "they" began to badger him to run for the Presidency. Dr. Gallup made a few soundings and discovered that he was far ahead of all other Republican Presidential possibilities. "It looks like I'm in for it," Dewey recalls saying to himself rather ruefully at the time. "If that many people want me elected, it is my duty to give them a chance." He held out for a while, but when the procession of supplicants began to clog the halls of his office, he saw that it was no good; he shouldered the cross.

The cold fact seems to be that Dewey became the nominal choice of the New York Republican Party for one of those reasons which make practical politics such a fascinating study for the layman. For years the New York delegation had gone to the national convention with its members hopelessly split, some favoring this man, some that. Last year the better minds decided that this was all nonsense and that it would be a good idea if everybody went to Philadelphia agreed on one man. Then, if *he* didn't go over on the first couple of ballots, the state chairman would be in a position to handle his delegation as a solid block in further negotiations. What happened, it seems, was that the dummy candidate decided to run in earnest, on a fine, expansive scale worthy of William Jennings Bryan. "We drafted this monkey," says one humble worker in the vineyard, "and, by Jesus, he took it serious."

This would not be a particularly alarming situation for the New York strategists if the primaries in other states hadn't made it clear that a good many romantic citizens were also inclined to take Dewey serious—so many, in fact, that at the moment it is quite possible that he will go to Philadelphia so firmly established as the People's Candidate that the boys in the back room, who would almost prefer to run Mr. Beebe, will have to climb on the band wagon. Incidentally, they will not be able to tempt him with the lesser rôle of the Vice-Presidency. Dewey says emphatically that he is not interested in anything but the White House, explaining to one interviewer that it would be impossible for him to live suitably in Washington on $15,000 a year. "I can't afford it," he said. "It costs money to be a Vice-President."

★ ★ ★

WHAT DEWEY WOULD be like in the White House can only be deduced rather arbitrarily from his history up to now. His early life in Owosso, as previously noted, was suitable but dull, and so were his years in college, where he won singing and debating contests, got an adequate B grade in his studies, but was on the whole practically indistinguishable from his contemporaries. Dewey's actual career, it might be said, dates from the summer of 1925, when, on a bicycle tour of France, he decided to grow a mustache. It turned out to be a dream—bushy, dramatic, an italicized swearword in a dull sentence. From then on, things began to happen. Later that year, he went to work prosaically for a law firm in New York, but he rose rapidly and by 1931, when he was twenty-nine, he was earning $8,000 a year. Furthermore, according to Rupert Hughes, whose biography of Dewey compares very favorably with some of Albert Payson Terhune's hymns to the collie, he "was handling most of the litigation in his office." This statement is rather crossly denied by fellow-employees of the period, but there may be prejudice here, and anyway he was doing all right.

The big break, however, came when he served on a case with George Z. Medalie and impressed him so vehemently that when Medalie took the post of United States Attorney for the Southern District of New York, he offered Dewey a job at a salary around $3,500 as one of the sixty assistants on his staff. Dewey, whose indifference to money is such that he can remember offhand how much he was making at any given day in his life, even for singing in choirs, politely declined that, as well as a subsequent bid of $6,000. He finally accepted only when Medalie had raised the ante to $7,500 and the position to that of chief assistant.

In the two years and nine months that followed, the United States Attorney's office successfully prosecuted such middle-sized kings of the underworld as Legs Diamond and Waxey Gordon, and a lot of minor nobility, including James Quinlivan, a vice cop whose moral fervor had netted him $80,000 in three years, and James J. (Cupid) McCormick, the clerk in charge of the Marriage License Bureau, where, it seems, the pickings were also very nice.

In 1933, Medalie resigned and for five weeks, until Martin Conboy succeeded him, Dewey was in charge of the office. During this period the newspapers casually referred to him as the Acting United States Attorney, a title to which Dewey objected vigorously. In a letter to the editors, he advised them that they'd better omit the word "Acting," and they did, so, when he went into private practice a month later, he was able to call himself a former United States Attorney. Once again, Dewey had made something look good on the record.

Dewey says he was immensely successful in private practice, estimating the take at between $50,000 and $75,000 a year, a figure which even his best friends consider imaginative. Except for this financial item, nothing much developed in the eighteen months he worked for himself, although they marked his first encounter with Lepke, a genuine crowned head, and his satanic prime minister, Gurrah. In this case the victory seems to have lain with the forces of evil, since the baking company which had employed Dewey to straighten out its labor difficulties was still paying tribute to Lepke and Gurrah when he retired. Talking of this now, the candidate pops his eyes and says, "Isn't it awful? They were so scared, they were even afraid to tell *me*."

The next step up the ladder, and a big one, was his appointment as Special Prosecutor, which came about in July, 1935, after the grand jury had finally broken with District Attorney William C. Dodge and asked Governor Lehman to appoint somebody to investigate racketeering and vice in New York. At the instigation of Medalie, who by this time regarded his protégé as one of the fanciest bloodhounds in the business, the Governor chose Dewey, though not before four other prospects had refused the job. His salary, which he set himself, was $16,695, the same as the District Attorney's. The expenses of his office, during the years 1935, 1936, and 1937, were $793,502.92, of which $117,994.63 came under the useful heading of "contingencies."

Dewey established his first offices in the Woolworth Building, where he set up elaborate defences against the hosts of darkness, including a twenty-four-hour police guard inside the building, secret entrances, and a special untappable cable connected directly with the main office of the Telephone Company. After examining some four thousand applicants, he picked four chief assistants, sixteen assistants, ten accountants, and nine investigators. Then, with the Governor and the Mayor, he called on the public to come forward with information on racketeering, assuring witnesses of protection. The first, and rather discouraging, fish to fall into this net was a nineteen-year-old boy whom Dewey's agents caught breaking windows, but soon the big ones began to come along.

The biggest unquestionably was Lucky Luciano, who, in the eyes of casual newspaper readers, soon came to bear the same relation to organized prostitution that the late John D. Rockefeller once bore to petroleum. Luciano's tentacles were everywhere, his income was fabulous, there wasn't a sporting lady in New York who didn't shiver in her chemise at the mention of his name. Rupert Hughes, giving a little shudder himself, called him "the deadliest and most evil genius in the whole country."

There are those, even among his enemies, who claim that Luciano never got a dollar from prostitution in his life, and it is known that he was doing nothing more deadly than making book at Saratoga when he was surprised to learn that Dewey had crowned him King of Vice. Nevertheless, sex being what it is, the trial was a tremendous artistic success. In addition to revealing the gay and provocative names which most of the girls had thought up for themselves, the testimony was gratifyingly explicit and gave the public a good working picture of the technical structure of a pretty complicated business. A lot of the entertainment also lay in the relations between Mr. Dewey and his staff and the witnesses who eventually won the case for the prosecution. From the beginning, the young women were treated with exceptional tenderness and chivalry, even though one of the investigators persisted in wearing gloves throughout the trial and several of them were rather ungallantly mystified when their clients insisted they were virgins. As the girls began to come through with the right kind of testimony, they were shown even more consideration. They were set up in apartments and hotels around town, given spending money, taken to the movies, on shopping trips, out to cocktails, and even to night clubs. This last practice, however, fell into disrepute when one of them, in the company of an assistant prosecutor, was observed by the opposition having a fine, though somewhat incoherent, time at Leon & Eddie's on Fifty-second Street. This incident went on the record, where it did not look good at all.

It was after the trial, though, that the prosecutor really showed that his heart was in the right place. In order to protect them from the vengeance of any possible surviving vice kings, two of the girls were given a trip abroad, spending four months in England and France with all expenses paid. Two others took a studio in New Rochelle and got $50 a week each for ten weeks while a writer from *Liberty* interviewed them. They also got $500 bonuses. With this money, the ladies bought a car and went to California, where they opened a filling station, whimsically christening it The Rooster. Contented letters came back to the prosecutor's office, reporting that business was fine. "We're selling more gas already than the other two stations near us," wrote one of the partners. "Regards to Mr. Dewey."

While the money kept coming in, everything was lovely between these far-flung witnesses and Uncle Dee, which was their pet name for the scourge of the underworld. When it stopped, however, and the Dewey office was unable to help *Liberty* sell their life stories to Warner Brothers for a movie, the girls began to get rough. In the middle of March, 1937, Luciano filed a motion for a new trial with affidavits from Nancy Presser, Mildred Harris Balitzer, and Cokey Flo Brown, in which they repudiated their previous testimony. Miss Presser said that she had spent most of her time in the prosecutor's office drinking liquor and listening to people shouting that they "had to get Lucky." Miss Brown went even further. Her testimony against Luciano was all made up, she said. Why, she had never laid eyes on the man in her life.

In spite of the fact that the motion for a new trial was denied, this ingratitude was discouraging, and so was the common report that most of the ladies had gone back to their regular work as soon as the heat was off. Mr. Hughes, it is true, wrote that one of them had "become a blooming bride after a year of hard work and clean living," but less roseate authorities were pessimistic. In fact, Samual Marcus, counsel for the Society for the Prevention of Crime, was able to dig up Stone-Faced Peggy at an address on West End Avenue, where, with six assistants, she was established in a penthouse from which she was sending out cards to her old clients, announcing the arrival of "the latest fall neckwear." This enterprise, according to Mr. Marcus, was partially financed with money Peggy earned as a Dewey witness.

The rest of Dewey's term as Special Prosecutor never rose to the dramatic level of the Luciano trial. Restaurant, poultry, and baking empires were overthrown, but, generally speaking, it was dry stuff, with no sex appeal and not much gunfire. It was not until December 31, 1937, when Dewey took office as District Attorney, that the fun began again. Richard Whitney, Jimmy Hines, Fritz Kuhn, and Lepke were all men of substance in one way or another, and lent themselves well to florid treatment both by Dewey and the newspapers.[1]

The Hines case—the only one, incidentally, which the District Attorney prosecuted in person—was probably the best, with its rumors of bodies done up in concrete and sunk forever in the East River; its suggestion, always agreeable to the public, that every member of Tammany Hall is on the payroll of the underworld; and its remarkable cast of characters, including the beautiful Hope Dare, who handled Dixie Davis's laundry, and the fantastic Abadaba, who could do quadratic equations in his head.

In this case, too, Dewey was conspicuously gentle with the witnesses for the People. Not only was Davis permitted to leave his cell and go visiting whenever he felt like it, but later, when the first effort ended in a mistrial, he and two other witnesses, George Weinberg and Harry Schoenhaus, were removed from the Tombs—they had been complaining about the heat—and shipped out to a country club on Long Island, where they learned to play badminton. When that got tiresome, the District Attorney fixed them up with a private house in White Plains. It was here that Weinberg ungratefully shot himself with a cop's gun, to the irritation of the owner of the property, who claimed it had a bad effect on real-estate values.

For everybody except Weinberg, who was dead, and Hines, who got from four to eight years, the case ended happily. Davis was given a year, but the sentence was shortened on the ground that he had theoretically served half of it while held as a witness; Schoenhaus got a suspended sentence; and the District Attorney's office, which apparently had a persistent enthusiasm for belles-lettres, encouraged

Hope and Dixie to write their memoirs for *Collier's*. They got $6,300 apiece. The policy game, according to reliable reports from Harlem, is still running just about the way it always was.

The Whitney and Kuhn cases also had their points (Lepke was rather an anticlimax because of the annoying circumstance that the G-men got to him first), but defalcation and propaganda are never as interesting as vice and gambling, and relatively they attracted less attention. Dewey's expenses as District Attorney from January 1, 1938, to the present have been $2,146,509.03, including $201,183.44 for "contingencies."

While all this was going on, Dewey heard the call to run as Republican candidate for Governor in the fall of 1938. He devoted over a month to the campaign, but was defeated by Lehman by a margin of approximately 67,000 votes. Undeterred by the fact that he had won only one elective office in his life, Dewey made formal announcement on December 1, 1939, that he was a candidate for the Republican nomination for President of the United States. Since then there hasn't been much of interest happening in the District Attorney's office, and during the past six months the boss has been absent some sixty-five days, though still, of course, on the payroll.

PEOPLE WHO HAVE watched Dewey perform in court sometimes wonder how the same technique would work in larger fields. His manner before the bench is as exasperating as it is in private. A distinguished attorney, who suffered from it painfully in the Hines trial, says that the District Attorney seems to feel that any lawyer who would stoop to defend a man indicted by the Dewey office must either be a crook himself or else corruptly allied with criminal interests. If a ruling is unfavorable to the People, Dewey will rise from his chair, slow and aghast, the blood mantling his neck, and cry, "Do you mean to say that the Court will not allow the District Attorney of New York County," etc., etc. During the first Hines trial, while the policy broker Spasm Ison was on the stand, Dewey sat slumped in his chair, pretending to read a Harlem dream book. Occasionally, without rising, he would drawl, "I think I'll object to that," and once, to Justice Pecora's indignation, he varied this formula. "I suppose it won't do any good," he said wearily, "but I think I'll object."

It is also part of his system to make the jurors feel that they are part of the prosecution, not a difficult feat with a blue-ribbon jury, which usually imagines that it has been divinely appointed to convict, anyway. When opposing counsel scores a point, Dewey turns to the jury and beats his breast to let them know that the People are being crucified. When an attorney for the defence says anything derogatory about him or any member of his staff, he objects thunderously to "this insult to the representatives of the People of New York," a classification, of course, including the jury. Sometimes, when things aren't going too well for his side, he is apt to stifle a yawn and saunter out of the courtroom for a smoke and a chat with the reporters.

Dewey's most annoying mannerism, however, is drinking water. He is one of the greatest water drinkers of our time, estimating himself that he gets away with more than three quarts a day, and he has learned that it is a wonderful way to harass the opposition. While Stryker was examining key witnesses against Hines, Dewey made many leisurely trips to the water-cooler near the jury box, filled himself a Lily cup, and ambled back to his table, looking bored to the edge of imbecility. This finally worked on Stryker to such an extent that the next time Dewey got up to get a drink, he waved him back to his chair, poured out a cup himself, and carried it politely over to the prosecutor's table. There can be no question that The Boy has mastered the art of getting on people's nerves.

After the second Hines trial, Dewey announced that he didn't propose to go into court again until after the election, but his technique is almost as effective in private life. His vanity is enormous, a fact of which he is aware and even rather proud (he once refused to appoint an otherwise capable man, saying seriously, "Why, he's as arrogant as I am"). When he was chosen to run for District Attorney on a ticket with LaGuardia, the Mayor suggested that it might be wise if he didn't have much to say to the papers until they had planned their campaign. "I can't do that," said Dewey. "My public will want to hear from me." Recently, when somebody asked him if he wasn't afraid that John T. Cahill's mounting reputation as a

United States Attorney might come to eclipse his own, Dewey was reassuring. "No, I don't fear that," he replied earnestly. "After all, the public knows there was only one Lindbergh."

Last year, a former United States Attorney named Green was nominated by the Republicans to run against Mayor Kelly in Chicago. Green was the prosecutor who sent Capone to Alcatraz for income-tax evasion, and consequently he had a local reputation as a gangbuster almost equalling Dewey's. Since his campaign against the corrupt Kelly-Nash machine was based on the need for divorcing crime from politics, the same war whoop that Dewey had been finding so useful in the East, Green's backers thought it would be helpful if the New York prosecutor came to Chicago and made a speech endorsing their man. Dewey declined after some thought. "There's only one thing that would pull Green through," he said, "and that's if I went out there." "But if I did," he continued, "everybody would know what had happened. I think the people of Chicago would resent having me come out there and elect their Mayor."

Dewey reached his peak, though, in the reply that went back to Anthony Eden, who, on his trip here in December, 1938, said that he would like to meet New York's celebrated crusader. The man who tried to arrange the interview got a brief telephone call from Dewey's office. "I have your message to Mr. Dewey," a voice said. "He has asked me to tell you that he will be glad to meet Mr. Eden if he will call at the District Attorney's office on Centre Street."

THE ADVENT OF the Deweys would certainly mean a new era of simplicity in official Washington society. Mrs. Dewey, who once sang in a road company of "George White's Scandals," is probably not temperamentally opposed to a little gaiety around the place, but lately she has grown increasingly conscious of her responsibilities as the candidate's wife. Political topics are taboo with her and she is fairly cautious on all others, so conversation is something of a strain.

Dewey himself is simply a man with no time for comedy or other irrelevancies. His life outside his work is a little like the interval between rounds in a prizefight—a period of rest, therapy, and reflection about what to do next. He gets up at the same time every day, eight-thirty, and eats the same breakfast. His lunch, which he usually has at his desk, never varies either, consisting of fruit salad, a chicken sandwich on white bread, milk and coffee, cheese and crackers. He lets himself go at dinner, but not recklessly. He limits himself strictly to one package of cigarettes a day and, since repeal, two highballs at a sitting. During prohibition he never drank or allowed alcohol in his house. If he was offered a drink at a party, he would smile tolerantly and say, "No, you go ahead and have a drink if you want one. That's your business. None for me." He plays pennyante poker with a nickel limit, and usually wins. His chauffeur, who used to have a job driving an old lady around, is right at home with him, because Dewey hates speed and objects to anything over fifty miles an hour, even in the open country.

The candidate is a great man for getting his sleep and always bundles Mrs. Dewey up at eleven-thirty and takes her home, no matter what's happening. He hasn't been inside a night club since his appointment as Special Prosecutor. To make up for this, the Deweys organized a private dancing group among their friends, hired an instructor and a small orchestra, and met regularly at one another's apartments for dancing parties. They did this for a season or two and then gave it up. It may have been too exclusive.

Dewey is terribly down on sculpture, but he says he likes all the other arts and is sorry he hasn't the time to get at them any more. He used to go to the opera quite a lot (he admires Wagner especially) and to the Sunday concerts at Town Hall almost every week. That's out now and so is the theatre. The only play he saw this season was "Ladies and Gentlemen," with Helen Hayes, whom he likes, though not as much as Ina Claire. When it comes to books, he reads history, biography, and mystery stories, volunteering that he's read just about all of Edgar Wallace. The only books currently visible in his office are *Who's Who in America* and "Debate Outlines on Public Questions." Dewey has even given up his own singing except for rare duets with his wife and a rich, baritone solo now and then in the bathtub, where he sings the Prologue to "Pagliacci," but he still gets to church. When interviewers ask his press secretaries how often he manages to get there, they say, "Not as often as he'd like to—about once every month or so." When they ask Dewey the same thing, he thinks it over for a while and answers, "Not as often as I'd like to—about once every month or so." Incidentally, while the candidate has only two official publicity men, at salaries of $6,500 and $5,000 a year, practically everyone in the office these days is cooperating with the Republican Party, including many of the Assistant District Attorneys. Considered on a man-hour basis, it is probable that the people of New York are spending $500 a week to send their prosecutor to the White House.

In winter the Deweys live in an eight-room apartment at Fifth Avenue and Ninety-sixth Street, which has nothing remarkable about it one way or another. Their elder son, Thomas, Jr., who is seven and a half, goes to a private school, although both his parents can hardly contain their admiration for the public-school system. John, four and a half, hasn't started yet. For the past three years, the family have been spending their summers on a 300-acre farm near Pawling, which Dewey bought last year. Before that they went to Tuxedo, until Dewey discovered that his neighbors led a "manicured existence." "Between you and me," he says, "that Tuxedo crowd is a bunch of snobs. I want my children to grow up with farm children." At Pawling, Dewey gets up early to go riding with Lowell Thomas, who more or less sets the social and intellectual pace for the colony. After that, he has the standard breakfast and then plays golf, shooting around a hundred, usually with Carl Hogan, a Madison Avenue furniture dealer and probably Dewey's closest friend; Kenneth C. Hogate, publisher of the *Wall Street Journal;* and Ralph Reinhold, publisher of an architectural magazine called *Pencil Points.* He plays earnestly, watching his opponents like a hawk so they won't try to chisel on their scores. Sometimes he plays softball with Thomas's Nine Old Men. He used to pitch, but he always tried to strike out the batter, and, as the game is played mostly for fun, they shifted him to second base. There is quite a lot of visiting around at Pawling, but no cocktail parties or other rough stuff. Altogether, it is a simple, earnest, and healthy way of life. How it would look to the British Ambassador or someone like Mrs. Longworth, there is no way of telling.[2]

Dewey's speeches have been described as the best that money can buy, and they are delivered in a voice that even Mr. Stryker has been obliged to admit is "quite an organ," but up to now nobody

seems exactly sure what he has been talking about. Generally speaking, he is apparently for everything that's good and against everything that's bad, which naturally includes most of the activities
of the administration. In spite of this vagueness—Raymond Clapper
has written in the *World-Telegram* that most of the Dewey policies are
about as mysterious as love—his campaign has been an astonishing
success. As a candidate, if you care to listen to his admirers, he is a
cinch for the White House. They see him as America in microcosm—
the small-town boy who demonstrated to the people not only that
the cities were as wicked as they had dreamed but also that wicked-
ness is helpless when confronted with rustic purity. He is the hope
of the world, the Plumed Gang-Buster. Berton Braley, a poet who
once accompanied the Ford Peace Ship to write odes to Mr. Ford,
has summed the District Attorney up lyrically:

Let Dewey do it! And Dewey did.
Dewey's "magic" was simply that
He did the job he was working at!
But do we duly do honor to
The work of Dewey? We do! We do![3]

To his critics, this picture seems a little too rapturous. Some have
complained that a man who spends a good part of his first year in
office running for Governor and even more of his second and third
running for President can't exactly be described as doing the job he
is working at. Robert Moses, a forthright man, said frigidly that it
seemed to him Mr. Dewey had "no manifest experience or probable
qualification for the job," and Mayor LaGuardia, returning thoughtfully from a visit to "Abe Lincoln in Illinois," dismissed all the current Republican aspirants with the word "phooey." The Arab in
William Saroyan's play called "The Time of Your Life" probably
came closest to getting at what a good many people have been trying to say about the Boy from Owosso in his reiterated refrain: "No
foundation. . . . No foundation. . . . All the way down the line."

May 25, 1940

THE CUSTOMER IS
ALWAYS WRONG[1]

JUST AS THE advance agent for a circus is not likely to be disturbed by even the largest elephant, so his metropolitan equivalent, the Broadway press agent, can look on the most succulent actor and still remain composed. This is a natural condition, since both actors and elephants, observed for any length of time at close range, are apt to seem no better than anybody else. It is remarkable only when the publicity man, who after all is paid to exploit these phenomena, makes no attempt to hide his good-natured derision.

There are a good many press agents in New York who operate on a sort of man-to-man basis with their clients; Richard Sylvester Maney, the most prosperous gnome of the lot, is the only one who persistently treats them with the genial condescension of an Irish cop addressing a Fifth Avenue doorman. This comparison isn't altogether arbitrary. Most doormen are more ornamental than cops, and practically all actors are more beautiful than Maney, but fundamentally, like the cop, he is a more impressive figure and they know it. A few conspicuously high-class performers, such as Maurice Evans and Noel Coward, have reached a state of precarious equality with their employee, but the rest are kept strictly in their places.

Mr. Maney's manner toward his inferiors is firm, though not unkind. Playing with them in one of those interminable games of chance that serve to keep him from being even richer than he is, he seldom bothers with their actual names.

"All right, actor, it's your turn," he will shout impatiently when some Thespian appears to him to be dawdling, and "actor" in his mouth is an Elizabethan word, with low and foolish connotations. Being a gentleman, he is more restrained on the whole with the ladies of the profession and even greets them from time to time with what he probably imagines are terms of endearment. "Thanks for the baubles, my peculiar witch," he once said politely, to Miss Grace

Moore, for whom he was working at the time and who had given him some pretty cuff links in a timid effort to melt his spectacular indifference. Miss Moore was enchanted.

He has a little more respect for producers, perhaps on the ground that they are occasionally men of some slight substance, though even here his admiration can hardly be called slavish. His notorious love affair with Billy Rose, who once recklessly employed him to exploit his vast and quite incomprehensible enterprises, has been discussed in print far too often to be repeated now, but many other producers have paid handsomely to be insulted both in the newspapers and privately.

"Mr. Harris has finally combed the last Cossack out of his curls," Mr. Maney remarked genially in the *Tribune* by way of announcing that Jed Harris, after a series of noble but discouraging experiments with the Russian drama, was again prepared to grapple with our native product. He was also impolite to his sombre young master during office hours. Like many another man of large affairs, Mr. Harris lived with the dream of eventually getting a little order into things, and for this purpose he introduced an elaborate system of interoffice memoranda for the use of his staff. These were supposed to constitute a dignified and permanent record of what went on in the Harris organization, but for some reason Mr. Maney found this idea irksome. Memoranda began to appear bearing such messages as "To: Mr. Harris. From: Mr. Maney. Re: What time is it?" and presently the whole system collapsed from sheer overproduction. A sign also turned up one day on the door behind which Mr. Harris dreamed his majestic and turbulent dreams. "Where the grapes of wrath are stored," Maney had printed neatly. Insofar as he was capable of admiring anything except a mirror, however, Mr. Harris cherished his queer employee.

Once, during one of Maney's several operations with Herman Shumlin, he watched with disgust while his usually sensible colleague labored with the production of a spectacle called "Sweet Mystery of Life," in which the actors fumbled about in the gloom, dwarfed by acres of scenery. It flew closed like a door, as Maney sometimes describes this occupational mishap, and Mr. Shumlin turned to his press agent for consolation. He made a mistake. "'Sweet Mystery of

Life,' indeed!'" retorted that rough diamond. "It was the triumph of lumber over art."

Another producer to suffer from Maney's basic inability to disguise his feelings was Courtney Burr, who once asked him whether a simple dinner coat or tails would be more appropriate for one of the Burr openings.

"You better wear your track suit," said Maney, and this, it turned out, was a prophecy.

Even Gilbert Miller, a famous cosmopolite, failed to awe Maney or shake his lofty integrity. One day, in a proud but misguided moment, Mr. Miller offered his hired man a shapely little announcement for the press which he had framed with his own cultivated hand. Maney read it through impassively and gave it back. "It isn't English," he said. Meekly, Mr. Miller made it English.

THE PROBLEM OF why so many sensitive and arrogant people continue to employ a man who is almost certain to hurt their feelings sooner or later is an interesting one. It would be easy to say that Maney is the best press agent in town and let it go at that, but somehow it seems too simple. He isn't indispensable. There are other boys in the business capable of handling publicity with about the same competence and doing it much more politely and quietly, without nearly so much wear and tear on delicate egos. The secret lies somewhere in the complex and difficult riddle of personality. It is profitable to be associated with Maney, but it is also quite an experience in its peculiar way—perhaps not unlike drinking a very dry Martini, which is rather shocking at first but develops its own special glow as you go along. Almost all producers who have worked with Maney find it hard to put on a show without the curious extra flavor he adds to their lives.

This is by no means a triumph of sheer physical charm. Maney is not a handsome man. His wide face is pure Celt. He looks like a tough Irish altar boy who has grown up to be a popular Second Avenue bartender. He has no eyebrows worth mentioning and forgotten fights—invariably lost—have blurred the classic detail of his nose. Usually, as the evening wears on, he has a tendency to settle inside his clothes, like a turtle in its shell, and his eyelids come down to hood his eyes. A habit of having his dusty hair cut very short makes his head seem even rounder than it is. His body has the solid, humorous rotundity of a Teddy bear's. Last year *Time*, in a rare spasm of felicity, called him a "roustabout George M. Cohan."

Maney's social behavior ranges from a wild truculence, when he lowers his head and bellows like a bull, to an equally furious gaiety, when community singing seems to charm him most. He particularly admires a noisy anthem called "My Dream of the U.S.A.," which involves banging glasses on the table, usually breaking them. At the match game, the standard entertainment at a restaurant called Bleeck's Artists' and Writers' Club and mathematically the most absurd form of gambling ever invented, Maney's vehement offer to play anybody for twenty fish can easily be heard in the *Herald Tribune* editorial rooms next door. There is seldom a dull moment and, in spite of all the tumult, almost never one when people feel like getting up and moving to another table.

By contrast, it is always a little startling to meet Maney in polite evening dress, supervising one of his own openings. Courtesy sits on him like a shroud, and for some reason he seems a good deal smaller than usual. Even on these grim occasions, however, the basic Maney isn't totally absent. He gets as many terrible shows as the next man and, while he doesn't enjoy them economically, he takes a certain sardonic interest in their effect on the public.

"How do you like it?" he asked a tactful but honest young woman during the first-act intermission at one such night not long ago.

"Well, that act seemed a little slow, Dick," she answered reluctantly, "but I'm sure the others are much better."

"That was supposed to be the good one, my deluded squaw," said Mr. Maney, and chuckled like a ghoul.

Meeting one of the authors of this same sad misadventure after the final curtain, Maney offered his fatherly comfort and advice. "Take to the hills," he muttered hoarsely.

THE MOST FASCINATING thing about Maney, however, lies in something rich and strange he has done to the English language.

This curious form of speech is one of the small miracles of the town and was once even imbedded in a play when Ben Hecht and Charles MacArthur transplanted its author intact to the stage in "Twentieth Century." The probabilities are that it was born in the first place as a form of compensation. Maney was properly brought up by a devout mother to whom blasphemy was as shocking as second-story work. To spare her pain, the child throttled his vocabulary but as he grew older, the natural fury and exasperation in him mounted and, although his speech remained as pure as a radio announcer's, his fundamental outlook on life got to be as blasphemous as hell. An outlet was necessary before the little boy blew up and so there gradually came into existence a system of invective that *sounded* like swearing but was in fact as innocent as Mother Goose. Robert Louis Stevenson was operating on the same principle when he created the most satisfactory gang of pirates in literature and never permitted one of them to say anything that couldn't safely be read to an eight-year-old boy.

This theory is probably as good as any, but however it happened, Maney today is the world's greatest master of disinfected epithet. While other and lesser men monotonously employ such clichés of displeasure as "son of a bitch" and "bastard," his range is practically infinite. His clients and acquaintances escape the stigma of illegitimacy, but few other qualities or conditions are spared them. He is surrounded by Comic Spaniards, Unfortunate Aztecs, Foul Turtledoves, Penthouse Cagliostros, and even more fascinating compounds. He seldom repeats himself. The well is deep and undefiled.

People who really know Maney submit to these caresses without resentment and usually with a certain amount of pleasure and admiration, although now and then a touch of bewilderment creeps into things, too. A young man who had been wanting to meet him for some time finally got his wish, but his report of his experience was a little plaintive.

"I can't seem to understand anything Mr. Maney says," he confessed. "Is this usual?"

It is only when Maney gets outside his own circle, however, that the real fuss is likely to begin. One night, in the company of an actor and some other negligible character, he set out on a tour of the drink-ing places in a strange and forbidding section of the town. Time passed agreeably, but at last, although nobody was prepared to go home, it began to look as if everything else was closed up. Maney ap-proached a native of the district, a colored citizen, conceivably on his way to work.

"Where can we get a drink around here, my vile Corsican?" he asked amiably. The dark stranger, though appearing more baffled than annoyed, swung nervously and Mr. Maney bounced on the pave-ment. This was clearly an occasion when simple blasphemy would have been less provocative, and there have been several others, so that for the most part Maney confines his night life to places where he is known and understood. With the enthusiastic cooperation of their proprietors, he has banned himself for varying lengths of time from many resorts, including the Stork Club and Twenty-One, where he feels that the average customer doesn't appreciate fancy rhetoric even when it comes up and spits in his eye.

In one case, the coolness between Maney and a certain fashionable pump room arose because he referred to its proprietor as an inflated busboy; in another, he approached an unknown but stylish icicle in a white tie and advised him to stop tossing his money around like a drunken sailor, a remark generally felt to be in restraint of trade. He reached the depths, however, as the result of a sincere effort to be polite. Entering a restaurant one day at the cocktail hour, he stopped to speak to a rich and beautiful young matron seated near the door. What he said was merely jocular, but it was misunderstood, and when Maney got to the bar his companions urged him to go back and apologize. He agreed and started out on this courteous errand, but somewhere along the way Dr. Jekyll began to fade and the man who reached her table was unmistakably Mr. Hyde. "Listen, my painted Jezebel," he began. The late Percy Hammond sometimes said with awe that his friend Maney had a distinctly voodoo personality.

Maney's talent is by no means confined to calling peculiar names. His most casual pronouncement has an air about it, a quality of invention and balance and study. "Dames who put ginger ale in Scotch highballs should be submitted to the bastinado and reduced

to moccasins," he remarked, offhand one night on this important
subject, and visitors to his untidy headquarters over the Empire
Theatre are greeted with pleasant extravagance. "Ah," the proprietor will shout warmly, "a spent runner staggers into the blockade,
a Blackfoot arrow protruding from his back!" In "Twentieth Century," Hecht and MacArthur put a pretty line into the mouth of
the character representing Maney. There is some talk about a Mr. and
Mrs. Lockwood, who are occupying Drawing Room A. "Mr.
and Mrs., hell," says the pseudo-Maney. "It's Romeo and Juliet,
hacking away at the Mann Act." While not genuine, this is an almost
perfect example of Maney's verbal technique, being balanced in
structure, florid in conception, and containing a useful classical reference. So fascinated was Billy Rose with some of his employee's
remarks that gradually he came to appropriate them as his own. In
a recent and rather unaccountable address to the Harvard Business
School, Mr. Rose described his feelings at the opening of "Jumbo."
"I stood on the Rubicon, rattling the dice," he told the enchanted
students, who couldn't be expected to know that this comment had
originally appeared in Maney's program notes some five years before. Mr. Rose has also quoted himself as having observed that
"Jumbo" would either make Rose or break Whitney, another *mot*
that was born elsewhere.

The literary bas-relief that ornaments Maney's speech, incidentally, is quite authentic. He is a formidable student, especially of
Shakespeare and other antiquities. On an "Information Please" program last spring, he delivered a good part of the prologue to "The
Canterbury Tales" and would have been delighted to furnish the rest
if he hadn't been restrained by the master of ceremonies. At his most
typical, Maney sounds a good deal like a circus barker with an LL.D.

THE REPOSITORY OF all this charm and learning and fury was
born forty-nine years ago in Chinook, Montana, a whistle stop on
the Great Northern with a population in those days of some five hundred. Today he describes it nostalgically as "a nest of mangy Crees,"
and adds that it has the reputation of being the coldest damn place in
the United States. From saying so a good many times, Maney has
almost come to believe that he was the first white child born there

and also that up to the age of twelve he preferred to converse in the Indian tongues. These things, however, seem rather unlikely. His father owned the local hardware store, but his heart was really in politics and he ran doggedly for everything, finally winding up as a trustee in the public-school system. His other innocent ambition was to make a musician, specifically a cornet player, out of his smoldering offspring. Maney blew the cornet from the time he was seven until he was twelve without developing much except a tendency to have a rather lopsided face. His mother finally put a stop to that.

"I'll have no monster on this ranch," she said, and the musician laid down his instrument without regret.

In 1906, Maney's father set out in a box car containing his family, his furniture, and eight horses for Seattle, where he took up contracting and his son went through high school and entered the state university. In the summer, Maney drove a dump truck for his father and in winter he studied, admiring the liberal arts and graciously tolerating everything else. Nothing in particular has survived from this period. Maney was not an athlete and his social life appears to have been placid. From time to time he made fifty cents working as an usher at the Moore Theatre, owned by John Cort, and after he was graduated with a B.A. in 1913, he persuaded Mr. Cort to give him a job.

A mist obscures the next thirteen years, and our glimpses of the principal actor are dim and intermittent. He was one of four advance agents for Anna Held in her "All-Star Jubilee," though not the man who thought up the celebrated milk bath.[2] In fact, as he remembers it, the tour progressed through such backward country that nobody got any baths at all, including Miss Held. At one time he lived with, and on, an enterprising associate who had collected $3,000 in damages for falling down an elevator shaft. At another he operated an electric baseball scoreboard in a saloon and at still another he was manager of a theatre on upper Broadway at which the leading attraction was a nervous performer who held a fork in his mouth and tried to catch potatoes thrown from the gallery. Both Maney and this unusual artist lasted exactly a week. Once, for a brooding moment, he found himself back under his father's roof in Seattle.

When everything else failed, he turned to a humiliating trade.

"Whenever I couldn't eat any other way, I looked around for a door to guard," he says. There were a good many doors. He was visible to his fashionable friends taking tickets at various theatres, but particularly at the Morosco, where he wore a Cossack uniform weighing fourteen pounds. He was rescued from this public degradation by Bronco Billy Anderson, a star of the silent pictures, who, dreaming of better things, put on an opera called "The Frivolities of 1920" and employed Maney to publicize it for him. Accompanying this dubious charade to Boston, he fell in with a Shubert press agent fantastically christened A. Toxen Worm and through him at last entered the more or less respectable fringes of the profession. Sponsored by Mr. Worm, he was soon associated with the firm of Jones & Green, producers of "The Greenwich Village Follies," and finally, in 1927, he went to work for Jed Harris, succeeding S. N. Behrman and Arthur Kober, neither of whom found himself able to cope with that small, dark man about whose head the lightning played. In this fashion, by way of many strange back doors, Mr. Maney came to Broadway.

Before he did, however, he had been through one of the most singular experiences of his life. Back in 1919, when he was living an idle, carefree life with the man who fell down the shaft, Maney spent some of his abundant leisure contributing odds and ends to a sports column run by a friend. These compositions were informed as well as sprightly, for Maney knows almost as much about baseball as he does about Shakespeare, and at length the word got around that he was a weighty expert on all matters dealing with recreation. Almost before he knew it, and certainly without any particular volition on his own part, he found himself the forty-dollar-a-week editor and staff of a highly specialized publication known as the *American Angler.*

Up to then all the fish that Maney had known intimately had been cooked; he neither knew nor cared how they got from the stream to the kitchen, and his opinion of anglers was low. Nevertheless, he was a conscientious man and he did his best. "Keep your flies in the water—trout don't live in trees," he advised his readers in one early issue, and a little later he wrote thoughtfully, "It has always been my contention that in a piano tuner, to a greater degree than in any other artisan, is concealed—possibly congealed—that quality which marks the successful fly-fisherman. Did you ever watch a piano tuner plying his painstaking if promiscuous art? No? Then do so at your first opportunity." Maney went on for quite a while in this vein, to the confusion of the innocent fishermen.

The Great Trout-Fly Symposium, however, was a tremendous success. Looking for something to fill his yawning columns, Maney hit on a very nice problem for his single-minded readers. "If you were condemned to go through life with but three trout flies, regardless of weather, season, or locality, what three would you choose?" he asked them provocatively. The response was immediate and almost overwhelming. Dr. Henry Van Dyke wrote from Princeton, "If I were required to limit my trout-fly book to three flies (which upon the whole would not be an altogether bad thing) I should choose (1) Queen of the Water, (2) March Brown, and (3) Royal Coachman." The Doctor was remarkably brief. Most of Maney's readers spread themselves happily. "To limit myself to three flies is unthinkable," wrote one O. W. Smith, "though I might get along with five if allowed several sizes, for, in my judgment, size is a more determining factor than pattern. When the water is clear and low, as is often the case in August, a tiny 'Professor' will take the fish, whereas . . ." This rhapsody filled an entire page and was accompanied by a photograph of the author, his hat bristling defiantly with flies of every conceivable size and shape. Several of Mr. Maney's correspondents were appalled at the idea of trying to get through life so grotesquely handicapped, but with one exception they all agreed that it was a good, interesting question. The solitary dissenter was a Mr. Louis Rhead. "I think the question very foolish," he replied crossly.

After a while the atmosphere around the *American Angler*, with its strangely possessed visitors and the almost tangible memory of dead fish haunting the corridors, began to get on the editor's nerves, and the breaking point came one day when a meek but persistent contributor drifted in looking for an assignment. "Go interview a successful trout, you underwater Boswell!" roared Mr. Maney, the veins rather unpleasantly corded in his neck.

The writer vanished, but he was back again in a couple of days, and to Maney's amazement and horror he had done exactly what he was told. "An Interview with a Successful Trout," purporting to be a submarine conversation with a bright fish, appeared in the *American Angler* for April, 1919, and it is one of the most nerve-racking specimens of prose in the language. A brief sample of the hero's remarks is certainly enough:

> "My friend Gorumpp, the bullfrog, keeps me pretty well informed about current events out of the water. He sits on a log and makes observations all day long, but at time he comes down here below for a visit. I love him as a companion although I would devour him were he conveniently smaller. You think it strange that I would like to dispose of a friend? As a matter of fact, I wonder how long I could be powerful and handsome unless I were to catch something a good many times a day. The minnows—a principal part of my diet—are engaged all day long in capturing ephemerids and cyclops, and various other kinds of things which in turn are catching something else.
>
> "I suppose that right is might, and if it were not right for me to be here I might be lost altogether. I asked Rulee [the local fairy] about it, and she says that one thing catches another, clear down to the microbes, and that microbes catch each other. Your Molière or Shaw might have written about the sentimental features of the subject."

There was something about this educated talk that convinced Mr. Maney that he had had about enough, and when the anglers invited their lovable old editor to judge a fly-casting tournament in Chicago, he quietly turned in his resignation and returned to Broadway, where fish are sensibly kept in iceboxes and don't talk.

ONCE HE WAS established as a New York press agent, Maney's progress was rapid. By the end of his third year he had represented such solid and memorable productions as "Broadway," "Coquette," "The Royal Family," "The Front Page," "Serena Blandish," and "Fifty Million Frenchmen." He had also perfected his attitude toward the theatre and the press. For the most part, Maney avoids the

traditional milk-bath, tanbark, and stolen-jewelry approach to his
trade, although he once abetted Ben Hecht and Gene Fowler when
those two relentless elves announced that they were going to lie in
separate coffins in a funeral parlor to celebrate the decease of an exhibit called "The Great Magoo," and he was responsible for an advertisement calling for one hundred genuine noblemen ("Bogus counts,
masqueraders, and descendants of the Dauphin will get short shrift")
to act as dancing partners at Billy Rose's Fort Worth Frontier Cen-
tennial. At the instigation of Mr. Rose, who never felt that he was
quite sufficiently in the public eye, he even announced that an elephant would be shot out of a cannon as the first-act finale of "Jumbo."
This was meant to be facetious, and it was taken that way by everybody except the editor of *Vanity Fair*, who sent a reporter around to
get a blueprint explaining how this prodigy was to be accomplished.

Such elementary pranks as these, however, haven't had much to
do with Maney's success. He manages to get practically everything
he writes—about six thousand words a week—printed somewhere
or other, partly because it is invariably accurate, partly because it
is written a good deal better than most of the material an editor
would be likely to get from members of his own staff, but mostly
because it sounds so little like publicity. This isn't altogether intentional. Maney tries to turn out rich and beautiful prose about the
work of the performers whom he genuinely admires—Helen Hayes,
Maurice Evans, Ethel Barrymore, Tallulah Bankhead, and a few
others—but there is a stubborn block between his enthusiasm and
his typewriter, and what comes out is almost invariably tinged with
derision and a suggestion that the theatre is a pretty comic business
at best. Miss Hayes is his darling, but she is just as likely to find herself described as a scampering Columbine as the next girl. This
frivolous tone, while a little dismaying to actors who dream of themselves as serious artists, is a relief to dramatic editors, who spend most
of their days ploughing through thinly disguised advertising matter, and they print it gratefully.

The same flavor is evident in the capsule biographies which turn
up in the programs of Maney attractions. Other press agents approach this routine task without much spirit, confining themselves
to simple lists of the plays in which their subjects have previously

appeared. Maney's notes, however, are a nice blend of the irrelevant, the scurrilous, and, with an air of reluctance, the foolish facts in the case. At one time or another he has written, "Brenda Forbes has a scar on her left wrist, weighs 120 pounds, and emerged from her cocoon to play the serving wench in 'The Taming of the Shrew.'" . . . "Frances Comstock was born during a blizzard in 1913, has sung in many of our toniest bistros, and over the air has given her lyric all for assorted toothpastes, lubricants, and juices." . . . "Alfred Drake sprouted as a baritone when the Steel Pier at Atlantic City was supporting a vagrant opera company. He was billed below the cinnamon bears." . . . "Donald Cameron got under way as a Roman rowdy, with spear, when Margaret Anglin came to grips with the Bard at the Hudson." . . . "Nadine Gay is a fugitive from a Fanchon and Marco unit." . . . "George Lloyd was last season understudy to a corpse."

Maney has also commented from time to time on the theatre in general. "Producing is the Mardi Gras of the professions," he once wrote sourly in the *Times*. "Anyone with a mask and enthusiasm can bounce into it." Somewhere else he paid his indignant respects to actresses. "All female stars have one thing in common: after you stand on your head to arrange an interview, they break the date because they have to go and get their hair washed." Of his own part in all these goings-on, he says, "The press agent is part beagle, part carrier pigeon, and part salmon (the salmon only goes home to die)." In fact, of all the people connected with the trade, the critics are about the only ones who have escaped his sinister attention. For obvious reasons, Maney treats these peevish but powerful men with mittens on, and if it remains a mystery to him how most of them got where they are, he keeps it politely to himself. He is an expert on all the curious feuds and phobias that afflict them and he is careful to seat them (fifty on first nights, seventy-five on second nights) where they will be as nearly happy as their twisted natures will permit. "It is not always possible for the first night press list to embrace the reviewer for *Racing Form* or the *Princeton Tiger*," he once remarked when pushed a little too far, but he is usually a model of discretion.

It is doubtful if this irascible behavior would work for everybody, but it has paid Maney handsome dividends. During the past five years he has handled the publicity for an average of eleven shows a season, out of which four could be described as hits. Considering that the total Broadway output during this period ran to something like eighty offerings a year, of which about fifteen were hits, and that some fifteen agents (there are fifty all told) were passionately competing for the business, it is evident that Maney has been doing all right.

For the information of posterity, his exact record has been as follows: In the season that opened in the fall of 1936, he had four hits out of six productions; in 1937, a discouraging year, only one out of eleven; in 1938, five out of thirteen; in 1939, five out of fourteen; and, last year, out of the ten shows he handled, five were definitely successful, including "Arsenic and Old Lace" and the two winners of the Drama Critics' prizes, "Watch on the Rhine" and "The Corn Is Green," all three of which are still doing very well.

So far this season, Maney's average is exactly .500. A dismal vehicle called "The More the Merrier" came and went, causing no more than a slight local irritation, but "The Wookey," although not conspicuously admired by the critics, seems assured of a substantial run, largely for patriotic reasons. His further plans include a Maurice Evans production of "Macbeth," in which there are rumors that Maney himself will play the Third Witch; "Clash by Night," by Clifford Odets, with Tallulah Bankhead; and "Anne of England," with Flora Robson, which was due to arrive this week.

It isn't easy, even for Maney himself, to figure out exactly what income all this represents. Press agents are paid from $150 to $300 a week for each play, and Maney's salary is usually up near the top. Thus, at the peak of last season, with six shows running simultaneously, his office was taking in at least $1,200 a week, and throughout the season the average was probably around $800.

Maney doesn't get all this wealth himself, however. In 1937, after a period of bickering of no conceivable interest to anybody except another press agent, the less prosperous members of the trade, already weakly banded together in something known as T.M.A.T. (Theatre Managers, Agents, and Treasurers), affiliated themselves with the tough and powerful Teamsters' Union of the American Federation of Labor. While not openly directed against Maney or anybody

else, this maneuver was designed to prevent any man from representing more than one show at a time without employing qualified
assistants—men, that is, who had themselves been active press
agents on Broadway within the preceding three years.

Maney, who up to then had been getting along handsomely without assistance, offered a certain amount of resistance to their demands. With a few almost equally fortunate colleagues, he retained
Morris Ernst, an attorney not without his own grasp of publicity
values, to preserve as much as possible of the status quo. Mr. Ernst
went raging into battle.

"I shall never deliver this little group to the tender mercies of the
teamsters," he promised his clients at a luncheon at the Algonquin,
and they went away reassured. Some four weeks later, however,
Maney and his friends were slightly dismayed to find themselves
good and regular members of T.M.A.T. and very much at the mercy
of the merry teamsters.

"I have a dim suspicion that somebody may have sold me out,"
said Maney upon being informed of this shotgun wedding, but on
the whole he accepted his defeat philosophically. By the terms of
the final agreement, he was obliged to hire one assistant at $75 a
week as soon as he had two plays; to raise this salary to $100 when
he got three; to employ a second man at $75 for his fourth, raising
him to $100 for the fifth; and to hire still a third at $75 for the sixth.
This was as far as it could go, since the union ruled arbitrarily that
no agent should be allowed to represent more than six shows simultaneously. While Maney's payments to his staff have run up to the
limit of $275 a week, they probably average $100, so that organized
labor costs him about $5,000 a year. Nevertheless, the chances are that
the season of 1940–1941 netted him at least $25,000, or approximately
twice the amount made by his nearest competitor.

His remarkable preëminence in his field was demonstrated in a
backhand sort of way once last year in the cooking column conducted by Lucius Beebe in the *Herald Tribune*. Mr. Beebe published
a picture of Maney solely on the ground that all that week he hadn't
phoned.

★　★　★

MANEY HASN'T ANY private life in particular. He is married and theoretically lives with his wife and stepson in a house in Westport, but he isn't there much. When he isn't on the road, engaged in preliminary tub-thumping, he gets to his office at ten in the morning, even on those occasional days when he feels as if he had eaten a bomb, and works grimly through until five or six. After that he has dinner somewhere and then, after calling professionally at a box office or two, he drops into Bleeck's or one of its equivalents, looking for a match game or perhaps just somebody to shout at. When he gets home, either to Westport or his room at the Parc Vendome in town, it is usually somewhere between two and six and he goes to bed. Sometimes it is even later than that. Coming in one morning from an especially merry gathering several years ago, he was astonished to find his stepson, Jock, neatly dressed and about to go out.

"Where do you think *you're* going at this ungodly hour?" asked Maney sternly.

"To school," said the child.

The weekends, in fact, are about the only time his wife really has much chance to observe him, and he spends them lying around in his pajamas, either reading about Napoleon, whom he admires even more than Helen Hayes, or else simply licking his wounds. In spite of the Westport homestead, purchased largely so that Mrs. Maney can raise horses, he loathes the country and avoids it whenever he can. This is partly because he has hay fever and partly because people keep trying to include him in their futile and dangerous games.

This rather restricted program, not to mention the continual association with actors and other inferior and disreputable companions, might depress another man, but Maney has no wish to change his lot. He has had offers from Hollywood and at least one enterprising publisher has tried to extract a book of reminiscences from him, but he has turned them all down. Scornful, indignant, frequently beside himself with rage, he is at the same time in a state of almost perfect inward adjustment. Just as Joe Louis can go into cold transports of fury in the ring while still finding there the whole explanation and justification of his existence, life in the theatre irritates Maney to the border of insanity, but perversely he loves every minute of it and he couldn't conceivably exchange it for anything else. He is doing precisely what he wants to. In spite of all the thrashing around, he may well be the most contented man in New York. It is only fair to add that he denies this base charge even more passionately than he denounces fish.

October 11, 1941

A VERY ACTIVE TYPE MAN~I[1]

A FAIR BIBLICAL precedent for Ralph Ingersoll might be found in the career of Saul of Tarsus, who, somewhere on the wild road to Damascus, was accosted by the Spirit and straightway became St. Paul the Apostle. Ingersoll was Ralph McAllister Ingersoll, a grandnephew of Ward McAllister, and he became plain Ralph Ingersoll, a devoted follower of Franklin D. Roosevelt; he was an ornament of the capitalist press, and he became the editor of Marshall Field's *PM*, a journal of salvation; he was a Yale man and a hypochondriac, and he was made whole. His conversion in its final stages took place in the offices of Time, Inc., where such miracles are neither frequent nor particularly encouraged by the management.

The change, perhaps, was not as drastic as the one reported in Holy Writ, since the new Ingersoll has not entirely put away worldly things. The *Social Register* still lists him as a member of the Union and Racquet Clubs, and his private life, which involves a small swimming pool and a terraced apartment, hardly fulfills the New Testament ideal. Nevertheless, in the light of his origins, he is at least mildly baffling to his unregenerate friends. It is even possible that he sometimes baffles himself. When the Ingersoll of today discusses the Ingersoll of the Coolidge and Harding administrations, it is almost as if he were talking about somebody else. "In those days I had a reputation for being rather enthusiastic and naïve," he is apt to say wonderingly, referring to his dead youth in the dead past.

Like St. Paul, Ingersoll not only sacrificed the regard of the fashionable world when he renounced it to take up prophecy but he also failed to appeal at once to the lowly. As a matter of fact, there was a considerable period during which he was energetically stoned by both sides. His old associates, the men of property, naturally had a tendency to think of him as a renegade—if not actually a member of the Communist Party, then at least a fellow-traveller. The conservative

daily press was either hostile or derisive and did its best to bar his
Red rag from the newsstands. The magazines of bourgeois opinion
were full of dark speculation. "The liberal sprinkling of Party members on the staff is difficult to explain," said the *Nation* cautiously, but
Eugene Lyons, in the *American Mercury*, sounded *his* warning loud
and clear. *PM* is "loaded with Stalin's past and present buddies," he
wrote. "In its tabloid format the sheet has only four columns. Is
there a fifth?" Others hinted that the policies of *PM* were dictated by
its editor's psychoanalyst, who, they said, had also chanced to be
employed in the same capacity by Mr. Field. Benjamin Stolberg, an
agitated journalist, once informed an upper-class dinner party that
Ingersoll was actually on the Moscow payroll.

All this, of course, was more or less to be expected. Some of his
other early detractors, however, must have come as something of a
surprise. The American Communist Party, friendly at first, cooled
rapidly when *PM* began to attack the Soviet-Nazi non-aggression
pact and to campaign for all-out aid to Great Britain. Soon it was
calling Ingersoll a political adolescent and, taking a tip from the
distracted Stolberg, distributing handbills which charged him with
being subsidized by a man across the sea, although its candidate was
Churchill rather than Stalin. The C.I.O. adopted a rather similar line
and one of its affiliates, the Newspaper Guild, objected to a labor
policy which Ingersoll considered notably liberal and enlightened.
There was even a certain amount of skulduggery on *PM*'s own
staff, which embraced many shades of political opinion, all vehement. At one time, the Comrades and their sympathizers are said to
have conspired to hand the paper over to the Kremlin, and while
this putsch was either suppressed or imaginary, it left some bitterness
behind. An early brickbat from *PM* to General Franco inflamed the
Coughlinites, while its vigorous pro-British and anti-German policy
stirred up the Bund to such an extent that it threatened Ingersoll
with personal violence and did, in fact, make one partially successful attempt to dismantle a *PM* photographer called Platnick. In addition to all this, a United States Army roster of publications
unsuitable for the tender military mind once listed *PM*, along with
the *New Masses* and the *Daily Worker*, in the dangerous group, be-

low the *New Republic* and *Social Justice*, which were just considered silly.

This widespread unpopularity, while disconcerting to a man who thought of himself as a friend of labor and a patriot, was probably not as hard to bear as the indifference or ingratitude displayed by *PM*'s chosen public. In his first prospectus, Ingersoll announced that he would address the "most intelligent million of the three million who now read the *Daily News* and the *Daily Mirror.*" He proposed to do it without appealing unduly to anybody's baser nature. There was no provision for a gossip column, and the aberrations of café and Hollywood society, if not ignored altogether, were to be treated with no rude smacking of the lips. Stockbrokers and sporting types would have to look elsewhere for their childish amusements, since *PM* had no intention of humoring them with market reports or late racing results. Such stimulating features as Advice to the Lovelorn, Embarrassing Moments, and Bright Sayings of Children were to be omitted and comic strips would not be stressed. Finally, *PM* was to take no advertisements, thus depriving the housewife of a whole world of dreams. The essence of Ingersoll's editorial policy, again according to the prospectus, was simple: "*PM* is in business to tell as much of the truth as it can find out—because it believes journalism's function in a democracy is to seek truth in contemporary life and to print it without fear or favor."

It was a high-minded project but overoptimistic. Either because five cents seemed like too much to pay for the truth or else merely because of something incorrigibly frivolous in human nature, a persistent notion that perhaps journalism's real function in a democracy is to find out what Tommy Manville is up to, the intelligent million who were supposed to drop everything and read *PM* kept right on with the *News* and *Mirror*. As a result of some spectacular promotion, the paper started with a circulation of nearly two hundred and eighty thousand, but within three months this had dropped to forty-five thousand. Since then it has risen slowly to a point where its editor triumphantly claims a hundred and fifty thousand readers. Even Ingersoll, however, concedes that at least two hundred thousand are needed before *PM* can pay its own way, and the present figure is generally believed to represent an operating loss to Mr. Field of more than half a million dollars a year. Since, however, four-fifths of this is presumably absorbed in Mr. Field's income tax, the cost of running *PM* is hardly a matter to cause him any particular concern.

ANOTHER MAN MIGHT have been discouraged by this combination of abuse and neglect, even though he got it free, but Ingersoll has obviously been having the time of his life. His decision to leave the *Time* organization in April, 1939, was at least partly dictated by a prejudice against obscurity. Nearly forty, he found himself "an editor making $45,000 a year but practically unknown." A little more than a year later, in charge of his own paper, Ingersoll had become one of the least anonymous editors in the world. He wrote almost nothing that didn't carry either his name or his initials—sometimes his pieces were even signed at both ends—and his employees obligingly mentioned him from time to time in their own copy. There were also pictures— Ingersoll aboard a sneering dromedary in the Sahara, Ingersoll stripped to his underdrawers in a Soviet railway station, the mighty Kremlin itself with an arrow showing the very gate through which Ralph Ingersoll went in.

"You don't think we're overdoing this?" he once asked an associate.

"Well, no," said the man.

Also, to employ that most celebrated of newspaper clichés, he got to meet a lot of interesting people. In the course of two excursions abroad he was granted private audiences with Chiang Kaishek, Stalin, Churchill, and many others only slightly less exalted. In Hawaii, five months before the Pearl Harbor disaster, Lieutenant General Walter C. Short, a prophet now somewhat in eclipse, told him that war with Japan was imminent, and in Singapore the Admiral of the China Fleet added that the attack would undoubtedly come on December 15th; in London he found the British authorities helpful ("I felt that I was getting the same coöperation as a Notre Dame quarterback"); in Turkey he reported that he was "a dizzy lion" with the diplomatic corps; he flew from Egypt to the Rock in a British general's plane. A framed letter in his office greeted him cordially as

"Dear Ralph" and bore the initials of the President of the United States.

All this was gratifying, but even more so was the wonderful bustle which presently began to surround his activities. While Ingersoll has lost much of his enthusiasm for the money-changers, he has never really ceased to admire their technique, especially when it comes to saving time. "When I started *PM*, I figured I had about five years of maximum energy left," he remarked the other day with his habitual outside-Ingersoll detachment, and he is determined not to waste a minute. Before he was firmly grounded by *PM*'s stockholders, he used to fly his own blue Fairchild monoplane, roaring down out of the sky at a hundred and twenty-five miles an hour with his briefcase under his arm; after that, until conserving rubber got to be his patriotic duty, he drove a Lincoln Zephyr as though pursued by all the yelping imps in hell (his chauffeur, once a dirt-track racer himself, said that nothing in the old days could quite compare with rounding a corner with Ingersoll, "a very active type man," presiding at the wheel).

He handles his appointments like a Morgan partner or a dentist, so that a three-o'clock man coming out of his office is neatly calculated to meet the three-thirty man going in. Staff conferences last exactly forty-five minutes and then disband, if necessary in the middle of a sentence, thus saving untold sums in the course of a year. Even the dull intervals of transportation from his Lakeville, Connecticut, house or his New York apartment to the office in Brooklyn are not lost. "I've got so I can work, eat, and sleep in the back seat of my car," he says happily. "I also have very fine business conferences there, because people have to stop talking at the end of the trip." In his private correspondence he is hostile to pronouns. "O.K. Can do. When want to see?" he wrote recently to a man who had asked for an interview. He dictates almost everything and at prodigious speed. When he was getting his current book on Russia ready for the printers, he used three stenographers working in relays and for a while averaged eight thousand words a day, which were then whisked magically away by a special courier. His social life these days is substantially limited to an occasional quick drink at the Stork Club at two or three in the morning and his exercise to glum calisthenics for reducing purposes. He sleeps about seven hours a night, resentfully. It is a full life, though peculiar and not, of course, for everybody.

The greatest thing about his present position, however, is that for the first time he is able to say exactly what he wants. Previously, on the New York *American* and on various magazines, including this one, he was restrained by the editorial prejudices of other men, who were usually, in his private opinion, either cynical or frivolous or uninformed, or all three. For nearly seventeen years his talent was politely suppressed—there was an exasperating theory that he was more valuable as an executive than as a writer—and at the end of them he was dangerously swollen with words. Then the great day came and they were miraculously set free. Publishing theories, economic and social gospels, old indignations and enthusiasms, millions of flashing and turbulent words poured out of him in the most impressive deluge since the Johnstown Flood. The fact that some of them were contradictory and others misunderstood, even the realization that they were being read by considerably fewer people than he had anticipated, depressed him only mildly. He had waited a long time, but at last he had a journalistic identity of his own and he was molding public opinion. Ingersoll regards his career up to now with modest satisfaction, and he is probably justified. Few men of our time have risen to fame as crusaders in the face of such an aggressively respectable background.

THE TOT WHO was to edit *PM* was born in New Haven on December 8, 1900. His father, Colin McCrae Ingersoll, was Chief Engineer of the New York, New Haven & Hartford, and behind them both stretched a long line of Connecticut statesmen, including a governor and a Minister to Czarist Russia. Robert Ingersoll, who may or may not have embraced Christianity on his deathbed, also belonged to the family, but he was an Illinois offshoot and apparently his outrageous ideas were not held against the orthodox Episcopalians of the local branch. The editor's mother, of course, was a niece of Ward McAllister, a fact no longer as fascinating to her offspring as it once was. In 1906, his father was appointed chief engineer of the Department of Bridges of the City of New York, and the family moved to a brownstone house at 44 East Seventieth Street. Ingersoll's memories of his childhood are unusual in only a few particulars. Because his father had supervised the designing of the Queensboro Bridge, he was the first boy over it, crossing high in the air on a catwalk, but he diminished this magnificent accomplishment by being sick at his stomach. He caught the SOS from the Titanic on a homemade crystal set, but subsequently lost the set when a vagrant current escaping from it almost electrocuted his father. Once, a butler hired from an employment agency for his sister's coming-out party got drunk and announced firmly that he was just as good as anybody else, giving Ingersoll perhaps his first inkling of the class struggle.

On the whole, however, his early days were quiet. He went to the Kirkmayer School, on East Sixtieth Street, and drilled with the Knickerbocker Greys. Most of his free time was spent on roller skates, in vacant lots, or on roofs, from which he thoughtfully dropped water bombs on the passers-by. When he was twelve, he was given a typewriter and composed one rather prophetic story. It was about a German invasion of New York, and Ingersoll saved the city. He decoyed the Huns into the Park Avenue railroad tunnel and blew them up.

When the United States entered the first World War, Ingersoll, then in school at Hotchkiss, dreamed of running away and enlisting, and did indeed get as far as a bar on Forty-second Street. He was intercepted by his parents when he went home to pack, however, and the fall of 1918 found him in the Sheffield Scientific School at Yale. Here he became a cadet in the Students' Army Training Corps, but his record was not particularly distinguished. Because of his training with the Knickerbocker Greys, he started out as a sergeant, but within two weeks he had been broken twice. He was demoted to a corporal when he got his commands mixed up and a company of implacable humorists he was drilling climbed the Yale fence and wound up facing a blank wall; he was reduced to the ranks when a man in his squad fainted and the commanding officer, for inscrutable military reasons, decided that Ingersoll had put him up to it. He was a private thereafter until he was graduated, when he got his commission as a second lieutenant in the Officers' Reserve Corps. Military experts, however, are not necessarily made on parade grounds, and today Ingersoll is one of the foremost strategists in the business. In *PM*, he has outlined plans for crushing Hitler in the Mediterranean, beating

Japan in six weeks (subsequently revised), and only last summer, flying over Pearl Harbor, he was able to note in his diary that it looked very vulnerable to him. "It is such a compact target for bombers," he wrote, and added with a kind of sombre pride, "I worry about so many things."

His non-military activities at Yale were modest, too. He won a medal for wrestling in the novice heavyweight class, but otherwise, though large and willing, he was not athletic. Nor was he particularly social. He belonged to no fraternities and devoted his leisure to a small club he founded himself, called 360 Temple Street, that being where it was. The club's insignia was a little golden flask but the orgies were limited to playing bridge and driving rapidly from Chapel Street to Savin Rock in a bright-blue Pierce-Arrow which belonged to one of the members. The only time Ingersoll really achieved any prominence on the campus was when he wrote a letter to the *Yale Daily News* (then edited by a beetle-browed infant called Henry Robinson Luce), accusing the faculty of firing a biology professor because he didn't share their pro-German sympathies. For some reason, perhaps because it was reprinted on the front page of the New York *Times*, this bugle call came to the attention of President Hadley, who promptly sent for the author.

"I don't see why I don't dismiss you," he said.

"I do," Ingersoll remembers answering. "You don't dare. There'd be too much stink about it."

Incredibly, President Hadley didn't fire him, or even order him shot, and for a while Ingersoll was almost as important as a football player or William Lyon Phelps.[2] It was all rather like a dream.

THE TWO YEARS following Ingersoll's graduation in 1921 were a little mixed up. He worked as a mucker in a mine in Grass Valley, California, where he joined his first union and established the impressive record of handling fifty-six tons of ore in an eight-hour day. He went abroad and flew from Paris to Rome, a trip that took him only one day longer than it would have if he'd made it by train. One summer he took a course in short-story writing under Blanche Colton Williams at Columbia.

"Ever since then clichés have nauseated me," he says. "Including my own."

Then he went back to the mines, this time in Bisbee, Arizona, and Sonora, in Mexico. The short-story course had left its mark on him, however, and he wanted to write. He always had, in fact, the engineering course and the mining being no more than a concession to his father, who was probably the first member of the vast conspiracy to keep Ingersoll from getting his thoughts down on paper. He had been promoted to division engineer in the Sonora mine, but he resigned and came back to New York.

The idea was to get a job as a reporter, but it wasn't as simple as it sounded. For several weeks he made the rounds of the newspaper offices, but he got to see nobody more imposing than an assistant city editor on the *Herald Tribune*, who got up quietly after five minutes and never came back. Ingersoll broadened his field to include magazines and one day found himself talking to Glenn Frank of the Century Company, who was obviously under the impression that his guest was somebody else.

"What's your book going to be about?" he asked politely.

"Mining," said Ingersoll, who up to that moment hadn't thought of writing one.

"That's fine. I want to read it," said Mr. Frank.

In four days Ingersoll was back with an outline and the first four chapters of "In and Under Mexico." Even in those days composition came to him with none of that grotesque torment of the spirit which afflicts less fluent men. When the book was finished, the Century Company obligingly published it, but, although it was angrily denounced by the mining journals, who accused Ingersoll of being disrespectful to pit-head society, it was received impassively by the general public.

Finally he got a newspaper job in a manner more true to life than morality. He found himself sitting next to a Hearst executive at a dinner party, and the next day he went to work as a reporter on the *American* at a salary of $22.50 a week. During this period two things happened to Ingersoll that were to have a considerable influence on his future. Although he worked seven days a week and usually had signed stories on the first page, the Hearst organization declined to raise his salary. From his reasonable indignation grew a dim suspicion that he was being exploited and that conceivably other workers were, too. It was the first imperfection he had noticed in the capitalist system. Also, about that time, there was a pressmen's strike and for a while the New York papers combined in putting out an eight-page daily, which gave the news in capsule form, carried no advertising, and pandered to none of its subscribers' morbid appetites. From that time on, he says, *PM* was always somewhere in the back of his mind.

Ingersoll left the *American* in a fine burst of moral indignation. Because of something rather innocent and bumbling in his appearance that seemed likely to disarm suspicion, he was sent out to do a series of articles on the Veterans' Bureau, an organization that had been persistently tossing other Hearst reporters out of the window. Ingersoll got his facts, wrote what he considered an accurate and impartial piece, and was feeling moderately pleased with himself generally until he picked up the paper and saw what his employers had managed to do with his material. It was a vicious attack on the Bureau and a complete distortion of everything he had written. The next morning Ingersoll went into action. First, he brought down Martin Dunn, the city editor, with a long, looping uppercut to the mid-section, and then he went to look for Victor Watson, the managing editor. Mr. Watson, a prudent man, was not in his office, however, and Ingersoll never got another chance at him, because the next day he was out of work.

He spent the following year as a freelance writer, covering a wide range of subject matter. His first work was turned out for a magazine provocatively known as *I Confess*, and it dealt with the reminiscences of a rather sporty débutante. In it Ingersoll, writing in the first person, described how he narrowly escaped being seduced at a Beaux-Arts Ball. He was not, however, exclusively preoccupied with sex, and his next piece was written for the *Saturday Evening Post* and covered some of the technical problems of the early radio. He wrote several more articles for the *Post* and then, following a fashion of the period, he sailed off to the Riviera, where he took a villa for seventy-five dollars a year and wrote a novel. He recalls this project with dim embarrassment.

"It was about two women," he says bleakly. "Bad subject for me, I guess. Anyway, nothing came of it."

Discouraged and a little alarmed to find himself living on his capital, a thing respectable people don't do, he came back to New York and began again to look for a regular job.

The story of how Ingersoll first got to be employed on a magazine, which happened to be the one you're reading, has its maniacal aspects. He came to call on the editor in a handsome, light-gray flannel suit and for a while the two talked guardedly. Ingersoll got a strong impression that his companion was painfully depressed by the idea of hiring anybody, particularly him. Presently, in fact, the editor abandoned the whole subject of employment and embarked on the story of his own past, which appeared to be voluminous. He was lit with a strange vivacity and his gestures grew wide and convulsive. Finally, in the middle of some unlikely story about his experiences on a paper called *The Stars and Stripes*, he swept his arm passionately across his desk and knocked an open bottle of ink into his caller's lap. With the help of a secretary, Ingersoll was blotted off, but it was plain that he was practically ruined and the situation itself remained untidy. The editor looked at his handiwork glumly and then seemed to come to a painful decision.

"All right. When can you come to work?" he said.

"What?" said Ingersoll, to whom things were obviously happening rather rapidly.

"When can you come to work?" repeated the editor impatiently. "I guess you'd better come Monday. I'll give you fifty dollars."

Through his confusion, as the door closed behind him, Ingersoll heard his new employer addressing the secretary.

"Jesus Christ," he cried with furious amazement, "I hire anybody!"

Ingersoll worked on this magazine for nearly five years, winding up as a managing editor. He is remembered by pioneer members of the staff as an untidy man of formidable energy—the creator of elaborate systems for simplifying office routine, the author of prodigious memoranda on every subject under the sun, a valuable authority on the fashionable doings of Park Avenue and Long Island. His desk was a pharmacist's treasury of pills, disinfectants, and hair-restorers, for he was convinced that his health was precarious and it was obvious that his hair was getting thin. He was not always easy to understand, because he had a tendency to lisp and some of his other consonants were rather blurred. Once a conference dissolved helplessly because everybody was under the impression that Ingersoll was saying "Thor" when he was, in fact, talking about a man called Thaw.

"I'll have no mythological characters in this magazine," said the editor sourly.

Like practically everybody else in those wonderful days, Ingersoll was profitably involved in the stock market and he spent a good deal of time talking to his broker on a curious attachment called a Hush-A-Phone, which made his voice sound even more muffled and ghostly than it was.

All this time, of course, he was yearning to write, but the authorities were not especially coöperative, and in the end he had to be content with a football column signed "Linesman." He took this seriously, bustling off to Yale, Harvard, and Princeton (the power football played by the big, tough schools didn't interest him), as picturesquely draped with blankets, flasks, binoculars, and assorted pelts as a man in *Esquire*. Later he watched in agony as the hired assassin on the copy desk mutilated a prose chiefly remarkable for its patient struggle to find synonyms for the word "football" and its rather frantic admiration for a young man named Albie Booth.

Ingersoll left this employment amicably enough in 1930. He felt he needed more scope and he was not averse to more money, and since both these were offered him by the management of *Fortune*, he resigned and joined Luce in his chromium-plated tower in the Chrysler Building. He was generally regretted by his former associates, who not only had liked him but also were never again to see a colleague who put on striped trousers and a top hat as a matter of course when he went out to report the Easter parade. Only the editor remained mildly sardonic.

"Ingersoll was a great man for system," he observed once. "If I gave him a thousand dollars a week just to sit in an empty room, before you know it he'd have six people helping him."

★ ★ ★

TIME, INC., WAS wonderful—an opium-eater's vision of a magazine office. For anybody who *was* anybody, salaries began at $10,000 (Ingersoll got $15,000) and ended in the stars. All God's chillun had stock, and the air was full of stupendous projects, as queer and impalpable as dreams. A special timesaving language was even employed, which first ran familiar words together and then printed them backward. The atmosphere was moral, energetic, and quick with hope, combining perhaps the best features of Yale and Heaven. Ingersoll fitted into it beautifully.

He was employed first as an associate editor of *Fortune*, which was going through difficulties because of the depression. It was Luce's theory that the public had a legitimate interest in the affairs of private corporations. Since, however, most of these affairs were a mess, a good many big businesses were reluctant to be investigated, even by a magazine that cost a dollar and could be classed as a moderately big business itself. It was Ingersoll's job to reassure them, and he did this so successfully—swooping down on the impressionable tycoons in his blue monoplane—that within a year he had been made managing editor. This lasted for five years, during which he was encouraged to write articles on such assorted subjects as William Randolph Hearst, Burlesque, the Gold Standard, and the Continent of Australia. He was having a hell of a time generally. He kept an ant palace in his office and he studied this world in microcosm attentively, forming his own opinions of human behavior. Moreover, in these benign surroundings, the nervous indigestion which had plagued him for years gradually passed away.

Late in 1935, when Ingersoll was vice-president and general manager of Time, Inc. (in charge of reorganization and other miracles), somebody dug up a dummy for a picture magazine, which had previously been dismissed as impracticable by Luce and relegated to the files. Ingersoll thought well of it in principle, both as an artistic enterprise and as a possible money-maker, and undertook to resell it to his employer, who at that time happened to be spending his honeymoon in Cuba, where he was devoting a good deal of his time either to reading aloud or else to taking setting-up exercises, both under the supervision of his bride. There is no record of precisely what emotions stirred in the groom's bosom as a plane winged out of the northern sky and discharged Ingersoll, bearing the revised dummy of the publication that was soon to be known as *Life*.

"I sold it to Harry and Clare right there on the beach," he says, with some satisfaction.

This was probably the high point of his career with the Luce organization. He was made publisher of *Time* in 1937 at a salary of $45,000 plus stock bonuses that were calculated to be worth a million dollars in the end, but for a while his relations with his employer had not been on quite the old glad, confident basis. In a rather sweeping memorandum written to himself during that year (it has always been customary on *Time* to address yourself formally, in triplicate), Ingersoll said:

I think this country is a swell place but I do not think it is nearly good enough. I think the majority of people who live in it get bad breaks. I believe not only that the wretched conditions in which these people are born and live and work are unhealthful to the welfare of the country, but also that a hell of a lot of it is unnecessary. Right-minded men can, and must, do something about it, each to his own trade. My trade is journalism.

Luce, according to Ingersoll, was not quite prepared for this brand of salvation. "Harry had a different idea of a journalist's functions. He believed that a journalist should be amoral—with no responsibility except to be accurate and able to hold the attention of his audience. We drifted apart."

These warring concepts of publishing morality reached a climax in an incident that is probably best described by Ingersoll himself in another memorandum that it is hard not to italicize here and there:

Harry takes the institution of choosing the man of the year for the cover of *Time's* first January issue very seriously. He is very clear about his policy on cover subjects. They are the people who make the most noise. Moral values are not to be considered. Harry had it all out years ago when he put Al Capone on the cover of *Time,* and the Methodist customers screamed like hell. Harry argued right back at them that the cover of *Time* implied no en-

dorsement; it simply represented the appraisal of the editors of
Time as to who was most "newsworthy."

All right. Came the time when I was publisher at *Time* and
the man of the year—the most newsworthy one in the world—
was obviously Adolf Hitler. And *Time* had a very striking color
photograph of Adolf in his khaki uniform—not deifying him
but making him look very solid and clean and respectable.

It began to worry hell out of me. It was about the time the
first atrocity and concentration camp stories were coming in
from Germany, and I felt very strongly on the subject of Hitler.
I did not see how *Time* could put this dignified picture of him
on the cover without conveying some kind of tacit endorsement. The words for what I felt are hard to find—this was before the world was clear on a lot of subjects—but what I felt was
more than a simple dislike. Anyway, I kept on worrying until I
decided to see if I couldn't find a picture which expressed what
I felt.

I began asking around, but it was December before I stumbled
on a hell of a fine lithograph of a Catherine-wheel with naked
bodies hanging from it and down in one corner a tiny little man
playing a hymn of hate on an organ, and the man was Hitler. It
said about what I wanted to say: that Hitler indeed rated the cover
of *Time* on newsworthiness—but he rated it because he was a
little man who had done such terrible things.

By the time I found this lithograph Harry was off some place
and I was alone running the shop. The editors of *Time* fell into
violent disagreement over my proposal to substitute the lithograph for the colored portrait. In the end I arbitrated by agreeing
with myself and putting the lithograph on.

The day Harry came back, I went up to see him and instantly opened the subject of the cover. I said I have done something you may not approve of, Harry, because it violates a
long-standing tradition of *Time*. But before you tell me whether
you do or do not approve I would like you to know how I felt
about it and why I did what I did—and I told the history of the
choosing of the man of the year cover.

It was in Harry's room on top of the Time-Life Building,

and we were quite alone. When I got through the fairly simple tale, Harry became visibly emotional, flushing and getting that cold set look he gets when he is very angry. We sat looking at each other for about a minute and then he said simply, "Spilt milk: let's not discuss it."

They never did and, as far as Ingersoll can remember, they never again talked frankly about any other editorial problems, either. Ingersoll, as a matter of fact, had just about outgrown Time, Inc. He was practically ripe for the great apocalypse.

(This is the first of two articles about Ralph Ingersoll.)

A VERY ACTIVE TYPE MAN ~ II

THOUGH THE PHYSICAL appearance of *PM* was determined nearly two decades ago when Ralph Ingersoll (then Ralph *McAllister* Ingersoll) fell in love with a little advertisingless daily put out by the newspapers of New York during the pressmen's strike of 1923, its spiritual character took much longer to form. Until 1930, when Ingersoll went to work at Time, Inc., it had never occurred to him to bother his head about politics (he cast his first Presidential ballot in 1932, when he was just as old as the century) and his education even thereafter was not especially rapid. He became a New Dealer largely through the influence of Archibald MacLeish, a poetic colleague on *Fortune*, but for some time he continued to admire much that was considered obsolete both by Mr. MacLeish and the President of the United States. He was convinced that right-minded men were under some obligation to improve the lot of their fellows, but the means remained rather vague. By 1936, according to a memorandum he wrote at the time, his feeling about Hitler was "more than simple dislike," but it was still short of the true crusader's zeal.

His ideas, however, were getting clearer and clearer, and in the spring of 1937 he took a month off and went up to his farmhouse in Lakeville, Connecticut, for private meditation and prayer. The result was not only a new Ingersoll but also the prospectus for a new paper. This inevitably covered a good deal of ground, since Ingersoll, a thorough man, felt obliged to describe not only a new philosophy of journalism but also the manner in which he proposed to staple the pages together. The essence of it, though, was to be found in a paragraph which the author must have admired, since he still reprints it from time to time at the masthead of *PM*:

We are against people who push other people around, just for the fun of pushing, whether they flourish in this country or abroad. We are against fraud and deceit and cruelty and we will seek to expose their practitioners. We are for people who are kindly and honest and courageous. We respect intelligence, sound accomplishment, open-mindedness, religious tolerance. We do not believe that all mankind's problems are soluble in any existing social order, certainly not our own, and we propose to crusade for those who seek constructively to improve the way men live together. We are Americans and we prefer democracy to any other principle of government.

Henry Luce, the proprietor of Time, Inc., to whom Ingersoll showed this battle cry along with the rest of his prospectus, was so impressed by it that he offered him a year's leave of absence with pay (he was getting forty-five thousand dollars a year) for further conversations with the Holy Ghost. There were dark rumors at the time that Luce's enthusiasm for Ingersoll's idea was so intense that he even experimented briefly with a similar enterprise of his own. The facts are not altogether clear. A tabloid called *Newsdaily*, somewhat resembling both *Time* and the embryo *PM*, was indeed issued shortly thereafter at Hartford, apparently as a rehearsal for a subsequent appearance in New York. Its bills were paid for three months by Time, Inc., but Luce's name was never officially connected with it and, after it expired, Ingersoll himself seemed unsuspicious.

"Just a coincidence, I guess," he was apt to say when prodded for an opinion.

Anyway, he took the leave of absence, although it was the spring of 1939 before he got around to it, since, during 1938, Time, Inc., underwent one of its strange, magnificent upheavals and Ingersoll volunteered to stay until things got straightened out. He was not totally inactive on his own project, however. He set up an organization called Publications Research, Inc., in an office on Forty-second Street and hired a man called Stanley to reduce his dream to its approximate cost basis. Mr. Stanley's first estimate was that an initial investment of five million dollars would be required, and even though his employer summarily cut that down by two million, it still sounded like a lot of money.

In April, 1939, Ingersoll finally left *Time* (it was called a leave of absence but there was an understanding that if he could finance *PM* he wouldn't be back), and rented a couple of rooms in the Time-Life Building. Before he could raise three million dollars or any other sum, it was obvious he had to have something to show potential investors, and he set out to produce a dummy issue of *PM,* along with a list of hypothetical contributors.

There are two versions of what happened next. Ingersoll says he got the dummy out in his own office, almost exclusively with the help of his old colleagues on *Time,* and was ready to go to work on the public in June. The *American Mercury,* which has always been inclined to take a rather theatrical view of life, printed its own account on the occasion of *PM*'s first appearance on the stands. It frankly suspected the worst:

> The mystery begins, appropriately, with a writer of detective yarns, Dashiell Hammett. After "The Thin Man" came *PM.* In November, 1938, in a suite at the Plaza, under the firm name of Publications Research, Inc., Mr. Hammett started to interview applicants for a nebulous newspaper that later jelled as *PM.* Gossip in newspaperdom (published and otherwise) mentioned such names as Dorothy Parker, Donald Ogden Stewart, Heywood Broun, Ruth McKenney, Lillian Hellman, Kenneth Durant, George Seldes, etc., as interested in the project or possible participants. . . . Right or wrong, the public impression grew that a mouthpiece was being fashioned for the influential Stalinist-liberal elements in New York and Hollywood, the so-called Anti-Fascist People's Front.

There can be no question that Mr. Hammett lived at the Plaza, where he interviewed quite a lot of hopeful journalists, or that he rewrote at least half of a dummy which, in its final form, contained departments signed by him as well as Mrs. Parker and Miss Hellman, or even that Ingersoll at the time was considerably impressed, if not intimidated, by his gifted friends. Otherwise, however, there seems little reason to suspect a Communist plot of any considerable dimensions. Ingersoll may be inclined to minimize the part played by the so-called People's Front in influencing *PM*'s policies and choosing its personnel, but on the whole it is likely that the spider web at the Plaza was largely a myth.

Like most stories that involve the raising of large sums of money, the financing of *PM* makes moderately dull reading. A firm of Wall Street brokers undertook to sell Ingersoll's stock for him but nothing much came of it, and he dispensed with them when Edward J. Noble, now in charge of Station WMCA but then busy making Life Savers, talked about subscribing the full amount. In September, 1939, when the war broke out, however, Mr. Noble withdrew and Ingersoll, after cutting his three-million-dollar estimate in half, decided to do his own peddling.

"I just went around ringing doorbells," he says, dismissing in this homely phrase a series of flights in his private blue monoplane during which he ranged the skies from the Thousand Islands to Key West, equipped with a directory of the local millionaires.

"Anyone would think this was a dumb idea," a dispassionate spectator has observed, "but it worked like zippo."

The largest single contribution had been two hundred thousand dollars from Marion Rosenwald Stern at the time the aviator got around to Marshall Field, who appeared on Ingersoll's list because "he had almost backed a paper a couple of times before." This historic meeting seems to have been undramatic, though productive. Mr. Field spent an hour going over the dummy and then signed up for a sum equalling Mrs. Stern's. The total amount had to be raised by January 15th or all bets were off, and Ingersoll got under the wire on the eleventh.

"The last days were like hitting oil," he says. "All the doubtful prospects came flocking in at once. We could have—and should have—recapitalized to take in much more dough." As it was, approximately one million dollars had to be turned down, in what must have been a daze.

In addition to Mr. Field and Mrs. Stern, the original list of stockholders included John Hay Whitney, Garrard B. Winston, Lessing Rosenwald, Philip K. Wrigley, Max Schuster, Mrs. Louis Gimbel, George Huntington Hartford II, and Ingersoll himself. Miss Hellman, Mr. Hammett, Dorothy Thompson, Archibald MacLeish, and Herman Shumlin were also represented, but only for nominal sums.

"I just lent them some money to pay the electric-light and tele-phone bills and got it back in stock," Miss Hellman says airily of her interest in this vast project.

In an article in the *Saturday Evening Post*, written at the time Mr. Field was starting his Chicago *Sun, PM's* larger backers were de-scribed as "an impressive array of fat cats . . . of an unsuspicious nature." Ingersoll denies this indignantly.

"We had a meeting before *PM* started," he says. "They understood everything perfectly. Matter of fact, they signed a document."

This, it seems, agreed that Ingersoll was to be given not only a five-year contract at thirty-six thousand dollars a year but also "com-plete, absolute, and exclusive power to formulate editorial, advertis-ing, circulation, production, and promotion policies."

THE FIRST ISSUE of *PM* was published on the eighteenth of June in the year 1940 of the Christian Era. For about six months prior to that, the public had been assaulted with one of the most vehement promotion campaigns since Lydia Pinkham's Vegetable Compound ("We offered 'em everything except a twenty-dollar bill with each copy," said the circulation manager with disgust), and obviously a large-scale miracle was indicated. What appeared, unfortunately, was just another tabloid newspaper, and not a very good one. As prom-ised, there were no advertisements, but the theory that this would free the writers for special crusades and revelations not possible in a kept press didn't seem to work out. *PM* carried about the same news as the other papers, but rather less of it and a good deal later. There was some emphasis on doings in labor circles, an unusually complete radio guide, and a lot of artistic, though whimsical, photographs, many of which were devoted to *PM's* adopted baby, a toothsome morsel called Lois. The early editorials, obviously attempting to rec-oncile the isolationism of the Party line with the interventionism of the New Deal, were more confused than incendiary, and merely succeeded in irritating both sides.

On the whole, *PM* plainly hadn't much to say, and its manner of saying it was sometimes unfortunate. Ingersoll had long had a no-tion that cold, objective journalism was a myth and his employees were encouraged to express their personalities. They did.

"They'd climb right up on your lap and muss your hair," said an early reader, and Ingersoll himself now concedes that the reaction from the old austerities may have gone too far. "*PM* was misconstrued as an invitation to the emotional," he says. "May have been somewhat guilty myself."

According to the editor, there were also difficulties in the circulation department. First of all, the other papers, suspicious of *PM*'s promise not to compete for advertising, ganged up to keep it from getting a regular position on the newsstands (it was apparently entitled to the one once occupied by Macfadden's *Graphic*); then they conspired to prevent the independent distributors from delivering it in the suburbs. Ingersoll burst into Mayor LaGuardia's apartment at two o'clock one morning to demand his rights, and after that things improved, though they were still far from perfect.

The most serious collapse, however, took place in *PM*'s own offices, which were not equipped to handle about a hundred thousand subscriptions which turned up during the last couple of weeks before publication, largely as the result of an almost supernatural campaign conducted by Harry Scherman, the president of the Book-of-the-Month Club. An overworked, or languid, or merely contemptuous employee solved this problem by direct methods—he bundled up all the cards bearing 'the subscribers' names and tossed them in a laundry hamper, where Ingersoll himself found them some ten days later. For two weeks, *PM* was able to dispose of an average of two hundred and twenty-five thousand copies a day, though where they went was practically any man's guess. After that, however, circulation dropped rapidly and finally reached a low of forty-five thousand. The crisis came at a stockholders' meeting on September 12th.

This gathering obviously hoped to eliminate Ingersoll and along with him an editorial policy which, however perfectly it may have been understood in May, now in September had a distinctly murky aspect. The mistake the stockholders made was in underestimating the extent of Marshall Field's own conversion to progressive idealism. Before they could say "categorical imperative," he had bought out their interests for twenty cents on the dollar and made it clear that he was prepared to stand a loss of a million dollars a year until the dawn of the millennium or any reasonable facsimile.

This was quite a triumph for Ingersoll, and he went back to his office in Brooklyn with his mind free to concentrate on getting out a successful paper. This, however, was a more complicated project than it sounds. Ever since that early but somehow unforgettable day when Ingersoll had considered calling his product *Newspaper*, presumably on the ground that the logical name for the best egg is *Egg*, there had been a strong atmosphere of original thought around *PM*. Ex-employees, trying to define the special quality of the goings on there, usually give up and fall back on what seem to them characteristic incidents. One man recalls, as in a dream, that after *PM* had at last been glumly adopted as the name for the new journal, the editor still looked thoughtful. "All right," he said finally. "Now, what's it going to be—morning paper or afternoon?" Dashiell Hammett, who was hired briefly to edit copy because Ingersoll admired his writing and hoped that *PM* might come to sound like it, remembers a photograph an employee called Weegee brought back from the Bronx. It was taken in the flooded basement of a clothing store and it showed the proprietor submerged to his waist in muddy water, embracing a wax dummy who seemed to resemble the Duchess of Windsor. For some reason, Ingersoll was bewitched by this odd scene and insisted that it had to be printed immediately.

"It's wonderful!" he said. "It's got everything!"

"Sure," said Mr. Hammett in the manner of Sam Spade, and moved away.

"Hammett is dynamite," said Ingersoll later, recalling a relationship that somehow or other failed to work out.

Another worker still dreams of a staff meeting he attended after he'd been on *PM* less than a week.

"What about you?" said his employer, turning on him dramatically in the midst of a large silence. "You in favor of firing Ben Hecht?"

The victim doesn't recall how he voted on this proposition; he just recalls a wild, momentary sense of power.

These meetings, which were held three nights a week and

included everybody except the office boys, were usually odd and occasionally painful. As in the case of the disposal of Mr. Hecht (who, in the end, just rather drifted away, murmuring the word "collegiate"), a general vote was taken on all matters of policy. It was academic, however, as the editor listened impassively and then did whatever he had intended to do in the first place. He justified this technique once to Mr. Hammett.

"I've got to have yes men," he said, "but I like to know what they think."

There were also sessions when a marked copy of the previous day's paper was produced and a few passages, conspicuously not in the manner of "The Thin Man," were read aloud for the sake of the culprits' morale. The strangest meeting of all, perhaps, occurred just after Ingersoll had decided to adopt his policy of all-out aid to Britain, come what might.

"Of course," he explained politely, "anybody who doesn't agree is at liberty to take a leave of absence for the duration."

The staff thought this over for a moment and then one of them raised his hand.

"Will we have to wear white feathers?" he asked.

This leave-of-absence technique, incidentally, soon got to be so basic a part of Ingersoll's labor policy that it picked up a name and a definition now commonly used by the Newspaper Guild in its disputes with *PM*. This name was borrowed from an employee called Fromer and the definition is a succinct account of what happened to him. Mr. Fromer was "fromerized," or, in the full, lovely phrase, "suspended by pay check until dead." Since Mr. Fromer obligingly became a lower-case verb, twelve other *PM* employees have been fromerized for one reason or another, and there has been considerable bitterness all around. The Guild's theory is that a publication either dismisses a man or it doesn't; Ingersoll's is that he is within his rights in firing a man with pay, or fromerizing him. It is an interesting controversy.

This was somewhat the atmosphere to which Ingersoll returned from his triumphant meeting with the stockholders. He also returned firmly convinced, first, that *PM* had better pass some kind of miracle right away and, second, that America ought to be in the war, for he had long since made his choice between the New Deal and the Party line. He had been writing a series of vigorous editorials advocating increased aid to Britain, but after the September blitz he decided that secondhand information wasn't enough and that he'd better go to London and see for himself. He flew there by Clipper, via Lisbon, arriving somewhere on the Dorset coast on October 20th.

INGERSOLL WAS IN England—in and around London—for just two weeks. He saw the extent of the September damage, interviewed Winston Churchill, Ernest Bevin, and Claude Cockburn, and went through a few blackouts and raids on his own account. He wrote nothing on the spot, but when he got back to New York he described all these experiences in a series of articles, which appeared first in *PM* and then, expanded to roughly sixty thousand words, in a book called "Report on England."

These made exciting reading at the time (*PM*'s circulation put on fifty thousand while they were running) and a lot of them still seem as good as any reporting that has come out of the war. Ingersoll is not a stylist in the sense that his ear automatically selects one arrangement of words as preferable to another as long as they mean the same thing. He is uneasy both with humor and in the subjunctive mood, and his moral sense can lead him into something dangerously close to parody. In "Report on England," for instance, there is this description of wartime shenanigans in a fashionable hotel:

> It is peopled with very cosmopolitan people. A Negress and a distinguished-looking Englishman. A handsome young lady smoking a cigar. Monocles are in female as well as male eyes. . . . There is a jazz band to play for this company and a number of the dancers have had too much to drink. The color of the faces is high and the note of the conversation slightly hysterical. Many are drinking champagne. "Those who are about to die" must raise their glasses once more. One last fling before the leave expires. That is the way it was in 1918. And here are these people acting out the same part. Only the point is, with the exception

of the occasional young aviator looking at it all in some bewilderment, these people are not about to die. . . . What is about
to expire is not the breath in their bodies but their property
rights in banks and mortgages. What it about to end is life as
they knew and lived it as "the international set"—the people
who are always in Cannes and Biarritz at the right time of year
in the right hotels.

Even allowing for the rapidity of newspaper composition, this may
well be one of the really singular passages in the language, combining
the more diabolical features of Evelyn Waugh and Mrs. Humphry
Ward.

On the other hand, given facts that speak for themselves or a scene
that needs no moral embellishments, Ingersoll can write moving and
even eloquent English. A visit to an air-raid shelter, the sight of a
British fighter plane in action, the sound of a flight of enemy bombers overhead and the anti-aircraft guns stabbing up after them—all
these are described in tight, declarative sentences and short, exact
words. Ingersoll has often said that he doesn't believe in objective
journalism, but it is just possible that he is primarily an objective
journalist, and a very good one.

THE WINTER OF 1940–41 was a reasonably quiet one on *PM*.
The tempo of Ingersoll's campaign for intervention was speeding
up (once he devoted his front page to a wishful headline, "We're in
It!," and from time to time he announced that he was personally embarrassed by the country's behavior), but so was the tempo everywhere, and his voice was not particularly loud in the mounting
chorus.

In June, 1941, however, Germany invaded Russia and a month
later Ingersoll had embarked on one of the most ambitious projects
of his career. On July 11th, he set out from San Francisco on a cir-
cumnavigation of the globe. This 30,000-mile excursion, by air, boat,
and train, took exactly ninety-eight days, beating Nellie Bly by almost four weeks and Magellan by a good two and a half years. His
main objective, of course, was Moscow, but he also visited Hawaii,
the Philippines, Singapore, Bangkok, Rangoon, Chungking, Kuib-

yshev, Rostov, Baku, Cairo, Istanbul, Alexandria, Malta, Gibraltar, and other way stations, all large in history.

Like his London adventures, everything that happened to Ingersoll on his trip around the world appeared first in a series of articles in *PM* and then, expanded, in a book, this time one called "Action on All Fronts." It was like his first in that it combined excellent visual reporting with rather overpowering social indignation, the latter usually in the form of random entries taken from his diary. A remarkably graphic account of the bombing of Chungking, for instance, followed almost immediately upon some rather vague moral reflections in which he noted severely, "A drunken Chinese woman is not a pretty sight." This book was also composed at top speed, a fact which conceivably accounted for what appeared to be either a notable lack of continuity in the author's thought or else a rather peculiar sense of values.

"Jennie walked with me in the moonlit, crenelated station and we talked politics and personalities," he informed the diary in the course of a sentimental tribute to his Russian secretary. "I felt fine. But by midnight I had talked myself out. Baku smells of oil." Of Turkey, he remarked, "An intensely patriotic government, it has effected such various reforms as unveiling the women and building a very fine broad-gauge railway." In Istanbul he came upon a breath of home and the past: "Thence to Miss Carp's apartment to meet the U.S. Consul—Latimer, Yale '24." His interview with Stalin, however, was slightly anticlimactic. The conversation was strictly off the record, though Ingersoll later reported the essence of it indirectly, and there was little he could do but describe the man he had come twenty thousand miles to see. "He looks exactly like his pictures," wrote the traveller, "but older and grayer. It startled me, his looking so much like his pictures."

Ingersoll was appalled by the poverty and ignorance he saw in Russia, but rather impressed both by its military establishment and the implications of its long-range economic program. Strangely enough, this temperate judgment failed to appeal very strongly either to Park Avenue or Union Square—the former was simply confirmed in its opinion that Ingersoll was a Comrade in thin disguise; the latter was surer than ever that he was, and always would be, a political Penrod, far too ingenuous for the true complexity of the Marxist dream. It is probably the essential tragedy of Ingersoll's publishing life that he has spent so much of it in the middle.

In a sense, Pearl Harbor was rather a problem to Ingersoll, leaving him gratified but bemused. It put America in the war, but there seemed a good chance that it might also put *PM* out of business. He had been running a paper passionately committed to intervention, and consequently, on the morning of December 8th, he found himself substantially without an issue. For almost exactly two months after that *PM* was no better morally than anybody else, and it was certainly no better journalistically. As a matter of fact, perhaps because of *PM*'s military reputation (it had always been hell on colored maps and intricate strategy), the circulation actually rose, but it was a nervous time just the same. Then, on February 9th, the Normandie burned at her pier in the North River and, miraculously, *PM* had one of the best stories of the year all set up and ready to use.

As early as January 2nd, a reporter named Edmund Scott had been sent out to get on board the Normandie and investigate the possibilities of sabotage. For a man of an ingenious nature, these proved to be practically unlimited. Introducing himself hoarsely to the authorities as an ex-convict, Mr. Scott was presently in possession of a cut-rate union card and quite free to wander where he chose, looking for something that might be blown up. The French liner, it turned out, was an arsonist's dream, with open barrels of excelsior, oily waste, and other combustibles obligingly placed wherever they would be handiest for even the most incompetent firebug.

"She would have been a cinch," Mr. Scott is said to have observed, with a faraway look in his eye. The story was not used until after the fire, on the ground that it was a "blueprint for sabotage," but thereafter the representatives of *PM* ran wild. Muffled and furtive, they approached defense plants from Bay Ridge to Deal Beach, and as often as not they got in. A reporter from another paper, incidentally, got so far into *PM* with no questions asked that he was able to sit down at the editor's desk and write the story of his adventures. The tone generally, however, was less frivolous.

"I wouldn't be surprised if three of my reporters got shot today," Ingersoll said once at the height of this campaign. None of them did, but it made quite a feature just the same. *PM*'s circulation, as noted, had been rising since Pearl Harbor, but the sabotage stories really clinched it. The figures jumped to a hundred and twenty thousand and kept on going up. Today they stand at a hundred and fifty thousand or a little better and the outlook is very reassuring. Ingersoll has been optimistic since birth. In the bleak days when he was struggling along with fifty or sixty thousand readers, he was encouraged by their extraordinary loyalty.

"The subscribers have always been an awful nuisance," he says of them with fond amusement. "Even when *PM* was at its worst, they went around buttonholing friends, trying to get them to take it seriously. They behaved like a kind of sect."

Now, of course, he is triumphant, confident that *PM* has finally passed out of its experimental stage and found its rightful position in American journalism. Apparently, this is a combination of Cassandra and Ida M. Tarbell (*PM* has exposed not only the Standard Oil Company but also the *Saturday Evening Post*, syphilis, life insurance, Charles A. Lindbergh, the Aluminum Trust, the *Daily News*, William Randolph Hearst, and *Social Justice*). Ingersoll, however, prefers to express this idea a little differently.

"There will always be room in America for a Paul Revere," he says.

PHYSICALLY, THE POST-APOCALYPTIC Ingersoll is not so different from the one who was graduated from Yale in 1921 and then spent most of the next seventeen years in the employ of magazines dedicated either to humor of an airy and disassociated nature or else to the greater glory of the American tycoon. Intense moral activity, combined with long hours, has taken about forty pounds off him, but he still weighs something like a hundred and ninety, and they are distributed with agreeable symmetry over a height of six feet and two inches. He dresses like any Yale man of his special vintage—white shirts with buttoned collars; subdued ties, usually in bands of solid color; double-breasted suits of that distinguished shapelessness which has always been Brooks Brothers' unique contribution to American tailoring. He walks with a sort of brisk shamble and in general he has an air of having been rather loosely and casually assembled. His eyes protrude a little and so does his lower lip, in a modified Hapsburg pout. His skin is pale, with a yellowish tinge, in memory of old sunburns. His usual expression is one of intense and distant concentration, as if he were perpetually looking for the right words for a rather difficult idea, and, indeed, such expressions as "I tried to understand," "I tried to get the picture," and "I tried to make sense out of him" figure largely in his conversation. His hair is thin and recently he has shaved off a mustache which was once notably dashing and profuse.

He is only mildly receptive to humor at best, and somewhat hostile to it when *PM* is involved. The fact that Sam Goldwyn instinctively refers to his paper as *MP* amuses him only slightly, and a suggestion that it be called *RI*, as a tribute to the number of times it contains its editor's byline, naturally strikes him as less than a gem of wit. When he is told, for at least the twentieth time, that somebody, in an effort to capture something earnest, progressive, but on the whole invincibly stuffy about his staff, had described them as "a bunch of young fogies," he just smiles patiently. Because of the ruthless demands of his profession, he breakfasts late and then lunches on two dry Martinis, a cup of black coffee, and a chain of mentholated cigarettes. For some reason or other, this reminded one interviewer of the Borden family, whose habitual breakfast of cold mutton soup, bananas, and cookies is thought by some to account adequately enough for the Fall River massacre.

"You eat like this all the time?" he asked respectfully.

"Sure," said Ingersoll. "I got to get back to the plant."

His outside enthusiasms are strictly subordinate to his professional duties. His place in Lakeville—a hundred acres of pine forest and a 1790 farmhouse, with such low rooms that he usually braces himself against the ceiling with one hand while talking—probably means most to him, and he spends a good deal of time dreaming of such improvements as a method of heating the swimming pool directly from the oil burner or else cutting doors that will lead him like magic from his bathroom out onto the rolling Connecticut hills. He is chiefly attended in this Eden by his cook, a Virgin Islander called Elizabeth Shepherd, who sometimes refers to *PM* with awe or some other emotion as "Mr. Ingersoll's million-dollar enterprise." In town he lives in a terraced apartment on East Eightieth Street, which he shares with an Airedale bitch called Shadow, who has been down to street level only once or twice in her pampered life. For a while he used to give parties there for the *PM* staff—a pinball machine and other gambling devices were installed—but this gaiety, though democratic, used to put the host to sleep and after a while it was discontinued.

Although once a determined squash player, he considers all games these days a waste of time. "I am one-thousand-per-cent sedentary," he says, "but I like to drive cars and fish." The only record of Ingersoll the fisherman comes from Havana, where he once went out for marlin with Ernest Hemingway and Herman Shumlin. This sport apparently involves a very definite technique: to get a marlin, you hook him immediately, while sailfish and such should be permitted to nibble at the bait. It is quite possible that this is either uninformed or backward. In any case, Ingersoll, though up on the method through his reading, was mistaken about the quarry. He thought, and insisted, that he was after sailfish. The rest of this story, perhaps, had best be told in the words of a man who got it more or less directly from somebody else:

"The hired captain (an emotional and enthusiastic fisherman, which was why Hemingway had him) nearly went nuts all day watching Ingersoll let the marlin nibble his bait and then get away. He tried over and over to explain to Ingersoll that these were marlin and not sailfish, but nothing came of it. At the end of the first day the captain was just baffled. On the second he kept muttering all afternoon, looking at Ingersoll. The next day, when they went to the boat, the captain was missing. He finally showed up, hardly able to stand. He'd got drunk and been beaten up in a bar, a thing that hadn't happened to him before, at least with Hemingway. He stood on the dock, moaning and cursing in Spanish and pointing at Ingersoll. Hemingway finally persuaded him to take them out, but it was quite an afternoon. Every now and then the captain would point at Ingersoll and begin to cry. Ingersoll never knew what it was all about, and he kept right on letting the marlin get away. Hemingway and the captain talked Ingersoll over in Spanish most of the afternoon."

Plenty of stories like this could be told about Ingersoll, for his life unquestionably contains a good many oddities of which he is not aware, since he is romantically and more or less exclusively preoccupied with his vision of himself as a crusading American journalist. He thinks of the brief history of *PM* as "the god-damndest dog fight, both internally and externally, in the history of publishing," and of himself, as its editor, somewhat as a voice in the wilderness, with rather a monopoly on publishing morality.

"In a world that was cynical, corrupt, and full of fraud," he has written, referring to the early days, "*PM* believed in people and refused to resign itself to corruption and fraud."

This is not a dream confined exclusively to the dreamer. There are a lot of people who think that Ingersoll is hot on the trail of salvation, if not already in charge of it, and others who feel that he is gifted far beyond most editors in the business. An editorial in an Illinois paper recently tossed him a typical bouquet.

"Ralph Ingersoll is so brilliant a writer that he can command 'most any salary he wants," observed the author, clearly of a folksy disposition. "He . . . is a dynamo at arousing public opinion along democratic lines."

The greatest tribute, however, probably came from the President's wife, who, on March 30th, wrote in her syndicated column: "I wonder if *PM* is becoming to you as interesting a paper as I find it. There is barely a day when some article in it is not worth reading from beginning to end." These sentences were indignantly removed from the version of "My Day" appearing in the *World-Telegram*, but they were printed out of town and gratefully reprinted in the interesting paper itself.

Such views of *PM* and its editor are even more widely held across the sea. An American writer of some prominence himself was recently entertaining two visiting Englishmen—a major in the Army and a well-known artist.

"Anybody you'd particularly like to meet?" he asked them in an attempt to break up one of those transatlantic pauses that sometimes fall.

"Well, this chap Ingersoll," said one of his guests. "But I don't imagine . . ."

"Ralph Ingersoll?" said the American. "Sure. I don't know if he's free, but I'll phone him."

"You *know* Mr. Ingersoll?" said the other, clearly lost in a new world. "You mean one just rings him up?"

May 2 and 9, 1942

LITTLE SURESHOT

U P T O T H E night she opened in *Annie Get Your Gun*, Ethel
Merman had appeared in nine Broadway shows, for a total of
2,754 performances, over a period of sixteen years. To get the rather
numbing facts out of the way as quickly as possible, this means that
her vehicles have had an average run of 306 performances, or about
thirty-eight weeks; that she has been working more than half the
time since she started on Broadway; that she has had seven hits out
of nine tries (it is often said that she has never had a flop, but *Stars in
Your Eyes* cost its producer, Dwight Wiman, a little over $200,000, and
Red, Hot, and Blue did not make Vinton Freedley especially rich or
happy either), and that she has been seen on the stage by something
like three and a half million people. In the theatrical world, where
soaring dreams are so apt to replace tiresome realities, the figures on
exact income are always open to suspicion, but it seems likely that
she has made more than two and a half million dollars, principally
from her salary, which started at $350 a week in *Girl Crazy* and has
risen now on a percentage basis to $4,500, and from eight full-length
moving pictures which paid her something like $35,000 each. How
much of all this she has been permitted to keep is, of course, something between Miss Merman's God and the Bureau of Internal Revenue. (Without any allowance for exemptions, she is entitled to
$57,893 out of her gross income of $277,400, but she has always been
very bright about money and she will certainly wind up with a lot
more than that.) Anyway, for a girl who was making $35 a week in
1929 as a secretary in Astoria, she is undoubtedly doing all right.

She has had a consistent popular success that has not even been
approached by any other star, musical or dramatic, in her time, and
the talent responsible for it is simultaneously one of the simplest and
most baffling in the theatre. The most desirable qualities in a musical-
comedy star are obviously grace, humor, beauty and a voice, not nec-

essarily in that order. It is naturally nice for a girl to have all four, but one in a superlative degree will do, as in the case of Beatrice Lillie, who is not a beauty in spite of her rather menacing British elegance, and whose voice is scarcely tuned for pleasure, but who is just about the funniest woman in the world, largely because practically all human aspirations seem to strike her as absurd. It is even possible to get along with none of the accepted gifts at all, substituting for them some quality so hard to define that it is usually just called personality. Helen Morgan's talent, for instance, fitted no pattern. She was not beautiful nor very bright and her sad little voice belonged in a speakeasy, providing synthetic tears for the synthetic gin. All she had was the faculty of communicating a vague, enormous melancholy, but it was enough, at least for the peculiar temper of her time. Unorthodox triumphs like hers, however, are rare; the quadruple threat is the ideal.

The fact that Miss Merman can triumphantly carry a show all by herself is an imposing mystery, since, at first glance, she would seem to be even more limited than most of her sisters. Ethel Merman is 5 feet 5½ inches tall. When she first appeared on Broadway she weighed 118 pounds, but now 130 seems more probable. She has an abundance of black hair; long-lashed, dark-brown eyes; a nose that has a rather Jewish cast, although she is not, and a generous mouth that is usually ajar, displaying handsome teeth, a little out of line along the bottom row. These conventional details, however, haven't much to do with what really makes her a figure of rare and irresistible humor on the stage before she even opens her mouth. It is partly a matter of structure and arrangement. Artists, in an attempt to impose some kind of order on the human body, have stated that, ideally, the female head is one-seventh the length of the whole figure, though in fashion drawing this is reduced to one-tenth for the purpose of achieving that unearthly grace. Working from photographs, since it is hardly practicable to apply a ruler to a lady piece by piece, statisticians have estimated that Miss Merman's head accounts for a little more than one-sixth of the total, making it measure about a foot, or nearly four inches beyond the length attained by less ambitious girls. Since the width is proportionate, it can safely be said that she has an almost record face. To borrow a useful phrase from Ring Lardner, it is a sleeper jump from her hairline to her chin and another one from ear to ear. The features on this plane are whimsically designed. The arching brows she offers to the public are a little higher than the ghostly traces of her own and give her a perpetually astounded air, heightened by her bright, round eyes, and her mouth, squared off by art, likewise expresses a constant, pleased surprise. Nature obviously intended her to have a rather inexpressive face and the look of intense vivacity that usually adorns it is as comic and unnatural as the look of glassy distinction worn by the odd celebrities in those whisky advertisements.

Her figure diminishes rapidly from her wide, square shoulders to her pretty feet so that, as one critic noted, the effect is curiously foreshortened, as if you were looking down at her from a stepladder. She walks with a rather jaunty swing, an appearance of elbowing her way through a crowd that may have been borrowed originally from Jimmy Durante, but now has a bustle unmistakably her own. Sometimes it amuses her to waddle like a duck, usually when the scene would normally call for classic grace, and now and then she kicks one foot up in the air in queer, perfunctory gaiety.

Miss Merman's voice somehow defies studious analysis. One critic, generally more at home at the Metropolitan Opera House than the Imperial Theatre, recently spoke of it with respect. "It is a big, well-focused contralto," he began carefully. "You might say it goes on a straight line." At this point, however, his educated manner deserted him. "Hell, it's quite an organ," he said. "Got ping, you know what I mean. I guess she's got leather or something down there." Others have mentioned her exact pitch (when she sharps or flats it is invariably for her own humorous purposes), her extraordinary sense of rhythm and the enunciation that, without the hideous grimaces that usually disfigure the precise vocalist, still makes every intricate syllable clear all over the house. Whatever her qualities, she acquired them without training, never having taken a formal lesson in her life. She has never learned to breathe according to the rules, simply doing so whenever she happens to feel like it, and she has had no experience with those elocution-class favorites like "The rain in Spain falls gently on the plain" that are guaranteed to make any young woman talk like Lynn Fontanne.

Of everything she has sung, up to *Annie*, Miss Merman has named *I Got Rhythm* as her favorite fast song, *Mississinewah* as the funniest song generally, *I Get a Kick Out of You* as the ballad that affected her most, and *Eadie Was a Lady* as the best character piece. A good many people might dissent mildly from this selection, especially from the omission of *You're the Top*, which certainly involved the greatest amount of stylish reference ever crowded into one lyric, but they were all fine songs and the words from them still bring back very cheerful memories to those who first heard that stirring and jubilant trumpet in the days when we were all certainly in far better shape.

While Miss Merman has certainly been fortunate in her authors, she has a firm mind of her own and hasn't hesitated to veto ideas that don't appeal to her. Once, for instance, Cole Porter thought it might be a good idea to incorporate some topical references in a song. The show was in a late stage of rehearsal and anyway she wasn't much impressed with the news item he had in mind.

"Listen," she told him firmly, "I'm not going to go louse up my lyrics just because some big dope *did* something."

When she refused to appear in *Sadie Thompson* the only show she ever declined, her objections were largely based on a difference of opinion with Howard Dietz about lyrics. He had a verse that amused him involving the word Malmaison, but Miss Merman was not convinced.

"What's it mean?" she asked.

He told her that Malmaison was a famous kind of lipstick and she went away, but obviously still doubtful. The next day she came back and delivered her ultimatum.

"Hey, Howard," she said. "That Malmaison. I asked twenty-five other dames and none of them ever heard of it either. It goes out."

It didn't, but Miss Merman did. About the only time she has ever lost in such a contest, in fact, was when she was in Hollywood, and the forces of purity proved too much for her. "One look at you and I get hot pants" was nervously altered to "One look at you and I get that way" and "feet" was substituted in a line that once ran genially: "Oh, she started a heat wave, by making her seat wave." Neither of these alterations struck her as an improvement, but, after all, she wasn't God.

"A clambake," she is wont to say tolerantly these days, referring to the moving-picture industry, which, in its turn, is said to have found her behavior a little relaxed for its rather anxious social life. She kept on shouting "You said it, sister," at the icy, elevated stars, and once on a cheerful impulse, she nailed an important actor's clothes quite fast to his dressing-room floor.

The events that led up to her present celebrity are really not terribly interesting. The facts seem to indicate that she was born on January 16, 1909, though today she is apt to say plaintively and without a great deal of conviction that it was really 1912. Her father, Edward Zimmerman (she intelligently dropped the first syllable long before she got to Broadway), was a bookkeeper of German extraction who could play the piano a little, and her Scotch mother, Agnes, from whom she got her middle name, was a choir singer who still fondly claims that her daughter could carry a tune when she was two; they lived in a two-family house in Astoria which, Miss Merman says, was "real country in those days, more like an orchard." It had nothing in particular to recommend it to a little girl, however, except the old Famous Players-Lasky Studios, which had a high fence around it through which it was sometimes possible to get a glimpse of the happy actors at work. Now and then, on a good day, Alice Brady would drive up in the longest, shiniest car you ever saw.

Miss Merman's voice was notable practically from the moment she was born—"That's Ethel," people in the next room would say with assurance whenever she opened her mouth—and in 1917, when she was nine, or maybe five, she was taken out to Camp Mills to entertain the troops, making the twenty-four-mile trip rather magnificently in an ambulance. The song she remembers best may have been dimly prophetic of her future tastes: "Since Maggie Dooley Did the Hooley Hooley." She also sang around the neighborhood, at lodges and political clubs, where sometimes the management held gold pieces over the contestants' heads and made their awards according to the volume of the applause. She did all right, though so far singing had not occurred to her as a profession. Her career at Public School No. 4 and Bryant High, where she took a secretarial course, seems to have been just about like anybody else's.

On Saturday afternoons she and her friend, Alice Welch, used to come to New York, have lunch and then go to the Palace, where she sometimes whispered, though without any particular envy, "Gee, I bet I can do as good as *that*."

She began to come to life in 1928, when she went to work as secretary to the late Caleb S. Bragg, president of the B. K. Vacuum Booster Brake Company, and a sportsman of some renown, having been an automobile racer in his day and the owner of the Gold Cup speedboat called *Baby Bootlegger*. Most of Mr. Bragg's dictation was terribly dull, being concerned with the affairs of his insanely named company.

"What would I know about vacuums and boosters and all that stuff?" says Miss Merman now, explaining how it often happened that she left a good deal of technical detail out of her employer's letters. "He'd read on and say; 'Look, Ethel, didn't I give you more than this?' 'Well, I didn't hear you,' I'd tell him. 'Maybe it's this Pitman system.'"

Some of the correspondence was more rewarding, however, for he would often write to quite interesting people. Irene Delroy, Vincent Bendix, George White. Big Shots. She likes to tell you that these days she meets such people socially, without giving it a second thought. Once she found herself rather crazily mixed up in Mr. Bragg's private life. A bunch of the girls from the office had been invited out to spend an afternoon on his houseboat, *Masquerader*, which was at anchor in Manhasset Bay. "We were just asked out to float around and stuff," she says, "stuff" being probably the most useful word in her vocabulary. "He had a lot of other people—you know, like Ruthie Selwyn—really there for the week-end but we were just an outing for the help." That would have been the end of it if her host hadn't decided to give some of the girls a spin around the harbor in one of his speedboats. *Crusader*, its name was. They were on the way back when *Crusader* hit a piece of driftwood and capsized, and the help were thrown into the water. Miss Merman had on her big, black Milan hat and a rather nice dress and she was more concerned about them than her safety. "I'm all right," she called irritably from the oily water. "Just get me out of this." She and her companions were taken back to the houseboat, dried off, fitted out in a bunch of silk pajamas that Mr. Bragg happened to have lying around and asked to stay for dinner. "What else could he do with us while our stuff was drying out?" she asks reasonably. Anyway, she sat next to Miss Selwyn, who was a producer, and she told her about her vague dreams at the Palace. "I told her I got burned up because I knew I could do as good as a lot of people you see on the stage." Possibly to help her host out of what must have looked like an untidy situation, Miss Selwyn promised that Miss Merman would appear in her next show, and though nothing came of that, the fact that the great were so accessible gave Miss Merman an idea. She had been doing quite a lot of semi-professional entertaining at night (she was often so tired at the office in the morning that she had to go lie down in the ladies', telling the other girls to wake her up if anything important, conceivably Mr. Bragg, happened to turn up) and she decided to ask her boss to give her a letter to George White, the producer of *The Scandals*.

It has been said that she wrote the letter herself and Mr. Bragg just signed it, which seems a little unlikely, but anyway it got written and she took it to Mr. White. It was a discouraging interview, because he had no second sight and apparently saw just a not remarkably pretty girl who wanted a job.

"What do you do?" he asked.

"I sing," said Miss Merman firmly. "I'm a singer."

"Well, all I can give you is a job in the line," he told her. "Frances Williams is doing all the singing this year."

"Nope. Not in any line," she said and left him in disgust.

The beginnings of her professional career are a little blurred by distance, and since the details are probably typical of what a lot of other girls had to go through to get on Broadway, they can be covered briefly. Early in 1929, while she was still working for Bragg, she got a job through a girl she knew at a place called Little Russia, West 57th Street, where she was heard by an agent called Lou Irwin. Aware that she had something though he wasn't precisely sure what, he got her a six months' contract at $200 a week with Warner Brothers, who, however, seemed to have no interest in singers and used her only once and then as a dramatic actress, when she was set to chasing around on a jungle set, for what purpose she can no longer recall. By one of those arrangements that are clearer in the cinema than in life, Warner's finally said she could sing elsewhere during her contract, amiably agreeing to keep her on the payroll when she was idle, and she went to work at Les Ambassadeurs, a night club conducted under the mad auspices of Clayton, Jackson and Durante. She hadn't much to do (she was just one of the girls, along with Arlene Judge and a couple of others, and she only got $85 a week) but it was better than wearing your can off sitting around a movie lot, and Durante said she was okay, which was quite an accolade in those days. This engagement, however, was cut short by an attack of tonsilitis, and she spent two theoretically convalescent months singing at a club in Miami Beach.

It is a little hard to say precisely what happened when she got back from Florida, partly because so much went on in so short a time that the actual sequence is almost impossible to straighten out. Roughly, however, it might be said that she took her first real step toward stardom one night when she met a pianist named Al Siegel at a party. She was asked to sing and did so willingly, rendering a piece forbiddingly called *Smile, Darn You, Smile.* Everybody just seemed rather depressed, except Mr. Siegel, who asked her to come and see him the next day. At that and several subsequent meetings, he worked out special arrangements for her, emphasizing a rhythmic beat that was intelligently suited to her voice and personality. Soon after that she was booked at the Pavilion Royale at Valley Stream for a week-end appearance. Siegel played the piano for her and, apparently because of her new style, for the first time in her life she stopped the show. After she had duplicated this performance a few times, people began to talk and she and Siegel (Irwin seems to have disappeared at about this time) were besieged with offers, finally accepting one at the Brooklyn Paramount for six weeks at $600 a week.

It was at this point, according to Siegel, that her sense of comedy first became apparent. The trouble up to then had been that her rather strident voice and personality didn't lend themselves to singing ballads straight—somehow or other it was hard to feel that she took all that moonlight and stuff very seriously. Intelligently determined to turn this liability into an asset, Siegel says he took a song called *Little White Lies* and made an arrangement in which the second chorus was a slight burlesque of the first. It worked like magic and to some degree established Miss Merman's permanent outlook on love, which might be summed up as "All right, get tough with me and I'll shoot you." Siegel also credits himself with perfecting the now hackneyed sustained-note device, whereby she hung on where she was while the orchestra played the melody. Shortly after accomplishing these miracles, Siegel joined Irwin in oblivion. The stories about this, like everything else having to do with those days, are vague and contradictory. It is certain that Siegel became seriously ill, but whether or not Miss Merman was guilty of ingratitude is still a matter of controversy on Broadway. His own argument, presumably in the affirmative, will be presented when he will publish his book. Hers, available at the moment, is rather cryptic. "I haven't mentioned that Siegel's name in fifteen years," she says, looking out the window.

It was at the Paramount that she first came to the attention of Vinton Freedley who was then casting *Girl Crazy.* "I heard about some Astoria girl who could sing as loud as hell," he says, "and I went over to the Paramount to hear her. She came out wearing a short black dress all messed up with bows and ribbons and a lot of jet, and her hair was even wilder than it is now, but she was quite a singer." Afterward he went backstage and asked her how she would like to be on Broadway, and the next afternoon she turned up at his office, wearing the same awful dress. Though he was vaguely dismayed, he took her down to the Alvin for an audition with George Gershwin and with his approval decided to put her in the show. They wrote in a nice tough girl called Kate, and since it was Miss Merman's first appearance in a musical, they gave her a couple of scenes to get used to things. Then, when the show had been running for twenty minutes, she swaggered out on the stage in a flame blouse and black skirt, leaned up against a bar, and began to sing *Sam and Delilah.*

Later in the show she sang *I Got Rhythm,* and the next morning everybody knew she was in, for good.

Unlike Tallulah Bankhead, who, offstage and on, is always and emphatically Tallulah Bankhead, Miss Merman has two personalities. In the theatre she is Annie Oakley, Panama Hattie or whatever part she happens to be playing, and such is the vehemence of her portrayal of these noisy, domineering girls that some of her colleagues are prone to credit her with similar qualities in private life. "I know Ethel gets terribly cozy with the audience," one of them remarked thoughtfully a little while ago, "but you can't help feeling that she's never been introduced to the cast." This comment came as the result of some little skirmish about precedence, and it is probably true that Miss Merman is somewhat touchy about anything she regards as an attempt to swipe her scenes. Once, in *Red, Hot and Blue*, Bob Hope lay down on the stage in the middle of one of her numbers and began to make funny faces. In the intermission Miss Merman went up to the stage manager in a fury. "Listen," she said, "if that son of a bitch does that again, I swear to God I'm going to lie right down on top of him." Paula Laurence, once a dear friend, began to do something Ethel didn't like in the *Mississinewah* song and again Miss Merman sought out the management, offering it the alternative of seeing that Miss Laurence behaved herself, or her own resignation. Miss Laurence is inclined to be philosophic about this episode. "Well, she was the star," she says, "and if she'd wanted me to paint my nose red, I guess I'd have had to. And don't think she wouldn't either," she is apt to add, throwing syntax to the winds.

For one such detractor, however, there are a dozen people who admire her with no reservations at all, and nobody has ever denied her uncanny efficiency on the stage. Absolutely nerveless herself, she is a wonderful first-night performer and a great help to more restive members of the cast. "Just remember if any of those dopes out there could do as good as you, they'd be up here doing it," she told a nervous young actress on one such occasion, and she never loses her presence of mind when some little catastrophe overtakes her on the stage. In one scene in *Annie* she fires her gun in the air and a stuffed bird falls on the stage. One night, in Boston, she raised the gun and pulled the trigger, but there was only a faint click. The bird, however, fell as scheduled.

"What do you know?" said Miss Merman, picking it up with a pleased expression. "Apoplexy."

She is also a remarkable study, both on words and music, and astonishingly quick to grasp her business in a scene—just show her once, everybody says, and she's got it cold.

To anybody who knows Miss Merman only around a theatre, her private personality is apt to seem a little dim and muted. Without her spirited makeup, her face has a rather plump and matronly air, and the celebrated voice, scaled down to conversation, is simply the pleasant speech of Astoria, the Long Island accent somewhat overlaid with grace notes she has picked up in the wider world.

She is an extremely hard girl from whom to extract unorthodox facts. Having given out what might be called the standard interview for sixteen years and to every publication with the possible exception of the Princeton *Tiger* and the *Daily Racing Form*, she is inclined to stick to it, probably on the sensible ground that it has always worked all right. The old anecdotes, like the one about George White and the letter, or a probably apocryphal story about how once, in her innocence, she applied for a passport to get from Astoria to New York, keep turning up and there is something about the way she tells them that suggests she has cast them in a permanent form, for the ages. Miss Merman seems vaguely aware of this herself.

"But I guess you've probably got that in the stuff," she will say to a reporter, referring to the old clippings with which she has learned that most of them are equipped. Even if he agrees that he has, however, she usually tells it anyway, being clearly skittish about getting off the beaten path. "They've printed some damn silly stuff about me," she complains, and indeed they have, from Lucius Beebe on down.

Miss Merman's apartment is a ten-room duplex on the twenty-first and twenty-second floors at 25 Central Park West, where she has lived for thirteen years, and it, also, has something of this same quality of protective coloration. The furniture, assembled for her by Mrs. Oscar Hammerstein II, is expensive and handsome, but it has a curiously impersonal air, as if each room, including the children's nurseries, had been transplanted intact from a window display in Sloane's. On the piano, there are autographed pictures of President Roosevelt ("To Ethel Merman, Franklin D. Roosevelt") and George Gershwin ("For Ethel—a lucky composer is he who has you sing his songs—George"); on the walls there are several correct land-scapes and street scenes and quite a few crayons and water colors of the lady of the house, which are more in the nature of dreams than resemblances; and in the study upstairs there are a good many books which Miss Merman frankly says she has no intention of reading. She is apt to pause over one little picture in a back room. "Kind of interesting," she says. "All made up entirely of canceled postage stamps." It is, and very ingeniously. There is a wading pool for the children on the terrace and a magnificent view of Central Park and all the clean, expansive towers that throng that part of town. Miss Merman believes in entertaining her friends in her home. "I say they aren't real friends, if you have to take them out to some night club," she says, with the air of having said it once or twice before.

In 1940 she was married to William J. Smith, a radio theatrical agent, and though this match was widely chronicled as made in Heaven ("She thinks *My Bill* is the greatest number she's ever met. And *My Bill* is not a song," wrote a lady in the *News*, summing up the general confident rapture), but it lasted only two months, when she apathetically permitted him to sue her for desertion. Soon after that she married Robert Levitt, promotion manager of Hearst's *Journal-American*. Mr. Levitt, a slight, rather handsome man of 35, accepts his position as the husband of a reigning star with composure. "When these dames come around asking questions about Ethel," he says, "I want to tell them to drop dead, but they work this fellow-newspaperman racket on me, and what the hell." His account of their romance is brisk. They met at a party at Dinty Moore's, while she was in *Panama Hattie* and, in the end, since he was the extra man, he was detailed to take her home, though his heart wasn't in it because up to then theatrical people had bored him silly. She made him get out of the cab somewhere along the way to buy her some chewing gum, and altogether, by the time they got to her apartment building, his opinion of her was not high. There was a big snowdrift in front of the door and he started to get out and help her, but suddenly decided against it and just let her plow through by herself. Somehow this experience drew them together and, after a courtship rather complicated by the fact that each thought the other liked to stay up all night and had to make a terrific effort to keep awake, they were married. "I guess I like her best when she's pregnant," Mr. Levitt has remarked, recalling those interminable nights. "Then we can just sit around and listen to the radio or play gin." Miss Merman, incidentally, is quite a gin-rummy player. During the war, when Levitt was a lieutenant colonel at Camp Shanks, she went to call on him once and got in a game with his commanding officer. It was the old-fashioned kind of rummy, with cards all over the table, but Miss Merman caught on quickly and gave the general the trimming of his life. "I tried to explain to Ethel beforehand that he always won," her husband says, "but I guess she didn't get the idea. She was a great help all around. The perfect Army wife." He has also commented on the poise with which she handles the birds she brings down in *Annie*. "I brought her home a couple of pheasants *I* shot once," he says, "but Ethel wouldn't put them in the icebox. We had to throw them away because they made Little Sureshot here sick at her stomach."

The Levitts have two children, Ethel Jr., who is three and a half and Robert Jr., who is ten months. Ethel Jr. is called Little Bit, because when she was born her father, usually not a sentimental man, decided that she was a little bit of Heaven. So far the child takes this designation impassively, though once in the elevator she was overheard discussing it with a fellow tenant. "My name is Little Bit," she said cryptically, "but they call me Ethel Merman the Second for short." Usually she is more forthright. When her mother's vivacity gets too much for her, as it sometimes does, she has been known to say, "Let's get out of this. It's too noisy with *her* in here," and at a matinee of *Annie* in Boston she got up and left her seat early in the first scene after watching her mother shoot a bird off another lady's hat. "That's all," she observed nervously and could not be persuaded to return. Though Miss Merman is fiercely devoted to both children, Bob at the moment is her darling. As she is terribly anxious to tell everybody, he weighs twenty-five pounds and thirteen ounces, an amount certainly adequate for anyone twice his years, and his legs are so fat ("I got a new fat brother," Little Bit is apt to inform callers) that the standard rubber pants won't fit him and he has to have special ones made, his father fortunately having a friend in the business. He is a solemn child, reticent about showing strangers his six teeth, and his famous mother often practically knocks herself out to get a smile out of him.

If actresses were to be classified by their avocations, Helen Hayes might be defined as the Causist Actress, Tallulah Bankhead as the Sporting Life Actress, and Gertrude Lawrence as the Burke's Peerage Actress, Miss Merman, in her present phase at least, would have to be labeled the Domestic Life Actress. Now and then she gets to a night club for a little while after her show, usually to the Barberry Room, a quiet place where people aren't likely to bother her by asking for autographs or spilling drinks, but she leaves early, after a bottle of beer or a couple of glasses of champagne, because she likes to be up early in the morning to play with the children. Sometimes she has lunch at "21," probably with some of the girls—like Dorothy Fields, who helped write the book for *Annie*, Leah Werblin, whose husband is Miss Merman's agent, or Regina Crewe, a motion-picture critic—and she eats heartily, being especially fond of pot roast and potato cakes. These, however, are just about her only dissipations. The rest of the time, when she isn't being interviewed or doing guest shots on the radio for $2,000 each or hanging around shops, she spends at home. It might strike a good many people, especially those who remember her when she used to be an almost permanent fixture at the Stork Club or Toots Shor's, as a rather dull life, but apparently she is having a hell of a time.

Miss Merman's wardrobe and its accessories, to amplify the shopping, have been investigated in what appears to be some detail by an expert, whose report may be illuminating to other ladies: "For fourteen years Miss Merman has been getting her clothes from Wilma, at 4 East 57th Street, who specialized in theatrical stuff, usually with fur on them somewhere, of the kind favored by her current customers—Betty Hutton, Lana Turner, Alice Faye and like that. The first things she bought were two custom-made gowns for her debut at the Plaza; an apple-green, mink-trimmed, low-cut job at $550, and a black-velvet, balloon-sleeved, pencil-skirt number with ermine ascot at $495. She still has them both. She also got a white-net silk, embroidered with rhinestones and 'extra-fine' sequins, appliqued with silver and gold thread, off the shoulders, for an opening night six years ago. These are the only made-to-order things she ever had, however, and she is not really a very lucrative customer. She likes dresses to cost $39.95, $49.95, or $60 or $70 at the most, getting terribly suspicious if they cost over $100. All her selections are from the ready-to-wear—off the hook. Apparently they just turn her loose like a puppy and forget about her. She confines herself almost exclusively to black and navy, but goes nuts with wild hats, jewelry and fussy shoes. The shoes come from Bonwit Teller, and the jewelry from Lou Freedman, who makes it for her specially. She is very proud of it. In addition to the star sapphires, aquamarines, etc., she has a bracelet, about an inch and a half wide, which spells out Ethel A. Merman, the letters in baguette diamonds, the period after the A-for-Agnes in rubies. All it needs is to flicker on and off."

Miss Merman's immediate future, of course, is secure, since *Annie* gives every indication of running to its $47,000-a-week capacity forever, paying her her usual 10 per cent and even the remote years can hardly give her much concern, since she has made a modest fortune and has always guarded it ferociously. Her money is in stocks and she scrutinizes the accounts from her brokers, as well as her box-office statements, as intently as, the Astoria housewife, she might have gone over her grocery bills. Now and then, however, she worries about what is going to happen to her when her voice gives out and she can no longer shout a big musical to glory. She has played with the idea of being a straight actress and Moss Hart, she says, has a play for her whenever she gets around to it, but she has never really succeeded in picturing herself in a role that would require her to identify herself completely with a company of actors, saying lines that were supposed to be taken seriously. The whole notion of the dramatic stage, in fact, seems to strike her as pretty silly. Last year her husband was offered a chair in journalism at the winter session of Rollins College in Florida, and he suggested that she might like to teach theatre at the same time. The idea just about killed her.

"Theatre?" she said, laughing merrily. "What the hell do I know about all that stuff?"

Life, July 8, 1946

They Write as I Please

Parodies

BOO, BEAU!

After reading altogether too much of this sort of thing

WENDELL'S, *ON DIT,* will show the way this fall with their new suit, called the Simplex. This is a five-piece felt *ensemble*—coat, trousers, waistcoat, hat—and it is expected to solve one of the most bothersome problems of getting dressed, since it will be delivered to the customer *already buttoned.* The buttons, as a matter of fact, will be sewed right into the buttonholes. Their places will be taken by zippers, permitting the suit to be opened along the side, somewhat in the manner of a Parker House roll, and laid out on the floor. The customer, of course, will simply lie down on the opened suit, insert his arms and legs into the proper apertures, and zip himself up; $760, made to order. . . . The old peaked-versus-notched-lapel controversy, incidentally, will rage again this winter. DeMilne, however, seems to have hit on a happy solution with a French broadcloth dancing suit with one peaked lapel and the other rounded in the conventional British fashion. . . . Mason, I am informed, has overcome that old bugaboo, the Ascot tie, by simply painting the whole thing in oils on the front of your shirt. This delicate task has been assigned to a Mr. Lodi, who for several years has been designing murals for state capitols. . . . Willock & Freeman are selling a wooden leg which they tell me is capable of holding between three and four quarts of whatever you want. Amusing for men with wooden legs. . . . Singleton offers an ingenious suit in which the bottom has been removed from the breast pocket so that you can pull the slack of your shirt through the hole. The effect is said to be much the same as that obtained by carrying a handkerchief. . . . Cloth-topped shoes are in again, and are to be worn a good deal in the South this winter. Way down, so to speak, upon the *soigné* river. . . . Pigalle's have their new fall fabrics in, and

will make you any sort of suit you like for a million dollars. . . .
Gentlemen do not wear earrings.

November 8, 1930

SPINSTER

AUTHOR'S NOTE: This article is an abridgment of all the stories called "Spinster" which have been published in the last thirty years.

EVERY SPRING, WHEN I was a child, Miss Mimley came to our house for a week or ten days "to do the mending." Under her patient, skillful fingers an old silk rumpelot of my mother's would be transformed into a bathing suit for me or a brilliant reefer for my father.

In spite of the rich fabrics and fashionable designs which passed endlessly through her hands, however, I recall seeing Miss Mimley herself in only one costume. This consisted of a battered top hat, given her by our local congressman; a faded Mother Hubbard; and a pair of hip-boots. She also carried a heavy sword-cane, a wistful elegance which I found infinitely pathetic.

She invariably appeared at our front door at exactly nine o'clock, an anxious little figure with a mouthful of pins. We had known her for years, of course, but she never entered the house without dropping her eyes timidly and murmuring: "Mimley on the mending, folks."

BEFORE I WAS born, village rumor had linked Miss Mimley's name with that of the cashier of the bank. He had, it was understood, "behaved very badly," on several occasions attempting to push Miss Mimley off cliffs or into the water. Eventually, discouraged, she had broken the engagement. Sometimes I have thought that this experience may have accounted for the gentle apprehension which always lurked in Miss Mimley's eyes.

Above everything else Miss Mimley was proud. When she was working at our house we always invited her to have meals with us, but invariably she refused. She would, however, accept small gifts of food—eggs, biscuits, and potatoes—from my mother after the meal was over, storing them carefully in her top hat. Sometimes at Christmas my father was able to persuade her to add a few nuts or raisins and a little of the blazing plum pudding to her modest store. For some curious reason she never ate any of these things in our presence, but took them home every night to the Italian section, where she lived, somewhat meagrely, in a piano box.

LIKE ALL THOSE who live vicariously, Miss Mimley was an indefatigable gossip. She was an almost official repository of disreputable secrets. Old Major Moffat was in the habit of beating his wife.

"He left-jabs her silly," said Miss Mimley, giggling.

Once, I remember, she came to me in a state of high excitement.

"They say," she whispered, "that that Henderson woman shot Garfield!"

This was at the time Garfield was shot.

"Really!" I gasped.

Miss Mimley nodded.

"He spoke out of turn," she said.

A little while ago my mother sent me a clipping from our country paper. Miss Mimley was dead. They had buried her in her top hat. I think she would have liked that.

June 20, 1931

HANOVER-ON-HUDSON

*[Impressions of a Parent After Reading Two Hundred and
Eight Boarding-school Catalogues]*

THE HANOVER COUNTRY School is situated on a wooded
knoll overlooking six suits of long woollen underwear. Each
student is also required to bring one (1) napkin ring and an eighteen-
hole golf course where all work and no play makes Jack a representative American citizen.

The students are supervised at all times by a capable faculty
consisting of Professor F. Dwight Bohn, Amherst '88, Princeton
'88, Harvard '88, D.D., LL.D., M.D., Ph.D., who has had many
years' experience as an educator in the row of beautiful pines which
flank the campus. It is from these pines that the Hanover Country
School takes its name.

Pupils with permission from their parents may smoke at all times
in the long panelled study hall, which, in the past, has seated such
notable Americans as Henry Wadsworth Longfellow, Jim Tully,
A. E. Housman, Rabindranath Tagore, and Henry Wadsworth
Longfellow.

A spirit of sturdy American independence is inculcated in the
younger boys by marching them down to the lovely little lake which
adjoins the medieval chapel and throwing them in. They drown.
Students who own polo ponies are allowed to entertain them in their
rooms not more than twice each term. Parents, however, are re-
quested not to send students opium or race horses. Rates for the
school term are $2,000, exclusive of board and tuition, and payable
in advance. This figure includes transportation between Des Moines
and Utica.

While studies come first, the spiritual life is by no means neglected,
and revivals are conducted every evening by the Rev. William Sunday, himself an old Hanover boy. The school also boasts units of the

Boy Scouts of America, the Y.M.C.A., the B.P.O.E., and Henry Wadsworth Longfellow Lodge 1080, A.F.&A.M.

The curriculum is based upon an extensive survey of the best modern educational methods. The boy is early taught to use and respect his hands. The courses include Manual Training, Manual History, Manual Spelling, etc. It is the faculty's dearest wish to make every Hanover graduate a representative suit of long woollen underwear.

July 4, 1931

EDWARD DAMPER

*[A Composite Book Jacket Written After Studying the
Publishers' Blurbs on More Than a Million Fall Novels]*

WHEN EDWARD DAMPER wrote his first novel, "Vile Counterpoint," at the surprising age of eleven, many critics, both in England and America, attributed it to William Faulkner. Far from being gratified by this tribute, however, the tot was furious.

"For a dime," he wrote William Lyon Phelps, who was then editor of *St. Nicholas*, "I'd knock your ugly teeth down your throat."

"Vile Counterpoint" was followed in quick succession by almost a hundred other novels, each considerably more repellent than the last, until in this, his latest book, the publisher feels that the young author has richly fulfilled his early promise. Certainly there is no more disturbing chapter in contemporary fiction than that in which Charlie Sands cuts up old Mrs. Bundy and mails the pieces to the members of the Supreme Court.

Mr. Damper, who is now sixteen, was born, whimsically enough, on an escalator at Bloomingdale's, and his subsequent life has followed an even more unconventional pattern. Searching for literary material, he has been successively a pickpocket, a pawnbroker, a pearl-diver, and a private detective, following for some devious reason of his own every conceivable profession beginning with a "p." He has been married five times, to the Misses America for the years 1926 to 1930 inclusive. The comparative brevity of each of these experiences can probably be attributed to a wistful quality in Mr. Damper's character which somehow made each new Miss America seem infinitely more vivid and desirable than the last. The novelist lives in an abandoned freight car on a siding near Rockville Center, L.I., where he devotes much of his time to an interminable dispute with the railroad officials, who keep trying to move the car somewhere else.

Mr. Damper likes women, money, and alcohol, and his favorite sport is bee-snatching. He has a Pekinese called Scottie, which he beats for amusement. He composes on the typewriter, using one finger, and goes pretty slow except when it comes to the physiological monosyllables. He could write *them* under water.

November 26, 1932

DEATH IN THE RUMBLE SEAT

With the Usual Apologies to Ernest Hemingway,
Who Must Be Pretty Sick of This Sort of Thing

MOST PEOPLE DON'T like the pedestrian part, and it is best not to look at that if you can help it. But if you can't help seeing them, long-legged and their faces white, and then the shock and the car lifting up a little on one side, then it is best to think of it as something very unimportant but beautiful and necessary artistically. It is unimportant because the people who are pedestrians are not very important, and if they were not being *cogido* by automobiles it would just be something else. And it is beautiful and necessary because, without the possibility of somebody getting *cogido*, driving a car would be just like anything else. It would be like reading "Thanatopsis," which is neither beautiful nor necessary, but hogwash. If you drive a car, and don't like the pedestrian part, then you are one of two kinds of people. Either you haven't very much vitality and you ought to do something about it, or else you are yellow and there is nothing to be done about it at all.

IF YOU DON'T know anything about driving cars you are apt to think a driver is good just because he goes fast. This may be very exciting at first, but afterwards there is a bad taste in the mouth and the feeling of dishonesty. Ann Bender, the American, drove as fast on the Merrick Road as anybody I have ever seen, but when cars came the other way she always worked out of their terrain and over in the ditch so that you never had the hard, clean feeling of danger, but only bumping up and down in the ditch, and sometimes hitting your head on the top of the car. Good drivers go fast too, but it is always down the middle of the road, so that cars coming the other way are dominated, and have to go in the ditch themselves. There are a great many ways of getting the effect of danger, such as staying in the middle of the road till the last minute and then swerving out of the pure line, but they are all tricks, and afterwards you know they were tricks, and there is nothing left but disgust.

The cook: I am a little tired of cars, sir. Do you know any stories?

I know a great many stories, but I'm not sure that they're suitable.

The cook: The hell with that.

Then I will tell you the story about God and Adam and naming the animals. You see, God was very tired after he got through making the world. He felt good about it, but he was tired so he asked Adam if he'd mind thinking up names for the animals.

"What animals?" Adam said.

"Those," God said.

"Do they have to have names?" Adam said.

"You've got a name, haven't you?" God said.

I could see—

The cook: How do *you* get into this?

Some people always write in the first person, and if you do it's very hard to write any other way, even when it doesn't altogether fit into the context. If you want to hear this story, don't keep interrupting.

The cook: O.K.

I could see that Adam thought God was crazy, but he didn't say anything. He went over to where the animals were, and after a while he came back with the list of names.

"Here you are," he said.

God read the list, and nodded.

"They're pretty good," he said. "They're all pretty good except that last one."

"That's a good name," Adam said. "What's the matter with it?"

"What do you want to call it an elephant for?," God said.

Adam looked at God.

"It looks like an elephant to me," he said.

The cook: Well?

That's all.

The cook: It is a very strange story, sir.

It is a strange world, and if a man and a woman love each other, that is strange too, and what is more, it always turns out badly.

In the golden age of car-driving, which was about 1910, the sense of impending disaster, which is a very lovely thing and almost nonexistent, was kept alive in a number of ways. For one thing, there was always real glass in the windshield so that if a driver hit anything, he was very definitely and beautifully *cogido*. The tires weren't much good either, and often they'd blow out before you'd gone ten miles. Really, the whole car was built that way. It was made not only so that it would precipitate accidents but so that when the accidents came it was honestly vulnerable, and it would fall apart, killing all the people with a passion that was very fine to watch. Then they began building the cars so that they would go much faster, but the glass and the tires were all made so that if anything happened it wasn't real danger, but only the false sense of it. You could do all kinds of things with the new cars, but it was no good because it was all planned in advance. Mickey Finn, the German, always worked very far into the other car's terrain so that the two cars always seemed to be one. Driving that way he often got the *faender*, or the clicking when two cars touch each other in passing, but because you knew that nothing was really at stake it was just an empty classicism, without any value because the insecurity was all gone and there was nothing left but a kind of mechanical agility. It is the same way when any art gets into its decadence. It is the same way about s-x—

The cook: I like it very much better when you talk about s-x, sir, and I wish you would do it more often.

I have talked a lot about s-x before, and now I thought I would talk about something else.

The cook: I think that is very unfortunate, sir, because you are at your best with s-x, but when you talk about automobiles you are just a nuisance.

October 8, 1932

PRIMO, MY PUSS

[EDITORS' NOTE: The following curious fragment, bearing the title "How I Lost to Max Baer, by Primo Camera, as told to Alexander Woollcott," was found in a wastebasket in the *Saturday Evening Post* offices.[1] A note scrawled in the margin said "*Highly dubious collaboration!*" and was signed "George Horace Lorimer."[2] We are able to reproduce it here through the courtesy of a charlady who picked it out and flew right over from Philadelphia to show it to us.]

A T THE CONCLUSION of that not especially memorable set-to in Long Island City when fifty thousand enchanted cretins watched the faintly orchidaceous Mr. Baer wallop the bejesus out of your correspondent, a certain William Brown, of the New York State Boxing Commission, was seen leaving the arena in what can be described only as a pet. Those nearest to the departing solon were able to discern that he was shaking his head and muttering to himself as if in considerable agitation. It is unreliably reported that Mr. Brown's concluding remark, as he snuggled into his wool fascinator and fared forth into the night, presumably forever, was: "Hell, I thought they was only one bum in there! It turns out they was two!"

Oddly enough, my blossoms, the captious fellow had somehow got it into his head that Mr. Baer and the oversigned were not prizefighters at all, but, rather, what that acidulous pundit, Mr. Thornton Wilder, is wont to describe as "a coupla stumblebums."

Somehow or other Professor Brown's tempered admiration for my person recalls a day in London, shortly after my encounter with that resolute horizontal, Mr. Philip Guedalla★, when Miss Rebecca

---

★MARGINAL NOTE: "Author perhaps means Phil Scott. Think Guedalla a poet. G. H. L."

West, in one of her vehement descents upon the mildly astonished capital, had occasion to pause at a little bookstore in Threadneedle Street.[3] Thumbing over the ragged volumes, thick with the dust of a century of desuetude, the fascinated lady chanced to come upon a small blue book, bearing in faded gilt letters the vaguely ribald legend: "Report of the East Chicago Vice and Crime Commission, 1909–1910." Miss West dealt briefly and adequately with the proprietor, a bibulous antique who hoarsely asserted that the article in question was a pearl beyond any price, and then, clasping her treasure to her bosom, she scampered forthwith to her eyrie over the Serpentine to examine it at her leisure. The report itself proved something of a disappointment, being a rather dispirited account of forgotten anatomical skullduggeries in the Middle West, and the lady was about to cast it firmly from her window when her eye happened to fall upon the title page, where a childish hand had written an almost illegible inscription. Bending forward, in the fading light, Miss West was finally able to decipher the spidery lines, and when she did so, her eyes filled with warm and happy tears.

"To Harpo Marx," she read, "on his third birthday, from his little friend and admirer, William Lyon Phelps."

And this, in turn, brings to mind a tiny drama which, only last week, came to enliven the placid byways of our own Fifty-seventh Street. It was high noon and the walks were prettily thronged with shoppers when, without warning, a street-cleaner of singularly mournful aspect collapsed weeping at the very feet of my informant, a whilom journalist called Swope. True to the traditions of his peculiar craft, this fellow at once sought to learn the cause of the creature's misery, and was fantastically rewarded when he did indeed come upon the truth. It seems, my pretties, that the hapless wretch had just spied an elephant.

TO RETURN, HOWEVER, to the ostensible purpose of these somewhat desultory memoirs, it was, I think, in the eleventh round of our considerably less than Homeric conflict that Mr. Baer, animated by a sudden and rather repulsive vivacity, visited upon your indignant correspondent a succession of blows which left him, for the moment at least, both breathless and passionately disinclined for

further combat. Seeking to avoid young Master B.'s repellent attentions, he sank gently to his haunches, and in that discreet position
became for the first time aware of the remote details of his Gethsemane, and in particular of those legends adorning the atrocious
hoardings which form a sort of idiot palisade about the crest of the
arena. It was with varying emotions that he learnt from them that a
crib blanket called the Snuggle Bunny might be procured right at
our own Best's; that a certain cereal manufacturer, not many miles
away, confects a shattering compound known as Airy Fairy Kwik-
BisKit; and—'clare to goodness—that Arnold Constable is advertising a crêpe-de-Chine undergarment called the Didy Pantie. It was at
this point that your correspondent made up his mind not to get up.

January 5, 1935

TIME . . . FORTUNE . . .
LIFE . . . LUCE

S AD-EYED LAST MONTH was nimble, middle-sized *Life*-President Clair Maxwell as he told newshawks of the sale of the fifty-three-year-old gagmag to *Time*. For celebrated name alone, price: $85,000.

Said he: "*Life* . . . introduced to the world the drawings . . . of such men as Charles Dana Gibson, the verses of . . . James Whitcomb Riley and Oliver Herford, such writers as John Kendrick Bangs. . . . Beginning next month the magazine *Life* will embark on a new venture entirely unrelated to the old."[1]

How unrelated to the world of the Gilson Girl is this new venture might have been gathered at the time from a prospectus issued by enormous, Apollo-faced C. D. Jackson, of Time, Inc.

"*Life*," wrote he, "will show us the Man-of-the-Week . . . his body clothed and, if possible, nude." It will expose "the loves, scandals, and personal affairs of the plain and fancy citizen . . . and write around them a light, good-tempered 'colyumnist' review of these once-private lives."

29,000 die-hard subscribers-to *Life*,★ long accustomed to he-she jokes, many ignorant of King of England's once-private life (*Time*, July 25 *et seq.*), will be comforted for the balance of their subscription periods by familiar, innocent jocosities of *Judge*. First issue of new publication went out last week to 250,000 readers, carried advertisements suggesting an annual revenue of $1,500,000, pictured Russian peasants in the nude, the love life of the Black Widow spider, referred inevitably to Mrs. Ernest Simpson.

Behind this latest, most incomprehensible Timenterprise looms, as usual, ambitious, gimlet-eyed, Baby Tycoon Henry Robinson

---

★Peak of *Life* circulation (1921): 250,000.

Luce, co-founder of *Time*, promulgator of *Fortune*, potent in associated radio & cinema ventures.

"HIGH-BUTTONED . . . BRILLIANT"

Headman Luce was born in Tengchowfu, China, on April 3, 1898,
the son of Henry Winters & Elizabeth Middleton Luce, Presbyterian
missionaries. Very unlike the novels of Pearl Buck were his early
days. Under brows too beetling for a baby, young Luce grew up inside the compound, played with his two sisters, lisped first Chinese,
dreamed much of the Occident. At 14, weary of poverty, already re-
specting wealth & power, he sailed alone for England, entered school
at St. Albans. Restless again, he came to the United States, enrolled
at Hotchkiss, met up & coming young Brooklynite Briton Hadden.
Both even then were troubled with an itch to harass the public. In-
toned Luce years later: "We reached the conclusion that most people
were not well informed & that something should be done. . . ."

First publication to inform fellowman was *Hotchkiss Weekly Record*; next *Yale Daily News*, which they turned into a tabloid; fought
to double hours of military training, fought alumni who wished to
change tune of Yale song from *Die Wacht am Rhein*. Traditionally
unshaven, wearing high-buttoned Brooks jackets, soft white collars, cordovan shoes, no garters, Luce & Hadden were Big Men on
a campus then depleted of other, older Big Men by the war. Luce,
pale, intense, nervous, was Skull & Bones, Alpha Delta Phi, Phi
Beta Kappa, member of the Student Council, editor of the *News*;
wrote sad poems, read the *New Republic*, studied political philosophy. As successful, less earnest, more convivial, Hadden collected
china dogs, made jokes.* In 1920 the senior class voted Hadden
Most Likely to Succeed, Luce Most Brilliant. Most Brilliant he,
Luce sloped off to Christ Church, Oxford, there to study European
conditions, take field trips into the churning Balkans.

---

*Once, watching Luce going past, laden with cares & responsibilities, Hadden
chuckled, upspoke: "Look out, Harry. You'll drop the college."

BEST ADVICE: DON'T

Twenty months after commencement, in the city room of Paperkiller Frank Munsey's *Baltimore News*, met again Luce, Hadden. Newshawks by day, at night they wrangled over policies of the magazine they had been planning since Hotchkiss. Boasted the final prospectus: "*Time* will be free from cheap sensationalism . . . windy bias."

In May, 1922, began the long struggle to raise money to start *Time*, Skeptical at the outset proved Newton D. Baker, Nicholas Murray Butler, Herbert Bayard Swope, William Lyon Phelps. Poohpoohed *Review of Reviews* Owner Charles Lanier: "My best advice . . . don't do it." From studious, pint-sized Henry Seidel Canby, later editor of Lamont-backed *Saturday Review of Literature*, came only encouraging voice in this threnody.

Undismayed Luce & Hadden took the first of many offices in an old brownstone house at 9 East 17th Street, furnished it with a filing cabinet, four second-hand desks, a big brass bowl for cigarette stubs, sought backers.★

★In return for $50 cash, original investors were given two shares 6% Preferred Stock with a par value of $25, one share Class A Common Stock without par value. 3,440 Preferred, 1,720 Class A Common were so sold.

170 shares of Class A Common, 8,000 shares of Class B Common, also without par value, not entitled to dividends until Preferred Shares had been retired, were issued to Briton Hadden, Henry R. Luce, who gave one-third to associates, divided remainder equally.

In 1925, authorized capital of Time, Inc., was increased to 19,000 shares; of which 8,000 were Preferred, 3,000 Class A; as before, 8,000 Class B.

In June, 1930 (if you are still following this), the Preferred Stock was retired in full & dividends were initiated for both Common Stocks. Corporation at this time had 2,400 shares Class A, 7,900 Class B outstanding.

By the spring of 1931 *Time* had begun to march, shares were nominally quoted at $1,000. Best financial minds advised splitting stock on basis of twenty shares for one. Outstanding after clever maneuver: 206,400 shares Common.

In 1933, outlook still gorgeous, each share of stock was reclassified into 1/10th share of $6.50 Dividend Cumulative Convertible Preferred Stock ($6.50 div. cum. con. pfd. stk.) and one share of New Common Stock. New div. cum. con. pfd. stk. was convertible into a share and a half of New Common Stock, then selling around $40 a share, now quoted at over $200.

JP Morganapoleon H. P. Davison, Yale classmate of Luce, Hadden, great & good friend of both, in June contributed $4,000. Next to succumb: Mrs. David S. Ingalls, sister of Classmate William Hale Harkness; amount, $10,000. From Brother Bill, $5,000. Biggest early angel, Mrs. William Hale Harkness, mother of Brother Bill & Mrs. Ingalls, invested $20,000. Other original stockholders: Robert A. Chambers, Ward Cheney, F. Trubee Davison, E. Roland Harriman, Dwight W. Morrow, Harvey S. Firestone, Jr., Seymour H. Knox, William V. Griffin. By November Luce & Hadden had raised $86,000, decided to go to work on fellowman.

"SNAGGLE-TOOTHED . . . PIG-FACED"

Puny in spite of these preparations, prosy in spite of the contributions of Yale poets Archibald MacLeish & John Farrar, was the first issue of *Time* on March 3, 1923. Magazine went to 9,000 subscribers; readers learned that Uncle Joe Cannon had retired at 86, that there was a famine in Russia, that Thornton Wilder friend Tunney had defeated Greb.

Yet to suggest itself as a rational method of communication, of infuriating readers into buying the magazine, was strange inverted Timestyle. It was months before Hadden's impish contempt for his readers,* his impatience with the English language, crystallized into gibberish. By the end of the first year, however, Timeditors were calling people able, potent, nimble; "Tycoon," most successful Timepithet, had been coined by Editor Laird Shields Goldsborough; so fascinated Hadden with "beady-eyed" that for months nobody was

---

Present number of shares outstanding, 238,000; paper value of shares, $47,000,000; conservative estimate of Luce holding, 102,300 shares; paper value, $20,460,000; conservative estimate of Luce income from *Time* stock (shares earned $9.74 in 1935, paid so far in 1936, $6.50; anticipated dividend for full year, $8), $818,400; reported Luce income from other investments, $100,000; reported Luce bagatelle as editor of Time, Inc., $45,000; reported total Lucemolument, $963,400.

Boy!

*Still framed at *Time* is Hadden's scrawled dictum: "Let Subscriber Good-kind mend his ways!"

anything else. Timeworthy were deemed such designations as "Tom-tom" Heflin, "Body-lover" Macfadden.

"Great word! Great word!" would crow Hadden, coming upon "snaggle-toothed," "pig-faced." Appearing already were such mad-dening coagulations as "cinemaddict," "radiator." Appearing also were first gratuitous invasions of privacy. Always mentioned as William Randolph Hearst's "great & good friend" was Cinemac-tress Marion Davies, stressed was the bastardy of Ramsay MacDon-ald, the "cozy hospitality" of Mae West. Backward ran sentences until reeled the mind.

By March, 1924, the circulation had doubled, has risen since then 40,000 a year, reaches now the gratifying peak of 640,000, is still growing. From four meagre pages in first issue, *Time* advertis-ing has now come to eclipse that in *Satevepost*. Published *Time* in first six months of 1936, 1,590 pages; *Satevepost*, 1,480.

NO SLUGABED, HE . . .

Strongly contrasted from the outset of their venture were Hadden, Luce. Hadden, handsome, black-haired, eccentric, irritated his partner by playing baseball with the office boys, by making jokes, by lack of respect for autocratic business. Conformist Luce disap-proved of heavy drinking, played hard, sensible game of tennis, said once: "I have no use for a man who lies in bed after nine o'clock in the morning," walked to work every morning, reproved a writer who asked for a desk for lack of "log-cabin spirit."

In 1925, when *Time* moved its offices to Cleveland, bored, rebel-lious was Editor Hadden; Luce, busy & social, lunched with local bigwigs, addressed Chamber of Commerce, subscribed to Symphony Orchestra, had neat house in the suburbs. Dismayed was Luce when Hadden met him on return from Europe with premature plans to move the magazine back to New York. In 1929, dying of a streptococ-cus infection, Hadden still opposed certain details of success-formula of *Fortune*, new, beloved Lucenterprise.

OATS, HOGS, CHEESE . . .

In January, 1930, first issue of *Fortune* was mailed to 30,000 subscribers, cost as now $1 a copy, contained articles on branch banking, hogs, glassblowing, how to live in Chicago on $25,000 a year. Latest issue (Nov., 1936) went to 130,000 subscribers, contained articles on bacon, tires, the New Deal, weighed as much as a good-sized flounder.★

   Although in 1935 *Fortune* made a net profit of $500,000, vaguely dissatisfied was Editor Luce. Anxious to find & express "the technological significance of industry," he has been handicapped by the fact that his writers are often hostile to Big Business, prone to insert sneers, slithering insults. In an article on Bernard Baruch, the banker was described as calling President Hoover "old cheese-face." Protested Tycoon Baruch that he had said no such thing. Shotup of this was that Luce, embarrassed, printed a retraction; now often removes too-vivid phrasing from writers' copy.

• Typical perhaps of Luce methods is *Fortune* system of getting material. Writers in first draft put down wild gossip, any figures that occur to them. This is sent to victim, who indignantly corrects the errors, inadvertently supplies facts he might otherwise have withheld.

• *March of Time* in approximately its present form was first broadcast on March 6, 1931, paid the Columbia System for privilege, dropped from the air in February, 1932, with Luce attacking radio's "blatant claim to be a medium of education." Said he: "Should *Time* or any other business feel obliged to be the philanthropist of the air to continue to pay for radio advertising it doesn't want in order to provide radio with something worthwhile?" So popular, so valuable to the studio was *March of Time* that it was restored in September of the same year, with Columbia donating its time & facilities. Since then *March of Time* has been sponsored by Remington-Rand typewriter company, by Wrigley's gum, by its own cinema *March of Time*, has made 400

★Two pounds, nine ounces.

broadcasts.* Apparently reconciled to philanthropy is Luce, because time for latest version will be bought & paid for by his organization.
• No active connection now has Luce with the moving-picture edition of *March of Time*, which was first shown on February 1, 1935, appears thirteen times a year in over 6,000 theatres, has so far failed to make money, to repay $900,000 investment. Even less connection has he with *Time's* only other unprofitable venture. Fifty-year-old *Architectural Forum*, acquired in 1932, loses still between $30,000 and $50,000 a year, circulates to 31,000.
• *Letters,* five-cent fortnightly collection of *Time's* correspondence with its indefatigable readers, was started in 1931, goes to 30,000, makes a little money.
• For a time, Luce was on Board of Directors of Paramount Pictures. Hoped to learn something of cinema, heard nothing discussed but banking, resigned sadly.

FASCINATING FACTS . . . DREAMY FIGURES . . .

Net profits of Time, Inc., for the past nine years:

1927	3,860
1928	125,787
1929	325,412
1930	818,936
1931	847,447
1932	613,727†
1933	1,009,628
1934	1,773,094
1935	$2,249,823‡

---

*By some devious necromancy, statisticians have calculated that *March of Time* ranks just behind *Amos & Andy* as most popular of all radio programs; reaches between 8,000,000 and 9,000,000 newshungry addicts.
†Hmm.
‡Exceeded only by Curtis Publishing Co. (*Satevepost*): $5,329,900; Crowell Publishing Co. (*Collier's*) $2,399,600.

In 1935 gross revenue of *Time-Fortune* was $8,621,170, of which the newsmagazine brought in approximately $6,000,000. Outside investments netted $562,295. For rent, salaries, production & distribution, other expenses went $6,594,076. Other deductions: $41,397. Allowance for federal income tax: $298,169.

Time's books, according to Chicago Statisticians Gerwig & Gerwig, show total assets of $6,755,451. Liabilities, $3,101,584. These figures, conventionally allowing $1 for name, prestige of *Time*, come far from reflecting actual prosperity of Luce, his enterprises. Sitting pretty are the boys.

LUCE . . . MARCHES ON!

Transmogrified by this success are the offices, personnel of *Time-Fortune*. Last reliable report: *Time*, 308 employees; *Fortune*, 103; Cinemarch, 58; Radiomarch, 10; *Architectural Forum*, 40; *Life*, 47. In New York; total, 566. In Chicago, mailing, editorial, mechanical employees, 216. Grand total Timemployees on God's earth, 782. Average weekly recompense for informing fellowman, $45.67802.[2]

From first single office, Timen have come to bulge to bursting six floors of spiked, shiny Chrysler Building, occupy 150 rooms, eat daily, many at famed Cloud Club, over 1,000 eggs, 500 cups of coffee, much bicarbonate of soda. Other offices: Cinemarch, 10th Avenue at 54th Street; Radiomarch, Columbia Broadcasting Building.

Ornamented with Yale, Harvard, Princeton diplomas, stuffed fish, terrestrial globes are offices of Luce & other headmen; bleak, uncarpeted the writer's dingy lair.

• Heir apparent to mantle of Luce is dapper, tennis-playing, $35,000-a-year Roy Larsen, nimble in Radio- & Cinemarch, vice-president & second largest stockholder in Time, Inc. Stock income: $120,000.

• Looming behind him is burly, able, tumbledown Yaleman Ralph McAllister Ingersoll, former Fortuneditor, now general manager of all Timenterprises, descendant of 400-famed Ward McAllister. Littered his desk with pills, unguents, Kleenex, Socialite Ingersoll is

Time's No. 1 hypochondriac, introduced ant palaces for study & emulation of employees, writes copious memoranda about filing systems, other trivia, seldom misses a Yale football game. His salary: $30,000; income from stock: $40,000.

• Early in life Timeditor John Stuart Martin lost his left arm in an accident. Unhandicapped he, resentful of sympathy, Martin played par golf at Princeton, is a crack shot with a rifle or shotgun, holds a telephone with no hands, using shoulder & chin, chews paperclips. First cousin of Cofounder Hadden, joined in second marriage to daughter of Cunard Tycoon Sir Ashley Sparks, Timartin is managing editor of newsmagazine, has been nimble in Cinemarch, other Timenterprises, makes $25,000 a year salary, gets from stock $60,000.

• $20,000 salary, $20,000 from stock gets shyest, least-known of all Timeditors, Harvardman John S. Billings, Jr., now under Luce in charge of revamped *Life*, once Washington correspondent for the Brooklyn *Eagle*, once National Affairs Editor for *Time*. Yclept "most important man in shop" by Colleague Martin, Billings, brother of famed muralist Henry Billings, is naïve, solemn, absent-minded, once printed same story twice, wanted to print, as news, story of van Gogh's self-mutilation, drives to office in car with liveried chauffeur, likes Jones Beach.

• Fortuneditor Eric Hodgins is thin-haired, orbicular, no Big Three graduate. Formerly on *Redbook*, boy & girl informing *Youth's Companion*, Hodgins inherited Pill-Swallower Ingersoll's editorial job two years ago when latter was called to greater glory, higher usefulness, still writes much of content of magazine, is paid $15,000; from stock only $8,000.

• Doomed to strict anonymity are *Time-Fortune* staff writers, but generally known in spite of this are former *Times* Bookritic John Chamberlain, Meistersinger Archibald MacLeish. Both out of sympathy with domineering business, both irked by stylistic restrictions, thorns to Luce as well as jewels they. Reward for lack of fame: Chamberlain, $10,000; MacLeish, $15,000; each, two months' vacation.

Brisk beyond belief are carryings-on these days in Luce's chromium tower. *Time*, marching on more militantly than ever, is a shambles on Sundays & Mondays, when week's news is teletyped to Chicago printing plant; *Fortune*, energetic, dignified, its offices smelling comfortably of cookies, is ever astir with such stupefying projects as sending the entire staff to Japan; new whoopsheet *Life* so deep in organization that staff breakfasts are held to choose from 6,000 submitted photographs the Nude of the Week; so harried perpetually all editors that even interoffice memoranda are couched in familiar Timestyle,★ that an appointment to lunch with Editor Luce must be made three weeks in advance.

Caught up also in the whirlwind of progress are *Time, Fortune's* 19 maiden checkers. Bryn Mawr, Wellesley, Vassar graduates they, each is assigned to a staff writer, checks every word he writes, works hard & late, is barred by magazine's anti-feminine policy from editorial advancement.

COLD, BAGGY, TEMPERATE . . .

At work today, Luce is efficient, humorless, revered by colleagues; arrives always at 9:15, leaves at 6, carrying armfuls of work, talks jerkily, carefully, avoiding visitor's eye; stutters in conversation, never in speechmaking. In early days kept standing at Luce desk like butlers were writers while he praised or blamed; now most business is done by time-saving memoranda called "Luce's bulls." Prone he to wave aside pleasantries, social preliminaries, to get at once to the matter in hand. Once to interviewer who said, "I hope I'm not disturbing you," snapped Luce, "Well, you are." To ladies full of gentle misinformation he is brusque, contradictory, hostile; says that his only hobby is "conversing with somebody who knows something," argues still that "names make news," that he would not hesitate to print a scandal involving his best friend.

Because of his Chinese birth, constantly besieged is Luce by visiting Orientals; he is polite, forbearing, seethes secretly. Lunch, usually in a private room at the Cloud Club, is eaten quickly, little attention

---

★Sample Luce memorandum: "Let *Time's* editors next week put thought on the Japanese beetle. H. R. L."

paid to the food, much to business. He drinks not at all at midday, sparingly at all times, takes sometimes champagne at dinner, an occasional cocktail at parties. Embarrassed perhaps by reputation for unusual abstemiousness, he confesses proudly that he smokes too much.

Serious, ambitious Yale standards are still reflected in much of his conduct; in indiscriminate admiration for bustling success, in strong regard for conventional morality, in honest passion for accuracy; physically, in conservative, baggy clothes, white shirts with buttoned-down collars, solid-color ties. A budding joiner, in New York, Luce belongs to the Yale, Coffee House, Racquet & Tennis, Union, & Cloud Clubs; owns a box at the Metropolitan; is listed in *Who's Who & Social Register.*

Colder, more certain, more dignified than in the early days of the magazine, his prose style has grown less ebullient, resembles pontifical *Fortune* rather than chattering *Time.* Before some important body he makes now at least one speech a year, partly as a form of self-discipline, partly because he feels that his position as head of a national institution demands it. His interests wider, he likes to travel, meet & observe the Great. Five or six times in Europe, he has observed many Great & Near Great. Of a twenty-minute conversation with King Edward, then Prince of Wales, says only "Very interesting." Returning from such trips, he always provides staff members with 10 & 12-page memoranda carefully explaining conditions.

Orated recently of conditions in this country: "Without the aristocratic principle no society can endure. . . . What slowly deadened our aristocratic sense was the expanding frontier, but more the expanding machine. . . . But the aristocratic principle persisted in the United States in our fetish of comparative success. . . . We got a plutocracy without any common sense of dignity and obligation. Money became more and more the only mark of success, but still we insisted that the rich man was no better than the poor man—and the rich man accepted the verdict. And so let me make it plain, the triumph of the mass mind is nowhere more apparent than in the frustration of the upper classes." Also remarked in conversation: "Trouble is—great anti-social development— is the automobile trailer. Greatest failure of this country is that it hasn't provided good homes for its people. Trailer shows that."

MILESTONES

Good-naturedly amused by Luce tycoon ambitions was Lila Hotz, of Chicago, whom he married there on Dec. 22, 1923. In 1935, the father of two boys, Luce was divorced by her in Reno on Oct. 5. Married in Old Greenwich, Conn., without attendants, on Nov. 23, 1935, were Luce, Novelist-Playwright Clare Boothe Brokaw, described once by Anglo-aesthete Cecil Beaton as "most drenchingly beautiful," former wife of elderly Pantycoon George Tuttle Brokaw.

Two days before ceremony, "Abide with Me," by new, beautiful Mrs. Luce, was produced at the Ritz Theatre. Play dealt with young woman married to sadistic drunkard, was unfavorably reviewed by all newspaper critics.*

In a quandary was Bridegroom Luce when *Time's* own critic submitted a review suggesting play had some merit. Said he: "Show isn't that good. . . . Go back. . . . Write what you thought." Seven times, however, struggled the writer before achieving an acceptable compromise between criticism, tact.

A MILLION ROOMS, A THOUSAND BATHS . . .

Long accustomed to being entertained, entertaining, is Mrs. Luce, intimate of Mr. & Mrs. A. Coster Schermerhorn, Bernard M. Baruch, Jock Whitney, glistening stage & literary stars. Many were invited last summer to 30-acre estate in Stamford to play tennis, croquet, swim; many more will be when Mrs. Luce has finished her

---

*Of it said Richard Watts, blue-shirted, moon-faced *Tribune* dramappraiser:

"One almost forgave 'Abide with Me' its faults when its lovely playwright, who must have been crouched in the wings for a sprinter's start as the final curtain mercifully descended, heard a cry of 'author,' which was not audible in my vicinity, and arrived onstage to accept the audience's applause just as the actors, who had a head-start on her, were properly lined up and smoothed out to receive their customary adulation."

new play, "The Women,"★ when *Life's* problems, budding policies have been settled by Luce.

Many, too, will come to 7,000-acre, $100,000 Luce plantation, near Charleston, S. C.; will sleep there in four streamlined, prefabricated guest cottages. Given to first Mrs. Luce in divorce settlement, along with $500,000 in cash & securities, was French Manoir at Gladstone, N. J., where Luce once planned to raise Black Angus cows, to become gentleman farmer.

Described too modestly by him to Newyorkereporter as "smallest apartment in River House,"† Luce duplex at 435 East 52nd Street contains 15 rooms, 5 baths, a lavatory; was leased furnished from Mrs. Bodrero Macy for $7,300 annually, contains many valuable French, English, Italian antiques, looks north and east on the river.[3] In décor, Mrs. Luce prefers the modern; evasive is Luce. Says he: "Just like things convenient & sensible." Says also: "Whatever furniture or houses we buy in the future will be my wife's buying, not mine."

WHITHER, WHITHER?

Accused by many of Fascist leanings, of soaring journalistic ambition, much & conflicting is the evidence on Luce political faith, future plans. By tradition a Tory, in 1928 he voted for Alfred E. Smith, in 1932 for Herbert Hoover, this year for Alfred M. Landon. Long at outs with William Randolph Hearst, it was rumored that a visit last spring to California included a truce with ruthless, shifting publisher. Close friend for years of Thomas Lamont, Henry P. Davison, the late Dwight Morrow, it has been hinted that an official connection with the House of Morgan in the future is not impossible. Vehemently denies this Luce, denies any personal political ambition, admits only that he would like eventually to own a daily newspaper in New York.

★Among backers are sad, ramshackle George S. Kaufman, high-domed fur-bearing Moss Hart.

†Smallest apartment in River House has six rooms, one bath.

Most persistent, most fantastic rumor, however, declares that Yale-man Luce already has a wistful eye on the White House. Reported this recently Chicago's *Ringmaster*, added: "A legally-minded friend . . . told him that his Chinese birth made him ineligible. Luce dashed to another lawyer to check. Relief! He was born of American parents and properly registered at the Consulate."

Whatever the facts in that matter, indicative of Luce conscious-ness of budding greatness, of responsibility to whole nation, was his report to *Time's* Board of Directors on March 19, 1936. Declaimed he: "The expansion of your company has brought it to a point be-yond which it will cease to be even a big Small Business and be-come a small Big Business. . . . The problem of public relations also arises. *Time*, the Weekly Newsmagazine, has been, and still is, its own adequate apologist. Ditto, *Fortune*. But with a motion-picture journal, a nightly radio broadcast, and with four magazines, the public interpretation of your company's alleged viewpoint or view-points must be taken with great seriousness." Certainly to be taken with seriousness is Luce at thirty-eight, his fellowman already in-formed up to his ears, the shadow of his enterprises long across the land, his future plans impossible to imagine, staggering to contem-plate. Where it all will end, knows God!

November 28, 1936

FUTURE CONDITIONAL

(*Mr. Noel Coward Carries on During a Period of Considerable Stress*)

I MAGINE THAT there must have been a general feeling that my conduct during the Revolution of 1940 was deplorable. From my point of view, however, it was a period of the most excruciating tedium, and to this day I haven't the slightest idea why social upheaval should invariably be attended by extreme personal inconvenience to those whose interest in it is, to put the thing mildly, academic. I remember that I was at the Ritz with Gertie and Ivor and an odd little object whose name I have utterly forgotten when word came that the crowds had sacked Buckingham Palace. Gertie, of course, gave the sort of polite and negligible squeal which I'm sure she felt was expected of her under the circumstances, and the anonymous little man turned quite beige with terror. I was somewhat startled for an instant myself, until I looked at Ivor and saw that he was shaking with laughter.

"How very trying for the Queen," I said.

"So typical of them to drop in just at lunchtime," he replied.

The whole thing, as a matter of fact, was manifestly absurd, but it was tiresome, too. The night before, I had gone to bed with a slight chill, and in the idle hours between ten and midnight I had written a play. It was called "The Thunderbolt," and in its flamboyant way I thought it was amusing. Both Gertie and Ivor were delighted with it, and Basil[1] planned to start rehearsals at once. The Revolution, however, put that out of the question. In addition to the fact that all the available stagehands in London were far too busy with their preposterous raping and looting to have any time left for anything so humdrum as shifting scenery, it was almost impossible to find a theatre that might not be blown up at any moment. Gertie was quite definite about refusing to run the risk of a degrading liaison with a bomb.

"It's always so desperately untidy, darling," she said.

And I could see myself that it would be a nuisance to have my most passionate embraces embalmed forever in falling plaster. Mother, of course, was perfectly splendid about everything, and wanted to scamper directly off to the Communist headquarters and put a stop to all this nonsense once and for all.

"Just you let me talk to them, Noel," she said.

I am perfectly sure that the dear old creature would indeed have gone to call upon the agitators, and it is by no means impossible that she would have put down the Revolution single-handed. There was also the possibility, however, that they might have paid the final abashed tribute to superior eloquence and cut off her head. We decided to wait a little while, at least until the first rapturous novelty of mass homicide had worn off.

AT LAST THINGS quieted down to a certain extent, and on December 16th, 1940, Gertie and I opened in "The Thunderbolt." It was, I suppose, a fairly macabre little piece—the whole thing took place over a weekend at a smart English houseparty; Gertie played the part of a gay young countess, with suggested overtones of drugs and nymphomania; I was her lover and at the same time the husband of a wealthy and far too durable old horror called Lady Pigeon. In the end, and in a deliberately understated scene, it became advisable for us to cut Lady Pigeon up into quite small pieces, stuff her in a trunk, and ship her off on a goods train. It was my intention, of course, to accentuate a basically horrible situation by superimposing upon it urbane and witty dialogue. Thus, for instance, while we were happily dismantling Lady Pigeon, Gertie said, "Of course, you know that all this is frightfully ungallant of you, don't you, darling?" And I replied that after all I'd always understood that an Englishman's home was his abattoir. I realize now that we may not have chosen precisely the most tactful time for this pleasing confection, since it represented a point of view no longer altogether fashionable. I had, however, no idea of what actually was in store for us.

Gertie opened the first scene beautifully, although I have never been convinced that the best way to suggest morphine addiction is to hop up and down as though one were infested with mice. However, she was playing well within herself and when, on my wife's first entrance, she turned and said to me, "What, isn't the old bitch dead yet?" I naturally expected the audience to laugh. However, there wasn't a sound, and a little later, when I had to say that the only reason I didn't go to work was that I didn't want to take the caviar out of some poor man's mouth—certainly one of the most amusing lines in the play—there was a noticeable commotion in the gallery. It was utterly ghastly, and the second act was even worse. I seemed to be the special object of their displeasure, and there were boos and catcalls every time I opened my mouth.

The thing culminated grotesquely in the third act. For some time rustic humorists had been throwing pennies and dubious vegetable matter on the stage, and we had managed to disregard them. Finally, however, there was a loud, metallic crash and a small hand grenade bounced across the stage and stopped directly at my feet. With singular presence of mind, I picked it up, tossed it into the trunk (which already contained the hypothetical residue of Lady Pigeon), and slammed the lid. There was a vehement explosion, filling the stage with small pieces of trunk, papier-mâché pieces of Lady Pigeon, and an excessively dismal smell, but fortunately nobody was hurt. In the face of such petulant criticism as this, however, it seemed unwise to continue the performance and I rang down the curtain.

Later, in a short curtain speech, I was able to thank the audience for one of the pleasantest evenings of my life, and although there was certainly no reason to suppose that they were susceptible to irony, it was a satisfaction. I needed satisfaction because my play was assuredly one of the most agonizing failures in the history of the English stage, and I knew it would take me at least a week to finish another.

May 8, 1937

SHAKESPEARE, HERE'S YOUR HAT[1]

(A New Play by Mr. William Saroyan, in Book Form,
With the Customary Prefatory Notes by the Author)

T HIS PLAY IS a masterpiece. It is young, gusty, comical, tragic, beautiful, heroic, and as real as a slaughterhouse or some dame fixing her hair. It could only have been written in America, by an Armenian boy who is an artist and a lover and a dreamer. All at once. All mixed up. It could only have been written by Saroyan.

Other people write plays, but they are no good. I go to them and I sit there and think, "My God, this is lousy! It was written by a man in an English suit of clothes who makes fifty thousand dollars a year, but it is not alive. It is dead. It stinks." A man making fifty thousand dollars a year doesn't write about Life; he writes about other people who make fifty thousand dollars a year; he writes about a bunch of rich corpses and, generally speaking, he is a rich corpse himself. Not me, though. Not Saroyan. This play is lyric and simple and alive. It says just exactly what it means. When the boy in this play dynamites his grandmother because he needs some money to get gin, that is something real. When he puts a nickel in the piano for music, that is real, too. When he meets the society girl and says "How's chances, sister?" and she answers "O.K., Mac," that is a real, lovely, and heart-breaking thing.

In the plays about the rich corpses, it takes three acts and about sixty thousand dollars' worth of scenery to get around to a beautiful and natural request like that, and half the time nothing comes of it, either.

II

I am a warm, rich, and passionate human being and very few things are too much for me. Not even dramatic criticism. When a man writes in a newspaper or a magazine that he doesn't understand this play or is bored by it, that is all right with me. It is hard to imagine anybody not liking something that is as eloquent and native and true as a child running after a butterfly or a colored man scratching himself, but I do not get sore. I am just sorry for the crazy bastard.

III

The following are excerpts from some of the reviews published in the New York press:

RICHARD WATTS, JR., *Herald Tribune:* It is a darling play . . . but we must not ignore the Chinese.

BROOKS ATKINSON, *Times:* Lit with the same ineluctable fire that once informed the witches and the cauldron on the heath.

JOHN MASON BROWN, *Post:* Challenges the best of Aristophanes, Gogol, Pirandello, Racine, and the Song of Solomon.

SIDNEY B. WHIPPLE, *World-Telegram:* Either Saroyan is crazy . . . or I am. A child has done this horrid thing.

IV

This play was written in an hour and a half with a quill pen I generally keep in a little bowl of bird shot. For a man like me, an original, talented, profound, sensitive, and humorous Armenian, a typewriter is an artificial barrier standing between the living brain and the clean paper. It is not for me, as the airbrush was not for Michelangelo and the adding machine was not for Euclid.

At that time I was working in Hollywood, where all authors use typewriters. "The greatest play in the world is right there on those keys, if you can only figure out how to hit them in the right order," one of them said to me. He was a man who made forty, fifty, a hundred thousand dollars a year, and he went around with a falcon on his wrist. I would rather use the quill pen. Me, personally.

V

Generally speaking, the American theatre is the aspirin of the middle classes. People go to a play because they want to get in out of the rain. Or because they have a date with some rabbit in it later on. Or just because they happen to know the press agent and don't have to pay. It is not that way with me. I go because I love Life. That is an important statement and I want to repeat it: *William Saroyan loves Life.*

In the theatre today, except in this play of mine, what you see is not Life. It is a drawing-room compromise with Life arrived at by a man who has never had to sleep in a silo or eat birch bark or trap mice to make himself a hat or any of the other brave, haunting, and sometimes foolish things people do when they don't happen to have been born on Park Avenue or in Newport, Rhode Island.

The cure for the American theatre is more plays like this one. More plays by Saroyan.

THE TIME OF *WHOSE* LIFE?

(*A dormitory at Groton, just before vespers. Three of the boys—Jones Minor, Ferris Major, and Tilden Elliott III—are changing from their rugger togs into their vespers togs. They are breathless and wondering, enchanted with a sweet world that also holds things like ginger beer and scones and "Esquire" magazine. Ferguson Nicholson, the housemaster, a tall, thin man, noble because of the pain in his heart, is sitting in one corner, reading "Variety" and drinking a dry Martini. In another corner an old graduate, mad and very dirty, is throwing cards into a hat. A scrubwoman comes in. A lifetime of toil, including six years with the Shuberts, has not quenched her brimming and precious spirit.*)

SCRUBWOMAN (*compassionate, supernatural; the Earth Mother*): How about sweeping up around here, gents? Get some of the fug out of the joint.

JONES MINOR: Sweep. You won't sweep the torture and despair of Life from the heart with a broom. . . .

FERRIS MAJOR: Or the beauty of it either.

OLD GRADUATE (*Lost in his eternal dream of the past*): Dissolute and damned. Both the student body and the faculty.

HOUSEMASTER: Elliott.

ELLIOTT: Yes, sir?

HOUSEMASTER: Go down to the Greek's and get me two ham sandwiches and a billiard ball.

ELLIOTT (*uneasily*): What for?

HOUSEMASTER (*watching the scrubwoman; fascinated by the unique, all-female, and mysterious experiences once enjoyed somewhere in the world by this scrubwoman*): Ham on white. British mustard.

ELLIOTT (*still puzzled, but going out dutifully*): A cue ball?

HOUSEMASTER: No, the red one. (*To the scrubwoman; waving the cocktail-shaker*) Martini?

SCRUBWOMAN: No thanks, pal. The Head don't like us to drink on duty.

HOUSEMASTER: You're missing a lot. *I'm* always drunk. The days and nights are whittling me away, and—(*He breaks off as the Headmaster, a quiet, grave man, carrying a bridle, comes into the cubicle.*) Were you looking for something, sir?

HEADMASTER (*genially*): Ah, Nicholson. Fried again, I see. (*With a change of mood, sternly*) Ferris Major!

FERRIS MAJOR (*springing up, dynamic, translated*): Sir?

HEADMASTER: Is there a polo pony in this room?

FERRIS MAJOR: A what, sir?

HEADMASTER (*going to a closet, opening it, and discovering a polo pony*): As I thought. You know the rules, I believe, Ferris. No polo ponies or young women in dorm after four o'clock.

FERRIS MAJOR (*in a low voice, accepting his doom*): Yes, sir.

HEADMASTER: This means a birching, of course. (*He goes out, leading the polo pony; fatal, inexorable, the Scourge of God.*)

OLD GRADUATE (*throwing the ace of spades at the hat*): Dissolute and damned. Both the student body and the faculty.

HOUSEMASTER (*still preoccupied by the scrubwoman; the strange, illicit, bygone adventures of the scrubwoman*): I drink to your unconquerable spirit, Mrs. Le Bogan.

SCRUBWOMAN: My name ain't Mrs. Le Bogan.

HOUSEMASTER: Then Guinevere or Héloïse. In any case, I drink. To your ancient sins, Faustine.

SCRUBWOMAN: Listen, what the hell you talking about?

HOUSEMASTER (*wearily*): I don't know. What do any of us talk about? Love. Happiness. Towering injustice everywhere. The game with St. Paul's. (*Furiously, draining the Martini*) How the hell do I know? What do *you* talk about?

SCRUBWOMAN (*sly, roguish, Salome, old but not regenerate*): Jeez, I dunno, Mister. Harry K. Thaw. The time we burned up the city of Chicago. Shooting Garfield. All like that.

HOUSEMASTER: Life! The terror and the wonder and the beauty of it. (*Gathering momentum*) Life! *Life!* LIFE!

(*As he goes on, Elliott reënters with the sandwiches and the billiard ball; the scrubwoman wrings out her mop and starts to wipe up the floor; the old graduate opens another pack of cards and begins throwing them at the hat; Jones Minor and Ferris Major gather up their hymnals and prayer books; the polo pony trots in through the door and back into the closet. Life has come full circle.*)

OLD GRADUATE (*sombre, triumphant; his opinion of everything borne out*): Dissolute and damned. Both the student body and the faculty.

(*From the courtyard the bell for vespers sounds, very wonderful and sad. The curtain falls.*)

January 13, 1940

SHAD AMPERSAND

A Novel of Time and the Writer, Tentatively Based on
"Cass Timberlane, a Novel of Husbands and Wives"

CHAPTER I

The city of Grand Revenant, in High Hope County and the sovereign state of Nostalgia, has a population of 34,567, according to the official census taker, a vast and bumbling liar, receiver of puny bribes and secret high acolyte of the poems of Algernon Charles Swinburne.

Grand Revenant is 49.6 miles from Zenith and 99.2 from Gopher Prairie.

It was founded in 1903, a year that also saw the birth, at Kitty Hawk, N.C., of a strange, boxlike contrivance that held the bright seeds of death for Coventry and Nagasaki and other proud cities, half the world away.

Its pioneer settler was old Cornelius Ampersand, a prodigious seducer of Indians along the thundering marge of Lake Prolix and on the cold, improbable trails that lead from Baedeker and Larousse to Mount Thesaurus. Corn was a He-Man, a Wowser, a High Anointed Member of the Sacred and Splendiferous Tribe of Good Scouts, and if his thin, despairing wife often wept alone in the night, nobody knew—except perhaps her two or three hundred closest friends.

In the years since old Corn raped his last squaw (and how those golden girls would giggle in the dusk!), Grand Revenant had grown like an angry weed in the fertile soil of the prairie.

Factories came—Wilson & Fadiman, who ravaged the little, firm-breasted hills for copper for moot points; Trilling & Cowley, who made the smoothest, shiniest, most astoundingly complicated little instruments for determining tension and slack (it was hard to say what everybody did before it was possible to determine slack to one-ten-thousandth part of an inch); Mencken & Nathan, who manufactured Hortex and were said to have the seventh largest mangle in the state of Nostalgia.

Stores were born—the Mad Mode Mart, Avis Cormorant, prop. (Miss Cormorant was a nymphomaniac and, very discreetly, a German spy, but her chic was the despair of her rival, Elsie Drear, who was a virgin and an Episcopalian); Blitberg's Department Store (*"Nous l' Avons!"*), which sold everything from needles to yachts, and if one or two salesgirls died each week from a strange and terrible disease called Dreiser's Botch, there was surely no kinder or merrier man in all Revenant than old Sam Blitberg; Dirge & Mouseman (Mrs. Mouseman, née Birdie Jump, was that object of almost inconceivable grandeur, a former inmate of the *Social Register*), where you could buy, for very little more than it would cost to build supernal beauty or to stamp out Yaws, rare stones of devious and bloody history.

Other noble monuments—the Revenant Museum of Art, which boasted a Modigliani and a Dali and a whole roomful of Grant Woods, but which was chiefly notable for its swimming pool which was as deep and blue as a lake; Revenant Junior High School, which regularly and gratifyingly beat the upstart team from East Hemingway in the annual marathon, and if very few of her graduates could tell you who wrote "Thanatopsis" or even "Mantrap," they usually proved astonishingly nimble at selling not too aqueous real estate and beautifully shiny automobiles, which often ran quite well; and, always and most particularly, Mme. Moriarity's bowling parlors, where the nickering males of Revenant betook themselves for curious delights, which sometimes they even actually enjoyed.

Churches sprang up, to the glory of a Fat God, whose other names were Baal and Moloch and Ahriman and Samael and Progress and Rugged Individualism.

Hotels and restaurants—the Revenant Inn, which travellers had been known to compare favorably with the glittering Bellevue-Stratford in Philadelphia, but at which there was no room for the Indians whose doomed campfires had once glowed where now its flying towers mocked the sky; Doug's Hotburger, where the cop on the beat, a cold and melancholy man, dropped in nightly to sigh: "Geez, you take my wife. A good woman, I guess, but no get-up-and-go to her like some of these peppy society dames. And *talk!* Golly! One of these days maybe I'll have to shut the ole girl up." At six o'clock one bitter January morning, he did, very neatly and irrevocably, using the old .44 service revolver with which he had sworn to uphold the law; the Heyday Grille, where Doc Kennicott and George Babbitt and Sam Dodsworth and all the glorious he-male company of competent seducers (about once a year, Babbitt conducted a fumbling, inconclusive experiment with some derisive young woman in a canoe) and two-fisted drinkers (sometimes, uneasily, they had a cocktail before lunch) met every Friday to bumble cheerfully: "Well, I dunno what you other, uh, homo sapiensi-buses think, but it strikes this not-so-humble observer that this lil ole burg is sure goin' straight to the twenty-three skiddoos." Solemnly, they agreed that Grand Revenant could not compare in splendor with Zenith and Gopher Prairie and Paris and New York; secretly, they knew that she was strange and beautiful beyond all the other cities of the earth.

CHAPTER II

Shad Ampersand, old Corn's grandson lived in a neat $26,500 bungalow called Christmas Past, on Revenant Heights, overlooking the brisk, aspiring town. He was a tall, ramshackle hayrick of a man of fifty-six, copper red (a testimony, it was whispered, to old Corn's prowess with the squaws) and sad of eye, like a water spaniel or an early Donatello. An admirer of loneliness and rye whiskey and thin, hawk-vivid girls, who listened with vast politeness while he explained such recondite matters as Arbitrary Microcosm, Limited Frame of Reference, Elementary Symbolism, and Dated or Synthetic Idiom, about all of which they knew precisely nothing and most enthusiastically cared even less.

Sitting on his tiny porch on one of the brightest, briefest, and most poignant of all October afternoons, Shad was very weightily considering the profound mystery of Sex.

"I'm not one of these highbrow geezers like W. Somerset Maugham or John Q. Galsworthy," he plondered heavily, "and it sure gives me a pain in the ole bazookus to hear some long-haired so-called intellectual claiming that love and marriage and kiddies and everything a dumb ole roughneck like me has come to hold most sacred is nothing more nor less than something called the Biological Urge."

"Hey, you don't have to talk to *me* like that," said Trenda Boneside sharply. "I'm not the Pulitzer Prize Committee."

She was a small, fierce kitten of a girl, who had lived for nineteen eager, sniffing years with her parents on a farm in Remnant, just across the state line.

"M? Nope. See what you mean," he said placatingly. She was a passionate white flame on a cigar-store lighter. He tried to imagine her cooking his breakfast. Tried and most conspicuously failed.

"No, you don't at all," she snapped at him, this brisk fox terrier of a girl. "You listen to me, Shad Ampersand. I'm not one of those old girls of yours—Carol or Leora or that awful Dodsworth woman, whatever *her* name was."

"Fran," he said humbly.

"Fran. Well, anyway, I'm not. Maybe that old hillbilly talk was all right for them, and even the *American Mercury*. But with me you can just talk like anybody else."

"M."

"That's another thing!" she cried furiously. "That 'M'! What the hell is that supposed to be? The name of a moving picture?"

"Gee, Tren," he sighed. "It's only an experiment in phonetics. You know, how to get something down the way it really sounds. As I was telling ole Doc Bongflap . . ."

Now she was really a tigress.

"'Bongflap,'" she wailed. "I've known you for a long time, Shad Ampersand, and I've certainly heard some terrible names—Vergil Gunch and Roscoe Geake and Adelbert Shoop—but that's the worst ever. Nobody in the world was ever called Bongflap."

"Well, maybe not, but, drat it, when an author wants to suggest how a character . . ."

"I know all about that," she said, "and I know all about Charles

Dickens, too, and you both make me sick. My God, even *Tarkington* wouldn't call anybody Bongflap. Or Timberlane, either, for that matter. Timber*lane*. Timber*line*. Even Hansen and Chamberlain ought to be able to get that one, but I think it stinks. I keep thinking it's Tamberlane or Timberleg."

"Aren't we getting a little off the subject, Tren?" he said mildly.

"I don't know. What *was* the subject?"

"Well, uh, love."

"Oh, *that*," she yawned. "What about it?"

"Well, uh," he fumbled. She was a laughing brook of a girl, cool, diamond-bright, a wanderer in secret loveliness. He dreamed of her in a gingham apron, cooking his breakfast. Golly! "Uh, I thought we might get married," he whinnied. It was so perhaps that Paris whispered to Helen before they came to the City of the Topless Towers, so the Roman gave his soul to Egypt's queen on the dreaming bosom of the Nile. She looked at him and suddenly her heart was in her eyes.

"Shad!" she cried, and now she was a bell.

"Wife!" he clamored through their urgent kiss, and miraculously it was a word in nowise stained with use.

CHAPTER III

The little orange cat called Pox stretched languorously in Shad Ampersand's lap.

"I know you're lonely since your wife, Trenda, left you last November to join Blight Grimes, the polo player and nimble seducer, at his hotel in Chicago, Illinois," she mewed. She was a very fetching device of a cat, an explanatory butler at curtain rise in a Lonsdale comedy.

Shad scratched her ears and thought: I should have known all along about Tren and Blight. The time they went away together for a week back in March and Trenda said—oh, she was very innocent and airy about it!—that they'd just gone up to Alaska to look at polo ponies; the time I found them upstairs in bed and they said they were just lying down because their feet hurt. I must have been pretty credulous, he decided, and Pox blinked her copper eyes in sardonic agreement.

"You're damn right," she purred, "but now, of course, she has delirium tremens and this Grimes character isn't exactly the kind of man you can picture running up and down stairs with paraldehyde and strait jackets. There's a strange streak of cruelty in him."

He nodded, but he was thinking despairingly: I must have failed her somehow. Maybe I was wrong to want to keep her here in Christmas Past pasting up scrapbooks for an old galoot like me— Blight, doggone his hide, was only forty-nine and lithe and puissant as a sword—when she ought to be running around with kids her own age, going to the movies and coming out with her head all full of stars and dreams (as a matter of fact, he knew she loathed the movies), having a soda with the Gang at Bleeck's and feeding nickels into the juke box for "Smiles" and "Margie," maybe even being kissed, in sweet and childish innocence, in the back seat of a Chevrolet.

"Pope Hartford," said Pox, who was also a mind-reader.

"M?"

"Pope Hartford," repeated the cat irritably. "You might as well stick to the period. And while I think of it, you can lay off that 'M' with me, too."

Anyway, he had failed her, his lost and golden girl, and she was in Chicago with Blight. He looked at his watch. 11:46. Probably they were back from the theatre now and up in their suite and Blight was slipping the little silver-fox cape from her shoulders.

"His heart contracted," murmured Pox.

"M, uh, I mean what?"

"Don't keep making me say everything twice for God's sake. 'His heart contracted.' That goes in there somewhere. In parentheses. After the second 'and,' I should say. It's one of your mannerisms, though not a very fortunate one. Also, you seem to have forgotten that she's on the sauce, if you'll pardon the expression."

Trenda spifflicated, swizzled, tiddly. He knew it was the truth, but the thought was a sharp agony, an unthinkable desecration, as if he saw the slender, terrible beauty of the Samothrace deep in foul mud and marred with the droppings of obscene and dreadful birds.

"I think you're overreaching yourself there," said Pox. "Too many modifiers, and it's a pretty elaborate image. After all, you aren't Henry James."

"Golly, Pox—"

"Ah, the hell with it. Let it go. It's your stream of consciousness, thank God, not mine."

In his despair, his cold, unutterable loss, Shad Ampersand began to think of all the world, and Pox looked at him sharply for a moment and then hopped off his lap and left the room. Shad thought: Marriage. A man and a woman—him and Tren, Romeo and Juliet, Philemon and Baucis, Ruth and, and, drat it, who *was* that guy—anyway, they fell in love—oh, Tren, sweet, we *must* have been in love the night we read "Gideon Planish" until the stars went out!—and they promised to love, honor, and obey—golly, the most beautiful words in the English language, except, of course, maybe some parts of Shakespeare—till death you did part. But then something happened. One day they woke up and the magic was gone. (He and Tren were having breakfast, Homogenized Virtex and Spookies, and suddenly, appallingly, she cried, "Shad! I'm going away with Blight! Right this minute! He's going to take me to London, Paris, Berlin—Gee, I've always wanted to see the Taj Mahal and all those cute little Androgynes or whatever you call 'em—and we're going to take along a sleeping bag, you know, like in that book I read some of, and camp right out on the biggest darn ole Alp we can find." He had burbled, "Gee, that sounds mighty interesting, Tren. Yes, sir. Like to take a little trip sometime myself," but the Spookies were ashes in his mouth.) Anyway, it always ended—either in the hideous, clinging slime of the divorce court, or else—and this was unutterably worse—in the terrible, icy vacuum of indifference, the final, shameful acceptance of infidelity. ("You ought to get yourself a girl, Shad," she had told him one night; as usual, she was sitting on Blight's lap, knitting a newfangled sock. "Why don't you call up Avis Cormorant? *There*'s a cheerful little giver for you. Or maybe one of those Piutes you say old Corn was always talking about." He had almost struck her then.) It was this, this modern cynicism, this flat denial of marriage, not the Communists or the Fascists or the Technocrats or even the hot-eyed disciples of Fourier and Adam Smith, that was destroying America.

In the ultimate scheme of things, the continuing marriage of Tren and Shad Ampersand, or, if you chose, of plain Helen and Robert Lynd, was more important than—

"Hey," said Pox, putting his head around the door, "I wouldn't disturb you, except you didn't seem to be getting anywhere in particular with that editorial. Anyway, she's back."

"Who?" spurted Shad, though his heart obliteratingly knew.

"Who the hell did you think?" said Pox scornfully. "Little Round Heels. With a hangover I could swing on by my tail."

She came in then, with a glad, unsteady rush, a broken cry, into his waiting arms, and if she was damaged, if she was no longer the bright, imperious child his dreams had known, but something harder, wiser, and infinitely sad, he had no eyes to see.

"Tren, baby!" he whispered fiercely in her hair.

"Shad!" she breathed, and gave him the ruined glory of her smile. After all, she thought, stroking the remembered kindness of his cheek, you always have to figure that the old skeezix is practically indestructible, there ought to be plenty of books still batting around in him for all the endless years to come.

"Nice going, sister," murmured Pox, and most discreetly shut the door.

October 27, 1945

TO A LITTLE GIRL AT CHRISTMAS[1]

*(How a Famous Question Might Be Answered if It Were Asked Today and
Mr. Westbrook Pegler Happened to Be Writing Editorials for the "Sun")*

YOU'RE DAMN RIGHT there is a Santa Claus, Virginia. He lives down the road a piece from me, and my name for him is Comrade Jelly Belly, after a poem composed about him once by an admiring fellow-traveller now happily under the sod.

In a manner of speaking, this Jelly Belly is in the distributing end of the toy business, and I guess the story of how that came about has its points for the social historian. Mr. Claus is understandably a reticent man, but the facts would seem to be that he was born quite a while back in the Red Hook section under the appetizing monicker of Sammy Klein. His mother was employed in a celebrated bucket of blood known as the Haymarket, also in what you might call the distributing end, and his father was any one of a number of slick operators, though the weight of evidence would seem to point to Police Lieutenant Becker of fragrant memory. How his mother happened to name him Sammy Klein is not known to this deponent, but there is a suspicion that she got it off the front of a clothing store she was in the habit of looting. It is not my way to speak ill of the dead, Virginia, but you'd have to go a long way to find a scurvier pair than the two who spawned the tot we're discussing.

In his youth, Jelly Belly did a short stretch of military service with the Hudson Dusters and the Dead Rabbits, two pinko front organizations of the period, and then passed on to the less perilous profession of rolling lushes in the subway. According to surviving court records, an operative in this classification, variously known as Sid Kline, Saul ("Fingers") Klem, and K. Stein, was arrested no less than thirty-seven times between 1908 and 1916, and stored in the poky for periods ranging from ninety days up. This was presumably Santa Claus.

So much, Virginia, for our hero's boyhood. In 1917, as you probably remember, a sick college professor in the White House ranted us into what he called a war to make the world safe for democracy, and Jelly Belly had one of the first numbers they pulled out of the bowl. This, however, was one rap he knew how to beat, and young Klein sat out World War I in a hospital for the criminally insane, having prudently assaulted a six-year-old girl on the very day his draft board invited him to call. He was pardoned in 1919 at the special request of the Assistant Secretary of the Navy, whose name happened to be Franklin Delano Roosevelt, and who even then displayed a strong affinity for the unbalanced.

It was at this time that Jelly Belly changed his name to Santa Claus, partly to escape from his too vivacious past and partly because he had just become a full member of the Communist Party and needed an alias with a sanctimonious flavor. His affiliation with the toy business began soon after that. When F.D.R. sprung Jelly Belly, or Santa Claus, from the loonybin, he went to work for the New York *Times* as a bushwhacker in the circulation department, his job being to mess up delivery boys from the rival *Herald*. This was naturally an employment highly to his taste, but when one boy died as the result of his attentions, it seemed sagacious to move on. It was in this manner that he came to F. A. O. Schwarz, where they made him first a shipping clerk and then the driver of a truck. The rest of the story—the prearranged hijackings that proved profitable enough to set Santa Claus up in the toy business for himself, the deals with Henry Agard Wallace, Felix Frankfurter, and his old friend Roosevelt that permitted him to pick the taxpayer's pocket to the tune of about eighty million dollars a year—is too complicated and dirty for a lady of your tender years. The important fact is that there *is* a Santa Claus, Virginia—a fat old party, with nasty habits and a dirty white beard, who, for reasons best known to himself, likes to go around either wholly undressed or else in an ill-fitting red suit.

TODAY, JELLY BELLY enjoys what is sometimes called the odor of sanctity, being generally regarded as a hell of a fellow by little children, soft-headed women, and the kind of deep thinkers who openly profess their opposition to the sterilization of all Communists. My own information is somewhat different. Jelly Belly gets around even more than Eleanor the Great, and I can't speak for his activities in other parts of the country. In my neighborhood, however, it is a matter of common knowledge that the burglary rate never fails to hit its peak at Christmas. No one has ever been caught for any of these misdemeanors, but the evidence in each case is always the same—a few shoddy toys in a stocking on the mantelpiece, and a mink coat or a pearl necklace missing from the hostess's effects. One victim I know said she wouldn't mind so much if the toys were any good, but they are just the cheap, tasteless junk that crooked labor unions have been turning out ever since the Great Brain decided to sell out his country to the lazy and incompetent.

I could go on for a long time telling you about Jelly Belly, Virginia. I could tell you, for instance, how the gross old slattern who passes herself off as his housekeeper would be described in less respectable pages than these by quite another word. Or I could tell you how he is a member of the Westchester Commuters Association, the National Association of Dahlia Growers, the Society for Improving the Condition of the Poor, and any number of other thinly disguised Communist organizations. Or I could even tell you with what drooling pleasure he beats his eight undersized reindeer, whose cruel whip sores I have seen with my own eyes. But these are probably not good things for a little girl to know. Youth is a time for innocent dreams and illusions, Virginia, and I don't believe I could live comfortably with myself if I destroyed yours. Yes, Virginia, there is a Santa Claus. There is old Jelly Belly.

December 24, 1949

Some Troubles I've Seen

Casuals

STORY OF THE BIBLE IN TABLOID[1]

"Pastors will do well to watch the methods of the newspapers."
—*RELIGIOUS MAGAZINE.*

THE NEXT THING, we assume, is a new edition of the Bible with headings and blurbs as follows:

CHASED FROM LOVE-NEST
"She Tempted Me!" Cries Adam, Blaming Beautiful
Snake-Charmer

BRUTAL AXE MURDER
Fiend Amuck in Nod—Victim's Brother Missing

FLOOD
World Inundated Last Night, Says Wireless From Noah's Ark

LOTTA PEP—This photograph of a salt statue of a woman was discovered by refugees on the plains of Sodom. Did last week's holocaust cause it? See J. B. Lot's story on page 3.

TRIED TO STAB OWN SON, SAY POLICE
Alienists Lay Old Man's Attempted Sacrifice of Kiddie to
Religious Mania

ROW OVER WILL
Esau Tells Court Brother Gypped Him Out
of Dad's Blessing—"Applesauce!" Counters Jacob. "He Sold
It For a Stew."

KISS IN A BEDROOM?
Potiphar Has Boy Seer Held on Wife's Complaint—
"Jilted Her" Joe's Alibi

BOY IN BULLRUSHES
Adoption Hinted for Waif Found by Beauty, She Says,
on Way to Bathing Beach

JEWS PERSECUTED
Threaten Reprisals If Pharaoh Camp, K. K. K.,
Keeps Up Lynchings

MY AMAZING ADVENTURES IN SEARCH OF THE PROMISED LAND
Revealed by the Famous Gang-Leader, Moses, Who Tells for
the First Time the Inside Story of the Servitude, Getaway and
Wanderings of the Famous Israelite Cult, Together With
Secrets of the Red Sea Disaster, Wilderness Manna and Other
Miracles, and the Truth About the Ten Commandments.

MOTHER-IN-LAW HER CUPID
Engagement Announced of Boaz, Big Butter and Egg Man,
and Girl He Met in Cornfield

ROOFTOP ROMANCE OF THE KING AND BATHING BEAUTY
How Her Little Dip Charmed Royalty's Roving Eye and
Made Her a Merry Widow, as Told by the Fascinating Bath-
sheba, Uriah's Ex-Mate and, Rumor Says, David's Next.

WEDS 700TH WIFE
Famous Songwriter and Wisecracker Jilts Mrs. Sheba for
Cabaret Cutie

These samples have but scratched the surface of the Scrip-
tures. Imagine what a live newspaper could do with the New
Testament!

February 13, 1926

ON WORKING THAT LINE
INTO THE CONVERSATION

A T THE MOMENT I was pretty sick of listening to Anne discuss what is known to her as her vermifuge appendix, so I was reading the car cards. Just across from where we sat was one advertising a drink alleged to be both non-alcoholic and refreshing.

"I'll bet," I said, pointing to it, "that that's neither beer nor there."

"Really?" she said vaguely and continued a surgical reminiscence not in the best possible taste.

Anyway there isn't much use talking to Anne, whose idea of humor ranges from something that takes place in a Turkish Bath to a good forty-foot massacre. I decided to save it for the party.

We arrived and I found I was taking Mrs. Windle in to dinner. There was wine and I saw my chance.

"Wouldn't it be nice," I said, "if they could have got a couple of kegs of beer instead of this lousy dago red? The only trouble is the beer you get nowadays is neither . . ."

I became aware that Mrs. Windle was talking to someone else but I wasn't discouraged.

The conversation turned to books and someone made a comparison between Ernest Hemingway and Tom Beer. Instantly I darted into the breach.

"In other words," I said, "Hemingway is neither Beer . . ."

"Nor anybody else," finished the girl with the teeth. "He's an artist in his own right."

I was checked but not routed. Once more I sat back in ambush for my opportunity. Time and again I thought I had it only to be cheated by some idiotic detour. I decided to take the thing into my own hands. With infinite subtlety I led the conversation round to prohibition. At last my opening came.

"For my part," said the girl with the teeth, "I think we ought to have light wine and beer. What do you think about beer, Mr. Gibbs?"

They'd fallen into the trap. I had them.

"Well . . ." I think I permitted myself a chuckle, "I'm afraid that most of it's neither *here nor there*."

There was a silence. I saw Anne's fingers tighten lovingly around a carafe. Suddenly I *knew!* In a daze I rushed from the room, from the house. Two weeks later they found me upside down in a snowdrift.

February 25, 1928

THE MAN AND THE MYTH

SANTA CLAUS WAS born in Latvia on May 8, 1831. As far as we can learn from history there was nothing particularly remarkable in the circumstances surrounding his birth. His parents were poor peasants, eking out a miserable existence by growing eggplants in the thin Latvian soil. Some authorities, of course, contend that the mother was in reality a duchess of the royal blood who had been abducted by wolves a few hours after her birth and then left on a mountain side by the languid animals. Apparently, however, there is nothing to substantiate this theory; my own research indicates that it was just made up out of whole cloth by a neurotic woman tired to death of putting eggplant seeds in holes.

The Clauses were damn poor people. Since their marriage they had been downtrodden literally as well as figuratively by a rapacious nobility who used to come riding through the fields, taxing people and stepping on eggplants and stealing kisses from the comely peasants. As there is nothing in history to indicate that Mrs. Claus was comely, even at the top of her form, however, it seems likely that we can dismiss any idea of a bar sinister in the child's paternity.

NOR WAS THERE much in Santa Claus' early youth to indicate the tremendous destiny for which he was destined. He went to school in the morning with the other children, but except for a rather precocious talent for zoology he was even a little backward. In the afternoon he helped his parents by carrying the smaller eggplants and fooling around with the kindling. In the evening he studied by the fire, scratching pictures of strange animals on the bottom of the coal scuttle with one of his mother's hairpins. In the light of his future career it is perhaps significant that most of these drawings took the form of horned animals. His father and mother, tired by their work in the fields and the incessant frivolity of the nobility, took little

interest in the child's pastime. Every now and then his father, emp-
tying the scuttle into the stove, would glance casually at the bottom
and say, "Well, that's a hell of a looking cow," but in the main they
were indifferent. The significant thing about this story, of course, is
the fact that there are no reindeer in Latvia and, while it may be that
the youth really was drawing cows—well, there are things in this old
world that the wisest of us know very little about. Take ferris wheels,
for instance.

THE BOY GREW older. He developed into a stocky youth (in later
life he was to be stout) with a short brown beard and eyes alight with
mischief. He also developed into a pronounced zoöphile, bringing
home and caring for many curious Latvian animals. At one time,
we are told, he had a whole bathtubful of limpets, which he fed
through straws. It was in fact this passion for fauna which led to his
break with his family and perhaps first set his feet on the trail to
greatness.

It seems that one day when he was up re-thatching the roof,
which had burned off the previous night (a favorite practical joke of
the nobility, by the way), his attention was attracted by a strange
peeping and yammering. Investigating, he was amazed to find a family of red-winged blackbirds comfortably ensconced in a nest built
into the side of the chimney. Here was a piece of luck! The young
man leaned over to capture his prize, but in doing so his foot slipped
and he and the nest were precipitated down the chimney and onto the
Claus hearth. The eggs were broken but young Claus paid little attention to them. He sat on the hearth and stared blankly up at the opening far over his head.

"Well, I'm damned," he is said to have murmured. "Some little
aviator!"

He had acquired a new interest in life. From that moment his
time was divided equally between his animals and sliding down the
chimney. The elder Clauses had become more or less resigned to
finding animals in the most unexpected places, but this latest phase
of their son's development proved a little too much.

"Snakes in my bed I can stand," Mrs. Claus would say plaintively, "and them lizards in the bathtub, but when it comes to him popping down the chimney every time a body turns her back—well, frankly it gives me the jimmies."

The young man promised to reform, but his mother was adamant.

"Either you leave this house or I do," she said firmly.

Santa Claus left the house. He left Latvia and established himself in Paris which was then, as it is now, the Mecca for the hot young blood of the world. Ah, Paris!

UNLIKE MOST OF the valiant, pitiful army of young dreamers who yearly besiege the City of Lovers in search of fame and fortune, Santa Claus was not long in want. He soon found a field for his unique talents in the employ of a collection agency which, when it had exhausted all the usual means of approach, would lower young Claus down the chimney on a rope. Usually when the occupants had recovered from their astonishment, they would find that they had paid their bill and the young man had vanished.

From time to time he was also a go-between in many intrigues and was on terms of the greatest familiarity with some of the most notorious demimondaines of the period. It was about this time, possibly in a revulsion of feeling against the loose standards of the nobility, that he married a girl of the people, a girl as poor as himself but with the light of high dreams in her eyes. There were no children.

HIS FORTUNE WAS not really established, however, until he entered the employ of a great department store which had recognized a highly lucrative source of publicity in this novel method of delivery. It was this firm which conceived the idea of some distinctive conveyance to run on a network of wires above the city. Santa Claus himself, still smarting from the memory of his parents' contempt for his "cow" pictures and with the love of animals firmly rooted in his heart, suggested papier-mâché reindeer and a sleigh, an idea which was enthusiastically adopted by the merchants.

The rest—the uncanny spread of the legend of a great red sleigh soaring over the world loaded with toys and driven by a stout, white-haired little man in a red coat—is largely the result of intelligent publicity. It is, in fact, another story about another and perhaps even greater man. It is the story of Ira Dedletter McGee, Public Relations Counsel.

December 22, 1928

ANSWERS-TO-HARD-QUESTIONS DEPARTMENT

To the Editors of The New Yorker, Sirs:

Recently we have received a number of requests from our readers concerning the exact editorial requirements of THE NEW YORKER. May we have an article from you concerning this and any other information for writers which you may care to include?

Yours sincerely,
THE WRITER'S DIGEST
A Journal for Ambitious Literary Folk

GENTLEMEN:

I have taken your request up with the rest of the staff, but I can't see how the answers I got are going to help you at all. There seemed, as a matter of fact, a disposition to confuse the "exact editorial require-ments," for which you asked, with the purely personal requirements of the individual editors to whom I spoke. I don't think, for exam-ple, that it would be of much assistance to your subscribers to know that one editor of THE NEW YORKER only asked to be allowed to go quietly mad in a hollow tree. Nor that another would be completely happy if people would stop leaning against his door and whistling dead marches. The answers were all like that—the vital, immediate requirements of a group of men and women who have been banged, whistled, rivetted, and generally chevied about for more than five years—not much help to ambitious literary folk one way or another.

With only these answers to go on, at best my message to your subscribers will have to be more or less negative. I myself have only the vaguest idea as to what sort of manuscripts THE NEW YORKER wants. I have, however, a pretty clear idea what it *doesn't* want, and I take great pleasure in passing this information, in tabulated form, along to you for what it is worth.

1. Unlike many of its contemporaries, THE NEW YORKER does not use epigrams. Such items, for example, as "The truly unhappy man is he whose bigness is too little for big people and whose littleness is too big for little people" are no good. It's no good sending them in. The editors just give them to the officeboy, an ex-spy, who chews them into pulp and swallows them.

2. Jokes, Pointed Paragraphs, Quips from the Shoulder, etc. See Epigrams.

3. There is a certain detachment here about fables, parables, and philosophic conversations among the illustrious dead. An editor, opening a manuscript and encountering the phrase "The scene is in Heaven," or observing that it is concerned with characters called "Mr. Wiseman" or "Miss 1930," *always* puts on his hat and goes out to lunch. In this connection I might also observe that, for THE NEW YORKER'S purpose, funny names do not make funny stories, and the above procedure is also followed in the case of manuscripts dealing with people called Joe Boopus or Miss Glitch. All these manuscripts, incidentally, are collected at the end of each day and placed in a sort of hopper which tears them up, bales them, and puts them out on the sidewalk in one insanely complicated operation.

4. Some of the editors still read parodies of "Alice in Wonderland," "The Night Before Christmas," "Samuel Pepys' Diary," etc.; others don't. With the thing on this rather hit-or-miss basis I don't know just how to advise your readers on this point.

5. While THE NEW YORKER is anxious to keep abreast of recent developments in science and invention, I cannot conscientiously advise your readers to submit contributions on technical subjects. In writing this paragraph I am inevitably reminded of an author who came into the office about three years ago with an article on the

Construction of Thermostats. This piece, in twelve parts, aroused the interest, or perhaps the native obstinacy, of one of the editors, who suggested that it be revised with a view to making some of the more involved parts comprehensible to the layman. The new version unfortunately fell into the hands of another editor, a lady, who shared her colleague's interest but felt herself baffled by certain words and phrases—such as "thermostat"—still remaining in the manuscript. She asked for a second revision. The thing went on in this manner, until, at the time of the author's death a month ago, thirty-four versions had been submitted without, however, achieving a form satisfactory to *all* the members of the staff. At the present time I understand that a surviving son is prepared to carry on the work. The difficulty in this case, of course, lay in the editors' congenital inability to cope with machinery, a quality which has not diminished with the years.

6. Sex. See Machinery.

7. THE NEW YORKER does not favor what is known as the "surprise" ending. Final paragraphs in which a character, previously unidentified, suddenly turns out to be a water spaniel, or a child, or President Hoover, do not surprise the editors. They are tired and saddened when they think of the number of trees that must be cut down to make paper for this sort of thing, but not surprised.

WHILE THE ABOVE summary does not pretend to be exhaustive, I feel that it ought to give your readers at least a general idea of the sort of material that is *not* suitable for THE NEW YORKER. What *is* suitable, as I said before, is another and far more intricate matter. My own feeling is that, even if I knew, I would be doing your readers a poor service by telling them. Life would be a pretty dull business without a certain amount of struggle. At least it seems that way to me.

Sincerely yours,
MR. WINTERBOTTOM
for THE NEW YORKER

SIMPSON[1]

SIMPSON CAME TO live with me about six months ago, when my sister decided to get married and left me with an apartment far too large for my rather monastic needs. He was recommended to me by a man in my office, who said that he was honest and wouldn't make much noise. At the time, I thought this was just what I wanted.

I saw Simpson the day he moved in. He had two old cardboard suitcases, and three cases of books. He explained to me shyly that he was a great reader.

"I'm almost halfway through Macaulay right now," he said. "I try to do that with all the important writers. Read right through them, everything they ever wrote."

I could imagine Simpson inching his way, like a corn-borer, through shelf after shelf of fancy leather bindings, and the idea made my head ache.

"That's fine," I said. "That way you're sure you won't miss anything."

He stared at me with an expression of dreary imbecility.

"Yes," he said, "and with the classics you know what you're getting. It isn't like all this sex truck people write nowadays."

My sister's room has its own bath, and a private entrance out into the hall where the elevators are. The walls are painted bright green, and the single window looks out on the side of the building next door, which is six feet away and quite uninteresting. I pointed out all these horrors to Simpson, but his mind was obviously on Macaulay, so I left him.

FOR SIX MONTHS after that, I never saw Simpson. He existed for me only as a thin, occasional rustling, like mice in the baseboard: the turning, I supposed, of those interminable and dreadful pages. Every Saturday morning, a white envelope slid out under Simpson's

door. It contained his rent, and from time to time a meek complaint. "Dear Gibbs: Some people threw something out in the court
last night and it broke my window. I wonder if I could trouble you
to mention it to the superintendent? J. S."

It was a curious thing about Simpson that not only did I never
see him, but apparently nobody else did. My maid said that he was
never there when she went in to make his bed and clean the room.
I even asked the elevator men, but they plainly regarded Simpson
as a character I'd invented for my own private and mysterious entertainment. Indeed, Simpson became a jocose legend with them, so
that all the unsolved crimes in the neighborhood were laid at his
door. "Prolly," they said, when the cordial shop underwent its
weekly burglary, "prolly this friend of yours done it. This Simp-
kins."

Even my friends refused to believe in Simpson's existence, or at
any rate in his gender. Once or twice inquisitive people opened his
door, ready to pretend that they had mistaken it for the bathroom,
but Simpson was never there. It was sometimes evident from a
smoldering cigarette in an ashtray, or a depression in the bed, that
up until that moment he *had* been there. But Simpson in the flesh,
never. I think he used to hide in the closet.

EVENTUALLY THIS EERIE and invisible fellowship began to
get on my nerves. I even dreamed about Simpson. I remember
dreaming that I burst into his room one night, determined to learn
his dreadful secret, and found him stretched out, cold and unpleasant, on the bed. He had starved to death, after gnawing the red-
and-gold bindings off a complete gift edition of the Leather-stocking
Tales.

Then, last week, when I had really begun to doubt if Simpson
had any existence except in my morbid imagination, we met again.
I was having breakfast when he appeared silently in the doorway.

"Well, hello," I said when I had recovered from my amazement.

"Hello," said Simpson. He blinked at me owlishly, and then gave
a short, embarrassed laugh. "Well," he said, "I finally finished the
Macaulay."

"Really?"

"Yes," he said, "and now I'm starting on Scott. You know, Sir Walter Scott."

I nodded.

"I don't know, though," he said with a sort of feeble combativeness. "I'm afraid he's pretty light."

We stared at each other helplessly for a moment, and then Simpson turned away.

"He seems pretty light to *me*," I heard him say sadly, as the door of my sister's room closed behind him.

August 20, 1932

LUNCH WITH A RIPSAW[1]

ABOUT ONCE EVERY six months, Uncle Adam asks me to lunch. I have always found these invitations a little bewildering, because it has always been only too clear that he regards me with a mixture of disapproval and alarm. Uncle Adam has never bothered to conceal his opinion of me; indeed, from things he has said to other members of the family, I imagine that the thought of me is a small but persistent irritation, lurking at the back of his head. The other night, according to my sister, who was dining with him and my aunt, he broke abruptly and gloomily into some talk about the depression.

"He keeps a cat," said Uncle Adam.

"Who?" asked my sister, a little startled.

"Oliver, of course," said Uncle Adam. "Doesn't surprise me a bit."

I have never owned any sort of animal in my life, loathing them. The truth, I suppose, was that Uncle Adam had actually heard of a man who kept a cat, and somehow it seemed perfectly in keeping with his conception of my character. This is very true of most of Uncle Adam's ideas. He believes exactly what he wants to, about everything.

OUR LUNCH BEGAN after a fashion that has almost come to be a ritual with us.

"You're smoking too much," said Uncle Adam. "Probably drinking a lot, too."

There followed the usual autobiography of Uncle Adam, who by neither smoking nor drinking had managed to make two and a half million dollars selling lumber. At my age, he had been supporting four people (in contradistinction, I suppose, to one cat), and getting up at five o'clock in the morning to cut down trees.

"Think of that!" said Uncle Adam. "I'd like to see *you* getting up at five o'clock in the morning," he added with satisfaction. "Probably kill you."

It being beyond debate that getting up at five o'clock in the morning to cut down trees would finish me off in a week, we went on to the menu. Uncle Adam ordered a bowl of graham crackers and milk, which he would presently reduce to a soggy mash, a little dismaying esthetically but easily the nutritive equivalent of a full-course dinner. I asked for a tomato-juice cocktail, eggs Benedict, and coffee.

"Débutante lunch," said Uncle Adam. "No wonder you're thin. What you need is roast beef and milk and plenty of greens."

"I'm not especially hungry," I said apologetically.

"Cigarettes," said Uncle Adam, and passed on to what might conceivably be regarded as a subject of common interest. My aunt was well, although she felt the cold. It didn't surprise Uncle Adam that people felt the cold, living in steamheated apartments. My apartment was probably kept at ninety degrees Fahrenheit. What use, by the way, did a bachelor have for an apartment? Why didn't I try the Allerton or one of those places? They were quite cheap, he understood, and there was plenty of companionship.

"I guess that's the trouble," I said.

"What?"

"I mean they've always seemed a little institutional to me."

"Mean they won't stand any nonsense," said Uncle Adam, implying in the word everything from modern painting to delirium tremens. "I guess that's it, eh?"

At a point I always collapse in the face of this sanctimonious browbeating.

"Well," I said weakly, "they have a radio in every room, too."

"What's the matter with the radio?" said Uncle Adam. "I have one."

God knows he has. It is concealed inside a grandfather's clock, and guests wander uneasily around his living-room trying to track down its eerie bellowing.

AFTER THIS, THERE remained no logical reason that I shouldn't move into the Allerton, so I steered Uncle Adam off on the theatre. He had seen almost everything, and they were all nonsense, ranging

from "Autumn Crocus," which was more or less innocuous nonsense, to "Dinner at Eight," which was malignant nonsense and
ought to be suppressed. The trouble was that America had no moral
standards any more. Heaven only knew what was going to become of
the country now that the Democrats were in. Socialism next, most
likely, and free love. Free love was Uncle Adam's favorite nightmare,
although it was a slightly misty term in his mind. He imagined, I
think, that all women were to be the property of the state, so that
citizens could order them from their congressmen, like seeds. We
touched, briefly and inevitably, on nudism, which Uncle Adam considered unappetizing. It was a small step from there to books. He read
nothing, it appeared, except detective stories.

"Only thing you can read that isn't full of sex," he said.

With a kind of feeble combativeness, I said that any full course of
reading ought to include something besides detective stories.

"Nonsense," said Uncle Adam. "Some of the most important men
in the country read 'em. Wilson, Roosevelt. As a matter of fact," he
said, "I read 'em myself."

By this time we had reached dessert, and almost the end of our
conversational rope. Uncle Adam asked with some hostility about
my plans. I was going to Bermuda for a vacation.

"Tourists and kept women," said Uncle Adam, putting Bermuda
in its place.

We parted a little while after that, Uncle Adam to sell lumber, I
to lie down and collect what remained of my mind.

I DIDN'T HEAR even indirectly from him until I got back from
Bermuda; then I lunched with my sister. She had seen Uncle Adam,
and had been told all about our lunch.

"He's had a nervous breakdown," he had said, referring to me,
"and he's taking some woman to Bermuda. Told me so himself."

February 4, 1933

OUTWITTING THE LIGHTNING[1]

T HERE WAS AN article in the *Saturday Evening Post* a while ago about how to keep from getting hit by lightning. I don't remember much that it said, because our cook was reading a serial in the same issue about a girl who fell in love with a jai-alai player, and took the magazine up to bed with her every night, so that I didn't get very far with the lightning article except to learn that you mustn't stand around under trees, and I knew that already.

It reminded me, though, of the times my aunt and I used to have with thunderstorms when I was a child. My aunt's major obsession is cats, which she thinks climb up on people's beds at night and smother them, but lightning comes next. I have heard that the fear of lightning is congenital, but I doubt it, because I can't remember that it ever bothered me until I went to stay with her on Long Island.

On the South Shore, storms come up very quickly. The clouds mount, purple on black, in the west. There is a stiff, hot wind that turns up the under sides of the leaves, giving everything a strange, end-of-the-world effect, and the next thing you know you're in the middle of it. Sometimes, of course, the storms go rumbling and flashing out to sea, but not often, and when they do, they're as likely as not to come back treacherously from the east, where you least expect them. These storms are hardest of all for my aunt to bear. They put her in a sort of double jeopardy and her nerves go all to pieces, so that she usually ends up sitting on a raincoat in the cellar.

I WAS ABOUT eight when I had my first experience with Long Island lightning. I was sitting on the floor cutting out the wings for a cardboard airplane with a pair of scissors when my aunt came in the room. She was wearing a pair of my uncle's rubbers and her head was wrapped in a towel, because thunderstorms always made it ache. She looked unusual and mildly deranged, like the White Queen. When she saw me, she gave a negligible squeal.

"Put down those scissors!" she said.

"They haven't any points," I said hastily. My mother was almost as theatrical about scissors as my aunt was about cats, her theory being that an enormous number of people committed involuntary hara-kiri every year by falling on the points.

"It isn't the points," said my aunt. "They're *steel*. Put them down before—oh, *dear!*"

There had been a violent crash just then, apparently directly outside the window. My aunt leaned against the door, shuddering.

"My, but that was close!" she gasped. "It must have hit one of the maples."

I got up and ran to the window, but there wasn't much to see. The rain was coming down straight and blinding, and everything looked very queer in the yellow glare. The trees seemed all right, though.

"I don't see—" I began, but she caught me by the shoulder.

"Come away from that window," she whispered fiercely. "Do you want to get killed? Never, *never* stand near a window when there's a thunderstorm."

IT WAS A bad storm and it lasted all afternoon. By the time it had gone muttering off to sea, I knew everything that you mustn't do during a thunderstorm.

In the first place, you mustn't use the telephone. If it rings, don't answer it. In spite of uninformed persons who imagine telephone receivers are rubber, they are made of steel. Touch one, and up you go. My aunt's explanation of that is quite simple: anything steel (and all the metal in the house automatically becomes steel with the first gathering thunderheads) attracts electricity. When it attracts enough, it blows up, along with anyone imprudent enough to be attached to it. My aunt's horror of the telephone extends to everything else that works by electricity. No matter how dark it gets, she never turns on the lights; she uses candles. If she happens to be in her car when a storm breaks, she turns off the switch and sits there,

to the confusion of traffic, until it is over. This is purest agony, because the car is steel too, and liable to go wham with her at any
moment.

Next to steel, water is the most dangerous thing in a thunderstorm. It conducts electricity. This is a somewhat vague term in her
mind. She doesn't mean that water conveys electricity from one
place to another. She means, in a large way, that any body of water
becomes impregnated with electricity at the outset of a storm and
stays that way until it is over. Anyone foolish enough to get in it is
briskly and competently electrocuted. This theory applies equally
to our bathtub and to the Great South Bay, except that the bay, being larger, holds its electricity longer. She considers it very unwise
to go swimming for at least an hour after a storm is over.

Draughts are another thing. In spite of the shattering violence of
which it is capable, lightning strays like smoke along the faintest
current of air. When a storm begins, she shuts and locks every
door and window in the house. That makes everyone pretty hot
and uncomfortable, but it doesn't do much good. There are always
strange breezes around her ankles, any one of which may easily
carry a bolt which will demolish the house. The fireplace is the
most perilous source of draughts. It is an open, almost suicidal invitation to destruction, and she avoids it carefully. As a matter of fact,
a fireplace had very nearly been the end of my grandfather, who
had been sitting in front of one when a ball of fire rolled down the
chimney and out on the hearth, where it oscillated for some time,
looking at him, before it rolled thoughtfully away and disappeared
in the cellar.

THAT IS ANOTHER of the perils of lightning: its ability to assume practically any form you can think of. It can be a bolt, or a
ball, or even a thin mist, luminous but deadly. You can take all the
negative precautions you want—avoiding metal and draughts and
water—but it will get you anyway if it's in the mood. There is only
one positive cure for lightning, and that is rubber. My aunt has the
utmost faith in rubber, which she thinks confers a sort of magic immunity. If you wear rubber, lightning can't get at you, not even if it
strikes in the same room. Like all her precautions, however, even

that has one miserable flaw. You have to be *all* rubber. If there is a single chink, however small, the lightning gets in, and you're done for. When a storm gets really bad, my aunt always spreads one rain-coat on the floor and sits on it. Then she puts another one over her head, like a tent. She sits that way until the storm is over, when she reappears tentatively, a little at a time. It always seems to astonish her mildly to find the rest of us alive and unsinged, but I think she puts it down mostly to luck, and is convinced that in the end we'll pay for our mad and unprecedented recklessness. It is a tribute to her training that even now, with the first far-away roll of thunder, I think so too.

August 9, 1933

A MAN MAY BE DOWN

IN JUNE, AFTER a series of small mishaps of no conceivable interest to anybody, my friend Munson vanished from the speakeasies. He gave up all alcohol except for the hypothetical three-and-two-tenths per cent in the new beer, which of course may be drunk by the bucket without inducing either gaiety or grace, but only a sort of gassy stupefaction, very dismal to behold. In the succeeding three months, I have followed his uninteresting experiment with the greatest care, and can only say that it all seems to have been a very tiresome mistake.

In the first place, the advantages have been negligible. His health, he says, is a lot better. A well man gets out of his bed in the morning, shaves with a firm hand, and eats a hearty breakfast—several eggs, I believe, and some ingenious form of patented bran. He goes to work whistling, and spends the day in a fine executive lather, making instantaneous decisions regarding the disposition of small pieces of paper with a vigor and clarity that his old dissolute self would have viewed with amazement and derision. At four o'clock in the afternoon, he feels about the way he did at ten in the morning; there is no sensation of being about to fall over backward, like a tree, or of listening miserably to the slow ticking of an inward bomb.

Where once he roared dangerously through the streets, pursued by all the yelping imps in hell, or in the daylight crept along nervously, obsessed with calamity, he drives now surely and evenly, contemptuous of traffic. On Saturdays and Sundays, he scampers vivaciously around a tennis court, or plunges carelessly into the most uproarious surf. His epidermis is brown, his eye clear and candid, his hand steady. If the occasion arose, probably he could thread a needle.

Financially, too, Munson is fine. His salary lasts from Friday to Friday, and there is a small but growing balance in the bank. In the old days, the first sight to greet Munson's coppery Sunday-morning eye was a miserable litter on the table beside his bed, consisting of his watch, his keys, several incomprehensible memoranda scrawled on the covers of match folders and about four one-dollar bills, torn halfway across. These would be the sole residuum of his rather comfortable salary; the rest he had spread generously across Fifty-second Street, like the clues in some disreputable paper chase. Munson has bought a new car, with hundreds of cylinders, and a great many clothes which enhance the new glories of his physique.

SOBRIETY HAS ALSO brought an unfamiliar simplicity and order into Munson's relations with women. Formerly, he was what might be described as "the marrying kind," although I use the term in a rather special sense. He never actually achieved the altar, but after midnight Munson was in the habit of asking almost anybody to marry him. It was quite automatic with him, a sort of tic, but it always led to embarrassment and frequently to bitterness, there being ladies unworldly enough to imagine that marriage with Munson might be feasible and even mildly agreeable. I think it was only the superlative nature of Munson's hangovers that kept him from having more wives than Solomon. As it was, though, they could never get at him to pin him down. He'd sit with them at lunch the next day, white and far-away, while the subject was tentatively approached.

"Of course"—humorously—"I don't suppose you remember what we were talking about in Tullio's last night?"

"No," Munson would say, intent on his private desperation. "Look, I wonder if you'd mind very much if we got the hell out of here. I'm sick as a dog, and I better get some air."

They never got anywhere with him, but as I've said, it complicated his life. Now his whole attitude is brisk and fraternal. "He keeps thumping his stomach at you, and talking about his serve," one lady said, wrinkling her pretty nose.

In that there is a clue to the whole tragedy of Munson's sobriety. He has turned, I fear, into an extremely dull man. The old Munson was outrageous at times—a liar and a bankrupt and the enemy of order—but I liked him. He was a man living on a volcano who had no confidence in any tomorrow, and gave you and the moment all

he had. The new Munson, this sepia changeling with the hard stomach, leaves me cold. There is something nastily calculating in his eye,
and I don't approve of his new interest in time and money. The old
Munson never looked at a clock or a check; at eleven o'clock, the
spirit of the new Munson almost visibly gets up and leaves the
room, although his body remains for a reluctant half-hour, yawning
and squirming; and he has developed a certified accountant's eye
for a ten-cent error in addition.

None of these things, however, are as bad as the dismal change
temperance has effected in his conversation. The old Munson never
told a story the same way twice. On Monday he would tell you that
he had been arrested for driving seventy-four miles an hour down
Fifth Avenue, and had spent the night in jail. On Tuesday it had
become ninety miles, and he had climbed out of his car and magnificently destroyed the policeman. Munson used to say that nothing ever happened to anybody that would make a good anecdote
without at least a little embroidery. The new Munson is scrupu-
lously truthful, and nothing he says is worth a moment of your attention. This dreary punctiliousness hasn't affected only his own
conversation; it has become an almost intolerable nuisance to his
friends.

"The first time Theodore Roosevelt was elected President," I
began the other night, when Munson raised a protesting hand.

"As a matter of fact," he said distinctly, "Roosevelt was only *elected*
once. He first *became* President in 1901, upon the death of McKinley."

WITH IT ALL—with his money and his health and the peace that
must come from being able to recall his entire day from breakfast to
bed—I don't think Munson is a happy man. The nature of life in
New York makes it impossible to avoid people who vehemently are
not on the water-wagon, and it seems that they pick on him.

"I hear you're supposed to be funny," they shout. "Say something funny."

He's hounded, too, by friends who bring up his wayward past.

"Do you remember the time you brought that *very* odd girl to
Mother's party?" someone will ask. It leaves him cold with distaste
and, embarrassment, and the worst of it is he's quite helpless. The gift

of repartee left Munson the day he drank his last Martini. He can only sit there, smiling uneasily and wishing they were all in hell. It is strange to me that a man of Munson's background should persist in trying to make sense out of drunken talk, but he does. He leans forward, full of anxious politeness, listening to their tangled nonsense, and making dreadful sensible little comments from time to time.

"I really think you ought to wait and see how you feel about it in the morning," I have heard him say earnestly to a dreary bore who was threatening to jump in the bay. The old Munson would have given him carfare and his benediction.

Lately, though, there has been a troubled light in his eye, and the other night he made really quite an encouraging remark just before he left me.

"You know," he said, "I've been living the life of a hunted animal."

I think perhaps Baby is coming home.

September 23, 1933

WIT'S END[1]

THE BED WAS burning quite briskly when Henry Martin woke up. For a moment he lay there coughing, and then automatically leaned over and switched on the bed lamp. Thick yellow smoke was pouring from a small crater in the mattress beside him, and one corner of the pillow seemed to be on fire, too, burning fitfully in rings that glowed and widened and disappeared. The room was full of smoke which smelled a good deal.

"*Now* what the hell?" said Mr. Martin. He said it with more resignation than anger, because life had accustomed him to small disasters and they caused him little more than a passive irritation.

By the time he had decided that he must have gone to bed with a cigarette in his hand, the fire had grown to quite imposing proportions, and it was uncomfortably hot on the bed. Although he was still rather more than half-asleep, Mr. Martin saw that something had better be done. He swung his legs over the side of the bed and felt his way into the bathroom through the smoke. It was a hotel bathroom and there was only a small tumbler on the shelf. There had been a pitcher once, but it had cracked long ago and the maid had taken it away. Mr. Martin filled the tumbler and, returning to the bedroom, flung it on the mattress.

There are places in the world—mines or oil fields or peat bogs or something of the kind—where fires have been burning underground, secretly and evilly, beyond the memory of the oldest inhabitant. Nothing can be done about them. It is the same way with a mattress. The water only had the effect of sending up a cloud of steam even more dismaying than the smoke. After a moment of indecision, the crater glowed as ruddily as ever, and even put out, here and there, vague tongues of flame. Mr. Martin tried two more tumblers of water, without much hope and certainly without any perceptible effect on the blaze. Then he went to the telephone.

"This is Mr. Martin in 8-B," he said when he had jiggled the operator into sleepy and resentful attention. "My bed's on fire."

IT HAD BETTER be explained here that Mr. Martin enjoyed rather a peculiar reputation with the night operator. She saw him very seldom, because his work—he was a construction engineer on a railroad—got him up very early in the morning, and it made him go to bed early, too. But the few times she *had* seen him—late at night and lit with a strange vivacity—had established him in her mind as a practical joker whose whimsy was scarcely to be distinguished from dementia. More like a nut, as she explained nervously to the manager the night that Mr. Martin, returning from the Beaux-Arts Ball arrayed as a voodoo priest, had stopped at the desk and put a curse on her in an alarming dialect which he declared to be the speech of the Island of Haiti.

The operator, half believing that Mr. Martin had dressed himself up purely for this singular jest, was both unnerved and indignant. Coupling this experience with a few more of the same kind, she was thenceforth determined to meet Mr. Martin on his own ground, and now, when he called up to say that his bed was on fire, she only laughed airily.

"Ha, ha," she said, "that's a good one, Mr. Martin." And then, suddenly and deliciously inspired: "That's a *hot* one, I *must* say."

She hung up, giggling. Mr. Martin looked doubtfully at the receiver in his hand.

"Damn girl's gone crazy," he said, putting it slowly back on the hook. He looked at the bed again. By this time there was quite a definite blaze, and flaming streamers were dropping to the rug, where they lay smoldering. The smoke, too, was nearly intolerable. Mr. Martin thought for a moment of running out in the hall in his pajamas and calling for help, but decided it would probably start a panic. He picked up the telephone again and jiggled the hook. There was no answer.

"Oh, damn," said Mr. Martin. Looking down at the bed, he felt a more utter helplessness than he had ever known in his life. Here was he at three o'clock in the morning with a bonfire on his hands, and nobody would pay any attention. He could lie down on the bed and burn up, and nobody would do anything about it. He took the receiver off the hook and laid it over the mouthpiece. He let the squealing go on for several seconds before he put the receiver to his ear. The operator was there, awake and annoyed.

"Sa–ay," she said, "what's the big—"

"Listen," said Mr. Martin. "This room is on fire. F–i–r–e. Burning up. If somebody doesn't do something, the whole damn hotel is going to burn up. You send a boy up here right away with a fire-extinguisher. Understand?"

There was a pause before the operator answered. She still sounded skeptical, and disagreeably bright.

"All righty," she said. "I'll send somebuddy."

"Quick," said Mr. Martin.

IT WAS ALMOST five minutes, though, before there came a knock at the door of the outer room. Opening it, Mr. Martin discovered a small boy who stared at him with an expression of dreary idiocy. He had no extinguisher.

"What was it you wished, Mr. Martin?" he asked.

A curling streamer of smoke, drawn by the open door, billowed out from the bedroom, and Mr. Martin waved his hand at it.

"Fire," he said.

The idiot child stepped through the door and peered into the bedroom. He saw the bed.

"Jeez, Mr. Martin," he said. "Your bed's boining."

"I know," said Mr. Martin wearily. "I just got out of it."

"Jeez, Mr. Martin, did you set it on poipose?"

"Yes," said Mr. Martin. "I was cold. Now you go get an extinguisher. Hurry."

The boy was gone so long that Mr. Martin, standing in the hall and rubbing the tears from his eyes, had begun to conclude that there were no extinguishers in the hotel, and had almost decided to begin throwing his clothes out the window, when the boy reappeared, pulling an enormous cylinder which bumped hollowly along the empty corridor. They dragged it into the bedroom, and the boy seized the hose and pointed it at the blaze. Nothing happened.

"Look here," said Mr. Martin, suddenly suspicious. "Do you know how to work that thing?"

"Well—"

"You turn it upside down," said Mr. Martin gently. "Here, let me take it."

Finally, between them, they put the fire out, incidentally dousing the rugs, pictures, lamps, and a pile of Mr. Martin's best shirts, which were lying on a chair waiting to be put away. The boy started to go.

"Wait a minute," said Mr. Martin. "I've got to have some place to sleep. Is there an empty apartment on this floor anywhere?"

"I don't know, sir. You'd have to ask downstairs, Mr. Martin."

FOR THE THIRD time, Mr. Martin went to the telephone and explained about his fire.

"I'll have to have another apartment," he said.

"Couldn't you stay there just for the night?" the operator asked. "We could get you another room in the morning."

"What do you want me to sleep on?" he asked bitterly. "The floor?"

"Oh, that's right," she said. "The bed burned, didn't it?"

"Yes," said Mr. Martin. "Quite beautifully."

"Well," doubtfully, "I'll have to ask the manager."

"Good God," said Mr. Martin. "Don't you even know where there's an empty room in your hotel?"

"I'll have to ask the manager," she repeated primly.

While he waited for the manager, who would unquestionably be cross and reproving, Mr. Martin felt the first premonitory chill of the pneumonia which was presently to carry him off.

October 21, 1933

MARS[1]

THERE WERE A great many sad and irrational and embarrassing things about the Reserve Officers Training Camp where I spent the last summer of the war. We were all in preparatory school then—most of us somewhere between fifteen and eighteen. We were lambs, but the harsh military winds were not perceptibly tempered in our favor. During our first week there, for instance, the whole battalion was lined up, injected with diphtheria antitoxin, and then marched seventeen miles under the July sun. This came under the heading of "toughening you men up," and it succeeded to the extent of weeding out the unfit, twelve of whom collapsed and had to be taken back to camp in a Ford truck. For some reason I was not one of the twelve, but I can still remember the last few miles of that march, with the dusty road unsteady under my feet, like a diving board. It is conceivable that this experience toughened me up, but I doubt if it contributed much to my enthusiasm for the martial spirit.

Nor did I ever grow to enjoy our sham battles, which were conducted in a neighboring cornfield, where the hard stubble lacerated (and again presumably toughened) our stomachs as we stalked the hypothetical enemy. These events were further enlivened by Lieutenant Gilhooley of West Point and his associate demons, whose pleasure it was to spank down with the flats of their swords any dorsal curves which they imagined might be visible to the foe. This pastime seemed to me simply painful and humiliating; bombing practice, on the other hand, filled me with terror. It was our firm belief that the Mills bombs we used had been condemned by the government because of faulty timing mechanisms, and while obviously this could not have been the case, the boxes they came in were stencilled "Not for active service." No other explanation suggested itself to us, nor was any advanced by the authorities, who had that

passion for small, unnecessary mysteries which seems to character-
ize the military mind.

As I remember it, in using a Mills bomb, you were supposed to
pull out the firing pin, and then count ten before throwing it. This,
of course, was designed to prevent the Germans, a cunning and
unsportsmanlike people, from picking it up and throwing it back. I
can't forget my horror, after I had pulled the pin, standing there
with that deadly (and possibly defective) mechanism, waiting for
the premature crash which would be my last memory this side of
the grave. As a matter of fact, a good deal of the time I didn't wait
to complete my ten, but threw it wildly at three or four, leaving an
interval in which, as Gilhooley always pointed out, the German
army could easily have picked up the horrible thing and mailed it
back to me.

There were other things, too. There was the Y.M.C.A. hut,
linked forever in my mind with limp Hershey bars, smoke, bridge,
and songs, repeated to insanity, most of which pictured the war as
an immense and rather good-natured football game. There were in-
spections and fatigues and getting up at six and beans on tin plates,
but above everything else there were the West Pointers who directed
our maneuvers, and there was Lieutenant Gilhooley in particular.
He was a small red man, brisk as a fox terrier, with a loud voice and
a simple vision of paradise as a boundless parade ground with all the
cherubim in step. He was the epitome of the "army spirit" and, although that was sixteen years ago, I can remember that I never
disliked anyone so much in my life.

ONE OF OUR first experiences with Lieutenant Gilhooley was
typical. We were digging trenches and a boy called Summers suddenly struck a sharp rock and tore off a fingernail. Gilhooley saw him
stand up (we were digging lying on our stomachs, being technically
under fire).

"Hey, you," he shouted, "get down there!"

"I've hurt my hand, sir," said Summers.

"For God's sake," said Gilhooley, "you're supposed to be a soldier
now. The Germans ain't going to stop the war just because some
nice little boy cuts his fingers. Get down."

This is probably a silly story, because I told it once to another army man, who seemed to feel that Gilhooley had behaved with quite unprofessional restraint. He should, it appeared, have shot Summers on the spot. I have met enough army men since then to understand this point of view, but at the time it seemed somewhat drastic.

Summers, who was really an almost chronic victim of West Point efficiency, had another experience, so strange and indelicate that I wouldn't be surprised if it haunts him even now, in the high noon of his thirties. It is apropos here because it, too, resulted from the R.O.T.C.'s determination to recreate the conditions of actual warfare. Two or three times during the summer we were allowed a weekend leave of absence, which we usually spent in Philadelphia, where then, as now, the opportunities for entertainment were limited and drearily innocent. In spite of this, and our extreme youth, it was the official theory that we spent our leaves in the wildest debauchery, in line with established military tradition. Accordingly, returning cadets were always asked a question which most of us found flattering, though vaguely comic. The army wanted to know if we had had occasion to visit any ladies during our absence, though the precise wording was considerably more direct. "Been with a woman, Jack?" they asked coarsely.

Summers took his first and only leave the second week we were there, and on his return repaired obediently to the doctor's tent. When he came out, he appeared to be in a sort of stupor, and it was a little while before we could find out what had happened to him. Finally, however, it developed that Summers had been asked the usual question and, in his awful, his incredible innocence, he had answered in the affirmative. Thereupon, to his considerable discomfort and amazement, the authorities had briskly treated his case in accordance with U.S. medical regulations on the subject. It developed that he hadn't had the vaguest idea what they were talking about, so that even if they'd given him time, I doubt if he would have thought to explain that the lady in question was a maiden aunt with whom he had spent the Sabbath blamelessly in a Philadelphia suburb.

FROM THE BEGINNING, Gilhooley—to get back to him—disliked me almost as much as I did him. This was because of a foolish remark I made the first time we met. I'd been excused from some minor fatigue by the camp doctor, and Gilhooley found me lying in my bunk.

"I thought you were supposed to be on duty," he said suspiciously.

"I'm sick," I said. "The doctor excused me, sir."

"Sick, hell," he said. "You're sick like all the rest of this bunch of bastards around here. Lazy. That's the trouble with this country. Too much mollycoddling."

I *was* sick, as a matter of fact, and irritable.

"Or maybe it's just too much virility," I said.

He reported me for that, but it must have been a little short of mutiny, because they let me off with only a short explanation of the relative positions of private and officer. It was something like your relation to God, only a little more complicated and arbitrary. However, I had criticized Gilhooley's passionate and only faith, and for the rest of the summer he did his best to make up for it. This was good enough, though, because he was thorough and ingenious, and after all, like God, he had certain advantages.

Owing to unfortunate physical peculiarities, it is impossible to wrap a puttee around my leg and expect it to stay there. Gilhooley got me for that. And he got me for the dust he could always find on my buttons or my shoes or hidden in the bore of my gun. He got me for my spirited but unorthodox performance of the manual of arms, and he got me for talking in ranks, but he was best, he was really superb, when it came to guard duty.

Our camp was high in the Pennsylvania hills and there wasn't much reason to suppose that German spies or anybody else would try to get in. An occasional local drunk or a tramp might, but he had very little idea of what was expected of him, and hardly qualified as enemy patrols or scouting parties or whatever it is you're supposed to watch out for in the trenches. We had about sixteen sentries on duty all day and all night, and it was evident something had to be done to keep them amused and to give them some experience of actual front-line conditions. The West Pointers did their best to meet this situation, impersonating German scouts with great enthusiasm.

I was on duty at about two o'clock one morning when I heard a rustling in the undergrowth surrounding my post.

"Halt! Who is there?" I called. ("Who goes there?" unfortunately is only in books.)

There was some more rustling.

"Who is there?" I called again and, still following the fancy catechism in the army regulations, "Stand or I fire."

The rustling stopped and a dim figure rose in the underbrush. It seemed to be Gilhooley.

"The battleship Maine on wheels," it said.

He had me there, because there is nothing in the army regulations to cover humor, however sorry. The answer to "Who is there?" was "Friend" or "Foe" (you shoot them, I think, if they say "Foe," which seems reasonable). The answer to "Friend" was "Advance to be recognized." I said that.

Gilhooley advanced. I recognized him.

"You had a call to shoot me then," he said. "You'd shoot a German if he tried to get comical with you, wouldn't you?"

I supposed I would.

Mysteriously, he seemed to be in a genial mood.

"Shoot 'em first and find out afterwards," he said. "That's the old army game."

"Yes, sir," I said. There hadn't been any chance of my shooting Gilhooley. We only had blanks.

"Never mind the 'sir.'" His good humor now was almost overpowering. "Say, some ball club those Red Sox got this year. Take that Carl Mays . . ."

We talked for a while about baseball, and the mystery of Gilhooley's sudden friendship grew even deeper. Among other things, it developed that I thought Carl Mays was celebrated for making home runs.

"Well," he said finally. "I got to be going."

I came to attention.

"Say," he said, flashing his light on me, "what's the matter with that gun you got there?"

"Nothing that I know of," I said. "It was all right when I came on post."

"Well, it ain't now," he said. "You got the bolt all hanging loose. Here, let me take it a minute."

Trustfully, I put it in his hands, and Lieutenant Gilhooley underwent a sombre transformation. He glared at me as he blew the little whistle that called the corporal of the guard.

"You're under arrest," he snapped. "God, suppose I'd of been a German . . ."

IN THE NEXT war, which, of course, will be upon us before the snow flies, it will be my dearest dream to meet Gilhooley again. I'd like, I think, to be on post, and to hear him again, rustling in the underbrush.

"Who is there?" I'd call.

"The battleship—" But he'd get no further than that, because it is always best to shoot first and ask afterwards. You get into the spirit of these things.

June 23, 1934

EDEN, WITH SERPENTS[1]

THE GUESTS IN Dr. Hardy's Sanatorium sat on the porch in the pleasant sunshine, talking cheerfully. They may have been a little handicapped because Dr. Hardy wouldn't let them talk about their symptoms, and this naturally was the topic which concerned them all most passionately, but on the whole they were contented, and quite pink with regular hours and simple food. It must be understood that Dr. Hardy's was something rather special in sanatoria, since it dealt with neither advanced alcoholics nor persons of really marked peculiarity. Some of Dr. Hardy's guests, it is true, were there because they drank too much, but it was the genteel alcoholism which comes from years of excellent living and not the vulgar collapse which follows a good ten-day bender. It must be admitted, too, that some of the guests were a little odd, but they were odd in interesting and subtle ways, and could be relied on not to get tough. The guests, as Dr. Hardy himself put it, were simply ladies and gentlemen who found themselves a little exhausted by the tempo of modern living, and had come to this quiet mountain retreat to rest. The treatment was consistent with this refined description. No lumpy and contemptuous young men threw medicine balls at these fortunate people, no one flung them on tables and hammered their stomachs, no one asked them to run or jump or wave dumbbells. They were allowed to smoke, and when it seemed advisable therapeutically they could have a little drink. Each morning after breakfast those who felt up to it went for a short stroll over the countryside while an attendant, equipped with restoratives, called their attention to scenery of conspicuous merit. Actually it was a lovely country, marred only (and very rarely) by encounters with native children who could not be persuaded to share Dr. Hardy's opinion of his guests and were apt to say so, rotating their fingers humorously at their temples. After lunch, everyone lay down for a little while, and then attended classes in occupational therapy. Each guest had his private studio, and in it he followed his own creative bent, playing the piano, or painting, or making extremely useful little objects out of wood and clay. Most of these, unfortunately, had to be destroyed upon the guest's departure, since there was no considerable local market for "occasional" tables and hand-painted pottery. Some of the more arresting specimens, however, were preserved for the inspiration of future guests, and were often said to compare very favorably with the work of professionals. Late in the afternoon there was tea, and then dinner, and in the evening bridge or backgammon. If you wanted to, you could just read, and there were a great many books, though none of a morbid character. At ten o'clock everybody went to bed, and the lights went out. This Eden was available for a hundred dollars a week, not counting extras.

ON THE DAY the Awful Thing happened, eight gentlemen and ladies were sitting in the sun. They were alike in that they were all middle-aged and of a respectable and even elegant appearance. There was nothing, indeed, to distinguish them from any similar group on the porch of an expensive resort hotel. Perhaps the cigarette trembled a little in Major Fortnum's hand, but this surely is not strange in elderly gentlemen and no necessary symptom of alcoholism. Mrs. Charlie Goodenough was very pale, but, as everyone understood, she was recuperating from a distressing experience, having only just been divorced from a "rotter." Mrs. Goodenough never condescended to define this term, and so she was a source of delightful speculation to the other guests, who credited Mr. Goodenough with bedtime eccentricities that would have amused Caligula. She had a right to be pale if anybody had, the guests agreed. The other six looked as normal as you or I, and a great deal stronger.

They were sitting there, talking languidly and watching the big yellow sun drop closer and closer to the roof of the garage, when there was the sound of a car laboring up the hill. As they watched without much interest, a battered taxicab appeared on the crest, shifted its gears, and rattled slowly up the driveway to the front door. In view of the fact that more than one hundred and fifty miles of difficult road lay between Dr. Hardy's and New York City, this was a remarkable apparition and the guests were troubled. Although, as I have said, there was nothing actually *wrong* with any of them, they regarded it for a moment with a vague mixture of apprehension and dislike, and no one, it was clear, quite wanted to be the first to recognize it officially. Finally Mr. Purcell cleared his throat.

"Looks like a taxi," he said.

A slight tension seemed to leave the other seven.

"A New York taxi," said Mrs. Minor, a lady who often felt as if she were floating. "How very odd."

An unpleasant face appeared at the driver's window of the cab and regarded the guests.

"This Hardy's?" it said.

"This is Min-a-wonk-it Lodge," said Major Fortnum coldly, this term, which is the Indian word for Tranquillity, being deemed a more appropriate name for a place that was, after all, far more like a club than a sanatorium.

"Hardy runs it, though, don't he?" persisted the face, which clearly had no patience with technicalities.

"Yes," admitted Major Fortnum. "What do you want?"

"*I* don't want nothing," said the face. "I just got a couple of customers for you."

"Customers?" said Mr. Purcell.

"Yes," said the face. "Wait'll you see 'em."

He chuckled to himself as he got down from his seat and walked around the cab.

"They're a couple of honeys," he said, and opened the side door of the cab. Nothing came out, however, and the driver bent forward and peered inside.

"Come on, gents," he said.

At length there was a stirring inside the cab, and presently two empty bottles rolled out, followed by a young man in evening dress, who sat down on the running-board.

"That's *one* of 'em," said the driver.

He leaned into the cab again and tugged, and this time produced a tall, thin man, also in evening dress. Both men were unshaven and dishevelled, and it was clear that they had been drunk for a long time.

"This is Hardy's, Jack," said the driver, supporting the tall man with difficulty.

"What in hell's Hardy's?" said the tall man, speaking slowly but with great clarity.

"The booby hatch, Jack," said the driver. "Where you told me to drive you."

"Oh," said the tall man, and regarded the guests with interest.

His companion, however, appeared to be disagreeably affected by these remarks, for he rose from the runningboard.

"I'm not going to any god-damn asylum," he said, and he turned and began to run swiftly, although unsteadily, down the road.

The tall man looked after him.

"Here, you," he said to the driver. "Go bring him back. Let go of me. I'm all right. You get him before he gets lost."

"I ain't chasing no drunks in these mountains, Jack," said the driver sullenly. "I do my regular work. That's all."

"Get him before I kill you," said the tall man, so venomously that the driver released him, and started down the road.

"O.K., Jack," he said, over his shoulder, "but I'm telling you—"

"*Get* him," said the tall man.

During all this, none of the guests had been capable of speech. Mrs. Minor was the first to recover.

"Hurry, Major," she whispered. "Go and find Dr. Hardy before something dreadful happens."

"I'll go," said Mr. Purcell, and he was gone before Major Fortnum could get out of his chair.

The tall man advanced on them, smiling.

"Might as well sit down and wait," he said. "Charles can run like hell. Probably have to chase him halfway back to New York."

He sat down in Mr. Purcell's chair, next to Mrs. Minor, who recoiled.

"Christ, what a head!" he said, and clasped it in his hands. "What do you have to do around here to get a waiter?"

"Young man—" began Major Fortnum.

"Never mind," said the tall man hastily. "I can drink it this way."

He took a flask from his pocket and held it out to them. They looked at him, too frozen for speech, but he was not abashed.

"Allie oop," he said, and drank. There was a silence while he looked about him reflectively.

"Never thought *I'd* wind up in one of these," he said, "but you never know. As a matter of fact," he added politely, "none of you are exactly what I expected, either."

Major Fortnum was the first to comprehend this unfortunate compliment.

"Young man," he said, "I think you'd better go. You're drunk."

"Drunk as a monkey," said the tall man affably. "That's what the joint's for, isn't it?"

AGAIN NONE OF the seven could answer him, and they sat there, watching the road desperately for Dr. Hardy, who conceivably could cope with this dangerous and degraded man. While they watched and waited, the tall man fell asleep, leaning almost imperceptibly against Mrs. Minor's quivering shoulder.

They had given up all hope, resigned to live forever in their shameful nightmare, when Dr. Hardy appeared at the top of the hill. He was accompanied by the taxi-driver, and supported between them, walking a little erratically, was Charles. Even at that distance he seemed to be protesting.

They were still a little way from the porch when Mrs. Goodenough could contain herself no longer.

"Dr. Hardy," she called, "this man is drunk."

"I know," said Dr. Hardy grimly. He released Charles, and walked up the steps.

"Here," he said, shaking the tall man's shoulder. "Wake up."

The tall man opened his eyes, and apparently recognized authority.

"What kind of a way is that to treat a patient," he demanded indignantly.

"I'm sorry," said the Doctor, "but you'll have to go."

"Go?" said the tall man. "Hell, I just got here."

"I'm sorry," said the Doctor.

"I come here voluntarily," said the tall man, acquiring momentum and pathos. "*Voluntarily*, by God! To be treated for an unfortunate condition, and I am turned away. Turned away to die."

"You aren't going to die," said the Doctor, tugging again at his shoulder. "Come on, now."

"All right, Sour Puss," said the tall man, getting up in sections. "I'll go. Come, Charles," he said darkly. "There is no room at the inn."

With this Biblical reproach, he left them, and staggered out to the taxi, which already contained Charles, though in a somewhat tangled condition. At the door he turned and looked at the stricken guests.

"The hell with you!" he shouted at them suddenly. "You drunkards!"

He got in and the door closed, and they watched the dreadful cab roll away. The last thing they saw as it reached the crest of the hill was the tall man's pale and maniacal face framed in the rear window. He seemed to be still shouting at them.

Mrs. Minor had one of her attacks. She rather annoyed them all by being the first to think of it.

April 20, 1935

THE HUNTRESS[1]

E VEN NOW, IN the comparative security of a city of seven million people, I sit dreaming of Miss Sellers, the most dangerous
woman in the world. For three years Miss Sellers was, in a sense, my
employee, although she kept me in a steady panic, and I had neither
dignity nor grace in her presence.

At that time, I was the editor of a New England weekly newspaper, dedicated to the social activities of the community, which were
repetitious, and the interests of the Republican party, which were corrupt beyond belief. Miss Sellers was my reporter, a heritage from
my predecessor, and certainly the most successful practical joke of
his negligible career. She was a native New Englander, which, next
to being a Jukes, is of course this world's surest guarantee of great
peculiarity.[2] She weighed about two hundred and fifty pounds, and
as a rule she wore a rusty red garment, shapeless and without sleeves,
like an old-fashioned nightgown. Her face was large and gray and
sparsely bearded, and it glistened continually with perspiration. Her
eyes protruded and never winked. Her hair was arranged, Japanese
fashion, in a tower of diminishing black buns, which sometimes contained an exhausted flower. On the whole, it is impossible to describe
her more graphically than to say that she resembled the late William Jennings Bryan, unkindly made up to play Madame Butterfly.

It was Miss Sellers' simple duty to report to me, in pencil on
ruled sheets of yellow paper, the weddings, births, deaths, and other
minutiæ of a community of three thousand people. She did this, I
am obliged to admit, acceptably enough, being particularly eloquent in her obituaries, which were written more or less from the
triumphant point of view of the earthworm. Unsolicited, Miss Sellers
also contributed other articles, largely of an editorial nature and
directed principally against the Catholic Church, of which she disapproved. These, however, were somewhat controversial in tone,

having to do with vast papal conspiracies to take over the county government, and they were not printed. She also contributed poetry, and, country newspapers being what they are, some of this *was* printed. It, too, was dark and menacing, and, being largely incomprehensible, gained the paper a considerable reputation for profundity among the simple lobstermen. I have lost what copies I ever had of these compositions, but one at least persists in my memory. It was called "Sardak Y Noval," which Miss Sellers, being pinned down, condescended to explain was the name of a "mythical pool." It began:

> *Down through the depths of the depthless,*
> *Narrow and sombre and cool,*
> *Down in the heart of the heartless,*
> *Oh, where is the soul of the pool?*
> *Oh, silence is golden, while silver is sound*
> *As the motto proverbial saith,*
> *But the silence of Sardak, that stillness profound,*
> *The silence of Noval is . . . DEATH!*[3]

I can still remember it all, but this, I think, is enough to convey the essence of Miss Sellers' gloomy gift.

NONE OF THESE extra activities, of course, had the slightest bearing on Miss Sellers' value to me as a journalist. It also happened, however, that she was the victim of a series of delusions which made my contacts with her matters of the greatest anxiety and embarrassment. Her paramount idea was that almost all men, not too near the cradle or the grave, had carnal designs upon her person. This is certainly not a novel fixation, and I suppose it has its pathos, but Miss Sellers' precautions against unavenged rape were so bizarre and elaborate that they deserve to be noted. In the first place, she had procured (in an interview which must have mystified the village doctor) a "certificate of chastity," stating that Edith Sellers had been examined and found to be a virgin; in the second, she had picked up, God knows where, an enormous old revolver, minus both hammer and ammunition, with which to threaten any wretch too passionate or abandoned to be disarmed by the certificate. Both these articles were kept in the side pocket of her Ford runabout, and both figured freely and forbiddingly in her conversation.

This, too, would have been harmless enough from my point of view, except that, of all men, Miss Sellers was most inclined to suspect the editors who employed her, apparently expecting them to demand a sort of journalistic *droit du seigneur* in exchange for her salary. The certificate and the revolver, indeed, became commonplaces in our interviews, and I was threatened with them daily, though never directly.

"Just let any of them try their dirty monkey tricks on me," Miss Sellers would say, staring at me with unmistakable menace.

I learned from the villagers, who were largely exempt from Miss Sellers' suspicions and therefore inclined to find her diverting, that one previous editor had become so unnerved by these persistent innuendoes that he had resigned and, in his anxiety to get as far as possible from Miss Sellers, had bought a candy store in Austin, Texas.

Eventually it became clear, even to Miss Sellers, that I was unlikely to attack her, and our relationship entered an even more embarrassing phase. She decided that a great, but purely platonic, love had sprung up between us. This spiritual kinship involved the writing (on her part) of a sequence of poems, not primarily designed for publication, and many references, ingeniously but much too thinly disguised, to the dear new bond between us. It was Miss Sellers' hideous fancy to pretend that she was writing a book, in which the principal characters were designated simply as "the boy" and "the girl." To make it even easier, "the boy" was the editor of a newspaper, while "the girl," a poetess of considerable power, worked for him as a reporter. On the slightest provocation, or none, and certainly in any company, Miss Sellers would outline the latest chapter in this work. Once, I remember, "the boy" was dying of pneumonia (almost all the chapters contained a satisfactory amount of sickness and catastrophe) and "the girl" brought him around with a sonnet. As a *roman à clef*, it had an enormous vogue among the happy villagers.

Our love also involved telepathy. Occasionally, in the newspaper office, I would answer the phone, to hear that unmistakable voice—Miss Sellers always spoke in the tone generally reserved by elderly ladies for children or small animals.

"Hello," it would say.

"Hello, Miss Sellers."

"You *knew!*" There would be a sound which I could picture only as Miss Sellers blowing hard into the mouthpiece. "Isn't it marvellous!"

"Oh, I ought to know your voice by this time, Miss Sellers."

"Oh, *no!*" More blowing. "Oh, it's *much* more than that!"

The final confirmation of our psychic tieup, however, came one evening when I was working late at the office. There was a frosted-glass panel in the door, and a strong light in the hall, so that anybody standing outside cast a sharp shadow on the pane. Looking up suddenly, I saw an outline that, from the triple bun on top to the gigantic waist, could have belonged to only one person in the world.

"Come in, Miss Sellers," I said hopelessly.

Miss Sellers came in, pale with some delicious blending of fright and rapture.

"It's uncanny! It frightens me," she cried. "Why, you *felt* me out there!"

I looked at the lighted panel, and at Miss Sellers, but I knew it was no use.

"Yes," I said, "it frightens me too."

A little after that, I resigned from the paper myself, partly because of Miss Sellers, and partly because I had no real interest in misleading the taxpayers. I left quietly, almost furtively, and I didn't see Miss Sellers. A few months ago, however, I got a letter from her. Our romance, it appears, has left no scars. Indeed, she didn't even mention it, being too preoccupied with news. There was a new editor after I left, an extremely disagreeable man, who had tried to take away her pistol and cause her "other troubles." Miss Sellers didn't specify just what these "other troubles" were, but I gathered that he'd tried to have her committed. He hadn't succeeded. In fact, the victory was magnificently with Miss Sellers. The editor had been driving along in a storm when a branch was blown down on his skull, fracturing it. He wasn't dead, but he was in the hospital, and nobody believed he'd ever be the same. Miss Sellers said that this was obviously the hand of God, and seemed to be somewhat alarmed at her own powers. In the meantime, there is a new editor—"a rather delicate boy." She hopes that he's stronger than he looks. So do I.

August 3, 1935

WAFERS ARE EXPLODED

IN THESE PERPLEXING days, when every man seems threatening to become my brother or better, almost my only comfort is in an anonymous English author who, in 1841, wrote a little book called "Etiquette for Gentlemen: with Hints on the Art of Conversation," published by Messrs. Tilt and Bogue of London. With his first sentences this nameless arbiter brings back to the world a forgotten order and security. Marvellously reassuring, for instance, to a man who had thought all privacy lost in the brotherhood of man is his comment in the chapter called "Introductions": "You should not introduce anybody, even at his own request, to another, unless you are quite sure the acquaintance will be agreeable to the latter. A person does himself no service with another when he obliges him to know people he would rather avoid." You didn't, in this happy society, have to meet dull people; in fact, it was rather hard to get to meet anybody at all. "If in the course of a walk in company with a friend, you happen to meet, or are joined by an acquaintance, do not commit the too common, but most flagrant error, of introducing such persons to one another." It is pleasant to think of this fashionable trio as they strolled through the town, Mr. A. irritably involved in two unrelated conversations as he struggled to avoid the flagrant error of introducing Mr. B. to Mr. C. The Master, however, goes even further. "Never introduce morning visitors, who happen to meet in your parlor without being acquainted, to one another," he says. "If *you* should be so introduced, remember that the acquaintance afterwards goes for nothing; you have not the slightest right to expect that the other will again recognize you." Here, of course, was the perfect escape from dismal fellowship: it seemed very unlikely that you'd ever be introduced to anybody, but even if you were it was presumably because of some flaw in your host's breeding, and was much better ignored.

In spite of this withdrawn attitude, however, my Englishman was no snob. He didn't care much about meeting his inferiors, but he had no special objection to acknowledging that they were alive. "If an individual of the lowest rank, or without any rank at all, takes off his hat to you, you should do the same in return," he observes democratically. "The two best-bred men of their time, Charles the Second and George the Fourth, never failed to take off their hats to the meanest of their subjects." Nevertheless, he could be haughty enough when the time came for it. "If you meet a fop, whose self-consequence you wish to reprove, you may salute him in a very patronizing manner; or else, in acknowledging his bow, look somewhat surprised and say, 'Mister—eh—eh?'"

On dress my man was also an encyclopedia, although, perhaps because of the patrician excesses of his day, he appeared to deal mostly with small blemishes and oddities of pigmentation. A man with a red nose, for instance, must "dress so that the eye, instead of being shocked by the strangeness of the defect, will be reconciled, if not charmed, by the graceful harmony of the colors." Or: "If you have weak eyes, you should wear spectacles. If the defect be great, your glasses should be colored. In such cases . . . green spectacles are an abomination—blue ones are respectable, and even *distingué*." And finally: "Almost every defect of face may be concealed by judicious use and arrangement of hair. Take care, however, that your hair be not of one color and your whiskers of another."

Passing quickly over the chapter called "Visiting," in which my friend contributes little except the comment that it is inadvisable to discuss literature in a house of mourning, we come to "Letter Writing," which is much more helpful, and contains again that note of elegant hypocrisy which must have made his day tolerable to the sensitive. "Always remember," he says, "that the terms of compliment at the close of a letter—'I have the honor to be your very obedient servant,' etc.—are merely forms, 'signifying nothing.' Do not avoid them because of pride or a dislike to the person addressed." There is a bitter wisdom (and perhaps the hint of a personal scar) when he writes, "In letters of every description, even those to the most intimate friends, there is need of the utmost caution in expressing sentiments and opinions. . . . If their affections do not change, your opinions may, and the evidence of change may be an inconvenient document." At the end of this chapter, the author descends to technicalities: "In general correspondence," he says, "wafers are now entirely exploded. Letters to gentlemen should be sealed with red wax. In notes to ladies employ colored wax but not perfumed."

THERE ARE MANY other chapters—one on "The Dinner Table," in which the cultivated host is advised never to apologize, even if all hell seems to be breaking loose in the pantry, and another on "The Ball Room," telling the young dancing man that nothing is more preposterous than to eat in gloves—but it is in his "Hints on Conversation" that the writer is at his best, and I offer these samples without further comment:

If you get entangled in a dispute with some learned blockhead, you may silence him with a few extemporary quotations. If that does not convince him, he will be so stunned with amazement that you can make your escape and avoid the unpleasant necessity of knocking him down.

Never commend a lady's musical skill to another lady who herself plays.

Most women . . . wish to obtain a reputation for intellect and an acquaintance with science. You therefore pay them a real compliment . . . by conversing occasionally upon grave matters, which they do not understand, and do not really relish.

Do not allow your love for one woman to prevent your paying attention to others.

Nil admirari, the precept of stoicism, is the precept for conduct among gentlemen. All excitement must be studiously avoided. When you are with ladies, the case is different. Among them, wonder, astonishment, ecstasy and enthusiasm are necessary in order to be believed.

Never ask a lady a question about anything whatever.

When you are going into company, it is of advantage to run over in your mind beforehand the topics of conversation which you intend to bring up and to arrange the order in which you will introduce them. You may also run through the details of the few very brief and sprightly anecdotes which you are going to repeat, and also have in readiness one or two brilliant phrases or striking words which you will use upon occasion.

For one who has travelled much, to hit the proper medium between too much reserve and too much intrusion on the subject of his adventures is not easy. Such a person is expected to give amusement by pleasant histories of his travels, yet in moderation: he should not reply to every remark with a memoir commencing, "When I was in Japan."

A constant flow of wit is excessively fatiguing to the listeners. "The wit of the company, next to the butt of the company," says Mrs. Montagu, "is the meanest person in it."

Punning is now decidedly out of date. It is a silly and displeasing thing . . . within the reach of the most trifling and often used by them to puzzle or degrade the wise.

Surrounded by my clever friends—fatigued by their witticisms, degraded by their puns, and bored by their memories of Japan—I often think of this pleasant society, gone forever from the world, in which all the ladies were skillful musically, and the gentlemen, stoics underneath, displayed only wonder, astonishment, and ecstasy as they spoke to them of the gravest matters. Then I wish that I were another man in another time—a man perhaps of whom it could be truly said, "He never asked a lady a question about anything," a time when I could politely hide my troubled face in some judicious arrangement of hair.

February 29, 1936

RING OUT, WILD BELLS

WHEN I FINALLY got around to seeing Max Reinhardt's cinema version of "A Midsummer Night's Dream," and saw a child called Mickey Rooney playing Puck, I remembered suddenly that long ago I had taken the same part.

Our production was given on the open-air stage at the Riverdale Country School, shortly before the war. The scenery was only the natural scenery of that suburban dell, and the cast was exclusively male, ranging in age from eleven to perhaps seventeen. While we had thus preserved the pure, Elizabethan note of the original, it must be admitted that our version had its drawbacks. The costumes were probably the worst things we had to bear, and even Penrod, tragically arrayed as Launcelot in his sister's stockings and his father's drawers, might have been embarrassed for us. Like Penrod, we were costumed by our parents, and like the Schofields, they seemed on the whole a little weak historically. Half of the ladies were inclined to favor the Elizabethan, and they had constructed rather bunchy ruffs and farthingales for their offspring; others, who had read as far as the stage directions and learned that the action took place in an Athenian wood, had produced something vaguely Athenian, usually beginning with a sheet. Only the fairies had a certain uniformity. For some reason their parents had all decided on cheesecloth, with here and there a little ill-advised trimming with tinsel.

My own costume was mysterious, but spectacular. As nearly as I have ever been able to figure things out, my mother found her inspiration for it in a Maxfield Parrish picture of a court jester. Beginning at the top, there was a cap with three stuffed horns; then, for the main part, a pair of tights that covered me to my wrists and ankles; and finally slippers with stuffed toes that curled up at the ends. The whole thing was made out of silk in alternate green and red stripes, and (unquestionably my poor mother's most demented stroke) it was covered from head to foot with a thousand tiny bells. Because all our costumes were obviously perishable, we never wore them in rehearsal, and naturally nobody knew that I was invested with these peculiar sound effects until I made my entrance at the beginning of the second act.

Our director was a man who had strong opinions about how Shakespeare should be played, and Puck was one of his favorite characters. It was his theory that Puck, being "the incarnation of mischief," never ought to be still a minute, so I had been coached to bound onto the stage, and once there to dance up and down, cocking my head and waving my arms.

"I want you to be a little whirlwind," this man said.

Even as I prepared to bound onto the stage, I had my own misgivings about those dangerously abundant gestures, and their probable effect on my bells. It was too late, however, to invent another technique for playing Puck, even if there had been room for anything but horror in my mind. I bounded onto the stage.

The effect, in its way, must have been superb. With every leap I rang like a thousand children's sleighs, my melodies foretelling God knows what worlds of merriment to the enchanted spectators. It was even worse when I came to the middle of the stage and went into my gestures. The other ringing had been loud but sporadic. This was persistent, varying only slightly in volume and pitch with the vehemence of my gestures. To a blind man, it must have sounded as though I had recklessly decided to accompany myself on a xylophone. A maturer actor would probably have made up his mind that an emergency existed, and abandoned his gestures as impracticable under the circumstances. I was thirteen, and incapable of innovations. I had been told by responsible authorities that gestures went with this part, and I continued to make them. I also continued to ring—a silvery music, festive and horrible.

If the bells were hard on my nerves, they were even worse for the rest of the cast, who were totally unprepared for my new interpretation. Puck's first remark is addressed to one of the fairies, and it is mercifully brief.

I said, "How now, spirit! Whither wander you?"

This unhappy child, already embarrassed by a public appearance in cheesecloth and tinsel, was also burdened with an opening speech of sixteen lines in verse. He began bravely:

"Over hill, over dale,
  Through brush, through brier,
Over park, over pale,
  Through flood, through fire . . ."

At the word "fire," my instructions were to bring my hands up from the ground in a long, wavery sweep, intended to represent fire. The bells pealed. To my startled ears, it sounded more as if they exploded. The fairy stopped in his lines and looked at me sharply. The jingling, however, had diminished; it was no more than as if a faint wind stirred my bells, and he went on:

"I do wander everywhere,
Swifter than the moone's sphere . . ."

Here again I had another cue, for a sort of swoop and dip indicating the swiftness of the moone's sphere. Again the bells rang out, and again the performance stopped in its tracks. The fairy was clearly troubled by these interruptions. He had, however, a child's strange acceptance of the inscrutable, and was even able to regard my bells as a last-minute adult addition to the program, nerve-racking but not to be questioned. I'm sure it was only this that got him through that first speech.

MY TURN, WHEN it came, was even worse. By this time the audience had succumbed to a helpless gaiety. Every time my bells rang, laughter swept the spectators, and this mounted and mingled with the bells until everything else was practically inaudible. I began my speech, another long one, and full of incomprehensible references to Titania's changeling.

"Louder!" said somebody in the wings. "You'll have to talk louder."

It was the director, and he seemed to be in a dangerous state.

"And for heaven's sake, stop that jingling!" he said.

I talked louder, and I tried to stop the jingling, but it was no use. By the time I got to the end of my speech, I was shouting and so was the audience. It appeared that I had very little control over the bells, which continued to jingle in spite of my passionate efforts to keep them quiet.

All this had a very bad effect on the fairy, who by this time had many symptoms of a complete nervous collapse. However, he began his next speech:

> *"Either I mistake your shape and making quite,*
> *Or else you are that shrewd and knavish sprite*
> *Called Robin Goodfellow: are you not he*
> *That . . ."*

At this point I forgot that the rules had been changed and I was supposed to leave out the gestures. There was a furious jingling, and the fairy gulped.

"Are you not he that, that . . ."

He looked miserably at the wings, and the director supplied the next line, but the tumult was too much for him. The unhappy child simply shook his head.

"Say anything!" shouted the director desperately. "Anything at all!"

The fairy only shut his eyes and shuddered.

"All right!" shouted the director. "All right, Puck. *You* begin *your* next speech."

By some miracle, I actually did remember my next lines, and had opened my mouth to begin on them when suddenly the fairy spoke. His voice was a high, thin monotone, and there seemed to be madness in it, but it was perfectly clear.

"Fourscore and seven years ago," he began, "our fathers brought forth on this continent a new nation, conceived . . ."

He said it right through to the end, and it was certainly the most successful speech ever made on that stage, and probably one of the most successful speeches ever made on any stage. I don't remember, if I ever knew, how the rest of us ever picked up the dull, normal thread of the play after that extraordinary performance, but we must have, because I know it went on. I only remember that in the next intermission the director cut off my bells with his penknife, and after that things quieted down and got dull.

April 4, 1936

BEAUTY AND GUTZON BORGLUM[1]

A T ABOUT FOUR o'clock the telephone rang, and Mr. Pettifer answered it. He said "Yes?" in a rather gruff, clipped voice, because he liked to think of himself as a busy man, with no time for foolishness. The voice at the other end was richly cultivated, with something in it of the sound of little bells.

"Mr. Austin Pettifer?" it said.

"Yes."

"This is Miss Myrna Haskell's secretary. Miss Haskell wondered if you'd possibly be free for cocktails on Friday afternoon."

Mr. Pettifer skimmed over the leaves of his desk calendar. On the line for five o'clock on Friday afternoon was the word "Dentist," printed in his secretary's neat, business-school hand. He crossed it out impatiently.

"Why, certainly," he said. "I'd be delighted."

"That's splendid," said the voice. "At half past five, then. The Ritz, of course."

When she had hung up, Mr. Pettifer leaned back and thought pleasantly of Myrna Haskell. Miss Haskell was a figure of some consequence in the city. She was young and beautiful and rich, and she was known to be amiably disposed toward the arts, although her direct connection with them was limited to a few short stories which had first appeared in the smartest of all possible magazines and then had been reprinted in a little book called "Cherubim and Terrapin." Mr. Pettifer didn't think much of these stories, largely because they dealt with a world outside his experience, where, it seemed to him, people dropped far too readily into French, but, after all, Miss Haskell's private struggles for self-expression had very little to do with the splendor of her social life. At her parties you were sure to meet the most interesting, or at any rate the most bizarre, figures of the day—the surrealists, the sensitive young men who took pictures of strange objects from even stranger angles, the unpunctuated novelists, and the unregimented poets; everybody, in short, who was doing interesting things in a way they'd never been done before. It was also nice to know, as Mr. Pettifer *did* know from the society columns in the papers, that this creative element would be leavened by a delegation of the rich and respectable—solid men of enormous affairs, names that were very old in the city.

Mr. Pettifer wondered momentarily why he had been asked to such a fashionable assemblage. He had met Miss Haskell just once, in the lobby of a theatre, and it had seemed to him then that her mind was only partially on his judicious estimate of the play. It was just possible, he thought, blushing a little at the arrogance of the idea, that she had read a few of the little book reviews he had had in that great woman's magazine of which he was an associate editor, and that she had been impressed by them. He found this explanation comforting, and gradually came to believe it.

AT EXACTLY A quarter of six on Friday, Mr. Pettifer presented himself at the desk at the Ritz, and soon he was in the elevator, with permission to call on the ineffable Miss Haskell.

A tidy maid opened the door for him, took away his hat, and guided him into the living room. This was a noble and arresting chamber, because one of Miss Haskell's protégés had been turned loose in it with no instructions except that he contrive a fitting background for her personality. Mr. Pettifer, however, was conscious neither of the glass nor the chromium nor the queer, writhing pictures on the wall; he realized only that he was alone, and he wondered miserably if he had come too early, or, far worse, if it could be the wrong day altogether. He was sitting there, worrying about these things and glancing furtively at Miss Haskell's clock, which had no hands but only two golden balls revolving in an empty face, when the lady herself appeared in the doorway.

Miss Haskell was very beautiful and strange. In his innocence, Mr. Pettifer was astounded that any human being could grow eyelashes an inch long, and he was interested in her costume, which appeared to be a pair of pajamas, but pajamas incredibly frail and mysterious, and impossible to imagine upon any young woman who merely wished to go to bed. Her hair was decidedly blue, and this, too, Mr. Pettifer considered unusual. Miss Haskell, in fact, looked almost exactly like an advertisement in *Vogue* or *Harper's Bazaar*.

She came in and gave him her hand, and spoke to him with an accent that belonged to no especial locality, although there was a good deal of English in it, and some French.

"How do you do?" she said. "It was so kind of you to come."

Mr. Pettifer, feeling idiotic, said not at all, it had been kind of her to ask him.

"*Mais non!*" she cried. "When I think of how busy you must be . . ."

Her voice trailed away, as if it made her a little faint to think how busy Mr. Pettifer must be, and she sank into a chair.

"Do sit down," she said, recovering at last. "Wouldn't you like a Martini?"

"Thank you."

"I suppose you want it sweet?" she said with a tiny expression of distaste. "All you Americans seem to like your cocktails so sweet."

The "you Americans" startled Mr. Pettifer a little, because he remembered quite clearly that Miss Haskell had come from his own native Pennsylvania, where her father had done very well in the cement business. However, there didn't seem to be much to do about it. Mr. Pettifer had a sweet Martini. Miss Haskell had a sherry, which he felt resentfully was probably drier than all hell.

There was a little silence while Mr. Pettifer sipped his Martini and found it even sweeter and more unpleasant than he'd expected. Miss Haskell contented herself with merely looking fashionable. At last she spoke.

"How is your little magazine these days?" she asked.

Mr. Pettifer, thinking of those two million readers sprawled between New York and Bangkok, said that it seemed quite satisfactory, all things considered.

"Of course, I'm sure you have a perfectly enormous circulation," she said. "I sometimes wonder, though, if it wouldn't have been better if you hadn't been *quite* so successful."

"I'm afraid I—"

"I mean it so often seems to me that you're getting just a little too popular. A little, well, vulgar." She paused and sighed. "But I suppose one *has* to be a little vulgar these days. *C'est l'esprit de l'âge.*"

Mr. Pettifer felt annoyed but helpless. By implication he had been called a vulgar American, but there was something about Miss Haskell and her attendant scenery that made him feel that perhaps this was only too true. Indeed, just then he felt obscurely like a large and rather dusty horse.

For a moment they both sat and thought sadly about the vulgarity of Mr. Pettifer's magazine, then Miss Haskell smiled.

"Well, I imagine it can't be helped," she said charitably. "And anyway that isn't what I wanted to talk about. I suppose you've been wondering why I wanted to see you."

He had indeed.

"I thought," she said, "that it might be fun if *I* wrote a little article for your magazine."

"That would be fine," said Mr. Pettifer feebly. He realized suddenly that there wasn't going to be any cocktail party at all; that Miss Haskell, in a creative mood, was simply in the habit of sending for editors and telling them about it, just as he himself might have sent for a man to fix the icebox. It was an interesting idea. It was also interesting to think how Mr. Pettifer's editor, an impatient man, would be affected by an article in which every third word would undoubtedly be in French, while the rest, from his point of view, might just as well be.

"I'm not sure whether you'll want it or not," she said with pretty modesty, "especially as it's about a man that I don't imagine you or Mr. Higgins—it *is* Mr. Higgins, isn't it?—has ever heard of."

"Well, that might be a difficulty," said Mr. Pettifer. "Who is it?"

"Gutzon Borglum," she told him. "Perhaps I'd better spell it for you. But he's really quite a well-known sculptor."

A little after that Mr. Pettifer went down in the elevator and out into the street, where he got into a taxicab. As he rode down Madison

Avenue, he thought somewhat about the well-known sculptor, but mostly about Miss Haskell's mind. For some reason he was never able to explain, it made him think of confetti.

September 10, 1938

A FELLOW OF INFINITE JEST

BARDOLPH MARTIN WAS the last of the fashionable literary humorists. Upon his death, which could hardly be far away, since practically everything imaginable was wrong with the old horror, nothing would be left of the art form to which he had given his life. Written comedy would survive vestigially in sad little collections of jokes in holes and corners of the newspapers and great national magazines, and books would continue to be composed dealing with eccentric domestic life in the suburbs or with persons engaged in bizarre occupations of one kind and another. For the rest, however, the wit available to the public would be found only on television and moving-picture screens, and on the stages of a few doomed theatres.

It was an appalling prospect, and the members of the great man's family were fully aware of their responsibility. On the cold February afternoon in 1960 with which this narrative has to do, these people—his wife, Perdita, and his two children, Cyril and Ariadne, who were twenty-two and seventeen, respectively—were sitting in the living room of their apartment at Park Avenue and Eighty-second Street, discussing a situation that simultaneously concerned them all acutely and bored them to the threshold of the madhouse.

"I assume," said Cyril, "that there really is some point in all this? I would be the last to deny that Father is the incomparable spokesman for intelligent bewilderment in a time of chaos and that his style combines the best of Flaubert, Henry James, and several other writers whose names escape me for the moment. It only occurs to me to wonder whether this is a particularly interesting accomplishment."

"You are questioning the most sophisticated critical opinion of our time," said Ariadne sardonically.

"I suppose I am," he replied. "All I know is that I find him almost unreadable. God knows, I try, but a paragraph is generally enough. I am happy, of course, to confess that I have no sense of humor whatever."

"Really, Cyril," said his mother, "you know you have an extraordinarily fine mind."

"I'm afraid there's not much connection," he said. "As a matter of fact, it may easily be that cultivation excludes an appreciation of humor, or at least Father's peculiar brand of humor."

"How would you define that, exactly?" asked Ariadne. "I've often wondered."

"It's hard," he admitted, "but I should say that the essence of it lies in a horridly winsome confession of his inability to deal with social situations that would present no real problem to a properly brought-up child of ten. Theoretically, I suppose, an insistence on one's lack of breeding combined with a certain amount of literary agility is entertaining. I'm sorry to say that I find it vulgar."

"And dull," said Perdita.

"And dull," he agreed.

THERE WAS A silence, in which each of them thought with disgust of Bardolph Martin's indomitable archness and his apparently inexhaustible capacity for self-revelation.

"Well," said Ariadne, at length, "whether we like it or not, the fact remains that we are in no position to permit Father to stop working. You understand I have no interest in the loss that it is generally supposed his retirement would mean to the English-speaking world. That is a ludicrous idea, naturally. Far from owing it to humanity to see that he goes on, I suspect that we would be performing a distinct public service in causing him to desist. As you say, he is an extremely common old man, and I am aware that his influence is deplorable, especially on the young. It is even necessary to consider the possibility that he might inspire a successor."

"You are morbid," said Cyril.

"No," his sister replied. "I am simply prepared to face the worst. However, we seem to be straying a little from the point. What I am trying to say is that, while it would be aesthetically desirable to put an end to Father's career, from our own selfish point of view it is unthinkable. You are both charming and I flatter myself that I am not wholly repulsive, but unhappily none of us is equipped to earn even an adequate income, much less the kind of money that would be required to maintain this establishment, which I, for one, find extremely comfortable. It is essential, therefore, that Father go on, and that we continue to assist him as we always have."

"I suppose you're right," said Cyril, "but I'm not sure that I can stand it."

"I'm afraid you'll have to," she said. "We all will. It was decided a long time ago, when Mother made up her mind that it was her duty to supply her husband with literary material, and deliberately cast us all as domestic comedians."

"Blame it all on me," said Perdita bitterly. "I am old and far from well and quite accustomed to ingratitude."

"Nonsense," said Ariadne. "Cyril and I went into it quite voluntarily. In the beginning, when I was playing an idiot child, it even struck me as rather fun. It certainly saved me a great deal of bother at school. We lived for almost a year, if you remember, on my inability to grasp arithmetic. It was nearly as successful as the series about Mother trying to balance her checkbook."

"That wasn't as easy as you seem to think," said Perdita. "It entertained your father—or at least it was useful to him professionally—to imagine I couldn't add. On the other hand, he had an almost pathological regard for money and he was apt to be very unpleasant about errors of more than five dollars. The same thing was true of his feeling about the way I operated a car. It served his debased artistic purpose to think that I was a hopelessly incompetent driver, but, actually, dented fenders and traffic tickets brought out the worst in his nature, which was, frankly, unspeakable. It was probably just as well that I was really an excellent mathematician and a very skillful driver, since it was consequently possible for me to provide the necessary comic effect without any actual financial loss."

"My own early contributions weren't really difficult at all," said Cyril. "I was away most of the time at school and camp and college, and very little was required except an amusingly illiterate letter once a month or so. Even as a boy, I was considerably more intelligent than Father, and I understood almost at once the kind of naïveté he wanted. As you know, he is at his best when he can write about us with the tolerant amusement of a man of the world set down mysteriously in a suburban boarding house. In their way, I imagine my letters had an almost epic vulgarity. He was enchanted with them and so, of course, were his editors and the public."

"When you come to think of it, those were really golden years," said Ariadne. "The demands of upper-middle-class humor were remarkably simple. The formula was always the same. There was a man who couldn't replace a burned-out fuse and a woman who couldn't cope with a checking account, and usually two children whose curious blend of precocity and innocence led them to do and say all kinds of embarrassing but laughable things. We were attended by a succession of servants and pets—mainly dogs—and it was amazing how quickly they understood what Father wanted of them. I am suspicious of all generalities, and I hesitate to say that the more primitive the mechanism the more rapidly it can be expected to grasp the fundamentals of humor, but the fact remains that we were seldom without the services of a supporting and highly remunerative cast of dialect comedians and neurotic animals. Almost infinite variations were possible, of course, but the prevailing atmosphere was always one of placid imbecility. We were quite happy collaborating with Father in those days, and—"

"I wasn't," interrupted Perdita. "You forget I was obliged to read what your father wrote, frequently in manuscript, and, furthermore, to listen to my friends discussing it. I don't think I am hypersensitive, but I can assure you that I often tired of the role of village half-wit."

"I can see that that might make some difference," said Cyril. "Not to mention the fact that you were married to him—a condition naturally repugnant to any fastidious woman. Life was unquestionably hard for you then, but I'm sure you'll admit that it got much worse."

"It did indeed," said Perdita.

"There was an abrupt change in popular humor," said Cyril. "Suddenly people had had enough of the old simplicities, and the author was obliged to turn to what, in his innocence, he believed to be more adult themes. The family he wrote about, which up to then

had been preoccupied with what you might call comic-strip dilem-
mas, was whisked almost overnight into a new and terribly complicated world. The central problem that confronted them now was sex,
with special emphasis on the married state. The change was very
difficult for Father, who had previously given little thought to sex,
being afflicted with the congenitally low vitality that is, I suppose, an
indispensable condition of humor."

"In many ways it was a very odd marriage," murmured Perdita.

"We were aware of that," said Cyril, "and you had our deepest
sympathy. However, taxing as this new kind of comedy may have
been for Father, I think there can be no question that it was infinitely more so for the rest of us."

"My part in it was particularly humiliating," said Perdita. "In
the early stages of his latest phase, if you remember, your father
wrote almost exclusively about a couple who had been married for
twelve or fifteen years. The point, of course, was that the husband
had begun to take a dim, disgusting interest in other women, and
the wife was obliged to employ various tedious stratagems to save
her marriage."

"Why is it," asked Ariadne, "that the wives in Father's fiction are
permitted no sexual exploits of their own?"

"Don't be silly," said Perdita. "For one thing, in spite of what you
may have read in the reviews, your father's humor has little or no connection with reality; for another, his vanity is such that I'm sure the
idea would never enter his head. Anyway, my position as the leading
actress in all this detestable nonsense was nearly intolerable. Your father, as you can hardly have helped noticing, is a man of little taste and
practically no personal charm, and as a result the women he chose to
supplant me temporarily not only came from a rather inferior order of
society, with all that implies in the way of callous butcheries of the
English language, but they were also singularly unappetizing in appearance."

"Mrs. Memuer," said Ariadne, "and those really extraordinary
teeth."

"She was by no means the worst," said Perdita. "What conversations we had—or, rather, what a conversation, because, of course, it
was always essentially the same. In a way, it was entertaining to

think that the real comedy, as distinguished from that which appeared in your father's subsequent reports, lay in the incredible difference between what I said and what was really going on in my head. Nothing, you can be sure, would have gratified me more than to see your father and Mrs. Memuer slope off to Bermuda, and nothing, I liked to think, could have been more surprising to her, or more irresistibly comic, than his behavior when they got there. However, I knew my duty, commercially speaking, and the scenes that actually took place among us were precisely as ghastly as they are in print. All this went on for several years. I doubt if any woman has ever made more gruesome sacrifices for art."

"Poor Mother," said Cyril.

"I suffered," she said, "but I consoled myself with the thought that it was bringing in approximately eighty thousand dollars a year. Before taxes, of course."

"My own Gethsemane came later," said Ariadne, "but I can't help feeling that it was almost equally distressing. By that time, Father was obsessed with the speech and behavior of the younger generation. I was little use to him in my natural condition, because, unhappily, I'd been to the wrong schools and I'd never even met anybody who talked the way he'd been led to suppose all teen-agers did. I also dressed with a certain modesty or decorum, partly because I'd been taught to do so and partly because I had no real wish to be mistaken for a cowhand, and that was a disappointment to him, too. My tastes in music, literature, and entertainment were immature but not wholly corrupt, and, finally, my relations with young men, while extensive, were hardly picturesque by his standards. Somewhere or other— conceivably from Mrs. Memuer—he'd picked up the idea that nowadays adolescents are paired off irrevocably at a very early age, and habitually employ such current vulgarisms as 'boy friend,' 'girl friend,' and that king of backstairs abominations 'going steady.' As you know, my conduct bore little relation to that. It seemed to me that the fundamental purpose of a reasonably personable young woman was to better herself socially and financially. I had been operating on that principle, accepting only those invitations, from young men of established position, that obviously held some promise for the future, when suddenly, like Mother, I realized my obligations, or perhaps where my best interests lay. It seems unlikely that you have forgotten what followed."

"You did very nicely," said Cyril. "As I recall it, you were pinned, ringed, and publicly signed, sealed, and delivered in almost every imaginable way and by persons whose origins were inscrutable, to put it mildly. You talked in a manner that was exceedingly repugnant to your mother and to me; your costumes were suitably cheap and hideous; and the house was littered with comic books, phonograph records, and magazines containing articles celebrating the genius of Elvis Presley, the late James Dean, and other public figures I happen to know you really considered grotesque. I found it a little difficult to get along with your invariable suitor, perhaps because he was so unmistakably all that you were pretending to be, but I, too, understood that Father was stuck with a series, and I coöperated to the best of my ability."

"I have never done so many things that were foreign to my natural disposition," said Ariadne. "In the current idiom, I suppose I am what is called a square. I turned myself into a hep cat, and, for Father's benefit, I forced myself to say things like 'See you later, alligator.' That, and the run-down moccasins and the tight blue trousers, which did very little for my figure, such as it is, seemed cruel and unnecessary punishments. Frequently, I struck myself as a martyr."

"You were heroic," said Cyril. "As a matter of fact, we all were. As much as anything else, I represented the old man's political phase. The general idea could hardly have been more idiotic. In some moment of more than usually muddled inspiration, Father got the notion that it might be funny to do a collection of articles in which a young man would represent the reactionary point of view while an elderly and successful author would speak for this brave new world—a phrase, of course, that has turned up here and there before. It made no more sense than all his other ideas, but who am I to argue with our bread and butter? In any case, the pieces took the form of a series of conversations between him and me. In the course of them, I found myself defending lynching, non-union labor, Senator McCarthy, government control of the press, and all manner of other absurdities. I got myself engaged to a dull and murderously plain young woman of unimpeachable background; I even joined the

National Association of Manufacturers. Father's tone in these dis-
cussions was naturally one of almost overpowering irony—he
talked, you might say, rather like a popular English professor in a
second-rate college. I tried to sound as if I had been written by J. P.
Marquand, with a little assistance from Sinclair Lewis. It was the
most exhausting experience of my life."

"I can't deny that you were awful," said Ariadne, "but, like Mother
and me, you really hadn't much choice."

"There should be some way out," said Cyril. "I speak, of course,
only for myself, but I doubt if I am physically up to another impersonation. You have to face the fact that only God knows what Father
will think of next."

"It can hardly be worse than what we've endured in the past,"
said Perdita.

"I think you're underestimating Father," said Ariadne. "He's capable of practically anything."

THE THREE UNHAPPY people, confronted with what seemed
to be their insoluble dilemma, sat for some time in silence. It was
clearly necessary that the great man go on, since all of them were
substantially unemployable; on the other hand, there were just as
clearly limits to the capacity of the human spirit for assuming roles
that promised to grow increasingly intolerable. Suddenly, however,
Cyril had what was always subsequently regarded as a stroke of genius.

"Insurance!" he cried. "Father must carry some insurance. But
how much?"

"A good deal more than he is worth," said Perdita.

"That would be about ten cents, if you ask me," said Ariadne.

"I am serious," said Cyril. "Specifically, how much?"

"I have always been rather vague about these things," said Perdita. "It never seemed precisely in good taste to inquire how much
a man is worth dead, even your father. But I think I remember
some talk about three hundred thousand dollars."

"Of course, it isn't a fortune," said Cyril. "But still . . ."

"Surely you can't mean what I think you do," said Perdita.

"You think not?" said Cyril.

At that moment, halting footsteps were audible in the hallway, clearly those of a man whose days, in any case, were numbered.

"I must say I feel just a little embarrassed," said Ariadne, and, as the door opened, she had the grace to blush.

April 13, 1957

So-So Stories

Short Stories

FEUD

W HAT A DAME!" said the callboy, finishing his apple and throwing the core over his shoulder. "No sooner do we figure Baldy's checked in at the yard—I'd stopped in at his place to call him for the six-o'clock Fresh Pond—than I'm laying there on his sofa and she's pouring me out a hooker of rum."

The yardmaster yawned.

"Some night one of them shacks is going to get home early and kick your teeth in," he said.

"Nuts to them," said the callboy.

"All right," said the yardmaster, "I'm only telling you."

It was eight o'clock. All the regular car floats had come in and the Brooklyn interchange yard was quiet except for the occasional cough and scuffle of a switch engine on the hill. Nothing was scheduled now until the midnight freight from New Haven got in with a train of refrigerator cars to be loaded on the floats and towed across New York Harbor to Greenville, where they'd be turned over to the Pennsylvania.

"Stick on the phones, Al," said the yardmaster. "I'm going to lay down a while."

He took off his coat, balled it up into a pillow, and put it on the table. He had scarcely laid his head on it before he seemed to be asleep. The callboy sat down at the yardmaster's desk and put his feet on the edge. He picked up the outside telephone and presently was connected with a lady called Myrtle, to whom he was able to speak frankly.

"Why don't you lay off them tramps?" said the yardmaster without opening his eyes.

"You're a fine guy to be talking about tramps," said the callboy. "How about that big Swede I seen you with at the Coliseum? How about that dizzy jane—"

"All right. All right," said the yardmaster. "Skip it."

He turned over and this time actually slept. The callboy took a folded copy of the *Journal* out of his pocket and turned to "Popeye the Sailor."

At nine o'clock there was a ring on the direct wire from Greenville.

"Bay Ridge," said the callboy. "O.K., Greenville, let's have it."

"Penn floats five-o-three and five-o-six, tug twenty, leaving Greenville at—make it nine-o-five. Thirty-eight cars, one livestock for Manhasset," said the receiver hollowly.

"What the hell kind of time is this to be sending out floats?" said the callboy indignantly. "Don't you guys ever give nobody a break?"

"What's the matter, dear?" said Greenville solicitously. "Was you asleep?"

"All right, wise guy," said the callboy, and hung up the receiver. It would take the floats about three-quarters of an hour to cross the harbor. When they got in, he would have to sort out the waybills, print destination cards from them, and then go out on the floats and tack the cards on their corresponding cars. In the dark this was a disagreeable and even a dangerous job. It was slippery on the icy floats, and the cars were lined up in three rows with barely enough space for a thin and active boy to move between. A checker carried his flashlight in one hand and a railroad spike and the stack of cards in the other. He kept the tacks in his mouth. Expert checkers were usually able to finish the floats before the switch engines came and began to pull the cars off, but sometimes the engines didn't allow enough time and the checker had to flatten himself against one row of cars while projections on the moving row scraped across his back. Livestock cars were worse because they were moved at once, and you could be sure the engines would be coupled on and pulling almost as soon as the floats were fast in the slips.

"Lousy bastards," said the callboy, referring to the Pennsylvania Railroad.

At nine-thirty he went over and shook the yardmaster.

"Come out of it, Jake," he said. "Floats on the way. They got cows."

When the tugboat captain came in the office with the waybills, they found that the livestock car was far back in one of the middle rows, which, for a technical reason, is the most inaccessible position possible.

"That's perfect," said the yardmaster bitterly.

"Don't tell me about it," said the tugboat captain. "I don't load floats."

AS THE CALLBOY went down the yard toward the bridges, he could see that the two floats were already fast. The switch engines, then, were probably on their way down from the upper yard. He had arranged his cards in order, meaning to tag the cars in rotation, but now he decided to tag the livestock first. They'd switch that right out and take it away. He could get the others in the yard later if he had to. Float 503, which had the cattle car, was in the right-hand slip and he climbed up on it, lighting his flashlight. The passageway between the cars was even worse than usual because there was a thin sheen of ice on the deck of the float.

"Oh, sure," he said bitterly, starting to worm his way back to the livestock car. Its number was PRR 637601, and presently he picked it out with his flashlight. As he started to hammer on his card, there was a stirring and grunting in the dark interior, and a piebald face peered at him through the wooden bars. The callboy looked at it nervously.

"Go on, beat it," he said, "before I spit in your eye."

He waved at the cow with his spike and it disappeared, snorting. The callboy put his flashlight up to the bars, illuminating the interior of the car. Eighteen or nineteen cows were standing together at the far end, their heads lowered, their eyes incandescent in the beam from the flashlight. He swung the flashlight around until it came to the floor of the car directly in front of him. Another cow was lying there, pressed against the side of the car. The callboy poked it gingerly with his spike.

"All right, on your feet, sister," he said.

The cow was motionless, however, and he poked it harder. Nothing happened, and he thrust his light through the bars and studied the cow more closely. It had, he saw now, a curiously flat and rigid appearance, and its eyes were closed. He focussed the flashlight on its ribs, and saw that there was no motion. The cow was dead, and there were indications that it had been dead for some time.

"Ain't *that* something," said the callboy. He took a last look at the cow, and then squirmed back through the alley between the cars. The switch engine was just rumbling up on the lead to the bridge when he came out, the conductor waving it on with his lantern. The callboy went up to him.

"Better hold it up, Eddie," he said. "One of them cows is stiff. I'm going in now to tell Jake."

"Yeah?" said the conductor. "Well, we ain't got all night."

"You got all night if Jake says so," said the callboy, and went away, whistling.

"FIND IT ALL right?" asked the yardmaster when the callboy came in.

"I found it," said the callboy, "but it ain't all right. One of 'em's dead."

The yardmaster swore.

"Did you look at it good?" he asked.

"I smelled of it," said the callboy simply.

"O.K. Go out and tell them shacks to pull five-o-three, switch out the cow car, and shove it back on the float. They can drag the rest of the cars up the yard. I'll talk to them dummies at Greenville."

The callboy went out, and the yardmaster spun the crank on the direct wire to Greenville.

"Hello, Maloney? Harvey. Listen, lug, I ain't running no tannery."

"Tannery?" said Greenville, and laughed with a light assumption of bewilderment. "What do you mean you ain't running a tannery, Mr. Harvey?"

"You know god-damn well what I mean," replied the yardmaster. "I mean I ain't got no use for any dead cows."

"Dead cows?" said Greenville, still seeming bemused. "What dead cows?"

"Nuts to you," said Harvey. "One of them cows is dead, and the tug is taking it back as fast as I can switch it out."

"Oh, *them* cows," said Greenville. "Well, I'm afraid there's some mistake, Mr. Harvey. Them cows were in number A-1 shape when they left here. Prolly them gorillas of yours broke their necks switching them."

"This cow has been dead a week," said Harvey. "It stinks."

"They were fresh as daisies when they left here," said Greenville. "I seen them myself."

"Never mind about that," Harvey said. "I'm only telling you the car is on its way back."

Greenville became official.

"You know we can't accept any dead cows, Mr. Harvey," he said. "You know we can't be liable just because you take some poor damn cow and bust its neck switching it."

It was clear to the yardmaster that he was up against a more active mind, and he abandoned the unequal struggle.

"I'm only telling you," he said, and hung up.

PRR 637601 MADE four trips back and forth across the harbor that night. Harvey persistently refused to accept it at Bay Ridge; Greenville politely insisted that the cow was in perfect condition when it left him, that Harvey had broken its neck, and that he was now transparently trying to foist the damages on the Pennsylvania Railroad. The car came over with every consignment from Greenville, and each time it was switched out and sent back with the returning load. The yard crew, which had at first been inclined to regard all this as a humorous variation of their routine, grew bored at length and complained that the cow was deteriorating rapidly and had indeed begun to affect their digestions. The surviving cows also appeared to suffer, from their morbid ferrying, and lay trembling and panting on the floor of the car.

At six o'clock the Long Island dispatcher at Jamaica called Harvey.

"What in God's name are you monkeys doing down there?" he demanded.

"Doing, sir?" repeated Harvey, who by this time had the sense that his mind was ticking like a bomb.

"Yeah. I got eight interchange reports here, and the same damn car on every one of them. Penn 637601. It don't seem possible that you've got the same car from the Penn four times, and sent it back four times. I mean, it don't make sense that you've been shipping the same car back and forth across the harbor all night, but I'm damned if I know what *else* to make out of it."

"No, that's right," said Harvey.

"Well, for God's sake, *why*?" said the dispatcher. "You ain't do-ing it just for the fun, are you?"

"No," said Harvey wearily. "It's on account one of them damn cows is dead."

"What?'

Harvey explained at length and bitterly about the dead cow, and the evidence that it had died while under the jurisdiction of the Pennsylvania Railroad, if not a long time before. The dispatcher lis-tened, but not sympathetically. At the end, he said, "Well, I guess you finally gone screwy, Harvey, put that ain't the point. Who's got the car now?"

"It's here," said Harvey hopelessly. "It just come in again on the five-thirty."

"All right, get out there and dump that damn cow in the harbor. Then pick up the car and put it on the first freight you got out of there."

"But—"

"Never mind 'but.' God almighty, you want *twenty* dead cows on your hands? You think it's good for them other cows to be riding around the bay all night with a stiff?"

"Yeah, but the Penn's got no right—"

"We'll take care of the Penn. You get after them cows."

"Yes, sir."

He called a brakeman and they went down to the float and found the car. Harvey broke the seals and pulled open the door, and, while the rest of the cows shuffled nervously, they rolled the dead cow out onto the float and then pushed it off into the water. It sank for a few seconds and then came up again, ten yards away, bobbing and twist-ing in the dirty current. Harvey watched it till it was out of sight, then he turned and looked gloomily across the harbor to Greenville, where the Pennsylvania humorist was probably already aware of his victory, and prepared to make the deadly most of it.

January 4, 1936

THE COURTSHIP OF
MILTON BARKER

MILTON BARKER, THE car checker, stood at the window, looking out at the freight yard. It was mid-April. A thin rain was blowing in from New York Harbor in little gusts and showers, filling the usual melancholy of the yard with further desolation. The dirt and cinders between the ties had turned to gray mud, and the smoke from a switching engine, idle in one of the leads, was flattened down by the rain and trailed off along the ground. The intricate steel towers that held the machinery for handling the car floats stood up dimly against the sky. Ben Rederson, the old switchman, went by with a lighted lantern, although it was only three o'clock in the afternoon.

"God," said Milton Barker, and rubbed the pane where his breath had clouded it.

The yardmaster looked up from the waybills he was checking.

"Some day, ain't it," he said.

"For ducks," said Milton, who was no man to slight a ritual.

"Yeah."

"You got no kick coming, sitting there on your fanetta," said Milton bitterly. "Take *me*, now."

"I been out in plenty rain worse than this in my time," said the yardmaster. "Say, when I was braking on the Santa Fe . . ."

Milton yawned.

"O.K., Pop," he said. "You already told me."

There was a potbellied stove in the middle of the office and a battered kettle on top of it. Milton took the kettle down and looked inside.

"You want coffee?"

"It's a pity one of you guys couldn't wash that pot once in a while," said the yardmaster. "It's got a cake inside of it, like in a pipe."

"You drunk worse things, Pop," said Milton.

He found a tin cup and a paper bag full of sugar in one of the lockers along the wall and took them to the stove. The coffee poured black and thick. Milton carried his cup over to the window and sat down.

"How you like to be in Pom Beach, Pop?" he said, and when the yardmaster didn't answer, he found peace in the *Daily Mirror*.

After a little while a telephone bell rang.

"Get that, will you, Milty?" said the yardmaster.

"Get it yourself," said Milton, who was reading with some dismay that Miss Lupe Velez, weary of tinsel, had decided to immolate herself in a convent.

"Listen, you," said the yardmaster.

"All right, all right," said Milton, and reached over and picked up the telephone, though without removing his eyes from a photograph of Miss Velez, taken in an earlier and more secular mood. "Harbor Yard."

The telephone chattered and Milton, abandoning the paper, wrote as he listened.

"Circus train . . . Layton & Crowley . . . Five P.M. from Greenville . . . To lay over until nine A.M. . . . Yes, sir. . . . Yeah, I got it."

He hung up the receiver and looked at the yardmaster.

"Well, can you tie that?" he said.

"Circus train?" asked the yardmaster.

"Yeah. Layton & Crowley. That ain't one of the big ones, is it?"

"Nah. A mud show. Plays like Lowell and Attleboro, them places."

"Well anyway."

"Five o'clock from Greenville? That means the float ought to get here around seven. Tell the yard crew it goes up in number three on the Hill."

"O.K."

"And listen, Milty . . ."

"Yeah?"

"It ain't like the 'Follies,' see? I wouldn't be figuring on nothing if I was you."

"You ain't talking to me, Pop," said Milton, and he went out to find the yard conductor.

THE CIRCUS TRAIN arrived on the float at half past six and by seven the yard engines had pulled it up on the Hill, where it was to lie until the following morning. Milton Barker, who had observed the cars sharply as they were pulled off the float, was able to report that nine of them were boxcars which presumably contained animals and stage properties, and that the tenth was a passenger coach which had its curtains drawn but must nevertheless contain the ladies and gentlemen of the cast.

"It cert'n'y *smells* like a hell of a cheap circus," he now told the yardmaster, staring up toward the Hill, where the circus train lay between two lines of empty boxcars.

"It's them elephants," said the yardmaster. "No matter what you do."

Milton nodded. The commonplace aspect of the boxcars and their outrageous fragrance had left him feeling cheated and slightly empty. He took a pair of shears out of a table drawer and began to cut the picture of Lupe Velez out of the *Mirror*. Suddenly there was a knock at the yard-office door.

"C'min!" he shouted, following the agreeable contours of the nun-to-be with the shears.

The door opened, letting in a gust of rain from the yard, and he looked up with annoyance.

"Say, how's for . . ."

He got no further because there were strangers in the doorway—two women and a man—and it was clear that they were not native to his world or even anything he could hope to classify from his previous experience.

The man, who was carrying two empty buckets, was sheathed in a purple suit. It was an opium-eater's dream of a suit, with lapels that rose vivaciously into two points that menaced its wearer's ears; the openings of the pockets ran up and down instead of crosswise and they were trimmed with braid; the trousers, which constricted him too lovingly, terminated in a pair of long, narrow suède shoes, turning up at the ends like little skis. Beneath the upper part of these antic vestments he wore a checked vest of hellish design. His face was pale and, in relation to the rest of his body, much too large. The expression it wore was arrogant but harassed—Monseigneur taunted by the rabble. Like his two companions, he was damp from head to foot, and in the sudden warmth of the yard office he had begun to give off a frail steam.

The two ladies each carried a bucket. They wore dresses which remained defiantly frilly in spite of the rain, and spoke somehow of the indolent South. Their faces, above this girlish finery and beneath two hats that were identical garlands of drenched flowers, were somewhat surprising. There was a prettiness about them, but it had a furious quality, a sort of triumphant ferocity. The ladies indeed looked as if they had just dispatched an enemy in a manner that had given them some dark pleasure and as if presently they hoped to do so again. They were almost exactly alike and it seemed reasonable to Milton to suppose that they were twins or at least sisters.

"Was there something I could do for you?" he asked cautiously.

The three came forward and surrounded the stove.

"You the yodmaster?" asked the man in a hoarse whisper.

"No," said Milton. "Him."

"Oh," said the man. "One of the shacks told us we could get some drinking water."

The yardmaster pointed to the washroom door.

"Hep yourself," he said. "You folks with the circus?"

"Yeah," said the man. He paused, clearly trying to think of something to say about the circus.

"Go on, halfwit," said one of the ladies. "Get the water."

"All right, Mildred," said the man sadly. "You don't have to holler."

She looked at him sombrely, and he picked up the four buckets and disappeared into the washroom.

There was a silence in the yard office while the ladies steamed and brooded in front of the stove. Suddenly the air was filled with the smell of singeing cloth.

"*Now* what the hell?" said one of them, sniffing sharply.

"It's your skirt, Babe," said the one called Mildred. "It's on the stove."

"Well, for God's sake," said Babe, though without, any special emotion. With one accord, the ladies drew back from the stove and sat down on the edge of the table by the window. Their sultry eyes swung around the yard office and rested at last on Milton.

"You," said Mildred. "What do you do here? What's your job?"

"He's just the clerk," said Babe wearily. "Forget it."

"Well," said Mildred, "he's better than the other one. That other one is dead, if you ast me."

"Say," the yardmaster began, but he was chilled by their bleak and impersonal stare and subsided.

"Listen," said Mildred to Milton. "You know where's a drink around here?"

"I told you it's just the clerk," said Babe. "He wouldn't know. Strictly a dummy."

"Gin or whiskey," said Mildred. "I wouldn't care."

"Well," said Milton slowly, "there's no bars around here. You could ast at the lunch wagon. If they knew you."

"They know *you?*"

"Sure."

"What do they carry?" asked Babe.

"Only grappa. It's some kind of a Greek drink."

"Oh, my God," said Mildred. "Well, all right. Get two of them. Two bottles."

"Well . . ."

"It's all right. We'll give you the dough."

"It ain't that," said Milton. "It's only I oughtn't to leave the yard."

"We'll take care of the yard," said Babe. "You get the what's-this."

"You don't have to worry," said Mildred. "I'll handle any trains."

They watched him as he shrugged into a raincoat and went out the door. "Hurry back, dear," said Mildred.

Babe looked at the washroom door.

"I think that bum is drowned," she said. "Your husband. I think he fell in."

"Well, that would be O.K.," said Mildred.

★ ★ ★

WHEN MILTON CAME back with the grappa, Mildred and Babe were still sitting on the table, and the man was standing by the stove. The four buckets, full of water, were on the floor outside the washroom. The yardmaster was finishing a story. "So when she found out I didn't have no money, she threw my shoes out of the window, right in the hobber." He looked at them, shaking with laughter. "Right in New York Hobber. I liked to died."

"You ought to be ashamed of yourself," said Babe coldly. "An old dope like you."

"Hello, dear," said Mildred to Milton. "Did you get it?"

"Yes," he said. He took the two bottles out of the paper bag and put them on the table. The man picked one of them up and held it against the light.

"What is it?" he asked. "Mule?"

"Grappa," said Milton.

"What's this grappa?"

"You ought to know," said Mildred. "You're part Greek or something, ain't you?"

"Ah, don't be like that, Millie," said the man. "I only ast him a question."

He took the cork out and held the bottle up to his nose.

"It don't smell much."

"Well," said Milton, "a bomb don't smell either."

"Listen, you can't drink that stuff in here," said the yardmaster.

"Why not?" said Mildred.

"The superintendent is liable to show up any time," he said. "He's regularly down here every time we get a circus train."

"Ah, tell him—"

"No," said the man. "Wade a minute. Wade a minute. What would he do?"

"Plenty," said the yardmaster. "Drinking on railroad property."

"He can't do nothing to me," said Babe.

"You want to try and tell that to the railway cops?"

"Oh," said Babe. "Well, O.K."

She looked at the four buckets.

"Say, who's going to carry them things?"

"Milty," said Mildred promptly. She put her arm through his. "Ain't you, Milty? Babe and I can each take one of the bottles and you and Stupid can carry the pails. We'll have a little drink up at the train."

"Say, I'd like to," said Milton, "but I better not leave the office, had I, Pop?"

"I don't care what you do," said the yardmaster. "I don't even care if they cut your throat."

"See," said Mildred. "He says it's O.K. Come on, Milty."

"Better leave me hold your watch," said the yardmaster.

It was raining even harder as they started across the yard toward the Hill, where the circus train lay. The floodlights on the float were enough to throw a pale gleam along the rails, but the ties were invisible, half drowned in the muddy water. Milton picked his way along them expertly, but he could hear Babe and the man with the other two pails stumbling and cursing up ahead in the darkness. Mildred came last and she too seemed to be having trouble and spoke sullenly about it.

"You need to be a duck or something," she said.

"Walk where I do," Milton told her. "Keep on the ties. I should of brung a flashlight."

"That's right," she said bitterly. "Now is when to think about it."

They were halfway up the Hill when she pulled at his sleeve.

"Let them go on ahead," she said.

"Why, what's the matter?"

"I ain't taking drinks to all that mob," she said. "There's fifty of them in that car. We wouldn't get no more than a smell. We better drink it right here."

"Listen," he said, with a daring that rather astonished him. "All them boxcars alongside your train. They're empty. How about if we go and sit in one of them for a while?"

"We-ell . . ."

"We could have a little talk," he said carelessly. "Just the two of us."

"Why, Milty," she said, and laughed unreasonably in the darkness. "All right. Whatever you say."

"Come on," he said. "Let's get going."

They reached the top of the Hill and started down the black aisle between the circus train and the empties.

"We better get far enough away from the passenger car," he said. "Some one of your friends might be coming out."

"My!" she said.

THEY HAD TO walk single file between the cars. Mildred went ahead and Milton followed her with the buckets. It was very dark and the strangling smell of the animals was heavy in the air. Suddenly the night was split by hideous laughter; it was inhuman; the laughter of the demented or the damned.

"Hey," said Milton. "What's that?"

"It's only Robert Taylor," she said.

"What?"

"The hyena. We call him Robert Taylor."

"Oh."

At last he stopped before one of the boxcars. The door was open and he peered inside.

"This one looks all right," he said. "It's got some hay in it."

"You think we come far enough, dear?" she said with a giggle.

"I guess so."

"O.K. Hep me up."

He boosted her in the car and then swung in himself, leaving the buckets outside on the ground. The car had apparently contained bricks, because the floor was covered with broken fragments and little piles of straw. Mildred kicked a pile of straw together against the wall facing the open door and sat down on it with a sigh.

"My God," she said, "am I ever pooped."

He sat down beside her on the straw.

"Say, this is all right, ain't it?" he said.

"Well, it's prolly better than the rain." She picked up the bottle and pulled out the cork with her teeth.

"This had better be good," she said.

She drank in the darkness and gave a little shiver.

"You sure that Greek didn't make no mistake, Milty," she said. "Like giving you kerosene or something?"

"Let me see it," he said, and drank cautiously. "No, that's the grappa all right. It don't taste very hot, but it's got a wallop."

"I'll be right here waiting for it," she said. "Give us a cigarette, huh?"

The match lit up the interior of the boxcar and even threw a brief yellow light on the car across the way. Milton noticed that the door of that was open, and there were bars across the opening. The car seemed to contain some kind of cage. In the flare of the match Milton thought he saw vague shadows, stirring enormously.

"What's in there?"

"Some one of the animals," she said indifferently. "I wouldn't know."

"Oh."

Mildred drank again, deeply and this time without apparent displeasure.

"Maybe you was right about this stuff," she said. "I begin to feel like I might live."

"You better take it a little easy," he said. "It's stronger than you think if you ain't used to it."

"Listen, Milty," she said. "You know what happened the last guy told me that? They had to scrape him up off the floor."

"I'm only telling you," he said.

She drank again.

"No, that ain't bad stuff at all," she said gratefully. "I got to remember to get some more of that stuff sometime. What did you say its name was?"

"Grappa."

"Grappa. I like it. Hey," she said with a sharp note of inquiry in her voice. "What seems to be eating *you?*"

Milton, who had put his arm cautiously around her shoulder, withdrew it.

"Nothing," he said uneasily. "I only thought you might find it more comfortable."

"Well, for the love of God," she said. "Milty the Raper."

She laughed coarsely at this exhibition of poor taste and in the darkness Milton blushed.

"All right," she said, relenting. "Go on, put it back, Milty. I ain't sore. It's only you surprised me."

They sat for a little while in silence, in tentative embrace. Mildred's face, lighted intermittently when she drew on her cigarette, seemed relaxed and peaceful, almost amiable. Milton, his eyes more accustomed to the darkness, could see the cage in the other car quite clearly now. There really was an animal in it, a big animal, pacing soft and deadly behind the bars. He could hear the sound of its heavy breath and the creaking of the cage when it threw its weight against the bars. The cage seemed to Milton a frail and ridiculous barrier for an animal that had really made up its mind to get out.

"Say, what *is* that over there, anyway?" he asked nervously.

Mildred glanced at the cage.

"It looks like the lion," she said. "Yeah, that's what it is. Say, is he ever a crazy bastard."

"How do you mean 'crazy'?" asked Milton with anxiety.

"He gets in these crazy spells," she said. "You dassent get near him. Like the time he chewed up this fellow's arm."

"He did?"

"Like hamburger," said Mildred with satisfaction.

"He didn't ever get loose, did he?"

"Not yet. But he can give those bars hell when he gets in one of these crazy spells."

The lion had apparently noticed their voices, because he had stopped walking up and down in the cage and was standing facing the door. Milton could see his wild and luminous eyes searching the darkness. A growl, low and distant like the roll of a train on a faraway bridge, began to stir in his throat. He was rapidly developing all the symptoms of a crazy spell.

"He ain't going to bother us," said Mildred, noticing that Milton seemed tense. "He's practically a tame lion compared to some of them."

She drank again and then laid her head on Milton's shoulder.

"Listen, Milty," she said, and now unexpectedly there was pathos in her voice. "I guess you think I'm just a tramp, don't you? I guess you don't think much of a girl that would drink this grappa, laying around with a fellow in a boxcar. I guess that's what you been thinking about me, ain't it, Milty?"

"I ain't given the topic so much as a thought," said Milton gallantly, though with a wary eye on the lion.

"Shut up before I spit in your eye," said Mildred, addressing the lion, which had begun to growl in earnest. "Listen, Milty, you try being a living statue off and on for ten years, and see how you like it. When I think the number of times I been Fame leading that Goddamn horse. Maybe I ain't always been a plaster saint, but what the hell kind of a life is that for a girl, I ast you?"

She drank, moodily.

"Nobody is calling me no tramp," she said furiously. "That louse in Wilmington. I guess he ain't passing no more remarks about people being tramps."

"Who?" said Milton.

She must have been a volatile girl, because now she laughed merrily.

"This fellow in Wilmington," she said. "Say, that was comical! This fellow was in the act, too. He was the General—you know, sitting on the horse—when I was Fame. Well, one night we all get stiff in a bar and this fellow called Babe and me a tramp. We didn't say nothing at the time, but the next night when he's the General and I'm Fame and Babe is some kind of an angel or nimp or something laying on the ground behind the horse, she takes this big pin and sticks the horse in his backside. Well, I'm hardly out of the way before he's down off the stand and like a bat out of hell for the exit. The General can't hardly keep on a horse staying still, so he gets tossed off in one of the boxes. He busted four ribs.

"Well," she said, with another of her dark and inexplicable changes of mood, "I ain't a tramp, and I don't want to have to tell you again, Milty, that's all."

"But I didn't—"

"Let it pass," she said magnanimously.

The rumble in the lion's throat had been growing steadily stronger and now it deepened into a passable roar. He flicked his paw tentatively at the bars, which rattled ominously.

"Pipe down, you," said Mildred.

"Say, maybe we better—"

"You, too, Milty," said Mildred, speaking with some difficulty because the neck of the bottle was in her mouth. "Both of you. Pipe down."

There could be no mistake this time about the lion's roar, and he lunged heavily against the bars.

"Well, for God's sake," said Mildred disgustedly. She had been smoking a cigarette, and when the lion roared again she threw it irritably toward the cage.

"Lay down, screwball," she said.

As Milton watched with dismay, the cigarette curved through the air, between the bars, and hit the lion sharply on the nose. A little shower of sparks enveloped his head, glowed, and went out.

For a moment nothing happened, and then the lion exploded. They could see him only dimly, a black and monstrous shape, tearing at the bars, but his intentions were clear and awful. The roaring had given way to a strangled, deadly snarl, and sometimes he spit like a cat. Beneath these louder sounds Milton could hear the even more paralyzing groan and creak of the tortured bars. Mildred added her own frail voice to bedlam.

"Shut up, shut up, shut up!" she shouted. "Shut up, *shut up,* SHUT UP!"

"My God," whispered Milton, "he's breaking the damn thing down!"

She didn't hear him or, hearing, paid no attention.

"I'll fix the crazy bastard!" she cried passionately, and while he watched in agony she scrambled down out of the car and picked up one of the buckets of water.

Milton waited for no more. He vaulted down out of the car and fled desperately into the darkness. For a little while, as he ran, he could hear Mildred arguing with the lion, but presently all sound died away. It occurred to him that this might mean that the lion had got Mildred and was eating her. He thought of this gruesome possibility with horror, but there were other emotions, too.

★   ★   ★

WHEN MILTON BARKER got back to the yard office, haggard, panting, mysteriously encrusted with mud and straw, the yardmaster looked at him curiously.

"Well, you cert'n'y ain't wasting no time, Milty," he said admiringly. "How'd you make out? Them babies treat you all right?"

Milton gave him a secret smile, implying many fascinating things.

"What do *you* think, Pop?" he said darkly.

Somewhere down in the yard Robert Taylor laughed his mad, derisive laughter.

April 9, 1938

SOME OF THE NICEST GUYS
YOU EVER SAW

E XCEPT FOR THE bartender, Mr. Compton and the man in the green overcoat were alone in the bar.

"Then there was Bill Thaw," Mr. Compton was saying. "He was Harry's brother."

"I didn't know he *had* a brother," said the man in the green overcoat. "I thought just Evelyn Nesbit and all those rabbits."

"No, Bill was his brother," said Mr. Compton, "but he was O.K. He was an ace in the last war. In the Lafayette Escadrille. Say, that was quite an outfit."

"I guess it was," said the other man. "I wouldn't know. I was only about six. How about another whatever you're having there."

"Thanks," said Mr. Compton. "Black Label and soda. No ice."

The other man ordered the drinks. He had thin, reddish hair and a neutral face. There was a quality of detachment or suspended judgment about him that Mr. Compton found almost as discouraging as his overcoat. It was also clear that he wasn't much of a conversationalist.

"Yes, sir," said Mr. Compton after a pause. "Those were certainly the days."

"Days?"

"The last war," said Mr. Compton.

"Oh," said the man in the green overcoat. "You in it?"

"I didn't actually get over," said Mr. Compton. "I was in what they called a students' training corps. We were in a camp in Pennsylvania, near Philly. We were still there when they signed the armistice."

"Tough."

"Oh, it wasn't so bad," said Mr. Compton. "Some of the nicest guys you ever saw. Yale, Harvard, Princeton—all over the East."

The best memories of Mr. Compton's life came back to him, as they often did now in this other war. The unbroken line, the strict perfection of the companies passing in review; the good feeling of order and discipline, perpetuating themselves; the kind of guys you could trust with authority because, in a way, they'd been brought up to it. It hadn't worked out—maybe there were too damn many people in the world—but at the time it had seemed clear and simple. And somehow permanent.

"We used to go down to Philly on leave," he said. "It was always the Bellevue-Stratford in those days. Well, we had some kind of special uniforms—long pants, a jacket like those old four-button Brooks jobs, officers' caps, all that stuff. When you put on a Sam Browne belt—you weren't supposed to, of course, but most of us did—nobody knew what the hell you were. Some kind of foreign officers or the Royal Flying Corps or something, I guess. Anyway, nobody could figure it out, not even the Regular Army. Even the officers would salute us and of course we'd salute back. We made up a kind of foreign salute, just to make it harder."

"It sounds wonderful," said the man in the green overcoat.

"Sure. If they didn't salute, most of us would naturally just let it go, but I remember one guy—Eddie Montgomery was his name—who'd call them every time. The privates and noncoms, that is. 'God damn it, don't you men know enough to salute an officer?' he'd say. He'd even pretend to take their names. Used to scare the bejesus out of them."

"Yeah?" said the man in the green overcoat. "What became of him?"

"I don't know," said Mr. Compton. "I lost track of him after the war. I've lost track of most of them. I've often wondered, because they're the kind of guys we ought to have right now. I don't mean the kidding part; naturally, but officers that look like officers, so the men have some respect for them. You don't just get officers out of some damn poolroom. There's a type. There's a—a *tradition* involved."

"I guess there is," said the man in the green overcoat. There was no particular expression in his voice.

Mr. Compton finished his drink and buttoned up his overcoat.

"Well," he said, "I've got to shove off. Thanks for the drink. Night. Night, Al."

The other man nodded and watched him go out the door. At last he turned back to the bartender. "There's a fine son of a bitch for you," he said.

"Yeah," said the bartender indifferently. "You get 'em."

MR. COMPTON, OUT on the street, was unconscious of having left any criticism behind him. The clear sky pricked with a million stars reminded him of the Germans. It was just the night for them. He looked up at the thin, silver spire of the Chrysler Building towering on his left, a block or so ahead. That would probably be the way the bastards would come, if they did—over from Long Island, flying high and fast, in strict and orderly formation.

January 3, 1942

MR. JERMYN'S LOVELY NIGHT[1]

T HE LATE AFTERNOON sun disclosed nothing along the level beach but sea and sand and Mr. Billy Jermyn, who was merely sitting there, wishing he had a drink. Mr. Jermyn was sixty-two, a man with a face like Punch and a body like Santa Claus; his clothes were mostly antiques that had been scornfully discarded by guests on their departure from his wife's boarding house. There were no shoes on his feet, which were washed intermittently by the lazy October tide. He looked as dissolute and unpromising as a vacant house, but that was misleading, for he was in reality a very deep and rewarding personality.

As the sun went further down, a chilly breeze began to sift through the vacancies in Mr. Jermyn's apparel, and presently he got up and started stiffly up the beach toward the dunes. He was headed home—reluctantly, for it was almost certain that his wife would think up some foolish employment for him around the house—when the sound of hammering came faintly to his ears. Very soon, he identified it as coming from the old McCormick house, a vast and crazy barn, slowly staggering into ruin on the ocean-front property adjoining his own.

"Probably boarding up," said Mr. Jermyn to himself, and thoughtfully changed his course. It was barely possible that Fred McCormick, closing his house for the winter, would have some liquor lying around that it might be advisable to drink up, for one reason or another. He went up the front steps of the house and, finding the door open, into the living room. Mr. McCormick, a contemporary, had a mouthful of nails and he was busy with a storm window. It was evident to Mr. Jermyn that the idea of drinking up the remainder of his summer stock had already occurred to his friend, for there was a bottle of Old Overholt on the table and an expression of intense and mysterious irony on his face.

"Hi, Freddy," said Mr. Jermyn.

"Mmm," said Mr. McCormick, removing the nails from his mouth. "Drink?"

"All right," said Mr. Jermyn, and drank. "Boarding her up, eh?"

"That's right," agreed Mr. McCormick. "A very melancholy time of the year. Kind of different with all them summer people gone, ain't it? You better have another drink."

"Maybe I better," said Mr. Jermyn. "But I don't know about you, Freddy. You're soused already."

"That's right," said Mr. McCormick. "Listen, Billy, did it ever occur to you that it's very unusual for a considerable number of men to weigh exactly a hundred and sixteen pounds?"

"How do you mean?" asked Mr. Jermyn. "Why wouldn't they? It stands to reason."

"No. I mean all together, in the same place. Some ten or fifteen men in a *group*, weighing that."

"Oh," said Mr. Jermyn, suddenly enlightened. "You mean jockeys."

"Yeah," said Mr. McCormick. "Between nailing up these windows, I got reading a newspaper and that's what it says. In one of those little charts they print."

"For God's sake, haven't you ever been to a horse race?" exclaimed Mr. Jermyn. "That ain't what they weigh. That's only what the horse has to carry."

"It said right there, weight: one hundred and sixteen pounds," said Mr. McCormick stubbornly. "Along with the guy's name."

"That's right, but that ain't what they weigh personally. Most of 'em weigh less than that—like a hundred and ten or so. The club makes 'em put lead in their pants pockets or somewheres so they all come out even."

"What the hell for?" said Mr. McCormick. "You don't find any baseball club putting lead in the players."

"They got it all figured out," said Mr. Jermyn. "One or two pounds will make a hell of a difference to a race horse. They want all the races to come out as close as they can, so they put various weights on the horses, depending on how fast they're supposed to be."

"Listen, Billy," said Mr. McCormick. "I'm telling you that *all* these guys weigh a hundred and sixteen pounds. According to you, that would mean that the club figures these horses all run at exactly the same speed. You don't make very good sense, Billy. You better have a drink."

Mr. Jermyn drank, a long one this time, because he himself felt that there was some fallacy involved in his explanation of handicapping, though he couldn't put his finger on it at the moment. It also seemed a good idea to change the subject, since Mr. McCormick's face had taken on a rather sullen and menacing expression.

"Geez, I got the biggest damn blister you ever saw," said Mr. Jermyn, exhibiting the base of his thumb. "She must have had me chop damn near a cord of wood this morning."

"Yeah?" said Mr. McCormick. "Let's see it."

He considered Mr. Jermyn's thumb and then passed it back to him with a shrug. "You got a blister all right," he said, "but I don't know how *big* I'd say it was. Suppose I was to say I'd seen a bigger one in—in Joplin, Missouri, back in 1927. How are you going to prove that one way or the other?"

"All right, all right," said Mr. Jermyn pacifically. "I didn't come here to get in an argument about blisters."

"It ain't blisters. It's the principle," said Mr. McCormick. He picked up the bottle and finished it in one long swallow. "I noticed something about you for a long time, Billy. You talk too big. I guess you're the best friend I got in the world, but you talk too big. Generally speaking, I wouldn't call a man on the size of his blister—it could be as big as this house for all I'd care—but with you, I think you ought to learn to stick to the facts. I don't mind a *stranger* coming to my house and drinking my whiskey and pretending to know some subject he doesn't, whether it's jockeys or—or the President of the United States, but when it comes to my best friend trying to . . ." He picked up the bottle and seemed surprised to find it empty. "Wait'll I get another of these," he said.

Mr. Jermyn looked after him doubtfully. It seemed evident that his friend was in an irresponsible frame of mind. He remembered a night when Mr. McCormick had somehow managed to lose his teeth in the mechanical piano at Sweeney's and finally, in the confusion, the front part of the piano got broken and Sweeney got sore and called the Coast Guard. However, there was the whiskey and Mr. Jermyn didn't feel that his friend should be allowed to drink it alone.

"Last one," said Mr. McCormick, coming back with a bottle about two-thirds full. "We'll drink that and then maybe we'll go down to the village."

"Ah, you don't want to go downtown, Freddy. What the hell is downtown?"

"Freda," said Mr. McCormick simply, naming a lady of middle years but undiminished spirit with whom his relations had been warm though intermittent for some time. It had been Freda, in fact, who had suggested breaking the glass in the piano.

"What's the matter with Freda?" said Mr. McCormick, observing the obvious distaste on Mr. Jermyn's face. "I suppose she ain't good enough for you. I suppose you want everybody to weigh a hundred and sixteen pounds."

"She's a very fine woman," said Mr. Jermyn. "I just don't think we want to go downtown."

"What you need is a drink," said Mr. McCormick. "You horse lover."

For a while after that they drank in silence and with apparent amiability. Presently, however, Mr. McCormick remembered a grievance.

"You got no right to keep knocking Freda, Billy," he said. "Just because she's got diabetes."

"What the hell is diabetes?" said Mr. Jermyn with rather astounding gallantry. "I never give it a thought. Mussolini had syphilis."

"Yeah?" said Mr. McCormick glassily. "That what he died of?"

"For God's sake, Freddy," said Mr. Jermyn. "They shot him. You ought to know that."

"Who?"

"Paul Muni," said Mr. Jermyn. He was astonished and delighted with this educated reference and elaborated it, slapping his knee. "Mr. Paul Muni and his magic bullet," he said. "The Twentieth Century-Fox Brothers."

Mr. McCormick looked at him blankly. "We better get downtown," he said. "Wale I get my hat." He stood up, swaying, and went erratically into the bedroom.

Mr. Jermyn took another drink and then, hearing loud and ominous noises—a creak of springs and what seemed to be a groan—followed him unsteadily. Mr. McCormick was stretched across the bed and already he seemed to be asleep. Mr. Jermyn looked down on him for quite a long time, supporting himself by the bedpost. At last he made up his mind and swiftly removed his host's trousers and, carrying them over his arm, wandered back into the other room. Mr. McCormick had nailed up all the windows and the padlock for the storm door was lying on the table beside the bottle. Mr. Jermyn put the bottle in his pocket and picked up the lock. Then he turned off all the lights and went out on the porch. While he was struggling to fit the padlock through the hasps on the storm door, the key fell out and went tinkling down through a crack between the boards.

"Spilt milk," he muttered, snapping the lock shut. He went cautiously down the steps, counting them aloud, and started along the concrete walk that led to his own house. However, looking up for the first time, he saw that it was a fair and spacious night, pricked with stars and rich with promise, too fine a night for a man with almost half a bottle of Old Overholt in his pocket to go home to his wife. He turned off to the right at the next corner and headed south, where the lights of the village glowed cheerfully against the sky. Suddenly, as he quickened his pace, he remembered that he was still carrying Mr. McCormick's trousers and, rolling them carefully into a ball, he threw them as far as he could into the thicket of bayberry and poison ivy that lay along the walk.

"Some day you're going to *thank* me for this, Freddy," he said virtuously, and continued toward the village, where Freda and Sweeney and life itself would surely welcome him with wide, admiring arms.

November 10, 1945

NO ROOM IN THE INN[1]

"WELL, YOU FOLKS get settled all right?" asked Mrs. Jermyn. "Come on up. Sit down."

Mr. and Mrs. Crane left the sidewalk and climbed the little flight of steps that led to their landlady's porch and sat down on a bench against the wall.

"Everything is lovely, except the bathroom door sticks," said Emily Crane. "The downstairs one."

"I thought if Mr. Jermyn had a plane . . ." her husband began. He had felt depressed and rather ill all spring. However, there wasn't supposed to be anything the matter with him that a summer in the sun wouldn't fix. Well, it had started out perfectly.

"I'll tell him," said Mrs. Jermyn. In the clear, receding light, almost level on the dunes, her expression seemed to be sardonic. "You get accustomed," she said vaguely. The house that rose behind her, and on the other side faced directly on the sea, looked old, enormous, and dissolute in the twilight. George Crane knew that it was full of summer boarders, hanging like bats from the rafters. He also knew that Mrs. Jermyn was supposed to be quite a character on Fire Island, a description, of course, that implied an original point of view. As if I didn't have enough to put up with, he thought, aware of the irritation that had been burning in him like a low fever since March.

"It's so quiet here," said his wife. "Just the ocean."

Lights had begun to come on in some of the houses in the little settlement between the sea and the bay; the tall grass that crowned the dunes stirred with some weightless breath of air, and the swallows dipped furiously in and out of the pools of collecting darkness between the dunes. It actually was a moment of curious peace.

"Somebody's coming," said Mr. Crane, looking down the concrete walk that ran just behind the row of houses that faced on the beach.

"Yes?" said Mrs. Jermyn. "Well, they can't come here." Peering down the walk, she looked more than ever like the figurehead at the prow of a pirate ship. "I've even got the editor of the New York *Times* sleeping in the shower," she said, and laughed shortly.

"Really?" said Mrs. Crane, who was inclined to believe what she was told.

"Anyway, some newspaper fella," said Mrs. Jermyn. "Crandall. McCandlish. I don't know."

They watched the three figures, heavily laden with suitcases and bundles, that were toiling toward them down the walk. They were all young men, and as they came abreast of the porch, they stopped and looked around doubtfully. Even before they spoke, George Crane recognized a common quality about them—something borrowed from a juvenile in an English comedy, something proud and soft and mysterious. The boys were another thing that Fire Island was supposed to be noted for, he recalled. They had come there a few years ago, tentative as deer at a brook, and finding no hunters, they had stayed and multiplied incredibly.

"Is this Mrs. Jermyn's establishment?" said one of them, in a fluty voice. Not a juvenile this time, George Crane, decided—a butler.

"That's right," said Mrs. Jermyn impassively.

"Well, I'm Elliott Farber, and this is Mr. Linsey and Mr. Rodriguez."

Mrs. Jermyn looked at the other two, a handsome, supercilious boy and a rather theatrical Latin, and nodded, as if in some secret, derisive agreement with herself.

"Of course you got my telegram about the rooms?" said Mr. Farber.

"Telegram?" she said. "I don't remember any telegram."

"But I sent it last *week!*" he cried desperately. "I even put down the name of your house. Dune 'n' Oot—so amusing."

"I didn't get it," she said calmly, "or anyway, I don't *recall* getting it."

In his despair, Mr. Farber stepped off the walk and onto the little plot of ground that lay in front of the porch.

"But you *must*—"

"You're on my roses," said Mrs. Jermyn sharply.

He looked anxiously down at the barren ground under his feet. "Roses?"

"They haven't come up yet," she said. "Probably never will now."

"I'm so sorry," he said, moving hastily back onto the concrete. "Well," he said uneasily after a moment, "even if my telegram *didn't* come—"

"I couldn't say for sure," she told him. "Things get lost around here. Especially papers."

"I'm sure it must be around somewhere," said Mr. Rodriguez, producing a rather chilly and Continental manner. "In any case, you have the room?"

She gave him what perhaps she considered a regretful smile. "No," she said. "I'm full up. As I was telling Major McCane here, I just had to refuse an editor from the New York *Times*."

"I'm not—" Mr. Crane began, and stopped. He had intended to disclaim the armed forces and even to correct his name, but then for some reason he decided to let the conversation take its own odd and unpredictable course. In the silence, his wife bent forward to light a cigarette and a bright ribbon slipped from her hair and fell to the floor. He picked it up and absently put it on top of his own head, and Mr. Linsey and Mr. Farber gave him a sudden look of intense and delighted surmise. Mr. Rodriguez, however, was not diverted.

"It is *most* unbusinesslike," he said severely. "A week should certainly have been adequate notice."

"You could try down in the village at the hotel," said Mrs. Jermyn. "They often got rooms at the last minute."

"My friends and I had especially counted on being directly on the beach," he said, and in his distress, he, too, edged a little off the walk.

"The roses," said Mrs. Jermyn wearily. "I guess I'll have to put up some kind of a sign."

"I beg your pardon," he said, retreating. "As I was saying, we were really counting—"

Mrs. Jermyn interrupted him in a voice that seemed to hold the memory of an old sorrow. "I got my little dog buried there, too," she said. "Little Tandy."

Mr. Crane looked at her thoughtfully, but her face was still as bland and vacant as the moon.

"He passed away last year," she said. "In the hurricane."

"How unfortunate," murmured Mr. Linsey, or perhaps Mr. Rodriguez. "He was drowned?"

"No," said Mrs. Jermyn. "He was just blown."

"Oh," said Mr. Farber. His unhappy glance travelled to Mr. Crane's face, under its cryptic hair ribbon, but clearly he found no comfort even there. "Well," he said, after what must have appeared to him a suitable period of mourning, "all I can say is that it's terribly disappointing. About the rooms, I mean."

"I have never been so cross in my *life*!" cried Mr. Linsey, tossing back his rather unusual hair.

"It's too disgusting," said Mr. Rodriguez.

There was a helpless silence while the young men shifted their suitcases and tried to regain their worldly composure. Mrs. Jermyn, however, seemed to have decided that they were invisible, and presently they trailed reproachfully off into the falling night.

"I'm so sorry about your little dog," said Emily Crane, reaching out and retrieving her hair ribbon from her husband's brow. "You must miss him terribly."

Mrs. Jermyn's eyes were on the middle distance, perhaps on the silver bowl of the water tower floating over the village in mysterious suspension, and her expression was peaceful and remote. "What little dog, dear?" she asked gently.

Mr. Crane looked at her with affection and a touch of awe. It's just possible I'm going to like it here, he thought, aware for the first time of the slow, healthy pulse of the neighborly sea.

June 15, 1946

DARK CLOUD IN THE SKY[1]

T HE INHABITANTS OF the beach were divided into little colonies, formed in the spring and lasting intact all through the summer. The nucleus of each group was usually the family; during the week, it consisted of a mother and her children, with perhaps a vague female relative or two and occasionally a nurse; over the weekends, there was, of course, a father, and probably there were some guests, rather paler than the permanent company, so they required portable shade and frequent protective applications of oil and grease. Sometimes, as in the case of the Cranes and the Andersons, two or more families were united in a somewhat more complicated organism and became, in a sense, a society, with customs and legends.

One July afternoon, a bright Saturday, with the sand wavering in the sun and the sea flat blue to Portugal, the Cranes and Andersons were assembled around two striped umbrellas, under one of which sat Paul and Edith Vincent, a lively and rather fashionable couple who were visiting the Andersons. Mrs. Vincent was rubbing something from a bottle on her husband's back, tilting her head to keep the smoke from her cigarette out of her eyes and seeming, on the whole, quite hypnotized by this wifely ritual.

"Before I'd have hair growing out of *my* shoulders," she said, with faint disgust.

A little outside the circle, the four resident children, ranging in age from little Marcia Anderson, who was five, to Billy Crane, who was eleven, played one of their mysterious and interminable games, hampered only by the adult rule against throwing sand.

It was a scene of almost overpowering American domesticity, George Crane thought, the gentlemen recovering from the wear and tear of commerce in the society of their women and children; who were virtuous and designed for tranquil pleasures. "Anybody want to go in swimming?" he asked. "That's what you're really supposed to do on a beach."

"You go, George," murmured his wife, speaking from some deep dream of peace. "We'll watch."

"Yes, you can come back and tell us all about it," said Mrs. Anderson, rather dimly, because she was lying on her stomach.

"All right, the hell with you," he said. "I'll take the children. Marcia? Billy? You want to go swimming?"

"No, thank you, Mr. Crane," said the little girl politely, and his son ignored him altogether.

"A fine bunch," he said. "Bums and half-wits."

"That's right," said Mr. Vincent. "Edith, for God's sake why don't you cut your nails? You're not supposed to *scratch* that stuff into my back."

"Keep it still, then," she replied.

"Wait'll I finish this cigarette, George," said Mr. Anderson. "I'll go in with you."

"O.K.," said Mr. Crane, and sank back on the sand. I guess I really like it here better than any place in the world, he thought, and for the moment his delight in Fire Island, in this one place where life could be slowed to the almost forgotten tempo of childhood, seemed as much as he could bear. The distance from New York, by train and boat, was only forty terrestrial miles, but in spirit it was enormous. You ate and slept in the dark, untidy little houses that lay along the dunes between the sea and the bay, but most of your life was spent on the loveliest beach in the East, a narrow, sunny shelf that ran thirty miles along the Atlantic, from Babylon to Quogue, and here you just lay in the sun, and all the staggering complexity of your relations with others, the endless, hopeless bookkeeping of your personal morality with too many people, could be put aside for a little while. It was a state of wonderful irresponsibility, a time in which you belonged to nobody but yourself, on which there were no claims from the world. From this brief and quite unusual dream of himself as a happy man, George Crane was recalled by the voice of Paul Vincent. It had an urgent sound.

"What do you know!" he was saying. "Molly Burden!"[2]

Mr. Crane saw that he was pointing to a group, somewhat larger than their own, collected on the sand in front of the boarding house operated by Mrs. Jermyn. The crowd around her was made up of her boarders, and they were all familiar to him with the exception of one woman, who, from a distance, merely struck him as unpleasantly vivacious.

"Who?" he said.

"Molly Burden," repeated Mr. Vincent. "My God, you must know Molly!"

"She's a madam," said Edith Vincent placidly. "A childhood sweetheart of my husband's. Apparently she's quite well known in sporting circles. Or at least so he says."

"Oh, *that* one," said Mrs. Crane, scattering sand as she sat up. "Of course, I've read a lot about her. Show me. Where?"

Mrs. Anderson also came to life, rolling over on her side and shading her eyes with her book. "Really?" she said. "How extraordinary!"

"What's so extraordinary about it?" asked her husband. "It isn't as if you'd never seen a madam."

"I suppose I must have," she said, "but never one so widely publicized. And it does seem rather odd, right here on this beach."

George Crane thought it seemed odd, too, and in his present rather elevated and moral mood, an intolerance of city ways brought on by sun worship, he found the infamous Miss Burden's presence intrusive and somehow menacing. The last time she had been on an island, he recalled, she had been a guest of the Police Department. He said this aloud and his wife smiled at him tolerantly.

"You're quite a wit, dear," she murmured. "Why don't you just go quietly down and be witty in the water. Do you really know her, Paul?"

"She's a dear old friend," Mrs. Vincent assured her. "From the days when he used to be so terribly cute."

"You just attend to the back," said her husband. "I'll supply any necessary facts. Sure I used to know her, Emily. Want me to ask her to come over?"

"Why not?" said Mrs. Crane. "It might be a nice change. I think George is getting in a rut."

"The chance of a lifetime," said Mrs. Anderson.

"All right," he said. "You finished with me, Doctor?"

"All finished," Mrs. Vincent said. "You run right over and fascinate the nice old tramp."

He looked at his wife doubtfully. "If she *does* come over," he said,
"how about none of that stuff? After all, she's quite a girl in her
way."

"None finer," agreed Mrs. Vincent heartily.

"And she certainly knows all those kind of jokes."

"*That* kind of jokes," said his wife. "No, don't worry, dear. We'll
be terribly discreet."

"Of course we will," said the other ladies, smiling at him with
bright, inscrutable charm.

MR. VINCENT STILL looked doubtful, but he got up, and soon
he was part of the group that surrounded Mrs. Jermyn and the celebrated stranger, who appeared to greet him with enthusiasm. Mrs.
Vincent screwed the cap slowly back on the bottle of sun-tan lotion
and lit a cigarette.

"You don't know her yourself, do you, Edith?" asked Mrs. Anderson.

"Not personally," said Mrs. Vincent, "but Paul has told me a lot
about her. He has a very confiding nature."

"I've often wondered about these things," said Mrs. Crane. "You
know, how people get started in that business, and especially how
they get to the top, so to speak."

"It's one of the great themes of literature," said her husband. "Especially with the French."

"No, I mean *really*," she said. "How superior industry and imagination and all the other qualities of—of *lead*ership manage to assert
themselves."

"Oh, for God's sake," he said. "I'm going swimming." He did, in
fact, start to get up, but his natural curiosity proved too much for him
and he sat down again. After all, a woman who had conducted the
most notorious establishment of an era had a certain romantic interest.

"It's a dull story," said Mrs. Vincent, "and rather unlikely, like a
movie with an immoral ending. It seems she was born in Russia—
Rostov, I think—and, of course, a perfectly beautiful child and

incredibly poor. Lentils and beet soup and I suppose her feet done up in sacks."

"Yes, I'm sure sacks," said Mrs. Anderson. "You're doing fine, Edith."

"Not me," she said. "Paul. Anyway, one night, when she was just thirteen, she was standing on a corner in a terrible storm, not knowing where *anything* was coming from next, when a young Czarist officer came up to her and—"

"How old was *he?*" asked Mr. Anderson. "Fourteen?"

"I told you it was unlikely," she said. "Well, they got to talking and one thing sort of led to another and finally he took her to St. Petersburg or Petrograd or whatever they used to call it then, and there seems to have been quite an establishment. Caviar and vodka and that dance where they kick their feet out in front and naturally a good deal of love all over the place." She paused and looked out at the ocean. "I get a little mixed up here," she went on, "but I think it was the revolution. Anyway, he was killed and she had to flee to America. The rest apparently was just application and getting to meet the right people. I don't know the details—I never *have* understood how people go about expanding their businesses from retail to wholesale—but I suppose that Romanoff background had something to do with it. However, she did, and there she is. Frankly, I don't believe a word of it myself, except that I guess she's Russian, all right."

"She isn't really so terribly *active* now, is she?" asked Mrs. Crane. "For a while you heard so much about politicians and bank presidents and all that stuff, but lately I don't remember hearing about her hardly at all. Of course, we lead a very sheltered life down here."

"Well, I think Mr. Dewey made things rather tiresome for her a few years ago," said Mrs. Vincent, "and I doubt if she ever did get back to quite the old scale. It's hard to be sure, though, because Paul is my only source of information on that side of life and I'm afraid he's been rather cut off himself, poor thing."

Mrs. Crane and Mrs. Anderson looked at her rather speculatively at this, but her expression told them nothing, and Mrs. Crane kicked a discontented little hole in the sand with her toe.

"It must have been quite a place in the beginning, though," she said.

"It was indeed," said Mrs. Vincent. "All those rather important men and really such embarrassing situations. Paul says he'll never forget the night the Governor of North Dakota or South Carolina or one of those places was up there and one of the girls fell out of the window."

"How did she do that?" asked Mr. Crane with reluctant interest.

"Nobody seemed to know exactly. She and the Governor had, well, retired and then there was quite a lot of noise and the Governor came out to say that his friend seemed to have fallen out of the window. He was tight as a monkey, and Paul says that he kept yelling that it was the first time such a thing had happened to him in his life. He seemed quite indignant about it, as if it was some crooked old New York custom, but Paul says that Molly was magnificent. 'You just take it up with the United States Senate, Governor,' she told him, and after a while they managed to get him out the back way, down a service elevator or something."

"Goodness," said Mrs. Anderson. "What happened to the girl?"

"Apparently they had quite a time with her, too," said Mrs. Vincent. "Fortunately it wasn't very high up, only two floors, and she landed in an awning, but she did break a couple of ribs and, of course, she didn't have very much on. The policemen were very nice about it, being rather accustomed to the fashionable life, you might say, but some little doctor from the neighborhood had examined her first and kept on insisting that she ought to go to a hospital. Well, nobody knew what to do, because the girl was still drunk and quite cross with everybody, especially the Governor, and likely to say practically anything. Finally Molly called up another doctor, one she knew more or less socially, and he came over and somehow he convinced the first one that he was with the police and talked him out of sending for an ambulance. So it was all right. This other doctor, the new one, got the girl back upstairs and fixed her up and I suppose Molly squared the rest of it with her. Paul says that after a while one of the policemen came upstairs with his notebook and wanted to know what the diagnosis was, I suppose in case any trouble came up later. The doctor was very professional about it. 'This young lady has acute bronchitis, Officer,' he said. 'She also has some slight muscular lesion brought about by coughing, but nothing that a day or two in bed won't clear up nicely.' I guess that really must have been kind of funny."

"Well, it's quite a sophisticated story, however you look at it," said Mr. Anderson after a pause. "How you people do get around."

"Did," said Mrs. Vincent. "And only Paul. I'm embarrassed to say that I've never been in a bordello in my life."

Somewhere in the middle of the story, Mr. Crane had made up his mind that he wasn't amused by the Vincents. Most of the years since he had been out of college, it seemed to him, had been spent with men and women who had nothing in particular to offer but these disreputable little anecdotes, which, even when they were successful, reflected what struck him as rather vacant and depressing lives. I'm getting to be a hell of a moralist, he thought, but I'm just too damn middle-aged and respectable to enjoy hookshop reminiscences or to bother speculating about the domestic problems of the people who tell them. He knew that the Vincents were supposed to be a very stimulating couple; he just wished they'd go back to New York.

"He's coming back," whispered Mrs. Anderson, "and he's bringing her with him."

"Why, she's quite fat," said Mrs. Crane, with disappointment.

Mr. Vincent arrived at the umbrellas, accompanied by Miss Burden, who was not so much fat as simply strong and square. She wore a simple black bathing suit, with a modest skirt, which was in fetching contrast with her copper skin. Her face was round and undistinguished and characterized chiefly by an expression of great amiability. Mrs. Crane found it hard to think of her in connection with the Governor of North Carolina or South Dakota and young women who fell out of windows.

"This is Mrs. Bender," said Mr. Vincent "Mr. and Mrs. Crane. Mr. and Mrs. Vincent. And my wife."

"But I thought—" began Mrs. Anderson.

"I am here a Mrs. Bender," said Miss Burden, with amusement. "It saves the nice Mrs. Jermyn from bloshing. The initials on the baggage are also the same. M.B."

"Of course," said Mrs. Crane brightly. "Won't you sit down with us for a while?"

Miss Burden sat down and lit a cigarette in a long, black holder. There was a silence in which she looked thoughtfully at the three young matrons on the sand, and it occurred to Mr. Crane that she might be considering them for a livelier life. If she was, she rejected them almost at once.

"It is a lovely place here," she said, waving her holder at the ocean and the dunes. "So cute. So ontrobbled. Maybe some day I start up a little business."

"Business?" said Mr. Crane, startled out of what he had intended to be an attitude of chilly detachment.

The lady laughed merrily. "Oho, not the one you think of," she said. "Not *that* business. That is for New York, where fellas need some place they can go relax. Here you got a beach."

It was the first time Mr. Crane had thought of the beach in precisely that light and he looked at it rather blankly.

"Not *that* kind of a business at all," she said. "No. A restaurant. I am down in this place—what you call it? Snyder's? No. *Sweeney's*— last night with Mrs. Jermyn and the food is *tarrible*. It stinks. So I think what they need here is some place people can eat. High-class. Cheap. I am a hell of a cook, especially on some Russian specialties I got, like borsch. How *you* make borsch?" she asked suddenly, turning to Mrs. Vincent.

"Why, I don't know. I guess you just sort of take some beets . . ."

"You do not at all 'just sort of take some beets,'" said Miss Burden scornfully. "You first, very carefully, take a great big pot and you rub it inside with . . ."

Mr. Crane continued to hear her voice as she went on with her recipe, but no longer the words. He was thinking of something both profound and very trite about women, too hazy to define, but having something to do with their amazing adaptability, their instant identification with a moral climate. In any case, there was no longer an intruder on his beach, or even a stranger, and in just a minute he would go swimming with his old friend, leaving the ladies to their dull and innocent chatter, as he had so many times before.

June 22, 1946

SONG AT TWILIGHT

"He was getting along beautifully until he shot that pickerel," said Mrs. Crane.

"He did *what?*" said Mrs. Anderson. They had been discussing a man called Ed Herlicher, whom they had both known several years before—one of those rather mysterious young men who for a little while turn up everywhere in New York, spending a good deal of money and acquiring a certain reputation either as comedians or beaux, and then vanish back into the social underbrush from which they came.

"He shot a pickerel," said Mrs. Crane. "With a double-barrelled shotgun. It was one of those absurd stories, like the things that happen in Evelyn Waugh."

The seven people on the porch of the Cranes' oceanfront cottage looked at her hopefully, but she seemed to be overcome by the murmuring sea and the gentle evening air and leaned back with her eyes closed.

"Wake up, dear," said Mrs. Anderson. "Tell us the rest of it."

"That was all," said Mrs. Crane in an exhausted voice. "He shot this fish and that was the end of him."

"No, it wasn't," said her husband. "Not the way you told it to me before."

"Well, it was terribly silly," she said, reluctantly returning to the mortal world. "This Ed Herlicher got around a lot, you know, and one week-end Jimmy Betts asked him up to his place in the Adirondacks. He had a hunting lodge on a lake, and a lot of them used to go up there to fish and shoot and—oh, whatever people like Jimmy Betts do when they aren't annoying girls or going to football games. Give me a drink, George."

She held out her glass and George Crane filled it from the shaker.

"Where was I?" she asked. "Oh, yes. Jimmy's lodge. Well, they had a lot of childish ideas up there, but I guess the worst was about this fish. It was supposed to be the biggest fish of its kind in that part of the world and they kept seeing it all the time right off the end of Jimmy's dock or somewhere, but it was too smart for them and nobody had been able to catch it. It got to be a legend. You know, the way people go on about that kind of stuff in the *Saturday Evening Post*."

She seemed about to fade away again but her husband caught her eye and shook his head.

"All *right*," she said, "but that's really about all there was. Ed listened to them practically all one night and then early the next morning when he must have been still drunk he went down to the dock and when the fish came up, he shot it with one of Jimmy's guns. They couldn't even tell how big it had been because he blew it right in half. As I said, it was the end of him socially. They hardly talked to him for the rest of the week-end, and when he got back to town, it must have got around '21' and places that he wasn't, well, quite a gentleman because pretty soon he just disappeared. He may have shot *himself* for all I know.' She yawned and settled back in her chair. "I told you it was a pretty dull story," she said.

IN THE SILENCE, George Crane looked around at the cocktail party, which had been going on now for about an hour. It was apparently one of his failures. His wife was clearly in a mood when any social effort seemed to tax her unbearably, and his friends, Mark and Virginia Anderson, who could generally be relied on to keep a conversation in motion also had a rather limp and unpromising air. The other three were comparative strangers—a Mr. and Mrs. Derleth, whom he had known slightly in town and who had just taken a house a little way down the beach, and a man named Freddy Basker, a Princeton classmate of Mark Anderson's, who was out for the week-end. The Derleths weren't particularly hard to classify. They had usually gone to Black Point in the summer, but this year they had switched to Fire Island in the hope that the sea might do something for her asthma. Mr. Derleth had complained several times that he missed his golf, and Mrs. Derleth found herself unable to get used to the fact that no considerable trees grew on the island. There was a noble elm on her lawn at Black Point, much admired by artists, that had once cast its shadow on soldiers of the King. Nothing, however, was precisely clear about Mr. Basker, a hoarse, reddish man of about thirty-five, except that he was quite drunk and obviously willing to get a good deal drunker. From time to time, he had filled his glass, without urging from his host, but, except for a low, tuneless humming, that had been the extent of his activity. Mr. Crane was about to give them all up—he had had a good many drinks himself and the role of conscientious host had begun to bore him—when help came from an unexpected source.

"You know Mrs. Crane's pickerel reminds me of our raccoon, Amy," said Mr. Derleth, chuckling and addressing his wife.

"Oh, yes, tell them about that, Sam," she said. "It was awfully sweet. There was this little brook behind our house in Black Point and almost every morning . . . no, but you go ahead, dear."

"As my wife has told you," said Mr. Derleth, looking at her with faint disgust, "there's a little brook behind our place—empties into the Sound finally, I guess—and . . ."

Mr. Basker was sitting beside Mr. Crane, who suddenly found he could detect a sort of lyric in his guest's humming. "Empties into the *Sound*," hummed Mr. Basker. "You don't say. Into the Sound. Well, my God and my Jesus." Mr. Crane looked at him sharply but there was no particular expression on his face.

"And one winter morning," Mr. Derleth was saying when his host caught up with him again, "on my way out back to get the car, I saw this coon sitting on the bank, hell of a cute little specimen . . ."

"What sex?" hummed Mr. Basker, but this time he was audible to them all.

"I beg pardon?" said Mr. Derleth politely.

"Unimportant point," said Mr. Basker, waving his hand. "Let it go." He began to hum again.

"Anyway," said Mr. Derleth, "he was sitting there, and what do you suppose he was doing?"

"Well—" began Mr. Basker.

Mr. Crane cleared his throat. "What *was* he doing?" he asked hastily.

"He'd broken the ice with his little paws," said Mr. Derleth, "and he was sitting there washing his face. Looked just like my own Timmie. That's our little boy."

"How *cunning*," murmured Mrs. Crane, giving him a bright smile, and Mrs. Anderson also made sounds of sweet approval.

"Yes, sir," said Mr. Derleth, "and after that I'd see him practically every day. I guess he got used to me because after a while he didn't pay any attention to me at all. He'd just come down and break the ice with his little paw—"

"How thick?" Mr. Basker asked. He was leaning forward and his eyes had a bright, peculiar fixity.

"What?" said Mr. Derleth.

"I said how thick was this ice," repeated Mr. Basker. "Approximately? Couple of inches? A foot? What did he do? Take a rock to it?"

"No," said Mr. Derleth. "It was very thin, of course. He just had to tap it with his paw."

"How cunning," said Mrs. Crane, rather desperately. "How terribly, terribly cunning. But everyone says they're awfully intelligent."

Mr. Basker gave her a tolerant smile. "You keep out of this," he said. "You're just supposed to be the pickerel expert." He turned back to Mr. Derleth. "Then what did he do? After he got finished with washing his face?"

"How do you mean?" asked Mr. Derleth, whose geniality was beginning to show signs of strain. "That was all he did. Just washed his face."

"Oh," said Mr. Basker. "Well, it's a damn good story, anyway. You'll never have any occasion to regret *that* story, old man."

"*Well*," said Mrs. Derleth, but apparently he didn't hear her.

"Damn good story," he repeated and got up and poured himself another drink. He sat down again and for a little while stared out to sea first with concentration, then suddenly with a look of deep, inward pleasure on his face.

"Reminds me of a somewhat similar experience *I* once had with a couple of rats," he said at length. "You want to hear about the experience I once had with a wonderful couple of rats?"

"Sure," said Mr. Crane. "What about these rats?"

"It was when I had an apartment down on Tenth Street," said

Mr. Basker. "I wasn't married at the time, though God knows how that happened because I've been married off and on to various women since I was nineteen. It's a hell of a thing, you start marrying dames and the first thing you know, you begin marrying them *all*. It's like—like collecting almost any kind of stuff." He stopped and looked doubtfully at Mr. Crane. "Say, listen," he said, "what the hell was I talking about?"

"Rats."

"Rats?" said Mr. Basker and he frowned with brief perplexity. "Oh, sure. *Rats*. That's right. It was down on Tenth Street. I had this apartment down there and for a long time I kept missing—ah—tennis balls. Many as two or three a week sometimes." His rather coppery eye fell on Mrs. Derleth and he winked at her genially. "I used to ask girls up there now and then," he said, "and for a while I thought they might be taking them. But then I thought now what the hell would *they* want with tennis balls. Whatever about these girls, they weren't much for playing tennis. I remember an Agnes used to come up there—*you* remember Agnes, Mark . . ."

"I've *heard* about Agnes, Freddie," said Mr. Anderson. "You better get back to the rats."

"O.K.," said Mr. Basker. "The rats. Let me see. Well, after I decided it wasn't the girls, or even Virgin Birth—"

"Virgin Birth?" said Mrs. Crane.

"Some name like that. One of Father Divine's Angels.[1] Anyway, my cook. She was always taking stuff up to Harlem with her after she got through, but only out of the icebox. Not sporting goods. Well, I was ready to give up until one night I was lying in bed reading when I suddenly heard this noise—kind of a squeak and some scratching—in the corner. I looked around and there, by God, was one of the damnedest rats you ever saw. I figured he came out of the closet, which naturally emptied into the bedroom."

Mr. Derleth, looking slightly harassed, went over to the table and mixed himself another drink. Mr. Basker waited politely until he had finished.

"So I just lay there and watched," he said, "and what do you suppose the little son of a bitch did?"

"Listen, Freddie," began Mr. Anderson.

Mr. Basker ignored him. "I forgot to tell you there were a couple of tennis balls lying right there on the rug," he said rapidly. "Well, this rat went right up to one of them and gave it a little shove with his nose. Cutest thing you ever saw."

"How about another drink?" said Mr. Crane.

"Sure," said Mr. Basker and held out his glass. It was clear, however, that he had no intention of being diverted. "All right, I thought, this is the bastard that's been stealing my balls, but *how*? That's what I asked myself. *How* is he going to get it out of here? He can't take it in his mouth because it's too damn big and he can't carry it because his little arms are too short and I can't see him getting to work and eating it right there on the rug. *How the hell is that damn rat going to get that ball out of the room?* I asked myself. That was my problem. *How——*"

"He pushed it along with his nose, Freddie," said Mrs. Anderson. "That's easy."

Mr. Basker looked at her blankly for a moment and Mr. Crane had a momentary impression that the well had run dry. He was mistaken, for Mr. Basker's face suddenly cleared and he beamed at her delightedly.

"Mmmm," he said. "Well, I suppose he *could* have done that, but the point is, he didn't. I'll tell you what he *did* do, because I think it's terribly cute. And I'm sure Mr. and Mrs. Deluxe will back me up."

"Derleth," said Mr. Derleth.

"Derleth. All right, here's what he did, and stop me if you don't think it's terribly cute. He lay down on his side next to one of the balls and he reached out his little paws and took it right in his arms. Then he rolled over until he was lying on his back. Just like a kid with a damn doll. Just like——"

"Drink?" said Mr. Crane. "You better let me get you a fresh drink."

"No," said Mr. Basker. "You wait. Damn good story. Where—oh, yes, there he was on his back with the ball in his little arms." He bent forward and tapped Mr. Derleth on the knee. "*Then* what did he do?" he asked more hoarsely than ever. "Give you any number of guesses. It's hopeless."

"All right. I give up," said Mr. Derleth, who was nothing if not a good sport.

"You'd better," said Mr. Basker, "because he didn't do a damn thing. Not personally. He just lay there on his back and the first thing I knew, *another* rat came sniffing out of the closet. The female, of course. The little girl rat."

"Oh?" said Mrs. Crane.

"Certainly," said Mr. Basker firmly, "and pretty as a picture, too." He closed his eyes as if reviewing the scene and it was clearly hard on his composure because he choked and had to wipe his eyes. "And what did *she* do?" he said when he had recovered. "Well, sir, she went right up to this boy rat, the husband, and she grabbed the end of his tail in her teeth and, by God, she pulled him right across the rug, ball and all, and right into the closet." He looked around at the members of his audience and his expression was bland and courteous, that of a man only anxious to instruct and entertain. "In a couple of minutes," he said, "they came out after the other ball. Same thing all over again—he rolled over with the ball in his arms and she pulled him the hell out of the room. Damn if it wasn't the cutest thing you ever saw."

"Well," said Mrs. Derleth, after a considerable pause, "I guess we'd better get started if we're going to get any dinner. Come on, Sam."

She got up and produced suitable farewells.

"Good night," she said to the Cranes. "It's been so nice. Good-night, Mrs. Anderson, Mr. Anderson. I'm so glad to have met you."

Her little nod to Mr. Basker was admirable—containing just the correct mixture of ladylike tolerance and amusement. It was wasted on him, though, because by that time he was clearly lost in another of his foolish and disreputable dreams, humming to himself and tapping on the arm of his chair.

July 6, 1946

LOVE, LOVE, LOVE

G EORGE CRANE AND Mark Anderson had been throwing the
tennis ball back and forth for quite a while. There was a fairly
strong wind down the beach, and Mr. Crane, throwing into it,
found that he had developed a rather astonishing curve. If he threw
the ball directly at Mr. Anderson's head, it broke down and away,
off into the sand at his right. Mr. Crane felt a little like Mathewson,
an admiration of his boyhood, but Mr. Anderson, after sprawling in
the sand three or four times, tossed the ball irritably up under the
umbrella and sat down.

"You'll ruin your arm if you keep trying to throw curves with
that thing," he said when Mr. Crane had joined him.

"The wind took it," said Mr. Crane defensively. "It sailed."

"Listen," said Mr. Anderson, "I used to throw roundhouse curves
when I was six. I know what you were doing."

He lit a cigarette and Mr. Crane looked at him thoughtfully.
There had been something just a little wrong with his friend for the
last few weeks. By nature he was an amiable man, often entertaining in vague, unexpected ways, and remarkably easy to get along
with. Lately, however, there had been a distinct feeling of strain and
a kind of spiritual absence, as if he were turning weighty problems
over in his mind. At first, Mr. Crane had put this down to literary
abstraction, for Mr. Anderson was a writer, the author of two novels
having to do with mild sexual confusion in fashionable circles. He
had one of those polite, derivative talents that are often regarded as
terribly promising on the campus but never seem to come to very
much later. At the moment, he was living on the proceeds from his
second book, *Penelope*, the story of a constant but relentlessly talkative wife, which had been sold to the movies. Mr. Crane decided
now that there was nothing in his friend's career that could warrant
the deep and apparently permanent depression into which he seemed

plunged. Even if he was planning a sequel to *Penelope*, his writing required no dark and anxious searching of the soul; all it needed was a typewriter and sufficient energy to manipulate it.

"You sick or something?" Mr. Crane asked.

"No," said Mr. Anderson rather hollowly. "I'm O.K."

"The hell you are," said Mr. Crane. "My son has noticed it, too. He thinks you're in love with Mrs. Wilmot."

"For the love of God, George!" said Mr. Anderson with a visible start. "He really said that?"

"Sure," said Mr. Crane. "At breakfast. That's when he gets all his best ideas."

It was quite true that Billy Crane, who was eleven and observant for his years, had so diagnosed Mr. Anderson's malady, but his parents had merely put it down as one of the odd fantasies, brought on by persistent attendance at the movies, that seemed to throng their son's head. Mrs. Wilmot was a shapely blonde with china-blue eyes and a loping carriage, who lived in the boarding house operated by Mrs. Jermyn, a celebrated local character from whom the Cranes rented their cottage. Since Mrs. Wilmot also swam a rhythmic, eight-beat crawl and performed competently on the tennis court, her fascination for Billy Crane wasn't hard to explain. In addition to these gifts, however, she was a social thinker of intense and deadly solemnity—"She makes me feel like Mrs. Lucius Beebe," Mrs. Crane said once after a long afternoon of gentle political reproach—and it was difficult to imagine her appeal for a man like Mr. Anderson, who was apt to tire quickly of purposeful thought. However, there was clearly something here that needed further investigation.

"You're not in any kind of a jam, are you, Mark?" asked Mr. Crane in a tone that might easily be taken for humor.

Mr. Anderson had picked up the tennis ball and seemed to be trying to pry the cover off with his thumb. "Well, I guess you could call it that," he said at length. He tossed the ball away and clasped his hands around his knees. It had the look of a confessional attitude, and Mr. Crane was conscious of some foreboding. "I don't know, George," said Mr. Anderson. "I seem to get in the damnedest jams. Like the first time I was married. You remember that?"

"You're damn right I do," said Mr. Crane. It was, in fact, a story that still haunted him in the twilight of his thirties.[1] At the time, about fifteen years ago, Mr. Anderson had been a reporter on an obscure Long Island daily, a job which consisted mainly of hanging around the Country Courthouse at Mineola, collecting facts about the corruption of the Republican Party, which was enormous but about which his paper usually felt unable to print anything. This naturally left him a good deal of time for revelry of one kind and another, and when his grandmother died and unexpectedly left him the rather awkward sum of five hundred dollars, he decided to give a party that his colleagues would remember with gratitude long after he was gone. It was only on the afternoon of the party, after he had made all his other arrangements, that he discovered, to his dismay, that he had neglected to provide himself with a girl and had to pick one, by a system of hurried elimination, from his little leather address book. The name he finally chose was not altogether familiar to him, but in general any lady who appeared in its pages could be assumed to be presentable, articulate, and of a tolerant disposition, and when he went to collect her, this girl seemed suitable enough.

Almost at once, however, she proved to have been a serious mistake. The party—there were three other reporters and their girls—began at Canoe Place Inn, out in Southampton, where the four couples had such an exhausting evening that subsequently they drove down to the neighboring beach to recuperate with a swim and a nap. It was at their rather liquid breakfast back at the inn the next morning that Mr. Anderson's protégée began to behave strangely. He was having a wonderful time—his guests seemed to him people of almost unbearable humor and charm—and at first he was only dimly aware of the murmur of protest and anxiety from the lady on his right. As nearly as he could gather in his uplifted state, she was a respectable girl with a family to whom it would be impossible to explain an overnight absence. Call them up, he had suggested cheerfully, but she only wept at that and said she'd rather die. Somehow he managed to soothe her temporarily, but her misery persisted and even grew as the festive day wore on, and it came to a climax of despair when they stopped for dinner at a place called Rothmann's, in East Norwich. During this disturbing meal, she said, among other things, that her father would certainly kill both her and Mr. Anderson and that on the whole it struck her as a good thing. She sobbed hopelessly as she prophesied this double massacre and altogether presented a picture of such dank and abysmal tragedy that Mr. Anderson, gloomily conscious that his party was drowning in her tears, made his incredible mistake. If she would just let them enjoy the rest of the meal in peace, he had said wildly, they would go down to Oyster Bay afterward and be married by a justice of the peace whom he chanced to know. Since everyone had been drinking conscientiously for twenty-four hours, this idea was greeted with enthusiasm, and since in those days there were no necessary legal or medical delays, it was entirely feasible. At eleven o'clock that night, Mr. Anderson was drunker than he had ever been in his life, but he was also indisputably a bridegroom.

Recalling all this, Mr. Crane recalled, too, his friend's description of the following morning, when he woke up alone in his hotel room (his bride had been deposited with her parents in a scene that was vague but painful in his mind) staring at his coat, which was hanging on the back of a chair. "I just lay there about half an hour and looked at it," he had told Mr. Crane. "I knew damn well what was in it, of course—that piece of paper with a couple of lousy doves at the top—but I thought there might be some way I could just ignore the whole thing." The marriage license had been there all right, and the marriage itself, though never a domestic fact, remained a legal one, impossible for Mr. Anderson to ignore, for nearly a year. It had been dissolved, finally, when the present Mrs. Anderson, competently and derisively taking charge of his life, had arranged to clear up this foolish detail, too.

"You're a crazy bastard, Mark," said Mr. Crane, returning to the present.

"No," said Mr. Anderson. "Just polite. I always feel as if I have to do what women expect, especially if they raise hell about it. It's more or less that way now."

"Look, Mark," said Mr. Crane, "you don't have to marry Mrs. Wilmot. In the first place, you've got a wife. In the second, she's your intellectual superior. You're a political pinhead."

"Oh, my God," said Mr. Anderson, and looked so desolately out to sea that Mr. Crane was really concerned about him.

"What *is* all this, anyway?" he asked.

"I don't know," said Mr. Anderson. "Of course, it started with those walks."

The walks in question had caused a certain amount of discussion on the beach, but it had been mostly facetious. There had been very few days during the past few weeks when Mr. Anderson and Mrs. Wilmot hadn't set out resolutely in the sun, bound either for the neighboring settlement of Point o' Woods, a couple of miles to the east, or for the Fire Island lighthouse, which lay about twice as far to the west. The lady's effortless lope ate up the miles, and Mr. Anderson was quite a walker, too, and, in spite of a few lazy and worldly comments from Mrs. Anderson and Mrs. Crane, it was generally assumed that their purpose actually was exercise.

"I think you're all wrong about her, in a way," said Mr. Anderson. "I know she's a serious girl, but she's read a lot of other stuff, too."

"A lot?" said Mr. Crane. "She's read everything. She's a Quiz Kid."

"Well, anyway," Mr. Anderson went on, "we got to talking about writing and she said that *Penelope* surprised her."

"I can see that it would," said Mr. Crane. "All that adultery in the surtax brackets."

"That's what I thought she meant at first, myself," said Mr. Anderson. "But she was talking about the way it was written. You know, she actually seemed to know parts of the damn thing by heart." He looked uncertainly at Mr. Crane, whose expression gave him no help. "Of course, I haven't any illusions about the book, myself," he said defensively. "It's the kind of stuff women buy to read on trains. But she really had picked out the best parts of it—not the plot, but some of the casual, incidental stuff—and she seemed to know what I was trying to do. She said that some of it reminded her a little of *zuleika*, and while that's absurd, naturally, it *is* a fact that I'd been reading a lot of Beerbohm at the time."

Mr. Crane's face persistently remained as vacant as the moon, and Mr. Anderson threw a handful of sand irritably down the wind.

"You're a hell of a lot of help, George," he said.

"I'm sorry," said Mr. Crane. "I was just thinking of something. Go on."

"Well, you can't exactly help feeling flattered about a thing like that," said Mr. Anderson, "and, oh, hell, George, you know how these things are."

"She's a damn pretty girl," said Mr. Crane.

Another Mr. Anderson, a tough and experienced faun, for a moment rather shockingly replaced the literary personality.

"Yeah, I noticed that, too," it said, and vanished, grinning, giving way once more to a sincerely troubled man. "We used to sit down on the beach up around the lighthouse," said the customary Anderson, "and the first thing I knew she'd, well, sort of rearranged my life for me. It was just kidding at first—you know, what I ought to do if I was just starting out to write—but it got more and more serious, details and stuff, and after a while it seemed to be almost an accomplished fact. God knows, I don't remember really agreeing to anything."

"Such as what?" asked Mr. Crane.

"I know it's going to sound feebleminded to you, George," said Mr. Anderson, "but you've got to remember that it all happened very slowly. Well, it seems she's got this damn house down in Bucks County—part of her divorce settlement, I think. Anyway, one of those old stone jobs out in the country. It's all fixed up so you can move right in and she says it's a wonderful place to work—no neighbors, and just some old woman she knows about to keep the place cleaned up."

"It sounds perfect," said Mr. Crane. "You mean she wants you to go down there and write?"

Obviously Mr. Anderson hadn't intended to come quite so directly to the point, but he nodded reluctantly. "Well, yes," he said. "She thinks I ought to have a chance to at least *try* something different. I don't mean one of those indignant books called *Loan* or *Slag* or *Jute* or whatever the boys keep writing. Just an intelligent novel about the cl—kind of people I know. She thinks I've got the background and technique to get them down the way they really are. In a way, I'd like to, because it's something that's never been very convincingly done in this country."

"I guess you're right," said Mr. Crane. "The only thing I don't exactly understand is how Mrs. Wilmot fits into all this."

"That's the hell of it, of course," said Mr. Anderson unhappily. "I don't know, somehow or other she got the idea that Ginnie and I weren't getting along so well. Maybe I said I was under a little strain, trying to work around the house—as a matter of fact, I am—and that sometimes I felt as if I was in some damn kind of a rat race. Nothing more than that, certainly. Anyway, she said that if I got down to Bucks County I'd have a chance to think that out, too."

"She going to be there?" asked Mr. Crane. "I mean, to help you make up your mind or anything?"

"That's a hell of a thing to say, George," said Mr. Anderson indignantly. "Of course she isn't. She was just kind enough to offer me her house for a couple of months."

"I was only wondering," said Mr. Crane vaguely. "You ever happen to see a play called *No Time for Comedy*, Mark?"

"No. What's that got to do with it?"

"Nothing much," said Mr. Crane. "Except that maybe you ought to, because you're acting in it."

"How do you mean?"

"Same old plot," said Mr. Crane. "I forget exactly how it turns out. I think it's a very ingenious compromise. Guy decides to go back to his wife and write a *serious* comedy. Anyway, it's you."

"You've got the whole idea wrong, George," said Mr. Anderson. "I never really had any idea of—"

"Watch it," said Mr. Crane sharply. "Here come the girls."

MRS. CRANE AND Mrs. Anderson were almost upon them as he spoke, advancing treacherously from behind. Now they waved gaily and, reaching the umbrella, sat down gratefully in its shade.

"We've had a very interesting morning," said Mrs. Anderson. "Emily came over and somehow or other we fell asleep for quite a while, and then we had a mysterious caller."

"Who was that?" asked Mr. Crane, though for some reason he was sure he knew the answer before she spoke. He was not mistaken.

"Mark's female walking companion," said Mrs. Crane. "That Wilmot. I think she came to case the joint."

"Yes," said Mrs. Anderson. "She was very—what was that word I saw in a story a while ago? Crypty. Yes, she was very, very crypty."

"I think she wanted me to go," said Mrs. Crane placidly. "So naturally, of course, I just sat there. You never heard so much throat clearing in your life."

"Probably she just came to borrow something," said Mr. Anderson, with what struck Mr. Crane as a rather ghastly parody of unconcern.

"Oh, no," said his wife. "It was *much* more than that. It was hard to tell, but it was sort of as if she was working up to a property settlement or something."

"Or a real-estate deal," said Mrs. Crane. "She kept talking about some house she has in Bucks County. Four rooms, kitchen, and bath, and a very fine view of that part of Pennsylvania, which I understand is quite lovely in the fall. It wasn't exactly as if she wanted to sell it, though. I got the idea she was more interested in some kind of a trade. Of course, it was a terrible handicap to her, my being there, and nothing ever did get exactly cleared up."

"There was a lot of other stuff, too," said Mrs. Anderson. "We rather exhausted the house, and then she said that she thought happiness was terribly important. She seemed awfully vehement about it. She kept saying that you couldn't always tell if people were really happy or just resigned to living in a vacuum. I'm sure she didn't mean anything *personal*, but she kept peering around with those big flat eyes until we both got quite depressed. Emily said she'd be perfectly happy if she could figure out some way not to get sand in her scalp, but Mrs. Wilmot looked so hurt that in the end we agreed that practically everybody was miserable when you really got to know them. That seemed to cheer her up a lot."

"She mentioned you, too," said Mrs. Crane, after a short pause, pointing her toe at Mr. Anderson, who had been following this seemingly idle conversation with almost painful attention.

"Oh?" he said.

"She's worried about you, dear," said his wife. "Or at least about your work. She thinks it's peripheral."

"That's a hell of a word," he said.

"Hers," she assured him, "not mine. She also wonders how you can function as a social critic, even as well as you do, when you have your roots right in the system you're criticizing. Naturally, that's a quote, too. I said, Goodness, I didn't know, but perhaps you ought to get away from it now and then. Take a little trip or rent a room or something. She didn't exactly say, but I think she agreed with me, or at least she was being awfully intense about *something*. Anyway," she said, yawning and stretching one of her brown legs admiringly in the sun, "we had a lovely visit. I hope she'll come again."

Mr. Crane, who had also been regarding the ladies with astonishment not unmixed with horror, perceived that they had said all they intended to say publicly about Mrs. Wilmot, probably forever, and he got to his feet and picked up the tennis ball.

"All right, Mark," he said. "This time *you* can try throwing into that damn wind."

July 20, 1946

THE CELEBRITY

E VEN BEFORE THE boat from Bay Shore had docked, George and Emily Crane were able to identify Horace Giddings and his girl waving to them politely from the upper deck. They were somewhat paler than the other passengers and certainly a good deal more stylish.

"My God, he looks like an advertisement!" said Mr. Crane morosely. "I hope he hasn't got the idea this is Southampton."

"Oh, dear, I hope not," said his wife, "but he does look awfully select, doesn't he?"

"He does indeed," he replied, and thought, as he always did when Horace Giddings turned up in his life, that actors were apt to live stubbornly in the queer worlds of their dreams. If his guest had come expecting magnificence, as his appearance seemed to indicate, the week-end promised to be quite an ordeal for everybody. Fire Island was the utmost sun and sea could offer the troubled urban spirit, but socially it was a desert, hardly the place for a successful actor who naturally had known many fêtes, from Park Avenue to the Garden of Allah.

The passengers came off the boat and past the little booth where the captain's wife collected their fares, and soon Mr. Crane was relieving his guests of their baggage, which was extensive and rich.

"Goodness, you're *black*!" said the girl, when she had been presented as Miss Lilly Patton, also a toiler on the stage. "Horace, just look at them!"

She was a pretty child, with a surprising figure and candid eyes. Mr. Crane had heard rumors of a new attachment, and now his respect for his friend's judgment was somewhat tinged with awe.

"Well, they don't do a damn thing but lie in the sun," said Mr. Giddings in his handsome, melancholy voice. "They're locust eaters."

"That's right," said Mr. Crane, not entirely sure whether humor was intended. "Here, I'll put your stuff in the wagon."

Except for the equipment used by the fire department, and one or two delivery trucks, automobiles are not allowed on Fire Island, the inhabitants pulling their bags and provisions from the village to their cottages in little express wagons. It was into one of these, a sad relic with unmatched wheels, that Mr. Crane piled Mr. Giddings' two big bags and the dainty Mark Cross travelling case that belonged to his companion.

"We have to walk about half a mile," Mr. Crane said. "You still know how to walk, Horace? Or do I have to pull you, too?"

His guest was about to reply to that when they were interrupted by a young woman in a bathing suit who had a fearful but resolute air.

"You're Horse Giddings, ain't you?" she said breathlessly, and when he nodded, "I told my girl friend. 'That's Horse Giddings over there,' I said, 'standing with Mr. and Mrs. Crane.'"

There was a pause, in which she inspected him hotly.

"Well, whata you know," she said. "I seen you in a pitcher out here oney last week."

"It was that one called *Lovers Grow Cold*, Horace," said Mrs. Crane. "I thought it was awfully silly, but for a couple of days there were big posters of you all over the village. We were terribly impressed."

"I better get back and tell Tessie," said the young woman. "Gee! Horse *Giddings!*"

She scuttled away and Miss Patten sighed.

"It's like that wherever we go," she said. "Like bumming around with somebody with two heads."

Mr. Giddings smiled patiently, an indulgent adult confronted with the tasteless and rather intrusive humor of childhood.

"Well, we might as well start," said Mr. Crane, uneasily aware that the news of his guest's fame was already spreading through the village.

FOR A LITTLE while they followed the main street, past the drugstore; the market, conducted in those days of famine by a

sorely driven man; the combined newspaper stand and soda fountain, where the young of the community sat all day reading, but
never buying, comic magazines and languidly insulting their digestions with various chemical sweets; past the barbershop, which also
dealt with ladies' hair; the Community House, which contained
three of the island's five telephones and where there were movies in
the evening; and, finally, Sweeney's Bar and Grill, where every night,
but especially on Saturday, the natives and the summer colonists met
in troubled solution to drink and dance to the squeal and wallow
and thump of the juke box.

Mr. Crane explained all these points of interest to Mr. Giddings
and Miss Patton, and though they were polite enough, he felt that
they were somewhat dismayed. On the whole, it wasn't hard to understand. They had come innocently expecting an American Riviera, but they could probably have accepted a really desolate and
primitive scene almost as well, since that also would have been picturesque. This transplanted suburb, however, this street that might
have been anywhere, that really ran from coast to coast, visibly wilted
their theatrical spirits, or at least Mr. Giddings'; Mr. Crane still wasn't
quite sure about Miss Patton.

They turned left at the end of the street and followed another at
right angles, one of the many parallel walks that led south from the
bay to the sea. This thoroughfare also had a profoundly discouraging air. It was lined on both sides with thickets of bayberry and
poison ivy, from which occasionally there rose a little clump of
stunted and disconsolate pines; here and there, in depressions in the
sandy soil, stagnant pools had gathered, filmed with oil and over-
hung with whirling gnats, and between and behind the houses the
dunes rose, small, melancholy hills tufted with dry and bitter grass.
The houses themselves, wooden beach bungalows, were wildly diverse in pattern, but all small, ugly, and apparently deliberately designed to exclude both sun and air. Each also bore a little sign,
whimsically lettered, that testified to its owner's sentimental or
humorous fancy. Most of the names were dear and familiar to the
American littoral—Sans Souci, Casa Mañana, The Pines, Skylark,
Shangri-La, and endless combinations involving "sea" and "dune"
and "sky"—but others were products of a livelier wit.

"What the hell is Six and One?" asked Mr. Giddings irritably. "That supposed to be a local joke?"

"Six and One?" said Mr. Crane, following his guest's eye. "Oh. It's just the capitals. It's really Vi and I. The inmate and his wife, I guess. You get a lot of that."

"Mercy!" said Miss Patton. "Has your house got a name, too, Mr. Crane?"

"Yes," he said. "It's called The Gulls."

"Oh," she said, regarding him gravely. "I suppose you've got a lot of gulls out here?"

"What do you think he's got, for God's sake?" said Mr. Giddings. "Bison?"

"How should I know?" she said amiably. "I'm a Kansas girl."

They passed Dunroamin and Sandy Beds and Birdies' Rest and Taria Whitmore, a pun that appeared to fascinate Miss Patton, though Mr. Giddings merely looked depressed.

"There's my favorite," said Mrs. Crane, pointing to a house on her left that was simply labelled "EEEE." "It's a sort of intelligence test, really."

"I just give up, Emily," said Mr. Giddings. "Probably four dames live there who all begin with E. Is that it?"

"Four E's," murmured Miss Patton, and suddenly clapped her hands. "But goodness, of *course*! For Ease. I think that's *cute*."

"What?" said Mr. Giddings vaguely. "Oh. Sure. Listen, George, do you really live around here somewhere? I mean, within a couple of hours' walk?"

"It's right up there at the end," said Mr. Crane soothingly. "That house on the left."

"My, I can hear the ocean!" cried Miss Patton, and the sound of the waves was indeed audible to them on the still air. In the past month, this measured rhythm, a surge and withdrawal a little slower than the heart, had brought a curious peace to Mr. Crane, almost as if the nervous tempo of his life had mysteriously abated in sympathy. Clearly, however, it had no such effect on Mr. Giddings.

"You live right here on the ocean?" he asked. "How the hell do you sleep?"

"It's supposed to be very soothing, Horace," said Mrs. Crane. "Some of our guests hardly wake up at all."

"We can always drug you," said Miss Patton. "I have some little pills."

They reached the house, larger than most of those they'd passed, but still only a frame cottage of bleak, unpromising design.

"We might as well leave the bags downstairs and go right up on the porch and have a drink," said Mrs. Crane. "Unless, of course, anybody wants to change or anything first."

Nobody did, and they went up an exterior stairway that led up to a small, railed platform that faced directly on the sea.

"Why, it's lovely," said Miss Patton, confronted with clear blue to the end of the world, and even Mr. Giddings was stirred to compliment the Atlantic.

"Bloody good show," he said.

Miss Patton grinned. "He picked that up in the U.S.O.," she murmured to Mr. Crane. "*Journey's End*, I guess."

Turning to her with amusement, Mr. Crane saw for the first time that the porch was already tenanted. At the other end, sitting in a rocking chair against the wall, was his landlady, Mrs. Jermyn. She was being entertained by the Cranes' eleven-year-old son, Billy, who, his father noted, was dressed only in a face towel, rather casually wrapped around his meagre waist.

"Oh, hello," said Mr. Crane. "Mrs. Jermyn, this is Miss Patton. And Mr. Giddings. Billy, you go put some pants on. This isn't Africa."

"O.K., O.K.," his son said tolerantly, and departed through the screen door that led into the house.

"I just dropped in about the icebox," said Mrs. Jermyn. "My husband says you need a new part, but he's taped it up so you ought to get some kind of ice for the time being." She looked at Mr. Giddings with her yellow, inscrutable eyes and seemed to find him vaguely comic. "You're the actor, ain't you?" she asked. "Mrs. Crane told me you were coming. Ain't you been in a lot of Shakespeare?"

"Well, no," he said. "Not in New York."

"I don't know why I should have thought that," she said. "Except I got this actor over at my house now. Tremlyn Dorkins. You know him?"

Knowing how fiercely Mrs. Jermyn's mind resisted precise information, especially proper names, Mr. Crane felt sure that even if one of her guests was indeed an actor, he was certainly not called Tremlyn Dorkins.

"No," said Mr. Giddings. "I'm afraid I don't."

"Well, he plays a lot of Shakespeare," said Mrs. Jermyn. "Clowns and stuff."

"I'll get the drinks," said Mrs. Crane. "Martinis all right for everybody?"

Assured that they were, she went in the house, and a little silence fell on the porch.

"Take me down to the sea again, the lovely sea and the sky," murmured Mr. Giddings, at length.

"What did you say?" asked Mrs. Jermyn with surprise.

"It's a line of poetry that happened to come into my mind," he explained indulgently. "John Masefield."

"Well, more or less," said Miss Patton.

Mrs. Jermyn considered her for the first time. "You act, too?" she asked.

"A little," said Miss Patton. "But rather like Tremlyn Dorkins, I'm afraid. Mostly clowns and stuff."

"Oh," said Mrs. Jermyn. Mrs. Crane came back with the shaker and glasses, and soon they were all equipped with drinks.

"Where you putting these folks?" asked Mrs. Jermyn after a moment. "In the upstairs rooms?"

"Yes," said Mr. Crane. "Right up there under the roof."

"Well, that's nice," she said, and addressed Mr. Giddings. "You been inside yet?"

"No," he said, looking apprehensively upward. "What do you mean right up under the roof, George? There doesn't seem to be much space. I mean, on top of this floor."

"Well, it's deceptive," said Mr. Crane. "You'll find you can stand up all right. At least in the middle."

"It's a funny thing about this house," said Mrs. Jermyn. "The downstairs is all right—two bedrooms and a bathroom, where Mrs. Crane keeps little Billy and Vicky and their nurse—but up here they've got this big two-story living room in the middle and then on one side is the kitchen and the other is the Cranes' bedroom. The rooms you've got are upstairs on both sides. They each got a separate staircase."

"It isn't as hard as it sounds, Horace," said Mr. Crane. "Anyway, what's so funny about it?"

"Oh, nothing," said Mrs. Jermyn. "That is, it's only funny when I think of this Tremlyn Dorkins we were talking about."

"It's a lovely name," said Mrs. Crane. "But I don't quite see . . ."

"Well," said Mrs. Jermyn, "he's been coming down here a good many years, but this was the first time, 'long about 1928, I guess. Around the time of the Bloom."

"The what?" asked Miss Patton.

"The Boom," said Mr. Crane.

"The time of the Bloom," repeated Mrs. Jermyn. "In those days I used to live in this house myself and only go over to the big one to fix up in the mornings. Sometimes when I was full up over there, I'd let a few people stay here, downstairs and in them two rooms on top. Well, this Dorkins showed up one day and I wasn't going to take him at first, because you always have a lot of trouble with theatrical folks, but he was a friend of John Murray Anderson or Shubert or one of them, so I said, 'O.K., you and Mrs. Dorkins'—I forgot to say he had this blondie with him—'you and Mrs. Dorkins can have a room in the basement, anyways over the week-end.' I knew she wasn't any Mrs. Dorkins any more than you are."

Miss Patton, at whom this appeared to be directed, looked at her with admiration.

"How did you know that?" she asked. "I've often wondered."

"Nobody would have to marry that one, dear," said Mrs. Jermyn. "Not even an actor. Anyway, he said right off she wasn't his wife. I don't know. I guess he figured he might run into friends or maybe he'd want to come down again and didn't want a wrong impression. So finally I put them up in them two rooms."

"I don't like to seem dense," said Mr. Crane, "but I don't quite see why he wanted to bring her down here at all if—well, just if."

"Well, you know how these things are," Mrs. Jermyn said. "They wake up in New York with a hangover and they think maybe if they could get out on a beach or somewhere for a couple of days. They don't care where anybody sleeps, not at the moment, anyway."

"Oh," said Mr. Crane, bowing to a wider knowledge of the world inhabited by actors.

"That evening they went down to Sweeney's for dinner," said Mrs. Jermyn, "and I guess they had a couple, because when they came back they sat around for a while holding hands and stuff and I could see they'd kind of changed their minds about the rooms. Well, they weren't getting any help out of me. 'You made those upstairs beds,' I thought. 'Now you can just go lay in them.' About ten o'clock they go up, and after a while I see their lights go out under their doors, so I go to bed, too."

"The poor man," said Miss Patton. "And after playing all those clowns."

"Well, I put out the lights and went to bed," Mrs. Jermyn went on, "and I guess I'd been asleep for maybe about an hour when suddenly you'd think the house fell in. There was a big crash and then a bunch of little ones like the furniture tipping over and in between somebody kind of cursing and groaning. Well, I go out, and there's this Dorkins laying on the floor of the living room with the standing lamp down on top of him and a couple of these little occasional tables that had a lot of seaweed and shells on them laying around, too. He had a little cut on his head, I guess where the bulb hit him, but he ain't really hurt, only sore. 'What's the matter, Dorkins?' I said. 'You have some accident?' 'I only come down to get a glass of water,' he says, 'and the goddam lamp fell onto me.' 'You got a long way out of your way for the water,' I told him. 'You got a faucet right up in your room.' By this time, the girl is out there, too, and she's all full of how he may be bleeding to death. 'No, he ain't,' I said. 'He just tripped over the electric-light cord and the lamp come down on him. Anyway,' I said, 'you might as well go back to bed, because he's through walking for the night.' I was beginning to get kind of sore at them myself, but suddenly I looked at him in the middle of all that busted glass and seaweed and I got to laughing and pretty soon she begun to laugh, too. 'You keep away from actors, dearie,' she told me. 'They're always getting something loused up.' He started to tell me again about the glass of water, but she told him to shut up, and finally we patched some sticking plaster on him and got him back up to bed. The next day all he said was to ask me how much he owed me for the lamp, and I said forget it. It was my own fault, I told him, for leaving the cord hooked up over the back of a chair where nobody could help but bunk into it."

"So that's the way it was?" said Mr. Crane. He had known Mrs. Jermyn now for more than a month, and there were still recesses in her character that attracted him darkly.

"Yes," she said. "I must have forgot people might be moving around. The way I had it, it would have been like getting through bobwire into a trench."

For a little while the five people on the porch sat quietly, busy with their cocktails and their private reflections. The expressions worn by his wife and his landlady told Mr. Crane nothing, and Mr. Giddings appeared to be lost in some chill, Alpine dream of his own, but while Miss Patton's face was also composed, her eyes were fixed on her escort and they seemed to be full of a new and rather delighted speculation.

"Poor Tremlyn Dorkins," she murmured at last. "What a perfectly *terrible* show for him, poor dear!"

From the moment the boat docked almost until she spoke, Mr. Crane had been looking forward to the weekend with deep misgivings. Now, however, it seemed to him full of infinite promise, and he lay back peacefully to watch it take its course.

August 3, 1946

THE FOREIGN POPULATION

"T HAT WAS IN Manila," said Commander McLaughlin hoarsely. "Nineteen twenty-two or -three. Damn good-looking girl she was, too. In the end, I had to stop answering the telephone. I'd let Mrs. McLaughlin answer it, and then, of course, this girl would hang up. She'd just give a sort of gasp and hang up. It got to be one of our family jokes."

Looking at Mrs. McLaughlin, impassively knitting under the beach umbrella, George Crane saw no particular amusement in her plain, rather discontented face. It was obviously an old story to her and presumably also one familiar in theme, for already that afternoon the Commander had mentioned two other young women who had similarly embarrassed him in faraway corners of the world. He was a man in his middle fifties, a professional sailor since his graduation from Annapolis, and he looked correct and blankly handsome even in the informality of an old towelling bathrobe and with his white hair tangled and matted from the surf. He was spending the weekend with the Cranes' closest friends, Mark and Virginia Anderson, to whom he was somehow obscurely related, and he had been in charge of the conversation on the beach for almost two days. To George Crane, who always lost confidence in his own anecdotes after the first thirty seconds, there was a kind of gloomy fascination about a man who could go on for twenty minutes with some aimless fragment of personal reminiscence. He remembered a publisher he had once met and his description of a popular author whose readers had unaccountably begun to fall away. "The trouble with Charles," he had said, "is that he's got to the point where he thinks that everything that happens to him is interesting." It was clearly an opinion that the Commander had held all his life.

"Look at those kids," he said now. "You've got a wonderful

place for them down here on Fire Island. I've always said that the seashore was the only place to bring up youngsters. I remember in Honolulu . . ."

George Crane detached his mind from the story about Honolulu and considered the children—his own two, Victoria and Billy; the two young Andersons; and two others not immediately familiar to him by name—who were playing in the sand a little distance away from the umbrella. The center of social activity in the group seemed to be a boy of about twelve, burned black by the sun and crowned with a great mop of exultant hair. Mr. Crane had often noticed him before, both because of his startling resemblance to an African Bushman and also because he usually seemed to be at the bottom of the frequent disturbances that swept the juvenile colony. His name was Bronny, Mr. Crane recalled with an effort, and it had been reported by young Billy Crane that he had once been in the habit of charging the other children five cents a day to play with him, and getting it, too, because he had a strangely adult gift for organized gaiety. Like Elsa Maxwell, Mr. Crane thought irrelevantly.

It was hard to tell much about the game the children were play-ing at the moment, except that it involved some rather elaborate excavations in the sand and a good deal of squealing and falling down on the part of the Crane and Anderson girls, who were both six and more apt to grasp the spirit of an entertainment than its technical details. As he watched, Marcia Anderson picked up a handful of sand and threw it wildly at the sun.

"Hey," her father called. "None of that."

"Oh, pooh," she protested. "It wasn't *at* anybody."

"No throwing sand anywhere," he said. "You know that."

"O.K., O.K.," she said with terrible weariness, and sat down be-side her friend Vicky. "My family would just as soon nail me up in a box," she said.

"Mine would just as soon put me away in the garbage," Vicky agreed. They both looked hopefully at Mr. Anderson, but he wasn't impressed.

"That's right," he said amiably. "That's where you both belong. Right in the garbage."

Giggling, the little girls got up, and moved a little further down the wind.

BEHIND MR. CRANE, the Commander was still going on about Honolulu, focussing with pronounced nautical gallantry on Irma Mendelsohn, a remarkably pretty young widow who lived about a quarter of a mile down the beach and often came to sit with the Cranes and Andersons.

"Mrs. Fortescue?" he was saying. "I knew her very well. Damn brave woman. I hold no brief for anybody taking the law into their own hands, but if there was ever ample justification—"

"But there were a good many stories—" began Mrs. Mendelsohn.

"There were a hell of a lot more than ever got printed," he said, "but that's beside the point. Wherever you get a tremendous foreign population—"

"Foreign?" she said mildly.

"I mean native, of course," he said. "Anyway, wherever the whites are tremendously outnumbered, you get the same problem. It isn't always possible to handle it as—as *legalistically* as some of us might wish."

"No," she said. "I've heard it isn't."

As she spoke, Bronny and another boy, three or four years younger, came up from their fortifications and sat down near them.

"Did you have a nice game, Davie?" Mrs. Mendelsohn asked. "What were you playing? It looked terribly exciting."

"Oh, nothing," he said. "It was all right until those girls had to come butting their heads in."

"Marcia and Vicky?" she asked. "You have to remember they're so much younger. They don't always quite understand your games."

"They're little dopes," he said.

Mrs. Mendelsohn gave Mr. Crane an apologetic smile. "I'm afraid chivalry doesn't set in until quite a bit later, George," she said.

"I know it," he said. "Billy hasn't much use for women, either. As a matter of fact, they really *are* terrible dopes, those two."

"Is this your son?" asked the Commander resonantly. "A fine boy."

"Yes," she said. "My son, David. And this other one is Bronny. I don't think I know your last name, Bronny."

"Fairchild," said the boy. His voice was not impolite; he just sounded profoundly bored.

"Bronny's my best friend now," David told his mother. "Aren't you, Bronny?" He looked at the older boy with sober pleasure, as if to confirm the solemn fact of the alliance between them.

"Sure, I guess so," said Bronny.

"He's going to play with me every day now instead of those other kids," said David triumphantly. "He says I'm the best kid he ever saw for a Jew."

Mrs. Mendelsohn breathed sharply. In itself, the familiar slur was nothing to her, Mr. Crane knew, but the pride in her son's voice was clearly a shock. She half stretched out her hand to him, in protest or pity, but caught herself and dropped it. "That's very nice of him, dear," she said quietly.

There was an awkward silence and then, to Mr. Crane's dismay, the Commander beckoned to Bronny.

"Come here, son," he said.

Bronny got up from the sand and reluctantly came forward a step or two.

"Oh, please," Mrs. Mendelsohn began, but the Commander shook his fine head.

"I think you'd better apologize to this lady," he said to Bronny. "You're old enough to know that we don't say things like that in this country."

The boy remained silent, sullenly digging his toe into the sand, and Mrs. Mendelsohn laid her hand on the Commander's arm.

"Please," she repeated. "It doesn't matter at all."

"I'm sorry, but I think it does," he said brusquely.

Mr. Crane cleared his throat, but Mark Anderson spoke first.

"Oh, let it go, Bill," he said uneasily. "He's only a kid."

The Commander ignored him. It was clear that he already regretted his impulse but that it was impossible for him to retreat. Embarrassment made his voice even louder and hoarser than it was normally. "We're waiting for you to apologize to this lady," he said.

"What for?" muttered the boy.

"You know perfectly well. For what you called her little boy."

"Well, he *is* a Jew, ain't he?" said Bronny. "Why do I have to apologize for calling him what he is?"

"That's not the point," said the Commander. "The point is . . ." He stopped, and Mr. Crane waited with fascination. "The point is that there are certain things that decent people just don't care to hear," he said, "and that's one of them."

Bronny still hesitated and the Commander lost what was left of his self-control.

"Damn it!" he shouted, the veins dangerously corded in his throat. "You'll apologize because I tell you to!"

For a moment, the boy stared back at him defiantly but the voice of the quarterdeck was too much for him and he dropped his head. "All right," he muttered. "I apologize."

"That's all right, Bronny," said Mrs. Mendelsohn. "Now we'll just forget about it, shall we?"

"Yes'm," he said, but the look he gave her was hostile and subtly derisive. The scene had been alarming, though largely incomprehensible, to David, and he had watched it with a troubled expression, but now his face cleared.

"Come on, Bronny," he cried with relief, taking his friend's arm. "Now let's go back and play."

The other boy pulled away irritably. "No," he said, glancing at the Commander. "No, I can't now. I gotta go home."

"Ah, *gee!*" said David. "You said we could play some more."

"I told you I got no time," said Bronny. He didn't leave, however, but sat on the sand with his arms around his knees and stared stonily out to sea.

"Gee, Bronny," David began, but his mother interrupted him gaily.

"Goodness!" she cried. "It *is* late! I had no idea how late it was. I'm afraid we have to go home, too."

David looked doubtfully at his friend and then at his mother and there began to be a kind of comprehension in his face. He took her hand. "Well," he said uncertainly, "I guess I got to go. G'bye, Bronny. See you in the morning."

"I guess so," said Bronny, without turning his head. "S'long."

★ ★ ★

FOR A MINUTE after the Mendelsohns had left, there was a silence, and then the Commander gave a short laugh.

"Hell," he said. "I didn't mean to be tough on the kid, but I certainly wasn't going to sit here and let a woman take that kind of stuff."

Mark Anderson looked at him and shook his head. "You're really God damn near perfect, aren't you, Bill?" he said. "Sometimes I forget."

"What do you mean?" demanded the Commander. "Just because you're willing to stand by and see a woman—"

"That's right," said Mr. Anderson, getting up. "I'm a Jew baiter at heart. Well, I think I'll go for a swim. You coming, Ginny?"

"All right," said his wife.

The Andersons walked away along the beach toward the section roped off for swimmers, and the Commander looked after indignantly.

"That Mark has got to be a hell of a strange boy these last few years," he said at length.

"Strange?" said Mr. Crane. "How do you mean?"

"I don't know," said the Commander. "Strange. Ineffectual or something. Just not much character, I guess." He thought it over, frowning. "It's a funny thing," he said. "You see them all over the world. Christ, it seems to me I've seen some fellow like Mark in every bar in the world."

"Like Humphrey Bogart," said Mr. Crane.

"I don't mean drunk," said the Commander impatiently. "Just sitting there. Hard fellows to talk to." He struggled with an idea that was vague in his mind. "I don't know," he said helplessly at last. "You never can figure out what the hell they really *stand* for. He's like what's wrong with the damn country, some way or other."

The Commander dismissed Mr. Anderson with an irritable gesture, and for the first time seemed to notice that Bronny was still sitting near them on the sand. "What's the matter, son?" he called. "I thought you'd gone home."

Bronny concentrated on a hole he was digging beside him in the sand.

"I'm O.K.," he said.

"That's right," said the Commander heartily. "Don't let it get you. You've just got to watch your step sometimes, that's all."

"Yes, sir," said the boy. He stood up and slapped the sand briskly off the seat of his bathing trunks. "Well," he said, "I better go. I'm very pleased to have met you," he added politely.

"O.K., son," said the Commander.

For a moment they looked at one another without embarrassment and then Bronny turned back to the sea.

"Hey, Billy," he called to Mr. Crane's son, who was walking along the shore down toward the bathing beach. "You going in? Then wait a sec. I'm coming, too."

August 17, 1946

THE CAT ON THE ROOF[1]

IT WAS RATHER like an old Chaplin comedy. George Crane, who was on his innocent way to the post office, was just about to turn the corner that led into the main street of the village when there was a clatter and screech of metal, a violent collision, and he was flung off the concrete walk and into a little clump of stunted pines that grew beside it. He had been carrying his sun-glasses and they flew out of his hand and broke on the pavement; otherwise he was undamaged, though indignant. Extricating himself from the branches and shaking his head, he saw that his assailant was a rather astonishing blonde on roller skates, who seemed to be having troubles of her own. Her blue sweater and dungarees were heavily streaked with some pasty substance, and a pie plate, lying upside down at her feet, only partly concealed the remains of what must once have been a cake. The expression on her round, self-possessed face as she surveyed this wreckage, however, held only a casual irritation. She turned the pie plate over with one of her skates and inspected the blob of dough and icing on the walk.

"Like to buy a cake?" she said, addressing Mr. Crane in a tone not unlike the one with which Miss Tallulah Bankhead is accustomed to bewitch her admirers. "I think I can let you have one pretty cheap."

"You ought to watch where you're going on those things," he said irritably. "This isn't a rink."

She was a tall girl and the skates brought her eyes a little above the level of his own. She looked down at him with derisive apology.

"I'm sorry, baby," she said. "I guess I had my mind on the cake." She noticed the empty celluloid frames in his hand. "Hey, you broke your glasses."

"It's all right," he said. "They just came from the drugstore."

"I'll get you another pair."

"No, it doesn't really matter. They were only a quarter."

"I'll get you another pair," she repeated. An elderly, disreputable dog had wandered up while they were talking and now it began to lick the icing on the pavement.

"That's right, you crazy bastard," she said. "Go on. *Get* sick."

For a moment, they both watched the dog in silence. Mr. Crane felt a little uncomfortable. They were not far from the center of the village and it was the time of the morning when most of the ladies he knew did their marketing. It seemed inevitable that such an unusual scene would soon attract an audience.

"Well," he said, "I'd better be getting along."

She wiped her hand on the seat of her dungarees and held it out.

"You're Mr. Crane, aren't you?" she said. "Somebody pointed you out last night in the bar. I'm Deedy Barton."

"Oh, yes," he said, since she appeared to expect some recognition. They had parted and he was on his way back from the post office, however, before her identity suddenly came to him.

"Well, I'll be damned," he murmured.

For the past five years, Deedy Barton—she seemed to have no rational first name—had enjoyed a curious, inverted celebrity in New York. In the beginning it had been confined to more or less guarded items in the gossip columns. Mr. Crane, who was a conscientious student of spitball journalism, could recall their general tone: "Deedy Barton sooo sorry about who broke that mirror at the Stork," "That Barton girl and the milkman a daily twosome," "What well-known fire-insurance biggie was Deedy Barton too hot for the other yawning?" Gradually, however, her furious personality had lifted her above innuendo, and there were pictures and jocular though rather mysterious stories in the tabloids. Miss Barton had been permanently banned by the management of a night club for pushing a table over on a moving-picture actress (there had apparently been some discussion of comparative morality); in another bar, a young man, alarmed by her attentions, had sought refuge in the washroom only to find that she was indifferent to signs on doors; once she had disrupted a floor show with an impromptu number of her own that featured a song not often sung in public; after a courtship that had left a trail of broken glassware across the city, she had married a band leader but that had cooled in a little while and she had flung his clothes out of the window of their hotel at high noon; now she was divorced and there were rumors of an engagement to a musical-comedy star whose disposition was almost as festive as her own.

As far as Mr. Crane could recall, he had never seen Miss Barton in New York, but that was probably either because the places he frequented would have struck her as appallingly dull or else because their proprietors would have been reluctant to admit so uninhibited a guest. It seemed unlikely, however, that she could have escaped his notice long on Fire Island, where a celebrity of any kind was a matter of burning interest in the bars and along the beach. He concluded that she had just arrived, and, as he had once or twice before when complicated metropolitan personalities had descended on this Eden of lost simplicities, he considered her presence an intrusion, filling him with irritation and dismay. Well, he thought, it shouldn't be hard to avoid her. He spent most of his time on the beach and she hardly had the air of a sun worshipper.

During the next few days, he heard a good deal about Deedy Barton. A moral matron who had an ocean-front house reported that she was in the habit of swimming at night without the visible formality of a bathing suit; her dancing had caused comment at Sweeney's, where a certain amount of jungle abandon was not unknown and one night in the course of a musical argument there she had broken the glass front of the juke box with a bottle; a member of the Coast Guard had left his jeep temporarily unguarded and she had driven it six miles up the beach to Cherry Grove, where she was finally captured in the bar. There were other stories, too.

Mr. Crane had not seen her, however, and she was far from his mind when late one afternoon he and his wife were sitting on their porch, drinking a peaceful Martini with their friends, Mark and Virginia Anderson. The porch faced directly on the Atlantic and it could be reached by an exterior stairway from the sidewalk which ran along the inland side of the house. They were talking idly about their children—Mr. Anderson had a theory that progressive schools made them unfit to associate with the other, simpler children in the colony—when they heard footsteps on the stairs.

"Goodness, I wonder who that could be," murmured Mrs. Crane.

"I guess Mrs. Jermyn," said her husband. "I was telling her about the leak."

"I've been telling her all summer," she said.

They were all looking at the top of the stairs when Miss Barton made her entrance. She was wearing a black bathing suit that went very handsomely with her admirable figure and her flaxen hair and she was carrying a limp Angora under her arm.

"Hi," she said to Mr. Crane and held out an envelope. "I brought your glasses."

"You didn't have to do that." He opened the envelope and took out the glasses. They were an expensive pair, with heavy frames and Polaroid lenses. "They're much too good," he protested. "You'd better keep them yourself."

"What the hell, baby," she said. "I broke your others."

"Well, thank you very much." He introduced her to his wife and the Andersons and offered her a drink.

"I just had a couple at Sweeney's," she said, confirming a strong suspicion in his mind, "but O.K."

While he was pouring it, she put the cat down on the floor, where it crouched, lashing its tail and digging its claws into the matting.

"She's beautiful," said Mrs. Anderson. "What's her name?"

"I don't know yet. She's new. I got her yesterday when I was in New York. The shop was right next door to the glasses."

She took the cocktail from Mr. Crane and drank most of it in one swallow.

"I brought her out in a hatbox," she said. "She was good all the way until the boat. Then she got the top loose. Say, do you know a guy called McGonigle? C. P. McGonigle? Kind of fat, with a little mustache?"

"I don't think so," said Mr. Crane. "Why?"

"He was the one I just had the drinks with. He finally caught her on the boat. She was damn near in the engine."

She finished her drink and held the glass out to Mr. Crane, who filled it with a slight sense of misgiving. She really seemed quite drunk, and she had the unfocussed, rather wooden expression that he had learned boded no good in his friends.

"That's quite an operator, that McGonigle," she said. "Listen, I told him last night, you keep that up and I'm going to have to saw off those pretty hands of yours."

The other ladies laughed amiably but her face remained sullen, preoccupied with the memory of her trials.

"Well, he *kept* it up," she said, "so I had to push him in the poison ivy."

"But I thought you said you just had a drink with him," said Mrs. Crane.

"Sure," she said, "and I'm going to pick him up later at Sweeney's." Suddenly her personality seemed to undergo a distinct change for the worse. "So what?" she said, looking at them with gathering and unmistakable menace.

"Nothing," said Mrs. Crane hastily. "I admire your spirit. How about another drink? George, give Miss Barton another drink."

Oh, God, he thought, now we'll never get her out of here, but he filled her glass and put the empty shaker down beside him on the floor. There was a long silence. His guest's smoldering regard was fixed on the Atlantic and though her thoughts were impossible to guess, they were clearly dark. Mr. Crane, feeling rather oppressed, sought to fill the vacuum.

"Mark and I are playing tennis in the morning," he said to his wife. "You remember where I left those balls the last time?"

She started to reply, but Miss Barton anticipated her. Her voice was a little blurred but it held an almost overpowering derision.

"Tennis?" she said. "You boys play tennis? Spansy game."

"Well—" Mr. Anderson began.

"Spansy game," she repeated firmly. She stared at Mrs. Crane with a peculiar fixity, narrowing her eyes. "What do you want to put up with these two? All this tennis and stuff?"

"Oh, they're all right," said Mrs. Crane, laughing. "They just play tennis. That's as far as it goes."

"That's not what *I* hear," said Miss Barton, "but you ought to know." Somehow this comment seemed to restore her geniality and she smiled warmly at Mr. Crane. "How's about a little drink, baby?" she asked, holding out her glass.

"I'm sorry," he lied, "but that was the end of the gin. There may be some beer in the icebox."

"Beer," she said with distaste. "No, no beer. Well, I better go find that McGonigle." On her second attempt, she got up from the chair and looked around hazily. "Where's that damn cat?"

"Right over there," said Mrs. Anderson. "In the corner."

"Oh."

Miss Barton approached the cat, which was curled in a soft ball and seemed to be asleep. The ensuing scene was never precisely clear to anyone on the porch. Either Miss Barton's foot caught in a hole in the matting or else she simply stumbled; in any case, she lurched over into the corner and her foot came down on the cat, presumably on its tail. There were two screeches—one from the cat and one from its owner—a sound of claws on wood, and then, almost too fast for the eye to follow, a flowing streak of blue-black light, along the railing of the porch, miraculously up the side of the house, and onto the roof. When this violent action at last resolved itself into a static scene, the cat was sitting on the peak of the roof, beside the chimney, and Miss Barton was bending over a formidable scratch that extended from her ankle to her knee. The words she was using to some extent explained her metropolitan reputation.

"You'd better let me put some iodine on that," said Mrs. Crane sympathetically.

"No," said Miss Barton, "it's all right. Listen, how are we going to get that damn thing *down* out of there?"

They all looked helplessly up at the cat, which was staring out over the wide ocean and switching its tail.

"Here, kitty, kitty. Nice kitty," Mrs. Crane called sweetly but the cat, after giving her a flickering glance, decided to stay where it was. They all tried, employing many foolish blandishments, but the cat ignored them, its noble, disdainful face once more turned out to sea.

"I could borrow a ladder from Mrs. Jermyn," said Mr. Crane.

"No," said his wife firmly. "It's slippery up there and too steep anyway. You'd break your neck."

Mr. Crane was relieved, but the spirit of chivalry was strong in him.

"Perhaps if Mark and I—" he began.

"No, not him either," said Mrs. Anderson. "You'd never catch it anyway. I know cats. I think you'd better just leave it alone. It'll come down when it gets ready."

"I suppose it will," said Mrs. Crane. "It just looks so forlorn."

Miss Barton had been following their conversation with evident exasperation and now she addressed them scornfully.

"All right, you lousy tennis players," she cried, "you want to see *me* get that cat down?"

"How?" asked Mr. Crane. "I don't think you'd better try to go up there."

"Who said anything about me going up there?" she demanded. "You just wait here. I'll get the son of a bitch down."

She looked at them all with an expression that Mr. Crane found disturbing, glanced up briefly at the cat, which had gone back to sleep, and then turned and ran down the stairway.

"What do you suppose she's going to do?" asked Mrs. Anderson. "Lasso it?"

"Either that," said Mr. Crane, "or else she's gone for her gun."

They hadn't long to wait. Miss Barton had been absent less than two minutes when a sound that seemed to come from everywhere and nowhere rose and filled the evening sky. It started with a grumble from a sleepy giant, swelled to a moan, grew louder and more disturbing, and culminated finally in a yell from all nature, Whitman's barbaric yawp over the housetops.

"My God," whispered Mr. Crane with horror and a touch of awe. "She's turned in a fire alarm. There's a box right on the corner."

The horrid noise was repeated twice, shaking the world, and then there were other sounds—screen doors slamming up and down the street, the high, excited voices of children and the patter of their bare feet, older voices asking questions and shouting directions, somewhere in the distance a car starting, undoubtedly one of the fire trucks.

"Oh, *dear*," murmured Mrs. Crane in despair, "the whole village."

"Yes," he said hopelessly. The fires on the island were usually negligible—quickly extinguished blazes in a patch of marsh grass or a clump of sumac—but now and then a house caught, often from a kerosene stove, and this could be spectacular. Earlier in the season, there had been an alarm down on the Bay side and when the department arrived, the bungalow was a roaring bonfire and in the end nothing had remained but a brick chimney and a small desolation of broken crockery and twisted metal. The villagers, curiously torn between apprehension and hope, never missed a fire.

The tumult mounted and drew nearer—it seemed to Mr. Crane absurdly theatrical, like the shouts and murmurs of an offstage mob in a play—and presently the four on the porch heard the first of the trucks come sputtering to stop down below on the pavement. Mr. Crane got to his feet.

"Well, I'd better go down and start explaining," he said unhappily.

He was too late. Footsteps pounded on the stairs, and in a moment Miss Barton appeared at the top. She was accompanied by two of the volunteer firemen, both lifeguards with whom Mr. Crane had previously been on the detached and courteous terms suitable between a householder and a public servant. Now they both looked rather sardonic; one of them, he noted absently, was carrying an axe. He started to greet them, but Miss Barton was already in charge of the scene.

"There he is," she cried, pointing a shaking finger at the roof. "Oh, the poor baby!"

Her volatile character had undergone another of its queer changes and her voice was choked with tears.

"You go get him down," she wailed, seizing one of the lifeguards by the arm and shaking him passionately. "You go right up there and get him before he falls off!"

"Take it easy, lady," said the guard. "He ain't going to fall off. Cats don't fall off things." He turned to the man with the axe. "Go on down and get the little ladder, Charlie," he said. His companion vanished, though subsequent sounds indicated that he was having trouble with some congestion on the stairway. Looking around for the first time, Mr. Crane was horrified to see that the crowd had encircled the house and now stood on the beach in front of it, an almost unbroken rank, all staring up. Most of the faces were familiar; they all wore expressions of lively and delighted attention. Even as he shuddered, sure that for the remainder of the season and probably for a good many seasons to come his name would be linked with Miss Barton's and his decorous behavior hopelessly confused with hers, she wrote a climax to the crazy scene. Suddenly, still weeping, she threw herself into his arms with such unexpected violence that they both staggered backward, fought for balance, and then collapsed together on a battered army cot that stood against the wall. He fell on top and she struggled desperately to free herself.

"Baby," she cried in a clear, wild voice. "Cut it out! You got to let me *up*!"

He was too dazed to reply, but he could hear a sort of vast exhalation of astonishment and pleasure from the crowd and when he raised his head, he read the death of his reputation in the lifeguard's bright, sardonic eye.

A little later, after the man had come back with the ladder and retrieved the cat and the audience had dispersed and Miss Barton, suddenly recalling C. P. McGonigle, had left to track him down, Mr. Crane made another batch of Martinis, a good deal drier than the first. After drinking the second of them, he found that he could think of the afternoon with reasonable composure; it was not until the fourth, however, that he began to laugh.

August 24, 1946

CRUSOE'S FOOTPRINT

IT WASN'T A very promising day—a strange, level wall of copper-colored clouds was building up in the west and the wind from the ocean was driving the waves higher and higher up the beach. Since the previous afternoon, the radio had been reporting a hurricane on its way up from the Florida Keys, with storm warnings already flying as far up the coast as Hatteras, but the inhabitants of Fire Island, who had twice seen the sea come smashing over their dunes, had developed an irritable fatalism about the weather and paid little attention to these alarms that always sprang up in September. A few nervous people still moved back to town with the first breath of danger from the South, but most of them, confident that the storm would either whirl harmlessly out to sea or else that the Coast Guard would give them ample warning of its approach, stayed where they were, feeling reasonably safe and agreeably heroic.

It was a Sunday afternoon, and in spite of the radio and the threatening sky, the beach was crowded. The sun, seeming to shine with an extra and rather unearthly brilliance over the low barrier of clouds, heightened the gay colors of the ranked umbrellas and the blue sea, and in its light the tanned bathers also seemed to have a more than mortal glow. It was all as pretty and vulgar as a postcard, thought George Crane, who was lying on the sand in front of his summer cottage. He had just been rereading Henry James and felt in a rather supercilious and Continental mood.

"Let's take a walk," he said to his wife, who was spread out beside him on a blanket, inert but not quite dead. "Too damn many people."

"All right," she said amiably. "Where to?"

"I don't know," he said. "The lighthouse, I guess. We haven't been there for quite a while."

"It's a long way. Five miles."

"Three," he said. "And the sand is good and hard. It won't kill you."

They stood up and started down toward the edge of the water.

"Look at that tide," she said. "Do you think we'll be able to get back all right?"

"Sure. We can walk on the dunes if we have to."

They set out west along the beach. It was a walk they had taken many times that summer, almost precisely as often, in fact, as they had gone the other way, to the eastward communities of Point o' Woods and Cherry Grove, and Mr. Crane, familiar with the scenery, found his mind free to wander back over the summer so nearly gone. He'd had a good time, he decided. His closest friends, Mark and Ginny Anderson, were pleasant people, generally tranquil in disposition, and articulate without feeling obliged to prove it by holding too many interesting literary and social opinions. I am a very tolerant man, he thought, but God I get tired of these ambitious conversations. Their other acquaintances on the beach and the guests who'd come down for week-ends had also been entertaining on the whole, though there had been a few too gifted raconteurs among them and one or two who were clearly not adapted to the innocent monotony of life on a beach. There had been the trouble about Miss Deedy Barton's cat, and he remembered a man called Francis Bidwell who had come to visit the Andersons, trailing an impressive reputation for persuading ladies against their better judgment. Mr. Bidwell had been responsible for a rather difficult night at Sweeney's when he had attached himself much too purposefully to a girl who was generally conceded to be the property of one of the lifeguards. The guards had closed in quietly, moving as one man, and it had required the combined fascination of Mrs. Anderson and Mrs. Crane . . . He looked at his wife, who was wandering along the water's edge, still intent on finding the perfect shell that had been eluding her all summer.

"I must say I find you extremely companionable, Emily," he said, parodying the fashionably constricted accents of Noel Coward in *Private Lives*. "There isn't a part of you I don't know, remember, and love."

"My," she said. And then as a wave swept over her ankles and ran high up on the beach, "Look at that. I told you we were going to get caught in this damn tide."

"What do you care? You haven't anything on to get wet."

She ignored that and began to whistle "Can't We Be Friends?" for she had a sweet, melancholy taste in music. His thoughts went back to the summer just behind them and presently he began to laugh.

"Remember Mark and that damn woman?" he asked.

"Mrs. Wilmot?" she said, referring to a rather troublesome experience Mr. Anderson had had with a lady who had made up her mind that, as a writer, he was cramped by his family ties and had offered him her own house to work in. It was hard to say whether or not another promise had been contained in this suggestion, but anyway, between them, Mrs. Anderson and Mrs. Crane had fixed Mrs. Wilmot.

"No," he said. "The other one. That time at Sweeney's."

"Oh, yes," she said. "About the hair. That was funny."

It had been funny, too. There had been about eight of them sitting there at a table by the dance floor one Saturday night. They had been watching the dancers—there was a never-ending fascination for Mr. Crane in the wild abandon of the steps they did and the certainly questionable postures they assumed and its contrast with the cold, inscrutable expressions that they chose to wear—when they gradually became aware that Mr. Anderson was involved with a red-haired girl at the next table. She was very drunk, though no drunker than the three delicate young men she was with, and her passion for Mr. Anderson was open and explicit. Mr. Crane found that most of the conversation was still fresh in his memory.

"Listen," she had said, addressing them all, "I *love* this man." She had hitched her chair away from her own table and so was in a position to put her arm around her victim's neck. "You got such wonderful beautiful hair," she had said fondly. "What's your name, honey?"

"Anthony Comstock."[1]

"O.K. if I call you Tony?" He had said it was and she had proceeded even more directly. "Whyn't we go out to the bar, Tony?"

"Sure," he'd said, "but what about your friends?"

"Oh, *them!*" It had amused her to be frank about her friends, and they had looked down at their bracelets in embarrassment and delight. Just then, one of the lifeguards had come to claim her for a dance, and she had gone, though smiling back at him with unmistakable promise. During the dance, though Mrs. Anderson had urged him warmly to enjoy himself, he had changed places with Eddie Willard, who had been sitting across the table.

"Tell her you're John S. Sumner," he'd said.[2] "Just tell her you're crazy about sex."

The lady had come back but such had been her exertions on the floor that she walked in a daze and sat down without looking behind her. In a moment, however, her hand had gone out, found Eddie Willard's shoulder, worked its way lovingly up his neck, and come to rest at last on his head, which was as bald as an egg. For a moment, her fingers had tapped doubtfully, then incredulously, and then she had swung around and finding only a naked skull where she had expected wonderful, beautiful hair, her mouth had dropped open in dismay and she had given a small, ladylike scream.

"My God," she had cried with horror, "what's *happened* to you, Tony?"

The summer had been full of experiences like that—small, neat absurdities, in most of which, he reflected, his friends' behavior had been a credit to him. They were not humorists, thank God; they just seemed to show a certain presence of mind in unlikely situations. It occurred to him briefly that financial security sometimes has a good deal to do with charm; that the native Fire Islanders, that is, who were in the business of renting houses and selling food, might naturally be inclined to make humor easy for transients, and even that the soft, mysterious young men, who made up such a large part of the summer population and had practically no money at all, might also find it intelligent to tolerate the whims of the solvent.

He remembered another evening at the bar, when Horace Giddings, an actor who had been visiting him, had raised some doubt in his mind about the real quality of what might be called privileged wit. There had been a crowd nearly three deep at the bar and getting drinks to bring back to their table had been a tiresome problem. Mr. Giddings had solved it briskly. Throughout the room there were a good many tables whose occupants were all male though their gaiety held a note of birds, and Mr. Giddings soon adopted the practice of waiting until a round of drinks had been secured for one of these and then approaching it courteously.

"I'm sure you won't mind, old man," he'd say, putting down a dollar and picking up one of the glasses. "For a lady, you know."

The owner had usually confined his protest to a rather breathless "*Well*," and the whole idea had seemed funny enough at the time, but now Mr. Crane remembered it with faint embarrassment. It would have been fine if one of them had taken a poke at Mr. Giddings, he thought, but, of course, he'd known damn well they wouldn't. However, Horace was a special case, an actor's actor; generally his friends had been admirable. He had a brief, self-conscious vision of himself as a rather distinguished figure in the community; the senior member, you might say, of a pleasantly worldly group, augmented from time to time by urban celebrities, that still understood the value of the simple life and had adapted themselves to it gracefully, without perceptible condescension.

Mr. Crane was brought out of these agreeable thoughts by the thunder of a wave and then a rush of water across his knees. "That was a hell of a big one," he said, bracing himself against the backwash.

"I told you the tide was coming in," said his wife. "Want to turn around?"

"No," he said. "Let's go a little further anyway."

The wall of clouds had begun to cut across the bottom of the sun, which now shone level and blinding in their eyes. The wind had increased and the waves, which had been breaking on a bar about a hundred yards offshore, rolled across it, mounted as the still water piled up under them, hung suspended for an instant, and then broke tremendously, making the beach tremble under their feet. There had been more spectacular surfs that summer, but somehow none quite as ominous. These waves were not so much breakers as slow, enormous swellings of the sea. I don't know about any hurricane, he thought, but there's a hell of a storm out there somewhere. Mrs. Crane had been walking on a higher part of the beach, where

it was still dry, and suddenly she stopped and looked down at something at her feet.

"Hey," she called. "Somebody's shoes."

He joined her and found a pair of moccasins lying neatly side by
side on the sand. They were quite new and obviously feminine.

"That's funny," he said. "Where do you suppose . . ." He picked
one up and as he tilted it in his hand looking for a label, a woman's
wristwatch slid down out of the toe. "Saks," he said. "E.M.K. on
the back."

There were a pair of sun-glasses in the other shoe and they, too,
were impressive in design. From where they stood, they could look
along the beach almost to the end of the island. There was no one
in sight.

"We didn't pass anybody coming up either," Mrs. Crane said. "I
guess she must be lying up there behind the dunes."

"Not around here," he said. "Not unless she flew. Look."

The only footprints in the sand came from the east, from the direction of the lighthouse, and whoever made them had been wearing
shoes. Obviously the woman had sat down where they were standing
and taken them off. Beyond these clear marks, there were only two
or three bare prints in the sand, leading toward the ocean. As they
watched, a wave came hissing up and washed a print away.

"I'd better go and take a look anyway," said Mr. Crane uneasily.
He walked across the narrowing strip of beach and clambered up
one of the dunes. From the top of it, he could see the few houses
that made up a settlement called Lonelyville scattered along the
margin of the bay about a quarter of a mile away. No one was visible on the barren stretch of sand and marsh grass that lay between,
but the land was hummocked with smaller dunes and it was possible
that the woman was lying behind one of them. It was really absurd
to think so, though, not only because of the absence of footprints up
from the beach but also because the grass would have been wickedly
sharp for anyone walking in bare feet, and even on the height where
he stood the air was thick with gnats. He rejoined Mrs. Crane at the
edge of the water.

"No," he said. He looked again up the beach toward the lighthouse. There was always a chance that the woman had walked off

in that direction barefoot and that the waves had washed away her prints, but there were a good many things against it—the moccasins and the watch left so near the water with the tide coming in so fast, the threatening storm (the sun by now was almost buried in the clouds), the beach clearly empty for at least three miles.

"Well," he said. He handed her his own watch and his cigarettes and matches.

"She wouldn't still be out there, George," said Mrs. Crane.

"I'll just go out to where they're breaking," he said.

He started wading through the shallow, fast-running water. The footing was bad. There was a strong pull to the east, and the current was scooping out deep holes in the bottom. The ocean sucked at his knees, and shells, sliding along the bottom, pulled roughly across his ankles. As he got nearer to them, the waves began to seem enormous—tons of water lifting appallingly over his head, hanging in instant, incredible suspension, curling and crashing down in great smothered explosions. He struggled out to within four or five yards of where they were breaking, keeping his feet with difficulty and half-blinded by the spray as the wind tore it from the crests of the waves. The hell with it, he thought. Emily was right, there would be no chance of finding anything out here. He took another doubtful step and the bottom fell away under his feet, dropping him to his armpits in the water. As he turned to fight his way back, the current caught him and pulled him off balance, twisting him around so that again he was facing out to sea.

He saw the big wave coming and realized with horror that it was going to break almost exactly where he stood. For a moment he stood idiotic with panic and then he threw himself forward and began to swim desperately toward it. He knew at the last second he was too late—the water around him was running swiftly uphill, sucked upward into the base of the wave—and he threw his arms around his head and tried to go under it. He saw the wave coming down and then it hit him, shook him with fierce, wrenching blows, ground him down to the bottom and dragged him furiously along it, flung him up in a boil of white water, threw him somehow to his feet, only to pull him down and roll him along the bottom again, in a nightmare of shells and sand and strangling water. He got up in the shallow water at last and stumbled up onto the beach. He heard Mrs. Crane's voice, but the roar in his ears and the floating white lights were too much for him and he put his head down between his knees.

"Son of a bitch," he gasped finally. "That one *got* me."

"Yes," she said. "You all right now?"

"I guess so." He turned his arm over and found a long scratch from wrist to elbow. "God, look at that. You got the cigarettes?"

"They're up the beach," she said. "You stay here. I'll get them for you."

He smoked for a while in silence and then reached over and picked up the moccasins. "I guess the only thing to do is tell them at the Coast Guard," he said.

"I suppose so," she said. "Do you want me to go? It's up back of the lighthouse, isn't it?"

"That's right," he said. "No, we'll both go. Wait'll I finish this."

PRESENTLY MR. CRANE threw the cigarette away and got up, and he and his wife started off for the lighthouse, still about three-quarters of a mile down the beach. The sun had disappeared behind the clouds, which now formed a black band halfway up the sky, and the wind was blowing much more strongly off the sea. Mrs. Crane estimated the width of the remaining beach.

"We'll have to walk back on the dunes," she said.

"Yeah, I guess so."

He couldn't tell precisely what was in his mind. It seemed to him almost certain now that the woman was drowned and, in conjunction with his own experience in the water, the idea made him feel sick at his stomach. He was also disgusted with the emotions—an almost pleasurable excitement, a sense of self-importance, though he had certainly had no heroic intentions—that he had felt when he waded out into the surf. He found he was shaking as he transferred the moccasins from one hand to the other.

They had walked about a hundred yards when Mrs. Crane touched his arm.

"Isn't that a jeep coming?" she asked.

"Yes," he said. "Probably *that's* the Coast Guard now."

The car was bouncing along by the water's edge, occasionally throwing out sheets of spray. Mrs. Crane began to wave and it slowed and soon pulled up beside them. The driver was very young, a self-possessed boy, with flanking ears and a sharp nose. His blue shirt was open at his mahogany throat and he wore his uniform cap jauntily, on the back of his head. There was a girl in a brief, black bathing suit on the seat beside him, and she, too, was young and quite hand-some, though her face wore a sullen and arrogant expression, clearly habitual.

"Something the matter, Jack?" asked the driver.

Before Mr. Crane could answer, the girl leaned forward and stared at him with surprise.

"Look," she said. "That man has my shoes."

"Oh," he said, holding them out. "Are these yours? We found them on the beach. I was taking them to the Coast Guard Station."

She held out her hand silently and Mr. Crane gave her the moc-casins.

"I had some glasses and a watch," she said with no particular expression.

He had forgotten them but they were in his other hand and he extended them to her.

"Yes," he said, "we found them, too."

She inspected them carefully and there was a silence.

"Well, thank you," she said at last. "I'm sorry I haven't got my purse, but if . . ."

"For God's sake," he said with exasperation, "we thought you were drowned. We were on our way to get the Coast Guard."

She looked surprised. "Oh," she said. "I'm sorry. But, of course, that was absurd. I was just walking down toward the Point and this man picked me up—because of the storm."

"Naturally," he said, but she clearly suspected no irony.

"Well," she said. "It was very kind of you anyway."

The driver had been listening to them impatiently and now he addressed Mr. Crane. "How'd you come to cut yourself, Jack?" he asked.

"That? I got caught by a wave."

"You mean you been in?" His tone was incredulous. "You oughta have sense not to go in a day like this." He looked at them curiously. "Say, where do you folks live?"

"Ocean Beach," said Mr. Crane. "It's a couple of miles down the beach."

"I know where Ocean Beach is at, Jack. Listen, you ain't going to get there walking, the way this ocean is."

"Oh, we'll get there all right," said Mr. Crane, hoping he sounded airy. "We can walk on the dunes."

"Don't you folks ever listen to the radio?" said the driver. "There's supposa be a hurricane coming up. You'd be in fine shape caught on this beach in a hurricane. Come on, you better get in here. I'll run you down."

Mr. Crane protested, but without much conviction. The sky was definitely alarming now and the sea might easily be gathering itself for a really dangerous effort. He climbed in, followed by his wife, and they sat humbly together on the narrow seat in the back, hemmed in by tarry coils of rope and many cans of paint. As the car jounced along, throwing them from side to side and drenching them with spray, he felt as foolish as he ever had in his life. Gradually, however, his embarrassment and indignation were succeeded by an overpowering weariness, and when the jeep pulled up in front of his house, his head was on Mrs. Crane's shoulder and he was sound asleep.

September 14, 1946

THE CURIOUS INCIDENT OF THE
DOGS IN THE NIGHT-TIME

THIS IS A nice place, Freddy," said Harrington, looking around the noisy, crowded room. "You come here often?"

"I used to," said Goetz. "A few years ago, before I got married. Not any more. Ellen claimed it made her head hurt."

"Oh," said Harrington. "That's quite a thing, you getting married," he said after a pause. "That's certainly one nobody ever figured on. What's she like?"

"Ellen?" said Goetz. "She's a wonderful girl, Tom. I want you to meet her."

"Swell," said Harrington. "We'll have to get together sometime. I'll get Jane."

"Who?" said Goetz.

"Jane Inman," said Harrington. "But on second thought I guess not. She's no girl if your head happens to hurt."

The two men had been standing at the bar for about half an hour. When they came in, at seven-thirty, there had been no tables vacant, and the captain had suggested they have a drink while they were waiting.

"Why don't you gentlemen just stand right up here to the bar," he had said. "I'll let you know the first moment there is anything free."

They were on their fourth Martini now, and in the silence following Harrington's last remark they were both suddenly conscious of the passage of time.

"Listen." said Goetz. "We ought to be sitting down pretty soon. Where the hell is that waiter?"

"Over there," said Harrington. "Leaning up against some damn thing. Hey, captain." •

The captain moved slowly toward them. He had a pale, impassive

face and an air of having formed a rather low opinion of his surroundings.

"Gentlemen?"

"How about that table?" said Goetz.

"Yeah," said Harrington. "How about us sitting down one of
these days?"

The captain looked around the room, tapping his fingers on the
menu card in his hand.

"I'm sorry, gentlemen," he said. "I still got nothing free. I'll let
you know."

"You said that before," said Harrington.

"You gentlemen get the first table that's free."

"All right, see that we do," said Harrington.

"Yes, sir," said the captain contemptuously, and moved away.

"Now you got him sore," said Goetz.

"Good," said Harrington. "I'm sore, too. How about another
drink?" He tapped on the bar. "Hey, a couple more Martinis here."

"This is the one I don't need," said Goetz when the drink came.

"What do you mean you don't need?"

"The one that gets me drunk," said Goetz.

"What's the matter with that? What are you saving yourself for,
Freddy? You planning a career or something?"

"Career, hell. I got to get up in the morning. I *work*."

"No. You're saving yourself. I know you married bastards. You
plan ahead."

"That's right, Tom," said Goetz pacifically. "I'm planning a career. I want to be a waiter."

"You're too old," said Harrington. "You got to start young in that
business. You got to be born in a linen closet or some damn place. All
the really great waiters have been born in linen closets. It's like those
trunks in vaudeville."

He was interrupted by the return of the captain, who gave them
what he conceivably regarded as a smile.

"I got that table now, gentlemen," he said.

"Thank you," said Goetz, finishing his drink. "All right, Tom,
let's go."

"Just a minute," said Harrington. "I wonder if I could put a question."

"Yes, sir?"

"This gentleman and I were having a little argument. I wonder if you'd mind telling us if you happened to be born in a closet."

"Sir?" said the captain, looking at him sharply.

"Never mind, captain," said Goetz. "You just show us that table."

"All right, you drunken half-wits," said the captain's expression quite plainly, but aloud he only said "This way, gentlemen," and led them to the table, which was off in one corner of the room. At his signal, a waiter came up and handed them both a menu.

"We better have another drink first," said Harrington. "Bring us a couple of Martinis. No, you better make that double Martinis. Two *double* Martinis."

"Two double Martinis," said the waiter, and left them.

"That's a good man," said Harrington. "Knows how to take an order."

"Listen, Tom, how about taking it easy? You're getting pretty soused."

"You don't know what soused *is*," said Harrington. He concentrated on the menu, shutting one eye. "Say, what *is* all this stuff? What nationality?"

"Italian," said Goetz.

"Well, it's a terrible language," said Harrington. "You know what I want? Just some eggs. Some scrambled eggs."

"I'm going to have the *cacciatore*. They do that pretty well here."

"They do, do they?" said Harrington. "You know something about you, Freddy? You talk, like a God-damn tourist."

The drinks came and they gave their order.

"Some pretty interesting people used to come here, Tom," said Goetz. "The Baker Street Irregulars."

"Who?" asked Harrington.

"The Baker Street Irregulars. The Sherlock Holmes experts. *You* know."

"Oh," said Harrington. "Yeah, I guess I read about them. Woollcott or somebody. This where they met, eh?"

"They did when I used to come here. Here or someplace very much *like* here. Maybe they still do. Woollcott, Morley, Tunney, Elmer Davis, some guy called Starrett—oh, a lot of 'em."

"That's a lovely bunch of boys," said Harrington. "What did they do? All I remember is they wore funny hats."

"They used to ask each other questions," said Goetz. "You know, about the stories. Like the name of the dog in 'The Sign of the Four.'"

"Toby," said Harrington promptly. "A lurcher, whatever the hell that is. And it's 'The Sign of Four.' No second 'the.'"

"The hell it is," said Goetz.

"All right," said Harrington. "Look it up. 'The Sign of Four.' I got five bucks says no second 'the.'"

"I'll take your word for it."

"You better. All right, ask me another. Ask me anything. Any of the stories. No, I'll ask *you*. What's a Penang lawyer?"

"Cane," said Goetz. "Dr. Mortimer carried it in 'The Hound of the Baskervilles.' Dr. James Mortimer, M.R.C.S."

"All right," said Harrington. "How many orange pips? How many Napoleons."

"Five and six," said Goetz. "In that order. For God's sake, is that the best you can do? How about three stories with 'three' in the title?"

"Well, there's one with a funny word in it," said Harrington. "'Garribeds'? No, 'Garridebs.' 'The Adventure of the Three Garridebs.'"

"That's one."

There was a long silence while Harrington stared at the table-cloth.

"O.K., Freddy," he said finally. "You win on that one. I give up."

"'The Three Students' and 'The Three Gables,'" said Goetz. "You're a hell of an expert if you don't know that."

The two friends went on like that for some time. Goetz horrified Harrington by not remembering that the villain of "The Speckled Band" was called Dr. *Grimesby* Roylott, and somehow or other Harrington missed on the last name of Jefferson Hope's fiancée, which, of course, was Ferrier, but on the whole they did remarkably well. Time passed, and though the eggs and the *cacciatore* remained substantially untouched on their plates, the double Martinis continued to arrive and vanish.

"Listen," said Goetz suddenly at ten o'clock, "maybe they *still* come here."

"Who?" said Harrington.

"The Baker Street Irregulars," said Goetz, managing so many consonants very successfully, all things considered. "Maybe they're here right now."

"Those sons of bitches," said Harrington. "A lot they know about it."

"Sure they do," said Goetz. "They write articles."

"Not Tunney," said Harrington. "He's no writer. He just *reads*. Mostly Shakespeare."

"Well, all the rest, then."

They considered this briefly, and Harrington snapped his fingers. "Test 'em," he said.

"What?"

"We go up and test 'em."

"Find out they here first," said Goetz.

"Sure," said Harrington. "Find out. Ask *him*. Hey, waiter."

The waiter came over reluctantly, for he had been instructed to serve no more double Martinis and he saw trouble ahead.

"Sir?"

"You got a meeting here tonight, waiter?" said Goetz.

"Meeting?"

For a moment, the name of the Holmes admirers escaped Harrington. "Bunch of boys with funny hats," he said. "Ask each other questions."

"There's some fellas upstairs," said the waiter. "Some society. I don't know about the rest of it."

"Called Baker Street Irregulars," said Goetz. By this time, however, the Martinis had got in their work and his speech was somewhat blurred.

"Some name like that," agreed the waiter. "Some society."

"Whereabouts?" said Harrington. "What floor?"

"Right up at the head of the stairs," said the waiter, and then, belatedly grasping their intention, "It's a private party though, sir."

"It's all right," said Harrington, getting to his feet. "We're friends."

"Old friends," said Goetz, also rising. "Fellow-members."

"Well . . ." said the waiter doubtfully.

"Old, *old* friends. Don't give it a second thought," said Harrington. "Dismiss it from your mind. Here, let's have the check."

The waiter produced the check from somewhere inside his coat and added it rapidly. The total came to twenty-three dollars and twenty cents, and Harrington gave him three tens.

"O.K.," he said. "You keep that."

"Thank you, sir," said the waiter. There was still a doubtful expression on his face as his customers started across the room but he made no effort to detain them or to communicate with the captain, who would certainly have been opposed to the project they had in mind.

GOETZ AND HARRINGTON turned to the right when they left the dining room and started up the stairs.

"Listen," said Goetz when they were halfway up. "Who you going to be?"

"Be?"

"Yes. I just remembered they all pretend to be somebody. Some character in the stories."

"All right," said Harrington. "I'm Holmes. You're Watson."

"Too obvious," said Goetz. "Anyway, they must *have* a Holmes and Watson. Probably the president and vice-president."

"All right," said Harrington. "Mrs. Watson. Mrs. Watson and Mrs. Hudson."

"No," said Goetz. "It isn't that kind of kidding. You got to stick to the right sex."

"Mycroft and Pycroft," said Harrington. "Addison and Steele. Gallagher and Shean." He laughed immoderately, holding onto the railing along the wall, but Goetz was not amused.

"No, the hell with that kind of stuff, Tom," he said. "Listen, how about Gregson and Lestrade?"

"Those dumb bastards," said Harrington. "No. I tell you—

Moriarty and Moran. First and second most dangerous men in London."

"Good," said Goetz. "Which one you want? First or second most dangerous?"

"Moriarty," said Harrington. "First most dangerous. Naturally."

Since one of the two doors at the top of the stairs was labelled "Men," they turned to the other.

"After you, Professor," said Goetz.

"Thank you, Colonel," said Harrington, and flung open the door.

There were perhaps twenty men in the small room. They were sitting at a long table and they appeared to be engaged in some general and earnest discussion. They wore no hats. Except for the table and the chairs, there was nothing in the room but a small piano, off in one corner.

"Gentlemen," said Harrington. "The chase is on!"

A silence fell on the room, and then a small, red-faced man got up from the table and approached Goetz and Harrington. He had on a rather jocular suit, but his manner was formal. "Some mistake, fellows, I think," he said.

"Not at all," said Harrington. He waved his hand at Goetz. "Like you to meet Colonel Sebastian Moran, late of the 1st Bangalore Pioneers. I'm Professor Moriarty."

"Of Reichenbach Falls," said Goetz. "Who are you supposed to be?"

The red-faced man cleared his throat. "Well, I'm Ed Tracy, of Denver," he said, "but—"

Goetz looked inquiringly at Harrington. "How about it?" he said. "You know that one?"

Harrington shook his head. "Might be 'A Study in Scarlet,'" he said doubtfully. "One of the Mormons. I don't remember him, though."

"I told you these boys made it tough," said Goetz. "All right," he said to the red-faced man, who had begun to wear a hunted look. "We give up. What story?"

"I don't know what you fellows are talking about," said the man helplessly. "This is a private party."

"I know," said Goetz. "We just thought we'd drop in. Great admirers."

"Disciples," said Harrington. He spoke thickly, and Goetz was surprised to see that his face was pale and headed with perspiration.

"You O.K., Professor?" he asked.

"No," said Harrington simply. "Better sit down a minute. Better *lie* down."

He swayed visibly as he spoke, and Goetz caught his arm.

"You going to be *sick*?" he demanded.

Harrington shook his head and then rose to a kind of heroism in his extremity.

"No," he muttered. "Just a touch of enteric. Old trouble of mine. Ever since Ladysmith."

His appearance actually was alarming, and between them Goetz and the red-faced man got him to a chair at the table. The other guests looked at him with a mixture of apprehension and respect.

"What's the matter with him?" said one of them. "What'd he say he got?"

"Enteric," said Goetz. "The curse of our Indian possessions."

"Yeah? What does he do for it?"

"Whiskey," said Harrington in a much stronger voice. "Only known cure for enteric. The Fuzzies live on it."

A bottle and a glass stood on the table near him, and without waiting for an invitation he poured himself a rather staggering drink. After a moment's hesitation, Goetz did likewise. Then, suddenly and simultaneously inspired, they raised their glasses in the air.

"To the Woman," said Harrington solemnly.

"To the Woman," repeated Goetz. "To Irene Adler."

The two emptied their glasses and, still in unison, they sent them both crashing to the floor.

"Listen, fellows," said the red-faced man. "*Please.*"

AFTERWARD, GOETZ HAD no very clear memory of the rest of the evening. Sometimes, in the tormented and fragmentary glimpses he got, he seemed to be shouting at a table of men who retreated from him, gradually and indignantly, until he was left alone at one end with Harrington, who sometimes shouted, too, and sometimes just slept. Sometimes he must have realized that these were not Sherlock Holmes experts, as the waiter and his own romantic heart had somehow led him to believe, but instead simply the innocent conclave of roofing experts from the West that their appearance and conversation indicated that they were. If he did occasionally recognize this for the discouraging truth, however, he never did so for long, and there were considerable periods when, noisily abetted by Harrington, he tried to force them into the shape of the Baker Street Irregulars, harassing them with unanswerable questions about the second Mrs. Watson and the Diogenes Club and whether Holmes went to Oxford or Cambridge. Once, he recalled, a waiter had been summoned and there had been some talk about putting them out, but that mysteriously had passed and there had been an interlude of great good will, when scrawled cards and promises of future gaiety were exchanged.

Goetz's only exact picture, as a matter of fact, was of the end of the evening. Harrington, somehow miraculously resuscitated, was seated at the piano and they were both singing, and it was his impression that they had been doing so for some time. He had looked up suddenly—this vision was as sharp as a photograph—and seen, to his perplexity, a line of figures, led by the red-faced man, tiptoeing from the room. After that, there was only the empty room and Harrington shouting and banging on the piano. Roofers or Baker Street Irregulars, the guests had gone, and they were all alone. His memory stopped there.

September 18, 1948

THE LIFE AND DEATH AND LIFE OF
GEORGE WHITEHOUSE

ONE BRIGHT NOVEMBER morning, a Mr. and Mrs. George Whitehouse found themselves on board a train on their way to New Haven, Connecticut, where it was their purpose to attend a football game between Yale and Harvard. There was nothing especially striking about them, except, perhaps, the fact that though it was still half an hour before noon, George was quite drunk and exhibited a strange, unfocussed hilarity that went very oddly with his neat blue suit and normally respectable middle-aged features. He had had dinner the night before with some friends at the Yale Club, continuing from there to a fashionable saloon, where he was somehow inspired to make out a blank check for two million dollars on the November National Bank and to date it 1923, which, he rather cryptically stated, had been the last really happy year of his life. This, together with some subsequent part-singing, failed to amuse the management, and George and his friends went back to the Yale Club, where one of them had a room and also two bottles of whiskey.

It was nine o'clock on Saturday morning when George woke up, and ten before, with the assistance of what remained in one of the bottles, he felt sufficiently well to telephone his wife to meet him at Grand Central. When he joined her at the gate, he made no attempt to conceal his condition, feeling, indeed, that there was something picturesque, and even a trifle unearthly, about it. She was not in a very amiable mood, both because she had known some anxiety about him during the night and because she had loathed all games since she had been a student at Miss Spence's School and had been obliged to play far too many of them as part of her social education. However, to the best of her knowledge, her husband had never been drunk in the morning before in the twenty-four years of their marriage, and she managed to greet him with indulgence, if not altogether with approval, and they entered the train together and sat down.

The train was somewhere between Greenwich and Stamford, making good time through the level, orderly landscape, when a man named Henry Fraser, a vice-president of the rug company for which George was advertising manager, came down the aisle and stopped beside the seats occupied by Mr. and Mrs. Whitehouse. The men were not especially close friends, but George's sense of almost supernatural well-being had not yet abated and he welcomed Henry Fraser with some exuberance, addressing him, in fact, as "good ol' Bill."

"This is good ol' Bill," he said to Mrs. Whitehouse. "Bill, I want you to meet something—something rather repulsive, my wife."

There is no way of telling what led George to this particular choice of words; whether, that is, it was simply part of the same ill-timed and morbid facetiousness that had dictated his behavior in the matter of the November National Bank and the year 1923, or whether it lay deeper, being the result of some treacherous slip of the sub-conscious, for there can be no question that Mrs. Whitehouse was at times an extremely tedious woman. In any case, the words were out, and though both Fraser, who left almost at once to join friends in another car, and Mrs. Whitehouse, who necessarily remained where she was, indicated that they regarded his intention as humor-ous, there was some coolness between husband and wife for the duration of the trip, and also throughout the game, which, inciden-tally, Yale won, by a score of 31–21. Whitehouse slept heavily on the train coming back, and when they reached their apartment, on East Forty-ninth Street, he went promptly to bed, complaining of a sharp pain over his right eye. He felt much better on Sunday, and as his wife failed to mention the matter of the introduction, he con-cluded either that she had forgotten it or else that it had never hap-pened at all, his memories of the last thirty-six hours having at best a somewhat dreamlike quality.

IN THE COURSE of the following week, three brief items ap-peared in the so-called gossip columns of the New York press. The

first, by a man named Walter Winchell, asked bleakly, "What car-
pet biggy and his squaw are getting Renovated because he called
her a vulture?" The second, purporting to be a communication to
one Ed Sullivan from his secretary, said, "Dear Boss: As you pre-
dicted three months ago, the Gus Whitewaters will tell it to the
judge. She will testify he gets 'convulsions.'" The third was the work
of Danton Walker, conceivably a pseudonym: "Insiders say that the
Glenn Bridgehouses (she was Birdie Semple) are busting it up. Charge
will be that he's too 'impulsive,' which is one word for it."

All these comments were directly traceable to Henry Fraser,
who had actually been deeply impressed by the incident on the
train and had reported it the same night to a table of friends at the
Stork Club. The somewhat blurred and shifting form the anecdote
took in the papers (Mrs. Whitehouse's maiden name, for instance,
had been Bridget Summers and not Birdie Semple) can be attributed partly to Fraser's own highly liquescent condition at the time
he told it and partly to the persistent apathy to facts that unfortunately characterizes what has been described somewhere as spitball
journalism.

George Whitehouse read neither the *Daily News* nor the *Mirror*,
but he received clippings from each of them in the mail, undoubtedly
a further specimen of Henry Fraser's misguided humor.

THE NEXT VERSION of the story appeared about a week later,
in a column in the *Post* rather adroitly known as "The Lyons Den," its
conductor being a man named Leonard Lyons. This time, it read,
"Last night in the Cub Room, Bernard M. Baruch was telling about
the Yale-Lawrenceville football game, which he attended with Bea
Lillie and Gen. Dwight Eisenhower. It seems they were sitting next to
a prominent clothing executive and a B'way showgirl, both of whom
had been partaking freely from the flask of champagne he carried on
his hip. Finally, during an intermission in the game, the souse turned
and caught sight of his famous neighbors.

"'Say,' he said. 'Aren't you Tallulah Bankhead?'

"Miss Lillie smiled grimly.

"'I certainly am,' she replied. 'And I know you, too. You're old
George Q. Repulsive.'

"Needless to say, the magnate was somewhat taken aback."

Whitehouse, who did read the *Post*, felt a dim uneasiness when his eye fell on the word "repulsive" coupled with his own first name, but a hasty rereading convinced him that it could only be a coincidence, and he passed on to Mr. Lyons' next item, which explained that Edgar Allan Poe and the Duchess of Windsor had both resided at one time in the city of Baltimore, though not, of course, simultaneously.

THREE DAYS LATER, a department in the *Herald Tribune* called "Pitching Horseshoes," by Billy Rose, made its contribution to the billowing legend. It is Mr. Rose's sentimental or jocular custom to cast much of his material in the form of conversations with his wife, a former Olympic swimmer named Eleanor, whom he obviously admires deeply. This piece was no exception and George Whitehouse skipped hastily through the opening paragraphs, which seemed to have something to do with Mrs. Rose's jaunty habit of boiling eggs in a mink coat, until he came to what he judged to be the body of the story.

"George W.," it began, "was married to Connie, the kind of gal you dream about, if you're lucky. A real blue-plate special, and what was more you could see the steam come out of her when she looked at George. She loved the guy period exclamation point bang. In his way, George loved her back, but he had a lot of other things on his mind, one of which was trying to see how much neutral spirit a man could absorb before brush fires began to break out in his hair. For a long time, Connie put up with seeing lover come home every night just one jump ahead of the colored animals, but finally, when she began to spot hostile lipstick mixed up with the bourbon on his chin, she gave up the struggle and moved to a hotel where nobody ever saw funny little men, except the ones that ran the elevators."

At this point in the column, there was some further interpolated conversation. Mrs. Rose expressed the opinion that so far her husband's story impressed her unfavorably, and wished to know if eventually it had a point. Mr. Rose suggested she keep her hair on.

"After Connie left him," his story went on, "a lot of things happened to George, none of them good. He lost his job with the advertising company, his old friends picked up the habit of looking at their watches whenever he came into the bar, and his private zoo began to have more specimens in it than Bronx Park. George often thought of calling up Connie, but one look at the haggard, unshaven face that stared back at him from the mirror behind the bar always changed his mind, and if he did call anybody, it was another number in a part of town where laughter often breaks off into thin, high screams."

"Goodness," observed Mrs. Rose at this point in the column, and George Whitehouse couldn't help agreeing with her. Having sufficiently established the lamentable condition of his hero, Mr. Rose abruptly transplanted him to the stands at a Princeton-Yale football game, to which, it seemed, he had been taken by the one old friend still tolerant enough to put up with his mannerisms.

"From his seat high in the Palmer Bowl, George looked down on the well-dressed, prosperous crowd of which he had once been so happily a part, and alcoholic tears ran down his sunken cheeks.

" 'It's too late now,' he murmured and raised the ever-present bottle to his lips. He drank deeply and suddenly the whole world went black before his eyes. When he recovered consciousness, he was lying on the stone floor between the rows of seats.

" 'Doubtless a bum,' he heard a man above him say. 'How repulsive.'

"More than ever before in his life, George wanted to be dead, away from the cold contempt in that affected voice. He was, in fact, willing death with all his little remaining strength, when miraculously he heard another voice, dear and familiar to him.

" 'Mr. Bullmer,' it said with dignity, 'I want you to meet the man I love,' and then, as her companion drew back abashed, Connie knelt down and put her slender arm around her husband's neck.

" 'If you're ready, George,' she whispered, 'I think we'll both go home.' "

Mrs. Rose was apparently too stunned to comment either favorably or otherwise on her husband's prose, and George Whitehouse found it somewhat disturbing, too. At the moment, he was having breakfast with his wife, and presently he addressed her tentatively.

"You read this guy?" he asked, gesturing with his coffee spoon. "This Billy Rose?"

"Yes," she said. "I read it while you were shaving."

Her expression conveyed precisely nothing to him.

"Um," he said. "Quite a story. Well, I'd better be getting down to the office."

"Will you be home for dinner?"

"Naturally," he said, startled. "Where else did you suppose I'd be?"

"I was just thinking about the ordering," she answered vaguely.

"Oh," said George Whitehouse, and went off to his office.

THE RELATIONS BETWEEN the Whitehouses for the next few days might have been called mildly strained. Obviously, being in possession of the true facts, Mrs. Whitehouse must have known that they bore little resemblance to Mr. Rose's invention, or even Mr. Lyons', for it is to be presumed that she had read that, too. Nevertheless, from time to time George felt her eyes fixed on him with unmistakable speculation, and there was, or there seemed to him to be, a definite tightening about her mouth on one occasion when he had three cocktails before dinner instead of the two that were his habitual limit. On the whole, he thought, it was rather as if she knew him guiltless of the actual behavior suggested in the papers but still couldn't help suspecting that there was somehow more about him than met the casual eye. That is, Mrs. Whitehouse didn't believe for a minute that her husband was really a secret drinker or that he was in the habit of making mysterious telephone calls to disreputable neighborhoods or even of consorting with showgirls. It was simply that Mr. Rose and Mr. Lyons had implanted a small seed of doubt in her mind, so that she had come to consider him easily capable of these things, and perhaps worse, if not vigilantly watched. Altogether, for George it was a time of considerable uneasiness, and once or twice he was strongly tempted to force the issue by going out somewhere and, in his own archaic idiom, getting drunk as a goat.

The resolution of this untidy, preposterous, but still conceivably dangerous situation came from an unexpected source. On December

10th, in a magazine called the *Saturday Review of Literature*, a certain Bennett Cerf produced the following: "Mayor William O'Dwyer tells this one on himself. It seems Hizzoner was up at Baker Field for the Columbia-Army game when he spotted his friend, George Whitehouse, sitting with a very luscious young woman. Between the halves, the Mayor went over to greet the pair.

" 'I don't think I know your daughter, George,' he said genially.

" 'Daughter, hell,' said the rugged rugman. 'Bill, I'd like you to meet something rather exquisite, my wife.' "

When Whitehouse read this final variation to his wife, she colored rather unattractively and said, "How silly!" However, when he picked up the magazine again that evening, he noticed that the item had been clipped out, apparently with a pair of nail scissors, and some days later, at a cocktail party, when he was polishing off what must have been at least his ninth Martini, her glance at him was warm, untroubled, and even, mysteriously, perhaps just faintly touched with hope.

January 15, 1949

THE CRUSADERS[1]

O N THURSDAY, RALPH Breck insulted Ellen Major for perhaps the fifteenth time that month. She would never have
mentioned it to anybody herself, because she was that rather anachronistic and touching thing, a lady, and she wished to enjoy no special immunity on account of her sex. However, the walls of Breck's
office were thin, and his secretary, who was subsequently replaced,
was of a confiding disposition, and it wasn't long before the story
got around. It seemed that Ellen had gone in with the proof of an
advertisement for her employer's approval. The earlier part of the
conversation had been amiable, or at least inaudible, but Breck's
voice had risen toward the end. It had been rough and hectoring,
and punctuated with jarring laughter.

"He sounded even more horrible than usual," the secretary
testified.

Anyway, his final remark had been quite clear, and the secretary
was able to report it verbatim.

"What the hell do you think this joint is?" Breck had shouted.
"A Goddamn kindergarten?"

Ellen had left the office rather pink and with tears of vexation in
her lovely eyes.

Inevitably, this disagreeable episode soon came to the ears of
three of Ellen's fellow copy writers, all of whom regarded her with
respect, admiration, and hope untinged with vulgarity. This trio
was composed of Alfred Mitchell, who might easily have been a
poet in a sunnier climate and a more tranquil age; Henry Abbott,
who was perhaps the most promising of all the younger men; and
Elliott Fox, who had been very recently graduated by the Harvard
Business School. Each of the three had suffered in his time from
Breck's intractable disposition, which was, indeed, often indistinguishable from lunacy, but, being male, they were not disturbed by

the steady, unaccented flow of blasphemy, and occasional obscenity, that passed with their employer for conversation. They pitied him for his poverty of expression, but since they also had the highest regard for his judgment, they were able to condone it, and even to find some entertainment in it.

With Ellen, however, things were, of course, quite different. The three men had come of age in a time of ever relaxing social standards, when a good many pedestals had been almost chipped away, but it still affected them unpleasantly to realize that Breck was in the habit of speaking to Ellen almost precisely as he spoke to them. They accepted this circumstance without comment for some time, hoping that Ellen's obvious gentility, her valiantly if unsuccessfully concealed discomfort when certain words were employed in her presence, would cause Breck to mend his ways. Their hope was vain. It may have been that Breck, aware of Ellen's embarrassment, honestly tried to restrain himself with her but that, being a man of drastically limited vocabulary, he was able to find no other words for those he was in the habit of using. Or it may have been that, quite aware of causing pain, he took a certain adolescent pleasure in continuing to do so. In any case, instead of improving, his behavior toward Ellen deteriorated rapidly. Mitchell, Abbott, and Fox watched with dismay as Breck forgot himself with growing frequency and abandon, and as Ellen came to look more and more apprehensive and wistful. She had even, they couldn't help noticing, begun to lose confidence in those little mannerisms that had so endeared her to them all. For a long time, they hesitated to act, but Thursday's episode, coming, as it did, as the climax of a month of ever more aggressive assaults on her modesty, proved to be too much.

"I guess we're going to have to do something," Abbott said as the three gathered that night in a neighboring bar. "He can't go on treating her like this."

"I know," said Mitchell. "It isn't as if she was *any* damn woman. She *feels* that kind of stuff."

"You can count me in on this, fellows," said young Fox.

IT WAS AS a result of this conversation that the friends found themselves in the elevator on their way up to Breck's apartment on

Saturday night. They had had dinner together and discussed the line they planned to take in insisting that their employer conduct himself in a more decorous manner.

"We'll have to be firm," said Mitchell as the car creaked upward.

"Yes," said Abbott. "Did he seem surprised when you telephoned him? Do you suppose he knows what we're coming about?"

"I don't think so," said Mitchell. "I didn't tell him, of course. I just said we wanted to talk to him."

"Good," said Abbott. "It may be helpful if he's surprised."

"Does Ellen know anything about this?" asked Fox.

"I mentioned it to her," said Mitchell.

"Oh," said the younger man, looking at him with faint dislike.

The door of the automatic elevator opened, and so, presently, did that of Breck's apartment.

"Hello, boys," he said. "Come in. Throw your stuff any damn place. Sit down."

They did so, and looked around the room, which was, indeed, a rather accurate reflection of their employer's bizarre personality. He had taken the apartment furnished, they knew, but the expensive reticence of the sofas, chairs, tables, and lamps had long since been overlaid with manifestations of a less coherent taste. The walls were covered with pictures—photographs of Breck's friends, usually in dissolute postures and facetiously inscribed; paintings and engravings that ranged erratically from kittens at play and young women enjoying the sun to tortured El Grecos and smoldering Gauguins; a color proof of an advertisement that an unfortunate slip of the engraver's tool had turned into a classic of impropriety. Books, also wildly various in subject matter, were piled everywhere, and there was a snowdrift of papers down from the chairs and tables across the floor. The proprietor himself was rather perplexingly arrayed. He had on the bottoms of a pair of pajamas, slippers, and the remnant of a panama hat. It occurred to his guests that he looked annoyingly frivolous, considering the nature of their errand.

Drinks were distributed, and for a time they sipped them in silence.

At last Mitchell cleared his throat and addressed Breck. "I'm afraid we've got a little problem, Ralph," he said.

"Well, who the hell hasn't?" said Breck, looking at him impassively.

"It's a little hard—" Mitchell began again, but before he could get any further he was interrupted by a strange and violent commotion in the wall behind his head—a thin whine of gears and the clanking of heavy chains.

"Problems," said Breck when this had died away. "You think *you* got problems. You hear that God-damn thing?" He gestured at the wall. "The lousy elevator. It does that all night. Right beside my bed. The little white Jesus knows the last time I got in a night's sleep."

"It's quite a noise," said Mitchell.

"Son of a bitch if it isn't," said Breck. "It's driving me nuts, Al."

"Well," said Abbott after a decent interval, "we wanted to talk to you about the office. That is—"

"The office?" said Breck. "You don't have to tell *me* about that office. I've worked there for fifteen godforsaken years. I've turned into a sick and beaten old man in that office. I used to have an appetite, Hank. I used to eat like other men. What do I live on now? Soup. No stomach, no teeth. I lost them in that office."

"Maybe you need a vacation, Ralph," said Abbott.

"Sure," said Breck. "And who's going to run the stinking joint? Except for you boys, what have I got? Women and children. God on a velocipede, *women!*"

"Maybe it's a little tough on women, too, Mr. Breck," said Fox.

Breck gave him a brief, sardonic smile. "*Everything* is tough on women, my boy," he said. "They make a career of having things tough. You know what Mark Twain said about women?"

"I'm afraid I don't," said Fox.

"He said they were beautiful creatures with pains in their backs," said Breck. "He had it right."

"Still," said Mitchell. "Well, in the case we wanted to talk to you about—"

"I don't know what the hell case you're talking about," said Breck. "There are all kinds of cases. You take my God-damn sister Muriel."

"We wanted to ask—"

"She keeps getting herself locked up," said Breck. "As a matter of fact, she's locked up right now. I don't suppose you knew that?"

"No, I hadn't heard," said Abbott, "but—"

"Well, she is," said Breck. "Some place up around Bridgeport. There's nothing the matter with her. Just every so often she feels she has to put herself away in one of these joints. She gets feeling picturesque or some God-damn thing and she slopes off to one of these joints. I wouldn't give a damn—it's her dough—except she keeps telling them *I'm* crazy. Maybe I am. You don't eat or sleep long enough, *anybody* is apt to go nuts."

While he stared at them defiantly, the elevator went up and down again in the wall, clanking and groaning, sending a small, unpleasant vibration through the apartment.

"What we came up about, Ralph—" said Mitchell uncertainly when the sound had ceased.

"Excuse me, Al," said Breck. He picked up a little bottle from a table beside him and shook a pill out onto his palm. "Supposed to quiet me," he said when he had swallowed it.

"You ought to be careful with those things, Ralph," said Abbott. "You can get dependent on that kind of stuff."

"Yeah, I know it," said Breck. "But what the hell. Drinking is no good. I've tried that. I don't get drunk. I just get depressed."

"Well, you ought to watch it, anyway," said Mitchell.

"A man has to relax," said Breck. "One way or another. You know that, Al."

"I know," said Mitchell.

"It's tough, Ralph," said Abbott.

"It sure is," said Fox.

"I'm thirty-seven years old," said Breck. "Supposed to be the prime of a man's life. That's a laugh. Look at me. I live on soup and sleeping pills. For all I know, I ought to change places with Muriel."

"You do look kind of tired, Ralph," said Abbott.

"Tired?" said Breck. "God!"

"You ought to try and get some sleep, kid," said Mitchell.

"I don't know," said Breck. "Maybe I can. I feel as if maybe I might tonight." He yawned and closed his eyes, but opened them again almost instantly.

"But hell," he said, "you boys wanted to see me about something. What's on your mind, Al?"

"Ah, let it go, boy," said Mitchell. "We can take it up some other time."

"Sure, Ralph," said Abbott. "You just get your sleep."

"It wasn't important, sir," said Fox. "You get some sleep."

"Thanks," said Breck. "Perhaps I will. Well, good night, boys. Thanks for dropping around."

He yawned again as he showed them to the door.

IT WAS SOME time before a cab came, and as they waited for it on the curb, they avoided one another's eyes.

"Poor guy," said Fox, tentatively, at last. "I hope he gets some sleep."

"Sure," said Abbott. He paused and slowly shook his head. "He seems to eat all right, though," he said. "At least whenever I'm with him."

"You're damn right he does," said Mitchell. Then he, too, stopped and stared off down the street. "I wonder . . ." he began again.

"So do I," said Abbott.

"You wonder what?" asked Fox.

"If the son of a bitch has really *got* a sister," said Abbott. "So do I."

May 22, 1954

Wounds and Decorations

Theater and Film Criticism

WHAT HATH GOD WROUGHT?

(Ah, Wilderness!)

I F ANYBODY EXCEPT Eugene O'Neill had written "Ah, Wilderness!" I can't believe that it would have caused quite the flurry in our community that it has. It is a pleasant play dealing with the perplexities of young love among nice suburban people that, done a little more deftly, might easily have been contributed by Booth Tarkington. Most of the opinion I hear, however, passes from reverent wonder that Mr. O'Neill should stoop to comedy at all to the strange conclusion that he has written a superb one. I gave the Guild play my most studious attention, and could find very little in it to justify any such notion. The humor in every case is hung on the most dependable old pegs—on the fact that America in 1906 was shocked by such quaintly posturing fellows as Wilde and Swinburne; on the embarrassment of a father explaining sex to his son; on the genteel shrinking of the ladies of that period from profanity and alcohol; even, I'm sorry to say, on comic drunkenness itself. I am quite willing to admit that each of these notions was funny once, but there isn't one that hasn't been beaten into our heads through the years, and Mr. O'Neill's rather broad statement of them doesn't do much to offset their familiarity.

The play itself—a study, essentially, of a middle-class father's attempt to understand his "sensitive" son—seems very little more novel, and to me interesting only in that Mr. O'Neill should have abandoned his involved and cosmic ponderings for quite such trifling stuff. The year 1906 being a little outside the field of my accurate recollection, I am not sure just how faithfully the idiom has been preserved (although I suspect the use of the word "lousy," even by a harlot), but the writing generally exhibits that celebrated contempt for lightness and brevity which was appropriate enough in "Electra" but seems slightly trying in a comedy.

All the foregoing, of course, does not affect in the slightest George M. Cohan's superb performance as the father, which is almost in itself worth your trip to the Guild. Mr. Cohan is persuasive in the most unbelievable scenes—I mention again that painful exposition of the facts of life—and won my almost heartbroken sympathy for his patience with one of the most maddening families I've ever seen. The whole cast, as a matter of fact, does very nicely, especially Marjorie Marquis, as the wife, and Elisha Cook, Jr., who, as the troublesome son, convinced me that the Rubaiyat is a book much better kept out of the hands of the young.

It is difficult to disassociate "Ah, Wilderness!" from its distinguished author and sponsors, but really I can't believe that it's more than an engaging and not too professional comedy, to be recommended especially to those ladies who bustle into town for the matinées. Under the Guild's supervision, by the way, the curtain goes up at the rather unearthly hour of 8:20, and they're quite firm about having you there then; even, I imagine, if you have to bring the dessert and coffee.

October 14, 1933

MISS NICHOLS
AND THE DEMIURGE
(*Abie's Irish Rose*)

WITH THREE MEMBERS of its original cast, who obviously don't know when they've had enough, "Abie's Irish Rose" reopened last week at Anne Nichols' Little Theatre—turning up again just like a bad penny, or in this case probably more like a bad three or four million dollars. For some reason, conceivably because I didn't have to, I didn't see Miss Nichols' singular work fifteen years ago, when it first drove the critics so nearly out of their handsome heads. I read a great deal that they wrote, though, and it is a tribute to their accuracy that nothing that happened the other night surprised me in the slightest degree. There can be no question that it disturbed me, so that frequently it was only the restraining presence of the Hon. Alfred E. Smith (who seemed to be having a fine time) that kept me from lying down in the aisle and howling like a dog. But the whole performance—plot, dialogue, acting—was exactly what I'd been expecting. It had, in fact, the rather eerie quality of a repeated nightmare; the one, perhaps, in which I always find myself in an old well, thick with bats, and can't get out.

IT IS INTERESTING, or at any rate strange, to lie awake at night and wonder how the vision of Abie first came to trouble his creator. I like best to think of Miss Nichols, herself in some dim borderline of sleep, conversing with the Demiurge.

MISS NICHOLS: Of course we'll have to have a love story.
THE DEMIURGE: Of course.
MISS NICHOLS: I thought of a Jewish Boy—
THE DEMIURGE (*doubtfully*): Hmm.

MISS NICHOLS: I *know*, but wait a minute. A Jewish Boy *and* an Irish Girl!

(*There is a little sound in the darkness which might be interpreted as the Demiurge snapping its fingers.*)

THE DEMIURGE (*admiringly*): *Say*, I think you've got something there! And their parents won't let them get married?

MISS NICHOLS: That's it.

THE DEMIURGE: But they do anyway, and—but you *can't* mean—

MISS NICHOLS: Of course. They have a baby.

THE DEMIURGE (*excitedly*): And naturally that placates the parents, brings 'em together?

MISS NICHOLS: No. At least not right away. After all, we have to have three acts.

THE DEMIURGE: But I don't exactly see—

MISS NICHOLS: Well, it's a little complicated here, so you'd better listen carefully.

THE DEMIURGE: All right. Give.

MISS NICHOLS: I thought of having the Jewish Boy's father wanting the baby to be a little boy, so that it could carry on his name, while the Irish Girl's father wanted a girl, so that it could marry an Irishman and *change* its name. I guess that isn't very clear, and I'm not sure of the details, but that's the idea, generally speaking.

THE DEMIURGE: It's a tough one, all right. And which *is* this baby?

MISS NICHOLS: What do *you* think?

THE DEMIURGE: I'm afraid you've got me.

MISS NICHOLS: Oh, come. It can't be a girl and it can't be a boy, so it's *got* to be—

(*The Demiurge can be faintly heard scratching its head.*)

MISS NICHOLS: Goodness, but you're slow! I'll give you another hint. It begins with a "t."

THE DEMIURGE: A "t"?

MISS NICHOLS—"T," "w"—

THE DEMIURGE: *Twins!* Well, I'll be damned! A boy *and* a girl?

MISS NICHOLS (*complacently*): Naturally.

THE DEMIURGE: And so everybody is happy. Miss Nichols, this is genius! It ought to run forever. Please don't let me keep you from your work.

(*He vanishes in a respectful, though supernatural, manner and Miss Nichols springs to her escritoire.*)

May 22, 1937

THE KATZENJAMMER KIDS
IN WASHINGTON
(Washington Jitters)

WHEN I WAS a boy assassin in prep school, my English teacher used to say that satire was the political reformer's natural weapon. He said this specifically about "Gulliver's Travels," but we were also instructed to put it down in our little notebooks as a valuable generality. Unfortunately he forgot to state the supplementary proposition, which is that inept satire can easily turn in the hand and give the reformer himself a very nasty flesh wound. I got around to making this distinction for myself about fifteen years ago, when F. Scott Fitzgerald, a social commentator of the period, wrote something called "The Vegetable, or From President to Postman." This play, never produced as far as I know, pointed out how thoroughly a simple peasant, achieving high office, might confound the bureaucrats. It had no visible effect on the administration, but it dealt Mr. Fitzgerald an embarrassing though superficial blow in the reputation. There was nothing wrong with the idea in "The Vegetable;" the trouble was that as satire it was dull, heavy-handed, and, because Mr. Fitzgerald apparently knew nothing about politics except what he read on the front page of the *Times*, disassociated from the actual crisis.

The curious periodicity of the theatre brought a new version of "The Vegetable" to town last week. This time it is called "Washington Jitters;" it was written by two gentlemen called John Boruff and Walter Hart, and it is presented by the Theatre Guild, but it is still "The Vegetable." It is also, I'm afraid, dull, heavy-handed, and without perceptible value either as comment or entertainment. If it makes one or two acceptable points, they are made on the principle that a man throwing a handful of bird shot into the middle of Times

Square is bound to hit something or other, even if it is only the Paramount Building.

The idea, in capsule, is that Henry Hogg, a sign-painter, sitting down by accident behind one of his own signs, is mistaken for the head of a government bureau, and this error, by the simple alchemy of the theatre, is transmuted into fact so that as far as the rest of the cast is concerned he *is* the Coördinator of ASP. There is a little love story, trailing through the play like arbutus, but most of the goings-on are about the efforts of both parties to get Hogg's support in a fight over an impending bill. The possibilities here are obvious, and Mr. Boruff and Mr. Hart do their damnedest to realize every one. For them, however, the political situation is no more subtle than it would appear to be from the cartoons in the Hearst papers and so what we get at the Guild is not satire but burlesque, applied with a stuffed club.

It is my own opinion that "Washington Jitters" is as dismal and irritating a way to spend an evening as you can find this side of picking oakum, but I am aware that it has its supporters. The night I was there it was greeted jubilantly by many of the Guild's most fashionable subscribers, one woolly old imbecile even going so far as to say that it was the wittiest thing he'd seen in five years. I guess it will just have to be my word against his.

I have nothing in particular to say about the actors in "Washington Jitters." I suppose on the whole they were O.K., but it would have been hard for me to recognize even the talent of a Salvini in a group of people so enthusiastically bent on boring me to death. The same comment, I fear, will have to cover the scenery.

May 14, 1938

NICE PEOPLE

(*Kiss the Boys Goodbye*)

Jokes about the Southern Girl being presumably eternal, Miss Clare Boothe, the author of "The Women," has written a play consisting of them and got it acted out at Henry Miller's Theatre. Miss Boothe's hand, I might as well say right off, has lost none of its nice, sharp fingernails. The people who infest "Kiss the Boys Goodbye" belong to both sexes, but they are every bit as bitchy as the girls Miss B. wrote about last time. Right there on the stage we have a drunken Communist, an unfaithful husband, a lecherous producer of moving pictures, a Hollywood nymphomaniac, and Cindy Lou Bethany, who, when in a "snit," as they say in Georgia, would just as soon shoot you as look at you. I am sure that, in its way, the ability to produce an unlimited number of dreadful people is a kind of genius.

"Kiss the Boys Goodbye" deals with the great American dilemma: who is going to play Scarlett O'Hara in the movie version of "Gone with the Wind"? Given that idea—a good one, incidentally—Miss Boothe doesn't bother much about the form or substance of her play. For three acts she just devotes herself to a glossary of the Southern idiom, which I found impressive, and a commentary on manners and morals, which seemed to me appalling. Scandalized as I am, however, I have to admit that a great deal of it is very funny indeed, because Miss Boothe has an acute ear for the humor of the bright boys and girls who hate everybody, including themselves. But, to be even more stuffy than usual, I think it is hard to spend two and a half hours looking at a play in which it is impossible to sympathize with anybody. Furthermore, it seems to me that when an author, having run through her plot in two acts, spends the last one just throwing mud pies, her play cannot be called intelligent in a structural sense. The prosecution rests.

Miss Helen Claire, playing the Daughter of the South who shows the damyankees where they get off, gives a performance which for sustained comic violence I can only compare with the job Gertrude Lawrence did last year in "Susan and God." Most of the time she carries the play around balanced on her head, and I think she is wonderful. I also admired Sheldon Leonard, the most talented portrayer of seducers in our theatre, a man who gets right down to the point, and Millard Mitchell as a motion-picture director with gas on his stomach. Miss Benay Venuta, the lady with the remarkable name, is the Hollywood siren, and John Alexander is supposed to be Heywood Broun or Mark Sullivan or somebody. I guess it's kind of a special joke, and I wouldn't bother with it if I were you.

October 8, 1938

A NIGHT AT NICK'S

(*The Time of Your Life*)

A N EVENING IN the theatre with William Saroyan is rather like spending an evening with a drunkard—a talented, sentimental, and witty man, but tight as a mink. There are times when he is very funny, with a wild, rich invention that no sober man can equal, and there are times when he is eloquent. Unfortunately, there are also times when he gets to talking about his girl, and this is when you wish he would just put his head down on the table and go to sleep. Mr. Saroyan's girl is the human race. Speaking with the assorted voices of bartenders, bums, policemen, hoofers, and prostitutes, Mr. Saroyan interrupts his play again and again to explain that he and Life are sweethearts. The tone is rapt and dreamy, but the message may be a little monotonous. Life, he says, is so wonderful that it is hard to see why everybody doesn't love her as much as he does, how there can actually be people who hate her and like to see her unhappy.

I think it is a pity that the force of Mr. Saroyan's odd personality is such that hardly any editing can be done on his work, because in many ways "The Time of Your Life," at the Booth, is vital beyond most things you'll see in the theatre. The customers who go to Nick's Pacific Street Saloon in San Francisco are about the handsomest collection of derelicts in my memory, and they light the place with a fantastic kind of gaiety. "Did you ever try to herd cattle on a bicycle?" asks the strange character called Kit Carson. "Did you ever happen to fall in love with a midget weighing thirty-nine pounds?" Carson has had these unusual experiences himself, or says he has, and in him there is the essence of the author's humor, a quality unexpected, childlike, and often, though I'm afraid it doesn't sound so on paper, enormously funny. There is a man at Nick's who plays a pinball game all night long, as lost to the world as a gambler at Monte Carlo; there is a mad Arab who performs on a harmonica; there is a young man trying to call up his girl (unfortunately, Mr. Saroyan's romantic heart led him to end this episode on a note of almost perfect bathos); there is a policeman who feels he picked the wrong career, and a lady slummer who smokes a big black cigar. All these fascinating people, however, are more or less suspended in space, because the play in which their creator has chosen to present them is hardly a play at all, and the main characters in it haven't much to do beyond expressing his love and compassion for all the world.

It is, I suppose, a symptom of Mr. Saroyan's youth and excitable nature that for him a prostitute is still laden with various mystic and literary connotations. She is the perfect specimen of the "little people" with whom he is chiefly concerned, the ultimate victim of man's inhumanity. The thin thread of story in "The Time of Your Life" deals with an alcoholic philosopher who tries to give back to such a girl the dreams she had before she entered public life. It is ineffective dramatically mostly because these two are not so much people as animated sonnets, but partly, I'm sorry to say, because of the performance given by Julie Haydon, who is an actress of delicate and unusual talent and resembles a waterfront hooker about as much as I resemble the late William Howard Taft. The actor of the evening is Eddie Dowling, but not even he can give complete reality to a character who sometimes seems to be God but a good deal of the time just a man who has been drinking too much champagne on an empty stomach. The trouble with Mr. Saroyan, generally speaking, is his impression that the entire content of any man's mind automatically becomes a great play when produced on the stage; his virtue is that for rather more than half the evening you are apt to believe the same thing yourself.

"THE POSSESSED," BASED on some tangled themes from Dostoevski, turned up at the Lyceum to, I should imagine, the considerable embarrassment of that great man's admirers. Persistent friends of mine who went back for the second act tell me things got a little better as they went along. They could hardly have got any worse.

November 4, 1939

FATHER ON BROADWAY
(Life with Father)

THE LATE CLARENCE Day's father was apparently a very complicated man—violent, opinionated, upright, and logical, with the rather terrible logic of a mind that makes no concessions to the accepted hypocrisies of polite society. It is a mistake, I think, to say that he was merely typical of his time and class. Father was that, especially when it came to handling money, but he was a good deal more, too. The upper middle-class New Yorker of the eighties was more or less in awe of the clergy; Father never hesitated to argue with God Himself if he thought He was handling things inefficiently. His contemporaries had a powerful respect for culture, though preferring to leave the actual details of it to their wives; Father approached art and letters as he did everything else, with a furious determination to demolish them out of hand if they happened to conflict with his own prejudices. Most of all, he was a man who liked to get to the bottom of things, and perhaps the mainspring of his fierce behavior was his conviction that people were always trying to obscure the issue and mix him up.

This character came out in its three dimensions and certainly in full color in the books his son wrote about him. In the play done by Howard Lindsay and Russel Crouse there has been a very considerable simplification at, it seems to me, some sacrifice of vitality and depth. Father, as Mr. Lindsay and Mr. Crouse have recreated him at the Empire Theatre, is very funny, but he is funny on moderately familiar lines—a domestic autocrat perpetually outwitted by his wife, a turbulent eccentric firmly conventional at heart. I suppose it was necessary to reduce Father, both in size and complexity, for the purposes of the theatre, but I can't help feeling that Mr. Crouse and Mr. Lindsay have made everything just a little too easy. Somehow I don't believe that Clarence Day, Jr., would have done it quite that way.

Considered without relation to its source, however, "Life with Father" is undoubtedly one of the pleasantest comedies you will see this season. There are times when not a great deal seems to be going on (getting Father to the baptismal font isn't, after all, a very substantial theme) but mostly it is pretty wonderful. Mother trying to explain that if you exchange a china pug dog for a suit of clothes at McCreery's the suit obviously doesn't cost anything; Father getting hold of one of his son's letters by mistake ("Some woman claims she's been sitting on my knee," he says with mystified disgust); young Clarence and his brother laying Mother low with a dose of Beneficent Balm—all these are agreeable moments, and, on the whole, the cast makes the most of them.

Mr. Lindsay is not exactly my idea of what Father was like, but since the part he plays isn't either, this is probably fairly captious criticism. Dorothy Stickney, on the other hand, *is* my idea of Mother, and she is very appealing and competent about it, too. The four Day boys, all violently red-headed, seemed fine to me, especially John Drew Devereaux as young Clarence, perhaps even then observing his parents with a speculative, literary eye. The rest are engaging enough, though I thought there were accents here and there that were neither nineteenth century nor Madison Avenue.

"Sea Dogs," which blew into the Maxine Elliott, was hard for me to accept as a serious dramatic enterprise, undertaken for profit. The ship was on fire, the captain was drunk, and, from where I sat, the audience appeared to be either dead or asleep.

November 18, 1939

A STAR-CROSSED REVIVAL

(Romeo and Juliet)

R OMEO AND JULIET," that tragedy of Veronese café society, was produced last week at the Fifty-first Street Theatre by Laurence Olivier, who himself undertook to play the youngest of the Montagues. August Wilhelm von Schlegel, discussing this play about a hundred years ago (it makes no difference how I happened to dig up Schlegel), called it, not unpoetically, "a single, endless sigh," but there is something in the way Mr. Olivier and his associates have dealt with the fatal lovers that, while justifying at least the second of these adjectives, seems to call for another noun. I'm afraid that "yawn" may possibly be the word. Some of this sad effect should be laid to the acoustical properties of the Fifty-first Street Theatre, which can muffle even the prettiest diction, but most of it must be charged to the fact that a great many of the actors speak their lines with almost no indication that they either know or care what they're talking about.

Except in the most talented hands, "Romeo and Juliet" is one of the most dangerous of Shakespeare's plays. The text is intricate, full of some of the author's most baffling puns; in many respects, Romeo is little better than feeble-minded, while Juliet shuttles much too rapidly back and forth between troubled adolescence and brisk and competent maturity; and the plot itself is often uncomfortably close to absurdity. There are too many innocent misunderstandings and staggering coincidences, too many potions and poisons; in the end, far too many bodies cluttering up the Capulets' not so very quiet tomb.

All these drawbacks are not insuperable, or probably even very important when the extraordinary and radiant poetry of the love scenes is given its full value, but unfortunately it is here that the present version fails most completely. Mr. Olivier himself is the principal offender. Not only is he just as inaudible as any of his colleagues, but also he plays with a strangely preoccupied air, as if half his mind was still busy with his problems as director. His balcony scene, especially, has less the appearance of a man transported by love than that of an actor-manager automatically reciting blank verse while reflecting uneasily that the balcony really seems absurdly low, which indeed it does.

Pictorially, Miss Vivien Leigh is an almost perfect Juliet, childish and lovely, but professionally she is still a little too limited and monotonous for one of the most volatile heroines in the theatre. There are good performances, when you can hear them, by Cornel Wilde as Tybalt, Wesley Addy as Benvolio, Halliwell Hobbes as old Capulet, and Dame May Whitty as Juliet's nurse. Edmond O'Brien's Mercutio, notably in the Queen Mab speech, which enchants some people and just floors others, has more vivacity than seems strictly necessary, and I am somewhat at a loss when it comes to the scenery, since most of it reminded me painfully of the Venetian epidemic that struck the South Shore of Long Island in the great days of Calvin Coolidge. There is not much doubt that both Mr. Olivier and Miss Leigh have charmed enough people on the screen recently to assure them of a modest success now on the stage. They will owe it principally to the Misses Brontë and Mitchell, however. Shakespeare can't be credited with more than an assist.

May 18, 1940

WELL, I GIVE UP

(*The Beautiful People*)

WHEN THE CURTAIN goes up on William Saroyan's play called "The Beautiful People," at the Lycéum, it discloses a set that might have been executed by Salvador Dali, needing, in fact, only a rubbery watch and a couple of lamb chops. This scene represents, or, more precisely, non-represents, the combined interior and exterior of a decaying house on Red Rock Hill in San Francisco. It is relentlessly playful, rather pretty, and after a while I got awfully sick of looking at it. As far as I am concerned, this comment also applies to the play.

Detailed synopsis, as I have remarked here before, is a lazy and unsporting way of dealing with the drama, but I don't really see how else I can give you the special nutty bouquet of Mr. Saroyan's latest composition. At the beginning, then, Owen Webster, a backward boy of fifteen, is lying on his stomach across a table reading a letter. In a minute or two he gets up, goes to the piano, and plays "Wonderful One," *molto vivace*. Toward the end of this piece, he is joined by an offstage cornet, theoretically being played by a man in New York. This is an interesting effect, and I'm sorry that it is too complicated to explain here. Next, he climbs up on top of the piano and gets a book down from a high shelf. "Just a bunch of words," he says, throwing it away and picking up a copy of the *Saturday Evening Post*. After tearing three advertisements out of this great organ for reasons not entirely clear to me, he starts reading a story and presently is acting out a love scene with a girl in it called Eleanor. At this point, Miss Harmony Blueblossom, a spinster with a Southern accent, comes drifting in, and we really get going.

Owen, who seems to have unlimited confidence in his own charm, tells this unfortunate woman that he has written a book consisting of the single word "tree," that he has a brother in New York who plays the cornet (perhaps that explains the cornet), that he (Owen) dislikes Longfellow, and finally that the house is full of mice who admire his sister Agnes and often arrange flowers to spell out her name. This last touch is too much for Miss Blueblossom and she leaves. Owen, somewhat exhausted by his own humor, lies down and goes to sleep as the curtain falls.

When the next scene opens we discover the word "Agnes" spelled out on the stage in red, white, and blue flowers and are also permitted to meet the lady herself. Agnes, like her brother, is a rapid and eclectic conversationalist. One of the mice, it seems, is absent, and her theory is that it is either dead or hiding out in the Catholic church. We learn, too, that Agnes has spent the day in the public library reading up on hummingbirds in the Encyclopædia Britannica. They fly backward. After absorbing this dope, she got caught in a revolving door with a man called John and they fell in love. This dizzy flow is finally interrupted by the arrival of her father, a lovable old maniac, who differs from Jeeter Lester principally in that his favorite expression is "By the polestar and pyramid" instead of "By God and by Jesus." There may even be a clue here as to the basic difference between Mr. Saroyan and Erskine Caldwell. Anyway, after some more of the disjointed conversation apparently habitual in the Webster family, Owen goes out to look for the mouse and Agnes slopes off after John, presumably still caught in the door.

Right here I can see that we are never going to get through at this rate, so I'll have to condense Mr. Saroyan's plot rather drastically. In rapid succession, then, you will meet a Mr. Prim, the vice-president of a company which has been paying old man Webster somebody else's pension by mistake (from time to time, Mr. Prim toots on a penny whistle, a souvenir of a cruise he once took to Mexico); a drunkard, quite groundlessly described in my program as "a good companion;" a Catholic priest, who comes in to complain that little Owen has fallen into the pipe organ while chasing the mouse; the brother with the cornet; and a nameless and speechless character whom I rather liked. These people sashay in and out on their peculiar errands, of which the return of Owen with the wrong mouse is probably typical. He is a proud mouse and a bad mixer, says Agnes, all knotted with whimsy, and it was here, I think, that Mr. Gibbs turned to Mrs. Gibbs and mentioned God. All this and more, my friends, went into the play called "The Beautiful People," which I strongly suspect of being largely the bunk.

May 3, 1941

RESURRECTION MAN
(*Blithe Spirit*)

Noel Coward's characters have always been inorganic, supernatural, and strange, but up to now they have been presented as actual people, made out of meat and subject to the law of gravity. In "Blithe Spirit," however, Mr. Coward has given us honest ectoplasm and also, I think, an interesting paradox: it is really easier to believe in one of his heroines if you don't have to pretend that she is mortal flesh and blood. The shimmering, unearthly wit is much more plausible in a shade; the lively but quite disembodied preoccupation with sex is only natural in a lady made of mist; the airy freedom from all economic or political concern is reasonable enough in a girl who can no longer eat or vote. Generally speaking, it is a risky business for a playwright to tamper with the Beyond, but Mr. Coward is a special case—if anything, more at home with the shadow than the substance. The play at the Morosco is classified by its author as an "improbable farce," but from where I sat it looked at least as probable as either "Private Lives" or "Design for Living" and, if Father may bare his claws for a moment, not much more farcical than "Point Valaine."

Like most of the Coward works, "Blithe Spirit" is moderately hostile to synopsis: the stage always seems to be full of furious activity, but in retrospect the plot dwindles until it is hard to believe that it could have been spread out to consume rather more than two hours. In this instance, the facts in the case are even more meagre than usual. Charles Condomine, a popular novelist residing in Kent at a time emphatically not the present, arranges a séance in order to get material for a book he is writing. His success is beyond his eeriest dreams, since the medium, to her own proud astonishment, manages to produce the lovely, ashen spectre of his first wife. As this fashionable wraith (cerements by Mainbocher) is visible and audible to no one but Condomine, her presence inevitably leads to a certain amount of domestic confusion, and the second Mrs. Condomine, observing her mate addressing nothing, reasonably concludes that he is either drunk or a mental case. Eventually, though, she is persuaded that the premises are indeed bewitched, and the two ladies settle down to one of the most unusual struggles ever waged over any man, especially one of the booksy type. In the end, through some ghostly error, the living Mrs. Condomine is killed in an automobile accident and is also transported to the astral plane, leaving the exasperated artist with two spooks on his hands. This, in essence, is the story of the play called "Blithe Spirit," and, for Shelley's peace of mind, it is probably just as well he died when he did.

Given only this negligible material, however, Mr. Coward has written as deft, malicious, and fascinating a comedy as you could hope to see. His characteristic juxtaposition of peculiar words has never been neater ("You always had a certain seedy grandeur, Charles," one of the spectral damsels tells the hero in a typical love scene); his comic invention was never more brilliant or profuse ("As a matter of fact, she's rather good fun," says the first Mrs. Condomine, referring to Joan of Arc, with whom, along with Merlin and Genghis Khan, she often played bridge across the Styx); and seldom, I think, has anybody varied the ancient triangle with quite so much ingenuity and malignant charm. Altogether, with the exception of a brief stretch in the last act when Mr. Coward apparently decided that two ghosts ought to be twice as funny as one and the law of diminishing returns began to set in, "Blithe Spirit" seemed to me an almost pure delight.

Clifton Webb, as the haunted author, has just the correct wispy elegance and achieves, I should say, one of the best performances of his career, while Peggy Wood and a beautiful, languishing Briton called Leonora Corbett are deadly and sweet as the ladies from hell. Mr. Coward's most notable creation, however, a bouncy spiritualist who converses entirely in the hearty clichés of a games mistress or a Girl Guide, has been entrusted to Mildred Natwick, who gives it the works. John C. Wilson's direction is all the master could possibly have asked.

November 15, 1941

THE MANTLE OF MANTLE

[Author's Note: The following is intended to be a rhymed alphabetical review of the current theatrical season, but there are conceivably a few points about it that need explanation. In the first place, the metre may from time to time seem faulty or variable. This is partly because the titles of a good many plays are better adapted to theatre marquees than iambic tetrameter ("Yesterday's Magic" and "Hope for a Harvest" are, I feel, particularly unsatisfactory) and partly because of certain technical deficiencies of my own. I think the lines throughout can be made to come out all right if you work at them, but it may easily be too much trouble. In the second place, several plays, now gone and forgotten, are dealt with in the present tense. This has been done entirely for my own convenience, in order to produce rhymes. In the third place, a good many rather ambitious plays have been left out ("Jason," "Lily of the Valley," "Clash by Night," and a number of musicals) simply because they begin with the same letter as something else. Finally, it will be observed that several letters, specifically D, E, Q, and X, are in under false pretenses, while Z doesn't appear at all. This should be blamed on the season rather than on me, since, as far as I can remember, it failed to produce anything with those initials. Z is omitted altogether because I could think of no proper names fitting it except a few like Zeus, Zuleika, Zeppelin, and Zarathustra, none of which seemed suitable.]

A's "Angel Street," in which a louse
Plans to polish off his spouse—
Just, in fact, the school to go to
If your partner seems de trop, too.

B's "Blithe Spirit": Coward looks
At two quite handsome female spooks.
The lesson here, when all is said:
Don't raise the queer, unruly dead.

C's "Candle in the Wind," a sermon
Proving all that's vile is German—
Either that or that it pays
To be a girl called Helen Hayes.

The Drama Critics Circle, D,
Is quite a bunch, including me.
There is hardly any play
Some critic doesn't wish away.

E is Evans, whom the Bard
Might well reward with myrrh or nard.
Good King Evans' latest feat:
He made "Macbeth" a partial treat.

F's "The Flowers of Virtue," which
Will hardly make its author rich.
The scene is laid in Mexico,
Where life is real and life is slow.

"Guest in the House," a pretty G,
Is full of fragrant bitchery.
Little can be said at most
For ladies who seduce the host.

"Hope for a Harvest" (letter H)
Should not have gone upon the stage,
Though pregnant with the strong emotion
Aroused in some by soil erosion.

I is for "In Time to Come,"
A play both dignified and glum.

Too many wigs obscured the glow
Of Wilson, Lodge, and Clemenceau.★

J's for "Junior Miss," which yields,
From Benson, Chodorov, and Fields,
A warning clear to you and me
That little girls are TNT.

K is "Keep 'Em Laughing," pard,
With Gaxton, Moore, and Hildegarde.
It's guaranteed to be a solace
To those who used to love the Palace.

L, "The Land Is Bright," was rife
With murder, lust, domestic strife,
With jewels, gigolos, and gin;
Where Kauf left off, the Ferb set in.

M is for "The Moon Is Down,"
About a small, a captive town
Where Hitler's legions walk in dread
Because old ladies cut them dead.

"Nathan the Wise" must be our N,
A history of holy men.
Though duller plays I've surely seen,
I'd rather look at George the Jean.

"Of V We Sing," the only O,
Might titillate the Eskimo,
But for the residents of here
It's apt to seem a little drear.

"Porgy and Bess" will do for P,
Will do for you and also me;

★Well, *mispronounce* it then.

How oft, indeed, I long to know
The Happy Dust of Catfish Row.

Q is for how queer this doyen
Found a year with no Saroyan.
As soon expect a soundless sea
As no new masterpiece from he.

R's "The Rivals," just a lark,
Made bearable by Bobby Clark
But otherwise with sorrow filled
For Helburn, Langner, and the Guild.

S is "Spring Again," a comic,
Yielding genteel laughs (not stomach).
I'm sure your mother, if a lady,
Will like C. Smith and Mrs. Brady.

T's for "Theatre," something from
Something else by Mr. Maugham.
'Twas interesting to this beginner
To see live actors round Miss Skinner.

U's "Uncle Harry," which they say
Opened up just yesterday.
Until I see it, I can't tell
If it's terrible or swell.

"Viva O'Brien," for a V,
Was just as queer as it could be.
The management, God save us all,
Used sugar for a waterfall.

W's "The Wookey," who's
A better man than me or youse,
Though Frederick Hazlitt Brennan's drama
Was laid on lightly, with a hammer.

X is for that lovely play
That somehow, somewhere, got away.
The dream that someone dreamed one night
And then at dawn forgot to write.

"Yesterday's Magic" is our Y,
A grope, a groan, a miss, a try.
Mr. Muni'll make more moola
Out on the lot a-playing Zola.

May 23, 1942

WITH THANKS
(*Oklahoma!*)

OKLAHOMA!," AT THE St. James, is a completely enchanting performance—gay, stylish, imaginative, and equipped with some of the best music and dancing in a long time. Following the general design of Lynn Riggs's "Green Grow the Lilacs," produced here in 1931, also by the Theatre Guild, "Oklahoma!" is a good deal more than the customary musical rendering of a successful play, which is just a matter of employing two or three formidable stars, two or three hundred appetizing legs, a good dose of Pullman-car humor, and a plot so simplified or distorted that the original author could easily sit through it without being aware that he was in the presence of his own handiwork.

After rereading Mr. Riggs's drama (a very fine and original one, by the way), I can't see that the version at the St. James has omitted anything of consequence. Naturally, there is no special definition of character—though the villainous Jud (Mr. Riggs's Jeeter has been rechristened for obvious reasons) is still a complicated and repulsive piece of work—and there has been some tampering with the facts, especially at the end. On the whole, however, it seems to me that Richard Rodgers, Oscar Hammerstein II, and their associates have heightened rather than diminished their material. Certainly the score is more interesting, if not more characteristic of the old Indian Territory, than the cowboy ballads, from the "Git Along, Little Do-gies" and "Home on the Range" album, that studded the original; such additions as the ballet in which the heroine imagines her lover dead at Jud's hands are not only fascinating in themselves but also admirably in keeping with what Mr. Riggs was getting at; and the building up of such secondary characters as the Levantine peddler, firmly not the marrying kind, and Ado Annie Carnes, a sort of Topsie of the prairies, has been done so skillfully that it is hard to imagine how "Green Grow the Lilacs" got along with only offhand sketches of these lovely people.

There is, in fact, so much to admire about "Oklahoma!" that I don't quite know how to sort it all out for you. In "Oh, What a Beautiful Mornin'" and "Pore Jud," Mr. Rodgers and Mr. Hammerstein have turned out two songs that are making the members of my family wish more than ever that I could sing on key; the dances arranged by Agnes de Mille are not only lovely and appropriate but also have a humor to be found only now and then in this rather serious-minded art; and the settings by Lemuel Ayres, who may owe a small debt to Thomas Benton and Grant Wood, give the stage depth and brightness and the audience a conviction that these red barns and green fields and yellow roads must be what America really looked like at the turn of the century. The cast is a comparatively modest one—the principals are Betty Garde, Alfred Drake, Joseph Buloff, Joan Roberts, Howard da Silva, and Celeste Holm— but it has been superbly directed by Rouben Mamoulian and I feel nothing but the deepest affection for everybody in it. To the Theatre Guild, which made all these joys available, my gratitude is practically boundless.

April 10, 1943

BLACK MAJESTY
(*Othello*)

IN PRODUCING "OTHELLO" with Paul Robeson in the title rôle, Margaret Webster has done a good deal to clarify a play that has been agitating the commentators since the days of Dr. Johnson. Always undertaken in the past with fetching golden-brown and café-au-lait versions of the Moor, it appears now with a man unequivocally black, and the pieces of the puzzle, or most of them, fall into place. The great trouble with the previous renderings has been that Othello never seemed particularly alien to the culture in which he found himself; there were, of course, such lines as those about the sooty bosom and the old black ram, but the man himself was an annoying contradiction—a dark but prepossessing warrior, in no way really strange or deeply antipathetic to the Venetians. The play, executed in these diluted shades, wasn't much more than a cloudily motivated tragedy, in which a jealous hero was destroyed by an obvious and preposterous plot. Miss Webster herself once wrote that Iago was a flawless conspirator, and at the time I thought this a rather excitable way to describe a man who seemed to me nearly as incompetent in his villainy as Desperate Desmond.

In the light of the present performance, however, I have to admit that she may easily be right, though "flawless" is rather too strong a word. Iago is still remarkably casual when it comes to the mechanics of intrigue—to the involved nonsense about the handkerchief, the flimsy stratagem with Cassio and Bianca, and the reckless confidences to Roderigo and Emilia—but as a psychologist he is superb. The scene in which suspicion is first implanted in Othello's mind—almost completely implausible when the Moor is portrayed as a man proudly sure of himself and the devotion of his wife in a society of equals—is murderously convincing when he is shown as a Negro mercenary, aware of the scorn and hatred that surround him, already suspecting that the morals of Venice are not his morals, and seeming almost to welcome the proof of what he dreads. Working on such a mind, Iago is subtle, sure, and deadly. The accusation against Desdemona, which was absurdly transparent when addressed to a man of something approaching European sophistication, is a masterpiece of evil suggestion when Othello becomes a pure African, transplanted to a world whose values to him are both mysterious and corrupt. It is the mark of Iago's genius that he says nothing that Othello has not already said to himself, that he selects and utilizes only the horrors that are already in his victim's mind. Whatever else Miss Webster may have accomplished, it seems very unlikely that we shall ever see Othello played again by anyone but a Negro.

At the risk of exciting a great many high-minded people, I am obliged to say now that I found Mr. Robeson's performance rather unsatisfactory, considered sheerly as a piece of acting. His voice, like his physique, is majestic, but sometimes it seems to me to be employed for meaningless organ effects, and there is a tendency to give more than full value to celebrated lines. When Mr. Robeson says, "Put out the light—and then put out the light," each word is a separate tombstone and unfortunately the effect, on me at least, verges on humor. His range of facial expression is limited—a fixed glare and a tortured smile—and his gestures often don't really convey anything in particular. I doubt, however, if all this matters very much. His reading is admirably clear (as are those of all the cast) and he is ideal pictorially—a perfect mixture of the noble, the primitive, and the obscurely terrifying that explains the behavior of the other characters as it has never been satisfactorily explained before.

The riddle of Iago is the hardest, and perhaps it is still not quite cleared up. He has many motives, but none that seems sufficient in itself: he may suspect that Othello has seduced Emilia, but his references to it are vague and sardonic; he resents the preferment of Cassio but not, apparently, to any murderous pitch; he hates Othello, for his race as well as for his moral and physical superiority, but it is hard to see what he expects to gain by his destruction. All these are contributory factors, of course, but it is most probable that Shakespeare intended him as a representation of pure and fundamentally purposeless malignance, and that is the way the part is played by José Ferrer. It is for me an intensely interesting performance. Mr. Ferrer's Iago is many different men: a shrewd co-plotter with Roderigo, his contempt always genially masked; a hearty man of the world with Cassio; an obsequious courtier to Desdemona; a rough, dominating husband to Emilia; an honest friend to Othello. It takes intelligence and a very flexible acting style to fuse all these elements into a unified portrayal, and Mr. Ferrer, having both to a high degree, does it beautifully, and even, surprisingly, has the necessary authority to match Mr. Robeson's Othello. I'm not sure I understand how Iago came to be obsessed with the idea of Othello's ruin, but, granted the compulsion, his conduct is always logical and its course inevitable from beginning to end.

Uta Hagen's Desdemona didn't make much impression on me one way or the other, which is probably not Miss Hagen's fault, since Desdemona is about the dimmest of all Shakespeare's heroines, an intense, credulous girl who seems almost bound to come to some bad end. If I didn't know Miss Webster as an extremely conscientious woman, I might suspect her of some fairly routine casting in the other rôles. Cassio (James Monks) is a Yale man, presumably in the advertising business, and Bianca (Edith King) is a Bridgeport trollop, much too florid and blowzy for his educated, suburban tastes. Roderigo (Jack Manning) is typical of all the thwarted, comic lovers in Shakespeare, a tubercular, effeminate specimen, rather like the conventional rendering of Sir Andrew Aguecheek, and Brabantio (Averell Harris) is pretty much the standard model of a distressed Shakespearean parent, too. However, I liked Miss Webster's own Emilia very much. Her conflicting loyalty, to her husband and to Desdemona, is another hard problem presented by the play, but I think Miss Webster solves it with brisk intelligence. Her direction and editing (for almost the first time in my memory one of Shakespeare's gruesome clowns has been amputated, and I am still numb with surprise and gratitude) are as perceptive as they can be. Altogether, if you can get into the Shubert Theatre, you'd better see "Othello." It's a good play, and I doubt if you'll ever see it done any better.

October 30, 1943

SUCH NICE PEOPLE

(*The Glass Menagerie*)

In "The Glass Menagerie" (a lovely title), you will see a very touching play, made to seem even better than it is because of a really magnificent performance by Laurette Taylor. The story is simple enough in essence—a crippled girl looking for some kind of emotional release, symbolized, as you may have gathered, by a pathetic little collection of glass animals, meets a man, largely through the violent manipulations of her mother, is stirred by him to some faint sense of reality, and then watches him go off to meet another girl. Some of the implications, however, may be a little blurred. As the final curtain comes down, Eddie Dowling, who serves as a combination brother and interlocutor, tells the audience, "Here my memory ends and your imagination begins." I have applied my imagination to the probable future of the heroine, left alone with her menagerie, but the results don't seem to be very satisfactory. I can only suppose that Laura, which happens to be her name, simply retreated back into the misty half-life that had imprisoned her in the beginning. Objections like these are captious in any case, because the author, Tennessee Williams, has captured a brief but poignant period in four lives, no negligible accomplishment on any stage.

It is hard to know just what to write about Miss Taylor. The last time I saw her, I think, was as the cockney charwoman in a revival of "Outward Bound," and I thought then that she was probably just about the greatest character actress in America. This time, as a former Southern belle and a fiercely designing mother, she is incomparable. Her recollections of past glories, when she planned to marry a rich planter rather than the lineman for the telephone company who actually turned out to be her lot, are fine, hilarious parody. Her efforts to beguile the young man with her daughter's charms and then her indignation at him when it turns out that he is "going steady" with a girl called Betty rise to a very affecting passion of maternity. Throughout, she is warm, humorous, and, of course, as nearly perfect technically as a mortal actress can hope to be. Julie Haydon, as the crippled daughter, plays with all her usual ethereal charm. It might be said that her deformity, so vehemently stressed by the other members of the cast, looked too slight to me to really handicap her emotionally or socially—in fact, there were times when she appeared to forget to limp at all—but it may be that too much emphasis on an affliction is not advisable in the theatre. Mr. Dowling, doing triple duty, since he directed the piece, along with everything else, is offhand and Irish and altogether admirable. Personally, I can get along without characters who stand on one side of the stage explaining to me what is going on in the middle (on the theory that a really sound play is capable of explaining itself), but if there has to be such a man around, my candidate is Dowling. Anthony Ross, who breaks one of Miss Haydon's little animals (we won't go into the significance of that) and even persuades her to dance a step or two, is not, perhaps, quite up to the competition, but he gives a sensible, attractive performance, surely good enough, in view of all the other riches on display.[1]

Altogether, I think you'll admire "The Glass Menagerie." There are certainly times when things get a little vague and confused, and Mr. Williams and Mr. Dowling do not always seem to be precisely sure what is on each other's mind, but they have a lot of appealing things to say and their play is unquestionably superbly acted.

April 7, 1945

THE BOYS IN THE BACK ROOM

(The Iceman Cometh; Cyrano de Bergerac)

T HE CIRCUMSTANCES ATTENDING the appearance last week
of Eugene O'Neill's "The Iceman Cometh" were certainly
enough to intimidate the most frivolous critic. There was the illustrious author—except for Shaw, perhaps the only living Olympian—
returning from years of mysterious silence with a play that was vaguely
reported to be just a part of a far vaster project; there was the knowledge that this work, though possibly only a fragment, was still of
such dimensions that the acting of it could not be accomplished in
anything less than four and a half hours; there was the impression,
somehow confirmed by the cryptic title and by the fact that the reviewers were furnished with the text in advance, that the visible play
offered but a very small percentage of its author's total meaning and
would therefore require a concentration on everybody's part at least
adequate for deciphering the hieroglyphs on the Rosetta stone. Under these conditions, it was a little disconcerting to find that "The
Iceman Cometh," while an interesting play, was by no means com-
parable to its author's best efforts in the past, either in style or substance, and furthermore that, except for some possible ambiguity at
the end, it was no harder to understand than any work that attempts
to convey large general ideas in terms of specific and circumscribed
action. Mr. O'Neill's idea in this case is no more original or abstruse
than the discovery, not unknown to melancholy sophomores, that
life is insupportable without illusions; his treatment of it, however, is
so monumental, so clearly designed to merit words like "Greek" and
"symphonic," that it is no wonder that elaborate interpretations are
already being provided by the metaphysicians in the parish. For the
moment, we will stick to the facts.

The curtain at the Martin Beck goes up on the bar of a Raines

Law hotel in the summer of 1912. It is six o'clock in the morning and a dozen or so of the inmates are sprawled asleep over the tables. They are thus disposed, rather than being upstairs in their beds, because they are waiting for the arrival of Hickey, a sporty travelling salesman who turns up once a year on the proprietor's birthday to buy them drinks and to relieve the tedium of their lives with the horsy humors of the road. It is a scene of appalling squalor, though Robert Edmond Jones has made it tremendously effective theatrically, and it is not improved as, one by one, the lost men wake up and we are allowed to inspect them in more detail. Inevitably, since Mr. O'Neill is dealing with the fate of all mankind, the personnel is extensive, ranging from cheap whores and mad Nihilists to scarecrow remittance men and Harvard graduates sunk without a trace. All they have in common, except for chronic alcoholism and filth, are their sorry lies about the past and their boozy dreams of an impossible tomorrow, but these still are enough to distinguish them as living men, capable of at least some dim parody of the emotions of human beings, even including a kind of desperate gaiety.

Hickey turns up at last, but it is soon obvious that he is not the companion they have known in the past. It is bad enough for them to discover that he is on the wagon but far worse to learn that he is preaching a curious salvation. Peace can come to them, he says, as it has come to him, only when they have abandoned all their empty dreams. Before these illusions can be given up, however, it is necessary to put them to the test, and, one by one—sober, terrified, and dressed with pathetic care—the bums leave the shelter of the bar to make their doomed attempts to take up life again. When they come back, they are finally without hope, but peace has escaped them, too. Faced with the tragic truth about themselves, some wearily accept the idea of death, some are roused to a savage hatred of their companions, all begin to lose their last resemblance to men. In their extremity, however, they learn that Hickey has murdered his wife, whose illusions about his behavior had given him an intolerable sense of guilt, and that the peace he offered them was only a spiritual counterpart of the physical death he had already accepted for himself. At the last moment, stricken with remorse at the terrible effect of his compassionately meant interference with their lives, he allows them to think that he has been insane, and with enormous relief they go back to their bottles and their hollow, happy dreams.

This, of course, is only a bare summary of Mr. O'Neill's theme. There is also an almost intolerable mass of supporting detail, for each derelict in the bar is relentlessly determined to give his own personal history, often as many as three or four times. Obviously, there isn't room for all of these here, but a few may help to indicate the play's impressive range and, incidentally, since this review is necessarily a work of drastic compression, give a partial listing of the cast that supports James Barton in the tremendous central role. Harry Hope (Dudley Digges), the owner of the bar, has never stepped out of it for twenty years. It is his pipe dream, his special evasion of the fact of lost will, to imagine that he has sequestered himself because of his grief over his wife's death and that any day now he will go out and resume his old career as a wardheeling politician. Piet Wetjoen (Frank Tweddell) and Cecil Lewis (Nicholas Joy) fought on opposite sides in the Boer War, and it is their delusion that presently they will go back across the sea to an honorable old age. Willie Oban (E. G. Marshall), a law-school graduate, is the son of a convicted bucket-shop operator. The most hopeless alcoholic of them all, he dreams of straightening up and getting a brilliant job in the district attorney's office. Rocky Pioggi (Tom Pedi) is Harry's night bartender, and his illusion is of a peculiar and negative character. He is under the impression that although two agreeable girls turn over their earnings to him, he is not a pimp, for the excellent reason that he holds a regular job and prostitution is only a casual sideline in his life. Unlike the rest, Larry Slade (Carl Benton Reid), a disenchanted radical, appears to be without any hope whatever. He is, he says, through with the Cause and only waiting around to die. In spite of the fact that he is able to identify the real nature of Hickey's peace and to fight it for the others, he is finally obliged to accept it for himself, since, if I am not mistaken, he is the symbol of tragic omniscience (or the author) on the stage. Of them all, only Dan Parritt (Paul Crabtree), who has betrayed his Anarchist mother to the police out of motives very similar to those that led Hickey to shoot his wife, dies in the end. All through the play, he and the metaphysical drummer have had a curious sense of identity with each other, and when the truth about Hickey is revealed and he is taken off to the electric chair, the other man finds his parallel solution in suicide.

There are many more in the cast, but these characters—all superlatively acted, by the way—should be enough to establish Mr. O'Neill firmly in the company of William Saroyan as a wonderfully prolific inventor of damned and fascinating people. His other qualifications for the position of America's leading playwright, however, I'm afraid remain just about what they were before. The construction, the ponderous building up, over three acts, of a situation that is to be resolved by a much too abrupt theatrical trick at the end of the fourth, is at least questionable, especially when the trick is so executed that it can be interpreted in two ways by the audience. If, that is, my own impression is right and Hickey's insanity is feigned for the purpose of giving his companions back their drunken hopes, he is simply a misguided philanthropist who has sincerely believed right up to the last that peace can be found only in the final, absolute acceptance of defeat. If, on the other hand, he is really insane, he is only a figure of crazy malevolence and the point of the play is hard to imagine. This alternate explanation, while it can hardly be justified on reflection, is nevertheless one that seems to have been subscribed to by a great many reasonably attentive people, including at least one critic, after the opening night, so it is hard to credit Mr. O'Neill with wholly satisfactory craftsmanship from a sheerly theatrical point of view. He has erred even further, I think, in a certain obscurity of intention that seems to mark several members of the cast. The demented Nihilist, for instance, undoubtedly keys in with Hickey's own spiritual Nihilism, but the analogy is never clearly developed and all that appears on the stage is a sort of irrelevant, comic-supplement bomb-thrower. The same thing applies to a lot of the others—they are obviously meant to be essential pieces of the total design, but their exact relation to it is not sufficiently defined and they become merely atmospheric "characters," present for a scenic effect rather than for comprehensible artistic purposes. I'm sure, of course, that Mr. O'Neill could readily explain how each actor is vital to the pattern and the forward movement of his play, but it is certainly by no means apparent in the theatre, where, unfortunately, the playwright's secret mind is not on view.

In regard, finally, to the style in which "The Iceman" has been written, I can only say that there is little evidence of the lofty eloquence that distinguished "Mourning Becomes Electra" or even, indeed, some of Mr. O'Neill's lesser works. As several critics have pointed out, the locale of the play and the prototypes of the bums who appear in it have been taken from the author's own remote past. The assumption, however, that he has exactly recaptured the sound of their speech may be open to question, and it is my opinion that, while Mr. O'Neill is a superb reporter of behavior and even of processes of thought, the language he uses to convey them is actually non-realistic, being of the conventional dese-dem-dose school of dialect, which a certain kind of abstracted literary intelligence, from Richard Harding Davis to Thomas Wolfe, has somewhat arbitrarily decided is the language of the lower depths. It is odd but nevertheless a fact that a writer can often understand perfectly what is being said around him without really hearing the accent of the voice or the structure of the sentence, and I'm afraid that this is particularly true of Mr. O'Neill.

Inaccurate as his bums may be, however, I'm not sure that they are as painful as some of his more articulate types. Slade, the radical, who serves more or less as his author's spokesman, is naturally given some rather towering sentiments to express and perhaps he may be forgiven a certain grandiloquence, but there can be no such excuse in the case of the burlesque old-school-tie locutions employed by the British captain, the elaborate, pedantic witticisms of the fallen Harvard man, or the laborious Babbittries and really stupefying repetitions of Hickey himself. On the whole, in fact, I suspect that Hickey is the worst of all, and there were times during the now famous sixteen-minute speech when I felt a deep sympathy with the old saloonkeeper and his guests, who could only murmur hopelessly, "For God's sake, Hickey, give us a rest! All we want to do is pass out in peace."

LIKE FALSTAFF, UNCLE Tom, the White Rabbit, and a great many other picturesque figures on the stage, Cyrano is a character so heavily obscured by eccentric makeup that it is hard to evaluate the performance that goes on underneath. I would like to be able to tell you, for instance, just how José Ferrer's work in the current revival of Rostand's famous old absurdity differs from that with which Walter Hampden enchanted the nation for so many years; how much the part gains or loses from being played by a young, witty, and highly original actor rather than by one who brought to it a considerably more impressive physique, a louder voice, and an acting technique for which rococo seems the mildest word. I went to the Alvin, that is, full of the memory of Mr. Ferrer's really brilliant Iago last season and expecting somewhat the same miracle again. If any tradition was shattered, however, it was not especially evident to me. Mr. Ferrer is, I guess, rather more agile in the celebrated duel, more urbane and stylized in his encounters with his inferiors, and less florid and, since these are scenes that really call for ham, a good deal less effective in his romantic dealings with Christian and Roxane, but essentially his portrayal seems to vary very little from what I remember of Mr. Hampden's. There is something about a flaring putty nose and comic mustachios that defeats subtlety, and since subtlety is one of Mr. Ferrer's chief accomplishments, he is seriously handicapped when his physical appearance, not to mention his text, permits only the broadest imaginable effects.

The general level of the production at the Alvin is pretty high. Frances Reid makes a rather charming Roxane, girlishly hypnotized alike by a rolling ballad and a handsome face; Ernest Graves, as Christian, though a little wispy for a really formidable lover, combines, nevertheless, a dashing bearing with a suitably noble vacuity of expression; Ralph Clanton is pictorially good as the sinister de Guiche; Paula Laurence makes a neat, humorous duenna; and Hiram Sherman is probably as funny as possible in the silly, slapstick role of Rageneau. The scenery and costumes by Lemuel Ayers take full advantage of their colorful period, and the direction, especially in the more populated scenes, seemed to me stylish and resourceful. The play itself, which I was seeing for the third time, struck me as a great deal longer and more childish than it used to be back in the Coolidge administration.

October 19, 1946

CATECHISM
(*Little A*)

(The Critic Submits to a Brief Examination, for the Purpose of Discovering How He Arrived at the Opinion He Did.)

Q—APPARENTLY YOU didn't care for the melodrama called—called—(*The investigator searches some papers on his desk.*)

A—"Little A." At the Henry Miller. No, I didn't, particularly.

Q—Why?

A—I don't know. It just seemed rather—well, amorphous.

Q—Oh, come. Surely you can find a better word than that.

A—All right. Shapeless. Scatterbrained. Frantic, maybe.

Q—Perhaps we'd better be specific. Just what is this play about?

A—About? You mean you want the whole plot?

Q—No. Just very roughly.

A—Well, in the beginning, this guy and his wife are celebrating their nineteenth wedding anniversary. They've had another couple in to dinner and they're sitting around afterward and talking. Naturally, a lot of background stuff comes out. The guy is called Little A because his father was Big A, and, in a way, that's the whole story. Big A had been practically the works in this California town they live in—big businessman, big parlor comedian, naturally, the big seducer—and his son has always sort of lived in his shadow. You get that idea pretty clearly, because every time he opens his mouth, somebody sits on him, usually his wife. I thought Otto Kruger was damn good.

Q—Never mind Kruger. Let's get the story.

A—O.K. After the other people go, there's some kind of fuss about sending the cook to a conservatory for four years to study music. She's written a symphony or something.

Q—What?

A—Well, I guess not the cook. The maid. Anyway, he wants to send her to music school, but his wife says no. She is a hell of a difficult woman. Jessie Royce Landis. Then an old friend of his, a doctor, comes in, and they start to play chess. It isn't much of a game, because Little A is terribly depressed. It seems that in addition to everything else, he suspects that his son isn't his at all but his father's. He has some poison in a desk drawer and apparently he's been playing with the idea of taking it and getting out from under the whole business. Say, listen, you don't really want all this stuff, do you?

Q—I guess you might condense it just a *bit* more.

A—I thought so. In a little while the son, who has come home from college, insults the maid and then knocks Kruger down for butting in. It turns out somewhere in here that the boy really is Big A's son—and, incidentally, Little A's half brother, though we don't need to go into that—so Little A puts the poison in his wife's sherry. A form of moral criticism, you might say. At the last minute, though, he decides not to kill her; he figures it would be simpler just to leave town. Well, his wife doesn't want any part of that, on the ground that it would ruin her socially, and she hatches up this scheme to have him declared insane.

Q—That would be O.K. socially?

A—I don't know. I'm just telling you what happens. Anyway, she invites that couple from the first scene back again, and when he refuses to act in the local minstrel show and goes on to call her a whore, everybody can see she has quite a case, especially since his mother had been crazy for years before she died. Had enough?

Q—Oh, you might as well tell me how it turns out.

A—All right, you asked for it, but I'm afraid it isn't going to make much sense. She's going to have him committed and, as I've said, the evidence looks pretty bad for him, so he takes the gun—I forgot to say that Big A always kept a gun in his desk—and threatens to shoot her. There is a lot of talk in here and maybe my mind wandered a little, but somehow or other she gets it away from him and—boy, you'd never figure this one out, not if I gave you a week.

Q—No?

A—No. What happens is she's standing there, not three feet from him, and suddenly she pulls the trigger, and, by God, she misses him by a foot.

Q—Oh. That the end?

A—Certainly not. She misses her husband all right, but her son just happens to be coming downstairs at that moment, and I'll be damned if she doesn't get *him*. He just kind of gasps, "Oh, Mummy," and drops dead.

Q—I see. And what was your word for all this again?

A—Amorphous. I just couldn't seem to follow the damn thing.

Q—Yes. Yes, on the whole I think I see what you mean. Case dismissed.

January 25, 1947

LOWER DEPTHS,
SOUTHERN STYLE
(*A Streetcar Named Desire*)

A Streetcar Named Desire," by Tennessee Williams, is a fine and deeply disturbing play, almost faultless in the physical details of its production and the quality of its acting. It is hard to define it very satisfactorily for those who haven't seen it. Most of us at one time or another have come on some incident in the street, some scene of senseless brutality or intolerable humiliation, that struck us inescapably as the last act in a life. Usually, of course, we were mistaken, since the real climaxes are almost never identifiable, but still it gave the imagination, especially if literary, something to wrestle with, and often we got home with quite a story worked out in our heads. Mr. Williams' play might easily be the triumphant product of just such an experience. The last scene shows a woman being led away from a crumbling house in a nightmare street. She is not young, being in her middle thirties, but she is still handsome and she has a certain amount of style—Old South, as it happens, but still style—both in her manner and her dress. It would not be necessary to identify the two people with her as a doctor and an asylum attendant for anyone to see that she is quite mad. Obviously, any explanation for such a moment, for such a coincidence of smiling insanity—she is clearly delighted with her companions—and ruined elegance and unspeakable squalor, is faced with the danger of seeming either hopelessly inadequate or absurdly melodramatic. All I can say is that Mr. Williams has written a strong, wholly believable play that, starting in a low key, mounts slowly and inexorably to its shocking climax. I think it is an imperfect play, for reasons that I'll get around to in a minute, but it is certainly the most impressive one that has turned up this season, and I wouldn't be surprised if it was a sounder and more mature work than "The Glass Menagerie," the author's previous compliment to Southern womanhood.

Mr. Williams has placed "A Streetcar Named Desire" in the Vieux Carré in New Orleans, where it seems there is or was just such a car, as well as one labelled "Cemetery" and a neighborhood known as the Elysian Fields, life in this case being singularly obliging to art. The set represents the two-room apartment occupied by Stanley Kowalski, a young Pole somehow cryptically connected with the automobile business, and his pregnant bride, Stella, a fine, highly sexed girl, though the daughter of that most exhausted of all aristocracies, an old Southern family. It is possible that some scenic artist somewhere has contrived a more gruesome interior than the decaying horror that Jo Mielziner has executed for the Kowalskis, but I doubt it. It is on the ground floor (outside, a circular iron staircase winds up to another apartment, containing perhaps the least inhibited married couple ever offered on the stage); there is no door between the two rooms, only a curtain; the furnishings are sparse and dreadful; the desolate street outside can be seen through the windows, or, rather, through the walls, since Mr. Mielziner's design is by no means literal. It is a wonderful effect and, as the evening wears along, oppressive almost beyond words.

One spring morning, Stella's older sister, Blanche, turns up at this hovel. She is a strange girl, but at first there is nothing visibly wrong with her except a slight hysteria, which she tries to fight down with frequent surreptitious drinks of whiskey, and that grotesque and terrible refinement that Mr. Williams has carried over from his portrait of the mother in "The Glass Menagerie." She is fashionably appalled by the Kowalski apartment and the goings on in it, which include an incredibly seedy, brawling poker game, but this is nothing compared with the dismay she experiences at her first sight of her sister's husband. This is understandable, since, thanks to a peculiar combination of script and casting, this character emerges as almost wholly subhuman—illiterate, dirty, violent and even somehow with a suggestion of physical deformity, an apelike quality, about him. In addition to the personal disgust he inspires in her, Blanche is slowly forced to realize that her desperate pretending is no good with him; from the moment she comes in, he suspects the unbearable truth about her, and when she seems to be infecting her sister with her stylish ways, he drags it out into the light, with contemptuous brutality.

It is something of a tribute to Mr. Williams' talent that the story of Blanche's past can seem even momentarily credible. The two girls were brought up in an old house, apparently the conventional "decaying mansion," which he has chosen to call Belle Rêve, though they pronounce it "Belle Reeve." Like Stella, Blanche married, but it was a brief and tragic escape, since the boy was a homosexual who shot himself after his seventeen-year-old bride had discovered him in a situation that could hardly be misinterpreted. She went back to Belle Rêve, where she watched the awful, lingering deaths of three old women, and then, when the creditors had taken the house, went on to a town called Laurel, where she taught school and gradually, in a sick—or quite possibly, by this time, an insane—revulsion against death, took up with many men. The Laurel episode ended with her seduction of an adolescent boy (youth plus love, I gather, seemed to her the absolute antithesis of death, though, of course, some authorities might have diagnosed simple nymphomania) and with her expulsion from the town, where, in her brother-in-law's sardonic phrase, she was getting to be somewhat better known than the President of the United States.

By the time Blanche comes to her sister's apartment, she has manufactured a gaudy and pathetic substitute past for herself, full of rich and handsome suitors, who respectfully admire her mind, but Kowalski tears that down ruthlessly, without any special moral indignation but with a savage, obscene humor that is infinitely more torturing. He also gives her secret away to the one man—a poor specimen, but kind and honest—who might conceivably have saved her and then takes her, casually and contemptuously, himself. The end comes when she tries to tell this to her sister, who, unable to believe it and still go on with her marriage, consents to having her committed to an asylum. This is, I'm afraid, a pretty poor synopsis—there is no way, for instance, to convey the effect Mr. Williams achieves in his last act of a mind desperately retreating into the beautiful, crazy world it has built for itself—but perhaps it is enough to give you the general idea.

The reservations I have may easily be captious. Principally, it seems to me that in the emotional surge of writing his play Mr. Williams has been guilty of establishing a too facile and romantic connection between Belle Rêve and the Vieux Carré. Not knowing much about the South, old or new, it was hard for me to visualize the girls' ancestral home, except as something vaguely resembling the House of Usher, but Stella is written and played as a pretty, reasonably cultivated girl, in no sense unbalanced, and her abrupt and cheerful descent into the lower depths of New Orleans seems rather incredible. Mr. Williams attempts, though the evidence on the stage is against him, to portray Kowalski as a man of enormous sexual attraction, so that the very sight of him causes her to see colored pinwheels, but even that is scarcely enough. It is the same, to some extent, with Blanche; whatever the forces working against her may have been, her degradation is much too rapid and complete, her fall from whatever position she may have occupied in a top level of society to the bottom of the last level a good deal more picturesque than probable. As I say, it is conceivable that these transitions do occur in the South, but it is my suspicion that Mr. Williams has adjusted life fairly drastically to fit his special theme. The only other thing I might complain about (Blanche's arrival from Laurel, where apparently she had just been tossed out of a cheap hotel, with a trunkful of pretty expensive-looking jewelry and clothes perplexed me *some*, but I'm willing to let it go) is the somewhat strained and literary analogy that keeps turning up between the streetcars named for passion and death and the tragic conflict in the heroine's mind. Mr. Williams seems to me much too good a playwright now to bother his head with these ladies'-club mystifications. "A Streetcar Named Desire" is a brilliant, implacable play about the disintegration of a woman, or, if you like, of a society; it has no possible need for the kind of pseudo-poetic decoration that more vacant authors so often employ to disguise their fundamental lack of thought.

After all that, I'm sorry to say there isn't much room left for the compliments to the cast, though God knows they and, of course, Elia Kazan, their director, deserve all I can offer them. Briefly, Jessica Tandy gives a superb, steadily rising performance as Blanche; Marlon Brando, as Kowalski, is, as hinted previously, almost pure ape (his sister-in-law's description of him as "common" entertained me quite a lot, there in the dark), and though he undoubtedly emphasizes the horrors of the Vieux Carré as opposed to Belle Rêve, it is a brutally effective characterization; Karl Malden, as Blanche's unhappy suitor, gets a queer, touching blend of dignity and pathos into what you might call one of those difficult, *listening* parts; and Kim Hunter, as Stella, is sympathetic and restrained and very decorative indeed. The others, representing the inhabitants of that abandoned district, all seemed admirable and awful to me.

December 13, 1947

WELL WORTH WAITING FOR
(*Death of a Salesman*)

Though it seems to me that Arthur Miller still has a ten-dency to overwrite now and then, his "Death of a Salesman," at the Morosco, is a tremendously affecting work, head and shoulders above any other serious play we have seen this season. It is the story of Willy Loman, a man at the end of his rope, told with a mixture of compassion, imagination, and hard technical competence you don't often find in the theatre today, and probably the highest compliment I can pay it is to say that I don't see how it can possibly be made into a moving picture, though I have very little doubt that somehow or other eventually it will. The acting, especially that of Lee J. Cobb, as the tragic central figure, Mildred Dunnock, as his loyal wife, and Arthur Kennedy, as a son whose character he has lovingly and unconsciously destroyed, is honest, restrained, and singularly moving; Jo Mielziner's set, centering on the interior of a crumbling house somewhere in Brooklyn but permitting the action to shift as far away as a shoddy hotel room in Boston, is as brilliant and resourceful as the one he did for "A Streetcar Named Desire;" Elia Kazan, also, of course, an important collaborator on "Streetcar," has directed the cast with the greatest possible intelligence, getting the most out of a script that must have presented its difficulties; and an incidental score, by Alex North, serves admirably to introduce the stretches of memory and hallucination that alternate with the actual contemporary scenes on the stage. Kermit Bloomgarden and Walter Fried, to round out this catalogue of applause, are the fortunate producers of "Death of a Salesman," and I think the whole town ought to be very grateful to them.

The happenings in Mr. Miller's play can hardly be called dramatic in any conventional sense. Willy is sixty-three years old, and he has spent most of his life as the New England representative of a company that I gathered sells stockings, though this point was never exactly specified. Recently the firm has cut off his salary and put him on straight commission, and the income from that is obviously not enough for him to get along on, what with a mortgage, and insurance, and the recurring payments on an electric icebox, an ancient contraption about which he remarks bitterly, "God, for once I'd like to own something before it's broken down!" In addition to his financial troubles, his health and his mind are failing (he has been having a series of automobile accidents, basically suicidal in intent), and his two sons aren't much comfort to him. Long ago, he had had muddled, childish dreams for them both—the elder, in particular, was to be a famous football star, greater than Red Grange—but things didn't work out, and now one is a stock clerk, not interested in much except women, and the other, when he works at all, is just an itinerant farmhand. Willy's deep, hopeless recognition of what has become of him, of the fact that, mysteriously, society has no further use for him, has reduced him to a strange borderland of sanity, in which fantasy is barely distinguishable from reality. The only remaining hope he has, in fact, lies in some crack-brained scheme the two boys have for making a fortune selling sport goods in Florida, and when that collapses, too, there is clearly nothing left for him but to kill himself, knowing that at least his family will manage somehow to survive on the money from his insurance.

That is the rough outline of Mr. Miller's play, and it doesn't, I'm afraid, give you much idea of the quality of his work, of how unerringly he has drawn the portrait of a failure, a man who has finally broken under the pressures of an economic system that he is fatally incapable of understanding. There are unforgettable scenes: the interview in which he is fired by the head of the firm, a brassy young man, who plays a hideous private recording in which his little boy names the capitals of all the states, in alphabetical order; a sequence in the Boston hotel, when his son finds him with a tart and his love turns to hatred and contempt; a dream meeting with his brother Ben, who has made a fortune in diamonds in the Kimberley mines and stands, in his mind, as the savage, piratical symbol of success; and, near the end of the play, a truly heartbreaking moment when

Willy at last comes to realize that he is "a dollar-an-hour man" who could never, conceivably, have been anything more.

"Death of a Salesman" is written throughout with an accurate feeling for speech and behavior that few current playwrights can equal. It may not be a great play, whatever that means, but it is certainly a very eloquent and touching one. The cast, besides Mr. Cobb, Miss Dunnock, and Mr. Kennedy, includes Cameron Mitchell, Thomas Chalmers, Howard Smith, Don Keefer, and Alan Hewitt. They are all just what I'm sure the author hoped they'd be.

February 19, 1949

WHAT A WONDERFUL WAR
(*South Pacific*)

W HILE "SOUTH PACIFIC," the only musical, as far as I know, ever to be based on a Pulitzer Prize book, lacks the special quality of "Oklahoma!," a sort of continuous sunny gaiety, it has about everything else. Richard Rodgers' score, if not his best, certainly isn't far from it, and Oscar Hammerstein's lyrics, with one or two exceptions, are just as successful; the plot, a difficult combination of sentimental love, tragic passion, and the rowdy behavior of our armed forces, is admirably handled on all three levels; the performances, especially those of Ezio Pinza and Mary Martin, are practically flawless; and Jo Mielziner's sets, ranging from the cockeyed disorder of a naval base to the strange beauty of a tropical island, are executed with extraordinary humor and charm. Altogether, it is a fine show, and I wouldn't be surprised if it were still at the Majestic when another Presidential election rolls around.

I don't remember James Michener's stories very clearly (somehow I have a feeling that they weren't really especially memorable) but I do know that it never occurred to me that they might furnish material for a musical comedy, since, like most honest pieces about war, they hadn't much in the way of orderly design and an acceptable love interest was conspicuously missing. However, Mr. Hammerstein and Joshua Logan, who collaborated with him on the libretto in addition to serving as director, have taken care of all that with the greatest possible ingenuity. The principal theme now is the romance between an exiled French planter, who didn't, as I recall, appear at all in Mr. Michener's book, and a jaunty nurse from Little Rock, Arkansas, who did turn up in one of the stories, though in a rather different context.[1] The only obstacle to their marriage is the fact that he is the father of two children by a Polynesian wife, and though she has died, it is a circumstance that would probably make any young woman think twice.

The secondary plot has to do with a lieutenant of Marines and his affair with a beautiful native girl. This is doomed from the outset, partly because her mother is a disreputable old baggage, dealing in grass skirts and shrunken human heads, but mostly because he is a native of Philadelphia and a graduate of Princeton and, naturally, somewhat conscious of his glorious heritage. These two separate but parallel stories are firmly joined together in the end, when the two men undertake a suicidal mission against the Japanese (an English remittance man was the hero of this episode in Mr. Michener's version), in the course of which the Marine is killed but from which the planter comes back to the nurse, who by now has realized the error of her ways. As you can see, this is a fairly weighty narrative sequence, calling for a liberal administration of comic relief. I'm glad to say that the authors have been generously and happily inspired about that, too, creating any number of fine, tough characters and providing them with some wonderfully funny material, including a vaudeville number, featuring Miss Martin in an outsize sailor suit and Myron McCormick with a full-rigged vessel tattooed on his heaving stomach, that may be the best show-inside-a-show you ever saw.

Some time ago, in an interview, Cole Porter remarked that he wished to hell theatre critics would refrain from discussing music, on the ground that even the most educated of them wouldn't recognize the national anthem unless the people around them stood up. Having taken this advice to heart, I will confine my comment on Mr. Rodgers' score to saying that "Some Enchanted Evening," magnificently delivered by Mr. Pinza, seems to me a tremendously moving song; that "I'm Gonna Wash That Guy Right Outa My Hair" and "I'm in Love with a Wonderful Guy," as rendered by Miss Martin, and "There Is Nothing Like a Dame," as sung, or bellowed, by the naval personnel, strike me as being among the liveliest of Mr. Rodgers' and Mr. Hammerstein's joint efforts; and, to intrude one dissenting note in this rhapsody, that I wasn't particularly impressed by "Bali Ha'i," which sounded to me a good deal like any number of other songs celebrating exotic place names, or by something called "You've Got to Be Taught," a poem in praise of tolerance that somehow I found just a little embarrassing.

There is nothing, of course, to say about Mr. Pinza's voice, beyond the fact that no greater one has been heard on the musical-comedy stage. Since he is also an intelligent and imposing actor, his appearance in "South Pacific" is one of the pleasantest things that have happened to the theatre this season. Miss Martin, whose talents as a comedienne haven't had much scope, at least in New York, since she first enchanted us all with "My Heart Belongs to Daddy," has just what she wants this time, and I think her performance is a delight from beginning to end. Of the others, Mr. McCormick gives perhaps the funniest and most hideous female impersonation in history; Betta St. John is astonishingly lovely as a kind of Tonkinese Madame Butterfly; Juanita Hall, as her unspeakable mother, is not only an accomplished comedienne but also the possessor of another notable voice; and there are sound, attractive contributions by William Tabbert, as the faithless Princetonian, and by Martin Wolfson and Harvey Stephens, as a couple of irascible officers. The nine young ladies who represent Navy nurses didn't look very medical to me.

April 16, 1949

BROOK AND RIVER
(*The Member of the Wedding*)

"THE MEMBER OF the Wedding," Carson McCullers' dramatization of her novel, is unquestionably the first serious new play of any consequence to reach Broadway this season. It has a good many touching and rather difficult things to say; it often has a queer, fantastic wit, not unlike Saroyan's; occasionally it reaches something very close to poetry; and it is illuminated by a magnificent performance by Ethel Waters and two remarkably spirited ones by Julie Harris and a seven-year-old boy named Brandon De Wilde. In spite of all this, however, I'm afraid that the piece at the Empire isn't entirely satisfactory from a theatrical point of view. The principal trouble, I think, is that Mrs. McCullers has tried to transfer her book too literally to the stage; to crowd, that is, the whole mysterious desperation of adolescence into three acts, along with a fairly exhaustive discussion of the complicated theme of race relations in the South. The result is a curiously uneven work—sometimes funny, sometimes moving, but also, unfortunately, sometimes just a trifle incoherent and shapeless.

The heroine of "The Member of the Wedding" is a rather plain twelve-year-old girl who is known to an insensitive world as Frankie Addams, though she prefers to think of herself as F. Jasmine Addams, and she lives with her widowed father and their old Negro cook, Berenice Sadie Brown, who has one bright-blue glass eye, in a small town in Georgia. Frankie has a great deal on her mind (at twelve, for instance, she is five feet five and three-quarter inches tall and at the rate she's going she is gloomily certain that she'll hit a good ten feet by the time she's twenty-one), but the real root of her unhappiness is her terrible sense of being alone, separate from everybody else in the world, both children and adults. Primarily, this feeling is a symptom of her age, but as it happens she really hasn't

much of a social life, since the slightly older girls in the neighborhood have banned her from their club, and her only companions
are Berenice and a cousin some six years her junior, who is moderately silly even as little boys go. At this point, when Frankie's need
to attach herself to something or somebody is almost unbearable,
her brother drops in with his fiancée. They seem to her the two
most beautiful people who ever lived, and she decides to join them
on their honeymoon, which she vaguely pictures as a triumphal tour
around the world, going on forever. Berenice, who has had a wide
experience with matrimony, tries to explain that membership in
weddings is customarily limited to two, but Frankie's dream of being part of something at last, especially something that promises to
be not only strange and lovely but also infinitely removed from
Georgia, is too strong for cynical arguments like that, and she goes
ahead with her plans, which include the purchase of a red evening
dress, cut right down to the waist in the back. In the end, of course,
she is left behind, and though the bridal pair do their best to spare
her feelings, for a time she is desolate, even to the point of attempting suicide. Sad as it is, this disillusionment has the effect of putting
an end to Frankie's childhood, and in the last scene we find her
reasonably adjusted to her surroundings, being, in fact, about to go
for a ride on a moving van with a young football player and his girl.

Mrs. McCullers has a peculiar gift for creating characters im-
mune to the usual rules of human behavior, and it is possible to accept the fact that Frankie can be an almost total biological ignoramus
while living in a circle where practically nothing else is ever discussed, and while herself employing most of the popular terminol-
ogy. She is not exactly a girl who will bear examination in retrospect,
but in her presence I was bewitched by her and saw no reason at all to
suppose that wedding bells and sex would have any vulgar association
in her mind. Miss Harris may be overplaying this part a trifle from
time to time, once to the extent of introducing a cartwheel into it,
but on the whole I admired her performance and concur in the general opinion that she is one of the most talented young actresses
around today.

The two other major figures in the play are also very fascinating,
if not quite so original in design. Berenice was absolutely happy

with her first husband, but he died and since then she has been trying to console herself with the "bits and pieces" of him that she has
found in other men. She serves chiefly as a contrast to Frankie's in-
experience and as her only refuge in her distress. This is obviously a
role with disastrous possibilities, but the writing, except in one or
two places, is free from bathos, and Miss Waters' interpretation is a
miraculously balanced combination of rowdy humor and sorrowful
understanding. The cousin, played by young De Wilde, struck me as
one of the few completely believable little boys ever put on the stage,
and I felt a strong sense of personal loss when Mrs. McCullers, for
rather arbitrary reasons, decided to kill him off in her last act.

The racial subplot, which, as I say, seems to me only to confuse
and diminish the play, however much it may have been an organic
part of the novel, has to do with a young mulatto, Berenice's foster
brother, who knifes a white man while under the influence of mari-
juana and subsequently hangs himself in jail. His abrupt and violent
end, coinciding with the cousin's death from meningitis, provides
"The Member of the Wedding" with a lively, if lugubrious, conclusion, but somehow it also introduces an element of contrived
melodrama out of keeping with the delicate mood that has been so
successfully sustained throughout most of the evening.

The cast, brilliantly directed by Harold Clurman, also includes
William Hansen, Harry Bolden, Henry Scott, and James Holden. I
can't remember a more engaging group of supporting players, and
Lester Polakov's set, presumably representing a typical Georgia
kitchen, would astonish Jeeter Lester with its neat and airy look.

January 14, 1950

ELIOT AND OTHERS

(The Cocktail Party)

"THE COCKTAIL PARTY," by T. S. Eliot, is, I should say, the knottiest problem presented to local criticism since "The Iceman Cometh." It is obviously a work of considerable literary importance, but, regarded sheerly as a play, its merits and its chances for success in the non-experimental theatre seem to me debatable. In form, it is essentially an alternation of scenes of English comedy, so high as to be occasionally almost inaudible to the American ear, with scenes of religious mysticism whose meaning is sometimes clear but sometimes seems to lie about nine-tenths submerged, like an iceberg. The transitions from one mood to the other are oddly abrupt, and whether wit and poetry, so closely juxtaposed, haven't a tendency to diminish one another, at least in the minds of audiences unaccustomed to such emotional roller-coasting, is a hard question. The opening-night gathering at the Henry Miller was a special one, well aware of the stern challenge to its culture, but even in it the pangs of adjustment were evident from time to time, and I suspect that subsequent ones may be even more distressed.

Mr. Eliot's comedy, to investigate the two levels of "The Cocktail Party" a little more closely, is partly the kind of thing that Noel Coward might have turned out if that fashionable elf had enjoyed the benefits of a classical education and some decent intellectual companionship. There is the same facile exchange of insult, the same profuse and airy reference to titles and great estates, and the same intense but rather disembodied preoccupation with sex. Mr. Eliot, however, is a far more versatile humorist than Coward, and this drawing-room frivolity is often relieved by passages of authentic satire, on both manners and politics, that recall Evelyn Waugh at his murderous best, and even once or twice by a paradox startling enough to charm Shaw himself. Altogether, it is a fascinating performance, superior in style and intelligence to anything else being done now on either side of the Atlantic, and I like to dream that someday its author may so far demean himself as to write an entire play in this vein alone.

The loftier portions of "The Cocktail Party" are much harder to define. As I've said, there are times when the messages Mr. Eliot has to deliver are perfectly clear and the language in which they are clothed, if something more than the speech of common humanity, is still controlled and lucid. There are many other times, however, when his ideas seem swallowed up in his own subtlety and eloquence, and the effect is rather like listening to a brilliant man who has reached that point of intoxication when, while it is plain that his mind is a treasure house of profoundly important thoughts, the things he actually says are no more than fragmentary clues, majestic in sound and syntax, almost unendurably provocative, but impossible to piece together into a coherent whole. I haven't seen the script of Mr. Eliot's play, and it may easily be that what on the stage often appears to be a losing struggle to express the nearly inexpressible presents no difficulties to the attentive reader, who can, of course, always go back and try an elusive passage again. The condition of a man sitting in a theatre, however, is quite different, and there were measurable stretches in "The Cocktail Party" when I had only the vaguest notion of what its author was trying to communicate to me, and even some when I seriously doubted if he knew himself.

Like a great many plays of a fundamentally poetic nature, the plot of this one isn't easy to reduce to rational synopsis, but if you'll take my hand, I'll do my best. Edward Chamberlayne is a middle-aged London barrister, and soon after the curtain rises we hear him explaining to a mysterious guest at a cocktail party he is giving that his wife, Lavinia, has left him after five years of practically incessant bickering and he's damned if he knows whether he wants her back again. There are weighty arguments both for and against a permanent separation, all almost eerily sophisticated, but at length the stranger persuades him that Lavinia had better come home and announces that, indeed, arrangements have already been made for her to do so. There are other people intermittently present in the course of this scene, notably Julia Shuttlethwaite, who seems at this point to be no more than a remarkably addled and tedious old lady; Alexander Gibbs, a world traveller and gourmet and also visibly a nuisance; Peter Quilpe, an earnest young man, with advanced ideas about the cinema; and Celia Coplestone, a beautiful young woman to whom Quilpe is strongly attracted, both artistically and emotionally. The party finally dissolves (I am condensing rather drastically here, since most of the guests are in and out of Chamberlayne's apartment all night) and Miss Coplestone returns. It seems that she is her host's mistress and, aware that Lavinia has left, is happily confident that there is no longer any sensible impediment to their romance. When he reluctantly informs her that this is not the case, adding, presumably for the sake of her feelings, that he has been obliged to face the fact that he is getting on in years and would be of little further use to a girl, she is naturally agitated and tells him, among other things, that he reminds her of nothing so much as a man-sized beetle, capable of producing only a thin, scraping sound by rubbing his back legs together. They part more or less on this note. Soon after that, Lavinia returns and he is not astonished to find that she is exactly as awful as he had remembered—a tiresome, domineering woman, principally interested in breaking his spirit. Since her opinion of him is even lower, the reunion isn't a success, and soon they are both patients of the same psychiatrist, who, as you've probably deduced, turns out to be none other than the unknown guest at the party.

Mr. Eliot's second act is devoted to unravelling the difficulties of these three people, and by extension, I suppose, those of a whole ailing society. It is here that his mingling of comedy and mysticism reaches its height. The scene in which the doctor, abetted by Gibbs and Mrs. Shuttlethwaite, who appear to be in some sort of cryptic partnership with him, persuades the Chamberlaynes to give their marriage still another try is brilliantly funny, and its contrast with the interview that follows is startling, to put it very temperately. This has to do with the far more taxing case of Miss Coplestone, whose disappointment in Chamberlayne has somehow resolved itself into a sense of guilt and a necessity for atonement, not because of anything as elementary as sin but because of her tragic failure to hold the vision, the "treasure," she once had in her heart. The doctor suggests that she can forget her loss in a normal life, with a husband and children, but she has no wish to forget, since that would be the final loss, and he offers her the only other possible course, which is a life of austere and disinterested service. With his blessing, she goes off to join a religious nursing unit and eventually to meet her death by crucifixion in a primitive village somewhere in Asia. At a second cocktail party, given by the now peacefully adjusted Chamberlaynes, it is generally agreed that no other end could have fulfilled her destiny or satisfied her troubled spirit. Mr. Eliot's language throughout these final scenes is on an extremely elevated plane and I'm not sure that I caught more than a very small part of his meaning, but it is enough, I think, to indicate that "The Cocktail Party" is a highly diversified entertainment, calling for a certain amount of mental agility in the spectator, as well as some familiarity with the esoteric formulas of the Roman Catholic Church.

The English cast, directed by E. Martin Browne, is excellent throughout, and Alec Guinness, as the psychiatrist; Cathleen Nesbitt, as Mrs. Shuttlethwaite; Irene Worth, as Miss Coplestone; Robert Flemyng, as Chamberlayne; and Eileen Peel, as his wife, give really superlative performances, managing Mr. Eliot's intricate prose and sudden changes in mood with great style and every appearance of perfect ease. Raymond Sovey's two settings—a fashionable drawing room and a doctor's office—are as handsome as anything I've seen this season.

January 28, 1950

BOUQUETS, BRICKBATS,
AND OBITUARIES
(*Guys and Dolls*)

I DON'T THINK I ever had more fun at a musical comedy than I had the other night, when an association of strangely gifted men put on a Broadway epic known as "Guys and Dolls." There have been loftier moral and aesthetic experiences, like "Show Boat" and "South Pacific;" there have been more enduring musical accomplishments, like "Porgy and Bess;" there have been occasions when the humor was clearly on a more ambitious level, like "Of Thee I Sing;" there have been more sensational individual performances, like practically anything involving Miss Ethel Merman. There has, however, been nothing I can remember that sustained a higher general level of sheer entertainment than the operation at the Forty-sixth Street Theatre. In form and content, the closest thing to it was "Pal Joey," but even that fine essay in jocular corruption had its moments when I wished the cast would move on to something else. There were none such—for me, at least—in "Guys and Dolls." The credits on the program note that the piece was produced by Cy Feuer and Ernest H. Martin; that the book was adapted, by Jo Swerling and Abe Burrows, from a story by the late Damon Runyon; that the music and lyrics were the work of Frank Loesser; that the settings were designed by Jo Mielziner and the costumes by Alvin Colt; that the dances were staged by Michael Kidd; and that George S. Kaufman was responsible for the direction. There isn't a man on this list who hasn't my deepest admiration and gratitude.

I haven't any idea how closely the story Mr. Swerling and Mr. Burrows have chosen follows the original, since it is one of the holes in my culture that I have read very little Runyon, whose idiom I always suspected—wrongfully, I'm sure—of being more or less synthetic, like Milt Gross's approximation of the vernacular of the

Bronx, and whose plots, or at least the few with which I am familiar, leaned heavily on the old O. Henry switch at the end. Both these faults, if they are faults, are visible in the play version. The speech employed by the characters is a heightened parody, and not a very accurate one, of that used by the Broadway types, including a good many horseplayers, of my acquaintance, and the switch is certainly present, especially when the toughest gambler of them all turns up as a member of a mission band. I don't think these things make any difference, and it may even be that what were flaws in fiction are virtues on the stage, where broad strokes and slapstick techniques are practically obligatory.

Mr. Swerling and Mr. Burrows, to get down to a rough outline of the facts, are primarily interested in two romances—one between Nathan Detroit, the impresario of the oldest floating crap game in New York, and a blonde, to whom he has been engaged for fourteen years, who heads the floor show in a joint called the Hot Box; the other between the gambler mentioned above, whose name is Sky Masterson, and the young lady in charge of the mission. Detroit, who needs a thousand dollars to rent a suitable site for his crap game, makes a bet for that amount with Masterson, who gambles on his ability to persuade the girl from the mission to accompany him to Havana. He succeeds, but, yielding to a soft impulse brought on by love, gallantly denies that he did, thus enabling the boys to get on with their game. Somehow or other (the details would just mix you up), everything works out satisfactorily, at least from the feminine point of view, and the final curtain falls on a rash of weddings. It is as simple as that.

I can list only a few of the brilliant and hilarious things that ornament this framework. Vivian Blaine, as the nightclub singer, has two numbers, one explaining how emotional frustration can give a girl a bad cold in her head, and the other an indignant ditty known as "Take Back Your Mink" ("to from whence it came"), that are as funny and as impressively delivered as anything you'll hear this season. Isabel Bigley, as the evangelist, has a face, a voice, and a figure that are all astonishing, to put it mildly, and her material, especially two sentimental songs called "If I Were a Bell" and "I'll Know," and a frivolous duet with Miss Blaine labelled "Marry the Man Today," is well worthy of all these talents. There is a memorable scene in which fifteen or twenty gamblers are tricked somehow into the mission and presently find themselves carolling something called "Follow the Fold," and another, involving some excellent dancing, in which they are all happily congregated in a sewer, shooting dice. The guys and dolls, in addition to those already named, bear such names as Nicely-Nicely Johnson, Benny Southstreet, Harry the Horse, and Angie the Ox. They are all hoarse in their speech, disreputable in their ways, and seriously misguided in the matter of shirts and ties. The actors who impersonate Detroit and Masterson are Sam Levene and Robert Alda, respectively, and they are superb at capturing that indefinable blend of terrible sentimentality and brassy sophistication that characterizes the Times Square man of distinction. The others include Stubby Kaye, Johnny Silver, Tom Pedi, and B. S. Pully, and I found each of them awe-inspiring, too. Among the virtuous members of the company are Paul Reed, as a hardboiled detective; Netta Packer, as the commanding officer of the mission band; and Pat Rooney, Sr., who, as one of her lieutenants, sings a song, called "More I Cannot Wish You," that is one of the pleasantest things in the show.

December 2, 1950

THERE'S ALWAYS RODGERS AND HAMMERSTEIN

(Me and Juliet)

WITH THE EXCEPTION of a piece called "Allegro," which, you may remember, had something to do with the superiority of the old-fashioned general medical practitioner over the Park Avenue specialist, "Me and Juliet," currently visible at the Majestic, is the first play by Richard Rodgers and Oscar Hammerstein II that has not been adapted from a work by somebody else. The lesson here, I guess, is that these two great men, while practically incomparable when it comes to adjusting material from one medium to another, are somehow lacking in invention of their own. This offering of theirs benefits enormously from Jo Mielziner's very fine settings; from the work of Irene Sharaff, who has designed costumes that fall into a mood I frequently found remarkably attractive; from Robert Alton's dances, which, as usual, are ingenious and completely in key with what the authors are trying to get at; and from the cast, which, on the whole, shows a gaiety and humor that often make listless or perfunctory scenes seem a good deal more entertaining than they actually are.

The chief fault undoubtedly lies with Mr. Hammerstein, who has written a book in praise of the romance and eternal durability of the stage, and furnished lyrics to somewhat the same effect, but part of the blame must be attributed to Mr. Rodgers, whose tunes certainly lack his customary verve. These include specimens called "A Very Special Day," "Marriage Type Love," "It Feels Good," "No Other Love," "Keep It Gay," "I'm Your Girl," "We Deserve Each Other," and "The Big, Black Giant," the last of which, a sort of indignant tribute to the power of audiences to make or break shows, may easily be one of the most painfully self-conscious contributions to popular music. Some of these are, of course, effective, but the general level is apt to be a little dismaying to admirers of "Oklahoma!" and "South Pacific."

The story deals with a play within a play, a theme that has entranced quite a few dramatists in our time. A producer called Mr. Harrison, who is audible but never seen, has, it appears, put on a spectacle with the same name as the piece at the Majestic, and the action oscillates between what the audience sees of this production and what goes on backstage during run-throughs. This involves a triangular love affair in which a young chorus girl, a drunken electrician, and an assistant stage manager are mixed up; another romance, having to do with the principal dancer and another executive in the company; and an orchestra leader who is perpetually frustrated in his efforts to find a beautiful woman who has been writing him love letters. There is some comic business attending all this—a lobby scene in which the authors express their real opinion of audiences, a sequence when the girls and boys change from their costumes to their rehearsal clothes almost in the twinkling of an eye, and a dance that astonished even me—but it is hard to believe that there is enough to entertain the public forever, which is the established tradition of this firm.

The star of "Me and Juliet" is, I suppose, Isabel Bigley, lately of "Guys and Dolls," who is in charge of a large part of the sex and appears to be most highly regarded by the management, but my own favorite is Joan McCracken, whose behavior, especially in the dance referred to above, would surely intimidate all proper Bostonians, not to mention the inhabitants of the great Middle West. Among the other featured players are Bill Hayes, Mark Dawson, and Jackie Kelk. George Abbott is the director, and the chances are he got as much fun as possible out of an unpromising script.

June 6, 1953

SOMETHING TO REMEMBER US BY

(*Cat on a Hot Tin Roof*)

O<small>N THE WHOLE</small>, this has been a barren year in the theatre (it has, in fact, been so barren that there has been scarcely a play I couldn't imagine having written myself, suitably stimulated), and it is therefore a pleasure to announce that Tennessee Williams, well known to you, I'm sure, for "The Glass Menagerie" and "A Streetcar Named Desire," has written an almost wholly admirable play called "Cat on a Hot Tin Roof," recently unveiled at the Morosco.

The story Mr. Williams has to tell is hard to summarize very intelligibly, because it deals with emotions rather outside our common, or at least acknowledged, experience. The play begins with a scene between a young woman and her husband, who has withdrawn from any real participation in life. In college, he reached a kind of limited excellence as a football player, and had a never quite explicitly homosexual relationship with another student, which makes it impossible for him to accept a world that seems to fall so far and disgustingly (this word is Mr. Williams') short of his adolescent dream. Anyway, he has taken to drink and has injured himself in a childish and drunken effort to recapture the athletic splendors of the past. His wife loves him, but her physical advances are repugnant to him and he is much too remote to appreciate the desperate humor of her conversation. There is no conceivable method of communication between them, and although it appears to me that Mr. Williams' specific dilemma is a little bizarre, his underlying thought is just as simple as this: the profound and tragic mystery that every man is to every other man in the world, and even to himself.

The plot is not much more than a serviceable mechanism for conveying the author's ideas. A rich old man, the hero's father, has come back, on his sixty-fifth birthday, to the family plantation. While an erroneous laboratory report has led him to suppose that he still has a good many years to live, the fact is that he is dying of cancer, and when he finds that out, he is obliged to make a final settlement of his affairs. This involves choosing as his heir either a boy whom he recognizes as an alcoholic and probably a homosexual or a son who is a competent bore with five existing children and another imminent. In a way, Mr. Williams has stacked his cards a little too obviously, since his corrupted idealist is as picturesque and charming a figure as any the theatre has recently produced and his bore isn't much more than a standard low-comedy caricature. There is never any question about the old man's real emotional commitment, and I should say that in this particular, too much legitimate dramatic suspense may have been sacrificed for a kind of self-conscious literary integrity. Mr. Williams, that is, has in general scornfully declined to write anything that could possibly be defined as a "commercial" play, and has, indeed, turned out something that occasionally seems like a parody of one. There are villains, but they are far too ludicrous to concern anybody much. If you really care about who gets the ten million dollars and the twenty-eight thousand acres of the most fertile land this side of the Nile, the Morosco is not the theatre you're looking for. The play there has to do with what an extremely sensitive writer has been able to make of a fragment of human experience. Any resemblance it may have to "The Desperate Hours" or any other shapely exercise of the year is the result of a compromise that I'm sure the author deplores exactly as much as I do.

Overlooking its mistakes, which seem to me many and important, "Cat on a Hot Tin Roof" is unquestionably a distinguished play. The scene in the first act between the hero and his wife is an impressive tour de force (it amounts essentially to a half-hour monologue, in which a semiliterate woman gives the whole history of the disaster that has overtaken them both to a man who stopped hearing living people talk quite a while ago), and a subsequent encounter, between the hero and his father, is on a level that few playwrights can approach. Much of Mr. Williams' thought is permanently inscrutable to me, but I think he intends to suggest that the partial knowledge men have of one another is infinitely preferable to the truth, which no one can face without seeing all the illusions by means of which he's managed to sustain himself destroyed. In any case, it is a piece of writing to be respected, and it seems a long time since I've been able to say that of anything.

Critics are notoriously half-witted in their appraisals of performances, and I would like to report only that Barbara Bel Geddes understands the technique of her trade better than any other young actress I can name (this includes Audrey Hepburn); that Ben Gazzara, in a part that demands an odd quality of low vitality, plays the husband with what struck me as a decent regard for the author's intention rather than any consideration of his own growing reputation; and that Burl Ives, as the father, is believable even when he is talking about the time he was seduced by a five-year-old Arab girl, which must have been quite a trick, on the whole. Among the others are Mildred Dunnock, Madeleine Sherwood, Pat Hingle, and Fred Stewart. They play more than acceptably the parts that Mr. Williams neglected to write, and Elia Kazan's direction indicates only occasionally that he was aware he had a Master on his hands. Jo Mielziner and Lucinda Ballard did the scenery and costumes, in that order. They are very gifted people.

April 22, 1955

MIXED BAG

(*Inherit the Wind*)

In "Inherit the Wind," at the National, Jerome Lawrence and Robert E. Lee have contrived a rather peculiar mixture of literal journalism and theatrical invention. The play, that is, has the general outline of the Scopes trial in Dayton, Tennessee, in the summer of 1925, and it includes a good deal of the actual testimony given there, but the names have been thinly disguised (Matthew Harrison Brady for William Jennings Bryan, Henry Drummond for Clarence Darrow, Bertram Cates for John Scopes, and E. K. Hornbeck for H. L. Mencken) and the time and locale are carefully not specified. In theory, this should allow the authors to enjoy the best of two worlds. It permits, for instance, the introduction of a romance between the young defendant and the daughter of a fundamentalist divine; it makes it possible for the character representing Bryan to be mortally and dramatically stricken in open court at the climax of the trail; and it is useful in stripping away such superfluous accessory figures as Dudley Field Malone and Arthur Garfield Hays, who had an important hand in the defense, and making the contest solely one between the two famous principals. Since this method doesn't forbid the use of anything Bryan or Darrow really said, it might reasonably be supposed that the result would be theatrically superior to the original performance at Dayton.

The fact, however, is that, at least in my opinion, history has been not increased but almost fatally diminished by all this literary ingenuity. The love affair is pat, unlikely, and annoyingly irrelevant; the melodramatic conclusion of the trial is an overcalculated effect that is not altogether without its comic aspects; and the simplification of the plot, which includes the picturing of Dayton as a community composed entirely of backwoods religious maniacs, which apparently wasn't the case at all, makes the play a much too elementary study in black and white. The selection from the recorded testimony is even more disappointing. Some of the memorable lines inevitably survive, such as Bryan's "I am more interested in the Rock of Ages than the age of rocks," and Darrow's sardonic "I want those 'Amens' to be put in the record," but a great many much better ones have been left out and there have been a lot of theoretically humorous insertions that introduce almost precisely the wrong kind of comedy. The worst trouble, though, is that the deadly and inexorable logic with which Darrow exposed his opponent as an ignorant old windbag has been so cut and rearranged that it has no real accumulating force. Bryan is exposed, all right, and the courtroom spectators' initial adoration of him is gradually turned to a kind of reluctant derision, but the stimulus for their behavior is far from adequate. The cure for this, I should say, would have been the preservation of some of the things that really were said and done at Dayton and the elimination of many that weren't. Among my choices for oblivion would be a considerable amount of love, an entire bloodcurdling and demented sermon by the heroine's father, and almost all the speeches made by the character impersonating Mr. Mencken, who is presented as an incredibly pretentious, self-satisfied, and elaborately cynical young bore. These alterations might deprive the play of some surefire stage effects, but I have a feeling that they would at least assist it in saying the important things that now are blurred or lost.

As Darrow-Drummond, Paul Muni achieves what from the pictures I have seen appears to be an admirable physical likeness, and if his mannerisms are rather more abundant and picturesque than those generally attributed to the original, they are still safely on the right side of caricature, and on the whole it is a sound and intelligent portrayal. Ed Begley's Bryan-Brady is also a successful likeness, and, except for a fixed benevolent smile that is not apparent in any portraits of the Great Commoner, his performance is convincing, too, and even has a degree of pathos, for which he deserves far more credit than the script. Of the others, I thought that Tony Randall, in the Mencken role, did little to minimize the exasperating nature of his part, but, with occasional reservations, I admired Bethel Leslie, as the girl; Karl Light, as the accused biology teacher; Staats Cotsworth, as the minister; Louis Hector, as the presiding judge; and Muriel Kirkland, as Brady's troubled wife. Peter Larkin's two-level set (the courtroom and a street in the town) is one of the most satisfactory we've had this year, and the forty-odd extras who people it are a mad and terrifying lot.

April 30, 1955

TWENTY-TWO ACTORS IN SEARCH
OF PIRANDELLO
(Six Characters in Search of an Author)

I KNOW PRACTICALLY nothing about Luigi Pirandello, who has been described by George Jean Nathan as the most original playwright since Ibsen, but as I watched the revival of "Six Characters in Search of an Author" down at the Phoenix, I pictured him somehow as a well-fed man sitting on a balcony looking out over the Mediterranean, chuckling jovially into his spade beard, and manipulating the last quill pen to be employed in the twentieth century. The play is, I'm sure, a triumph of Latin ingenuity, full of a fine fantastic wit not often present in our local operations, but the truth is that my experience on Twelfth Street was rather painful, on the whole. This glum reaction—that I found the piece as redolent of the twenties and as remote from my present interests as the works of James Branch Cabell—can be traced somewhat to a stubborn hostility on my part to a certain kind of complicated literary archness on the stage. Even more of it, however, can be traced to the manner of the production, which I think is unhappily designed to blur and distort almost everything that Pirandello wanted to say.

Before we go into this point, it would probably be advisable to deal briefly with the facts. "Six Characters in Search of an Author," then, opens with a congregation of actors and their director, who are engaged in rehearsing a conventional play. Their labors are presently interrupted by the appearance of half a dozen lugubriously attired shades, the creations of a playwright who gave them their identities and embedded them in a dilemma, and then, after the exasperating fashion of his kind, discarded them in favor of something else. These callers consist of a man and his wife; a boy, who is their son; and three children—one of them a grown-up girl—who have been born to the woman out of wedlock. The story they have to tell is sufficiently harrowing. The father, it seems, is of an experimental turn of mind, and the three bastards are the result of his wish to find out what would happen if he threw his mate together with someone almost precisely as simple-minded as she is herself. Everything turned out very badly indeed. The legitimate son has become a frozen symbol of hate and disgust; his mother is little better than an idiot; one of the small children is about to fall in a fountain and drown; the other is already fondling the pistol with which he will eventually shoot himself; and their older sister is a prostitute, who is more or less surprised to find that her step-father is among the clients of the establishment in which she is employed. Naturally, the director is impressed with this synopsis, and soon his guests are acting it out for the benefit of his cast, with the idea, of course, of turning it into an acceptable play. That is the skeleton of the plot. Pirandello's accompanying message, to put it in terms that have been lifted almost intact from the text, has something to do with the reality of illusion as opposed to the illusion of reality. This is hardly a novel line of thought, but it is intelligently expressed, and the apathy I felt toward it can be laid only to its curiously maladroit presentation on the stage.

The great point to be made in a production of "Six Characters," I should say, is the contrast between the ghostly visitors' conception of their tragedy and the rendition of it that the professional players plan to give. This should be a reasonably subtle thing—a careful statement of the difference between the shapeless vitality of a true report on human experience and the neat falsity of the same material trimmed and tidied up by art. In the stage directions of the Edward Storer translation, which was used in the original New York production in 1922, it is said specifically that the actors' version of the "characters'" story "has not in any way the air of a parody." This is also true at the Phoenix, but only because "parody" would be an inadequate word for what goes on there, which is complete and outlandish burlesque. The scene, for instance, in which the young whore meets her stepfather at her place of business is reproduced by a middle-aged actress and a leading man obviously several years her junior, and their behavior closely resembles what I have occasionally seen in travesties of "Uncle Tom's Cabin." Inevitably, this has its broadly comic moments, but it seems to me that it is nearly fatal to the real intention of the play. Similar resolute kidding marks the conduct of the players-within-the-play throughout the evening. This is bad enough, but what is worse is that the same thing is often visible in the performances given by the "characters," who all too frequently slip into a dim rascality of their own. In spite of the considerable praise that has been accorded the Phoenix cast, as well as the new adaptation, engineered by Michael Wager and Tyrone Guthrie—the latter also directed—I can't help feeling that they are about as misguided as they could possibly be.

The large company engaged in this grim lark includes Natalie Schafer, Francis Bethencourt, Whitfield Connor, Betty Lou Holland, Kurt Kasznar, Katherine Squire, and Mr. Wager, and I see no object in discussing the various ways in which it seems to me each is mistaken. The costumes were designed by Alvin Colt and the almost non-existent scenery was handled by Klaus Holm.

December 24, 1955

SHAW WITH MUSIC
(*My Fair Lady*)

JUST ABOUT THE most brilliantly successful scene I remember seeing in a musical comedy turns up somewhere about halfway through "My Fair Lady," the adaptation of Shaw's "Pygmalion" at the Mark Hellinger. Eliza Doolittle, the Cockney flower girl whom Professor Henry Higgins is grooming to talk like a lady, suddenly manages to say "The rain in Spain falls mainly on the plains" with all its treacherous vowels intact, and so enchanted are her listeners that they go into a triumphant little tango by way of celebration. It is a moment that has practically everything—charm, style, wit, gaiety— and I will cherish it as long as I live. The rest of the play never quite achieves this magic level, but it is still all wonderfully entertaining, and extraordinarily welcome in a season that previously offered no musicals except two glum exploits called "The Vamp" and "Pipe Dream."

"My Fair Lady" is meritorious in every department, but probably its greatest accomplishment lies in its remarkable humanization of Mr. Shaw, who has been transformed from an amiable but fundamentally sardonic observer of human behavior into a beam-ing old sentimentalist, as warm and lovable as Santa Claus. The changes and elisions that Alan Jay Lerner has made in the text are surprisingly few, considering the peculiar demands of musical com-edy, but there is certainly a new sympathy for love. In "Pygma-lion," the approach, while by no means hostile, was still pretty chilly and vegetarian, giving the impression that the author was quite willing to tolerate sex but rather preferred to discuss the caste system. Mr. Lerner has remedied that. The science of phonetics and the general absurdity of hereditary aristocracy get into "My Fair Lady" all right, but the real emphasis is enthusiastically on romance. It seems to me that here and there something has been lost—Eliza's raffish papa, for instance, is a healthier and much less complicated scoundrel than he was in the original—but on the whole it is a highly intelligent and tremendously engaging piece of work. An only slightly smaller miracle has been accomplished with the songs, whose lyrics, by Mr. Lerner, if not precisely Shavian, are always cheerfully in key with the rest of the proceedings, and whose melodies, composed by Mr. Frederick Loewe, are as bright and stylish as everything else about the production. In addition to its pleasant sound, "My Fair Lady" is entrancing to look at. Oliver Smith's sets, ranging from the crazy squalor of Covent Garden to the icy grandeur of an embassy ballroom, are handsome, posterlike inventions, and Cecil Beaton's costumes—by far the best we've seen this year—show impressive wit and imagination. People really looked like something in 1912, I thought, surveying my neighbors in the opening-night audience, who seemed to have gone out of their way to dress in a singularly melancholy and uninspiring fashion.

As Eliza, Julie Andrews fulfills all the promise she showed last year in "The Boy Friend." The part, of course, could hardly be more gratifying to an actress, since the transition from the screeching Cockney slattern of the early scenes to the composed and majestic elocutionist of the later ones is almost guaranteed sorcery, but Miss Andrews goes far beyond the obvious effects. She turns very satisfactorily from a howling savage into a suitable companion for duchesses, but there remains a fine suggestion of incorruptible vulgarity smoldering somewhere inside. Even when her poise and accent are most implacable, she still seems just on the verge of a yell. It is a hilarious and at the same time singularly touching performance. Rex Harrison, who plays Higgins, is rumored to have resisted even the slightest tampering with the original text, and there are times when he appears to be condescending somewhat to Mr. Lerner's version of the role. Nevertheless, it is generally an attractive effort, and he talks his songs at least as effectively as a lot of actors would sing them. Stanley Holloway, as Doolittle, is marvellously funny in his rendering of two numbers called "With a Little Bit of Luck" and "Get Me to the Church on Time," and there are other valuable contributions by Robert Coote, as a stuffy bulwark of the Empire; Cathleen Nesbitt, as a handsome Mayfair matron; and Viola Roache,

Philippa Bevans, and John Michael King, in more or less subordinate assignments. Moss Hart has directed the cast of thirty-one with
his customary skill, and Hanya Holm has staged at least two dances
that struck me as being as lovely as dreams.

March 24, 1956

ENOUGH IS ENOUGH IS ENOUGH
(*Waiting for Godot*)

As the class has surely all been told, there have been strange doings lately at the John Golden Theatre. The curtain goes up on a stage barren of everything except a few mortuary slabs of concrete and a single blasted tree. It is the way the world will perhaps look when the bombs have finished with us—as chilly and disconsolate as some landscape on the moon. Into this desolation there presently stray a couple of bums, who also look as if they might be the survivors of some ultimate explosion. They are nicknamed Gogo and Didi, and their conversation is peculiar. They talk mainly about their melancholy lot—they are tired and hungry, their feet hurt, and bands of savage strangers set upon them at night and beat them up. This discourse has a certain graveyard hilarity, having, I suppose, something to do with the idea of infinite misery sustained with no dignity at all but only a kind of lunatic vulgarity. It is also remarkably hard to follow, since few lines are even remotely responsive to those preceding them. The only thing that emerges with reasonable clarity is that they have come to this spot to keep a rendezvous with someone named Godot, a cryptic figure whom they may or may not have met before and who somehow holds the key to their salvation.

They are getting practically nowhere with anything when they are interrupted by the arrival of a powerful and menacingly fashionable man named Pozzo, who is attended by a cowering and horribly emaciated slave with a rope around his neck. The tramps naturally find these newcomers fascinating, especially that quality in their relationship that makes the slave so obviously dread nothing in life so much as the prospect of losing his bonds. It is a very interesting scene, and it ends on a high note when Pozzo, to demonstrate that his debased creature can still think quite nicely, calls on him for a speech and he responds with one beginning:

> Given the existence as uttered forth in the public works of Puncher and Wattmann of a personal God quaquaquaqua with white beard quaquaquaqua outside time without extension who from the heights of divine apathia divine athambia divine aphasia loves us dearly with some exceptions for reasons unknown . . .

This goes on for almost a hundred lines more, and at its conclusion everybody closes in on the orator in an enthusiastic attempt to beat him to death. The remainder of the act is comparatively tranquil. The slave is revived and Pozzo leads him off. Gogo and Didi are embarking on another of their gloomy dialogues when a small boy enters to announce that Godot isn't coming after all. He can be expected without fail, however, the following evening. The partners accept this news with resignation, or at least without explicit dismay. The final lines of the act read:

> DIDI: Well, shall we go?
> GOGO: Yes, let's go. (*They do not move.*)

Since it is clearly impossible for me to go on like this much longer, I'll just say that the second act is substantially a duplicate of the first, the only important difference being that this time when Pozzo and his lackey turn up the former is blind, the latter is dumb, and both are visibly close to some common end. When the child appears again to say that Godot has been delayed, there is a conceivably significant exchange:

> DIDI (*softly*): Has he a beard, Mr. Godot?
> BOY: Yes, Sir.
> DIDI: Fair or . . . (*he hesitates*) . . . or black?
> BOY: I think it's white, Sir, (*Silence*)
> DIDI: Christ have mercy on us!

The concluding lines and directions are identical with those at the end of the first act.

SINCE THE AUTHOR of "Waiting for Godot," a follower and former secretary of James Joyce named Samuel Beckett, can hardly have written with no coherent purpose whatever in mind, a secondary and clarifying meaning certainly exists, and it seems to me that the most likely is also the simplest. Gogo and Didi, then, represent the great mass of lost men, and the savior who never comes for them is God. Apparently, in Mr. Beckett's opinion this deity is not only an eternal promise and an eternal betrayal but also an eternal waster of time and imposer of senseless disciplines. (Gogo and Didi *want* to go somewhere else and do something different, but they *have* to wait for Godot every evening by the tree.) Pozzo and his slave, by this same simplification, are just wealth and the artist who has been bought and destroyed by it. Wealth, it seems, is also to be destroyed. Neither of them, in any case, is particularly concerned with Godot, who is an opium reserved exclusively for the masses, as the samplers of my childhood used to say. I have struggled to extract some other and less sophomoric message from Mr. Beckett's play (several of my colleagues have said that the possible interpretations are almost endless), but I'm afraid that this 1934 Model of the Universal Allegory is the best I can do. All I can say, in a critical sense, is that I have seldom seen such meagre moonshine stated with such inordinate fuss.

This leaves us with the acting. Bert Lahr, who plays Gogo, has been quoted as saying that he has no idea what the damn play is about. His statement brings up the curious picture of a director, who presumably does understand his script, failing to share this useful knowledge with one of his stars, and it may be unique in the theatre. Mr. Lahr gives a fine, gaudy vaudeville performance, but I'm afraid his ignorance of the meaning of his part is only too accurately a fact, and the spiritual damage to the play strikes me as considerable. The others—E. G. Marshall, as Didi; Kurt Kasznar, as Pozzo; and Alvin Epstein, as his slave—are less boisterously entertaining, possibly because they *do* have glimmerings of comprehension now and then. It is a very sad and confusing situation all around.

May 5, 1956

DOOM[1]

(*Long Day's Journey into Night*)

PEOPLE OF HYPERCRITICAL or frivolous disposition are bound to find a great deal to complain about in Eugene O'Neill's massive "Long Day's Journey Into Night," at the Helen Hayes. It is approximately twice the normal length, not because so much time was really necessary to develop and explain the four tragic figures involved but simply because its author chose to repeat himself endlessly and also to drag in a lot of material neither particularly fascinating in itself nor perceptibly relevant to the story he had to tell. A moderately competent editor would have had little difficulty in cutting the manuscript in half, and the result would almost certainly have been an improvement. The play is often as barbarously written as it is possible for the work of a major writer to be. Somewhere in the course of the evening, the young man who represents Mr. O'Neill on the stage says of himself, "Stammering is the native eloquence of us fog people," and there is a considerable amount of stammering, not to mention a considerable amount of humor that has a very labored air, and of original poetry—as distinguished from the abundant quotations from Swinburne, Wilde, Baudelaire, and Dowson—that would have been rejected as vacant and pretentious by any judicious publisher. In answer to the obvious inference here, it might be said that neither the jokes nor the lyrical passages are fumbling by intention, as a means of indicating some poverty or vulgarity of the characters' minds. There are a few such, but for the most part the offending samples occur in the speeches delivered by two young men who are presented as authentic ironists and—potentially, at least—original and sensitive masters of the language. The failure is a curious one, and perhaps it can be explained only on the ground that while Mr. O'Neill clearly thought of himself as strongly linked with the Irish dramatists, he was almost totally lacking in their wit

and their feeling for poetic speech, and his attempts to incorporate
these qualities into his work were generally unfortunate.

Finally, it is hard to deny that the assorted dooms that close in on
the Tyrones during the sixteen hours covered by the play may stir a
customer here and there to some emotion other than the appropriate pity and terror. The mistress of the house has come to what
seems the inevitable end of a twenty-three-year struggle against
morphine addiction; her younger son is discovered to have consumption and is about to be packed off to a cheap sanatorium, presumably to die; the elder, a drunken failure, cries out that—with
half his heart—he has always hated his brother and worked to de-
stroy him as he has destroyed himself; and old Tyrone, an actor who
has betrayed his talent for the sake of popular success, comes at last
to confront the fact that the miserliness he learned in the frightful
poverty of his youth started them all on their various paths to ruin.
Every family, of course, has its vicissitudes, but the epic scale of
calamity here, the simultaneous termination of four major trage-
dies, is so far beyond common experience that some may find it too
shocking to accept at all, and others—the cynical, who are always
with us—may regard it only as a dramatist's instinctive heightening
and rearrangement of life into a form too recognizable as magnificently expert theatre to be deeply affecting.

In spite of all these objections, most of which strike me as reasonably valid, I think "Long Day's Journey Into Night" is an impressive play. It was written, as you doubtless know, in 1940, when
the author was fifty-two, and it deals with things that happened to
him and his family twenty-eight years before that. In essence, it is a
man's desperate effort to recall and explain the past, to reduce it to
some ultimate comprehensible order, to understand and consequently
forgive. In the play, it is suggested that to a certain extent this understanding and forgiveness existed in him at the time—that he
understood when he was twenty-three the strange insecurity, the
passion for owning land, that made his father save money by employing only the cheapest quacks for his family, and thus condemn
his wife to a lifetime of drug-taking and his son, conceivably, to
· death; the destructive balance of love and hostility in his brother's
heart; and even all the mingled factors, including an early devotion

to the Catholic Church, that made his mother's addiction incurable practically from the start. It is hard to believe that a boy of such an age and so situated would know anything but hatred and despair, and it seems likely that Mr. O'Neill gave his younger self quite a lot of extra penetration, but that is a minor point, as is the overskillful telescoping of many years of suffering into a single day. The play, I think, accomplishes its purpose. In a dedication in the printed version, the author expresses his gratitude for having been able to face his dead at last, and write of them with pity and forgiveness. He has done that, and he has made them understandable and pitiable to us, too. In the face of a formidable body of opinion to the contrary, I seriously question whether "Long Day's Journey Into Night" will survive as a major contribution to the drama of our time, but it is a courageous one, and I hope its writing gave its author peace.

The four principal performers are Fredric March, as Tyrone; Florence Eldridge, as his wife; Jason Robards, Jr., as the elder son; and Bradford Dillman, as his brother and, of course, the character representing O'Neill himself. All these parts are extremely difficult and exhausting, the Tyrones having been a singularly volatile family, even without the assistance of drugs and alcohol, and I can only say that every one is handled superbly. José Quintero, who directed "The Iceman Cometh" so brilliantly downtown last spring, has done equally brilliant work here, and David Hays' set, a living room hideous even by suburban 1912 standards, is a fitting graveyard for all mortal hopes.

November 24, 1956

OUT OF THE NOWHERE
(*A Visit to a Small Planet; My Fair Lady*)

THERE IS ENOUGH material in "A Visit to a Small Planet," by Gore Vidal, for roughly an hour and a half of fine, fantastic comedy. It is somewhat unfortunate that the play at the Booth is obliged to go on for about fifty minutes longer than that, forcing the author to fill in this considerable gap either by stretching out genuinely comic situations almost to the breaking point or by writing in scenes that seem to contain rather less humor than desperation. The extra stuffing, presumably to be explained by the fact that the script is an expansion of one that was originally employed on television, is frequently irritating, but it isn't really calamitous, and I'm sure that you'll have a very pleasant time with Mr. Vidal's cheerful little report on the day the Spacemen came. In neither style nor invention can "A Visit to a Small Planet" be compared with Noel Coward's "Blithe Spirit," which also dealt with supernatural callers but did so with a precise, sustained, and chilling wit certainly beyond Mr. Vidal's powers and probably even a trifle foreign to his natural disposition. Within its limitations, however, his play is a remarkably lively and agreeable piece of work, and it has the further merit of providing two highly—if not, indeed, outrageously—gifted comedians, Cyril Ritchard and Eddie Mayehoff, with parts just about perfectly suited to their talents.[1]

The story you are asked to contemplate is concerned with the dreadfully disturbing things that are going to happen sometime next summer in a charming old house belonging to a celebrated newscaster near Manassas, in Virginia. The trouble begins with the landing of a flying saucer on the lawn and the emergence from it of a fascinating stranger, whose name is Kreton. This man is not from Mars, a planet that, in fact, he regards as almost impossible socially, but from some immensity beyond our present poor conception of time and space, and he belongs to a race that, having abolished food and sex, along, of course, with death, inevitably has a good deal of time for travel. His own hobby, as it happens, is the Earth, whose inhabitants amuse him in many ways but especially in their unique capacity for violence. Having hoped to arrive in time for the Battle of Bull Run, he has come equipped with the appropriate costumes, including an extremely handsome Confederate uniform, but his navigation proved faulty, and though he hits the right place, the date, to his embarrassment, is nearly a hundred years off. Deprived of the quaint old war he came to look in on, he can think of nothing to do but start a nice new one of his own, and he has just about finished his arrangements when, happily, his superiors whisk him back to the infinite.

It is quite a plot, combining, as you can see, satire with fantasy, and on the whole Mr. Vidal has done very nicely with it. His achievements are fairly difficult to describe. One particularly enchanting scene, for instance, shows Kreton trying to arouse the proper martial ardor in a young man by singing him a medley of the most terrible war songs ever written; another, involving some interesting sound effects, demonstrates his ability to read a whole stageful of minds simultaneously; another finds him in an intimate conversation with a cat, agreeing with her, as I got it, that it is no more disgusting to eat mice than to eat bacon; and still another pictures a Pentagon general doing his desperate best to fill in— naturally, in quadruplicate—a set of official forms classifying his guest and explaining the purpose of his visit in suitable military language. I might go on with these notes indefinitely, but it is obvious that the quality of the original is almost completely lacking in them, and it seems both superfluous and unkind to tax you further. It is probably enough to say that while I could do without a few things, such as a burlesque newscast that struck me as at once tedious and familiar, and a couple of not too exhilarating sequences devoted to young love, I found most of the play considerably funnier than anything else that has turned up this year.

The performances given by Mr. Ritchard, as Kreton, and Mr.

Mayehoff, as the general, are in hilarious contrast. Although the action of the play takes place in 1957 and his own garb is that of 1861, Mr. Ritchard's conduct is basically that of a Restoration fop, and this wonderfully mannered elegance is the best of all attitudes for a man engaged in what can only be described as a slumming expedition. Mr. Mayehoff's technique is broader, being modelled more or less on that of the grampus, and no one is better equipped to impersonate a soldier whose tongue can never hope to keep up with one of the slowest minds in the world. At one point, for reasons that escape me now, he has occasion to imitate a mobile laundry unit, and not since Reginald Gardiner gave his famous impression of the sounds made by wallpaper has the art of mimicry reached a more peculiar height. The others in the cast, which Mr. Ritchard took the professional risk of directing himself, include Philip Coolidge, as the newscaster; Sibyl Bowan, as his empty-headed wife; and Sarah Marshall and Conrad Janis, as a pair of young lovers, whose sexual abandon Kreton finds very stimulating—a point of view I couldn't always share. They are all quite satisfactory in these subordinate assignments.

FOR BETTER OR worse, science has made practically everything possible, and so, the other night, after seeing Edward Mulhare as Professor Higgins in "My Fair Lady" I was able to go home, turn on the record-player, and hear again Rex Harrison's delivery of the same material. The result of this experiment, plus my memory of Mr. Harrison's physical appearance in the part, is that I can see little to choose between the two performances. On the whole, I should say that Mr. Mulhare's portrayal is a bit softer, broader, and more sentimental than his predecessor's, and while this probably removes the role still further from its Shavian original, it may conceivably be useful for musical-comedy purposes, since it makes the terminal romance— never, of course, intended by Shaw—somewhat easier to accept. My man remains Mr. Harrison, whose prickly intellectual seemed to me to offer a humor not always visible in Mr. Mulhare's younger, more winsome, and certainly prettier version, but it may be that this is just the captious opinion of a traditionalist and not to be taken very seriously. In any case, the charm and style of the play—unequalled, I should say, in the theatre in our time—are not perceptibly diminished, the continuing presence of Julie Andrews and Stanley Holloway being more than enough to guarantee that.

February 16, 1957

HOODLUMS AND HEIRESSES
(*West Side Story*)

WEST SIDE STORY" isn't, I'm afraid, an operation that will bring much comfort to those who still visit musicals in the wistful hope of seeing valor overcome a certain number of obstacles to capture beauty in the end; of laughing at a set of celebrated and generally reliable clowns; of listening to a collection of songs that can be reproduced more or less accurately in the taxi on the way home; of admiring costumes that create an atmosphere of expensive grandeur or simple charm, or both; and, of course, of gazing fondly on a score or so of cunningly constructed young women dancing merrily, all in a row. The men who collaborated on the work at the Winter Garden have other and sterner ideas, and their offering contains almost none of these delights. The story, as you've surely been informed by now, somewhat follows the tragic pattern of "Romeo and Juliet," and its characters are members of two racially hostile teen-age gangs, the Jets and the Sharks, in a section of town where the police usually find it expedient to patrol in pairs. The heroine is newly arrived from Puerto Rico, and, innocent of American ways and local tensions, she meets and falls in love with a young Polish-American at a dance. To even the most casual newspaper reader, the events that follow will be familiar enough, though still shocking. There has always been bitter feeling between the Sharks, who are Puerto Ricans, and the Jets, who consider themselves "Americans," however various and obscure their origins, and presently a "rumble" between the two gangs is arranged by their leaders. It is decided that this contest shall take the comparatively harmless form of a fist fight between two champions, but there are emotional complications, and the switch-blade knives are put to work. In a few minutes, two boys are dead—one of them the heroine's brother, stabbed, with classic inevitability, by her lover. The sorry story ends when he, in his turn, is killed by one of his victim's friends, and, in a finale that I should say is a good deal more Shakespearean than plausible, the two gangs unite to carry his body from the stage. Unlike Juliet, the heroine survives, but it is still not exactly what you'd describe as a happy ending.

My opinions of "West Side Story" are, I have to admit, very mixed. The plot, though certainly racking, seems to me strangely empty of real emotional content. Partly, this may be due to the fact that Shakespeare's ideas of what is permissible in the way of dramatic coincidence aren't easy to accept today, and it is hard to escape a feeling of patness and contrivance in the way each fatal encounter is arranged. It is also, however, almost equally the result of the difficulty of reconciling the characters who appear on the stage with their actual prototypes uptown. All my reading, vividly assisted by photographs, has led me to think of the members of juvenile gangs as vicious, senseless, and degraded. The boys and girls at the Winter Garden are tough all right, but somehow we are asked to believe that they are simultaneously rather winsome and picturesque, with essentially a high regard for chastity in the young women who accompany them, and even a certain delicacy and style in their employment of the English language. They are capable of murder in moments of great stress, but it is impossible to suspect them of rape, mugging, perversion, drug addiction, torture, or any other practices that would naturally be repugnant to the normal American boy. It is probably necessary to present them in this disinfected light in the theatre, but the whole conception is just beyond my powers. Asked to believe that significant tragedy and tender, doomed, not unliterary romance frequently exist among juvenile delinquents, I remain, I'm embarrassed to say, incredulous and unstirred.

In spite of this fundamental complaint, I found admirable and exciting things in "West Side Story." Jerome Robbins' choreography is almost unfailingly brilliant, especially in the tense and controlled ferocity of his handling of the "rumble" and in a number having to do with the lovers' dream of a kind of peace they'll never know. Leonard Bernstein's music has a wide and impressive range. It can be harsh and ominous, cheerfully antic, and really quite lovely, as the mood of the play shifts, and Stephen Sondheim's lyrics are intelligent and appropriate, though one excursion into the humor of delinquency struck me as something of an error. The sets and costumes, by Oliver Smith and Irene Sharaff, respectively, and the lighting, by Jean Rosenthal, do more than you'd believe possible to make squalor fascinating, and Mr. Robbins' direction, particularly considering that he was dealing almost exclusively with very young and inexperienced performers, is amazingly good. The leading actors, in some vague order of the prominence of their roles, are Larry Kert, Chita Rivera, Carol Lawrence, Mickey Calin, and Ken LeRoy. They seem extremely gifted.

October 5, 1957

THE DIMMEST VIEW
(*The Entertainer*)

In "The Entertainer," at the Royale, John Osborne, who
might conceivably be described as Her Majesty's sorest subject,
has accomplished the unusual feat of writing an extremely distressing but at the same time almost totally meaningless tragedy. The hero,
for lack of a better word, is a cheap music-hall performer named Archie Rice, and the story is concerned with the final stages of this
man's disintegration, which, by strong, practically bludgeoning implication, are identical with those of his unhappy country. Somewhere in the course of the play, Archie's daughter, striving to
capture the full flavor of her father's personality, calls him "a bastard
on wheels," and this, considering all the facts, would appear to be a
remarkably temperate judgment. A horror on the stage, where his
lack of talent is perfectly matched by the offensiveness of his material, Archie is nevertheless far more appalling in the bosom of his
family. He is a tireless boaster about his sexual prowess and, in order
to marry a young girl, proposes to divorce his elderly wife, whom
his ferocious contempt has reduced to hopeless alcoholism. He is
almost literally a murderer, since, in the hope of saving his dreadful
act, he drags his old father, who once had a great name in the profession, back to the theatre and certain death. And, in his less criminal
but just as odious moments, he is an interminable, whining bore,
full of political opinions that often have the air of being venomous
parodies of those held by Mr. Osborne himself; consumed with
scorn for the past, hatred of the present, and despair for the future;
and sick about equally with self-pity and gin, which, indeed, seems
to be the only retreat any of them have left from intolerable reality.

In an attempt to enlist some sympathy for Archie, or at least to
make him endurable to watch and listen to, Mr. Osborne suggests
from time to time that he is not wholly despicable. He is not self-

deluded, in that his contempt for the world extends to himself, and he has a kind of desperate gallantry, since in the end, offered the chance of a new life in Canada, he still prefers to stay where he is and carry on a struggle that he knows is doomed. There is something affecting in this refusal to accept life on any terms other than his own, but I'm afraid it isn't enough to redeem Archie for me. I could put up with the bastard in him, as I was happy to do in the case of the hero of Mr. Osborne's previous play, "Look Back in Anger," but the sheer mindless vulgarity is just too much. It is one thing to attack the state of the world, with particular reference to the British Isles, through the medium of a character whose speech has the bite of authentic wit and style; it is quite another to do so through one who is manifestly a semiliterate clown and whose opinions about anything, when they are coherent at all, must be regarded with intense suspicion. The basic trouble with "The Entertainer" may easily lie right there. The ideas it expresses are likely to drive a good many people straight back to the collected works of Rudyard Kipling, while the manner in which they are stated has a grating, jeering monotony guaranteed to exhaust nearly everybody.

None of these remarks, of course, is intended to reflect on the extraordinary range and brilliance of Laurence Olivier's performance as Archie. The play presents its central character alternately as a music-hall performer of a singularly repellent sort (it would be hard to say whether the jokes are more atrocious than the songs, or whether the dancing is more dismaying than either) and as a domestic catastrophe of imposing dimensions. In both these impersonations, Mr. Olivier is magnificent, capturing with amazing skill the bland, measureless vulgarity of the entertainer and the half-deliberate, half-unconscious cruelty of the family man. It all seems to me art applied to a fairly paltry purpose, but it is still art of a very high order. His principal associates—Brenda de Banzie, as his wife; George Relph, as his father; Joan Plowright, as his daughter; and Richard Pasco, as a surviving son (the assassination of another at Suez is announced during the play)—are also completely admirable, and Guy Spaull, Peter Donat, and Jeri Archer, portraying, respectively, two symbols of the solid worth that Archie loathes and the kind of nude that he has always found irresistible, make interesting and valuable contributions, too. Tony Richardson's direction of the difficult, episodic script is impressive; Alan Tagg's sets, featuring a backdrop of incomparable tastelessness, are exceptionally ingenious; and the occasional music provided by John Addison is hideously appropriate.

February 22, 1958

TRIPLE-THREAT MAN

(*The Music Man*)

TWICE IN MY life, for reasons that escape me now, though I'm sure they were discreditable, I allowed myself to be persuaded that I ought to take a hand in turning out a musical comedy. Both these ventures reached Broadway, though my connection with them had ceased long before that, and both closed with inconceivable rapidity.[1] A writer, I suppose, discovers the limits of his talent only through a system of trial and error, and, whatever else I may have learned from these two fiascoes, I came away from them knowing surely and forever that this particular form of art was not for me. This intelligence, in addition to serving a useful purpose—there is too little time for a man to waste any of it on lost causes—produced in me a feeling of nearly perfect detachment. It is an embarrassing fact that I seldom see a straight play, either a comedy or a drama, without the conviction that if I had been asked, I could have provided the author with several very valuable suggestions. A musical, however, is quite another matter. I have no idea how the damn things get there in the first place—by what weird midnight prodigies of collaboration—and I certainly have no coherent advice to offer anyone about fixing things up, being comparatively accomplished only in the construction of English sentences, a knack approximately as useful in these entertainments as the ability to knit.

This lack of the writer's habitual nagging instinct to improve, coupled with an indifference to the form as a means of personal expression, makes me, of course, the practically ideal (or totally disembodied) critic of all musical comedies, and we will proceed immediately to the one called "The Music Man," which is now turning thousands away from the box office at the Majestic. This piece, the all but unassisted work of Meredith Willson, who contrived the book, the music, and the lyrics, received about the most remarkable set of notices in my memory, being greeted by one stunned worshipper as one of the three most exhilarating experiences he had undergone in the theatre in twenty-six years, and by his colleagues as an offering comparing very favorably with "Oklahoma!," "Guys and Dolls," "My Fair Lady," and almost anything else you care to name. I myself have nothing against "The Music Man," regarding it, in fact, as an exceptionally cheerful offering, but it is not as good as all that.

As a composer, Mr. Willson, who was once a flutist with John Philip Sousa and has clearly never overcome his deep original passion for marching bands, has achieved a score that is distinguished chiefly by fine, swinging, brassy numbers that ought to enchant any musical taste, from the most primitive on up. There are, naturally, sentimental songs in their suitable places, and a barbershop quartet is occasionally employed to excellent comic effect, but Mr. Willson's heart really belongs to the horns and drums, and his work with them is—well, stupendous. As his own lyricist, he is again rather more successful when he is writing words to which people can go stomping around the stage ("Seventy Six Trombones," "Wells Fargo Wagon," "Pickalittle") than he is when he is asked to speak of love ("Till There Was You," "Will I Ever Tell You?," "Goodnight My Someone"). As a librettist, he is somewhat like Booth Tarkington in his loving regard for the American Middle West in the early years of the century and somewhat like the author of "Alias Jimmy Valentine" in his basic plot structure, since "The Music Man" has to do with a genial crook who mends his ways through the influence of a virtuous woman, the protagonists in this case being a peddler of nonexistent musical instruments and uniforms and the custodian of the local library. Altogether, it is a rousing, sentimental, highly professional show, a little short on verbal humor, perhaps ("I don't want to hear another poop out of you"), but otherwise most agreeable to the eye and ear, and certainly a welcome change from the semi-operatic renderings of semi-classical dramas that in recent years have disguised themselves far too often as musical comedies. Unlike most of my fellow art experts, I doubt very much whether an epic has really been visited upon us, but this is the extent of my disagreeableness for the moment.

The star of "The Music Man" is Robert Preston, who, except for a couple of revivals, has been previously featured on Broadway only in such trolls' work as "His and Hers," "The Tender Trap," and "Janus." There is no more comforting condition than omniscience, and I would like to be able to say that Mr. Preston's ability was apparent to me from the moment I first saw him. The fact is, however, that as I watched him going about his grisly employment (I didn't see him in the revivals), it never occurred to me that he was anything much more than just another actor. I was mistaken. Mr. Preston sings slightly better than Rex Harrison (he actually sings the few notes that lie within his range and merely opens and shuts his mouth the rest of the time), and his agility is greater, but, on the whole, his musical-comedy equipment is negligible. It doesn't matter at all. He has the two top things demanded by the stage—infallible technique and a unique personality—and these, in combination with a wonderfully picturesque role, make his performance one of the season's memorable events. As the young lady who sees to it that he really does outfit the local bugle corps (I'm not at all sure this was a good thing), Barbara Cook is demurely attractive and sufficiently melodious for two, and there are pleasant, talented contributions by David Burns, Pert Kelton, Iggie Wolfington, Dusty Worrall, and four gentlemen named Al Shea, Wayne Ward, Vern Reed, and Bill Spangenberg, who are prepared to sing "Good Night, Ladies" in close harmony on no provocation whatsoever. The dances, which I assume to be characteristic of Iowa in 1912, were staged by Onna White; similarly characteristic sets and costumes were designed by Howard Bay and Raoul Pène duBois, in the order named; and Morton Da Costa directed—very well, too, it seemed from where I sat.

January 4, 1958

CURTAIN CALLS

(A Miscellany of Critical Jottings)

N AT N. DORFMAN has contrived such strange and stately speeches for his characters in "Errant Lady," at the Fulton, that it is a wonder to me that actors were found who could remember them at all. They were, though, and there you are.

★ ★ ★

I HAVE ALMOST no reason to believe that "Alley Cat," by and with Alan Dinehart, will be at the Forty-eighth Street Theatre when this notice reaches you; nor, if it is, can I advise you to rush right around there and see it. It is the story of a man who finds his soul in Greenwich Village, a new high, perhaps, in improbability, but nothing much else.

from Straus, Sex and Psychiatry[1] (Errant Lady; Alley Cat),
September 29, 1934

★ ★ ★

"THE MOTHER," PRESENTING Alla Nazimova in the last drama written by Karel Capek, was a sad and embarrassing experience to the audiences (four) who came to pay their respects to these distinguished talents. The agony and bewilderment of a woman robbed by an incomprehensible civilization first of her husband and then of her five sons is, I'm sure, a high-minded theme, but the collection of spooks, supernaturally talkative, who debated it at the Lyceum conveyed no message to me except, conceivably, that a boring man makes a boring angel and that conversation in Paradise will be just as exasperating as it often is in Fifty-second Street. This beyond any question is the most discouraging thought the theatre has brought me this year and probably accounts in a measure for my distaste for Mr. Capek's play. Mme. Nazimova, cast as a female Job minus the boils, wrestled helplessly with her part and had my complete sympathy when, in the middle of the last act, she just lay down on the floor and apparently went to sleep.

from Some Troubles I've Seen
(*The Mother*), May 6, 1939

★ ★ ★

MR. MAURICE EVANS made his third appearance in "King Richard II" last week at the St. James Theatre, giving rise to a brief Shakespearean controversy in the breast of one critic, who has the greatest admiration for Mr. Evans, but a certain prejudice against looking at anything more than twice:

CRITIC: This King, this Gaunt, this Bolingbroke,
    This blessed plot, these tights, these wigs, this scenery—
    I've seen them all enough (I'd die pronouncing it).
HIS CONSCIENCE: Stay but a little while.
CRITIC: I'd give my program for a glass of schnapps;
    My stiff apparel for a layman's tweeds;
    My special seating for a little bar,
    A little, little bar, an obscure bar.
CONSCIENCE: O, God, defend your soul from such foul sin!
    Would you seem shameful in great Nathan's sight?
    Anathema to Watts or Brown?
CRITIC: Needs must I damn their eyes. I'd weep for joy
    To stand upon the sawdust once again—
    Dear dust, I do salute you with my hand.
CONSCIENCE: O thrice-misguided boy! Have you not heard
    That "Richard II" is the king of plays,
    And Evans king of all who've played in it?

That every repetition only shows
A greater glory? More reward?
CRITIC: I've heard all that, and still I say
Enough's enough. There's such a thing
As seeing Shelley all too plain,
Or in the humbler language of the street,
Three strikes is out.
CONSCIENCE: Perhaps you're right. Let's cop a sneak. . . .

(*The curtain comes down and they exit, heading west on Forty-fourth Street, toward a clean, well-lighted place.*)

CRITIC: Never did captive with a freer heart
Cast off his chains of bondage and embrace
His golden, uncontroll'd enfranchisement
More than my dancing soul doth celebrate
Its freedom from the Bard.
CONSCIENCE: Convey me to a bar, and then to bed.

(*They disappear arm in arm in the night, singing a rather obvious paraphrase of the "St. James Infirmary" blues.*)

from A Seal, Miss Barrymore, and the Bard (*King Richard II*),
April 13, 1940

★   ★   ★

IF "THE MAN Who Had All the Luck" held me in my seat for three interminable acts, it was largely out of incredulity, for in it Arthur Miller surely wrote one of the strangest plays of the decade. Since it is now deceased, a very brief synopsis should suffice. The first act was about a garageman who didn't know much about machinery; the second act was about a pitcher who was no good when there were men on the bases because he had been trained privately by his father in the basement; the third act was about childbirth and a mink farm where the mink were threatened with poisoning because there were silkworms in their fish. There was also some mention of a veteran of the first World War who got the Croix de Guerre when the boiler blew up in a whore house. A little shapeless, you might say.

from Apley in the Flesh (*The Man Who Had All the Luck*),
December 2, 1944

★ ★ ★

"L O C O," W H I C H   A L S O opened last week, is not reviewed in this department, at the express wish of Jed Harris, its producer. It cannot precisely be said that I was barred from the Biltmore, where this attraction was on display, since a recent statute provides that any decent, sober man, on presenting a ticket, must be admitted to a place of public entertainment. The facts were simply that Mr. Harris failed to supply the ticket and noted further that my presence in the theatre, however I got in, would cause him serious physical discomfort. The reasons behind Mr. Harris's reluctance to receive me as a guest, paid or otherwise, are not, I imagine, of wide general interest, and I will only say that they arose from the irritating circumstance that my profession permits me to discuss him freely with several thousand people, while his remarks about me are necessarily confined to the rather smaller circle of his friends. There is obviously an injustice here, somewhat similar to the injustice that limits a duck in its arguments with a man with a shotgun, and since I am aware of it, I refrained from trying to insert myself into the Biltmore by any of those ingenious stratagems that colleagues of mine, also outcast, have employed in the past. I can't help feeling, however, that there is some obligation on my part to furnish the readers of this magazine with at least a hearsay report of new endeavors on Broadway, and so I append here the consensus of critical opinion on the morning following the opening:

Atkinson, *Times:* "Incompetently written, large sections of it seem like a prolonged non-sequitur."

Barnes, *Herald Tribune:* "The piece is little more than garishly trivial."

Chapman, *News:* "'Loco' [is] about a model's measles; the play is spottier than she is."

Coleman, *Mirror:* "Jed Harris, whom we've always considered one of the theatre's top directors, has staged 'Loco' with all the corny touches of a third-rate summer stockman."

On the whole, it seems possible that Mr. Harris sent his tickets out to quite a lot of undesirable people.

from Out of the Library (*Loco*), October 26, 1946

★ ★ ★

A DRAMA CALLED "The Haven" opened, and closed after a brief run, last week. You are supposed to be polite about such operations, and I am prepared to be as polite as the next. Dennis Hoey, Melville Cooper, Valerie Cossart, Viola Roache, and Ivan Simpson were in it.

from Three in a Row (*The Haven*), November 2, 1946

★ ★ ★

IN PARIS, JEAN-PAUL Sartre is widely known as the founder of Existentialism, a philosophy rather obscure to most but which he himself seems once to have defined as the antithesis of nausea. His play called "No Exit," now at the Biltmore, has been described as a notable sample of this school, though to the casual eye nausea hardly enters into it one way or the other. No matter how you label it, however, it strikes me as little more than a one-act drama of unusual monotony and often quite remarkable foolishness. The scene, as you may have read, is a small, hideously decorated room off a corridor in Hell, and the characters, in addition to a demoniac bellboy, are a collaborationist, a Lesbian, and a young woman whose mortal past seems to have included adultery, nymphomania, and infanticide. Exasperated somewhat by the fact that the house furnishings offer neither mirrors nor toothbrushes, these three devote the evening to extracting one another's case histories, which are undeniably picturesque; to a triangular love affair, for which the only word is eccentric; and to a succession of reedy jokes about their environment, which are repetitious beyond belief. The general idea, I think, is that actual physical torment would be superfluous, since three such people could be relied upon to badger one another sufficiently throughout eternity without infernal assistance, and it is a proposition with which I am not inclined to argue.

For some reason, "No Exit" seems to have enjoyed a considerable success in both London and Paris. It is quite possible that the overseas temperament had most to do with that, since it has often been observed that small, doomed experiments flourish best on European soil, but I'm afraid some mention must also be made of the production. The principal members of the cast in this Broadway version are Annabella, Claude Dauphin, and Ruth Ford, and while Miss Ford's adulteress has a kind of throaty style, her companions appear to have decided that the Lesbian and the collaborator should be portrayed in a manner not unlike that employed by the actors in a spy play of the first World War—say, "Three Faces East." Paul Bowles' translation, which occasionally provides its French characters with such baffling Americanisms as "two-beet whore," is not particularly fortunate, either.

from Dream Boy (*No Exit*), December 7, 1946

★ ★ ★

"TIME FOR ELIZABETH," by Groucho Marx and Norman Krasna, was about a man who abandoned the washing-machine business and went to Florida, where he underwent such extremities of boredom that he turned right around and came back again. This work, notable for some of the flattest jokes and most appalling character actors ever assembled on the stage, was withdrawn after eight performances, leaving Otto Kruger and Katherine Alexander, who starred in it, available for more elevated employment. Unless Mr. Marx and Mr. Krasna, both of whom are associated with the cinema, wished to express a contempt for the

New York theatre at least as withering as the theatre's well-known contempt for Hollywood, I can think of no possible explanation of this enterprise.

from Fun With a Friend (*Time for Elizabeth*),
October 9, 1948

★   ★   ★

ANY MAN WHO will rhyme "Cressida" and "ambassador" is capable of practically anything, and that is exactly what Cole Porter has done in "Kiss Me, Kate," a strange mingling of William Shakespeare and musical comedy, at the Century. This is, in every sense, a wonderful show, and I can't think of a single sensible complaint to make about it. The story, radically compressed, has to do with a production of "The Taming of the Shrew" at a theatre in Baltimore. The leading man and woman were once married and they are still strongly attached to each other, though at one point he feels obliged to spank her so hard she can't sit down. Bella and Samuel Spewack, who wrote the parts of the book that Shakespeare didn't, have arranged things so that the action alternates between the private behavior of two people called Fred Graham and Lilli Vanessi and their performances as Petruchio and Katharine, and it makes a very nice framework for some of the best singing and dancing and the most uninhibited comedy that anybody has turned out for a long time. The plot also involves some complicated shenanigans on the part of a couple of gangsters, who are trying to collect a ten-thousand-dollar gambling debt from the hero; a subsidiary romance, between Bianca and Lucentio, who, of course, have secondary identities, too; and an even more drastic rearrangement of Shakespeare than Rodgers and Hart accomplished in "The Boys from Syracuse." I approve heartily of all these matters, especially the last, since it has always seemed to me that "The Taming of the Shrew" could do with quite a lot of editing, as well as a few good tunes.

All Mr. Porter's songs are excellent, taking you back to the great days of "Fifty Million Frenchmen" and "Anything Goes," but I guess the ones I like best are "So in Love Am I," whose nature is probably apparent from its title; "I've Come to Wive It Wealthily in Padua," a rather sardonic item sung by Petruchio; "I Hate Men," which Katharine delivers as if she meant it; "Too Darn Hot," which has something to do with the weather, particularly in relation to love; "Always True to You (in My Fashion)," a fine, tough piece, entrusted to a fine, tough girl; and "Brush Up Your Shakespeare," a sort of guide to the Works, sung by the gangsters and containing perhaps the most ingenious of all Mr. Porter's lyrics, including that maniacal coupling of "Cressida" and "ambassador." The dances, arranged by Hanya Holm, who was partly responsible for "Ballet Ballads" last year, are first-rate, too, and the people who execute them have enormous spirit and grace. Finally, Lemuel Ayers has designed some very handsome costumes and sets (they're also often pretty funny), and John C. Wilson, who directed the show, keeps everything moving at top speed.

As Petruchio, or Fred, Alfred Drake again demonstrates that he is one of the most useful men on the musical stage, since he is not only an extremely gifted singer but also an actor of unusual intelligence, who reads what Shakespeare there is left with a humor and authority not often found in more conventional versions. Patricia Morison, the Katharine-Lilli, is almost as good, playing that beautiful, indignant heroine with the greatest self-possession and singing her songs in a strong, clear voice. Of the others, Lisa Kirk, who is Bianca in the interior play, has a notable success with "True to You" and does a very attractive job with several other numbers; Harold Lang, as Lucentio, dances superbly, and, though not as well equipped vocally as he might be, still handles the music satisfactorily enough; there are two excellent comic offerings by Harry Clark and Jack Diamond, as the gangsters, and some admirable specialty dancing by Fred Davis and Eddie Sledge; and Denis Green, Annabelle Hill, Thomas Hoier, and Lorenzo Fuller are all effective in smaller parts. Altogether, I can't remember having such a consistently good time at a musical comedy since the night Miss Ethel Merman opened in that piece about Annie Oakley.

from Giraudox, Porter and Guitry (*Kiss Me, Kate*),
January 8, 1949

★ ★ ★

AT ONE POINT in "Anybody Home," at the Golden, the heroine complains that she is going mad because she has no social life. The reason she gives is that her husband is too preoccupied with his career to take her around, but the real one, I suspect, is that she is the damnedest bore in Westchester County, where the action of this gruesome piece takes place. While this harassed matron is unquestionably the leading nuisance on the premises, the members of her immediate circle—her husband, who is a political thinker of almost unparalleled imbecility; her admirer, a suburban rake and equestrian; and her sister, who seems to be some kind of reformed aviatrix—aren't far behind, and altogether "Anybody Home" is as stupefying an offering as we've had this season, not excepting "Grandma's Diary." It was written, if that's the word I'm groping for, by one Robert Pyzel and produced by his wife, Phyllis Holden, who also plays the principal part in it. Among the others in the cast are Lloyd Holden (Miss Holden's brother), Roger Clark, Katherine Anderson, Donald Curtis, and Emory Richardson. With the exception of Mr. Richardson, who gives a restrained and sensible performance as a Negro butler, they all ought to be arrested for disturbing the peace.

from Return of the Native (*Anybody Home*),
March 5, 1949

★ ★ ★

KATHARINE HEPBURN MOVED into the Shubert with Shaw's "The Millionairess" last Friday, and it is a wonder the roof is still on the old house, because it is doubtful if such a shattering performance has been visited on a New York theatre since Tallulah Bankhead appeared in her personal version of "Private Lives." Miss Hepburn is, of course, a talented and intelligent actress, and has demonstrated these qualities on many happy occasions in the past, but this time, I fear, she has made a mistake, and, as Mayor LaGuardia used to say of his own errors of judgment, it is certainly a beaut.

From the moment when she first bangs her way into her attorney's office, shouting her opinion of her husband and the world in general, breaking chairs, pacing the stage like an entry in a trotting race, and gesturing like a semaphore, she is a shining example of how not to play what is—in intention, at least—high comedy. The gymnastics include throwing herself in grotesque and what would appear to be painful attitudes on the floor or any available piece of furniture, arching her back until her spine seems sure to snap, hurtling up a flight of stairs as if, perhaps, the author's avenging ghost were hot on her heels, and giving such a convincing exhibition of judo that it is hard to believe her opponent's bones are not actually, instead of only theatrically, fractured. These acrobatics are sufficiently wearing—and even faintly embarrassing—to watch, but I suffered more from the manner in which the lady has chosen to deliver her speeches. This is rather hard to describe. There are, I should say, just two methods of attack: either the line is yelled *in toto*, threatening not only the star's vocal cords but also the hearing equipment of everybody in the first six rows of the orchestra, or it begins on a sort of purr or growl and winds up with a yell, a device that made me jump practically every time. Miss Hepburn's facial exertions are in keeping with both the gyrations of her body and the tumult of her voice—the lips drawn back to form a square in that famous wide and mirthless smile, or extended almost incredibly in maniacal laughter, or else compressed, below narrowed eyes, to indicate that her mind is occupied with complex and usually wicked plans. As I have noted, it is a shattering performance. I don't know about Miss Hepburn, but when I left the Shubert, I was barely a shadow of my former self.

As for the play, which was written when Shaw was seventy-nine, it is one of that great man's least auspicious works, having to do principally with the premise that money is apt to beget money, although there are a few sideswipes at marriage, medicine, and other topics that engaged that supernaturally versatile intelligence from time to time. The story, such as it is, concerns the heroine's efforts to find a man whose financial acumen is equal to that which she inherited from her father, who also left her thirty million pounds. Three men are involved in this quest—the husband, a prodigious athlete but otherwise a far from stimulating personality; an amiable man of the world, who is the seriously damaged loser in the wrestling match mentioned above; and an Egyptian doctor, who is helplessly attracted to the heiress because of her slow, strong pulse and carries her off in about as silly a scene as any Shaw ever wrote. These roles are taken by Peter Dyneley, Cyril Ritchard, and Robert Helpmann, in that order. Only Mr. Ritchard, who is about the most urbane actor now extant, is able to cope with and, in a sense, diminish Miss Hepburn's spectacular vitality. The two others, along with Campbell Cotts, as the lawyer; Genine Graham, as the athlete's Cockney fiancée; Bertram Shuttleworth and Nora Nicholson, as a couple of sweatshop operators, employed to demonstrate the mysteries of high finance; and Vernon Greeves, as a hotel manager, who performs much the same function, just look rather stunned. The settings, designed by James Bailey, are ponderous but undoubtedly suitable, and I am informed by an expert that a couple of the star's costumes are things of great beauty and style. The direction is credited to Michael Benthall, but I don't believe for a minute that any mortal man was reckless enough to try to cabin and confine Miss Hepburn's volcanic art.

from Of Women and Children (*The Millionairess*),
October 25, 1952

★   ★   ★

"THE BAT," THE joint work of Mary Roberts Rinehart and Avery Hopwood, turned up last week at the National. This is its third production and the third time I have been subjected to this most lurid of all melodramas. Seldom, I think, have there been more opening and closing doors, more mysterious exits and entrances, more claps of thunder, more pistol shots, more bloody hands thrust through broken windowpanes, more shrieking, more cases of mistaken identity. The plot is some foolishness about four hundred thousand dollars concealed in a secret room in an old, dark house; the characters, who are various, to put it mildly, include an elderly lady, her beautiful niece, her eccentric maid, and a group of gentlemen of whom none is precisely what he seems. The whole affair is just about as silly as it can be, but the chances are you will be entertained against your better judgment from time to time.

Lucile Watson, ZaSu Pitts, Shepperd Strudwick, and Harry Bannister are among those chiefly responsible for keeping things moving.

from The Devil to Pay (*The Bat*),
January 31, 1953

★ ★ ★

THE BLUEFISH WERE going crazy last week at Fire Island jetty: six- or seven-pounders, so thick you could walk on their backs, and so sore they'd hit anything—a jig or a plug or even, probably, your finger if you were sap enough to stick it in the water. You didn't even have to retrieve after a cast. You could just leave the lure lying on the bottom and give it a couple of twitches and pretty soon one of the silly bastards would be on. For this reason, I didn't see "A Red Rainbow," by Myron C. Fagan, on its opening night, Monday, but put off going to it until Wednesday, being led by my colleagues' notices to believe there was a fine chance that the damn thing wouldn't be around by then. As it happens, however, Mr. Fagan is a stubborn man, and his work was still visible at the Royale when I got there, playing to an audience composed mainly of service men, who watched it impassively over their bubble gum and, for the most part, devoted themselves to comic books in the intervals.

"A Red Rainbow" was exactly as described in the papers. The actors informed one another and such members of the public as chanced to be listening that the late Harry Hopkins personally sold the atomic bomb to Stalin, that the disaster at Pearl Harbor was directly engineered by the Roosevelt administration, that the Black Tom explosion in the First World War was set off by the heroine's father, and a lot more that might easily tax the credulity of Westbrook Pegler. In the end, one of them was shot—conceivably by Mrs. Roosevelt, though I didn't linger long enough to find out. It was all dreadful beyond your darkest fancy.

Now, about these blues. The best way is to get there around five o'clock in the morning and—But no, there is a place for everything.

from Mrs. Snyder Goes to London (*A Red Rainbow*),
September 26, 1953

★   ★   ★

IT WAS ONE of the management's very minor eccentricities that no curtain rose on "Sing Till Tomorrow," a drama about a discontented druggist which was revealed last week at the Royale. The setting was already visible when early comers took their seats, and it remained so exposed during the whole demented evening. If this maneuver was intended to suggest that the piece was not actually meant to be regarded as a play, I should say that it served its purpose, because never, in a career that has demanded my attendance at such unforgettable specimens as "Grandma's Diary," "A Red Rainbow," and "Popsy," have I seen anything quite equal to it in moonstruck incoherence of plot, in horrid abuse of the English language, and in a style of acting strongly remindful of that attributed to the King and the Duke in "Huckleberry Finn."

"Sing Till Tomorrow" opened with a pale and furious young man standing in a beam of light. "This is my play," he said. "My father is in it. Evie's in it. I'm in it." I report these four sentences with such care because, as far as I was concerned, they were just about the last comprehensible remarks made that night. Words, of course, continued to pour across the footlights, but while an alert ear could identify them individually, they appeared to make little or no sense in combination. It was clear that the author is a powerful master of elegant variation ("I think I shall depart elsewhere") and deliriously tangled metaphor ("Your pestle is a striped candy bar crushed at the base of the Pyramids"), but beyond that I could deduce almost nothing about the quality or content of his mind. The action wasn't especially helpful, either. At one point, the druggist seemed to be upbraiding a companion for entering a cold-storage bass in a fishing contest; at another, several characters stood at the forefront of the stage and pretended to cast bait out into the audience; at still another, a band of resolute cutups set a small, jocular fire in the drugstore and extinguished it with punch; and throughout the play, the pharmacist addressed his wife as "Son," an arch device that may be unique in the annals of the theatre.

The actors principally involved in this massacre were named John Marley, Michael Sheehan, and Eileen Ryan. As I've said, their performances were somewhat lacking in polish, but I find it hard to contain my admiration for their memories. Anybody who could read, retain, and subsequently deliver the dialogue of "Sing Till Tomorrow" could, I should think, readily do the same thing with a cookbook. There is always the chance, of course, that they were just making it up as they went along.

from Many Marriages (*Sing Till Tomorrow*),
January 9, 1954

★　★　★

LAST YEAR, HORTON Foote wrote a play, called "The Trip to Bountiful," that permitted Lillian Gish to give a remarkably sustained and touching performance as a woman who travelled to a small town in Texas in an attempt to get back the unrecoverable past. It also contained at least one other part that showed the type of astute and bitter observation of small-town American womanhood that used to be the special province of Mr. Sinclair Lewis. Jo Van Fleet was cast in that one, and I thought she played it beautifully.

This year, in "The Traveling Lady," at the Playhouse, Mr. Foote has done just about the same thing. There is a girl who shows up in Texas looking for a new life with her ex-convict husband (the unrecoverable past), and there is a terribly funny picture of a woman who is, I'm sure, the kind of "character" without which no hamlet in this great nation could hope to get along. This one, specifically, has a passion for hunting fireflies at night; she is as apt as not to invite total strangers to go swimming with her; and she is very likely to entertain you with her memories of the Civil War, which took place a good many years before she was born, as her daughter is in the habit of indignantly pointing out. She is a very fine comic invention, and Kathleen Comegys realizes practically every possibility she offers.

Unfortunately, a play goes with all this, and it is hard to have anything but a low opinion of that. From the minute the curtain rose, it seemed quite clear to me that the heroine would wind up with the clean-cut young man called Slim (one of my impossible dreams for the theatre is a play in which the boy named Slim doesn't get the girl), and I watched the means by which this was accomplished with a good deal of detachment. A scene in which the unregenerate man was momentarily freed from his handcuffs in order that he might sing a farewell ballad to his child, with suitable gestures, produced something a little stronger than detachment, and so did one in which an otherwise excellent actress, Kim Stanley, who has the misfortune to be cast in the title role, went on and on about the circumstances that led her to take up with a bum in the first place, but I see no point in being needlessly unpleasant. It is enough to say that Mr. Foote has substantially recapitulated himself, and I just wish he would stop.

In addition to Miss Comegys, the supporting players are Mary Perry, Jack Lord, Calvin Thomas, Helen Carew, Katherine Squire, Lonny Chapman, Tony Sexton, and a tot known as Brook Seawell, who would probably do a great deal better if the director, Vincent J. Donehue, would let her alone. The set was designed by Ben Edwards. I can imagine no more horrible place to live, but I guess that was the idea.

from Two to Forget (*The Traveling Lady*),
November 6, 1954

★   ★   ★

MAURICE CHEVALIER'S PROGRAM of songs and impressions, at the Lyceum, brings up a point that I think I've touched on irritably once or twice before. This is the notion, energetically fostered by nearly every Gallic entertainer I have ever seen, that Frenchmen are disgustingly proficient in the art of love. It is not primarily a matter of physique—though they are apt to be wiry little devils—but, rather, of superior technique and sophistication. The oily scoundrels, that is, understand that practically all women really like to get mussed up but that what you might call the light-hearted approach is necessary. Anglo-Saxons, a race of heavy breathers, are no good, because the girls are apt to get the idea that a pretty weighty transaction is taking place. Ugly words like "marriage" pop into their heads, and before you know it the whole thing is on a business basis. Either that or they just get to pushing and giggling, which, of course, is even worse. It takes a Frenchman to convince a woman that amour, conducted with an accomplished partner, is a fascinating game of chance and skill at which, happily, everybody wins. This is the theory. The truth, based on my own observation of many Gauls at work, seems to be that it is all quite a bit like girls' basketball. There is a lot of squealing and jumping up and down, but certainly not much in the scoring department.

I go into all this again because M. Chevalier is probably the outstanding proponent of the argument that his compatriots have got sex sewed up. Other topics are dealt with in his current bill, but his heart seems most clearly in the items having to do with this special skill. There is one that demonstrates how suavely a true Parisian can accost a lady on the street without getting arrested; there is another about a young couple on a bench in the park who continue to embrace right through a thunderstorm, which shows, I suppose, that you can never damp a Frenchman down; and there is a third that explains that an English gentleman never boasts of his affairs, a reticence that is just comic to the merry *boulevardier*. Ah, Paris, ho hum.

If you think that this elaborate digression has anything to do with a reluctance on my part to express my opinion of the entertainment at the Lyceum, I guess you've got a point. Along with the rest of the audience on opening night, I did my sentimental best to recapture something of the old spell, but it was melancholy work. The tilted straw hat and the jutting lower lip were still in evidence, and so were most of the famous mannerisms, including that miraculously persisting difficulty with the pronunciation of the simplest words, but the real magic was gone. Chevalier was part of a wonderful period in the history of the theatre, but it has ended now and he is sixty-seven. Some of the charm comes back to life when he sings songs like "Louise" and "Valentine," but most of the time there are only memories on the stage.

from Jeune Fille Fatale (*Maurice Chevalier*),
October 8, 1955

from SCHOOLMASTER JANNINGS—
RADIO ANNOUNCERS, PORTIAS, AND
FLAGPOLE-SITTERS[1]
(The Blue Angel)

IN THE AVERAGE picture, bum dialogue doesn't upset me unduly. For one thing, I have come to expect it, and for another, it usually seems to me that it goes nicely with the bum story and the bum acting. It would, for instance, be a pity to waste good lines on a piece about a young lady who falls in love with an All-America quarterback. It does get in my hair, however, when so fine a performance as that given by Emil Jannings in "The Blue Angel," at the Rialto, is blurred by foolish and irrelevant talk, badly synchronized. "So you take three lumps of sugar," observes one character a little while after her lips have stopped moving. "Some sugar daddy!" That is a good sample, and the situation isn't improved by the fact that everybody talks broken English, possibly out of deference to the star, whose English is so broken that it is practically unintelligible.

If you can overlook the talk, though, it seems to me that "The Blue Angel" merits your respectful attention. This is the story of a middle-aged German schoolmaster whose career is crowned and broken by his marriage to a beer-garden singer. Jannings is very fine and plausible—by far, I think, the best character actor in the movies—and Marlene Dietrich, the woman I happen to be in love with, is beautiful and rowdy as the singer.

Altogether "The Blue Angel" is one of those things you ought to see, but I can't help thinking it would have been a lot better a lot quieter.

December 13, 1930

FOOLISH BUT FUN
(*National Velvet*)

Enid Bagnold's "National Velvet," which was a charming and preposterous novel, has been made into just about the same sort of picture. The story of a twelve-year-old girl called Velvet Brown, who wins a horse for a shilling in the village lottery, makes up her mind to enter him in the Grand National, is obliged for complicated reasons to pose as a boy and ride him herself, and then, almost too rapidly for the human eye, wins the race by a neck, collapses (revealing her sex), and, though disqualified by the stewards, becomes a worldwide celebrity overnight, has, of course, more the shape of a lovely, childish dream than anything in humdrum life. It is, however, such an intelligent and high-spirited fantasy—Miss Bagnold is one of the few who can successfully place real people in unreal situations—that I cheerfully sat through more assorted absurdities than you'd think it would be possible to crowd into one winter afternoon.

In addition to the heroine, an enchanting little monomaniac with braces on her teeth, "National Velvet" contains such other unusual characters as Velvet's sister, who seems to have dedicated her life to a bunch of canaries; her mother, who once swam the Channel breast stroke and is now, I'm afraid, inclined to be rather dogmatic or stuffy about the brevity of fame; an ex-jockey who once had an accident and now is afraid to ride; and a wonderful little boy called Donald, who seems to be the most majestic liar in the world.

The picture is in Technicolor and, though the sea is much too blue, the grass too green, and the people all too pink, it is less bothersome than usual, and the sequences devoted to the running of the National (four and a half miles and thirty jumps) are very exciting and, for all I know, reasonably authentic. Elizabeth Taylor, who plays Velvet, is not only a serious and touching child but apparently also a considerable horsewoman, though I doubt if I'd mistake her for a boy at anything under half a mile. She is principally assisted by Mickey Rooney, Donald Crisp, Anne Revere, and Jackie Jenkins, whose interpretation of a demon infant is enough to scare the daylights out of you.

December 23, 1944

WHAT HATH WALT WROUGHT?

(*The Three Caballeros*)

Walt Disney, who started out with a couple of mice in simple arrangements of black and white, has got to the point now where he will settle for nothing less than an ambitious combination of living women and caricatured animals and a series of backgrounds that are half stylized drawing and half what appear to be photographs of picture postcards, all executed in Technicolor. I can hardly believe that it is a step in the right direction. "The Three Caballeros," which is the occasion for this complaint, is ostensibly a patriotic attempt to cement our relations with South America. Actually, it is a mixture of atrocious taste, bogus mysticism, and authentic fantasy, guaranteed to baffle any critic not hopelessly enchanted with the word "Disney." It is probably best to take these points up in sequence.

In the first place, a somewhat physical romance between a two-foot duck and a full-sized woman, though one happens to be a cartoon and the other pleasantly rounded and certainly mortal, is one of those things that might disconcert less squeamish authorities than the Hays office. Leda and the Swan have the endorsement of the libraries and art galleries; Leda and the Duck, executed purely for comic purposes in a moving-picture theatre, may just possibly be obscene. It might even be said that a sequence involving the duck, the young lady, and a long alley of animated cactus plants would probably be considered suggestive in a less innocent medium.

The bogus mysticism, generally speaking, goes back to "Fantasia," in which Mr. Disney went in for a lot of kaleidoscope effects—mostly colored globes that split and dissolved—that were rather arresting on the screen but could be criticized aesthetically as pretentious and meaning just about nothing. In this case, set against the drawn scenery, which often has the naïve charm of the illustrations in a child's book, and the photographed scenery, which is vulgar beyond belief, it has a somewhat irrelevant and preposterous air.

The fantasy is something else, being a legitimate extension of Mr. Disney's best zoological humor. There is a penguin who can't get warm and sails away to the tropics on a cake of ice, a very disagreeable little bird who wrecks trains for his private amusement, a donkey with wings who wins a race, though even more severely handicapped than that horse in "National Velvet," and a very funny scene in which Donald Duck is mysteriously compressed into conventional Aztec designs. I have no hope of making this last item clear. It is, however, the sort of thing Mr. Disney ought to be doing, instead of pretending he is either Salvador Dali or the operator of a magic lantern.

The only other notes I have to offer on this production are that Donald seems curiously subdued, something that often happens to a vaudeville headliner abruptly transplanted to a full-length show; that the legend of the Nativity is a little out of place in a piece principally concerned with lecherous birds and orbicular chorus girls; and that if anyone is inclined to believe that "The Three Caballeros" is likely to promote good will in this hemisphere, he may be mistaken.

February 10, 1945

BEST-SELLER

(A Tree Grows in Brooklyn; Here Come the Co-Eds)

ALTHOUGH IT RUNS rather more than two hours, "A Tree Grows in Brooklyn" covers only about the first half of Betty Smith's best-selling novel, ending with Francie's triumphant graduation from grammar school. Since I read this vastly overrated book fitfully, lying on a beach in the sun, my memories of it are far from exact, but as I recall it, the heroine had a considerable emotional life and the beginnings of a literary one after she got her diploma. It may be that Twentieth Century-Fox is saving this material for a sequel. I hope not.

The film, in this truncated form, is probably an accurate pictorial representation of Williamsburg a generation ago, but the behavior of the principal characters strikes me as unlikely in any time or place and also as more than a little tedious. Francie, for the benefit of those who somehow contrived to duck Miss Smith's book, is the thirteen-year-old daughter of a drunken singing waiter, whom she loves passionately, and his hard-working, practical wife, who is fiercely determined that her children shall have all the advantages she never knew. In addition to this rather standard literary pair, Francie has two much more fascinating relatives in a younger brother who is opposed to the family's nightly readings from Shakespeare and the Old Testament on the ground that they don't seem to make any sense, and Aunt Sissy, a wonderful blonde who calls all her husbands Bill no matter what their real names happen to be.

Francie herself is a rather trying child, given to those long, doughy abstractions and elaborate fantasies that mark, I suppose, the budding writer. She is especially difficult with her father, who also has an untidy mind, though in his case, of course, the alcohol may be a factor. Anyway, in spite of the private fog in which she moves, they manage to get Francie through school, and the picture ends with everybody straightened out, including the mother, now widowed, who gets herself engaged to a policeman, described by everyone as "a good man." This phrase, by the way, was applied to practically every male on the screen at least once, lending a certain monotonous, or tom-tom, beat to the dialogue.

The acting in "A Tree Grows in Brooklyn" is, I should say, a good deal better than the text. Peggy Ann Garner, an appealingly plain little girl, has the tough job of portraying the authoress's memories of herself as a noble and sensitive child and does it with an admirable gift for making synthetic pathos seem almost real; Dorothy McGuire, as the mother, has what the program notes describe as "one of the choiciest dramatic rôles" in years but handles it with dignity and restraint, even in a childbirth scene that might seem too graphic to Elmer Rice; James Dunn, as the mildest case of acute alcoholism I ever saw, is suitably Irish, with that special quality of gay futility which may explain why all Brooklyn loves a bum; and Joan Blondell, as Aunt Sissy, is almost perfect in this raucous part, though I found it a little hard to believe that such a dressy type could neither read nor write. Elsewhere in the cast, I observed Lloyd Nolan, Ted Donaldson, James Gleason, and John Alexander, all good men.

As a footnote to the above, I would like to say that I am getting very tired of literary authorities, on both the stage and the screen, who advise young writers to deal only with those subjects that happen to be familiar to them personally. It is quite true that this theory probably produced "A Tree Grows in Brooklyn," but the chances are it would have ruled out "Hamlet."

IN "HERE COME the Co-Eds," Lou Costello and his more serious accomplice, Bud Abbott, have quite a time in one of those comedies about lifting the mortgage on a girls' college. At one point, Mr. Costello swallows a pair of oversized dice and his friends shoot crap with him, observing the results through a fluoroscope; at another, he almost loses a hand when an irascible oyster snaps up at him from a stew; and in the end he finds himself playing basketball, in a very unusual blond wig, against a team of young amazons, all at least seven feet tall, who keep stepping on him. The humor, as you can see, is more or less physical, but it enchanted my son (nine and a half) and is recommended to similar customers with no hesitation at all.

March 3, 1945

Thoughts on Infinity

Personal and Professional Essays

LITTLE NEMO AND THE
CARDBOARD LION

THE REASON I approach the theatre as I do, with suspicion and a cold foreboding, is that for me it began with a cruel deception. In nineteen-six or seven there was—and for all I know there still may be—a theatre at the corner of Broadway and 110th Street called the Nemo. At about the same time in the Sunday *Herald* Winsor McKay was drawing a comic strip called "*Little* Nemo," dealing, as everybody remembers, with the adventures of the most fortunate child in the world.[1] No sooner did Nemo's head touch the pillow each night than he was transported to an agreeable dreamland where almost anything could, and did, happen. Each night for the approval of The Princess, who was as pink as a puppy's stomach and more beautiful than I can tell you, he outwitted a great many odd creatures, including a clown called Flip, a doctor in a red-and-white stovepipe hat, and a Zulu. (This was the peculiar era when comic strips were drawn for and usually about children; the idea of drawing them for stenographers and elevator boys, or even for the aesthetic appreciation of Gilbert Seldes, didn't turn up until much later.)[2] Anyway, to a child living in those days and in the God-forsaken purlieus of upper Broadway, the connection between "Little Nemo" and the cheerfully illuminated theatre on the corner was obvious and irresistible.

For a long time, because children couldn't go in alone and because my parents had their own ideas about the kind of entertainment suitable for the young, I was able only to stand wistfully on the sidewalk outside, watching the happy crowds on their way to see Little Nemo, miraculously translated into flesh and blood, outwitting Flip and the Doctor. Finally an aunt, younger than my parents and credited by them with an irresponsibility bordering on madness, yielded to my entreaties (why I wanted to go to the Nemo was obviously a mystery to her, but she was an amiable girl and seldom bothered people for explanations) and off we went. I can remember few details of that disastrous performance: it began, I think, with a troupe of performing dogs, and ended for me—of this, I *am* sure—with a mystifying scene in which a fat man spanked a young lady repeatedly with a board. I can remember clearly that I sat, tricked and furious, in the smelly dark.

THAT WAS THE first deception and the bitterest, but the theatre had by no means finished with me. A few months later, in Baltimore, I was taken to see "The Wizard of Oz;" I went with the complete approval of my parents, for it was guaranteed to be an antiseptic performance, containing, among other things, those Galahads of musical comedy, Montgomery and Stone.[3] Thinking of it in retrospect, I'm sure that for grownups "The Wizard of Oz" must have been charming, but for me it was just more perfidy and foolishness.

As I'd had about "Little Nemo," I had a perfectly clear picture in my mind of what I was going to see. Dorothy, L. Frank Baum's heroine, was a child of about my own age who went through a series of encounters with animated scarecrows, wizards, and talking animals which I was able to accept without believing; or perhaps without believing that similar experiences were possible for me, while not finally questioning that they did happen to her. There is, I think, such a period in almost every childhood, when we can accept simultaneously the reality of actual life and the reality of supernatural happenings in books. In any case, the characters in "The Wizard of Oz" were real to me and I knew what they looked like, and what I saw in the theatre that night was all wrong.

In the first place, Dorothy, although she wore a parody of the costume in the book, was definitely grown-up; not perhaps quite as antique as my parents, but certainly old enough to be excluded from any world in which I had the slightest part or interest. She also had a habit, unknown to the real Dorothy, of detaching herself suddenly from the events around her and singing a song. In the book, there was one particularly satisfactory chapter in which Dorothy rode a lion through a field of deadly poppies; in the miserable fiasco on the stage, not only Dorothy but the lion and even the poppies themselves (who also on inspection proved to be elderly women) burst suddenly into a repulsive song that had no possible bearing on anything that was going on. I loathed them all.

I really think, however, that that lion was my bitterest disappointment, although the Tin Woodman and the Scarecrow were bad enough. In the book, I had admired him enormously and envied Dorothy the grandeur of riding on a live lion, but this lion was a miserable fake, incapable of making anybody (except conceivably an adult) believe that he was anything more than just an actor dressed up, and certainly incapable of carrying the changeling Dorothy around on his back. I was sad enough to cry about him, and whenever I read the Oz books after that, it was never a living lion I saw, but a cloth-and-cardboard one, prancing idiotically on its hind legs.

Synthetic animals played an increasing part in my disillusionment about the theatre. Nana in "Peter Pan," for instance, was transparently not a Newfoundland, any more than the creature that swallowed the alarm clock was an alligator, or could sensibly have been regarded as an alligator by anybody under the age of ten. And a little later, the horses that raced in "Ben Hur" were real horses all right, though small, but they raced on a treadmill that was only too visible and audible even up where I sat disgustedly in the gallery.

It never let up, in fact, and presently I began to suspect that all so-called "children's entertainments" were designed to provide adults with a bogus and condescending nostalgia. Looking back, indeed, I can remember no approved entertainment of my childhood, except perhaps the circus and parlor magicians, that was anything but a violation of my private ideas, and it wasn't long before I formed a surreptitious attachment for the movies. For a while then I was happy. I never quite understood, I'm afraid, why the Emperor Nero kept chasing the pretty ladies, but at least they were real lions that ate the Christians, and they really ate them, too, sandals and all. The trouble was that the old doubt persisted and soon reappeared, and has grown stronger with the years. Even the movies, I suddenly found out, weren't very much like the books. It was only a little while ago, in fact, that I sorrowfully watched a Catherine the Great without a lover to her name, and a Nana (Zola, not Barrie) who was a good girl at heart, just misunderstood.[4]

May 25, 1935

WHAT EVERY BOY SHOULD KNOW

A COUPLE OF weeks ago a young man from N.Y.U. came to talk to me about the theatre, having been previously discouraged, it seemed, by most of my colleagues. He picked the same day that my son and some of his little friends had chosen to find out if you could build a snow man on a radiator, so it wasn't a very successful interview. We agreed that up to then the season had been disappointing and touched on a few other matters, but after a while the smell of damp childhood got to be too much for him and he went away, without getting what he really came for, which was material for a little essay on the happy life of a dramatic critic and how to get to be one. The children, for inscrutable reasons of their own, decided that he was an interpreter and were rather disgusted with him for not speaking several languages; I don't think he was very favorably impressed with them, either. In any case, the profound and searching things I had been prepared to tell him about my work never got said and, in view of the fact that there is nothing else of a theatrical nature on my mind at the moment, I might as well put them down here. Attached, then, are ten golden rules for the benefit of any young man who plans to spend his life inspecting actors and hopes to get paid for it.

I—*The Quick Fade, or Some Ethical Aspects of Ducking after the First Act.* This practice is frowned on by all virtuous reviewers. Just because a playwright has been dull and illiterate for forty minutes, it is not fair to assume that he's going to go on being that way the rest of the night, though I'm sure I don't see *why* it isn't. If the second act also appears to be the work of an idiot child, however, it is O.K. to go home. Thus, when I left "My Fair Ladies" at 10:25 last Sunday evening, I wasn't conscious of sin. There was enough suffering at the Hudson without adding mine.

II—*The Marginal Notation, or Hen Tracks in the Sands of Time.* The

most successful critics are always scribbling things in their programs, largely because it gives them an important and industrious
air. Also, it is interesting to try to figure out what you've written
afterward. Last week, for instance, I made a very helpful note during the second act of a drama called "They Walk Alone." "Lanchstr
get face stuck 1 these nights awful if," it seemed to say.

III—*Second-Story Men at Work, or Guarding the Koh-i-noor.* Now
and then the writer, brooding in the dark, thinks up an epigram so
concise and deadly that it is almost a complete review in itself. Naturally, there is a strong temptation to exhibit this pearl to his colleagues, who huddle on the sidewalk between acts like dusty crows
on a fence, but it is always resisted. The seasoned critic, in fact, never
offers anything but his second-best meditations to anybody before
he gets his piece written. This is an unnecessary precaution, since no
critic ever really thought another had any opinions worth listening
to, much less swiping, but it is part of the tradition and should be
respected.

IV—*The Well-Dressed Critic, or What God Would Wear.* To the
considerable annoyance of their wives and sweethearts, it is hell's
own job to get most reviewers into dinner coats for anything less
than Shakespeare or a $6.60 top. The working uniform, generally
speaking, is a well-worn gray suit, apparently stuffed with dead actors; a blue shirt; and a hat that can be sat on. This outfit is a form
of criticism in itself, a notice to producers that its wearer is no man
to be intimidated by any fancy stuff on the stage.

V—*Just Try to Beat Daddy to the Bar, or How About a Quick One?*
The intelligent critic is very wary about skipping across the street
for a drink between the acts unless he is going to give the show a
rave. If he pans it, the management's spies will instantly conclude
that he was drunk as a mink when he wrote his piece and probably
telephoned it in from a brothel. See also *"The Quick Fade."*

VI—*Hobson's Choice, or Whither Grandma?* About once a week
the average critic is asked to recommend a show suitable for an old
lady who has something seriously the matter with her head. This is
the only really insuperable problem to be met with in the profession, except perhaps moving west on Forty-fifth Street on a rainy
night. "Hellz-a-Poppin" is as good a choice as any, on the ground

that there is a chance it will either kill her off altogether or else leave her too batty to complain, but you can't count on it.

VII—*The Rueful Meeting, or Bygones Are Never Bygones on Broadway.* With a few exceptions, actors, playwrights, and producers have schooled themselves not to dismantle hostile critics in public. Some haven't, however, and the critic who knowingly frequents places where actors congregate deserves whatever he gets. After all, sensible bullfighters don't drink cocktails with the bulls.

VIII—*The Empty Chair, or The Bad Companions.* Even critics' wives sometimes get enough, and there will be times when you'll be faced with the problem of what to do with that extra seat. This is a very important matter, because, consciously or not, you are almost sure to be influenced by your companion's behavior. I know earnest and mournful young women who have almost persuaded me that Beatrice Lillie was silly, and frivolous little items who crowed so happily over Ibsen that I have often been tempted to look under them for eggs. The critics I know meet this dilemma in various ways. One man takes his physician, others take their relatives, many evade the issue by going alone. Altogether, the last is probably best, since it solves the problem of what to do with your coat.

IX—*The Critic as Sphinx, or What's Behind Nothing?* Simple-minded customers sometimes look at critics to see how they are taking the show. This is just a waste of time, because the veteran observer's outside appearance has little or nothing to do with his emotions. If he laughs, the chances are that he is amused by his own mysterious and dissolute thoughts; if he looks solemn, he is probably merely asleep. This protective inscrutability has to be cultivated by young critics, but after a while it gets to be second nature.

X—*The Mantle of Winter, or Edwin Booth Revisited.* Old critics frequently try to intimidate their juniors by going on about some performance of "Hamlet" they saw immediately after the Battle of Appomattox. This is irritating, but it can be ignored by the philosophical. Remember that in 1965 you will undoubtedly be just as tiresome about Maurice Evans, and that Time takes care of everything in the end, even the New York Drama Critics Circle.

A PRIMER FOR CRITICS

SEVERAL WEEKS AGO, on this platform and in a dangerously offhand spirit, I discussed some of the basic principles of dramatic criticism. These had to do exclusively with the *social* behavior of the critic at work—his proper conduct, that is, while sitting on his hands, observing the performance; his attitude toward his colleagues and the public between acts; his costume, his diet, and various other matters pertaining strictly to that half of his function which takes place in and around the theatre itself. This week, I would like to talk about the other half—the actual writing of the copy which will be printed and distributed to cultivated people everywhere. As before, there will be ten divisions, and here they are:

I—*The Critics Have a Word for It, or Behrman Is Urbane.* Because of publication deadlines, critical writing usually has to be accomplished at high speed, in a considerable lather of the spirit. This allows little time for the selection of the precise word—the adjective, in most cases, that will define the special quality of some particular talent, pinning its wings for posterity, like a bug on a cork. This midnight struggle for the *mot juste,* this terrible flogging of the static imagination, has driven many critics into retirement; those who have survived have done so by meeting the situation realistically. These farsighted writers, when they sit down to deal with a drama, are already prepared to take care of its personnel, at least as far as the adjectives go, because over the years they have chosen and memorized one definitive word for every man or woman of reasonable prominence in the theatre. Thus, of the playwrights, Mr. S. N. Behrman, as noted in the title of this section, is invariably urbane (to distinguish him from Mr. Philip Barry, who is merely witty), Mr. Eugene O'Neill is brooding, Mr. Noel Coward brittle, Miss Clare Boothe beautiful, Mr. William Saroyan antic, and so on, down to the Irish dramatists, all of whom, except Mr. Bernard Shaw, are tenderhauntingandpoetic, pronounced as one word. Mr. Shaw is impish. Of the actors and actresses, Miss Katharine Cornell, of course, is gracious; Miss Gertrude Lawrence, electric; Miss Helen Hayes, poignant; Mr. Victor Moore, lovable; and all the Barrymores, already legendary. A complete check list of these useful terms, suitable for framing, will be sent postpaid on receipt of a loaf of bread, a jug of wine, and Miss Carmen Miranda, for whom no adequate word has yet been coined—at least by me.

II—*Once Upon a Time, or the Sneak Preview.* In most publications, theatre reviews are supposed to take up a certain minimum amount of space, and this is often a severe test of the critic's ingenuity, for plays will sometimes come along about which he finds he has absolutely nothing to say. There are several ways of meeting this problem (one man I know seizes such occasions to discuss another play, in which he has some slight personal interest, having written it), but the most popular method is a complete synopsis of the plot, including whatever clever surprise the playwright may have thought up for his final curtain. This material can be introduced as early as the second paragraph and requires almost no preliminary gambit. "The story itself," writes the reviewer, making his mind a blank, "deals with a young couple who have come to New York from Racine, Wisconsin, where he has been employed as congestion manager in a rag works. The city is strange to them, and when she is arrested for peddling narcotics in the Barbizon Plaza and almost simultaneously discovers that she is pregnant, the husband in desperation telephones Walter Winchell. In the meantime . . ." All this, plus a paragraph saying that Miss Haila Stoddard is poignant and electric as the girl, Mr. John Emery poignant and electric as the boy, and everybody else adequate and electric in minor rôles, fills up two pages, and by 12:45 the critic is usually able to slope off quietly to a bar, his duty done.

III—*Songs of Social Significance, or God Bless Chiang Kai-shek.* Too often dramatists, a cynical crew, are in the racket merely for the dough and write plays as barren of moral or political content as Fannie Farmer's cookbook. It is up to the conscientious critic to remedy this situation. One good system involves the use of the hothouse parallel, or arbitrary coincidence, in which the writer points out that at the very instant that Mary is playing Chopin to Desmond in the conservatory forty-seven workmen are trapped in a coal mine in Tennessee. The clear implication is that Mary and Desmond ought to get right down there and dig them out, and it is certainly a stinging rebuke to the playwright and maybe even to Chopin for wasting his time on piano music. The best trick, however, is to credit the play with a secondary level on which the author's real purpose becomes apparent. The discovery that his neat little bedroom farce is in reality a ringing denunciation of capitalistic morality may astonish the innocent author, but this obviously isn't the critic's fault.

IV—*The Dissenting Opinion, or What Makes Horse Races.* It would be a very dull world, I'm sure, if everybody always saw eye to eye with everybody else, and the critic owes it to himself and his readers to come up with a startling disagreement at least once every season. Naturally, there are two choices available here. Either he can dislike and attempt to dismantle some brave and tender old piece of junk that all his colleagues are busily grooming for immortality or else he can salvage some little job that they have tossed in the ash can and jam his own personal laurels down over its ears. Both are almost equally satisfactory and if the box-office figures happen to bear him out in the end, he automatically becomes a major prophet and can ask for more dough.

V—*Tongues of Angels, or Please Come Off the Roof.* Style in the dramatic critic is a somewhat dubious blessing. Because of the rapidity with which he is obliged to compose, the writer can hardly expect to achieve both symmetrical prose and rational substance; it is either lovely balderdash or stumbling logic, seldom both. A review, for instance, that begins "Far away and very long ago, in the time of the last of the Caesars, there lived a woman whose rueful incandescence was destined to survive two thousand years" is hot stuff all right, but the chances are that it isn't going to be *about* very much. The critic in this case has decided to sacrifice information to syntax, and you can be reasonably sure that he is sitting at a desk where he can watch himself in the mirror. On the other hand, if the first sentence reads " 'Minnie Gaspard,' a drama by Adam Fox and Hugh Gimbel, directed and produced by F. Douglas Windboy, opened last night at the Bandbox, with a cast headed by Gloria

Bosquette and St. Clair Cummery," you are in for some pretty grim reading, but you will probably wind up with most of the facts. Some readers love beautiful words, strung like pearls; others are simply in the market for theatre tickets and want to find out what's what. You can't please them both. It is a very tough business.

VI—*Critics Should Be Heard but Not Seen, or Please Stick to the Subject.* A poet of sinister perception, writing in this magazine, once laid his finger on a very disquieting characteristic of the reviewer at work:

> *The critic leaves at curtain fall*
> > *To find, in starting to review it,*
> *He scarcely saw the play at all*
> > *For watching his reaction to it.*[1]

The average worker in the dark vineyard, in fact, is usually conscious of two plays—the one on the stage and the one represented by the behavior of his own arrogant and subtle mind. His temptation is to give the second a considerably better notice than the first, but this ought to be resisted. For some reason or other, readers just aren't interested in how critics arrive at their opinions. What burning memory of the past, for instance, what sad old scar makes Mr. X so skittish in the presence of plays touching on adultery is usually a matter of indifference to the public, though probably of the deepest interest to Mr. X himself. And the fact that Mr. Y, confronted with a Chinaman on the stage, is irresistibly reminded of his own travels in the mysterious East may charm fewer readers than he ever dreams. The average subscriber, mousing through a column on the drama, has no real wish to grapple with its author's personality or to listen to his reminiscences. He has to go through enough of that kind of stuff with his wife's friends.

VII—*The Black Arts, or Fools Rush In.* Very often, in the theatre, the curtain will go up to reveal a room differing in no important respects from a sample exhibit in the window of a furniture store, but the audience will applaud as if it had suddenly been vouchsafed a private glimpse of the powder room in the Taj Mahal. On other occasions, a female character will appear in a costume by no means as rich or peculiar as twenty to be observed in the first three rows of the orchestra, but she too will get her brief ovation. These are two of the small but exasperating mysteries that make a dramatic critic's life the burden that it is. It is up to him, in the pursuit of his duty, to comment on both scenery and costumes, but since he is neither an interior decorator nor a dressmaker, his remarks are usually very silly indeed and just serve to amuse all the pretty, sardonic ladies and the delicate young men who really know something about these recondite subjects. The only safe procedure that I can think of is a cautious retreat into generalities. "Greymalkin's settings contributed effectively to the sombre mood of Mr. Ramlett's play" is a good standard evasion when you're talking about scenery, and "Ilonka Fraschetti's gowns had a brilliant pictorial quality" ought to take care of the girls' dresses. As far as I know, neither of these statements means anything at all.

VIII—*The Hen or the Egg, or Who Does What?* To the unseasoned critic, the director's function is frequently at least as baffling as the scenery and costumes. A dramatist I know told me the other night about an unsettling experience he had during a rehearsal of his own most recent play. He was sitting in the dark auditorium beside his director when suddenly he observed that the man seemed to be on the edge of strangulation.

"What's the matter with *you?*" our friend asked anxiously. "You sick or something?"

"Certainly I'm sick!" yelled the director. "Look at that guy up there. Do you see what he's doing?"

The playwright looked up at the stage, where an actor was running through his part. Aside from that, he didn't seem to be doing anything in particular.

"What's the matter with him?"

"Matter with him?" gasped the director. "He is committing a cold-blooded, deliberate, ghastly, god-damn murder, that's what's the matter with him. *He's out of the triangle!*"

"Oh," said our friend.

If it illustrates anything, this aimless anecdote goes to show that there is more to the theatre than meets the casual eye, and the point where the actor leaves off and the director begins, or vice versa, is at best a matter of considerable guesswork with the critic. This problem, too, should be approached discreetly by writers who don't wish to seem uninformed to the people of the theatre, on the whole a vicious and unscrupulous crew when it comes to reprisals. "Tobias Gregg's direction, as usual, was crisp and imaginative" won't get you in any trouble, except with people who happen to think it stinks, and it is permissible to say he handles his crowds well, if there are any. Anything beyond that, however, is taking a chance, and anything at all about choreography is plain suicide.

IX—*Shakespeare and Stuff, or Hats Off, the Bard Is Passing By!* Foreign dramatists, both the quick and the dead, have to be handled with mittens, but Shakespeare is the worst, and it is a reckless critic who will admit publicly that his life would soil be supportable even if he never saw another Capulet. The commentators of more than three hundred years have picked the bones of the plays themselves moderately clean, but each revival is a ringing challenge to every reviewer's theatrical erudition. Like the horrible little guessing games that sprang up all over during the prohibition era, every new performance of one of the Bard's major works calls for a complete list, with comparative analysis, of all the actors who have ever played important parts in it, and, in the profession, a critic stands or falls by the number he can reel off without stopping. This, of course, is especially true of "Hamlet," any man who hasn't seen at least seven versions of this work obviously being a literary nonesuch who ought to be out covering fires. Whether or not the public appreciates the vast amount of Shakespearean research that is done on its behalf, however, is hard to say. Once, in a spirit of sacrilege, I named my own nine favorite Hamlets, suggesting that they might get up a ball team. The list was composed of Forbes-Robertson, Mantell, Hampden, Barrymore, Gielgud, Howard, Tinker, Evans, and Chance, and after a dusty afternoon in the Library, the most scholarly of the *New Yorker* proofreaders came back to report that as far as existing records showed neither Mr. Tinker nor Mr. Chance had ever played Hamlet in his life.[2] It may therefore be that the average reader doesn't know or care much one way or the other about the glorious traditions of the English-speaking stage. The *aficionados* are something else, though. Get funny with the Swan of Avon and they will snatch you bald-headed. I know.

X—Kneel to the Prettiest, or Oscars Aweigh! Somewhere in town the eighteen gentlemen and the solitary lady of the New York Drama Critics Circle met this week in a smoke-filled room in a hotel. They were assembled to choose the best play of the season, presumably Miss Lillian Hellman's "Watch on the Rhine," although, as I write this, Mr. William Saroyan's entry is still snorting at the post. In a week or two another group, the Pulitzer Prize Committee, will gather for the same purpose, and their choice may well be "Claudia," a clean, high-minded little piece, very suitable indeed for elderly gentlemen of a sentimental turn of mind. In the end, if you persist in following a career which can never lead to any good and whose practitioners are usually buried by their relatives furtively and late at night, you too will be confronted with this same responsibility. There is little I can do to guide you in your moment of terror and uncertainty. "Best," as employed by the gray brothers on the aisle, is a hard word to define. It doesn't mean the play at which the largest number of people are apt to have the most fun, or even the one at which the critic himself has been lifted most effectively out of criticism and into a state which might conceivably pass for pleasure. It means, as nearly as anything so intangible can be caught in print, the drama which most closely approximates a composite picture of the critical mind; that is, it may be daring but not vulgar, original but not eccentric, witty but not cynical, indignant but not subversive, dramatic but not lurid. Obviously, a very fine play, such as "Watch on the Rhine," can fulfill all these conditions. On the other hand, an equally fine one might violate most of them. The fallacy of criticism lies somewhere in this paradox. The trouble with the whole strange business, children, is that it has so very little to do with entertainment. I think that will be all for the moment. Write on one side of the paper. Try to keep your noses clean.

April 26, 1941

THE KINGDOM OF THE BLIND[1]
An Ex-Moving Picture Reviewer Considers His Ex-Job

FROM EARLY DECEMBER 1944, until this past September, I was employed to review moving pictures for a magazine of modest but genteel circulation. It was, a makeshift arrangement, brought about by the war, and long before the ten months were over, both the editors and I were aware that a mistake had been made. Nothing was actually said, but there was an air of constraint and embarrassment, rather as if we had both made up our minds to ignore the fact that I had suddenly developed a slight impediment in my speech, and when in a moody moment I resigned, everybody was visibly relieved. Since the subscribers gave no indication of either agreeing or disagreeing with anything I wrote, it seemed permissible to deduce that they hadn't bothered to read it. The only comment from the profession appeared in a screen writers' trade-paper on the Coast. It compared me sardonically with Marcel Proust, the idea being that I gave the impression of operating from an insulated cell, in a very fancy atmosphere of anemia and corruption. Since one of my colleagues was described as writing as if his upper plate had worked loose, however, it was possible to regard this as a compliment.

The purpose of this essay is to explain, as clearly as I can and while certain memories are still green, why it seems to me that the cinema resists rational criticism almost as firmly as a six-day bicycle race, or perhaps love. I am conscious of the danger of generalizing too freely from a very brief experience and also of stating some things that are both obvious and highly prejudiced. However, it's a chance I'll have to take, and it is my indignant opinion that ninety percent of the moving pictures exhibited in America are so vulgar, witless, and dull that it is preposterous to write about them in any publication not intended to be read while chewing gum. The exceptions to this indictment are the documentaries, which have, of

course, only very limited opportunities to distort life; frank melodramas, which have nothing to do with life and are therefore exempt from criticism; and the occasional pictures, one or two a year
at most, which defiantly photograph some recognizable fragment of
our common experience and generally lose a good deal of money.
They are so few that obviously no one could hope to find regular
employment writing about them, and consequently they can be
ignored here.

The explanation of the ninety percent is so elementary and it has
been offered so many times that it needn't detain us long. The cinema is a medium of entertainment economically feasible only if it
can be sold to an audience of probably a hundred million in this
country and God knows how many more in the rest of the hemisphere and across the sea. It must, of course, be intelligible to a vast
majority of these people. The common level of intelligence in the
world is presumably that of the normal adolescent, who has no need
or ability to relate the parts to the whole, or the present to the total
stretch of time. To him that is, a baby is a baby, cute and permanent; it has no future and there are no conclusions to be drawn from
it. (The persistent survival of Jackie Coogan as a middle-aged man,
with a divorce and thinning hair, incidentally, often has an unnerv-
ing effect on lady cinema patrons, though they are only vaguely
aware of him as a symbol of their own continuity.) The level of
formal education, of course, is even lower, so that any system of civilized reference is obviously out of the question. To get in a picture,
Homer and Emerson must first be suitably defined, in words of not
too many syllables.

The third factor that has to be considered in this universal audience is the manner of life to which it is accustomed; its incredible
extremes of wealth and poverty, its varying social concepts, and its
differences in language, technical progress, and even climate and
clothes. To some extent, Hollywood has succeeded in imposing its
own vision of life on the world, so that a cocktail party on Park
Avenue need no longer be entirely mysterious to an Eskimo. However, while the cocktail party has gone far beyond life in gaiety and
magnificence since people can be taught to accept almost anything
visually, it has been necessary to scale it down almost to imbecility

in behavior since nobody can be expected to recognize a system of conduct or conversation that has its roots in a more elaborate background than his own. The result of all this is that very little seen or heard on the screen is precisely a picture of anything.

As if these handicaps were not enough, a series of strict, external codes, governing their political and moral content, have been imposed on the films either by organized pressure groups or else by unorganized but highly vocal minorities with a taste for out-size fig leaves. This makes it impracticable to name political philosophies or explain what they stand for, to discuss religion in any terms conceivably startling to the inmates of a parochial school or a Baptist seminary, to speak disparagingly of any specific business, except perhaps dope-running or the white-slave trade, or to deal with sex in any way that might indicate that minor irregularities are not necessarily punishable by a lifetime of social ostracism and a lonely and untended grave. Hollywood, of course, did not frame these rules, but its own earlier excesses of vulgarity (not frankness or daring) were responsible for their existence in the first place, and it has not been noticeably heroic in combatting them up to now.

Given all these restrictions, whether imposed by financial considerations or the Hays (now Johnston) Office, it is inevitable that the moving pictures should be just what they are—an astounding parody of life devoted to a society in which anything is physically and materially possible, including perfect happiness, to a race of people who operate intellectually on the level of the New York *Daily News*, morally on that of Dayton, Tennessee, and politically and economically in a total vacuum. I know, of course, that there are a great many pictures, usually "sophisticated" comedies or glum dramas of the soil, that *seem* to exceed this definition. It is only an illusion, however, though often an extremely clever one. Close attention will inevitably prove that no rules have been broken, that no sinister worldling ever says anything that would be essentially surprising from your grandmother, that no doomed share-cropper ever really criticizes anything more specific than the climate.

★ ★ ★

HOW THE CONSCIENTIOUS reviewer writes about the so-called A pictures (those that cost more than a million dollars to produce) is a small but fascinating literary comedy. Aware that he is dealing with names that are household words from Newark to Bangkok, with minds that command up to five thousand dollars a week for their power and agility, and with budgets that rival the national debt, he gets an uneasy feeling that such massive vulgarity somehow requires massive treatment, though those are not perhaps quite the words he'd use. Pictures are good or bad to him, for he has his standards, but their quality, whatever it is, is on the grand scale, and his discussion of it takes on a very peculiar accent, enormous, educated, and fuzzy. He writes, you might say, rather the way Henry Wadsworth Longfellow used to look.

Generally speaking, however, he has space for only five or six hundred words and very little time to put them down. The result is that he has developed a very special vocabulary in which words come to transcend their exact and customary meanings—in which, in a sense, they are detached from the language and inflated like little balloons, and presently sent spinning, lovely, iridescent, and meaningless, into the wild, blue heaven of critical prose. "Luminous" is such a word. Coming from the typewriter of a skilful operator, it means that the performance given by a young woman who has probably gone through each scene from ten to twenty times with her director and still has only the vaguest idea what it is all about is strong, beautiful, humorous, tragic, and lit with something of the same strange, ineluctable fire that once burned bright in Duse and Bernhardt. It means, that is, everything and nothing; it is both the non-word and the all-word. "Taut" is another and says, in reference to an actor's work, that he is somewhat greater than Booth or Salvini, and, in reference to a story, that it is high time for "Hamlet" to move over. There are a great many of these wonderful words—"haunting," "lyric," "brave," "tender," "compassionate," and, above all, "poignant" occur to me in passing—and they are invaluable in imparting such a cosmic air to a conversation that it is never quite apparent just what precisely is being discussed. The only trouble with all this, in fact, is that, habitually so used, these words can no longer be employed in their original and limited sense.

The reviewer is also remarkably talented in summarizing the complicated but fundamentally non-existent plots that come his way. These, too, he inflates to several times their natural size, colors with vague but impressive suggestions of other meanings than those that appear on the surface, and also sets adrift in space. In speaking, for instance, of a tornado that has apparently only a simple, melo-dramatic intent, he is apt to write, "There is, it seems to me, a pro-found and urgent ["urgent," by the way, is another favorite all-word] symbolism in the storm that carries away Miller's house and drowns his bed-ridden aunt." The symbolism is very seldom explained, but it is apt to delude everybody, including the writer, into believing that a subtle analogy has been offered, unerringly detected, and stylishly exposed.

In addition to complimenting the players and magnifying the plot, it is, of course, the reviewer's duty to go into the difficult matters of direction and photography. The first of these, since the mass mating of minds in any Hollywood picture makes it practically impossible for the layman to tell who did what is usually conveniently dismissed by the use of a few all-words, or of phrases like "Mr. Desmond displayed great resource in his handling of nuclear mass," or "Mr. Drear's use of casual overtones is provocative, both of which I presume mean some-thing or other, though not to me.

Photography, on the other hand, is something actually visible on the screen and it is a good deal harder to brush off since the writer is confronted with an insanely complicated endlessly refined, and wickedly deceptive technical process, about which it is reasonable to assume that he knows about as much as he does about the inner workings of a seismograph. He has picked up a few useful terms like "lap dissolve" and "pan take," but for the most part he is obliged to rely on his personal artistic judgment, which, logically enough, since he is not an art critic, is apt to be unformed. He is a great one for "correct" or "striking" compositions, those, that is, that most closely resemble the paintings on sale in department stores, and he is a pe-rennial sucker for the studiously telling details—a dead and falling leaf, a face in a crowd, a hand slowly relaxed—that are all part of a sort of primitive emotional shorthand used by the films to trap the unwary. Since photography is the one thing that Hollywood handles with invariable competence, and often with considerable taste and ingenuity, it seems too bad that the reviewers are neither mechanically nor esthetically equipped to deal with it adequately.

ALL THAT I have written, of course, has probably passed through the mind of anyone who has given any appreciable thought to the cinema. It took me ten months of notable physical discomfort and mental confusion, however, before I really saw, in the terms set down here, the whole absurdity of what I was trying to do—to write, that is, for the information of my friends about something that was plainly designed for the entertainment of their cooks—and before I realized that I had no intention of ever doing it again. I once knew an educated and almost excessively cultivated man who really enjoyed reviewing the movies. He was, however, a special case, in that he was unfailingly amused in his wintry way by sex in what he was pleased to call its "contactual aspects," and the idea of an art form fundamentally based on the slow, relentless approach and final passionate collision of two enormous faces struck him as convulsing. He wrote about it all with a wonderful, maidenly distaste, and to the total bewilderment of the motion-picture industry, but he really had the time of his life. He was also a very valuable critic since, free from the terrible spell of Love, he saw a good deal that escaped his colleagues.

Saturday Review of Literature, November 17, 1945

ROBERT BENCHLEY: IN MEMORIAM

O NE AFTERNOON ABOUT two years ago, Bob Benchley dropped in at my home for a drink. It was at a time when my life had got more or less turned around backward, something apt to happen to a drama critic, and as usual I was still in my pajamas, though it was about six o'clock in the evening. The idea of not dressing till nightfall seemed rational enough to me, since I had nowhere in particular to go in the daytime, but it was a matter of some concern to my son, who was just eight, and attending a school where, it seemed, the other boys' fathers performed respectably, and suitably clothed, in their offices from nine to five. Apparently, the jocular explanation among my son's classmates who came to call on him from time to time was that I was a burglar by profession, and it caused him intense embarrassment. When Benchley finally got up to go, and I went to the door with him, it was more than the child could peaceably bear.

"Gee, Dad, you're not going to start going out in the street that way, are you?" he cried in dismay.

"No," I said. "I'll try to spare you that final humiliation."

It was hardly a notable remark, but it seemed to amuse my guest, who chose to regard it as somehow typical of my domestic life, and he laughed very gratifyingly thereafter whenever he happened to think of it. This anecdote, dim and aimless in itself, is illuminating only in that it shows how politely anxious, how delighted he really was to promote his friends, and I certainly wasn't an especially old one, to the pleasant company of fellow-humorists.

When you were with him, in the wonderful junk shop he operated at the Royalton in "21," or in less fashionable saloons which had the simple merit of staying open all night, you had a very warm and encouraging feeling that you were a funnier man than you'd previously suspected, the things you said sounded quite a lot better than they really were and, such was the miracle of his sympathy and courteous hope, they often actually *were* pretty good. He wanted his guests to feel that they were succeeding socially and he did his best to make it easy for them. The truth, of course, was that Benchley himself maneuvered these conversations, tactfully providing most of the openings for wit, but the effect was that people were mysteriously improved in his company, surprisingly at home on a level of easy charm of which nobody would have dreamed they were capable. This willingness to play straight man to amateur but hopeful comedians is rather rare in the world he inhabited, where it is not customary to give very much away, but he did it instinctively.

I have used the word "courteous" before, but it seems inevitable. He was one of the most courteous men I ever knew, in the sense that whenever he was aware of a feeling of insecurity or inadequacy in anyone he met, he was automatically their genial, admiring ally against the world. It committed him to a great many bores and some men and women who used him rather shamelessly, and he knew it all right, but he was helpless. Perhaps it was a price he had agreed with himself to pay for the luxury of knowing that he had failed very few people in kindness.

Most of the available anecdotes about Benchley have recently been put through the giant mangle operated by the gossip columnists, coming out in the form of an extremely depressing hash, and I have no intention of adding to them here. Anyway, his humor didn't fall very easily into formal patterns. He was enchanted once when a young woman employed to grapple with his wildly tangled affairs remarked quite unexpectedly, "Sniff. Sniff. Somebody in this room has brown eyes" (I have probably butchered that one as cruelly as the genius on *The Post*), and most of the things he said or wrote himself that reflected his personality most accurately had the same quality of almost-logic, the same chilly, fascinating little skid off the hard road and right to the edge of the swamp, where the mind goes down and doesn't come up.

Though a great many earnest students have tried, the nature of humor has never been very satisfactorily defined—there are too many tastes and nothing is terribly funny to everybody—and it is a reckless thing to try to put any writer into a neat and permanent compartment. It is especially hard for me with Benchley, because the extra fact of known personality inevitability gets into it, too. Rereading his pieces, that is, my judgment is influenced by a clear picture of how he would have looked telling the same story, punctuating it with the abandoned laughter that used to be so famous at opening nights, and assisting himself with gestures of quiet desperation.

It is also conditioned by another absurdity not apparent in the text. For the most part, he wrote about his own polite New England bafflement in the face of strange but negligible crises; the actual fact was that he led one of the most insanely complicated private lives of our day and did it, on the whole, with extraordinary composure. It is possible that this secondary information makes his stories seem funnier to me than they really are, so that my estimate of his talent may be a little high. I can't honestly say that he made me laugh more than any other humorist writing in his time—some of Thurber's maniacal experiences in Columbus, Ohio, still seem to me incomparable as examples of comic genius operating on what must have been an extremely favorable environment—but I think he was, by far, the most brilliant and consistent of the school, originating with Leacock, who performed such dizzy miracles with parody, *non sequitur*, garbled reference, and all the other materials of off-center wit.

He avoided with a very acute instinct the monotony that can come from a reiterated comic device and the disaster that comes from crossing the strict line which divides high comedy from awful foolishness. He was sure, wonderfully resourceful, and his style, really based on a lifelong respect for good writing, would have been admirable applied to anything. It was no secret, I guess, that his later appearances in the movies and on the radio bored and depressed him, though he was enormously successful at it, for he was dedicated to writing, and he suffered bitterly when, mistakenly or not, he decided that he couldn't do it any more, and never did.

IN COMMENTING ON him as a critic, an editorial note in *The New Yorker* said:

His reviews had a quality now largely missing in criticism in that they reflected a complete personality, genial, sensitive, informed, too mature and tolerant to care about the easy, rather discreditable reputation for wit that can come from hasty and intemperate ridicule. It was a weapon he didn't need anyway; his disapproval was all the more effective because it always seemed clear that his kind heart was far more anxious to admire and praise.[1]

That was true of all his work and, in a sense, of all his life. His death was a sad loss to thousands of people who never knew him; to his friends it still seems almost incredible. He took up so much room in so many lives.

New York Times, December 16, 1945

THE SECRET LIFE OF MYSELF

(An Essay in an Idle Week, with a Peck on the Cheek for James Thurber, Who Wrote "The Secret Life of Walter Mitty")

THE REHEARSAL WAS going very badly. For at least the fifth time, the leading lady had come to the line which was supposed to read, "From now on, darling, you'll have to be strong for us both," and simply shaken her head in pretty despair.

"It's no use, Max," she said at last to the director. "I simply don't *feel* this scene. It sounds so damn silly. I know it's supposed to be sophisticated comedy. 'One of Charles L. Bedrock's urbane and searching studies of a woman's heart.'" She laughed unpleasantly. "But nobody can tell me that any woman in her right mind is going to leave her husband for the *Wagner* Act. Especially to take up with a man who keeps on telling her what a terrible time she's going to have. 'I'm afraid I can't promise you anything for a long time but all my love and the clean satisfaction of a good fight.' For God's sake, what is that supposed to be? Churchill? I'm sure Bedrock is a great writer, but somebody ought to tell him he isn't Lillian Hellman."

They all looked at her helplessly, because it was obvious that the scene couldn't be played as Bedrock had written it. It was disastrously naïve in the way that often happens when a poetic and essentially cloistered talent attempts to deal with the affairs of the changing world.

"Perhaps you have some constructive suggestions, Miss Rembody?" said the director sardonically.

"No," she replied. "All I know is it stinks."

"God," he said. "I wish Wolcott Gibbs were here. He's only a drama critic, but I understand he's been called in a couple of times—secretly, of course—to advise Behrman and Robert E. Sherwood and a couple of others. I bet he'd know what to do."

"Perhaps I would, Max." The quiet, rather tired voice came from the back of the darkened theatre and it was a moment or two before the others could identify the speaker in the gloom. It was indeed Wolcott Gibbs, however, and as he spoke he came slowly down the aisle, furling his umbrella.

"I just dropped in for a moment to get out of the damn rain," he said, "but now that I'm here, of course, you're quite welcome to any assistance I can give. Would you mind trying that line just once more, Miss Rembody?"

"'From now on, my darling, you'll have to be strong for both of us,'" she began, responding automatically to his easy charm, as so many women had.

"I see," he said. "The idea, as I get it, is that you're prepared to give up your old life at the Stork Club and '21' to help your lover gather material for his book on the evils of the vertical hook-over system in the automotive industry."

"Whatever that may be," she said.

"But you're a little afraid not only of giving up financial security but also of the ridicule of all your old friends?"

"That's it," she said. "Isn't it silly?"

"Precisely," he said. "It's a basically preposterous situation. Even a Theatre Guild audience would laugh it off the stage. Let me see." For a moment he was lost in thought while they watched him anxiously. At last he snapped his fingers and turned to the director.

"You got your secretary here, Max?" he asked. "I can't guarantee that these are exactly the final lines, but at least it's something for Bedrock to work on. All right, Miss . . . ?"

"Grismund, Mr. Gibbs," she said rather breathlessly, for it was the first time she had met a critic in the flesh. "Yes, I'm ready. If you don't go too fast."

"Here we go, then," he said. "Instead of having Miss Rembody looking out of the window and saying that last line, she goes over to a little bar in the corner—you'll have to put that in, of course—and makes herself a cocktail. Very slowly and carefully, because she's trying to make an important decision. We see only her back for a minute, but when she turns around she has a glass in her hand and there's a curiously ironic little smile on her face. 'Marsden,' she says, or whatever the guy's name is, 'Marsden, did it ever occur to you that I'm a beautiful woman?'"

"Well, that's more like it," said Miss Rembody.

"Naturally, you're a little startled by that, Mr.—ah—van Drum, isn't it?—but you recover in a second. 'Of course, everyone knows you're the loveliest thing in New York, Bedelia,' you say, giving a little bow."

"As *I* understand this character," said Mr. van Drum, "he is one of those crusading journalists, like Quentin Reynolds or Ralph Ingersoll—you know, a sort of slouchy, Lincoln type. It seems to me that a sophisticated note like that is a little out of key. More for somebody like Coward, I'd say. Anyway, I don't see how I'm going to learn damn near a whole new part with the show opening this Saturday night."

There was dismay on every face, for not only was Forrest van Drum a notoriously slow study but it was also clear that this new conception of the part was fatally at variance with his rough-hewn appearance and his pleasant but unmistakably Middle Western ac-. cent. At last Darius Portaman, the old producer, who was an almost legendary figure in the theatre, sighed and shook his head.

"I'm afraid it's no go, as you youngsters put it," he said. "I think Mr. Gibbs is on the right track, but nobody else could possibly learn the part in time, unless"—his eyes lighted for a moment, but then he gave a rueful smile—"but, of course, that's out of the question."

"What?" said Miss Rembody.

"I was going to say unless Mr. Gibbs would consider taking it on himself, but I'm afraid that was just a dream. I'm sure his profession has taught him practically all there is to know about acting, but naturally he isn't an actor himself."

To everyone's surprise, Miss Rembody gave a delighted little laugh.

"Perhaps he isn't now," she said, "but he certainly was once."

"What do you mean by that, Miss Rembody?" asked Mr. Portaman. "I don't think this is exactly the time for levity."

"I'm not joking," she said. "It was a long time ago, when I was a very little girl. I had a brother up at the Riverdale Country School and one spring my mother took me up there for their spring play. It was 'A Midsummer Night's Dream' and Mr. Gibbs was Puck. I'm sure you'll laugh, but it was one of the most astonishing performances I ever saw in my life. He was only a boy, of course, but it was really brilliant—confident and gay and absolutely professional. I'm sure exactly what Shakespeare meant Puck to be."

"Is that so?" said Mr. Portaman. "Well, this is certainly a great stroke of luck. Think you could see your way to giving us a little hand around here, Mr. Gibbs? I'd certainly appreciate it."

"I don't know, sir," said the critic rather doubtfully. "I'm afraid a man's apt to get a little rusty after thirty years."

"Nonsense, my boy," said Mr. Portaman. "Acting is something in one's blood. Either you're born with it or you aren't. I've got a pretty big investment represented in this show—about four hundred and sixty-five thousand dollars, I think—and if I'm willing to take a chance on it, I don't see why you shouldn't be. After all, what have you got to lose?"

"Well," said Gibbs, with his melancholy but rather charming smile, "you can never tell about those sons of bitches in the Drama Critics Circle, but . . ." He gave a quick shrug, obviously having come to a decision. "Ah, the hell with them. The worst they can do is take away my membership, and I don't think they'd dare go as far as that. After all, I know where a good many bodies are buried. It's a deal, Mr. Portaman! I'd be delighted to play Marsden Barlock for you!"

"Thank God!" breathed the old man. "You've saved the day. Miss Grismund, take a note to arrange for Mr. Gibbs' Equity membership on your way home this afternoon. After all," he said with the ghost of a chuckle, "we might as well do these things according to Hoyle."

"That's right, sir," said Gibbs, taking off his overcoat and assuming the position on the stage rather irritably vacated by Forrest van Drum. "Now, where were we? Oh, yes, I've just said, 'Of course, everyone knows you're the loveliest thing in New York, Bedelia,' and now, Miss Rembody, you say—let me see—yes, you'd better say, 'Thank you, kind sir. And that's precisely why I can't go on with this. I don't wish to seem cynical, Marsden, but I can't help feeling that there is a certain absurdity in the spectacle of a beautiful woman, clearly designed for love, carrying one of those little signs in a picket line.' "

"By God, I think he's got it!" whispered the director, as the clear, unhesitating voice . . .

"For heaven's sake," whispered Mrs. Gibbs, tugging at her husband's sleeve. "*Now* what's the matter with you?"

"Eh?"

"I don't know," she said. "You were muttering and tossing around as if you were having a nightmare. You weren't really asleep, were you?"

"Certainly not," he replied. "May have just shut my eyes for a minute, that's all."

"Well, you'd better try to keep them open," she said. "After all, that's what you're supposed to be paid for, isn't it?"

"Oh, God, I guess so," he said, and focussed grimly on the stage, where Marsden Barlock was just clasping Miss Rembody in his arms and from the context it appeared that they had decided to take the midnight for Detroit. I still think it made more sense the way I had it, he thought, and if that van Drum can act, I'm Ty Cobb.

January 19, 1946

ONE UP, ONE DOWN

TRYING TO RUN down a rumor that there is some peculiar tradition of the stage which demands that the opening show of each new season shall be an almost unforgivable insult to the intelligence of the customers, I have just been back over the evidence for the past five years as submitted in this department—an egocentric project, if ever I saw one. Even excluding occasional vagrant midsummer enterprises, like the recent, dreadful exhumation of "Rip Van Winkle" at the City Center, which really are just expressions of a sort of hot-weather delirium, I find that the initial ventures of the season have presented a bloodcurdling picture indeed.

On August 31, 1942, the miserable entry was something called "I Killed the Count." Such, apparently, was my indignation with it that the record supplies neither the name of the author nor even any rational summary of what the damn thing was about. "The dullest exhibition you can imagine," I wrote, and trailed off feebly into a list of the doomed actors in it.

On September 1, 1943, "The Snark Was a Boojum" came to town. The notes on this are more or less incoherent: "A confused, vulgar, and tiresome little piece . . . never before, probably, has an audience been so relentlessly pelted with sad, moist old jokes or so cruelly bludgeoned with innuendo . . . to the bewilderment of an audience which clearly had no idea what the hell was up and to the disgust of my colleagues, who once again found themselves confronted with the old problem of writing a whole column about nothing."

The candidate on August 21, 1944, was "Song of Norway," and here the pattern was almost broken. I liked the music, which was derived from Grieg; some dances, staged by George Balanchine; and the rather pretty Scandinavian scenery, designed by Lemuel Ayers. The book, however, seems to have been the inevitable September

disaster. "Everything was all right," the review said, "as long as nobody talked."

Another musical mishap turned up on September 6, 1945. " 'Mr.
Strauss Goes to Boston,' " I wrote, "is typical of all the big, foolish
operettas that sidle hopefully into town around this time of year. It
seems incredible that anybody accustomed to wearing shoes could
sit through the pre-adolescent humors of Leonard Levinson's book
and the complex vulgarities of Robert Sour's lyrics without some
dim feeling of being beaten over the head with a bundle of old radio scripts."

Last year, on September 5th, an operetta was again the first offering
to reach Broadway. Richard Tauber, it appears, was "imbedded in an
almost incredibly childish operetta called 'Yours Is My Heart.' . . .
Fred Keating turns up, now and then, at his old tricks with vanishing
canary birds. I vanished without his assistance at the end of the second
act."

Last Wednesday, to bring this melancholy calendar up to date,
"The Magic Touch" opened at the International. It was falsely described as a comedy, there being no humor in it more complex than
the spectacle of a dignified matron sitting down in a chair full of
pins; it was acted with a good deal more enthusiasm than discretion; and it was in every sense a perfect successor to the casualties of
all those other falls. Since, barring some autumnal madness of your
own, there seems no reason to believe you will ever be exposed to
it personally, I will not burden you with the names of the performers,
the details of the plot, which are far from clear to me anyway, or
quoted proof of the really staggering illiteracy of the script. It is
enough to say that the losing streak has not been broken. The season of 1947–48 has opened; the night of September 3rd is history. I
wouldn't give it a second thought.

September 13, 1947

IN DEFENSE OF DERMATHERMY

SUNBURN, OR TAN, according to the most reliable authorities, is a morbid condition of the skin resulting from overexposure to actinic rays. It has been known to be fatal to humans and, in Australia, a certain species of rabbit is so embarrassingly susceptible to it that its ears drop off. These, however, are extreme cases. Far more often, the results are no more serious than rubescence, swelling, chills and fever, nausea, coma, exfoliation of the epidermis, or peeling, and minor hallucinations such as the impression that the sufferer has died and gone to hell. As far as science can determine, man is the only animal that deliberately and defiantly exposes himself to the sun for any other purpose than getting warm or dry; the only animal, that is, prepared to cook himself as a form of social or sexual decoration, or to imagine that he would, in some mysterious way, look *better* cooked. The prospect of appearing nude on a platter with an apple in his mouth, for instance, is undoubtedly repugnant to any sensitive pig. A man sizzling on an August beach differs from the pig in that he is alive, aware of his condition, and probably has a cigar rather than an apple in his mouth, but otherwise the resemblance between them is strong, and on the whole favorable to the pig, which is certainly younger, more shapely, and has, after all, the merit of being edible. Basically, the man's conviction that the painful, unnatural, and potentially dangerous charring of the frail envelope that, so to speak, holds him in one piece, gives him extra charm, especially to the opposite sex, is under the same delusion, that afflicts the female Ubangi when she distends her lower lip to the dimensions of a dinner plate. It is a demonstration that, in spite of the eons that separate him from his first home in the sea, man still does a lot of things that would seem foolish to the average fish. This, very briefly, is the case against self-mutilation by heat, and I can't deny that it is a strong one.

★　★　★

THE ARGUMENTS IN its favor may seem inadequate or frivolous, taken one by one, but I think the sum of them more than bal-
ances the scale. For the reader's convenience, I will tabulate them
numerically:

1. Young women of the better class are reluctant to take off their
clothes to any really interesting extent, unless they can somehow
assure themselves that they are doing it for some more virtuous reason than simply to stun or fascinate the male. In spite of all the grim
evidence to the contrary, a girl on a beach can always convince
herself that the sun is good for her ("You can get vitamins or something") and that the more of her person she can expose to it, the
healthier she is going to be. Men, and elderly or untidily constructed
members of her own sex, may attribute baser motives to her, but her
private conscience is clear. This, of course, is a very comforting state
of mind for her, as well as a distinct improvement in the landscape as
a whole.

2. A man with an impressive coat of tan may still be an almost
total physical wreck, a perennial bankrupt, and a stupefying bore,
but so powerful is the tradition that a well-bronzed skin postulates
health, wealth, and strange adventures in distant lands that his chances
for social, financial, and even amorous advancement are usually
excellent, especially in the pallid society of the boulevard and market place. A fine example of this is the cachet enjoyed by the sun-
burned male among the British, to whom he is almost a symbol of
the Empire.

3. To some extent, the combination of sun, sand, and sea actually
is conducive to health, since a certain amount of physical activity is
more or less inevitable. From time to time, the intolerable heat and
the busy flies are almost bound to drive even the leatheriest addict
down into the adjacent surf, to soak if not to swim, or off on brief,
salubrious walks along its edge. Also, every day is a tiny moving day
for families who live on the ocean, with a complex arrangement of
umbrellas, blankets, backrests, and children's toys to be set up each
morning and then bundled up and carried home each night. This is
enough exercise for any civilized human. There are men and women
who throw balls, wrestle, make love, drink cocktails, and otherwise

comport themselves recklessly, but they are extremists and apoplexy will get them in the end.

4. Mentally, a man sunning himself is in a remarkably happy vacuum. It is practically impossible for him to read, since newspapers blow away, and any book more difficult than a detective story is too much for his drowsy mind; he is incapable of rational conversation, since his thoughts are as enormous and shapeless as the clouds on the distant horizon; he can't even worry about the state of the world, since a worrier, generally speaking, needs facts to go on and in his warm confusion, he can't for the life of him remember what they are. Altogether, he is little higher in the scale than a shell, a crab, a gastropod, but much more tranquil and relaxed than any urban man can hope to be.

5. Socially, the advantages of lying in the sun are also considerable. As noted previously, ambitious conversations and foolish games are discouraged, and even if they do spring up, it is always possible to escape them simply by walking away or falling asleep, two forms of criticism hardly possible in a drawing room or a restaurant. Furthermore, the Society of Sun Worshippers is not only highly exclusive, being confined to those who have almost unlimited leisure on their hands (real tanning is no part-time job) as well as reasonably tough hides, but also, paradoxically, it is agreeably democratic, since there is nothing like a pair of bathing trunks to make a banker look like a bum and vice versa. This situation is frequently confusing to women, who often contract financially ridiculous alliances in the rosy delirium of summer, but eugenically it is all for the best, breeding the most spectacular physiques of the nation to produce a new race of supermen, or at any rate, lifeguards.

6. Even educationally, sun-bathing has its advantages, since the proper student of it almost invariably develops a thorough, if rather specialized knowledge of chemistry. The cosmetic industry has invented countless oils, greases, lotions, salves, and creams to promote a lovely, even glow while discouraging total incineration, and the real aficionado feels obliged to test them all, basting himself now with one and now with another formula, until at last he finds the perfect ointment of his dreams. It has been my own experience

that a man whom God intends to burn will burn even through a heavy coating of lard, but this is a minority opinion (like my conviction that the Giants will be leading the National League by Labor Day), and I guess it can be ignored.

7. This final point is, I'm afraid, more or less personal. After more summers in the sun than I care to count, my own skin is practically impervious to its rays. In the beginning, perhaps, there is some slight rubescence, followed by a gentle exfoliation, but after that, like Shadrach, Meshach, and Abednego, I am at home in the furnace, and by the Fourth of July the finished product is ready for the public.[1] In this condition, I have been variously described as a well-worn moccasin, a middle-aged Hiawatha, and, due to the simultaneous bleaching of my hair and darkening of my pigment, to a photographer's negative. I prefer, naturally, to think of myself as a viking, irresistible to any intelligent woman—but actually my appearance is unimportant compared with the spiritual change that goes on behind it. The winter man, pale, apprehensive, lost in the dark tunnel of months from November to May, gives way to a superior stranger—arrogant, remote, coldly amused by the sufferings of the unhappy week-end guest, whose soft white skin bubbles so comically, so like the pitch in the seams of a whaler, in the awful heat. The time comes too soon when the season is over, and my own skin fades from copper, to Mongol yellow, to the color of a wet newspaper—but while the sun is high I am inseparable in spirit from Sitting Bull and Cecil Rhodes and the Gaekwar of Baroda.[2] It is a brief illusion, but still the happiest I know.

Cosmopolitan, July 1949

"NON-GRADUATES, WE ARE GATHERED HERE . . ."

L ADIES AND GENTLEMEN:
   Looking, over this vast audience, composed of more than ninety-three per cent of the population of this nation, I am reminded of a remark once made to me by a friend who had just been graduated, with considerable relief on both sides, from Yale University.

"The only really useful thing I learned at New Haven," he said, "was how to sleep sitting up."

There is, of course, a certain amount of exaggeration here. College training obviously does other things for the young man or woman fortunate enough to enjoy it. It teaches him or her certain special accomplishments, or social graces, among which might be listed the knack of borrowing larger sums of money from more people and with infinitely less embarrassment than is usually possible to a product of secondary education; the capacity for indulging in elaborate and mysterious rituals, unequaled by anyone except perhaps a member of the Ku Klux Klan or an African head-hunter; and the ability to understand the delicate distinction that exists between an amateur and a professional football player. It also provides him ("him" from this point on will be understood to include both sexes) with a group of memories, usually having to do with alcohol, sex, or practical jokes, or possibly all three simultaneously, that will supply the major portion of his conversation for the rest of his life, and with a collection of friends who, being themselves overflowing reservoirs of precisely the same kind of reminiscence, can generally be relied on not to get up and leave the room at the first mention of old "Pig" Struther, or the day the boys from Kappa Sig put the broken glass in the swimming pool. None of these skills and memories and friendships can or should be minimized. They are the symbols of a gracious way of life, and I'm sure America would be a poorer land without them. It is not pleasant to think of a nation bereft of such great traditions as the one which decrees that any member of Skull and Bones who mentions a woman's name between seven-thirty and nine-fifteen at any bar shall be publicly branded with a "C" for Cad, or that other and even darker one that leaves a Hook and Bullet man caught shooting fish, with no alternatives but death or the Foreign Legion. No, if these things were lost, the light of civilization would burn more dimly from Maine to California. Without "Pig" Struther, we would be a dull and humorless people; without Skull and Bones, we might indeed be lost.

We are not here today to debate the value of a college education—for it is clearly invaluable—but to try to determine whether for people like you and me, who are without its advantages, life can still be endurable; whether in the stern race for survival you and I can hope to compete with "Pig" Struther and his friends. The odds are great, but the answer, my friends, is "Yes"! There are, in my opinion, two ways of achieving this end. The first, which may have occurred to some of you, is the simulation of a college education. This requires not only a considerable talent for mimicry, but also a good deal of personal bravery, for your true college man is apt to show small mercy to impostors. How well do I remember the fate of one poor friend of mine who recklessly attempted to pass himself off as a graduate of Hardin-Simmons when he had in fact gone directly into business on finishing at Groton. He was stoned—yes, my friends, stoned to death on the floor of the New York Stock Exchange! On the whole, all things considered, I am not inclined to recommend this method. If you are successful in your impersonation, the rewards, of course, are enormous, but the strain of carrying it out is incalculable—another unfortunate friend of mine lost his mind completely while striving to master a book of Harvard songs and cheers—and the result of exposure, as we have seen, may well be death, and a lonely and untended grave.

No, my advice to you here today is: Grasp the nettle! Bite on the bullet! Face, in short, the grim and unalterable fact that you are disadvantaged in the race, with the same courage that those who suffer from some grave physical disability are so often able to face their own particular misfortune! There is, in fact, much for us to learn from the crippled, the halt, and the blind, who, as we know, usually develop some extra strength or skill to make up for those they lack. It is in this way that the noncollege man must develop *his* faculties to the utmost to compensate for his lack of those "outward and visible signs of an inward and spiritual grace" which are, of course, the natural heritage of the fortunate alumnus of a great university. It may sometimes seem impossible to overcome by will alone, the seemingly insuperable handicap of not possessing a diploma, but it can be done. May I repeat that thought? *It can be done!*

If I may dip once more into my apparently inexhaustible fund of personal reminiscence, I once knew a man who never survived the eighth grade in Tombstone, Arizona, but was still able in later life to reach the position of Second Vice President in Charge of Complaints, Altercations, and General Abuse in one of the most famous mink dispensaries on the Eastern seaboard, and whose social career, thanks partly, of course, to a marriage with the proprietor's daughter, included membership in the Audubon Society, the New York Athletic Club, and the American Society for the Prevention of Cruelty to Animals—other, naturally, than mink. How, you may well ask, did this man come so far with such scant and even laughable equipment? I'd like to give you the answer in his own words.

"Every morning," he once told me with a smile, "I repeat a very simple formula, saying it over to myself ten times. 'I will so conduct my life today,' I tell myself, 'that any act of mine could well be adopted as a general rule of behavior at Princeton University.'" Obviously this is a high and difficult ideal, but it paid off in one man's case, and I see no reason to doubt that it will be equally successful with every man and woman here.

IN *WHO'S WHO in America*, which is, of course, a listing of our most distinguished citizens, the number of noncollege men is rather less than one in ten. This is a dark prospect for us to face, but there is, I think, still some comfort to be gained from this volume. While it is true that certain professions such as medicine, law, teaching, and the clergy are usually closed to the non-graduate, there are many others in which his handicap will be negligible, if indeed it exists at all. Few stage actors and actresses and almost no screen stars, for instance, are products of the higher learning; though many artists and musicians hold degrees, academic training is by no means essential in this field; and, hard as it may be to believe, the highly educated writer is the exception rather than the rule, as witness the careers of such eminently successful practitioners as Mr. Ernest Hemingway, Mrs. Eleanor Roosevelt, Mr. Walter Winchell, and Mr. Erle Stanley Gardner. None of these busy and gifted people went to college. Indeed, there is some question in my mind whether a thorough knowledge of the classics or a formal grounding in syntax would have benefited any of them, or whether it would have simply slowed them up. The figures on politicians are not readily accessible, but some brief research would seem to indicate that while most senators, diplomats, and members of the judiciary possess more than high-school training, it is not necessary or even customary for a congressman to get much beyond the eighth grade, and it is presumably possible to pass directly into Congress from kindergarten. In this connection, it might be interesting to note that though Mr. Thomas E. Dewey is a graduate of the University of Michigan, President Truman got his early education in the public schools of Independence, Missouri. He entered the Kansas City School of Law when he was thirty-nine.

No address such as this would be complete without some brief listing of men and women who did get to college but whose conduct thereafter was such that I think it can safely be said that, even among the anointed leaders of our thought and morality and social behavior, there have been, if you will permit the expression, "a few bad apples." Such a list might include Mr. Alger Hiss and Miss Judith Coplon, who are, momentarily, in the public eye; Mr. Richard Whitney, who not only went to Harvard but even stroked the crew there, and whose subsequent career certainly fell far short of these distinguished beginnings; Dr. John W. Webster, another Harvard man, who bludgeoned a colleague to death and then cut up the remains and concealed them in a vault under the Medical College; and Mr. Aaron Burr, who was graduated from Princeton with the highest honors and whose later history needs no discussion.

★ ★ ★

THERE ARE UNDOUBTEDLY many more, but these, I think, suffice to show that while college men are unquestionably superior to their fellows, it is still conceivably possible for one to turn out rather disappointingly. This is an idea that has sometimes given me comfort in my hours of despair, and I hope that it may do the same for you. Ladies and gentlemen, I thank you.

Cosmopolitan, June 1950

STUFF AND NONSENSE, MR. C.[1]

R EADING THIS DEPARTMENT—the first thing I do every morning after various necessary domestic chores, like putting out the cat—I have often been struck by the fact that Mr. Crosby seems to be under the impression that he leads a tough life. He is employed to look at, listen to, and write about stuff that usually appears to him to be the work of halfwits; he is supposed to criticize work that defies any rational criticism; and altogether he is an outstanding example of misapplied talent—a hunter out after rabbits with a machine gun. The point I would like to make is that this is mainly nonsense, or at least comparative nonsense. In theory, if not necessarily in the opinion of my colleagues, I am a critic myself, hired by an indulgent management to attend something like eighty shows a year and subsequently to record my impressions of them, in a reasonably fashionable and antic prose. Mr. Crosby is called upon for rather more volume (about two hundred pieces a year as opposed to thirty-five), but otherwise I should say that his sufferings are negligible compared with mine.

In the first place, his career permits him to operate in a stationary position, from an expensive arm chair, with his coat off, and presumably with something cold and stimulating in his hand. In my work there is nothing like this happy condition. As often as not, it is either raining or snowing when I set out on my appointed round, and even if it isn't, there are seldom any cabs in the slum area in which I live so that I have to progress dismally and circuitously from East to West underground, usually winding up somewhere in the mysterious catacombs underneath Times Square, where it is said many a man has been lost forever.

THE THEATER ITSELF, on an opening night, isn't a very comforting place for a nervous man. The old faces (and some of them

are getting very old, indeed) have the effect of a recurring nightmare: the off-stage conversation is loud and generally facetious, for
there is hardly a first-nighter who doesn't fancy himself as a humorist: the air is almost always either too hot or too cold and strongly
charged with the scent of alcohol, perfume and disinfectant; there is
rarely any adequate place to dispose of a hat and coat; and again there
is the anxiety about getting a cab in the end—a doomed project,
since only the first ten or twelve people leaving the theater are likely
to be so accommodated and there are those who, after years of experience, can run rings around an antelope. These are by no means
all the physical discomforts attached to my career—there is, for instance, the matter of trying to make notes on a program in the dark
which are apt to seem to say, "Why she keep that goat in the attic?"
on inspection the following morning—but they are probably enough.
It has sometimes occurred to me that managements would be well
advised to furnish each critic with a good stiff drink of something
or other on his arrival at his seat, but I'm afraid this idea will never
really take hold, the consensus among producers being that a writing man operates best in a state of faint uneasiness and melancholy.

So much for the disadvantages of going to the theater in the flesh
as opposed to getting one's entertainment from a box. I suppose it
might be reasonably held that the living stage is a more elevated medium than radio or television and that the artists employed on it are
likely to be more exalted than those who reach their audiences
through the same current that works the ice box and vacuum cleaner.
It is a point I have no intention of debating, beyond remarking that
for sheer and staggering ineptitude I will match a little number called
"Grandma's Diary" with anything that ever turned up on Mr. Crosby's set, not excluding those programs intended to be enjoyed while
boiling an egg.

THE GREAT BOON, the staggering privilege, that Mr. Crosby
enjoys is that he doesn't have to write about anything unless he happens to feel like it. The machine operates continuously; the deadly
surge of creation goes on night and day; it is up to him only to loll
there, watching and listening, sipping and smoking, making perhaps a legible little note from time to time, until it seems to him

that enough material has accumulated for a column. The writing itself may present certain difficulties (the only writer I ever knew who claimed that composition caused him no pain was a very bad one and is now employed, I think, in a filling station), but they are by no means unsurmountable, especially if the tone is to be one of well-bred distaste which, as practically every author knows, is the least taxing of all literary attitudes. In fact, in my frequent visions of Mr. Crosby at work, I see a happy man, abundantly supplied with quotations that need no editorial comment; synopses of plots that would seem elementary to an Eskimo; and, above all, with the inalienable right to discard anything that seems likely to turn into a dull piece.

It is far, far different in the theater. If it happens, as it frequently does, that the week's only production is a revival of "Two Gentlemen of Verona," executed by a group of people whose only real qualifications for the theater are enthusiasm and leisure, the unhappy reviewer has to deal with it doggedly and at considerable length, gaining himself a formidable reputation for boring the public to insanity. On the whole, it is a dog's life, compared with that led by Mr. Crosby, and I am delighted to have this opportunity to get the facts down on paper.

New York Herald Tribune, May 20, 1951

Coda

THEORY AND PRACTICE OF EDITING
NEW YORKER ARTICLES[1]

THE AVERAGE CONTRIBUTOR to this magazine is semi-literate; that is, he is ornate to no purpose, full of senseless and elegant variations, and can be relied on to use three sentences where a word would do. It is impossible to lay down any exact and complete formula for bringing order out of this underbrush, but there are a few general rules.

1. Writers always use too damn many adverbs. On one page recently I found eleven modifying the verb "said." "He said morosely, violently, eloquently, so on." Editorial theory should probably be that a writer who can't make his context indicate the way his character is talking ought to be in another line of work. Anyway, it is impossible for a character to go through all these emotional states one after the other. Lon Chaney might be able to do it, but he is dead.

2. Word "said" is O.K. Efforts to avoid repetition by inserting "grunted", "snorted", etc., are waste motion and offend the pure in heart.

3. Our writers are full of cliches, just as old barns are full of bats. There is obviously no rule about this, except that anything that you suspect of being a cliche, undoubtedly is one and had better be removed.

4. Funny names belong to the past or to whatever is left of Judge magazine. Any character called Mrs. Middlebottom or Joe Zilch should be summarily changed to something else. This goes for animals, towns, the names of imaginary books and many other things.

5. Our employer, Mr. Ross, has a prejudice against having too many sentences beginning with "and" or "but." He claims that they are conjunctions and should not be used purely for literary effect. Or at least only very judiciously.

6. See our Mr. Weekes on the use of such words as "little", "vague", "confused", "faintly", "all mixed up", etc. etc.[2] The point is that the average *New Yorker* writer, unfortunately influenced by Mr. Thurber, has come to believe that the ideal *New Yorker* piece is about a vague, little man helplessly confused by a menacing and complicated civilization. Whenever this note is not the whole point of the piece (and it far too often is) it should be regarded with suspicion.

7. The repetition of exposition in quotes went out with the Stanley Steamer:

Marion gave me a pain in the neck.

"You give me a pain in the neck, Marion," I said.

This turns up more often than you'd expect.

8. Another of Mr. Ross's theories is that a reader picking up a magazine called *The New Yorker* automatically supposes that any story in it takes place in New York. If it doesn't, if it's about Columbus, Ohio, the lead should say so. "When George Adams was sixteen, he began to worry about the girls" should read "When George Adams was sixteen, he began to worry about the girls he saw every day on the streets of Columbus" or something of the kind. More graceful preferably.

9. Also, since our contributions are signed at the end, the author's sex should be established at once if there is any reasonable doubt. It is distressing to read a piece all the way through under the impression that the "I" in it is a man and then find a woman's signature at the end. Also, of course, the other way round.

10. To quote Mr. Ross again, "Nobody gives a damn about a writer or his problems except another writer." Pieces about authors, reporters, poets, etc. are to be discouraged in principle. Whenever possible the protagonist should be arbitrarily transplanted to another line of business. When the reference is incidental and unnecessary, it should come out.

11. This magazine is on the whole liberal about expletives. The only test I know of is whether or not they are really essential to the author's effect. "Son of a bitch", "bastard", and many others can be used whenever it is the editor's judgment that that is the only possible remark under the circumstances. When they are gratuitous, when

the writer is just trying to sound tough to no especial purpose, they come out.

12. In the transcription of dialect, don't let the boys and girls misspell words just for a fake bowery effect. There is no point, for instance, in "trubble", or "sad".

13. Mr. Weekes said the other night, in a moment of desperation, that he didn't believe he could stand any more triple adjectives. "A tall, florid and overbearing man called Jaeckel." Sometimes they're necessary, but when every noun has three adjectives connected with it, Mr. Weekes suffers and quite rightly.

14. I suffer myself very seriously from writers who divide quotes for some kind of ladies club rhythm.

"I am going," he said, "downtown" is a horror, and unless a quote is pretty long I think it ought to stay on one side of the verb. Anyway, it ought to be divided logically, where there would be pause or something in the sentence.

15. Mr. Weekes has got a long list of banned words beginning with "gadget". Ask him. It's not actually a ban, there being circumstances when they're necessary, but good words to avoid.

16. I would be delighted to go over the list of writers, explaining the peculiarities of each as they have appeared to me in more than ten years of exasperation on both sides.

16. Editing on manuscript should be done with a black pencil, decisively.

17. I almost forgot indirection which probably maddens Mr. Ross more than anything else in the world. He objects, that is, to important objects, or places or people being dragged into things in a secretive and underhanded manner. If, for instance, a profile has never told where a man lives, Ross protests against a sentence saying, "His Vermont house is fall of valuable paintings." Should say "He has a house in Vermont and it is full, etc." Rather weird point, but it will come up from time to time.

18. Drunkenness and adultery present problems. As far as I can tell, writers must not be allowed to imply that they admire either of these things, or have enjoyed them personally, although they are legitimate enough when pointing a moral or adorning a sufficiently

grim story. They are nothing to be light-hearted about. "*The New Yorker* can not endorse adultery." Harold Ross vs. Sally Benson.[3] Don't bother about this one. In the end it is a matter between Mr. Ross and his God. Homosexuality, on the other hand, is definitely out as humor, and dubious in any case.

19. The more "As a matter of facts", "howevers", "for instances", etc. etc. you can cut out, the nearer you are to the Kingdom of Heaven.

20. It has always seemed irritating to me when a story is written in the first person, but the narrator hasn't got the same name as the author. For instance, a story beginning. "George", my father said to as one morning; and signed at the end Horace McIntyre always baffles me. However, as far as I know this point has never been ruled upon officially, and should just be queried.

21. Editors are really the people who should put initial letters and white spaces in copy to indicate breaks in thought or action. Because of overwork or inertia or something, this has been done largely by the proof-room which has a tendency to put them in for purposes of makeup rather than sense. It should revert to the editors.

22. For some reason our writers (especially Mr. Leonard Q. Ross) have a tendency to distrust even moderately long quotes and break them up arbitrarily and on the whole idiotically with editorial interpolations.[4] "Mr. Kaplan felt that he and the cosmos were coterminus" or some such will frequently appear in the middle of a conversation for no other reason than that the author is afraid the reader's mind is wandering. Sometimes this is necessary, most often it isn't.

23. Writers also have an affection for the tricky or vaguely cosmic last line. "Suddenly Mr. Holtzmann felt tired" has appeared on far too many pieces in the last ten years. It is always a good idea to consider whether the last sentence of a piece is legitimate and necessary, or whether it is just an author showing off.

24. On the whole, we are hostile to puns.

25. How many of these changes can be made in copy depends, of course, to a large extent on the writer being edited. By going over the list, I can give a general idea of how much nonsense each artist will stand for.

26. Among many other things, *The New Yorker* is often accused

of a patronizing attitude. Our authors are especially fond of referring to all foreigners as "little" and writing about them, as Mr. Maxwell says, as if they were mantle ornaments.[5] It is very important to keep the amused and Godlike tone out of pieces.

27. It has been one of Mr. Ross's long struggles to raise the tone of our contributors' surroundings, at least on paper. References to the gay Bohemian life in Greenwich Village and other low surroundings should be cut whenever possible. Nor should writers be permitted to boast about having their telephones cut off, or not being able to pay their bills, or getting their meals at the delicatessen, or any of the things which strike many writers as quaint and lovable.

28. Some of our writers are inclined to be a little arrogant about their knowledge of the French language. Probably best to put them back into English if there is a common English equivalent.

29. So far as possible make the pieces grammatical,—but if you don't the copy room will, which is a comfort. Fowler's English Usage is our reference book. But don't be precious about it.

30. Try to preserve an author's style if he is an author and has a style. Try to make dialogue sound like talk, not writing.

c. 1936

NOTES

"NOTES AND COMMENT" AND "THE TALK OF THE TOWN"

1. For most of the magazine's history, *The New Yorker*'s "Notes and Comment" and "The Talk of the Town" entries ran unsigned. Gibbs shared anonymous credit on this piece with John McNulty.

2. Gibbs's strident tone here suggests a lingering antipathy toward the newspaper coverage of the suicide of his second wife, Elizabeth, in 1930. Coincidentally, like the subject of this column, Elizabeth fell exactly seventeen floors to her death.

3. The German American Bund was a domestic pro-Nazi movement that sought to enlist sympathy for the Third Reich and keep the U.S. out of a European war. This piece was written following the Bund's high-water mark, an infamous rally of twenty thousand followers in Madison Square Garden on February 20, 1939. The reporter Dorothy Thompson (1893–1961) was so early and prominent a critic of National Socialism that the Hitler regime expelled her in 1934.

4. Fritz Kuhn (1896–1951) was the leader of the Bund.

5. Grover Whalen (1886–1962), known as "New York's Official Greeter" for his organizing of ticker-tape parades, was president of the 1939 New York World's Fair Commission.

6. King George VI and Queen Elizabeth of the United Kingdom conducted a highly publicized tour of the U.S. in 1939 to bolster Anglo-American relations on the eve of World War II.

7. The child in question was actually Gibbs's son, Tony (1935–). So enchanted was the American composer Celius Dougherty (1902–1986) with Tony's musings that he set them to music and called the song "Declaration of Independence." Published in 1948, it was recorded by Pete Seeger.

8. Gibbs later quoted this "Comment" in his production of *Season in the Sun*. He shared anonymous credit on it with E. B. White.

9. Bill "Bojangles" Robinson (1878–1949) acted with and danced alongside Shirley Temple in a number of movies in the 1930s.

10. Ward McAllister (1827–1895), the self-proclaimed arbiter of late-nineteenth-century New York society, devised the term "the Four Hundred" to refer to its most elite members.

11. Gibbs shared anonymous credit on this piece with Stanley Edgar Hyman.

12. Gibbs shared anonymous credit on this piece with Stanley Edgar Hyman.

13. Gibbs shared anonymous credit on this piece with Elizabeth Bullock.

14. Steve Brody (1861–1901) attracted widespread fame for claiming to have survived an 1886 jump from the Brooklyn Bridge.

15. Gibbs shared anonymous credit on this piece with Miguel Covarrubias.

16. On this second piece from April 11, 1942, Gibbs shared anonymous credit with John McNulty.

17. Gibbs shared anonymous credit on this piece with John McNulty.

Up from Amherst

1. Despite the tart tone of this profile, Gibbs and his subject, the actor and director Burgess Meredith (1907–1997), became good friends. Indeed, it was "Buzz" who directed Gibbs's *Season in the Sun.*

The Diamond Gardenia

1. "Van Bibber" figured in a number of stories by the veteran war correspondent Richard Harding Davis (1864–1916). In the very first issue of *The New Yorker,* the "Talk of the Town" was signed by "Van Bibber III." "Philo Vance" was the hero of a dozen highly successful crime novels written by S. S. Van Dine (1888–1939).

2. The widely read newspaper columnist Oscar Odd McIntyre (1884–1938) once wrote that Gibbs had been seen lunching at the Plaza. Upon McIntyre's death, Gibbs wrote in "Comment" that McIntyre had been sorely mistaken.

Lady of the Cats

1. Credit for this profile was shared with Eugene F. Kinkead.

Big Nemo

1. Tony's was a popular speakeasy and restaurant on West Forty-ninth Street. Its owner, Tony Soma, was a yoga addict who would often perform headstands for his guests.

2. Woollcott's reluctant dinner companion was actually *New Yorker* editor Harold Ross. "Mr. Connelly" is the Pulitzer Prize–winning author and Algonguin figure Marc Connelly (1890–1980).

3. "Sergeant Quirt" was one Seth Bailey, whose personal history is conveyed here. The pseudonym is that of one of two lead characters in the 1924 drama *What Price Glory?* by Maxwell Anderson and Laurence Stallings.

4. Balto (1919–1933) was a lead pack dog on a legendary 1925 sled run that delivered badly needed diphtheria antitoxin to Nome, Alaska.

St. George and the Dragnet

1. New York Stock Exchange president Richard Whitney (1888–1974) pleaded guilty to Dewey's charges of embezzlement. Dewey convicted Tammany Hall politico James "Jimmy" Hines (1876–1957) of selling police protection to gangster Dutch Schultz (1902–1935). Fritz Kuhn, leader of the German American Bund, is discussed in the notes of the "Notes and Comment" section; Dewey convicted him for tax evasion and embezzlement. The head of Murder, Inc., Louis "Lepke" Buchalter (1897–1944) approved Schultz's murder after Schultz asked the Mafia for permission to kill Dewey.

2. The outspoken daughter of Theodore Roosevelt, Alice Roosevelt Longworth (1884–1980) once likened Dewey to the bridegroom on top of a wedding cake.

3. The poet Berton Braley (1882–1966) was one of more than 150 pacifists who, funded by automobile pioneer Henry Ford, traveled to Europe in 1915 on a widely ridiculed mission to halt World War I.

The Customer Is Always Wrong

1. Gibbs personally chose this profile for the anthology *This Is My Best* (Dial Press, 1942), edited by Whit Burnett, founder of *Story* magazine. As with his profile of Burgess Meredith, this barbed look at the Broadway press agent Richard Maney (1891–1968) did not preclude a close friendship.

2. The "milk bath" of the singer Anna Held (1872–1918) was a publicity stunt hatched by journalist Max Marcin, who planted stories that Held bathed in milk every day and was being sued by a purveyor who wanted back payment for sixty-four quarts of his product.

A Very Active Type Man

1. The largely positive tone of this profile of Ralph Ingersoll (1900–1985) belies his fractious relationship with Gibbs, with whom he worked at *The New Yorker* from 1927 to 1930. By Ingersoll's account, Gibbs's second wife, Elizabeth, killed herself shortly after Ingersoll personally witnessed a "cruel tongue-lashing" that Gibbs had given her. "The tragedy," wrote Ingersoll's biographer, Roy Hoopes, "ended his relationship with Gibbs." Then, in the August 1934 issue of *Fortune*, Ingersoll published the first in-depth public examination of *The New Yorker*'s history, finances, and personnel. Though the piece was almost entirely respectful (James Thurber compared it to "a bouquet of roses"), Ingersoll enraged many staff members by estimating their salaries and spotlighting their foibles. He called Gibbs "slim, handsome, macabre"—a man who "hates everybody and everything, [and] takes an adolescent pride in it." It is generally thought that Gibbs's "Time . . . Fortune . . . Life . . . Luce," published two years later, constituted a counterattack of sorts.

2. The scholar and critic William Lyon Phelps (1865–1943) taught in the Yale English department for forty-one years.

Primo, My Puss

1. Max Baer (1909–1959) and Primo Carnera (1906–1967) both reigned as world heavyweight champions.

2. George Horace Lorimer (1867–1937) for many years edited the *Saturday Evening Post*.

3. The author and critic Rebecca West (1892–1983), one of the twentieth century's leading public intellectuals, was also an important contributor to *The New Yorker*.

Time . . . Fortune . . . Life . . . Luce

1. Oliver Herford (1863–1935) was a humorist and illustrator. The humorist John Kendrick Bangs (1862–1922) was editor of *Puck*.

2. Gibbs initially arrived at this preposterous number by running his finger across the top row of his typewriter keys, coming up with "$45.67890." When Harold Ross said the joke was too obvious, Gibbs changed it to "$45.67802."

3. The "Newyorkereporter" was probably St. Clair McKelway, who interviewed Luce for Gibbs's piece. Their colleague Eugene Kinkead worked his way into the Luce home to establish its true spaciousness.

FUTURE CONDITIONAL

1. "Gertie," "Ivor," and "Basil" are, respectively, Gertrude Lawrence (1898–1952), Ivor Novello (1893–1951), and Basil Dean (1888–1978), all of them Coward's friends and/or collaborators.

SHAKESPEARE, HERE'S YOUR HAT

1. Although Gibbs had intermittent respect for William Saroyan (1908–1981) as a playwright (see his reviews of Saroyan's *The Time of Your Life* and *The Beautiful People* in the "Wounds and Decorations" section), he did not feel similarly about the man himself. In his review of *Get Away Old Man* (1943), Gibbs referred to "William Saroyan's intensely public love affair with William Saroyan."

TO A LITTLE GIRL AT CHRISTMAS

1. Once a highly regarded Pulitzer Prize-winning columnist, Westbrook Pegler (1894–1969) became a rabble-rousing espouser of right-wing causes. The inspiration for this piece was likely a scurrilous attack on the journalist Quentin Reynolds (1902–1965) that Pegler had published a few weeks before. The resulting libel suit, led by famed trial lawyer Louis Nizer, yielded a then-record $175,000 in punitive damages against Pegler in 1954.

STORY OF THE BIBLE IN TABLOID

1. This piece, published while Gibbs was still at the *East Norwich Enterprise*, is his first known appearance in the magazine. Like many of his early submissions, it was signed "W.G."

SIMPSON

1. "Simpson" is actually Leonard Sillman (1908–1982), a Broadway producer with whom Gibbs shared an apartment at 21 East Tenth Street in Manhattan for seven months, after his sister Angelica had indeed moved out to get married. In his autobiography, Sillman wrote that all of Gibbs's assumptions about his odd way of life, though not strictly accurate, "were perfectly valid" under the circumstances. What Gibbs does not mention, but what Sillman did, is that the latter would often put the former to bed following nights of drunken revelry.

LUNCH WITH A RIPSAW

1. "Uncle Adam" is a thinly disguised version of Gibbs's brilliant but somewhat overbearing and distant uncle, George Gibbs (1861–1940), the brother of Gibbs's father, Lucius. Probably in deference to Uncle George—who had helped raise Gibbs and his sister, and who was largely responsible for getting Gibbs his job on the Long Island Rail Road—this sketch was originally signed "Oliver Borden."

OUTWITTING LIGHTNING

1. The "aunt" in this story is Elizabeth Vanderpoel Duer Harvey (1874–1952), the sister of Gibbs's mother, Angelica, with whom he spent many comparatively happy childhood summers in Merrick, Long Island. The piece was originally signed "Amos Andrews."

WIT'S END

1. More than once, Gibbs nearly killed himself under the circumstances depicted here. Ironically, it was not Gibbs, but his third wife, Elinor, who died from smoking in bed in 1963.

MARS

1. Gibbs drew on his experiences with the Student Army Training Corps at the Hill School for this casual. "Lieutenant Gilhooley" was probably his real-life commanding officer, one D. M. McAlpin.

EDEN, WITH SERPENTS

1. In *Sinclair Lewis: An American Life* (1961), Mark Schorer claimed that this story depicted a visit by Lewis to the then-famous sanitarium in Kerhonkson, New York, run by Dr. Fritz Foord (whose name Schorer consistently misspelled as "Ford"). But the piece was likelier inspired by a simultaneous stay there of Gibbs and St. Clair McKelway.

THE HUNTRESS

1. The subject of this piece was probably an otherwise unidentified "Miss Wuerst," with whom Gibbs worked at the *North Hempstead Record*. In a 1926 column he called her "that indefatigable huntress."
2. When Gibbs reprinted this piece in his 1937 collection *Bed of Neuroses,* "New England" and "New Englander" became "Long Island" and "Long Islander". The recidivism and "feeble-mindedness" of the extended and pseudonymous "Juke" family, who were studied in upstate New York by sociologist Richard L. Dugdale in the late nineteenth century, were often invoked as a defense of eugenics. In 1949, Gibbs titled a satire of a riotous meeting of the New York Drama Critics Circle "The Jukes Family Revisited."
3. This is actually a stanza from a poem that Gibbs published in 1919 in *The Hill Record*.

BEAUTY AND GUTZON BORGLUM

1. This casual is based on an encounter between Gibbs and Clare Boothe Brokaw (1903–1987), the future U.S. ambassador and wife of Gibbs's most famous profile subject, *Time* publisher Henry Luce. When she met Gibbs, around 1931, she was an editor at Condé Nast but eager for freelance assignments. In this instance, recalled Gibbs's colleague James Munves, Clare did indeed hope to write a profile of Gutzon Borglum. Although the incident does not figure in Gibbs's 1936 parody of *Time*, it may well have helped fuel the venom behind the piece.

A FELLOW OF INFINITE JEST

1. Except for his regular theater column, this highly autobiographical piece was Gibbs's last appearance in *The New Yorker*. "Perdita," of

course, represents Gibbs's wife, Elinor; the children, "Cyril" and "Ariadne" are his son and daughter, Tony and Janet (1939–2004). The "dull and murderously plain woman of impeachable background" to whom Cyril finds himself engaged is Tony's future wife, Elizabeth "Tish" Villa (b. 1935). "From his perspective, it was probably a pretty accurate description," she later said. "I've never pretended to be a great beauty, and by his standards I was certainly dull."

MR. JERMYN'S LOVELY NIGHT

1. This and the following eight stories make up Gibbs's *Season in the Sun* collection, later the basis for his Broadway play.

NO ROOM IN THE INN

1. In this and the other *Season in the Sun* stories, the four members of the Crane clan serve as counterparts to Gibbs's own family. "George" is Gibbs; "Emily" is Elinor; "Billy" is their son, Tony; and "Marcia" is their daughter, Janet.

DARK CLOUD IN THE SKY

1. When reprinted in Gibbs's 1946 anthology *Season in the Sun and Other Pleasures*, this piece was redubbed "Dark Cloud on the Sun."
2. Molly Burden was inspired by the famous New York madam Polly Adler (1900–1962), whom Gibbs knew from Fire Island. Among her more famous customers was Robert Benchley, Gibbs's friend and immediate predecessor as *The New Yorker*'s theater critic.

SONG AT TWILIGHT

1. "Father Divine" (1876?–1965) was a charismatic preacher based mainly in Harlem and Sayville, N.Y. who claimed to be God himself. St. Clair McKelway and A. J. Liebling dissected him in a two-part 1936 *New Yorker* profile.

LOVE, LOVE, LOVE

1. This flashback is derived largely from the circumstances behind Gibbs's first brief, unhappy marriage to Helen Galpin (1906–1985). Curiously, Gibbs assigns the history to the character of Mark Anderson, rather than to his own alter ego in the story, George Crane.

THE CAT ON THE ROOF

1. This story was based on an incident involving the café society fixture and socialite Leonore Lemmon (1923–1989), perhaps best known for her engagement to the actor George Reeves shortly before his death in 1959. Another unfortunate encounter with Lemmon can be found in the Introduction.

CRUSOE'S FOOTPRINT

1. Anthony Comstock (1844–1915) was so vigorous a foe of moral turpitude that in 1873 he formed the New York Society for the Suppression of Vice.
2. John S. Sumner (1876–1971) succeeded Comstock as head of the Society.

THE CRUSADERS

1. This story, Gibbs told fiction editor Gus Lobrano, was based on an incident in which he, James Thurber, and E. B. White confronted Harold Ross to "remonstrate" about his critical treatment of Katharine White. Probably out of respect for Ross, Gibbs waited until he had died before publishing this fictional version.

SUCH NICE PEOPLE

1. Anthony Ross (1909–1955) would later play "Horace Dodd," a barely disguised version of *New Yorker* editor Harold Ross (no relation) in Gibbs's *Season in the Sun*.

WHAT A WONDERFUL WAR

1. Gibbs was quite in error here, as Michener's friend Herman Silverman recalled in his memoir *Michener and Me* (Running Press, 1999). Gibbs, Silverman wrote, "didn't think the play bore any resemblance to Michener's book." Michener and Silverman were outraged. "We decided to call Gibbs and tell him what a jerk he was. We reached him at home and complained. To our gratification, Gibbs apologized and explained that he had used as his reference a paperback edition of Jim's book which omitted the two stories upon which the musical was based."

DOOM

1. Arthur Gelb (1924–), who covered Broadway for the *New York Times* at this time and had the chance to observe Gibbs at close range, wrote later that during this performance, Gibbs twisted in his aisle seat and tried as best he could to face the back of the auditorium, leaving abruptly during the second of the play's four acts. Asked why he had skipped one of the great dramatic works of the age, Gibbs curtly explained that O'Neill's merciless examination of a family destroyed by a mother's drug addiction and madness had "cut too close."

OUT OF THE NOWHERE

1. Along with the aforementioned Anthony Ross, Eddie Mayehoff (1914–1992) appeared in Gibbs's *Season in the Sun*. He played "Paul Anderson," who was clearly derived from the "Mark Anderson" of Gibbs's original stories.

TRIPLE-THREAT MAN

1. As noted in the Introduction, Gibbs was an early collaborator on *Dream With Music* (1944). But there is no record that he worked on another musical that actually reached Broadway.

CURTAIN CALLS

1. Gibbs would often weigh in on several productions in a single issue of *The New Yorker*. In many cases in this volume, not all of his critiques

within a given column have been reprinted. However, the original headlines have been retained, prefaced by "from" to indicate that the column has been truncated. Columns that have been abridged, but which clearly refer to the headline, lack this designation.

from SCHOOLMASTER JANNINGS—
RADIO ANNOUNCERS, PORTIAS, AND FLAGPOLE-SITTERS

1. As with his theatrical criticism, Gibbs would frequently dispose of several movies in a single column. His original headlines have been similarly retained here.

LITTLE NEMO AND THE CARDBOARD LION

1. The pioneering cartoonist Winsor McKay (1867?–1934) was also famous for creating the comic strip *Dreams of a Rarebit Fiend* and the groundbreaking animated short *Gertie the Dinosaur*.
2. The critic Gilbert Seldes (1893–1970) was editor of *The Dial*.
3. David C. Montgomery (d. 1917) and Fred Stone (1873–1959) were veteran vaudevillians who headlined a loosely adapted version of *The Wizard of Oz* on Broadway in 1903. Montgomery played the Tin Man and Stone the Scarecrow.
4. Sir James Matthew Barrie (1860–1937) was the creator of *Peter Pan*.

A PRIMER FOR CRITICS

1. The poet was E. B. White.
2. A reference to "Baseball's Sad Lexicon," a poem by newspaper columnist and Algonquin fixture Franklin Pierce Adams (1881–1960), which described the legendary double-play combination of Chicago Cubs shortstop Joe Tinker (1880–1948), second baseman Johnny Evers (1883–1947), and first baseman Frank Chance (1876–1924).

THE KINGDOM OF THE BLIND

1. This piece, when reprinted in *Season in the Sun and Other Pleasures*, was redubbed "The Country of the Blind."

Robert Benchley: In Memoriam

1. Gibbs himself wrote this.

Stuff and Nonsense, Mr. C.

1. One of the leading television critics of the 1950s, John Crosby (1912–
    1991) wrote most notably for the *New York Herald Tribune* and hosted
    the Emmy-winning series *The Seven Lively Arts*. Gibbs wrote this
    guest column for the *Herald Tribune* while Crosby was on leave.

Theory and Practice of Editing *New Yorker* Articles

1. In a note dated November 22, 1969, Katharine White described the
    background of these Gibbsian guidelines. Included among her col-
    lected papers in the Bryn Mawr College archives, it is reprinted here
    in full:

    This attached manuscript is not classified. It has been published
    previously in New York either in a newspaper or in *Printer's
    Ink*—I cannot remember where.
        This funny, wise, and completely inner-office memo titled
    "Theory and Practice of Editing *New Yorker* Articles" must date
    about 1936–37. It is a revealing literary document, written perhaps
    at my request or perhaps as his own idea, by Wolcott Gibbs when
    I was head of the Fiction Department and he was my right hand
    man and alternate or substitute as head of the Department during
    my illnesses or vacations. It was intended only to be read by new
    Fiction Editors on how to edit manuscripts to fit the magazine's
    practice, and particularly how to edit copy to fit Harold Ross's odd
    quirks and prejudices on subject matter and style. Gibbs and I were
    constantly trying out or training new editors at this period be-
    cause Gibbs wanted to give up editing and spend all his time on
    writing and theater criticism, and I wanted to move to Maine and
    work only at long distance. We also were always trying out new,
    young, first readers and young editors.
        The magazine's editing rules or suggestions and H. W. Ross's
    own prejudices were greatly altered before Ross died in 1951, but
    this was the way it was in the later middle thirties. Any biographer

of Ross or of Wolcott Gibbs would find this most illuminating and also, of course, anyone writing a book on the history of *The New Yorker* itself. As of 1969 and for many years back, since William Shawn has been editor, only the essential grammatical and bad style clauses would hold true of *The New Yorker* setup today, because outspokenness and subject matter bans have changed constantly with the times. But there is acute advice for any beginning writer here from one of the most talented and witty magazine editors, of all time. Remember that no editing change ever was made even from 1925 without the consent and approval of the author. The person referred to as "Weekes" was Hobart G. Weekes, then final page-proof Copy Editor, a key job. He was far more than a proof editor—an authority on style. He is still on the staff.

So far as I know this is a carbon copy of Gibbs's original typescript as it was found hidden away in my desk when it was finally emptied this year (1969) for the use of someone else. The original copy belongs to *The New Yorker* and will go with its files eventually to one of three libraries not yet decided on, so far as I know. It was Gibbs, himself, who put in two paragraphs numbered 16. How the memo was sneaked out to be published elsewhere, I don't know, but I can guess that this was done by an editor on trial who did not get hired permanently.

2. Weekes (1901–1978) was a year ahead of Gibbs at the Hill School. Gibbs once credited him with "my impeccable syntax."

3. Sally Benson (1897–1972) was a prolific *New Yorker* short story writer probably best remembered for her collection *Meet Me in St. Louis*, which was the basis of the hit Judy Garland film of the same title.

4. Leo Rosten (1908–1997), a.k.a. "Leonard Q. Ross," was a teacher and humorist whose best known work was *The Education of H*Y*M*A*N K*A*P*L*A*N*.

5. *New Yorker* fiction editor and writer William Maxwell (1908–2000) succeeded Gibbs as the resident editorial figure assigned to attend the magazine's weekly cartoon meetings.